Disarming the Nation

WOMEN IN CULTURE AND SOCIETY   *A series edited by Catharine R. Stimpson*

Disarming the Nation

Women's Writing and the American Civil War

Elizabeth Young

THE UNIVERSITY OF CHICAGO PRESS   CHICAGO AND LONDON

ELIZABETH YOUNG is associate professor of English at Mount Holyoke College.

The University of Chicago Press, Chicago 60637
The University of Chicago Press, Ltd., London
© 1999 by The University of Chicago
All rights reserved. Published 1999

08 07 06 05 04 03 02 01 00 99   1 2 3 4 5

ISBN 0-226-96087-0 (cloth)
       0-226-96088-9 (paper)

Library of Congress Cataloging-in-Publication Data

Young, Elizabeth.
    Disarming the nation : women's writing and the American Civil War / Elizabeth Young.
        p.   cm. — (Women in culture and society)
    Includes bibliographical references and index.
    ISBN 0-226-96087-0 (cloth : alk. paper). — ISBN 0-226-96088-9 (pbk.)
    1. American literature—19th century—History and criticism.   2. United States—History—Civil
War, 1861–1865—Literature and the war.   3. Women and literature—United States—History—
19th century.   4. American literature—Women authors—History and criticism.   5. United States—
History—Civil War, 1861–1865—Women.   I. Title.   II. Series.
    PS217.C58Y68   1999
    810.9′358—dc21   99-31518
                                                                                        CIP

To my mother and father

Contents

Illustrations

Series Editor's Foreword

In 1939, the film *Gone With the Wind* premiered in Atlanta, Georgia. The legendary novel on which it was based had appeared three years earlier, and its author, Margaret Mitchell, was a fierce defender of the traditional South. Indeed, as a child she had happily assumed that the Confederacy had won the Civil War. The theaters in Atlanta were segregated in 1939, and Hattie McDaniel, who was to win an Oscar for her role in *Gone With the Wind*, was forbidden to enter the privileged whites-only theaters. Even so, some African-American children were permitted to see *Gone With the Wind* in this venue. Dressed in "pickaninny" costumes, they were on stage as part of the entertainment for the white audience. Martin Luther King, Jr., then ten years old, was among them.

This chilling, ironic story is about many things, including, most certainly, the deep connections among gender, race, and America's representations of the nineteenth-century epic of Civil War. It is no minor coincidence that a Southern white woman had written a book instrumental to definitions of the War in the twentieth-century. Among other motives, she had wanted to repudiate an equally famous book by another white woman that helped to justify the necessity of the Civil War in the nineteenth century—Harriet Beecher Stowe and her 1852 novel, *Uncle Tom's Cabin*. Yet, in 1939 the celebration of the film version of *Gone With the Wind* excluded an accomplished black woman and included a young black man, but only in a demeaning role that catered to the racial fantasies about blacks held by white men and women alike. Despite this, the young man would go on to lead a civil rights struggle that would end legal segregation in America and, in doing so, inspire new representations of the Civil War.

Such connections are the subject of Elizabeth Young's astonishing, important, and wonderful first book, *Disarming the Nation*. Conventional wisdom, she argues, has accepted a literary myth about the Civil War that brings together the birth of the nation, whiteness, and masculinity. As a result, the canonical Civil War novel is "a book by a white man about a white man in combat" (p. 1). Incisively, lucidly, Young shows how shallow and narrow conventional wisdom can be as she explores the ways in which black and white women represent the Civil War, beginning with Stowe and ending with contemporary voices. These ways are far more numerous than we have realized. Women, she reminds us, did dominate the literary marketplace for Civil War fiction. Moreover, women actively participated in the War as nurses, laundresses, seamstresses, spies, and scouts.

As Young juxtaposes white and black women writers, she also demonstrates the intersections of race, gender, and sexuality in the construction of American identities. For example, when a Southern white man suffered defeat in a Civil War that freed black slaves, he was symbolically emasculated and made vulnerable to rape.

Young takes up cartoons, films, law cases, tourist sites, and the public spectacle of the re-enactment of the Civil War with equal suppleness and aplomb. Her focus, however, is on prose and prose fiction: the work of Stowe; Louisa May Alcott; Elizabeth Keckley, who was born a slave and later became a fashion designer and confidante of Abraham and Mary Lincoln; Loreta Janeta Velazquez, who masqueraded as Lt. Harry T. Buford in the Confederate Army; Frances Ellen Watkins Harper; and Mitchell, who inspired formidable counternarratives from such black women writers as Margaret Walker.

Their representations of the War vary wildly, depending on time, place, ideology, and circumstance. Northern and Southern white women have split as sharply as opposing armies. The Northern women, however, could nonetheless exclude black women from their rhetoric of national redemption and reconstruction. For African-Americans, the primary narrative of the War is a narrative of the struggle to end slavery, which was inseparable from the black men's battle to win the right to fight in the Union army. Ironically, the representation of the worthy black male warrior could still exclude black women. Harper, whose novel *Iola Leroy* appeared in 1892, had the additional burden of writing against the white backlash of the late nineteenth-century—the cult of the "Lost Cause" of the Confederacy, Jim Crow laws, the picture of black men as hypersexualized rapists, and lynchings.

Yet, these women have their commonalities. Each explores the doubled meaning of Civil War. As a bloody political event, it refers to a nation divided against itself, a war without. As a psychological event, it means a woman divided against herself, a war within. They are inseparable. Young is continually alert to the double meanings of the War's vocabulary. A border state is both a political unit located on the line between North and South

(Kentucky, for example) and a liminal condition that marks the threshold between two ways of experiencing and being in the world. For the Civil War
tore the fabric of women's lives apart, no matter what their region, no matter
what their race. Velazquez's story of cross-dressing, then, is "a literary fantasy
prompted by the real-life transformations of Southern white women during
wartime" (p. 161).

"Civil" also meant civility for both black and white writers. Yet, white
women writers experienced the war and writing about the war as a way of
freeing themselves from the stifling imperatives of being a civil, civilizing sex.
Young is devastatingly astute regarding Margaret Mitchell's construction of
the incivilities of female pleasure and Scarlett's sexual excitements in *Gone
With the Wind*. Excluded by racism from the imperatives of being the good
sex, black women writers found writing about the Civil War a strategy for
establishing and dramatizing their own codes of civility.

Disarming the Nation compels us to realize that women are still writing
about the Civil War, and, as a result, continuing to create memories and meanings that conflict with each other. By doing so, they are maintaining the life
of an America that is a site of perpetual contests over what it is, what it values,
and what history it will bank. "Then as now," writes Young, "women's fictions
of the Civil War are more divisible than invisible, and the war itself is less
unwritten than unending" (p. 23). Elizabeth Young now joins the company
of necessary guides to this America.

—Catharine R. Stimpson

Acknowledgments

I have had a great deal of assistance in the decade since I started thinking about women's writing and the Civil War. For indispensable financial and institutional support, I am deeply grateful to the National Endowment for the Humanities for a fellowship year, the Huntington Library for a research fellowship, Mount Holyoke College for a Faculty Fellowship and other forms of assistance, and the Andrew W. Mellon Foundation and the University of California at Berkeley for graduate fellowships and other funding.

Laura M. Green and William A. Cohen have overseen every aspect of this book from the start, and I could never have completed it without their brilliance and patience. I owe the project's initial incarnation to the supportive guidance of my dissertation director Carolyn Porter and committee members Susan Schweik and Mary Ryan. Others at Berkeley, particularly Elizabeth Abel, Catherine Gallagher, and Kaja Silverman, have also influenced my thinking on aspects of this project, as did an earlier group of teachers, Sacvan Bercovitch, Joseph Boone, and Sonya Michel. At Mount Holyoke College, my colleagues in the English Department and in Women's Studies, American Studies, and Film Studies have encouraged me as this project evolved toward book form. In particular, Nina Gerassi-Navarro and Amy Kaplan have greatly enriched the book, and Christopher Benfey and Donald Weber have offered valuable assistance along the way.

For very helpful readings of the full manuscript, I am grateful to Kathleen Diffley, Linda Kerber, Tania Modleski, Carla Peterson, and Laura Wexler. I appreciate the scholarly assistance of Kristina Brooks, Lois Brown, Elaine Ginsberg, Joan Hedrick, Elizabeth Leonard, Tara McPherson, Kathy Peiss, Charles Rutheiser, Karen Sánchez-Eppler, Jane Schultz, Barbara Sicherman, Cathy Stanton, Priscilla Wald, and Alfred F. Young. For various forms of personal and professional support over the years, I am grateful to Eytan Bercovitch, the late Gila Bercovitch, Brenda Bright, Cathy Davidson, Simone

Davis, Jill Frank and Larry Glickman, Judith Jackson Fossett, Leah Glasser, Carolyn Karcher, Kavita Khory, Candida Lacey, Susan Mizruchi, Mary Renda, Elaine Showalter, Terri Snyder, Trysh Travis, Susan Ware, and Ken Wissoker. Thanks to Sue Grayzel, Branwen Gregory, Karen Heath, and Roo Hooke for ballast, with particular gratitude to Lisa Hunter for constant long-distance support.

Portions of this project have been presented as lectures and conference talks and as lectures at the following venues: Five College Women's Studies Research Center, Harvard, Princeton, Southern Methodist University, the University of Maryland, and the University of Massachusetts. I am grateful to the organizers of these events and their audiences for stimulating responses. I have benefited greatly from the Northeast Nineteenth-Century Women Writers Group and its supportive community of feminist scholars. Librarians at Mount Holyoke College, Duke, Emory, Harvard, the Huntington Library, the University of Georgia, and the University of North Carolina and elsewhere made my work much easier. I thank Alan Thomas, Randy Petilos, Kathryn Kraynik, and others at the University of Chicago Press for their dedication to the manuscript throughout.

My deepest acknowledgments are to Awam Amkpa, my comrade in arms, and to my family: Alfred Young and Marilyn Mills Young, my first mentors in life and scholarship; Sarah Young and Noah Fortino-Young; and Jeff Goll, Davia Young, and Emily Young, my agent extraordinaire.

THE FOLLOWING MATERIAL was previously published in different form: part of chapter 2 appeared as "A Wound of One's Own: Louisa May Alcott's Civil War Fiction," in *American Quarterly* 48:3 (September 1996); part of chapter 4 as "Confederate Counterfeit: The Case of the Cross-Dressed Civil War Soldier," in *Passing and the Fictions of Identity,* edited by Elaine K. Ginsberg (Durham: Duke University Press, 1996); and part of chapter 5 as "Warring Fictions: *Iola Leroy* and the Color of Gender," *American Literature* 64:2 (June 1992).

Introduction

In a sermon he delivered shortly before the American Civil War began, New England minister Henry Ward Beecher declared that "manhood,—*man-hood,*—MANHOOD,—exercised in the fear of God, has made this nation." The literature of the Civil War regularly underscores and capitalizes on the generative power of masculinity. The most famous document of the war, the Gettysburg Address, captures this idea in its opening words, a succinct account of men giving birth to America: "Four score and seven years ago our fathers brought forth on this continent, a new nation, conceived in Liberty." Like Beecher, Lincoln offers a fantasy of national self-fathering, in which masculinity circulates as the literary lifeblood, as well as the literal canon-fodder, of the injured body politic. In the land of the self-made man, the story of national self-division—like the birth of a nation—apparently needs no mothers.[1]

Histories of the war and its literature elaborate these exhortations to masculine nation-building. From nineteenth-century commentaries to recent revaluations, historical discussions of the Civil War have focused primarily on its white male policymakers and soldiers, reproducing a narrative in which Lincoln, his generals, and their privates successfully labor to reunify the nation. In a complementary story of patrilineal self-generation, criticism of Civil War fiction foregrounds the works of white male writers, particularly those who represent white soldiers in battle. In this critical paradigm, a Civil War novel is a book by a white man about a white man in combat, a description whose touchstone is Stephen Crane's *The Red Badge of Courage* (1895). Crane's novel translates the scarlet letter of antebellum romance into the red badge of combat realism and, in turn, authorizes a twentieth-century American canon of works by and about white men at war. Thus one critic states that "[F]or most Americans, [the Civil War] represented the ultimate test of manhood" and asks, unironically, "What would our literary heritage be without *The Red Badge of Courage* (1895), *A Farewell to Arms* (1929), or *The Naked and the Dead* (1948)?"[2]

White women's fiction appears infrequently in this lineage, while African-American accounts of the war, male or female, are marked out of the Civil War canon almost entirely. Originated by *The Red Badge of Courage*, the Civil War novel as a genre passes a dual paternity test, emerging as the legitimate offspring of a war considered the province of male fighters and a war novel deemed the creation of male writers.[3]

Like most myths of origin, however, this one is highly suspect. Women, white and African-American, were key participants in the Civil War in civilian and combat arenas. Organizing massive support initiatives at home, women worked in the army as cooks, laundresses, nurses, spies, scouts, and soldiers. More fundamentally, as a conflict fought on United States territory, the Civil War definitively eroded the boundary between male "battlefront" and female "homefront." For black women, this boundary had never been in place, since a brutal slave system denied African-Americans the prerogatives of a peaceful homefront. The war provided new opportunities for black men and women, free and enslaved, to continue ongoing battles for survival and freedom. For white Southern women, by contrast, previously secure domestic spaces could become battlefields. The Confederate women whose homes were invaded by Sherman's troops, for example, found themselves in militarized arenas akin to the fields of Gettysburg and Antietam. As in other wars, moreover, the absence of men mandated new levels of female leadership at home and occasioned conflicts over appropriate gender roles for women. During the Civil War, women inaugurated a range of activities, from new political organizations to full-fledged riots, which interrupted the usual male gendering of the public sphere. As feminist historians have shown, gender configurations were in flux along with national and racial boundaries, and a fuller account of the conflict sees it not only as a war fought by women as well as men, but also and more fundamentally as a war over the meaning of gender itself.[4]

So too for the war's literary history. Despite the framing of the war as a literary touchstone for manhood, there is, in fact, no male canon of great American Civil War novels as such but, rather, a hole precisely where one ought to be. None of the most canonical authors of the immediate postwar period—Twain, Howells, James—fought at any length in the war; neither they nor the next generation of American naturalists wrote Civil War novels; and the most "authentic" of Civil War novels, *The Red Badge of Courage*, was a retroactive version of the war invented by a man born after it had ended.[5] The two most influential studies of Civil War literature, Edmund Wilson's *Patriotic Gore* (1962) and Daniel Aaron's *The Unwritten War* (1973), both struggle in revealing ways with this problem of male absence. Aaron expertly assesses the writings of well-known authors, almost exclusively white and male, for their representations of the war, with results that disappoint him. Looking within the self-perpetuating terms of the canon, he finds that the Civil War remains surprisingly "unwritten," and he concludes that while the conflict affected generations of writers, it was "not so much unfelt as unfaced."[6] Edmund Wilson's approach is more capacious. Conceding that the period of the American Civil War "was not one in which belles lettres flourished," he assembles an eclectic roster of diaries, memoirs, and journalism by lesser-known writers, works that "dramatize the war as the poet or the writer of fiction has never been able to do."[7] Not coincidentally, this more relaxed approach to canonical value allows for examination of more women writers, including Harriet Beecher Stowe, Julia Ward Howe, Mary Chesnut, and Charlotte Forten. Together, *The Unwritten War* and *Patriotic Gore* begin to suggest a different Civil War literary history. Aaron's emphasis on the "unwritten war" exposes a curiously impotent male canon, while Wilson's eclecticism begins to point toward an alternative literary genealogy—one less unfaced than effaced and more unread than unwritten.

Wilson's attention to the journals of Charlotte Forten, for example, points to a tradition almost entirely absent in the conventional criticism of Civil War literature: the extensive commentary provided on the war by African-American women. Such commentaries include, through the turn of the century alone, not only Forten's journals but also the memoirs of Annie L. Burton, Kate Drumgoold, Elizabeth Keckley, and Susie King Taylor; the poetry of Josephine Delphine Henderson Heard, Lizelia Augusta Jenkins Moorer, Effie Waller Smith, Clara Ann Thompson, Priscilla Jane Thompson, and Katherine Davis Chapman Tillman; the biographical writing of Octavia Victoria Rogers Albert and Frances Rollin; the letters of Harriet Jacobs; the oratory of Sarah Parker Remond; the journalism of Mary Ann Shadd Cary; the magazine fiction of Pauline Hopkins; and the fiction, poetry, oratory, essays, and correspondence of Frances Ellen Watkins Harper. The broader category of nineteenth-century Civil War texts created in part by black women, even if they did not themselves write, includes the dictated and otherwise mediated narratives of Mattie Jackson, Sojourner Truth, and Harriet Tubman. Works by and about black women, in turn, form part of a larger African-American literary conversation about the war. Men participating in this conversation ranged from established figures like Frederick Douglass, Martin Delany, William Wells Brown, and George Washington Williams, who published and lectured publicly about the war, to the many black soldiers who registered their responses in letters home. Together, these texts constitute a counter-genealogy of Civil War literature in which the central historical fact of the war for African-Americans—the end of slavery—took many literary forms.[8]

Equally divided among genres, white women's writing about the war was more sharply split along partisan lines. The best-known woman's war commentary is that of a Southern white woman, Mary Chesnut, whose diaries Wilson termed "extraordinary" and Aaron praised as "more genuinely literary than most Civil War fiction." Other Confederate women produced numerous literary responses to the war, both public and private, although publishing resources in wartime were so diminished that novels sometimes had to be printed on wallpaper. In a region whose cultural sensibilities favored the historical novel—Mark Twain famously blamed the Confederacy on the Southern popularity of Sir Walter Scott—fiction was a particularly welcoming genre for women. A few women novelists expressed ambivalence about the Confederacy. The novelist known as Marion Harland (Mary Virginia Hawes Terhune), for example, torn between her native Virginia and her Northern husband, wrote a Civil War novel, *Sunnybank* (1866), split between two female protagonists with contrasting partisan allegiances. Far more common and popular, however, were the numerous virulently pro-Confederate works published during and shortly after the war. Such novels included Augusta Jane Evans, *Macaria; or, Altars of Sacrifice* (1864), Sally Rochester Ford, *Raids and Romances of Morgan and His Men* (1864), Florence J. O'Connor, *The Heroine of the Confederacy; or, Truth and Justice* (1864), and Mary Tucker Magill, *Women; or, Chronicles of the Late War* (1871). Subsequent generations of Southern white women returned repeatedly to the Civil War in their fiction. Ellen Glasgow and Mary Johnston, for example, centered long novels on the battles of Civil War Virginia, while Grace King and Kate Chopin filtered the war through the Creole culture of Louisiana. White Southern women's literary interest in the Confederacy culminated in the most famous twentieth-century novel about the Civil War, Margaret Mitchell's *Gone With the Wind* (1936).[9]

In the North, where a more well-developed literary culture continued to thrive during the war, white women writers exploited publishing venues, producing poetry, fiction, and political pamphlets along with private diaries and letters. Northern women's works about the Civil War pursued diverse themes and found different degrees of visibility: Emily Dickinson's many unpublished poems from this era obliquely but powerfully register the impact of the war, while at the other extreme of circulation, Julia Ward Howe's poem "The Battle Hymn of the Republic" became, in song form, the rallying-cry of the Union cause. Several fiction writers began their careers during the war and returned repeatedly to it. Louisa May Alcott, for example, drew on her experiences as a Union nurse in *Hospital Sketches* (1863) and returned to wartime settings again in *Little Women* (1868) and *Work* (1873), each with a pro-Union New England focus. Rebecca Harding Davis, raised in the part of Virginia that seceded to become its own state during the war, depicted divided wartime loyalties in stories like "John Lamar" (1862) and "David Gaunt" (1862), and she centered her postwar novel *Waiting for the Verdict* (1867) on racial struggles in the war era. Two prominent abolitionists also focused their immediately postwar novels on the war's meaning for race relations: Anna Dickinson indicted the racism of the 1863 New York City Draft Riots in *What Answer?* (1868), and Lydia Maria Child introduced the war into the closing chapters of her novel of interracial marriage, *A Romance of the Republic* (1867). The most popular Northern white woman's Civil War novel, by contrast, seemed to evade racial questions entirely, focusing on the inner crisis of a white woman mourning the death of her brother in combat. Elizabeth Stuart Phelps's *The Gates Ajar* (1868) made its twenty-four-year-old author into an instant national celebrity.[10]

Indeed, while black women's Civil War writings had limited public visibility, white women not only populated but dominated the literary marketplace for Civil War fiction. During the war, the majority of the short and long fiction published about the war was by white women, as were many of the best-selling war novels from the 1860s onward. As one twentieth-century critic of the genre puts it, the "earliest general conventions" of war novels "grew from sentimental reactions to war of professional and amateur lady writers."[11] The influence of "lady writers" was not confined to the homefront but also reached soldiers in camp, to whom the Civil War brought new leisure time for reading; Boston publisher James Redpath launched his successful "Books for the Camp Fires" series aimed at soldiers with a volume of Louisa May Alcott's war stories.[12] From the start, women's fiction affected the political as well as literary culture of the war. Evans's *Macaria,* for example, was considered so incendiary in its support for the Confederacy that it was literally burned by military leaders in Northern army camps.[13] Most famously, the 1852 novel that had prompted furious political debate, as well as phenomenal sales, was credited with bringing on the war itself. Selling 10,000 copies in its first week and 300,000 in its first year, producing myriad spin-offs and rebuttals, *Uncle Tom's Cabin* had such a profound impact on sectional hostilities that Abraham Lincoln allegedly greeted Harriet Beecher Stowe as "the little woman who made this great war."[14]

Extending this alternative account of origins, this book analyzes women's writing about the American Civil War, from the 1860s to the present. I focus on six figures: Harriet Beecher Stowe, Louisa May Alcott, Elizabeth Keckley, Loreta Velazquez, Frances Ellen Watkins Harper, and Margaret Mitchell. Some of these women are virtually unknown, like Loreta Velazquez, author of a memoir about her masquerade as a Confederate soldier. Others appear in new guises, like Margaret Mitchell, whose *Gone With the Wind* I interpret through the lenses of the author's seldom-discussed interests in cross-dressing, blackface, and sexually explicit prose. Throughout, I juxtapose white and African-American women's voices, Northern and Southern. Two of the book's six chapters are focused on African-American writers, and chapters on white writers treat their work in conversation with African-American texts. I situate Stowe, for example, in relation to Sojourner Truth, Sarah Parker Remond, Katherine Davis Chapman Tillman, Susie King Taylor, and Anna Julia Cooper, and I highlight black critiques and revisions of *Gone With the Wind*. While the book centers on women, I also discuss men who influenced, responded to, or otherwise illuminate this writing, from literary figures like Paul Laurence Dunbar and Thomas Dixon to politicians like Abraham Lincoln and Confederate General Jubal Early. Emphasizing prose fiction, I include analyses of memoirs, diaries, letters, oratory, cartoons, songs, plays, films, memorabilia, and Civil War reenactments.

This project is heavily indebted to the insights of feminist literary criticism, but it addresses gaps in that field as well. While feminist scholars have developed a substantial body of interdisciplinary work on women and war, they have rarely taken the Civil War as a central framework, literary or historical, for interpreting women's writing.[15] In revaluing the privatized domestic sphere of nineteenth-century Northern white women's writing, for example, scholars have ironically contributed to a neglect of women's literary relation to this central public event of the nineteenth century. Nor have critics of African-American literature focused at length on the meaning of the war in black women's writing, although the centrality of emancipation in this literature implicitly brings the demarcating line of the war into view. The Civil War appears most fully in scholarship on white Southern women's writing, where it is symptomatic of the greater attention given the war in studies of that region as a whole.[16] Nonetheless, most criticism of nineteenth-century women's writing, like most accounts of nineteenth-century American literature as a whole, continues to divide the century into antebellum and postwar zones, with a gap where the war—and its women writers—would be. In the chapters that follow, I fill in this gap, identifying the war as an important presence in American women's writing across race and region, from the 1860s to the present. I argue that women writers were profoundly influenced by the Civil War and that, in turn, their writings contributed powerfully to cultural understandings of the war and its aftermath.

WHEN WE BEGIN Civil War literary history with women's texts at the center, the traditional account of that history seems not only partial but preemptive. If African-American women's writings have been left out of the war's literary history because of their presumed irrelevance, then white women's texts have been erased because of their perceived overabundance. "Woman has now taken to her pen . . . and is flourishing it with a vengeance," wrote a journalist at the beginning of the war.[17] Rather than simply ignoring women's writing, men's commentary about the Civil War was haunted by the specter of women with "flourishing" phallic pens. This imagery updated Hawthorne's famous lament about the "scribbling women" writers of antebellum domestic fiction to a later era, one in which new institutions of cultural authority and changing aesthetic norms marginalized women more fully than in the antebellum era. Under the emerging criteria of literary realism, women's interest in writing about war represented a flagrant violation of gender norms; war novels, like war itself, were ostensibly a matter for men. Male jeremiads about women's Civil War fiction angrily and anxiously defended these boundaries, repeatedly constructing the Civil War as a literary battlefront under assault by armies of inferior but powerful women.[18]

Such defenses are at work, for example, in William Dean Howells's responses to John De Forest's *Miss Ravenel's Conversion from Secession to Loyalty* (1867), the novel that next to *The Red Badge of Courage* holds pride of place in Civil War criticism.[19] In his initial review of *Miss Ravenel*, Howells praised De Forest for his divergence from Civil War fiction by women:

> [T]he heroes of the young-lady writers in the magazines have been everywhere fighting the late campaigns over again, as young ladies would have fought them. We do not say that this is not well, but we suspect that Mr. De Forrest [*sic*] is the first to treat the war really and artistically.[20]

In Howells's account, the Civil War story has been incongruously overrun by "young-lady writers," and the male literary battleground under siege becomes another example of what Nina Baym has called the American "melodrama of beset manhood."[21] In response to this siege, Howells erects a masculine aesthetic of war fiction, in which "really" and "artistically" are synonyms for "authentically." Despite such praise, however, *Miss Ravenel* was not a major success, and in an 1879 letter to Howells, De Forest lamented, "I don't understand why you and I haven't sold monstrously except on the theory that our novel-reading public is mainly a female or a very juvenile public, and wants something nearer to its own mark of intellect and taste."[22] De Forest focuses here on women readers rather than writers, equating "female" and "very juvenile" in his denunciation of the literary public. By 1901, the dependence of novels upon women readers has become the dependence of women readers upon novels, when Howells concedes that De Forest is "a man's novelist, and as men do not need novelists so much apparently as women, his usefulness has been limited."[23] Over nearly forty years, then, Howells and De Forest together narrate the reception of *Miss Ravenel* as that of a man's novel rejected because of the predominance of women, first as writers of fiction and then as readers. This defensive commentary preserves De Forest's lack of popularity as a sign of his value but only by ceding the field of Civil War literary production and consumption to women.

In this context, even the most "masculine" of Civil War novels, Crane's *The Red Badge of Courage,* can be read as an anxious allegory about the feminization of the Civil War literary marketplace. In its corrosively antiheroic depiction of a terrified young soldier, Crane's novel ironizes the statement of masculinity with which it concludes: "He felt a quiet manhood, nonassertive but of sturdy and strong blood. . . . He was a man."[24] Throughout the novel, as critics have noted, Henry's "manhood" is not quiet, sturdy, and strong, but closer to "an abject pulp" (76); by the end of the novel, the making of manhood in war is virtually inseparable from its unmaking. In particular, as Amy Kaplan has shown, *Red Badge* undermines masculinity through a constant dependence on spectacle and spectatorship: "For Henry to become a man or to have a self, he needs to imagine an audience watching him."[25] The novel so insistently privileges the spectatorial register of battle that Henry must generate a divided image of self-observation not only to fight—"Swift pictures of himself, apart, yet in himself, came to him" (55)—but even to have consciousness at all: "The youth awakened slowly. He came gradually back to a position from which he could regard himself" (34).

Extending this analysis, we can see visual spectatorship in the novel as linked to literary consumption and more specifically to the consumption of war stories by an audience close to Howells's despised "female" and "very juvenile public." In Crane's novel, war narrative, like masculinity, requires the presence of an audience to provide coherence. *Red Badge* begins with a vignette about the telling of war stories, in a description of a "certain tall soldier" who

> was swelled with a tale he had heard from a reliable friend, who had heard it from a truthful cavalryman, who had heard it from his trustworthy brother, one of the orderlies at division headquarters. He adopted the important air of a herald in red and gold. . . . To his attentive audience he drew a loud and elaborate plan of a very brilliant campaign. When he had finished, the blue-clothed men scattered into small arguing groups between the rows of squat brown huts. A negro teamster who had been dancing upon a cracker box with the hilarious encouragement of twoscore soldiers was deserted. He sat mournfully down. (5)

In this passage, identity is organized through the telling of war stories to an audience, a scenario that "swells" the speaker with an obvious masculinity. Yet the tale itself is fifth-hand and impossibly "brilliant," as unreliable and attenuated as masculinity itself. This unreliability surfaces more fully as Crane shifts from the fantasy of telling a war story to the fear of losing an audience. The image of the dancing "negro teamster"—the only black character in the novel—evokes the minstrel show, here captured at the moment when the audience leaves. As a double for Crane himself, the "negro teamster" offers a dual image of male powerlessness: not only rendered impotent by the flight of his audience—literally unable to stand erect—he is also, as an African-American, definitively disenfranchised from the privileges of American masculinity.[26] In its opening moments, the novel thus suggests that the successful consolidation of white masculinity through the telling of war stories is less than a paragraph away from emasculation.

Although this opening vignette locates the audience for war stories in other soldiers, *Red Badge* centers its anxieties about audiences on white women. Female characters appear only in the opening chapter of the novel, when Henry says goodbye to his mother and a would-be sweetheart. Later, in a moment of ebullience, he fantasizes reciting his wartime exploits to these same two women:

> [A]s he reviewed the battle pictures he had seen, he felt quite competent to return home and make the hearts of the people glow with stories of war. He could see himself in a room of warm tints telling tales to listeners . . . He saw his gaping audience picturing him as the central figure in blazing scenes, and he imagined the consternation and the ejaculations of his mother and the young lady at the seminary as they drank his recitals. Their vague feminine formula for beloved ones doing brave deeds on the field of battle without risk of life would be destroyed. (74)

This passage uses Henry's self-spectatorship—"He could see himself in a room"—to launch a pleasurable fantasy about women and war stories. Crane posits women as the central members of an admiring and ignorant audience, their "vague feminine formula" of war part of a sentimental culture of the homefront. As their fantasies are "destroyed" by Henry, these women will be gratefully humbled to the point of "consternation."

Elsewhere, however, women provide a less tractable audience for male narration. Henry's mother is less than supportive of military ambitions: "He had burned several times to enlist . . . But his mother had discouraged him. She had affected to look with some contempt upon the quality of his war ardor and patriotism" (7). While his mother fails to perform her authenticating role in the conventions of war, his potential sweetheart is presented in dangerous proximity to a far less inviting young woman: "A certain light-haired girl had made vivacious fun at his martial spirit, but there was another and darker girl whom he had gazed at steadfastly, and he thought she grew demure and sad at the sight of his blue and brass" (9). Together, the "contempt" of his mother and the mockery of the light-haired girl transform the later passage about "battle pictures," for they suggest that Henry's fantasy of female consternation disguises his fears about the possible cruelty of a female audience.

More brutally, Henry's female consumers threaten not only to reject but literally to consume him. Throughout *Red Badge,* Henry's abjection is his absorption. "Deeply absorbed as a spectator" (101), he both looks at and is absorbed by battle; on the verge of flight from battle, "He seemed to shut his eyes and wait to be gobbled" (36) while another soldier worries that the regiment will "git swallowed" (85). Like spectatorship, absorption is linked to women. In the earlier passage, Henry fantasizes happily that his "gaping" female audience "drank his recitals," but the ominous possibilities implicit in this image are later realized: "He fought frantically for respite for his sense, for air, as a babe being smothered attacks the deadly blankets" (31). Unable to consume even the air he needs to breathe, Crane is instead infantilized and smothered, implicitly by his mother. This moment of what one critic terms "maternalized engulfment"—one of many such images in Crane's fiction— carries the gendering of consumption to its logical extreme.[27] Howells's anxieties about women writers and readers here resurface in lethal form. In Crane's Civil War story, the most terrifying figure of all is the murderous mother, both the producer of explosive "ejaculations" and the ultimate female consumer.

As *The Red Badge of Courage* suggests, then, the critical account according to which De Forest or Crane "fathers" the war novel is a defensive one. Critics have not only masculinized but remasculinized the Civil War, constructing it as the apotheosis of literary masculinity from a perceived state of emasculation.[28] Rather than simply ignoring women, this remasculinizing account displaces the female author and reader from their foundational positions within the making of Civil War fiction. Reconceived as a central presence in the literary history of the war, women's Civil War fiction constitutes a rich field for cultural analysis.

We can begin to gauge the literary possibilities of the Civil War by focusing on the term itself. The name of the war was sharply contested from the start, with a profusion of nominal possibilities signaling mutually exclusive partisan views. Northern names like "Great Rebellion" and "War to Save the Union" emphasized the illegitimacy of secession; less commonly, terms like "War to Free the Slaves" foregrounded abolition. By contrast, Southern names like "Second American Revolution," "War of Southern Independence," and "War of Northern Aggression" invoked the legitimizing heritage of the American Revolution and framed the North as invading tyrant. After the war, the federal government officially adopted "War of the Rebellion," enraging white Southerners for decades. "It was not a rebellion, and we were not rebels or traitors," wrote one correspondent to the *Confederate Veteran* in the 1890s, an era of revived protest against this designation. "The 'War of Coercion,' or the 'War Against State Sovereignty' would express it; but the 'Rebellion,' never!"[29] Many Southerners favored "The War Between the States," thereby stressing that the conflict had involved two independent entities rather than one nation undergoing internal dissent. As one Southern senator declared during a 1907 Congressional debate about the name, "It was in no sense a civil war; it was a war between sovereign States."[30] Conversely, "Civil War" emphasized the unitary nation and evacuated any claims for the legitimacy of the Confederate government. The subsequent colloquial rise of "Civil War" thereby cemented a victory for Northern perspectives, reprising military triumph as linguistic hegemony.[31]

Regionally and racially partisan, the competing names of the Civil War also had distinct gender implications. "The War of Northern Aggression," for example, posited the Union army as metaphorical male rapist; more literally, the Southern campaign to replace "War of the Rebellion" with "War Between the States" was led by the white women of the United Daughters of the Confederacy.[32] Less obviously, the term "civil war" encoded a complex set of gender connotations. From "civus," of or pertaining to citizens, "civil" is both a description of political status and a set of behavioral norms. Politically, as the *Oxford English Dictionary* summarizes, "civil" describes "the organization and internal affairs of the body politic, or state" (hence civil rights, civil society). As a description of the state, "civil" is distinguished in military terms (civilian versus soldier) and legal ones (civil versus criminal). The political meanings of "civil" seem quite divorced from its second set of definitions as meaning polite, well-mannered, or well-behaved, often used as a disciplinary imperative (be civil; keep a civil tongue in one's head). Yet the disparate meanings of "civil" are closely related, as an excerpt from the *OED* definition of the term helps to bring into view:

6. Becoming or befitting a citizen . . .

7. Having proper public or social order; well-ordered, orderly, well-governed . . .

8. In that social condition which accompanies . . . citizenship or life in communities; not barbarous; civilized; advanced in the arts of life . . .

9. Educated; well-bred; refined, polished, 'polite'. . .[33]

In this semantic slide from citizenship to refinement, state and individual are implicitly linked by their relation to bodily regulation. On a spectrum of bodies large and small, the well-behaved body politic of civil society differs in degree rather than kind from the well-behaved individual body. The cluster of words that relate to civil—"civility," "civilize," "civilization"—follows from elements of this shared definition. "Civility" and "civilization" are the achieved states, behavioral and social, that result from being civil, while "civilizing" is the process that makes those states possible. The civilized person behaves civilly, is educated about civilization, and is an orderly member of civil society. In the variety of meanings that attach to "civil," the maintenance of order links the polite with the political.

Framing "civil" in this way highlights its relation to gender in nineteenth-century America. As John Kasson has shown, "civility" was a complex and important discourse in this era, encompassing manners, emotions, speech, clothing, household management, public behavior, and modes of cultural consumption.[34] The expression of civility in these arenas functioned most immediately in class terms, as identifying markers of middle-class identity. Like gentility and domesticity, civility was also intimately linked to gender, as a province over which middle-class white women had some authority. To civilize was to domesticate, an equation wherein white women were the civilizing agents of the culture and their training-ground the domestic sphere. In this role, white women were accorded a measure of social power but ambivalently so; their role in what Norbert Elias termed "the civilizing process" was both praised and ridiculed, just as "domestication" implied both comfort and constraint. Refinement could easily become confinement, as in the famous closing lines of Mark Twain's *Huck Finn:* "But I reckon I got to light out for the Territory ahead of the rest, because aunt Sally she's going to adopt me and sivilize me and I can't stand it. I been there before."[35] In a self-sustaining cultural dynamic, Twain's conclusion both dismisses female "sivilizing" as a mode from which Huck must flee and confirms its importance as a process that he, having "been there before," has already internalized.

Mocked as the agents of civility, white women were also disciplined as its objects. An elaborate network of formal prescriptions and informal customs policed female emotions and behavior in the name of civility. Against a model of female civility as restraint, the possibilities for transgressive excess were almost endless. For example, although women were expected to be consistently cheerful and to inspire cheerfulness in others, cheer could easily go too far. In an 1881 etiquette book's prohibition against female laughter in public, the horrors of excess female emotion converge with the hazards of unbounded social space: "Few things are more distasteful than a party of young women making themselves conspicuous in public places by loud talk and laughter." Other etiquette books took aim against female anger. An 1833 etiquette book condemned "an enraged woman" as "one of the most disgusting sights in nature," while an 1859 guide recommended that "terrible fits of anger" could be prevented in the following way: "A looking-glass held before her, to let her see what a shocking object she had made herself, would, we think, have an excellent effect." This emphasis upon mirrors suggests the importance not only of surveillance but of self-surveillance in the maintenance of female civility. The examples cited above are all from etiquette books written by women, and they rely upon mechanisms of self-spectatorship, whether psychologized as emotional self-scrutiny or literalized in the form of the mirror. If female civility highlighted a contrast between civil women and rude men, then it equally depended upon, and in turn created, an internal split between female excess and restraint. Both internally and externally patrolled, the line between civil and uncivil was not so much an absolute divider as an unstable boundary in need of constant fortification by women themselves.[36]

These dynamic contrasts were racially organized as well. In a racist culture that marked "civil" as "not barbarous," whites defined whiteness as the repository of civilization and blackness as its negation. Dehumanized and commodified, African-Americans were brutally excluded from the prerogatives of civility and used as figures against whom whites could demarcate their own access to and performance of these prerogatives. Slaves might be the objects of civilizing efforts by whites, thereby becoming "domesticated" and potentially a civilizing influence for others. Yet even the "good slave" was an unreliable cultural figure for whites, since his behavior might mask that of the traitorous rebel. In response to these racist stereotypes, African-African initiatives for power in both antebellum and postwar periods placed a high premium on civility and civilization. Elias Wood's *The Negro in Etiquette* (1899), for example, articulated a "gospel of civility" for African-Americans. More explicitly political than white versions of civility, African-American initiatives within this discourse, from literacy and education to manners and elocution, were a crucial component of the project of racial uplift.[37]

Black women were at the forefront of this project, forging black civility against both male "rudeness" and white racism. The yields of their work were substantial, particularly at the end of the century, when a flourishing and autonomous black women's political culture encouraged radical uses of civility. Ida B. Wells-Barnett, for example, radically redefined "civilization" as part of her attack on lynching. Yet like the dicta of white women's civility, black women's civility was also self-policing, at once opposed and renewed by the threat of its opposite terms. The combined obligations of emotional and racial uplift were great. As one turn-of-the-century conduct manual for young black women admonished, "If it be true that upon the womanhood of a race depends the manhood of that race, then the whole being of *our* women must be permeated by noble ideas, her fine taste enriched by culture, her tendencies to the beautiful gratified and developed, her singular and delicate nature lifted up to its full capacity." The rest of the guidebook, which was written by a black man, offered a relentless catalogue of prohibitions, warning young black women against the wrong kind of reading, fashion, hygiene, education, husbands, and almost every conceivable form of social misbehavior. With perfect disciplinary precision, this work was entitled *Don't. A Book for Girls.*[38]

Organized along these interlocking grids of gender, race, and class, civility profoundly circumscribed social and psychic possibilities for women in nineteenth-century America. Yet civility was always a contested discourse for women, stimulating what might be termed "civil disobedience"—albeit in a more expansive framework than that of Thoreau, who directed the term to men. The Civil War, as a concentrated moment of social flux, catalyzed and authorized multiple modes of civil disobedience for women. Northern white women, for example, expanded the boundaries of civilian identity through their participation in wartime relief efforts. Mary Livermore, a leader in the United States Sanitary Commission, recalled "the consecrated and organized work of women, who . . . bridged over the chasm between civil and military life."[39] Some Northern women focused not on "the chasm between civil and military life" but on the chasms within civil society that would separate male politics from female politesse. The Woman's National Loyal League, founded in 1863 by Elizabeth Cady Stanton and Susan B. Anthony, agitated for abolition by collecting signatures on a petition to Congress. Invoking the rhetorical tradition of "republican motherhood" developed during the Revolutionary War era, Stanton and Anthony declared, "[I]t is the duty of women to be co-workers . . . in giving immortal life to the NEW nation."[40] Still other Northern white women, however, violated civility not to speed abolition but to fight it. In the New York City Draft Riots, when new Union conscription laws prompted widespread racist resistance, white women were at the forefront of anti-black violence. The "inner civil war" that produced different political positions among Northern male intellectuals also prompted contrasting violations of civility among Northern women as well.[41]

Confederate women were no less disruptive than their Northern counterparts of the norms of civility. White women in New Orleans, for example, responded to the Union army's occupation of the city with rebellious gestures that included spitting at Northern soldiers. Like Northerners, Southern white women also targeted their own government, as in the bread riots initiated by poor women who rejected the official ethos of female self-sacrifice.[42] Already engaged in struggles for freedom, African-American women contested their exclusion from civil society, as well as civility, in a variety of ways. During the Civil War, for example, Harriet Tubman served with celebrated courage and skill as nurse, relief worker, scout, and spy, leading a famous guerrilla raid on the Combahee River area of South Carolina that freed more than seven hundred slaves. Already dubbed "General Tubman" by John Brown, Tubman used the Union army as a new weapon in her fight against slavery. Traditionally confined to the margins of national representation, an African-American woman crossed over race and gender lines to assume the "generalship" of the nation's army.[43]

Without political representation, however, activism offered a limited arena for women's expressions of civil disobedience. Despite her celebrity, Harriet Tubman fought the government for thirty years to receive financial benefits for her wartime service and later won them only because her husband had been a soldier; symbolic national leader, she was still political noncitizen. Susan B. Anthony acknowledged that the signature-collecting of the League was a default strategy, since "Women can neither take the ballot nor the bullet."[44] Northern-based feminist political initiatives were in crisis by the end of the 1860s, fractured by racism, and suffrage for all women remained nearly sixty years away. Some Southern white women translated their wartime activities more directly into postwar life, leading initiatives of Confederate memorialization. Yet these efforts relied on an iconography of female passivity alongside male heroism, one that moved away from involvement in organized feminism and toward the revival of Confederate manhood.[45]

Literary representation, by contrast, provided a far more capacious realm for women—white and African-American, Northern and Southern—to reinvent their relation to national politics. As the Civil War made new kinds of public activity possible for women, it also catalyzed a reconfiguration of literary possibilities for women writers. Nineteenth-century women writers wrote at length about war before 1861; in the thriving genre of historical fiction, for example, dozens of novels by women addressed the American Revolution.[46] The extreme scale, flux, and immediacy of the Civil War, coupled with new forms of female activism and expanded visibility in the wartime literary marketplace, encouraged women to write about their relation to national politics anew. This process, moreover, worked both ways: if women's Civil War writing inserted women in new ways into national stories, it also inserted the symbolic rhetoric of civil war into stories about women. As Margaret R. Higonnet has argued in an important essay on women's civil war fiction, the very idea of rebellion against the state prompts the possibility of sexual disorder. "Once a change in government can be conceived, sexual politics can also become an overt political issue," so that "civil war serves as emblem and catalyst of change in the social prescription of sexual roles." At the same time, the process works in reverse, such that "political relations acquire the color of gender."[47] In literary terms, the effect of civil war on women writers could be dual, moving outward toward national rebellion and inward toward psychic fracture.

When women writers addressed the American Civil War, then, the idea of "civil war" could extend far beyond an opposition between Union and Confederate armies. Most immediately, both North and South were themselves marked by internal dissent, as in border states with divided loyalties. The axis of civil conflict was consistently racial as well as regional, with struggles over black freedom pervading all regions. Class tensions fractured regional unity, with poor whites, for example, resisting official policies. Sexuality was a contested arena in both coerced and consensual modes: rape, for example, could be deployed as a soldier's weapon of war, but heterodox forms of sexuality like same-sex desire also found new expression. Potentially cross-cutting all of these axes of internal conflict were civil wars over gender. The Civil War could frame "battles of the sexes" and female insurrections, but in an era of "sister against sister," it could also generate conflicts between women across race, class, or region.

Moreover, for women writers representing the era, the Civil War could also prompt battles, both psychic and social, against civility. As Robert Penn Warren remarked, in a civil war,

> [A]ll the self-divisions of conflicts within individuals become a series of mirrors within which the plight of the country is reflected, and the self-division of the country a great mirror in which the individual may see imaged his own deep conflicts, not only the conflicts of political loyalties, but those more profoundly personal.[48]

Warren's prototypical "individual" is the white man, but his metaphor of a "great mirror" of national disorder has specific resonance for women under civility's external and internal modes of surveillance. During the Civil War, the mirror—long a pervasive figure for self-scrutiny in women's writing—could reflect a fracturing of female civility as well as national order.[49] In a nation turned upside down, uncivil behavior, such as laughter or anger, might find full expression, whether illicit or authorized. For white Southern women, for example, the aggressive adoption of a new nation, the Confederate States of America, could legitimate the assertive refusal of civility's norms. Conversely, for women writers denied access to the terms of civility, a civil war might be as much a battle for civility as a flight from it. For African-American women depicting struggles for freedom, for example, "civil wars" might center on the liberatory movement from coerced servility to chosen civility.

For any woman writer, finally, a civil war might address the very separation between two ostensibly separate spheres of "civility": private politeness and public politics. As the Civil War itself blurred the literal boundary between homefront and battlefront, so too could it reconfigure—in literary terms at least—the hierarchy that privileged white male citizenship over female civility. And as the war receded from lived event into literary memory, women writers could challenge official commemorations that excluded or trivialized them. Against a rhetoric of national reconciliation intent, as Kathleen L. Diffley has shown, on "making war civil," women could retain the more disruptive legacies of the war to foster their own ongoing incivilities.[50]

In this book, I argue that women writers fully exploited all of these symbolic possibilities in addressing the Civil War. The key to this body of writing is its use of the Civil War as multivalent cultural symbol as well as literal setting. The writers under discussion employ the idea of "civil war" as a metaphor to represent internal rebellions, conflicts, and fractures. The war functions as both historical ground and literary figure in their texts, with the declared antagonism between North and South providing an overarching metaphor for conflicts of gender, sexuality, and race within fictional plots. For the women at the center of these plots, the Civil War symbolically energizes a war within and against the terms of civility. At the same time, I argue, this metaphor is reversible, since the "civil wars" within these novels allegorically reconstruct the Civil War itself, entering into the process by which public understanding of the war had been shaped by fictional metaphors from the start. The texts under discussion take the idea of "civil war" as a point of departure to create new allegories of nationhood. Some writers exploit existing metaphors, such as the injured body politic, the divided house, and the regional romance; some appropriate iconic figures, like Abraham Lincoln and Jefferson Davis, or resonant sites, like Washington, DC, and the war's border states, for specific symbolic uses; and some invest wartime roles—soldier, nurse, spy—with new meaning for women. Together, these works divide the individual and reunite the nation, setting up a reciprocal metaphor between individual body and body politic. Through the rhetoric of internal dissent, women's Civil War fiction articulates reciprocal connections between fictions of nationhood and fantasies about gender.

Several conclusions emerge from my analysis. First, this study affirms the centrality of gender to the construction, political and literary, of nationhood. In these works, the rhetoric of the body politic is never ungendered, and that gendering is seldom stable; civil war emerges as a critical event in the unstable gendering of nationhood. Writing about the American Civil War, women intervened in the "foundational fictions," "invented traditions," "imagined communities," and other modes of nation-building that might otherwise exclude or disempower them. In their writings, the nation often becomes, symbolically speaking, feminized, transvestite, or protolesbian. Manifestly raising issues of gender and sexuality, such alternative nations are equally inseparable from racial formations, whether affirming or contesting racist norms. The resulting literary frameworks do not themselves undo the literal erasure of women from political power in nineteenth- and twentieth-century America, but neither do they leave that erasure intact. At the very least, these interventions into national symbolism render the iconic ironic.[51]

Correspondingly, these texts also shift the gender framework of the American literary canon. Two of the anchoring works of this study, *Uncle Tom's Cabin* and *Gone With the Wind*, have often been denigrated by critics; not coincidentally, both are written by women, populated by female characters, and addressed in large part to women readers. Inverting this traditional dismissal of the popular and the female, I argue for the centrality of these works to literary explorations of Americanness. Stowe and Mitchell created two of what Willie Lee Rose terms the four "most popular reading-viewing events in all American history," along with Griffith's *The Birth of a Nation* and Alex Haley's *Roots*.[52] Leslie Fiedler, in an extended study of these same four texts, identifies them as the "inadvertent epic" of American culture, consistently "rooted in demonic dreams of race, sex and violence."[53] Apart from Stowe and Mitchell, each of the women writers under discussion here is part of this "inadvertent epic," contesting each other as well as more traditionally masculinist literary versions of America. The contrasts between, for example, Elizabeth Keckley and Harriet Beecher Stowe, or between Keckley and Frances Harper, are instructive not only as variations within a subgenre of American women's writing, but also as competing versions of the larger literary project of representing the nation. As a study in women's writing, this is also an exploration of American national identity, and indeed my aim is to suggest that these two topics are related not hierarchically, as margin to center, but as overlapping circles.

Third, as a project in feminist theory, this book argues that women's Civil War writing presents a valuable opportunity to theorize the conceptual interdependence of gender, race, sexuality, and region in a concrete historical frame. At the center of this study is the conflicted intersection of gender and race.[54] For many white Southern women writers, for example, the very language of rebellion that authorizes white female insubordination is often organized through the subordination of black women. Northern white women's texts often reproduce this split, albeit more covertly, through their projection of white fantasies onto black characters. North and South, white women's Civil War texts confirm that white representations of blackness are often self-reflexive meditations on whiteness, or as Toni Morrison elegantly notes, "the subject of the dream is the dreamer."[55] Conversely, many of the African-American writers under discussion, rather than encoding fantasies of identification with white people, often register a desire for distance from them, whether overtly fighting slave mistresses or covertly challenging antislavery allies. Division between black and white women, explicit and implicit, is a major theme of this study, while the inseparability of gender from race is its constant framework.

So too is gender never unmodified by sexuality in these texts. Sexuality is consistently unstable in the disruptive Civil War moment recreated in these texts. Both lesbian possibilities and fantasies of male homosexuality surface, often in dynamic interplay with weakened heterosexual formations. Both orthodox and heterodox sexuality frequently operate as allegorical languages for describing national and regional relationships. The connection between gender and sexuality, like that between gender and race, may itself be in conflict: the text most openly protolesbian in expression, for example, is also the most openly antifeminist. In identifying a tradition of women's writing centered on the conflicts of civil war, I thus analyze the limits of such a project. While the authors under examination all share an exclusion from dominant discourses of nationhood, the terms of that exclusion vary significantly, making this a study not only of diversity within women's writing but also of conflict among women. As such, it tests the profound difficulties involved in invoking a taxonomy of "women's writing"—or of "woman" as category—even as it asserts the continued importance of using such a conceptual frame.

Fourth, these texts suggest that the axes of gender, race, and sexuality are divided not only in relation to each other, but also internally. Like the nation in turmoil during civil war, identity in these works both bifurcates into sharply demarcated zones and contains more ambiguous and liminal "border states." Gender, for example, is an unstable category whose key cultural constructions—femininity and masculinity—are so constantly in flux that the boundaries between them are open to continued dispute. Masculinity is mobile throughout these writings, moving across races and sexes. Images of "masculine women" have different implications in these texts: for example, masculinity may provide a language for imagining women's power, align with literal cross-dressing, or inaugurate protolesbian fantasies. As women are often represented through masculine imagery, so too are the men in these texts frequently feminized. The valences of feminization vary dramatically, from the valorized figures of Uncle Tom and the martyred Civil War soldier through the emasculated images of Ashley Wilkes and Jefferson Davis; Abraham Lincoln is both approvingly and pejoratively feminized. These texts suggest that in a world in which sexual and regional boundaries are volatile, masculinity is as much within the domain of female identity as femininity—if not more so.

Similarly, racial identities are constructed in surprisingly mutable ways in these texts. The hierarchical opposition of black and white is a central feature of this literature, but the terms of this opposition are mutually constitutive, with neither side stably in place. As this study brings masculinity into view, it also focuses on another dominant term: whiteness. In these texts, both whiteness and blackness are constructed categories often separated from white and African-American individuals, and these categories both conflict and combine. Such combinations are most obvious in the case of mixed-race characters, whose bodies literalize the civil war between black and white. Interracial sexuality—not coincidentally, the term "miscegenation" was coined during the Civil War—is a common theme in these texts, and it functions as a metaphor for as well as a linguistic product of the war's many transformations. Racial ambiguities in these texts are also a matter of disguised identity, as in the case of black characters who pass as white, and white characters who are presented in literal or metaphorical blackface; at the furthest reaches of racial cross-identification, characters whose skin is white are represented with putative traits of blackness. As blackness and whiteness dynamically define each other, moreover, they also consistently take shape in relation to other national and ethnic designations. These works include characters who inhabit or assume forms of identity outside the dichotomy of black and white, particularly those of Irish and Cuban nationalities. Such designations blur distinctions between race and ethnicity and further unsettle the unstable boundaries of whiteness. As masculinity and femininity criss-cross in these texts, then, neither whiteness nor blackness is necessarily what it seems.

Finally, these texts provide a model for analyzing conflicts within individual women. As these writers gloss fractures of national identity, so too do they bring into view some deep faultlines, social and psychic, in female subjectivity. These writers' articulations of rebellious self-division, for example, are often at odds with their stabilizing national allegories. Carnivalesque images of freedom from civility coexist in uneasy contradiction with disciplinary fantasies of civilizing the nation. Through the language of civil war, these writers thematize new forms of individual and national identity. Yet they often do so through rhetoric that reinforces internal division. From fractured national identity to split female subjectivity, this book is thus about "civil wars" in many senses: between North and South, black and white, and male and female, but also among women, within women, and between individual and nation.

This broad thematic scope has specific methodological frames. I do not offer a complete survey of women's Civil War writing; neither is this book a comprehensive study of the historical novel as a literary genre. It is, rather, a study of selected literary texts that, in illuminating key themes in women's literary relation to the Civil War, also bring into view particular historical moments. In the nineteenth century, such moments include the 1860s, the era of the war and its immediate aftermath; the late 1870s, the end of Reconstruction; and the 1890s, a period of major historical revisionism about the war. The twentieth-century discussions move toward and away from *Gone With the Wind* (1936), whose narrative draws from versions of the Civil War current in the preceding three decades and whose huge success necessarily marks a turning-point for subsequent Civil War discourse. The Afterword brings the discussion into the present.

In moving across almost a hundred and fifty years, I am mindful of the mutabilities of both historical memory and literary metaphor. As it shifts from lived experience into memory, the Civil War changes over time, becoming an increasingly attenuated presence. Yet there is no simple progression away from an immediate version of the war offered in the 1860s to increasingly remote war stories from later years. The Civil War is remote in some texts of the 1860s and urgent in, for example, many works of the 1890s and 1960s, when its memory and symbolism become freshly energized. The memory of the war is as much a political as a temporal phenomenon, and a Civil War novel of the 1890s is as much about the 1890s as it is about the 1860s—as this study is, of course, in part about the 1990s.

If memory is one form of shifting ground in this study, metaphor constitutes another. By definition, a metaphor is a literary figure of speech that effects an equivalence between two unlike terms; it is composed of two parts, the tenor, which is the thing being described, and the vehicle, which is the mode of description. More generally, metaphors may be visual or verbal, sustained in narrative form or framed in individual moments, organized through abstract images or structured by named icons. This study employs examples from all of these categories, taking the metaphoric implications of the Civil War as broadly as possible. It is a study of metaphor less as a specific aesthetic form than as a connective mode of representation, which brings together spheres—such as female psyche and male nation—that might otherwise be culturally distinct. As these texts offer literary renditions of history, so too do they situate metaphor historically. The history of the Civil War and the aesthetics of the literary metaphor intersect, in this study, in the sphere of cultural representation.

Finally, the focus of this book is fiction, though not in the strictest literary definition of the genre. Two chapters are anchored to works, by Elizabeth Keckley and Loreta Velazquez, that present themselves as autobiographical nonfiction. Yet fiction, more broadly conceived of, remains a defining term for all the works in this study. Both the Keckley and Velazquez texts contain elements of novelistic form: Keckley's includes elements of both war and sentimental fiction, while Velazquez's resembles the picaresque novel. More important, both texts were condemned as fictional, in the sense of inauthentic. In Keckley's case, this judgment was linked not only to her scandalous assertions about Abraham and Mary Todd Lincoln, for whom she had worked, but to her race. As an African-American, Keckley faced the mistrust of a racist culture that treated black authorship as an anomalous phenomenon in need of white authentication. For Loreta Velazquez, who claimed to have cross-dressed as a male soldier in the war, the charge of sensationalism was centered on her violation of gender norms. Condemnations of her autobiography implicitly equated an inauthentic text and an inauthentic gender. As I suggest in the Afterword, this anxious equation surfaces with startling similarity in today's cases of women who cross-dress in Civil War reenactments. From the 1860s to the present, women have been in the domain of Civil War fiction, whether they wanted to be or not.

The first chapter establishes the framework for these arguments through a reconsideration of *Uncle Tom's Cabin*, situating the novel at the nexus of both individual and national civil wars. Stowe's ethos of feminization, I suggest, is fractured by internal conflict, organized through the figure of Topsy. Moreover, in the topsy-turvy approach to and aftermath of sectional conflict, both Stowe and Topsy served as allegorical templates for competing versions of the Civil War nation. Chapter 2 addresses the implications of wartime topsy-turvyness in the fiction of one of Stowe's successors, Louisa May Alcott. Throughout her career (1860s–1880s), Alcott repeatedly recreates two cross-gendered figures, the feminized Civil War soldier and the masculinized female nurse. Together, these figures give voice to Alcott's own incivilities and offer an allegorical reconstruction of the postwar nation in which men are trained as little women.

In chapter 3, I turn to African-American women's Civil War writing of the 1860s, focusing on *Behind the Scenes; or, Thirty Years a Slave and Four Years in the White House* (1868), Elizabeth Keckley's memoir of her upbringing in slavery and career as fashion designer and confidante to the Lincolns during the Civil War. Foregrounding the "border states" of this text, I argue that Keckley wages a covert civil war against Mary Todd Lincoln and others through her symbolic representation of the production and consumption of clothing. Clothing remains a central theme in the next chapter, which examines narratives of women who cross-dressed as male soldiers in the war, particularly Loreta Velazquez's *The Woman in Battle* (1876), purportedly the memoir of a cross-dressed Confederate soldier. I argue that cross-dressing in this text is an explosive point of exchange, bringing together a nation split between regions and races and individuals divided among sexes and sexualities. Despite Velazquez's devotion to the Confederacy, her narrative inadvertently threatens the racial and sexual mythologies of the postwar South.

The contested racial legacy of the war at the end of the century informs the next chapter, which assesses Frances Harper's *Iola Leroy; or, Shadows Uplifted* (1892) in the context of contemporary African-American commentaries on the war. A radical challenge to the racist war mythologies that were to culminate in D. W. Griffith's *The Birth of a Nation, Iola Leroy* is also, I suggest, a novel about turn-of-the-century discourses of black civility. *Iola Leroy* suggests the heightened value of the discourse of civility for those denied access to it, but it also reveals the internal conflicts this discourse produces and is produced from. Chapter 6 picks up the inheritance of *Birth of a Nation* in the most influential twentieth-century account of the war: Margaret Mitchell's *Gone With the Wind* (1936). As in Loreta Velazquez's Confederate war story, identity is surprisingly mobile in Mitchell's novel, with whiteness and heterosexuality, as well as masculinity, open to transformation and masquerade. The result, I argue, is a novel whose central romance plot functions interracially, with Scarlett and Rhett engaging in a civil war that metaphorically interweaves racial as well as sexual fantasies.

In the Afterword, I turn briefly to three more recent examples of the ongoing entanglements between the Civil War and women. Two literary works, Rosellen Brown's novel *Civil Wars* (1984) and June Jordan's essay "Civil Wars" (1980), bring the metaphoric resonances of earlier women's texts into the present, as do the stories of women who cross-dress as soldiers in contemporary Civil War reenactments. Like women writers, these reenactors continue to reshape the meanings of "civil war" in ways startlingly similar to their nineteenth-century counterparts. Then as now, women's fictions of the Civil War are more divisible than invisible, and the war itself is less unwritten than unending.

ONE

⊰𝒯𝑜𝑝𝑠𝑦 - 𝒯𝑢𝑟𝑣𝑦

Civil War and *Uncle Tom's Cabin*

I

The most influential Civil War novel was written a decade before declared sectional conflict actually began. Abraham Lincoln's apotheosis of Harriet Beecher Stowe as "the little woman who made this great war" secured this status for *Uncle Tom's Cabin* (1852), but even apart from its presidential imprimatur, Stowe's novel holds a central place in the culture of the Civil War— as it does in nineteenth-century writings by women. As Elizabeth Ammons has argued, Stowe's influence on subsequent American women writers is "impossible to overemphasize," an influence already apparent to nineteenth-century critics of women's fiction. In her 1891 essay "Woman in Literature," for example, Helen Gray Cone gave special praise to Stowe. After the success of *Uncle Tom's Cabin,* wrote Cone, "the old sense of ordained and inevitable weakness on the part of 'the female writer' became obsolete. Women henceforth, whatever their personal feelings in regard to this much-discussed book, were enabled, consciously or unconsciously, to hold the pen more firmly, to move it more freely." If Lincoln credited Stowe with having unmade the nation, then Cone suggests that she had remade the woman writer.[1]

Unsurprisingly, in the genre that combines these two realms—women's Civil War writing—Stowe's impact is unavoidable. In the majority of women's writings about the war, *Uncle Tom's Cabin* makes an appearance, as passing citation, extended reference, or implicit intertext. Crossing gender, race, and region, these appearances are as visible in the writings of Stowe's enemies as of her allies. Stowe functions as a literary goad, for example, in Florence O'Connor's virulently pro-Confederate novel, *The Heroine of the Confederacy* (1864), which condemns "wealthy, ill-dressed, ill-bred Northern aristocrats who fill our hotels during the winter . . . and then return home to the North to write of 'Legrees' and 'Uncle Toms.'" For O'Connor, this condemnation becomes the foundation of Southern self-representation: "In future, we shall paint and draw our own [portrait], even should we be considered somewhat egotistic for so doing."[2] Stowe is equally catalytic in the more equivocal diaries of Mary Chesnut, written in the 1860s and heavily revised in the 1880s. In Chesnut's constant references to Stowe, the Northern writer is often aggravating, sometimes insightful, but always productive of Chesnut's own prose. "Without emulating Mrs. Stowe, how can I tell Wade's tales," she queries after a friend's visit; "And now for a document à la Stowe," another story begins.[3] Throughout the diaries, Stowe is Chesnut's indispensable interlocutor, as she is in much of women's Civil War writing. Any analysis of this writing, then, inevitably has two beginnings: the start of the war and the publication of *Uncle Tom's Cabin.*

To introduce my interpretation of this dual beginning, I would like to return briefly to the meeting between Lincoln and Stowe, an event that remains widely cited but strangely unexamined. For one thing, Lincoln's comment, while allegedly made in 1862, did not become widely known until 1897, the year after Stowe's death, when Annie Adams Fields reported in her biography of the writer that "It was left for others to speak of Mrs. Stowe's interview with President Lincoln. Her daughter was told that when the President heard her name he seized her hand, saying, 'Is this the little woman who made this great war?'"[4] At the time, no one recorded Lincoln's actual greeting—or, for that matter, Stowe's response. However, as Joan D. Hedrick notes, both the writer and her daughter Hatty, who was present at the meeting, were at least clear about the tone of the event. "I had a real funny interview with the President," wrote Stowe to her husband Calvin. Describing the meeting to her twin sister, Hatty was more forthcoming: "It was a very droll time that we had at the White house I assure you . . . it was all very funny—and we were ready to explode with laughter all the while . . . [When we got back] we perfectly screamed and held our sides while we relieved ourselves of the pent up laughter that had almost been the cause of death."[5]

What was so funny? Stowe had embarked for Washington with characteristic seriousness, concerned about the health of her son Fred, whose Union regiment was stationed there, and with Lincoln's commitment to abolition: "I am going to Washington . . . to satisfy myself that I may refer to the Emancipation Proclamation as a reality & a substance not to fizzle out at the little end of the horn."[6] She would shortly begin a new series of essays for the *Atlantic,* the "House and Home Papers," as an antidote for her own depleted resources, describing her wish for "a sort of spicy sprightly writing that I feel I need to write in these days to keep from thinking of things that make me dizzy & blind & fill my eyes with tears so that I can't see the paper . . .

It is not wise that all our literature should run in a rut cut thro our hearts &
red with our blood."[7] If she and her daughter barely kept from "laughing to
death" while with the president, Stowe was otherwise blinded by tears for the
Union dead.[8]

Whatever the president said to make mother and daughter laugh so hard,
however, we may interpret the "real funny" tone of the meeting between Stowe
and Lincoln as evidence of a more general peculiarity. Then as now, the rhetorical force of Lincoln's greeting relied on the absurdity, if not the outright
hilarity, of the idea that "a little woman" might have a formative impact on
a "great war." In antebellum America, war was to be made, literally and rhetorically, by men, as suggested in the exhortation by Stowe's brother Henry Ward
Beecher to "manhood,—*manhood*,—MANHOOD." As feminist critics have
shown, an alternative cultural rhetoric in this era capitalized upon femininity
rather than masculinity, privileging white women's ability to control the inner
spaces of household, mind, and heart. To Stowe's sister Catharine, for example, women were "the conservators of the domestic state," holding "grand office as the educator of the mind."[9] Despite the cultural influence of this rhetoric of domesticity, however, the nation's literal office-holders and voters were
men. Henry himself was an advocate of woman suffrage, but neither feminist
initiatives nor the influence of feminization fundamentally dislodged the actual
power vested in white men in nineteenth-century America.[10]

Yet if brotherly "manhood" trumped sisterly "feminization," these political
rhetorics were nonetheless closely related. Henry and Harriet once playfully
cross-dressed in each other's clothes, with Henry becoming "the 'very spit and
image' of Harriet" and Harriet appearing as "a more than passable Beecher
youth."[11] So too was there potential for gender cross-over between male and
female cultural spheres. In Lincoln's oratory, for example, the house is an image of some gender flexibility. Its masculine connotations emerge in the famous "House Divided" speech of 1858, which includes both "A house divided
against itself cannot stand"—a phrase adapted from the Gospels—and another house metaphor:

> [W]hen we see a lot of framed timbers, different portions of which we know have
> been gotten out at different times and places and by different workmen . . . and
> when we see these timbers joined together, and see they exactly make the frame
> of a house or a mill . . . we find it impossible to not *believe* that . . . all worked
> upon a common *plan* or *draft* drawn up before the first lick was struck.[12]

In this passage, the house is a metaphor for Lincoln's suspicions that proslavery
politicians were conspiring against him; its rhetorical intricacies together pre-

sent the house as a structure literally built by men, in the male worlds of politics
and commerce. Yet Lincoln's rhetoric of the house could also draw from the
feminized sphere of the household. In a speech from the campaign of 1860,
for example, he promised that "If the Republican party of this nation shall
ever have the national house entrusted to its keeping, it will be the duty of
that party to attend to all the affairs of national housekeeping."[13] This image
focuses on the inside rather than the outside of the house, its domestic economy rather than its commercial status. Within the male sphere of presidential
oratory, Lincoln could shift from the construction of the house by men to its
maintenance by women.[14]

While Lincoln's antebellum rhetoric potentially moved domesticity from
nation to home, Harriet Beecher Stowe exploited this meeting-ground in reverse, turning women's role as domestic "conservator" into activist critique of
domestic national politics. The success of *Uncle Tom's Cabin* was a phenomenon not only because it "set all Northern women crying and sobbing over the
sorrows of Sambo," as George Templeton Strong observed, but also and more
powerfully because it sent men into the world of the domestic novel, positioning them anew as sobbing readers.[15] Despite his frequent disagreements with
Stowe, William Lloyd Garrison acknowledged the "frequent moistening of
our eyes, and the making of our heart grow liquid as water, and the trembling
of every nerve within us" in response to the novel.[16] Stowe's meeting with
Lincoln attests to her novel's ability not only to liquefy male interiors but also
to propel its author into the inner chambers of presidential power. The First
Lady of domestic novels, she was now admitted to the White House itself,
a space that served as both the home of the President and the symbolic center
of the domestic nation.

Yet if Stowe's meeting with Lincoln suggests her passage over the threshold
separating male and female "houses," it also testifies to the lines of racial hierarchy structuring both forms of domestic space. As Stowe's celebrity derived
from her authority to represent the "sorrows of Sambo," her very access to the
president was inseparable from her privilege as a member of the white New
England cultural elite. This racial privilege comes more clearly into view when
contrasted with the meeting between the president and another celebrated
woman of the Civil War era: Sojourner Truth. Popular accounts of this 1864
encounter pictured Lincoln treating Truth respectfully and consulting her on
matters of policy; an 1894 painting of the event posed the two together, with
Lincoln sitting deferentially below Truth. As Carleton Mabee and Nell Irvin
Painter have shown, however, Truth was actually unable to secure an appoint-
ment with the president without the combined efforts of Lucy Colman, a
white abolitionist, and Elizabeth Keckley, the Lincolns' African-American

clothing designer and confidante. Truth was kept waiting for several hours before seeing the president, who probably conversed only briefly with her. On at least one other occasion, she was not permitted to attend a White House reception. Although both Stowe and Truth became cultural icons, known for their proximity to the president, Truth struggled against the closed door of a presidential house that was symbolically as well as literally white.[17]

Stowe and Truth held different amounts of power not only in their access to the president but also in their own relationship. Truth's public reputation grew substantially because of Stowe, whose 1863 *Atlantic* profile "The Libyan Sibyl" introduced her to a wide Northern audience. In keeping with abolitionist rhetoric, Stowe honored Truth through the stereotypical language of romantic racialism; Truth's singing, for example, "seemed to impersonate the fervor of Ethiopia, wild, savage, hunted of all nations." Stowe also turned Truth into an artistic object, the "living, breathing impersonation" of one statue and the source of another.[18] Immured in marble, the black woman came to life caricatured as a symbol of primitive courage. Animating Truth as slavery's "sibyl," Stowe simultaneously authorized herself. As Patricia R. Hill has shown, the Civil War was a period of prolific and self-aware literary production for Stowe, and this essay helped the writer consolidate her own status as political authority and cultural arbiter.[19]

Yet Truth consistently played an active role in the construction of her own image, manipulating the terms in which Stowe and other white women described her. During this period, Truth employed distinctive forms of self-representation, such as the *carte-de-visite* photographs of herself she began selling during the war and her "Book of Life," the volume in which she kept autographs of famous people she had met. As Carla L. Peterson argues, these photographs and autographs conferred considerable authority, if not authorship, on Truth herself.[20] Truth's dictated descriptions of her Civil War activities also suggest her agency. Here is her account of an 1862 pro-Union rally in Indiana, as dictated to white abolitionist Frances Titus:

> The ladies thought I should be dressed in uniform as well as the captain of the home guard . . . So they put upon me a red, white, and blue shawl, a sash and apron to match, a cap on my head with a star in front, and a star on each shoulder. When I was dressed I looked in the glass and was fairly frightened. Said I, "It seems I am going to battle."
>
> . . . As we neared the court-house . . . I saw that the building was surrounded by a great crowd. . . . But when the rebels saw such a mighty army coming, they fled, and by the time we arrived . . . not one was left but a small boy, who sat upon the fence, crying "Nigger, nigger!" We now marched into the court-house, escorted

by double files of soldiers with presented arms. The band struck up the "Star-Spangled Banner," in which I joined and sang with all my might.[21]

This story offers a struggle over representation centered on the iconography of the American flag, which became a highly politicized symbol of the Union during the war, celebrated in rituals that were often led by white women.[22] As this anecdote begins, white women costume Sojourner Truth in the colors of the flag, coercively animating her as a national icon—as her biographers had controlled her textually—and alienating her from her own mirror-image. Yet Truth turns the shock of her body's symbolic status into a foundation for militarized power. Alongside other soldiers, she joins the "mighty army" advancing triumphantly to the courthouse—an army so mighty that it diminishes racism into the impotent form of a small crying boy. At the end of the story, she turns the flag from imposed costume to chosen song, laying claim to her own vocal authority over "The Star-Spangled Banner." In this moment at least, she dictates her story politically as well as orally, reshaping her own iconic status through the iconography of the Civil War.

As the comparison between the presidential meetings with Stowe and Truth suggests, then, the Civil War that Harriet Beecher Stowe discussed with Abraham Lincoln was structured not only by regional conflict but also by less visible internecine tensions between fiction and politics, men and women, and black and white women; by the implicit contrast between the war as contemporary event and its later reconstruction through memory; and by the unresolved incongruity, within descriptions of Stowe's meeting with the president, between the pleasures of unrestrained hilarity and the pressures of self-restraint. These tensions all circulate, I suggest, in the legacy of *Uncle Tom's Cabin,* a legacy comprised not only of Stowe's original novel but also of the plays, songs, poems, toys, and other redactions it prompted. In this chapter, I take Lincoln's tribute to Stowe seriously, interpreting *Uncle Tom's Cabin* as a cultural artifact of, if not actually about, the Civil War. *Uncle Tom's Cabin* not only prepared for literal sectional conflict but articulated two other forms of "civil wars" more broadly defined. Two related forms of internal fracture, I argue, structure Stowe's novel and its reception in Civil War America: the psychic rebellions within nineteenth-century white femininity and the unstable rhetoric of the masculine nation at war with itself.

I begin with the faultlines within *Uncle Tom's Cabin,* arguing that Stowe's advocacy of feminization to combat slavery opens up an internal war against white women's civility. Like the national struggle, this internal war is organized along racial lines, with the racist fantasy of unruly blackness serving as the inverted counterpart to the constraints of white femininity. The emblem of this unruliness is the character of Topsy, whose importance remains surprisingly underexamined in the critical industry devoted to *Uncle Tom's Cabin.* As the novel's stage history helps to illuminate, Topsy constitutes a blackface projection of white femininity, in which inversion is at once utopian fantasy and demonized grotesque.

From Stowe's antebellum construction of Topsy, I turn to the rhetoric of "topsy-turvyness" within the political culture of the Civil War era. Briefly surveying this culture, I focus on an 1863 Confederate play, *The Royal Ape,* which represents Northern defeat through images of racial and gender inversion in the Lincoln White House and on the Civil War battlefield. Both antebellum and postwar responses to *Uncle Tom's Cabin,* I then suggest, similarly construct sectional relationships through metaphors of inversion, as effected by Stowe herself and enacted through her character of Topsy. I focus on three examples from the decade leading up to the war—from white Southerners, white Northerners, and black Northerners—to show some of the ways in which both Stowe and Topsy functioned as allegorical representations of the nation.

Finally, moving to the aftermath of the war, I compare two texts that articulate contrasting uses of Stowe and Topsy at the end of the century. In *The Leopard's Spots,* Thomas Dixon avenges the topsy-turvy Southern world created by Stowe, the Union army, and emancipation; in *A Voice from the South,* Anna Julia Cooper turns Stowe's own imagery of Topsy upside down. Internally divided from the start, *Uncle Tom's Cabin* stages civil wars that were later reproduced on a national scale in struggles over the memory of the Civil War itself.

II

As feminist critics have argued, *Uncle Tom's Cabin* articulates its attack on slavery through strategies of plot and characterization that center on the redemptive possibilities of feminization. The novel's ethos of what Jane Tompkins terms "sentimental power" privileges maternal love, compassion, and tears, but the potential for people to be feminized, and to feminize others, is not limited to mothers. This potential extends across generations to Little Eva, across gender to St. Clare, and across race to Uncle Tom, who functions, in Elizabeth Ammons's words, as the novel's "true heroine." Feminization is also closely linked to the novel's idealized domestic spaces of the Quaker living room, the little girl's bedroom, and the slave's kitchen. Replicating the psyche on a larger scale, these domestic spaces constitute a microcosmic model for resolving the national "house divided." Conjoining psyche, house, and nation,

Stowe advocates a feminization of American culture whose source is female sentiment and whose goal is abolition.[23]

Yet as critics have noted since the novel's publication, this sweeping vision of redeeming woman and redeemed nation is severely limited in racial terms. Stowe rejects slavery but replicates racial stereotypes, privileging light-skinned over dark-skinned black characters. Black women in the novel have unequal access to its ethos of feminization; as Hortense Spillers puts it, characters like Aunt Chloe and Topsy "are granted *no* vocality."[24] The role of black men in this vision is anxiously circumscribed and utterly restricted by novel's end. As one black newspaper summarized in 1852, "Uncle Tom must be killed, George Harris exiled! Heaven for dead Negroes! Liberia for living mulattoes. Neither one can live on the American continent."[25] This closed continental border also reflects Stowe's ambivalence toward contemporary uprisings in Europe, which she regarded as too violent. Her novel is thus domestic in a restrictive as well as expansive sense: enlarging the feminized household to the size of the male nation, she expels blackness, along with revolution, outside of domestic national space.[26]

Interpretations of *Uncle Tom's Cabin* have tended to separate these two strands of critique, celebrating the novel's gender dynamics or condemning its racial ones. My interest is in showing how the racial dynamics of *Uncle Tom's Cabin* operate *within* its vision of feminization. It is not only that the novel's depiction of black people is racist, but also that racial fantasies structure the internal operations of whiteness in Stowe's narrative. As Stowe stabilizes national conflict through the displacement of revolution, her model of feminization emerges only through her circumscription of internal forms of psychic rebellion. Countercurrents of uncontrollable female anger and unmanageable female comedy run throughout *Uncle Tom's Cabin*, with both impulses centered on African-American women characters. These characters constitute fantasies about white women as well as black women. As Toni Morrison observes, "The fabrication of an Africanist persona is reflexive; an extraordinary meditation on the self; a powerful exploration of the fears and desires that reside in the writerly conscious."[27] In *Uncle Tom's Cabin*, the fabrication of Topsy offers a reflexive commentary on the culture of nineteenth-century white women's America as well as the "fears and desires" of Harriet Beecher Stowe.

Throughout *Uncle Tom's Cabin*, black women threaten as well as fulfill the terms of Stowe's abolitionism. Maternal anger, for example, is central to Stowe's didactic project, and Eliza exemplifies the productive uses of such anger when she saves her son: "[S]tronger than all was maternal love, wrought into a paroxysm of frenzy by the near approach of a fearful danger."[28] Yet this "paroxysm of frenzy" may be less controlled, as in the case of Cassy, who shows "fierce pride and defiance in every line of her face" (501) and whose fury at being separated from her children causes a far more dangerous reaction: "It seemed to me something in my head snapped, at that moment. I felt dizzy and furious. I remember seeing a great sharp bowie-knife on the table; I remember something about catching it, and flying upon him; and then all grew dark" (520). Cassy's anger is so unconscionable that she literally loses consciousness; later, in fulfillment of this fury, she kills her newborn child rather than subject him to slavery. Reunited with her surviving children, Cassy is ultimately re-inserted into a more conventional plot, but the force of her anger cannot be so easily assimilated. As critics have noted, Cassy literalizes the story of *Jane Eyre's* Bertha Mason when she haunts Legree from his attic. Like Bertha, Cassy remains a threat to the overall narrative, signaling the hauntingly inadmissible excess within Stowe's plots of individual and national redemption.[29]

Closely aligned with this excessive anger are the novel's comic impulses, again expressed in or by its black female characters. Dinah "[scorns] logic and reason in every shape" (310), and her kitchen resists "systematic regulation" of any kind (312).[30] This illogic takes corporeal form in the character of Topsy. In her first appearance, Topsy stands before Miss Ophelia and St. Clare with her mouth "half open with astonishment at the wonders of the new Mas'r's parlor," her hair "braided in sundry little tails, which stuck out in every direction" and her clothing "a single filthy, ragged garment, made of bagging" (351). Open-mouthed, unkempt, and filthy, Topsy incarnates the black body as comic grotesque, in behavior as well as appearance. No sooner is she introduced than St. Clare orders her to perform:

> The black, glassy eyes glittered with a kind of wicked drollery, and the thing struck up, in a clear shrill voice, an odd negro melody, to which she kept time with her hands and feet, spinning round, clapping her hands, knocking her knees together, in a wild, fantastic sort of time, and producing in her throat all those odd guttural sounds which distinguish the native music of her race. (352)

A spectacle positioned for white amusement, Topsy is represented as an inhuman "thing." Her "black, glassy eyes" are to be seen rather than to see, and her voice makes "odd guttural sounds" rather than intelligible speech. The many stage versions of *Uncle Tom's Cabin* consistently highlighted Topsy's role as comic buffoon, with the character becoming, as Patricia Turner puts it, "the first truly famous pickaninny." The legacy of this characterization is one of incontrovertible racism.[31]

To understand Topsy, it is important to see her not only as the object of contemptuous humor for white audiences but also as a constitutive feature of white fantasy, as constructed in Stowe's novel and circulating throughout American culture in theatrical and other forms. Topsy exemplifies what Peter Stallybrass and Allon White, anatomizing forms of hierarchy, characterize as the "low-Other," a figure who is "despised and denied at the level of political organization and social being whilst it is instrumentally constitutive of the shared imaginary repertoires of the dominant culture." The "low-Other" consistently takes certain forms, such as the grotesque and the carnivalesque, that threaten dominant culture not simply by inverting its norms, but also by enacting its internal fantasies. This staging of fantasy, as Stallybrass and White argue, is inherently dynamic, at once recuperable and destabilizing. The relationship between discipline and carnival—the theoretical legacies, loosely speaking, of Foucault and Bakhtin—is one of mutual reinforcement, but also of mutual threat.[32]

Within *Uncle Tom's Cabin,* Topsy similarly challenges, even as she renews, social norms—a challenge encoded in her name. Like the idea of "the world turned upside down," "topsy-turvy," a term in place in Britain since the mid-sixteenth century, could connote a disruption of political order. In the United States, the term was commonly used to describe the disruptions of the American Revolution. Loyalist Peter Oliver, for example, lamented a "material World . . . turned topsey turvey" during the Revolution and predicted "a similar Rotation" of political hierarchies. For those who enjoyed such "Rotations," revolution could involve the deliberate inversion of political norms through their precise mimicry. John Adams, for example, described a habit among revolutionary patriots of "reversing the Picture of King G. 3d . . . One of these Topsy Turvy Kings was hung up in the room, where we supped."[33] In *Uncle Tom's Cabin,* forms of mimicry and rotation pervade every aspect of Topsy's daily life: "Her talent for every species of drollery, grimace, and mimicry,— for dancing, tumbling, climbing, singing, whistling, imitating every sound that hit her fancy,—seemed inexhaustible" (364). Topsy also takes the idea of inversion one step further, when she answers the question "Who was your mother?" with the claim, "Never had none" (355) and asserts that "nobody never made me" (356). Not simply the unruly child mocking her parents—like the patriots who rehang the portrait of King George—she admits no parental origins at all. The revolutionary Sons of Liberty have become nobody's daughter.[34]

Like her mimicry and "tumbling," Topsy's denial of origins enfolds angry resistance within comedy. African-American culture of this period includes numerous comic figures who encode resistance to slavery, from the trickster folktales featuring the wily Br'er Rabbit, which were later codified and reframed by Joel Chandler Harris, to the willed misbehavior of the child Frado in Harriet Wilson's *Our Nig,* whom Carla L. Peterson links to Topsy.[35] Topsy is a product of white fantasy, but within the racist framework in which she is delineated, she too incarnates resistance to white governance. This trait is emphasized by one English reviewer of the play, who declared that "At one moment she is stubborn, insensate, and unimpressionable—anon, she flies into an ungovernable, almost demoniac rage."[36] "Demoniac rage" is the dorsal side to Topsy's comedy, as the back of her own body belies her smiling face: "on the back and shoulders of the child [were] great welts and calloused spots, ineffaceable marks of the system under which she had grown up thus far" (355). One of the novel's reviewers aptly termed Topsy "a sort of infantine Caliban," an analogy that illuminates the political potential for resistance in her ostensibly comic behavior.[37] A recent theatrical revision of *Uncle Tom's Cabin* by African-American playwright Robert Alexander, *I Ain't Yo' Uncle,* brilliantly highlights such potential, turning Topsy into an inner-city African-American whose antisocial anger is the direct result of the racist society in which she has been raised.[38]

If Topsy is Caliban, however, then who is Prospero? The obvious candidate is the white male slaveowner who has made the "ineffaceable marks of the system" on Topsy's back. Such a figure is implicit in the opening scene of *Uncle Tom's Cabin,* when Harry, Eliza's young son, mimics his white master in a performance for white slavetraders: "Instantly the flexible limbs of the child assumed the appearance of deformity and distortion, as, with his back humped up, and his master's stick in his hand, he hobbled about the room . . . in imitation of an old man" (44). Harry takes "his master's stick in his hand," but in the case of Topsy, we can see Prospero in the form of Stowe's preferred magician-rulers: the white women, like herself, whose feminizing force will overturn slavery. Topsy's mimicry represents not only a "deformity and distortion" of the world of the white male slaveowner but an imitation of white femininity. As Cassy literally kills her child, Topsy rhetorically kills her mother, with both characters violating the novel's ultimate piety: its apotheosis of motherhood. In a narrative whose emblem of order is that of the civilizing mother, the figures of greatest disorder, both black, are the murdering mother and the matricidal daughter. Together, they offer a racially specific version of what Mary Russo terms the "female grotesque."[39]

We may interpret this grotesquerie as both particular to Stowe and representative of larger stresses within white New England middle-class women's culture. Stowe's advocacy of the redemptive force of motherhood drew on her status as mother of seven, but her actual experience of motherhood was marked by her own ill health, domestic obligations, financial worries, and fatal losses. When Stowe began *Uncle Tom's Cabin,* Hedrick suggests, she was fueled by her feelings of personal grief over the recent death of her son Charley as well as her anger at the injustices of slavery.[40] The author's presence can be tracked through her novel along different routes. Lora Romero, for example, argues that *Uncle Tom's Cabin* articulates a parallel between the suffering slave and the hysterical housewife, a parallel rooted in the author's episodes of nervous collapse.[41] W. T. Lhamon, Jr., suggests an identification between the author and the child Harry Harris, whom Eliza later cross-dresses as a girl and re-names "Harriet" to protect from returning to slavery.[42] Topsy offers another fictional mirror for Stowe, as suggested in an account of Harriet at age eight: "Harriet makes just as many wry faces, is just as odd, and loves to be laughed at as much as ever."[43] In her adult life, Stowe's comic misbehavior resurfaced in her descriptions of the black people with whom she had the closest relations: her women servants. Stowe wrote that she "had many frolics & capers" with one woman, Dine; she remembered another, Aunt Frankie, for her "hilarious hearty laugh."[44] Such phrases suggest that Stowe conceived of black women as her companions in comic release, a relationship she represented in *Uncle Tom's Cabin* through the figure of Topsy. One Southern critic noted that Stowe had "translated herself in fancy to the cottonfields of the South as a slave, and then interrogated herself as to how she felt."[45] In the self-reflexive narrative of *Uncle Tom's Cabin*, Topsy is one feature of Stowe's self-translation.

More generally, Topsy reveals the racial organization of emotional labor within the cultural ideal of domesticity. As white women's literal domestic workers, black women "domestics" potentially performed their emotional work as well.[46] In a culture that mandated civility for middle-class white women, black women could form a conduit for white women's psychic release and a screen onto which they could project their impulses toward incivility. In *Uncle Tom's Cabin*, Topsy is one such screen, reflecting white womanhood back to itself. In particular, Topsy's talent for mimicry exposes white women's propriety as constructed performance, destabilizing the white original from which she draws her copy. This mimicry, however, has its limits, since Topsy never appears as other than "the blackest of her race"; her behavior is distinct from other moments in the novel when characters successfully disguise their identities, such as Eliza's cross-dressing and George's impersonation of a Spanish nobleman.[47] Unlike Eliza and George, who pass up and out of the South, the ineffaceably black Topsy is one of "those low negroes" (356), associated with southward movement within the South itself; asked whether she understands the biblical Fall, she insists that she "came down from Kentuck" (368). As Diane Roberts, adapting the terms of Stallybrass and White, persuasively argues, the South functioned for Stowe as the "low-Other" of the national body politic, "'down there' the way the stomach, the bowels, and the genitals are 'down there.'"[48] Firmly located within the nation's lower depths, Topsy corpo-realizes white female rebellion pushed "downward" through psychic repres-sion, racial differentiation, and geographic displacement. Mimic of white women's propriety, she both voices fantasies of inversion and keeps them rec-ognizably at bay.

The theatrical history of the role of Topsy illuminates her relation to white women's fantasies. Theatrical incarnations of Topsy exemplified excess, both in the exaggerated content of the role and in her number of appearances on stage. As time went on, Topsies multiplied, and companies devoted to staging the play began to include two, three, or four Topsies. All of these Topsies were embodiments of white fantasy: until late in the century, Topsy, like the play's other black characters, was portrayed by white actors in blackface, and this tradition continued into the twentieth century with film versions of Topsy played by, among others, Judy Garland and Betty Grable. While theatrical stagings of *Uncle Tom's Cabin* were distinct from minstrel shows per se, they were a hybrid combination of minstrelsy and melodrama, and Topsy was one of the play's most direct links to the minstrel tradition. This link is forged in the novel when St. Clare explains his purchase of Topsy, "I thought she was rather a funny specimen in the Jim Crow line" (352); a major character in the minstrel show, the "Jim Crow" character symbolized a Southern plantation rustic, set off against his Northern counterpart, the dandy "Zip Coon." As endlessly proliferating figures of comic excess, stage Topsies exaggerated rather than invented the cross-racial fantasies of minstrelsy, fantasies that Stowe her-self had already set in place.[49]

Like other forms of blackface, this history offers a complex mixture of what Eric Lott has termed "love and theft" or the "dialectical flickering of racial insult and racial envy." Examining the all-male minstrel troupe, Lott's primary interest is in the instabilities of white masculinity revealed by minstrelsy.[50] The theatrical history of Topsy, however, suggests the importance of blackface for mirroring transgressive images of white femininity. Such transgressions moved in two directions. First, stage Topsies represented a vision of girlhood freed from femininity into masculinity. In general, theatrical adaptations of Stowe's novel focused on its men; Mrs. Shelby, Mrs. Bird and Rachel Halliday, for example, were all eliminated, undercutting Stowe's emphasis on the feminiz-ing force of women.[51] Consistently preserved in stage versions of *Uncle Tom's Cabin,* the character of Topsy furthered such masculinization. George L. Aiken, author of the most influential stage adaptation of the novel, originally conceived of Topsy as a boy, and although the character was scripted as a girl, Topsy was often played by a man.[52] The cross-gendered casting of Topsy reinforced the racism of the role, for it replicated what Patricia Morton terms the "defeminizing" assault of slavery, whereby black women were denied access to marriage, children, and other prerogatives of white femininity.[53] Topsy's defeminization also reinforced her availability for fantasies of white female rebellion. Loud, dirty, and impudent, the theatrical Topsy was so distant from the dictates of femininity that she was closer to bad boy than bad girl.

In Aiken's play, Topsy openly voices hostility toward adult femininity, in the form of her tirade against the light-skinned Miss Rosa:

> "I despise dem what sets up for fine ladies, when dey ain't nothing but cream-colored niggers! Dere's Miss Rosa—she gives me lots of 'pertinent remarks.' T'other night she was gwine to ball. She put on a beautiful dress dat missis give her—wid her hair curled, all nice and pretty. She hab to go down de back stairs—dey am dark—and I puts a pail of hot water on dem, and she put her foot into it, and den she go tumbling to de bottom of de stairs, and de water go all ober her, and spile her dress, and scald her dreadful bad! He! he! he! I's so wicked."[54]

Topsy's overt target here is the supposed class pretensions of light-skinned African-Americans. She later criticizes slaves who, she says, "seem to think yourself white folks. You ain't nerry one—black *nor* white. I'd like to be one or turrer" (25). Yet her explicit advocacy of intraracial class distinctions is inseparable from her implicit attack on the imagery of adult femininity, white as well as black. When she sends "Miss Rosa" tumbling, she travesties "fine ladies" who would dress and groom themselves to go to balls. Celebrating her own exemption from femininity, she leaves the figure of the "pretty" woman in literal as well as metaphorical hot water.

Too masculine, stage Topsies could also pervert femininity in a second direction, toward excessive female sexuality. The character was sometimes linked to the promiscuous heterosexuality associated with both black women, who were stereotyped as hypersexual "Jezebels," and actresses, who were linked to prostitutes.[55] The Union soldiers in Pittsburgh who came to see wartime productions of the play, for example, were invited there by the white actress who urged them, "Come and see me play Topsy!" The resulting performance, according to Harry Birdoff, capitalized on the sexual implications of Topsy:

> She made stage history the first night. When a roar from the house indicated that something was amiss, she discovered that her black tights and stockings had separated, the parting of the ways clearly apparent to the audience by generous strips of white skin. In a twinkling, Mrs. Wilkinson summoned her native ingenuity to the rescue. "Golly, Marse St. Claire," she ejaculated, "guess I must be mortifyin!"[56]

The racism at work in this moment is extreme, as Topsy becomes a variation on the "Jezebel" stereotype. Reinforcing racism, the anecdote also suggests one of its functions: the transgressive pleasures afforded to a white actress and her audience by the costume of blackness. The "parting of the ways" within the black pieces of the Topsy costume allows for the pornographic exposure of white skin, while the adoption of Topsy's speech brings the actress comic success through linguistic excess. The "mortifyin" moment becomes one of triumph for the white woman, in which the performance of outraged blackness energizes the enactment of outrageous whiteness.

In this anecdote, the audience for Topsy is male, but the career of the most celebrated Topsy actress, Caroline Howard, suggests the powerful connections forged among white women—author, actress, and audience—in the performance of the role. Caroline Howard's husband, George C. Howard, produced one of the major theatrical versions of the play, and she became famous for this role. As Topsy, Caroline Howard looked like what she was: an adult white woman in blackface, costumed as a child (figure 1). Within this context of obvious theatrical invention, she was said to bring a moving mixture of pathos and comedy to Topsy. In the words of a London reviewer, Caroline Howard was

> such a perfect embodiment of Mrs. Harriet Beecher Stowe's Topsy that one would imagine both ladies had studied from the same model . . . Her elf-like figure, and the strange, wild, screaming chant in which she sang the song, "I'se So Wicked," was something quite *sui generis* unlike anything we have before seen; but it seemed to us to realize the picture of the authoress, and we believe that it is a truthful representation of the original.[57]

The ambiguous language of this reviewer aligns not only Stowe and Howard, who seem to "have studied from one model," but also Stowe and Topsy. "A truthful representation of the original," Howard's Topsy realizes "the picture of the authoress," as if the original picture is of, rather than by, Stowe herself.

Stowe's own response to this performance, as described by a friend, extends these connections:

> I never saw such delight upon a human face as she displayed when she first comprehended the full power of Mrs. Howard's "Topsy."
>
> . . . I remember that in one scene "Topsy" came quite close to our box, with her speaking eyes full upon Mrs. Stowe's. Mrs. Stowe's face showed all her vivid and changing emotions, and the actress must surely have divined them. . . . There

FIGURE I.
Caroline (Mrs. G. C.) Howard as Topsy, sheet music illustration for "I'se So Wicked," 1854 (The Harvard Theatre Collection, The Houghton Library)

was but a slight wooden barrier between the novelist and the actress—but it was enough! I think it a matter of regret that they never met.[58]

The description records multiple transgressions for Stowe: her first (and only) attendance of her play in a public theatre, a setting she considered indecent; her particular investment in the representation of Topsy; and, most profoundly, her own identification with the actress, a member of a disreputable class. Stowe and Howard are at once mutual spectators, turning "speaking eyes" upon one another, and mutual actors, with one performing Topsy while the other shows "vivid and changing emotions." Blackface functions in this moment as a key feature of relations between white women, at once mirror and barrier. Howard's blackface mirrors back to Stowe, in literally made-up form, the self-translation at work in Stowe's original characterization of Topsy. At the same time, blackface separates the two adult white women from each other, constituting a blockage between Stowe and Topsy as firm as the "wooden barrier" between them.

Both within the novel and in its cultural spin-offs, Topsy's performance of inversion is most intimately related to the propriety of Little Eva and Miss Ophelia. Stowe neatly organizes the contrast between Eva and Topsy as that of "The Saxon, born of ages of cultivation, command, education, physical and moral eminence; the Afric, born of ages of oppression, submission, ignorance, toil and vice!" (361–62). Despite their symmetrical opposition, however, Eva and Topsy implicitly function as split selves within normative white femininity. This conjunction was literalized, in nineteenth-century American culture, in the form of the popular two-headed "Topsy/Turvy" doll. Patricia Turner describes this doll as "a pretty, well-dressed, blond-haired white doll [that] when turned upside down becomes a grotesque, thick-lipped, wide-eyed, sloppily dressed black doll."[59] Originating during slavery, Topsy/Turvy dolls gained popularity from *Uncle Tom's Cabin;* some versions were called "Topsy/Eva" dolls.[60] As Karen Sánchez-Eppler has argued, the topsy-turvy doll precisely enacts the complex interdependence of cultural constructions of white and black womanhood. The two dolls are conjoined but also "mutually effacing . . . To face one necessarily entails skirting the other."[61]

· The theatrical history of Topsy and Eva reinforces their ideological inseparability in other ways. A 1923 musical comedy called *Topsy and Eva* was centered on these characters, who were played by the two Duncan sisters, one in blackface. The Duncan sisters reprised their roles in a 1927 film of the play, which ends with an image of Topsy and Eva asleep in bed in an affectionate embrace. This sororal bond was closer still in the case of mid-nineteenth-century productions, when Topsy and Eva were often played by the same actress. In the Howard family productions, Caroline Howard played opposite her own daughter, Cordelia, as Little Eva. In the relation between the two Howards, the Topsy-Turvy doll turns over once again. Topsy was usually the repressed figure beneath the white girl's bottom, but in this case the woman who represented her had literally given birth to the theatrical Eva.[62]

While Topsy is implicitly conjoined with Little Eva in the novel's popular culture, her most sustained relation to a white woman within the novel is with Miss Ophelia. Miss Ophelia is an overt contrast to the angelic Eva, openly satirized in the novel for her political rigidity and for the hypocrisy that makes her unable to touch Topsy. Yet child and spinster are linked by their shared deviation from the role of mother, their status as "little" and "Miss" instead of "Mrs." Both have a topsy-turvy relation to normative white femininity, as symbolized by their close connections to Topsy. This connection was again made literal in the Howard family productions, in which Caroline Howard's mother played Miss Ophelia. As performed by the three generations of Howard women, Miss Ophelia, Topsy, and Little Eva constituted a genealogy of cross-racial fantasies in which Topsy was at once mother to the angelic white child and daughter of the censorious white spinster.

As Topsy constitutes the disruptive "bottom" to the doll-like Little Eva, so too does her intimate relation to Miss Ophelia raise the possibility of the spinster's own inversions. In Aiken's theatrical adaptation, the outer limits of such inversions emerge in a comic exchange between Miss Ophelia and a character named "Deacon Perry":

DEACON PERRY: Miss Ophelia, who is this young person?
OPHELIA: She is my daughter.
DEACON: [Aside.] Her daughter! Then she must have married a colored man off
    South. I was not aware that you had been married[,] Miss Ophelia?
OPHELIA: Married! Sakes alive! what made you think I had been married?
DEACON: Good gracious[.] I'm getting confused. Didn't I understand you to say
    that this—somewhat tanned—young lady was your daughter?
OPHELIA: Only by adoption. She is my adopted daughter.
DEACON: O——oh! [Aside.] I breathe again. (45–46)

The question of Topsy's origins returns here as one of paternal mystery. The issue is no longer "Who was your mother?" but who was Topsy's father, and the answer is that Miss Ophelia "must have married a colored man" in order to produce a child so "tanned." As critics have noted, the intimate pairing of Little Eva and Uncle Tom both invokes and domesticates the prospect of interracial sexuality.[63] In the closing embrace of *Topsy and Eva,* the conjunction of Topsy and Eva raises this prospect within a same-sex frame. In this exchange between Miss Ophelia and Deacon Perry, Topsy's presence retroactively catapults her "mother" into bed with a black man. In this moment at least, Miss Ophelia's inability to bring herself to touch black bodies seems motivated not by revulsion from black skin but by desire for it.

This exchange does not appear in Stowe's novel, but *Uncle Tom's Cabin* repeatedly situates Topsy as an overdetermined figure for Miss Ophelia's rebellion in other ways. So frustrated by Topsy's misbehavior that she literally shuts her up in "dark closets" (362), Ophelia is particularly incensed by the child's disingenuousness, as when, "during the time when the good lady's back was turned in the zeal of her manipulations, the young disciple had contrived to snatch a pair of gloves and a ribbon, which she had adroitly slipped into her sleeves, and stood with her hands dutifully folded, as before" (358). Like the confidence man, Topsy's ability to slip something up her sleeve while appearing "dutiful" marks a form of disorder more difficult to combat than overt lawlessness. Challenging Miss Ophelia's "zeal," Topsy also mimics it, turning the domestic project of neatness into the criminal impulse toward concealment. In another enactment of corporeal duality, Topsy is both the imp behind Miss Ophelia's back and the flip side to the other woman's sense of duty.

Reversing Miss Ophelia's behavior, Topsy also overturns it. This choreography of inversion is most fully enacted within the intimate setting of the white woman's bedroom:

> If Miss Ophelia . . . was so sanguine as to suppose that Topsy had at last fallen into her way, could do without overlooking, and so go off and busy herself about something else, Topsy would hold a perfect carnival of confusion. Instead of making the bed, she would amuse herself with pulling off the pillowcases, butting her woolly head among the pillows . . . she would climb the posts, and hang head downward from the tops . . . dress the bolster up in Miss Ophelia's night-clothes, and enact various performances with that,—singing and whistling, and making grimaces at herself in the looking-glass; . . . in short, as Miss Ophelia phrased it, "raising Cain" generally.
>
> On one occasion, Miss Ophelia found Topsy with her very best scarlet India Canton crape shawl wound round her head for a turban, going on with her rehearsals before the glass in great style,—Miss Ophelia, with carelessness most unheard-of in her, left the key for once in her drawer. (366)

In this passage, Topsy's "carnival of confusion" involves multiple inversions, with her upside-down head, "butting" amongst the "tops," serving as both cause and emblem of a world turned upside down. The imagery of the turban also aligns Topsy with a decadent orientalism, an orientalism that suffuses Stowe's descriptions of Louisiana as a whole; Florence O'Connor, in her Confederate novel, protested Stowe's impression that "we dream our lives away in quite an Oriental style."[64] In this moment, upright Miss Ophelia would seem to be at the further remove from turbaned Topsy, emblem of the orientalist South.

Yet the scarlet shawl is Miss Ophelia's own, hidden away as she had earlier closeted Topsy, and her unusual carelessness in leaving the key suggests a psychological desire for the shawl to be discovered and displayed. Through the passage as a whole, Topsy seems to enact Ophelia's own rebellions against femininity, wherein the symbolic night-clothes of the white woman's unconscious emerge in the costume and behavior of the unruly black child. This psychologized relation between the two characters is enhanced by the language of surveillance in the passage. Surveillance, the emblem of civility, is here as much internal as external, moving from "overlooking" to the self-scrutiny of the "looking-glass." Mirroring Ophelia's own "performances," Topsy provides a site upon which the white woman's inversions can be both reflected and displaced elsewhere.

Topsy's function as both mirror to and screen for Ophelia emerges even more clearly in a poem Harriet Beecher Stowe wrote based on this moment in the novel. "Topsy at the Looking Glass" was published in 1853 as part of *Pictures and Stories from Uncle Tom's Cabin,* a spin-off "designed to adapt Mrs. Stowe's touching narrative to the understandings of the youngest readers and to foster in their hearts a generous sympathy for the wronged Negro race of America."[65] The poem begins:

> See little Topsy at the glass quite gay,
> Her mistress has forgot the keys to-day,
> So she has rummaged every drawer, and dressed
> Herself out in Miss Feely's very best.
>
> Mark where she stands! the shawl of gorgeous red
> Wound like a Turk's great turban round her head;
> A finer shawl far trailing on the floor,
> Just shews her bare black elbows, and no more.
>
> With what an air she flaunts the ivory fan,
> And tries to step as stately as she can,
> Mincing fine words to her own shadow, "Dear!
> How very ungenteel the folks are here!"

These stanzas again seem to divorce sober Miss Ophelia from "gay" Topsy, whose costume is now identified in even more explicitly orientalist language as that of "a Turk's great turban." But the poem again erodes the contrast between the two, an erosion deepened by the context of performance. Topsy's "mincing" mimicry suggests the masquerade involved in the spinster's own performance of good behavior. When Topsy condemns the "ungenteel folks" of the South by speaking to "her own shadow," she recreates precisely her own relation as psychological shadow to Miss Ophelia. The visual imperative that opens the poem—"See little Topsy at the looking glass"—further draws the reader into this implied circuit of spectatorship, constructing the poem as revealing looking-glass for its audience as a whole. The illustration that accompanies the poem further develops these mirroring relations, twinning Topsy's delight at her mirror-image with Ophelia's horror at Topsy (figure 2). In this image, it is as if Topsy is herself a mirror for Miss Ophelia, drawing

FIGURE 2.
"Topsy at the Looking-Glass,"
illustration from *Pictures and
Stories from "Uncle Tom's
Cabin,"* 1853 (Harriet Beecher
Stowe Center, Hartford, CT)

back the curtain on the disorderly psyche that lurks behind the adult woman's
neat exterior. To complete this relay of reflections, Topsy seems to stare directly from the middle of the image, as if providing a mirror for the reader
of the text.

Having established these unstable mirroring relations, however, Stowe
abruptly swerves away from them:

But while that shadow only Topsy sees,
Back comes the careful lady for her keys,

And finds her in the grandeur all arrayed—
Poor Topsy will be punished, I'm afraid.

Now it is wrong, as every reader knows,
To rummage other people's drawers, and wear their clothes;
But Topsy is a negro child, you see,
Who never learned to read like you and me.

Closing off Topsy's rebellion, the poem's narrator safely reestablishes disciplinary and racial hierarchies in which both "you and me"—the presumably white narrator and reader—occupy a safe distance from the illiterate "negro child." The next two stanzas of the poem continue this distancing project, aligning Topsy's illiteracy with her lack of home, school, and Bible. In the poem's penultimate stanza, Stowe moves toward closure from a new direction, offering a general exhortation against plagiarism—"The copy by some clever school-mate penned, / The witty saying picked up from a friend"—which she aligns with the "borrowed plumes" of Topsy's misbehavior. The poem's ending distances Topsy still further, framing her as an object-lesson for white school-children whose crimes are certain to be discovered:

But none can keep such borrowed plumes as these
For some one still comes back to find the keys.
And so they are found out, it comes to pass,
Just like poor Topsy at the looking-glass.

Yet even as the didacticism of the ending cements Topsy as disciplinary object, Stowe's closing emphasis on the misbehavior of white children also brings the question of Ophelia's own masquerade back into view. Topsy will not be allowed to pass as Miss Ophelia, but in an uncertain world in which texts, sayings, and manners are all open to imitation, Miss Ophelia's propriety may itself be plagiarized "copy."

So too does the novel firmly, yet imperfectly, domesticate Topsy. After Eva's death, "The callous indifference was gone; there was now sensibility, hope, desire, and the striving for good" (443). As Rachel Bowlby notes, Topsy's psyche represents "an open field for civilized cultivation or colonization," and the remainder of her story bears out this potential.[66] Topsy returns to New England with Ophelia, where she "rapidly grew in grace and in favor with the family and neighborhood" and "became a member of the Christian church" (612). Publicity for theatrical productions of *Uncle Tom's Cabin* neatly captured

FIGURE 3. Detail from publicity herald for a theatrical production of *Uncle Tom's Cabin,* 1885 (The Harvard Theatre Collection, The Houghton Library)

this transformation, depicting before-and-after versions of Topsy unruly in the South and upright in the North (figure 3). In Stowe's novel, Topsy ultimately leaves the country when she is "approved as a missionary to one of the stations in Africa" (612). Provisionally admitted within the discourse of civility, Topsy has moved from uncivilized heathen to civilizing agent. She can extend the civilizing project to Africa, where it will become both an imperial invasion and a psychic attack on the "Dark Continent" of blackness. From her initial failures at self-surveillance, Topsy now joins the imperialist disciplinary project wherein, as Henry Ward Beecher triumphantly announced, "Christian nations rule the world . . . There is a Christian police around this globe!"[67]

As in Stowe's poem, however, the novel's ending is so intent on subduing Topsy that it has the contrary effect of suggesting her power. The narrator's final assessment of her expresses no little relief at her removal to Africa: "[W]e have heard that the same activity which, when a child, made her so multiform and restless in her developments, is now employed, in a safer and wholesomer manner, in teaching the children of her own country" (612). "Safer" in "her own country," Topsy still cannot be accommodated within America. As a fantasy of unruly whiteness as well as blackness, she remains an unresolved presence, in Stowe's text and in the proliferations of her image that followed. Even in the publicity image of Topsy "in the North," her brightly patterned clothing and direct gaze suggest the challenge she continues to pose to norms of female civility. In her antebellum war within and against the terms of white femininity, Harriet Beecher Stowe turns a fictional self topsy-turvy but then cannot quite set it upright.

III

I have argued that Harriet Beecher Stowe's model of feminization is internally fractured, generating a counternarrative of inversion both expressed in and displaced by the figure of Topsy. This internal conflict constitutes a war within civility, the discourse from which Stowe derives her authority but against which she also chafes. Stowe advocates civility in her belief in the civilizing authority of white women and in the self-civilizing practices of women toward themselves. Topsy threatens to undermine this project, even as she becomes its greatest exemplar. As a novel of civility, *Uncle Tom's Cabin* at once adheres to its restrictive framework and pushes against it. A decade before the actual Civil War begins, Stowe's novel articulates a form of "civil war" over white women's incivility, a war in which disciplinary and carnivalesque impulses conflict and combine.

Yet the connection of *Uncle Tom's Cabin* to "civil war" is not simply metaphorical. Stowe's novel cannot, of course, comment on the Civil War that followed; nor does its narrative actually advocate sectional conflict. The author carefully separates pro- and antislavery positions from sectional identities: her most powerful antislavery voice, little Eva, is a Southerner, while her slave-holding villain, Simon Legree, is from the North.[68] As a cultural artifact, however, *Uncle Tom's Cabin* has an intimate relation to the Civil War, including but extending beyond its contributions to sectional hostility. Prospectively and retroactively linked to the war, *Uncle Tom's Cabin* provided a point of departure for radically divergent constructions of national allegory. As I will argue, these reconstructions turn on the metaphorical possibilities of racial and sexual inversion, with a variety of texts using the figures of Stowe and Topsy to characterize the instabilities of the nation moving toward and away from civil war.

To understand the national implications of *Uncle Tom's Cabin*, we must first survey metaphors of the body politic in the Civil War era, as developed in oratory, journalism, cartoons, theater, and fiction. The governing metaphors of the American Revolution largely employed a generational scheme of filial rebellion, in which revolutionary sons rebelled against the patriarchal authority of Britain and then became "Founding Fathers" of the new nation. In antebellum America, the rhetoric of rebellion shifted from the vertical axis of revolution to lateral struggles between regions. While the language of fathers and sons continued to suffuse political discourse, competing metaphors of regional relation also configured race and gender along new lines.[69] Some Northern abolitionists, for example, equated slavery with feminized masculinity, an image exemplified in *Uncle Tom's Cabin* by Augustine St. Clare, who, as a child, is "more akin to the softness of woman than the ordinary hardness of his own sex" (239). At the same time, fears that a Southern "Slave Power" conspiracy was planning to extend slavery implicitly masculinized Southern aggression. Some Northerners pejoratively characterized the slaveholding South as a kind of American Africa, while abolitionists used the visual emblem of the chained black body, male and female, to attack slavery. Conversely, Southerners looking North alternately asserted the "manhood" of their region and identified it in feminine terms. Southerners sometimes represented themselves as metaphorical slaves to the North, but their defenses of slavery also aligned abolitionists with blackness. And in the movements for black emigration that informed both pro- and antislavery writing nationally, the assertions of white nationalism displaced blackness from the body politic altogether.[70]

Continuing this metaphoric profusion, the Civil War itself was represented in sustained national allegories that focused on siblings, spouses, and bodies. A comprehensive network of metaphors on both sides equated national fracture with the struggle of "brother against brother." The nation also appeared as an injured body, damaged either by secession and slavery (Northern version), or by the aggressive intolerance of the North (Southern version). While this injured body was male, both sides invoked the idea of liberty, iconographically female. For Northerners, Liberty and her sister icon Columbia were potentially militant symbols of the besieged Union, although not necessarily the emblem of slaves. Some Northern wartime illustrations, for example, adapted the iconography of the French Liberté, depicting Liberty wearing a Phrygian cap and armed with a sword to defend the Union. Southerners also claimed the idea of liberty—along with the inheritance of the American and French Revolutions—to authorize secession, but their most famous visual depictions of women, as in the commemorative 1864 painting *The Burial of Latané*, promoted more passive imagery of female mourning and sacrifice. Like the divided house and the injured body, women offered a wartime iconography that could go both ways, not only between South and North but also between militant warrior and damsel in distress.[71]

Less reversible was the rhetoric of divorce and marriage, which was used during the war to signify sectional conflict and emerged in the immediate postwar period as a central feature of what Nina Silber has analyzed as the "romance of reunion." The language of Northern victory relied centrally on gender metaphors that extended the antebellum rhetoric of a feminized South in several ways. Some Northerners represented the South as a land of gender inversion, where emasculated men were dominated by powerful women. More conciliatory images of Southern feminization imagined regional reconciliation as the metaphoric marriage between regions, in which the Southern "bride" was courted by her Northern groom. Some white Southerners contributed to this rhetoric, but others resisted it, constructing a nationalist iconography whose reactionary nostalgia actively thwarted regional reunion. For many ex-Confederates, the legacy of the "War of Northern Aggression" was one of continued male violation.[72]

In many of these metaphors of the Civil War body politic, women are central but voiceless. Emblematic women might sometimes be militant sword-carriers, but they were more often disempowered through metaphor. In an 1862 lecture, "The War for the Union," for example, Wendell Phillips declares that the Civil War is "a terrific war—not a war sprung from the caprice of a woman." However, he then turns to the iconography of female caprice to describe the warring South: "[T]he reason why I claim that Carolina has no right to secede is this: we are not a partnership, we are a marriage, and we have done a great many things since we were married in 1789 which render it unjust for a State to exercise the right of revolution . . . The right of revolution is not a matter of caprice." In this broken marriage, the South is not only disobedient but sexually indecent, for England is "holding out to the South the intimation of her willingness, if she will but change her garments, and make herself decent—[laughter]—to accept her under her care."[73] The context of performance cements the gender lessons of Phillips's metaphors, as the parenthetical laughter of the presumably male audience confirms the absurdity of either regional or sexual decency. The figure of the female coquette serves as a joke both to condemn uppity women and to cement homosocial relations between men.[74]

A more complex example centered on the representation of Abraham Lincoln shows the ways in which gender metaphors in Civil War rhetoric were inseparable from issues of race. During the war, Lincoln was caricatured for his perceived support of abolition in various ways, including symbolic "blackening." Opponents suggested that he had "African" origins, while a related strand of satire caricatured the president as Othello, "Blacked . . . all over to play the part." Similarly, an 1862 etching by Confederate sympathizer Adalbert Volck satirized Lincoln with the idea of his hidden blackness; entitled "Beneath the Veil," the image depicts the president as a man whose recognizably black features are revealed when he lifts an orientalist veil. An 1863 anti-Lincoln play entitled *The Royal Ape* extends such iconographies, conjoining racial caricature with a pejorative imagery of feminization to offer a sustained attack on Lincoln. Before returning to *Uncle Tom's Cabin,* it is worth examining this little-known play, written by a Confederate lawyer named William Russell Smith, at some length, for it suggests the complications and consequences of a wartime rhetoric of national masculinity turned topsy-turvy in both racial and sexual terms.[75]

The Royal Ape takes place during the first Battle of Bull Run, an early episode of Confederate triumph, and moves between the settings of the White House and the "Bull Run" battlefield in Manassas, Virginia. In both spheres, the prospect of Southern victory occasions radical threats to Northern masculinity. On the battlefield, one of Lincoln's advisors, Senator Henry Wilson of Massachusetts, encounters "Sambo," described as "a negro in grotesque Confederate uniform."[76] Wilson, an abolitionist, assumes that "Sambo" will welcome him, but the black man instead orders him at gunpoint to strip:

WILSON: You do n't mean to make me strip off my clothes? . . .
SAMBO: . . . Off wid 'em. Its warm dis ebnin', and you need n't be shamed. No body wont see you but me. You look like you needed wentilatin.
WILSON: I am the colored man's friend. I come here to assist you.
SAMBO: Well den, just gib me a good suit ob close!
WILSON: I sent this army to fight for you; do n't you want to be free? I bring you liberty and equality.
SAMBO: . . . I am already free. You know de law in dis new federashun, dat every nigger dat captivates a Yankee is to be free! So you see, boss, you are *my* prisoner—my *contraband.* (48)

This exchange imagines the black man as a loyal Confederate soldier whose greatest animus is against the abolitionist who aims to defend him. This racist fantasy both subdues Confederate anxieties about slave disloyalty and uses the slave to humiliate his misguided Northern supporter. Humiliation is expressed as racial reversal, with Wilson called "contraband"—the wartime term for escaped slaves claimed as the property of the Union army—and turned into the prisoner of the black man. The form of this reversal, the swapping of clothes, at once turns Wilson into a slave and signals his emasculation. A veiled threat of sexual violation also emerges at this moment, in the claim, both invitation and menace, that "No body wont see you but me. You look like you needed wentilatin." His trousers undone, Wilson is open to the assaults of both the Confederate army and the black man with a gun.

Meanwhile, at the White House, the prospect of defeat wreaks multiple forms of gender havoc. Like other critics of the president, Smith portrays the customary life of the Lincolns as one of royalist decadence: at the play's start, Abraham Lincoln seems insane, Mary Todd Lincoln appears hideous and shrill, and their eldest son, Robert, is a drunken wastrel sleeping with two of the White House maids. Defeat at Bull Run, however, turns customary dissolution into complete inversion, as detailed in the play's final act. Like Senator Wilson emasculated by his capture, Lincoln loses his potency:

> I, that was sev'n feet high, am suddenly
> Shrunk into seven inches; and my body,
> In its vast littleness, doth drag my soul down
> To its own dwarf'd proportions—for I fear,
> That if I should perceive an enemy,
> Armed with a straw, did he but glare on me,
> I would be driven to crawl into a crevice,
> Or hide me in a cupboard. (66)

With Abraham Lincoln shrunken to the "vast littleness" of seven inches and retracted into a cupboard, he loses the support of his followers. General Scott denounces Lincoln in suggestively gendered language:

> Thou cozening wench! with what abandonment
> I worship'd thee! with what idolatry
> I wrapp'd the mantle of thy fascinations
> About my captivated heart! So strives
> Th' insatiate bridegroom, in his honeymoon,
> To make it run perpetual . . . (68)

Scott's speech presents Lincoln as "cozening wench," female seducer and betrayer of his "insatiate bridegroom." The terms of his condemnation implicitly underscore the homoeroticism of military life—Lincoln and Scott are so close as to seem married—at the same time that they expel Lincoln to the metaphoric domain of femininity. From impotence to feminization, Lincoln has shrunk to "dwarf'd proportions" so small that they turn him into a "cozening wench."

Lincoln's shrinkage, moreover, is Mary Todd Lincoln's enlargement, as her authority assumes unnatural proportions. Throughout the Civil War, the First Lady was a highly unpopular figure North and South, condemned for her perceived extravagance and egotism.[77] *The Royal Ape* extends such criticism into a lampoon of her unnatural authority. Lamenting that "The house is topsy-turvy; fortune's fickle!" (70), Mary Todd Lincoln resolves to smuggle Lincoln from the White House; acceding, he declares that "I am ruled by you, / And would be ever led by one so true" (76). The symbol of this topsy-turvy world is Lincoln's disguise, a pair of striped pants that turns him into a ridiculous spectacle. Lincoln's loss of his own pants, like that of Senator Wilson, symbolizes emasculation, here accompanied by unnatural female tyranny rather than unexpected black authority. Like the character of Sambo in his Confederate uniform, Mary Todd Lincoln, described as sweating and shouting, is another version of the grotesque. In a Northern world turned topsy-turvy by defeat, the president takes his pants down because he is "ruled" by his tyrannical wife.

At the same time, Lincoln's son Robert carries the feminized connotations of flight to their next logical step: becoming a woman. When Robert turns to his lovers for help, each proposes to hide him beneath her clothes; as Kitty explains, "A woman's last resort (you know I doat) / To save her lover, is her petticoat" (77). Like his father, Robert Lincoln inverts gender norms. In this case, he also crosses class boundaries, hiding in the bottom half of a member of the "bottom" class. Robert soon comes even closer to the female body, when Kitty subsequently decides to cross-dress him:

> I'll pass you as a girl, at any inn;
> And make you like one as a pin to pin.
> 'T will not be hard, you are so delicate;
> Your cheeks are variant as a maid's; your lip
> Like to a ripe peach when the peel is off,
> Runs rosy nectar, and without disguise
> Might woo successful any pouting youth
> To struggle for a taste . . . (77–78)

A detailed blazon of Robert's neck, hands, eyes, and voice follows these tributes to cheek and lip. The impact of the whole is not only to feminize Robert but also to suggest that he is already excessively feminine. Cross-dressing will only render in female form the effeminacy that already undermines Robert's masculinity. This burlesque of Robert's masculinity also undoes his heterosexuality, since his lips "without disguise / Might woo successful any pouting youth." Indeed, Robert's effeminacy is a veritable guarantee of male courtship, for Kitty predicts that "the coldest youth, beholding you, / Would quick grow phrenzied and begin to woo." In the play's logic of feminization, Robert is the ultimate unmanned man, so lacking in masculinity that he not only faces male assault—like Senator Wilson dropping his pants for "Sambo"—but incites homosexual desire.

The final scene of *The Royal Ape* brings together the unmanning of the Lincolns *père et fils*. Cross-dressed, Robert leaves the White House with Kate and Kitty, utterly dependent on them to pull the strings, quite literally, of his newly female identity: "This whalebone skirt's a very awkward thing; / And this d——d corset keeps a-tightening! / . . . / Here, take my knife and cut the infernal things" (83). Having handed over his phallic knife, Robert reveals his masquerade to his parents, whose inversions are different in degree but not in kind from his; as his mother declares, "We're all dishonored by these antic capers" (85). The final lines of the play cement these associations between generations: Kitty and Kate explain to Mary Todd Lincoln, "We fix'd the Prince to aid in his escape," and Robert declares, in the play's closing line, "I play'd the *girl*, and dad, he play'd the *ape*" (85). The alignment between mother and maids signals their shared "fixing" of men, while Robert's line conclusively couples his unmanning with that of his father. The closing equation between "girl" and "ape" pithily aligns feminization and blackening as related metaphors through which white men in wartime are "dishonored."

The Royal Ape is, to be sure, an unusual text, both for the extravagance of its satire and for the bounded historical moment from which it emerges. Jubilant fantasies of Confederate victory would shortly give way to opposite iconographies. In the immediate postwar period, for example, Northern images of the defeated South pictured Jefferson Davis fleeing capture while allegedly dressed in his wife's clothes. With Davis represented as cross-dressed in defeat—an image to which I will return in chapters 3 and 4—white Southerners would struggle against their own vulnerability to inversion metaphors. Yet the very reversibility of *The Royal Ape*'s metaphors suggests their relevance to the rhetoric of the Civil War. The play demonstrates key features of bodily metaphor in Civil War discourse: the use of such metaphor to describe both "homefront" and "battlefront"; the importance of gender inversion as a trope for transformation; the inseparability of gender inversion from racial reversal, with black authority, in this case, prompting white emasculation; the proximity of both gender and race to sexual instability, with feminization here launching a trajectory from emasculation to homosexuality. And finally, the play brings into view the absent presence of women in Civil War narrative. *The Royal Ape* is fundamentally a story about relations between white men in a world organized by misogyny and racism, wherein the role of women is to vivify men as each other's objects of desire. Like Wendell Phillips's condemnation of the disobedient South as a petulant woman, *The Royal Ape* satirizes the North through gender metaphors in which women speak only in the voices of men's fantasies and anxieties about themselves.

Yet the reactionary metaphors of a text like *The Royal Ape* are not necessarily monolithic in their operations and results. As Joan Scott argues, gender metaphors in political rhetoric have multivalent meanings: "'[M]an' and 'woman' are at once empty and overflowing categories. Empty because they have no ultimate, transcendent meaning. Overflowing because even when they appear to be fixed, they still contain within them alternative, denied, or suppressed meanings."[78] In Phillips's condemnation of the female coquette, the very equation between the image of unruly femininity and the reality of an armed regional rebellion also makes possible the fantasy of lived female disobedience. Civil War rhetoric created new "family romances" of national order, but those romances did not necessarily cement patriarchal order. While the authoritative female characters in *The Royal Ape* are vilified, the play also enacts the potential that in a topsy-turvy world that gives black men guns and puts white men on their bottoms, women—from First Ladies to maids—might someday be on top.[79]

While there is no direct link between *The Royal Ape* and *Uncle Tom's Cabin*, congruent images of inversion saturated Southern representations of Harriet Beecher Stowe and her novel, before, during, and after the Civil War. From the start, white Southerners interpreted Stowe as an enemy of the South, equating her violation of regional boundaries with a transgression against gender norms. Thus George F. Holmes, condemning her in the *Southern Literary Messenger* for creating "unappeasable hatred between brethren of a common country," also proclaimed that "she has forfeited the claim to be considered a lady." The reviewer in the *New Orleans Crescent*, moving Stowe from nonlady to monster, declared that "There never before was anything so detestable or so monstrous among women as this." And William Gilmore Simms, demoting Stowe from monster to devil, asserted that "Mrs. Stowe betrays a malignity so remarkable that the petticoat lifts of itself, and we see the hoof of the beast under the table."[80] These attacks were leveled as virulently by women as by men. Louisa McCord, for example, published a furious critique of the novel in the *Southern Quarterly Review*, while an anonymous woman condemned Stowe, in a letter to the *New Orleans Picayune*, as "the man Harriet."[81] As Diane Roberts has shown, such white Southern tirades against Stowe articulated two related forms of gender anxiety. For some, Stowe "abdicated her gender to drift like a soul in a desert of deformed, sexually undefined bodies.

For others, Stowe had not masculinized herself so much as become a *fallen woman*: by speaking/writing in public, she displayed herself like a prostitute."[82] Whether seen as "the man Harriet" or a "shameless" prostitute, Stowe was constructed by white Southerners as demonic grotesque.

This language of assault both shared and complicated the terms of a later work like *The Royal Ape*. The masculinization of Stowe signaled anxieties about Northern tyranny, just as the emasculation of Lincoln would celebrate fantasies of Northern defeat. Moreover, for both figures, images of gender inversion were inseparable from racial conflict; the *New Orleans Crescent*, for example, thought Stowe would encourage "the bursting out of a slave insurrection." Another etching by Adalbert Volck, "Worship of the North" (ca. 1862), carried these congruent racial fears about Stowe and Lincoln into the war era. In this image, a black man sits atop a platform entitled "Negro Worship," surrounded by a crowd that includes both Stowe and the president, who is caricatured with African features. At this moment of Northern "Negro Worship," the devil Harriet "worshipped" in the same church as the Royal Ape.[83]

Yet devil and ape were not simply complementary metaphors. The vilification of Stowe expressed additional anxieties, for which there was no male equivalent, about feminism. As Holmes wrote in the *Southern Literary Messenger:*

> We know that among other novel doctrines in vogue in the land of Mrs. Stowe's nativity—the pleasant land of New England . . . is one which would place woman on a footing of political equality with man, and . . . would engage her in the administration of public affairs; thus handing over the State to the perilous protection of diaper diplomatists and wet-nurse politicians. Mrs. Stowe, we believe, belongs to this school of Woman's Rights, and on this ground she may assert her prerogative to teach us how wicked are we ourselves . . .[84]

The "school of Woman's Rights" is here a metaphoric source for both Stowe's gender inversion and her regional invasion. The result of her efforts is a state run by "diaper diplomatists and wet-nurse politicians," imagery that anticipates but redoubles the satire of *The Royal Ape*. For while the play effects multiple inversions, it also reinforces the assumption that the primary actors in a drama of war are men, however burlesqued. By contrast, attacks upon Stowe envisioned a future in which the woman-on-top might be not only grotesque First Lady but "wet-nurse politician," taking on phallic "hoof" to emasculate the nation as a whole.

As antebellum white Southerners anxiously depicted regional, racial, and gender inversions through caricatures of Harriet Beecher Stowe, they also reprised the connotations of her own emblem of inversion, Topsy. For the dual excesses ascribed by white Southerners to Stowe—masculinity and promiscuity—were also, I have suggested, implicit within her own construction of Topsy as "low-Other." This homology suggests two conclusions. First, the overlap between images of Stowe and Topsy affirms the centrality of these discourses of excess for characterizing white women's incivility in nineteenth-century America. In a closed metaphorical circuit, the fantasies Stowe herself had displaced onto Topsy were then relocated, in the novel's Southern reception, as fears about the author herself. Second, the overlap between author and character suggests the relevance of Topsy herself to competing constructions of national identity in this period. For example, in the *Southern Literary Messenger's* fury at Stowe "[asserting] her prerogative to teach us how wicked are we ourselves," the "wicked" white South sounds like Topsy being instructed by Stowe's Ophelia. In such contemporary responses to her novel, Stowe's own incorporation of the South as "low-Other" returns as the anger of Southerners at being treated as "low-Other" by the author herself.

The theatrical history of the novel again amplifies this echo. As the two-panel illustration of Topsy in the South and North makes explicit, theatrical adaptations of *Uncle Tom's Cabin* like that of George Aiken explicitly mapped Topsy's behavioral transformation onto her regional migration. In her before-and-after transition to provisional gentility, it is as if the regions themselves embody inversion and rectitude. Moreover, as Eric Lott has shown, the rivalry between Aiken's production and another adaptation of *Uncle Tom's Cabin* in the 1850s, both popular in the North, crystallized political conflicts then emerging in sectional form as Northern and Southern perspectives. Aiken preserved more of the novel's antislavery politics and more of its pathos, while H. J. Conway, sponsored by P. T. Barnum, turned the story into a proslavery plantation comedy. Topsy was a key figure in both versions of *Uncle Tom's Cabin* but to different effect. While Conway's Topsy was a comic centerpiece of his general portrait of happy slaves, Aiken's Topsy, as played by Caroline Howard and others, resonated with audiences as a symbol of the potentially unruly South.[85]

Two examples from just before the Civil War make this allegorical possibility explicit, employing Topsy to represent the white South in very different ways. The first is a Northern political cartoon, "South Carolina Topsey in a Fix," which expresses Northern anger at South Carolina for its encouragement of secession in six Southern states in early 1861 (figure 4). On a plantation porch, Miss Ophelia, holding an American flag missing several stars, chastises Topsy: "So, Topsey, you're at the bottom of this piece of wicked work—pick-

FIGURE 4. "South Carolina Topsey in a Fix," political cartoon by Thomas W. Strong, 1861 (Library of Congress)

ing stars out of this sacred Flag! What would your forefathers say, do you think? I'll just hand you over to the new overseer, Uncle Abe. He'll fix you!" Topsy's defense is, "Never had no father, nor mother, nor nothing! I was raised by speculators! I's mighty wicked, anyhow! 'What makes me ack so?' Dun no, missis—I'spects cause I's so wicked!" A slave listening in the background exclaims, "Hand us over to ole Abe, eh? Ize off!"

The cartoon's antisecession politics are inseparable from its racism, as it grotesquely caricatures slaves and scolds them for secession, a scenario that Shirley Samuels terms "blaming the victim."[86] Of particular interest here is the way the image adapts female figures from *Uncle Tom's Cabin* to a national allegory of the coming Civil War. With the flag on her lap and a liberty cap behind her, Stowe's Miss Ophelia merges with the American icon of Columbia, who was featured elsewhere in cartoons in the Civil War era. One Northern political cartoon from shortly before the war, for example, showed Lincoln dressed as "Miss Columbia" in the role of a schoolteacher attempting to discipline unruly students; another image, from the campaign of 1860, depicted Columbia spanking a naughty Stephen Douglas, as a bystander encourages her to "give him the stripes until he sees stars."[87] "South Carolina Topsey in a Fix" redoubles the punitive force of such images of Columbia with the disciplinary legacy of Stowe's Miss Ophelia. The effect is, on the one hand, to localize the national icon within a specific racial and regional drama and, on the other hand, to expand the field of authority over which Stowe's original character held sway. A fictional character crossed with a national icon, she now oversees not only the scarlet shawl worn by Topsy but the sacred cloth of the flag itself. Linking the flag with female authority, Miss Ophelia may also look toward the iconography of Betsy Ross, who would be retroactively mythologized, later in the century, as the nation's first flag-maker.[88]

At the same time, the cartoonist makes Stowe's Topsy into a symbol of white slaveowner rather than black slave. The cartoon's composition further enacts this double inversion: connected by color to the black slave behind her back, Topsy reverses color, as it were, in her frontal relation to Miss Ophelia, to whom she represents white rebellion. Topsy's words also shift in meaning, as in the *Southern Literary Messenger*'s lament; it is no longer the black child corrupted by slavery but her white owner impassioned about secession who is "wicked." These changes seem to invert the meaning of Stowe's Topsy. Rather than condemning slavery, the cartoon reproduces it on a national scale, situating both of its allegorical protagonists on a slaveholding plantation and turning the offstage president into menacing "overseer Uncle Abe." Despite this apparent contrast with *Uncle Tom's Cabin,* however, the cartoon is fundamentally faithful to Stowe's novel, for Topsy functions as a symbol of white fantasies in both texts. If Stowe's Topsy is a blackface emblem of white woman's incivility, then in this cartoon, she is a blackface symbol of white Northern anxieties about the impending Civil War.

A second image of the white South as Topsy presses the same trope in more radical directions. In 1859, Sarah Parker Remond, a free black woman from Massachusetts whose brother was noted antislavery orator Charles Lenox Remond, launched her own career as an antislavery speaker with a lecture tour in Great Britain. In a speech given early in the tour, Remond twice invoked *Uncle Tom's Cabin.* Condemning the slave South, she lamented both the miserable condition of slaves and the corollary impoverishment of white Southerners: "The five millions poor whites are most of them in as gross a state of ignorance as Mrs. Stowe's 'Topsey' in *Uncle Tom's Cabin.*" Later in the same speech, she cited a legal case involving Stowe's novel as an example of injustice under Southern law: "[I]n Maryland there is at present a gentleman in prison, condemned for ten years, because a copy of *Uncle Tom's Cabin* was found in his possession."[89]

Like "South Carolina Topsey in a Fix," Remond's speech inverts Stowe's

Topsy, but in different ways and to contrasting ends. Her opinions about Southern whites were indebted to the theories of a white Southerner named Hinton Helper, who argued that a slave labor system harmed poor whites and impoverished the Southern economy as a whole. In borrowing this argument, Remond positions her analogy between the white South and Topsy in an explicitly antislavery context, one that differentiates between white slaveowners and poor whites. Her second reference is to the situation of Samuel Green, a former slave, whose house was searched on suspicion of his involvement in antislavery activities; Green served five years in jail for possessing *Uncle Tom's Cabin* before he was pardoned.[90] In the shift from Mrs. Stowe's "Topsy" to Mr. Green's *Uncle Tom's Cabin,* Remond further recasts the significance of *Uncle Tom's Cabin,* using it not as a source of fictional black characters but as a material artifact in the struggles of actual black people for freedom. Moreover, Remond's presence on the lecture platform was itself a powerful emblem of these struggles. Displacing the figure of Miss Ophelia as national pedagogue, Remond herself dispels the image of the ignorant Topsy. The cartoon "South Carolina Topsey in a Fix" changes the context of Stowe's Topsy while sustaining her racist foundations. Remond's speech, by contrast, animates both the character and her creator in new ways, displacing white fantasy rather than simply converting it for new uses.

With the arrival of the war itself, Stowe and Topsy became templates for new forms of national allegory focused not on sectional conflict but on national reunification. During and after the war, *Uncle Tom's Cabin* continued to circulate throughout American culture. Traveling theater troupes devoted exclusively to the play proliferated after the war; there were nearly fifty traveling "Tommer" companies in the 1870s and as many as five hundred in the 1890s.[91] Many of these postwar productions gutted Stowe's antislavery politics. As Michael Rogin notes, these productions "promoted national reconciliation by celebrating the plantation, on the one hand, and intensifying racial division, on the other."[92] In the 1890s, however, other theatrical adaptations emphasized emancipation. According to Thomas Gossett, these versions brought the story into the war years, inventing scenes of Lincoln reading the Emancipation Proclamation and often ending with the arrival of the Union army in the South.[93] Publicity for these and later versions of the story firmly ensconced Stowe in this Civil War pantheon, aligning her with Lincoln, an unnamed slave, and the Emancipation Proclamation (figure 5). Such reinventions of *Uncle Tom's Cabin* retroactively consolidated the links among Stowe, the war, and black freedom that antebellum culture had already set in motion.[94] These retroactive consolidations were also interventions in contemporary racial struggles. In a period marked by virulent new forms of racism, from the segregations

FIGURE 5. Detail from an undated motion picture herald for *Uncle Tom's Cabin,* possibly 1903 (The Harvard Theatre Collection, The Houghton Library)

of Jim Crow to the sanctioned violence of lynching, Stowe's relation to the Civil War energized new controversy.

Two sharply different turn-of-the-century Southern commentaries suggest the range of this controversy, extending the strategies of antebellum commentary about Stowe and Topsy into new political contexts. First, for many white Southerners, the legacy of the Civil War was one of regional invasion and racial inversion. "It appears like the whole World is turn[ed] up side down," wrote one Confederate woman at the end of the war; William Middleton, a prominent Charlestonian, lamented "the utter topsy-turveying of all our institutions."[95] This sentiment was echoed forty years later by Myrta Lockett Avary in her pro-Confederate memoir *Dixie After the War* (1906). "[F]reedom as it came," Avary recalled, "was inversion, revolution. Whenever I pass 'The House Upside Down' at a World's Fair, I am reminded of the South after freedom."[96]

Thomas Dixon, the premier literary voice of turn-of-the-century Southern racism, avenged this perceived legacy of inversion through novels that simultaneously reanimated the Confederacy and dismembered Harriet Beecher Stowe. Dixon's trilogy of novels—*The Leopard's Spots* (1902), *The Clansman* (1905), and *The Traitor* (1907)—were extremely influential; *The Clansman* became the basis for D. W. Griffith's 1915 film *The Birth of a Nation. The Leopard's Spots* established the social matrix of the trilogy: a postwar white South politically emasculated by Confederate loss and sexually menaced by black men. Miscegenation is the ultimate enemy and the revival of Anglo-Saxon masculinity the goal. Dixon's hero triumphantly declares, "This is a white man's government, conceived by white men, and maintained by white men . . . we will not submit to Negro dominion another day, another hour, another moment!"[97] Updating and reversing the terms of *The Royal Ape,* the novel avenges regional and racial inversion as the perceived consequences of defeat.

Centered on the Southern erasure of "Negro dominion," the novel explicitly attempts to destroy the literary dominion of Stowe. While Lincoln's image had been rehabilitated among white Southerners by the turn of the century, many still vilified Stowe.[98] Dixon was inspired to write *The Leopard's Spots* after seeing a 1901 theatrical production of *Uncle Tom's Cabin;* his original title for the novel was *The Rise and Fall of Simon Legree.* The novel's portrait of the Reconstruction South represents an explicit attack on Stowe's novel, which one character alludes to as follows: "A little Yankee woman wrote a crude book. The single act of that woman's will caused the war, killed a million men, desolated and ruined the South, and changed the history of the world" (262). To counter this history, Dixon uses Stowe's novel against her, inventing characters named Simon Legree, George Harris (son of the first George and

Eliza Harris), and Tim Shelby (an ex-slave of Stowe's Shelby family), and burlesquing them. Tim Shelby is a Reconstruction politician who is killed after asking a white woman for a kiss. George Harris, now a Harvard-educated intellectual, turns to crime. This transformation of the novel's heroes into villains demonizes both black men and Stowe, ruining "the little Yankee woman" as she had ruined the South.

Simon Legree remains a villain, but Dixon reverses the meaning of his villainy, making him an opportunistic pro-black Reconstruction politician "posing as the representative of the conscience of the North" (143). As in *The Royal Ape,* Dixon feminizes his villain: during the war, Dixon's Legree evaded capture by Union forces when he "shaved clean, and dressed as a German emigrant woman. He wore dresses for two years" (85). Dixon uses Legree's cross-dressing to condemn the hypocrisy of Northern men, but this trope again exacts revenge against Stowe, since the emasculation of Legree is also the symbolic emasculation of the woman constructed as "the man Harriet." *The Leopard's Spots* suggests the difficulty for some white Southerners of countering a history of multiple reversals, wherein the inversions effected by racial emancipation and military defeat were themselves preceded by the assaults of an unnaturally "masculine" woman writer. In Dixon's virulently racist and misogynist project, the unmanning of Stowe is the necessary foundation for the remasculinization of the Southern white man.

For black women writing at the end of the century, by contrast, the postwar legacy of Stowe functioned very differently. As Sarah Parker Remond's 1859 speech shows, black women writers had long acknowledged Stowe's novel in a variety of genres; their antebellum tributes also included three poems by the young Frances Ellen Watkins Harper.[99] At the turn of the century, a large number of black women writers paid explicit tribute to Stowe. They included Eloise Bibb, Andasia Kimbrough Bruce, Olivia Ward Bush-Banks, Anna Julia Cooper, H. Cordelia Ray, Katherine Davis Chapman Tillman, and especially Mary Church Terrell, who wrote an extended encomium to the author, organized centennial celebrations in honor of her, and later urged black women to "show their gratitude and appreciation of the efforts made by Harriet Beecher Stowe in some substantial, outstanding way, for no author has ever done more with the pen for the cause of human liberty than she did."[100] Other contemporary texts by black women more indirectly registered the impact of Stowe, including Octavia Victoria Rogers Albert's collection of edited interviews with ex-slaves, *The House of Bondage* (1890), and Harper's novel *Iola Leroy* (1892).[101] Several contemporary contexts energized these tributes and allusions. Most immediately, renewed visibility for Stowe's novel kept the horrors of slavery in view, thereby serving as a weapon for the continuing struggle against anti-black violence in its new forms. In a period of growing white Northern indifference to black freedom, *Uncle Tom's Cabin* also offered a powerful reminder of white interest in black struggle. Finally, in an era of concentrated activism and literary production by black women, the legacy of Stowe could corroborate black women's own growing authority as political and cultural agents.

Like the very different Thomas Dixon, black women recast Stowe's dynamics of feminization. In contrast to the language of emasculation that structures *The Royal Ape* and *The Leopard's Spots,* these writings, like Stowe's novel, depict national feminization as female utopia rather than male nightmare. Recalling midcentury abolitionist commentary on the novel, Katherine Davis Chapman Tillman wrote in 1895 that "when 'Uncle Tom's Cabin' had been cried over by gray-haired men, blooming matrons, young folks and children, the battle [against slavery] was half won." Yet Tillman invoked Stowe's feminizing impact in the context of black women's activism. Appearing midway through an essay on "Afro-American Women and Their Work," this description is followed by tributes to Phillis Wheatley and Frances Harper.[102]

Recontextualizing Stowe's narrative, black women also identified *Uncle Tom's Cabin* as an important artifact in current struggles. Near the end of her 1902 Civil War memoir, *Reminiscences of My Life in Camp,* Susie King Taylor injected a commentary on *Uncle Tom's Cabin:*

> I read an article, which said the ex-Confederate Daughters [United Daughters of the Confederacy] had sent a petition to the managers of the local theatres in Tennessee to prohibit the performance of "Uncle Tom's Cabin," claiming it was exaggerated (that is, the treatment of the slaves), and would have a very bad effect on the children who might see the drama. . . . Do these Confederate daughters ever send petitions to prohibit the atrocious lynchings and wholesale murdering and torture of the negro? Do you ever hear of them fearing this would have a bad effect on the children? Which of these two, the drama or the present state of affairs, makes a degrading impression upon the minds of our young generation! In my opinion it is not "Uncle Tom's Cabin," but it should be the one that has caused the world to cry "Shame!" It does not seem as if our land is yet civilized.[103]

Taylor uses *Uncle Tom's Cabin* to condemn both the United Daughters of the Confederacy and the larger culture that would support anti-black violence. Her interrogatives shift the grounds for concern from the children who might see Stowe's drama to the quiescent would-be spectators of lynching and, finally, to the uncivilized land as a whole. This rhetorical shift both subordinates Stowe's drama to contemporary struggles and elevates Taylor's own relation to that drama. Like Sarah Parker Remond, Taylor uses *Uncle Tom's Cabin* to expand her own role as arbiter of national "shame," now shifted from slavery to lynching.

Such turn-of-the-century commentaries uniformly praised Stowe, surely a strategic necessity for black women consolidating their own authority as writers and reformers. Yet black women also contested the racial hierarchies implicit in Stowe's novel and in her cultural legacy—a legacy that, as in the advertisement for the motion picture *Uncle Tom's Cabin,* elevated a white woman above a kneeling black man. Praise of Stowe could encode critique, a possibility that emerges, for example, in the interstices of Anna Julia Cooper's *A Voice for the South* (1892), her radical call for racial and gender equality on behalf of "the open-eyed but hitherto voiceless Black Woman of America."[104] Cooper repeatedly invokes *Uncle Tom's Cabin* in "One Phase of American Literature," an essay in this volume on the literary representation of African-Americans. She praises the novel for having "revolutionized the thought of the world on the subject of slavery" (180). Criticizing white writers who attempt to portray black characters, she notes that "Not many have had Mrs. Stowe's power because not many have studied with Mrs. Stowe's humility and love" (186). As with writers like Tillman, the terms of this tribute evoke Stowe's own feminizing ethos, wherein "humility and love" result in social power.

Mrs. Stowe, is not, however, all-powerful, and as the essay nears its end, Cooper laments:

> I am brought to the conclusion that an authentic portrait, at once aesthetic and true to life, presenting the black man as a free American citizen, not the humble slave of *Uncle Tom's Cabin*—but the *man,* divinely struggling and aspiring yet tragically warped and distorted by the adverse winds of circumstance, has not yet been painted. It is my opinion that the canvas awaits the brush of the colored man himself. (222–23)

In this demand for black self-representation, Cooper implicitly renounces *Uncle Tom's Cabin.* The renunciation is centered on the status of "the black man as a free American citizen," who merits full authority as both author and literary subject. No longer the "humble" slave, the African-American man must be freed from both the institution of slavery and the literary confines of his representation by Stowe. Like Dixon, her political opponent, Cooper calls for remasculinization from the feminizing legacy of *Uncle Tom's Cabin*—in her case, however, for black rather than white men.[105]

While "One Phase of American Literature" offers an embedded critique of Stowe, another essay in the same volume, "Woman versus the Indian," implicitly returns to the legacy of Stowe's Topsy in the wake of the Civil War. As her book's title suggests, Cooper explicitly positions herself as a *Southern* woman, thereby revising the cultural equation of Southern with white perspectives and of Southern womanhood with white femininity. In "Woman versus the Indian," Cooper creates an alternative vision of the South's role in nineteenth-century history, representing the region allegorically as a misbehaving white girl:

> Every statesman from 1830 to 1860 exhausted his genius in persuasion and compromises to smooth out her ruffled temper and gratify her petulant demands. But like a sullen younger sister, the South has pouted and sulked and cried: "I won't play with you now; so there!" . . . Until 1860 she had as her pet an institution which it was death by the law to say anything about . . . And when, to preserve the autonomy of the family arrangements, in '61, '62 and '63, it became necessary for the big brother to administer a little wholesome correction and set the obstreperous Miss vigorously down in her seat again, she assumed such an air of injured innocence . . . [that] the big brother has done nothing since but try to sweeten and pacify and laugh her back into a companionable frame of mind. (104–5)

As political allegory, this is a scathing inversion of white norms. Cooper condemns the white South as a whining white girl, a characterization that recalls Wendell Phillips's metaphor of the South as petulant coquette. Yet Cooper uses this image to condemn the North as well, criticizing the Northern "big brother" who pacifies the postwar South into good humor rather than aggressively eradicating the effects of slavery. The postwar legacy of these complementary sibling failings is continuing racial inequality, or as Cooper sarcastically summarizes, "The Negro is not worth a feud between brothers and sisters" (108). This rhetoric updates Remond's characterization of poor white Southerners as Topsies, expanding such associations and situating them within Civil War allegory. In Cooper's version of the national family romance, the political rhetoric of unruly femininity serves to condemn the white body politic both North and South.

Revising Civil War history, Cooper's rhetoric also rewrites the racial imagery of girlhood, as that imagery had been organized through the figures of Little Eva and Topsy. While Cooper probably did not intend a direct revision of Stowe's characters, her imagery nonetheless offers an inversion of the racist cultural grid stabilized by Stowe, which opposed white and black little girls as emblems of goodness and badness. In *Uncle Tom's Cabin*, the rich white Southern girl, Little Eva, is the novel's preeminent civilizing force. Here, however, the rich white Miss South is so sullen and spoiled that it renders her grotesque: "[The South] grew so ugly, and kicked and fought and scratched so outrageously, and seemed so determined to smash up the whole business, the head of the family got red in the face" (105). "Obstreperous" and ill-tempered, Miss South is surrounded by father and brother, but not, in Cooper's three-page allegory, by any mother. Intractable and motherless, Miss South seems closer to Stowe's Topsy than to Little Eva, as if Cooper were inverting the Topsy-Turvy doll to put Little Eva on the bottom. In this inversion, little Miss South becomes Cooper's emblem of incivility.

By contrast, Cooper accords black women a central place in struggles for "civility to the Negro" (109). Highlighting the politics of manners, Cooper argues that courtesy shown to black women is the ultimate test of racism, for while "Any rough can assume civilty [*sic*] toward those of 'his set,' and does not hesitate to carry it even to servility toward those in whom he recognizes a possible patron or master . . . But the Black Woman holds that her femineity [*sic*] linked with the impossibility of . . . position or influence in her case makes her a touchstone of American courtesy exceptionally pure and singularly free from extraneous modifiers" (93). The recipients of "pure" civility because they cannot provide influence in exchange for courtesy, black women are also civility's agents. Since the "American woman is responsible for American manners" (86), she "can do this country no deeper and truer and more lasting good than by bending all her energies to thus broadening, humanizing, and civilizing her native land" (116). Like Taylor, Cooper attacks the nation as uncivilized and offers civility as national remedy. In Cooper's vision, the black woman is "free from extraneous modifiers" to be both the ultimate object of white civility and a powerful civilizing force of her own.

If little Miss South suggests a negative version of Little Eva, then Cooper's use of the discourse of civility reverses the iconography of Topsy, moving black women from fantasy figures of white rebellion to positions of agency. Cooper inverts what was already an inversion of whiteness, turning Topsy right side up and creating a vision of the nation feminized by the civility of black women. As the essay concludes, Cooper expands this vision even further:

> [W]hen race, color, sex, condition, are realized to be the accidents, not the substance of life . . . then is mastered the science of politeness, the art of courteous contact . . . then women's lesson is taught and woman's cause is won—not the white woman nor the black woman nor the red woman, but the cause of every man or woman who has writhed silently under a mighty wrong. (125)

Dissolving the racial boundaries that would keep black and white women at either end of the topsy-turvy doll, Cooper also includes men in her utopian model of civility's triumph. "The science of politeness" situates black women at the center of "woman's cause" and gives women the power to transform the new American nation.

Yet Cooper's powerful political vision has its own limits. While Cooper inverts the legacy of Topsy, the resulting model of black women's civility risks reproducing the limitations of the discourse that had produced Topsy in the first place. The black woman who becomes, in Cooper's term, a "powerful civilizing force" is then positioned to occupy Topsy's role at the end of *Uncle Tom's Cabin:* that of the imperialist "Christian police," disciplining incivility in other nations and in foreign regions of her "native land."[106] Continuous with the problem of imperial expansion is that of psychic contraction. Cooper appropriates a discourse of civility that operates by the repression of internal conflict, requiring a "low-Other" to discharge its psychic stresses. If Topsy is Stowe's "low-Other," who then will enact this role for the black woman "civilizing her native land"? Cooper burlesques the obstreperous "Miss South," but as with Stowe's creation of Topsy, the very rebelliousness she imparts to this female figure also suggests the potential for misbehavior suppressed within her maker. *A Voice from the South,* in other words, inverts the racial politics of civility, but it does not resolve its psychic pressures; as I argue in chapter 5, these pressures suffuse the fiction of Cooper's ally, Frances Ellen Watkins Harper. In this context, the Civil War that separates Cooper and Stowe historically unites them in a more metaphorical sense. For both writers, the fantasy of feminization, however it redresses a rhetoric of the masculine nation, can only heighten the civil wars within femininity itself.

With Cooper's model of black women's civility, then, we come full circle back to *Uncle Tom's Cabin.* The significance of *Uncle Tom's Cabin* to women's Civil War fiction, I have suggested, extends beyond the tribute paid to Harriet Beecher Stowe by Abraham Lincoln. Stowe's novel was engaged in "civil wars" long before the Civil War itself, both enacting and containing a war against civility whose emblem is the figure of Topsy. The novel's thematics of inversion, internally divided along racial lines, also inflected national metaphors of the body politic from its publication onward. Set against a national rhetoric that relied on embodiment to symbolize political inversion, both Stowe and Topsy were repeatedly reconstructed in allegorical terms. In widely divergent allegories, writers repeatedly recast Stowe's language of inversion along the axes of region, race, and gender. As Cooper's writing suggests, even the most radical of these recastings could not entirely resolve the contradictions of her text.

In the unresolved legacy of *Uncle Tom's Cabin,* Harriet Beecher Stowe's laughter in her meeting with Abraham Lincoln stands as a battle cry of incivility, not only for her own novel but for the stories that followed it. Restrained in the White House, her laughter echoes, in tones both angry and comic, in the works discussed in the following pages. Writing in 1851, Stowe herself could only look toward the possibility of the Civil War. For other women writers—working within, against, and around the terms Stowe had helped to establish—the Civil War itself would launch new possibilities for the representation of self and nation. To these possibilities I now turn.

TWO

A Wound of One's Own

Louisa May Alcott's Body Politic

I

Topsy-turvyness, I have argued, organizes both the narrative of *Uncle Tom's Cabin* and cultural responses to the novel and its author. Within the novel, inversion and incivility find form in the character of Topsy, while in disparate commentaries on the Civil War nation, both Topsy and Stowe become protean icons of inversion. For Stowe's most direct successors, the conflicts that energize *Uncle Tom's Cabin* took newly concrete form. In the writings of the first generation of white Northern women to address the Civil War, topsy-turvy female psyches are shaped literally and metaphorically by the warring nation.

The works of Elizabeth Stuart Phelps, for example, repeatedly interweave female rebellions against civility with the Civil War itself. Phelps's first published story, "A Sacrifice Consumed" (1864), focuses on the grief of a woman whose lover, a Union soldier, dies at Antietam; as she later recalled in her memoir, she was inspired to write it by "the women,—the helpless, outnumbering, unconsulted women; they whom war trampled down, without a choice or protest . . . to them I would have spoken."[1] Catalyzed by her desire to give voice to women "trampled down" by war, Phelps's literary career was dominated by a novel on this theme. In her best-seller *The Gates Ajar* (1868), a young woman, Mary Cabot, learns to accept the death of her brother, a Union soldier, through the support of her Aunt Winifred; the influence of Stowe, Phelps's idol, suffuses the novel's representation of maternal values and feminized Christianity. Yet, as in *Uncle Tom's Cabin*, the redemptive project of Phelps's novel wars with an impulse toward female incivility, registered as Mary's initial refusal to accept her brother's death. A deacon admonishes her, "I am sorry to see you in such a rebellious state of mind"; when he counsels acceptance, she retorts, "I am *not* resigned." While the narrative overtly charts the disciplinary victory of faith over protest, a moment late in the story offers a glimpse of Mary's "rebellious state of mind." Playing with her young niece, Faith, she launches into a series of impersonations: "I was her grandmother, I was her baby . . . I was a roaring hippopotamus and a canary-bird, I was Jeff Davis and I was Moses in the bulrushes."[2] In this moment, the leader of Confederate rebellion, Jefferson Davis, energizes Mary's own playful boundary-crossing. However fleeting, Mary's impulse toward unbounded mimicry, infused with the iconography of the Civil War, suggests the ongoing persistence of internal incivilities within Phelps's narrative of female self-silencing.[3]

The "civil wars" hinted at in *The Gates Ajar* emerge in their most sustained, complex, and revealing form in the fiction of Phelps's New England contemporary, Louisa May Alcott (1832–1888). The "little woman" who wrote *Uncle Tom's Cabin* and the creator of *Little Women* shared the culture of abolitionist New England; in her journal, Louisa May Alcott listed *Uncle Tom's Cabin* as one of her favorite books. Feminist critics have stressed Stowe's influence on Alcott. Sarah Elbert, for example, underlines their common commitment to the "redemptive power of women," and Elizabeth Ammons identifies their shared emphasis on "women's alternative morality." For less sympathetic readers, the commonalities between Stowe and Alcott are a suffocating and racist sentimentalism: *Uncle Tom's Cabin*, writes James Baldwin, "is a very bad novel, having, in its self-righteous, virtuous sentimentality, much in common with *Little Women*." In *Goodbye to Uncle Tom,* J. C. Furnas is harsher still, conflating the two women and their literary creations in his description of Stowe herself as "a character created by Louisa M. Alcott: the ugly duckling gradually evincing talent in a Yankee context, committed to a world where women doughtily make do because men are shiftless . . . Call her Jo March with a small-boned skeleton, curly hair, many children, and a touch of megalomania."[4]

Whether positive or negative, these evaluations implicitly share a focus on Stowe's most visible literary legacy: her fictional creation of a feminized world. But Alcott, I suggest, is Stowe's heir in a second sense as well: in her representation of civil wars within women. Alcott, like Phelps, inherits from Stowe both a topsy-turvy self and a feminized nation and the corresponding tension these models establish between carnival and discipline. In contrast to Stowe and Phelps, however, Alcott shapes these impulses from her own direct participation in the Civil War.

In 1862, at the age of thirty, Louisa May Alcott went to work as a nurse in a Union army hospital in Georgetown. In so doing, she became part of a widespread social transformation occasioned by Civil War nursing. Thousands of nurses participated in the war, including Clara Barton, whose tireless battlefront efforts helped to make her a national celebrity, and Mary Livermore, whose leadership was instrumental in the massive relief efforts of the United States Sanitary Commission. As Jane E. Schultz has shown, nurses not only contributed significantly to the Union cause but also found their own lives transformed in the process.[5] This was certainly true for Louisa May Alcott, who served as a nurse for less than two months before contracting typhoid fever but was profoundly affected by this experience for the rest of her life. The mercury prescribed for her cure permanently ruined her health, causing chronic pain and significantly contributing to her death at age fifty-six. So too did Alcott's exposure to the war profoundly affect her work, beginning with the thinly fictionalized book she published about her nursing experiences, *Hospital Sketches* (1863). This volume helped to launch her career as a professional author, while the war years and their aftermath were her most important period of literary development. The Civil War became a defining presence in her writing for the next twenty-five years, in texts ranging from *Little Women* (1868–69) to *Work* (1873) to her last novel, *Jo's Boys* (1886).[6]

Throughout her literary career, I suggest, Alcott returned to the war to reimagine the relation between women and nationhood—or, more specifically, between the disorderly body of the woman author and the diseased body politic of the country at war. This nexus of disruptive and disrupted bodies centers on two Civil War figures: the wounded male soldier and the female nurse. First appearing in *Hospital Sketches,* the suffering soldier is marked by and praised for his proximity to femininity. In this text, moreover, Alcott offers a second Civil War figure who blurs gender designations. Even as she valorizes the injured soldier for his feminine characteristics, she also relocates the traits of masculinity within the figure of the female nurse.

This permeable boundary between masculinity and femininity, I argue, has a dual significance in Alcott's fiction and, in turn, in the larger nineteenth-century culture her work illuminates. First, read in conjunction with Alcott's journals and letters, *Hospital Sketches* aligns the masculinized nurse with the author herself, offering a commentary on her own battles against gender propriety. In Alcott's internal "civil wars," the Civil War functions symbolically to reveal and realign the faultlines of femininity in nineteenth-century America. Throughout *Hospital Sketches,* the vocabulary of carnivalesque gender confusion represents an embattled form of access to masculine agency. Alcott's figure of the masculine nurse, like her own self-representation as "topsy-turvy," articulates an inverted relation to the sexual and racial norms of white femininity. Through metaphors that simultaneously masculinize and "blacken" both herself and her fictional nurse, Alcott turns the white female psyche into a site of metaphoric inversion and insurrection.

Second, Alcott, like Stowe, uses feminization to intervene in contemporary constructions of nationhood. Interpreted in the context of political rhetoric about the body politic, the figure of the feminized Civil War soldier serves as a point of a departure for the reconstruction of the wounded postwar nation. Alcott begins this reconstruction in *Hospital Sketches,* experiments with it in stories like "My Contraband" and "A Hospital Christmas," and develops it fully in *Little Women* and its two sequels. In the *Little Women* trilogy, Alcott looks toward a body politic disciplined and led by white women. Alcott, like Stowe, finds a productive cultural fantasy in the idea of feminization, but she both contracts the racial boundaries of feminization even further than Stowe, into a nearly all-white world, and she expands its regenerative force more fully into psychic domains. In the national allegories of the *Little Women* trilogy, Alcott privileges female self-mastery as a metaphorical model for male development and fantasizes a reconstructed nation in which men become little women.

In Alcott's Civil War writings, in short, a reciprocal metaphor connects gender and nation: the national conflict symbolizes individual struggles against gender norms, while such internal civil wars allegorically reconstruct the warring nation. These two metaphorical trajectories are closely related, at once complementary and contradictory. In both cases, Alcott brings together fictional plots with historical events and individual bodies with the larger body politic. Yet her negotiations of internal and national disorder, like those of Stowe, are also at odds with each other in their contrasting uses of carnival and discipline. In narrating the split female psyche, Alcott celebrates the pleasures of carnivalesque inversion; yet in addressing the divided nation, she foregrounds the uses of disciplinary order. The tension between these two projects suggests the difficulty of reconceiving the relation between women and nationhood when the primary weapon of national transformation—female discipline—all too easily rebounds upon women themselves. In feminizing the Civil War body politic, Alcott simultaneously sets the white woman author at war with herself.

II

Feminist critics have excavated Alcott's writings of the 1860s with rich results. Her many sensation stories of this decade, published anonymously or pseudonymously, offer openly rebellious accounts of female defiance in plots involving deception, adultery, murder, and drug addiction. The sensation stories allowed Alcott imaginative scope denied her in her signed fiction, with the disguise of the pseudonym often echoed in plots involving theatrical masquerade. In "Behind a Mask; or, A Woman's Power," for example, a scheming actress pretends to be an innocent governess to gain access to a fortune; an obvious revision of *Jane Eyre*, the story presents "woman's power" as the ability to operate "behind a mask," and femininity itself as a strategic masquerade. In bringing what Elaine Showalter terms the "alternative Alcott" into view, however, critics have paid less attention to what was a central event in Alcott's life in this decade, as it was in America as a whole: the Civil War. Contemporary with her sensation stories, *Hospital Sketches* engages similar questions of split female subjectivity but along different rhetorical lines. If femininity for Alcott is a form of gothic masquerade, it is equally a matter of metaphorical "civil wars," internal conflicts that predate but are newly energized and transformed by the Civil War itself.[7]

Hospital Sketches is the first-person account of the experiences of one Tribulation Periwinkle, a nurse for the Union army. The book's six chapters chart her decision to work as a war nurse, her journey from Boston to Washington, her daily activities as a nurse, her impressions of Washington while forced to convalesce, and her comments on life in a wartime hospital. Thinly fictionalized, the origins of the text lie in a series of letters Alcott wrote to her family about her own experiences, which she then adapted into sketches appearing in four installments in the spring of 1863 in the Boston abolitionist newspaper *The Commonwealth*. The sketches were then published in book form in 1863 and reprinted along with other stories in 1869.

At the center of *Hospital Sketches* is the chapter entitled "A Night," whose tone is far more serious than that of the rest of the volume and whose narrative, the most sustained subplot of the text, focuses on the death of a soldier named John. Modeled on a dying Virginia blacksmith nursed by Alcott, John at first seems a conventional model of heroic masculinity in wartime. A figure of "broad chest and muscular limbs," he is described approvingly by the narrator as "so genuine a man."[8] Yet Alcott's characterization subtly redefines the masculinity of the mortally injured soldier. To begin with, although John is only a year younger than Periwinkle, his masculinity is strangely childlike: "Although the manliest man among my forty, he said, 'Yes, ma'am,' like a little boy" (41). Further, what makes Periwinkle praise John as the "manliest man" is not only his boyishness but his womanliness: his smile is "as sweet as any woman's" (39), and when he says goodbye to his favorite companion, "They kissed each other, tenderly as women" (44). This image is, in turn, part of an implicit narrative of romance between the two men, who have "a David and Jonathan sort of friendship" (38). When John dies, the other man is accorded the status of mourning spouse: "Presently, the Jonathan who so loved this comely David, came creeping from his bed for a last look and word" (44).

Taken together, these descriptions of John effect two related transformations of the language of military masculinity. In terms of sexuality, they articulate the homosociality of the battlefield in implicitly homoerotic terms. Alcott's language is akin to Walt Whitman's famously homoerotic paeans to the dying men whom he met while serving as a Union Army nurse: "Many a soldier's loving arms about this neck have cross'd and rested, / Many a soldier's kiss dwells on these bearded lips."[9] In terms of gender, however, Alcott diverges from Whitman, for she locates homoerotic masculinity *within* a framework of femininity, such that love between men is described in female terms ("tenderly as women") and soldiers behave like affectionate little women. "Sweet," "comely," and "tender," John—like Stowe's Uncle Tom—is as much heroine as hero. In Alcott's metaphorical translation of female traits into male bodies, the best man in the wake of battle behaves like a woman.

At the same time, in an apparent reversal of this feminization, Alcott also suggests that the best woman for the hospital is surprisingly like a man. The feminine name Tribulation Periwinkle would seem to suggest that the nurse is quintessentially female. Specifically, the nurse is a maternal figure, and throughout *Hospital Sketches*, maternal imagery abounds, from Periwinkle's first assumption of "as matronly an aspect as a spinster could assume" (21) to her general feeling of "a motherly affection for them all" (32). Yet as the idea of "assum[ing]" a matronly aspect suggests, such maternal femininity is unstable, and it has the status of adopted performance, rather than innate identity, throughout the text. One of Alcott's first tasks is to bathe injured soldiers, an activity that precipitates a tentative impersonation of motherhood:

[T]o scrub some dozen lords of creation at a moment's notice, was really— really—. However, there was no time for nonsense, and . . . I drowned my scruples in my washbowl, clutched my soap manfully, and . . . made a dab at the first dirty specimen I saw. . . . I took heart and scrubbed away like any tidy parent . . . Some of them took the performance like sleepy children . . . others looked grimly scandalized, and several of the roughest colored like bashful girls. (23–24)

The tone of this passage—like much in the opening chapters of *Hospital Sketches*—is lighthearted, but here as elsewhere, a humorous tone softens a more painful theme. In this passage, Alcott attempts to navigate the shock of her encounter with male bodies through metaphor. Initially unrepresentable ("really— really—"), the moment is negotiated by a series of gender crossovers, whereby soldiers are "like bashful girls" and Periwinkle acts "manfully." The infantilization of men is here, as in the depiction of John, preliminary to a renegotiation of gender: men become "sleepy children" on the way to becoming "bashful girls." Meanwhile, the role of mother—"like any tidy parent"—is precisely enshrined as *role*, its identity as constructed as the gender and generation of soldiers.

Elsewhere in the text, Periwinkle intermittently abandons this performance of maternity. Though she leaves for Washington "as if going on a bridal tour" (6), she more closely resembles a soldier on his tour of duty. Requesting a nursing position at the start, she declares, "I've enlisted!" (4), and she describes her teary farewell to her family in masculine terms: "I maintain that the soldier who cries when his mother says 'Good bye,' is the boy to fight best" (6). As Jane Schultz notes, in the book's opening chapter, Periwinkle "aligns herself with male consciousness, claiming public and literary citizenship."[10] Periwinkle's allegiances are to masculinity, as she later declares explicitly: "I have a fellow feeling for lads, and always owed Fate a grudge because I wasn't a lord of creation instead of a lady" (68). Rather than incarnating an innate femininity, then, Periwinkle's nursing seems less a form of mothering than a means of soldiering.

More lad than lady in her approach to war, Periwinkle is also more soldier than nurse in her experience of military service. Occurring only six weeks after her arrival in hospital, Periwinkle's illness might seem to signal a failure of strength, linking femininity and illness in pathologizing combination.[11] Yet *Hospital Sketches* defines female illness differently, implicitly equating the female nurse who falls ill with fever with the male soldier delirious from his war injuries. Immediately following the death of John, the first words of the next chapter transfer the question of the soldier's ill health to Periwinkle herself, as a doctor informs her, "My dear girl, we shall have you sick in your bed, unless you keep yourself warm and quiet" (47). What links Periwinkle's suffering most directly to those of soldiers is its psychic register. When her illness worsens, she finds that "Hours began to get confused; people looked odd; queer faces haunted the room, and the nights were one long fight with weariness and pain" (60). Such symptoms strongly echo those of the men hospitalized alongside John, such as a New Jersey soldier "crazed by the horrors" of the war: "[H]is mind had suffered more than his body; some string of that delicate machine was over strained, and, for days, he had been reliving, in imagination, the scenes he could not forget, till his distress broke out in incoherent ravings, pitiful to hear" (35). Periwinkle's "odd" people, "queer" faces, and "confused" hours reprise such painful hallucinations. If the origins of her illness diverge from those of soldiers, its effects converge with theirs in the domain of the psyche.

Periwinkle's symptoms seem closest to those of the Civil War soldier whose wounds, deracinated from their physical origins, now reside wholly in the psyche: the amputee. As Periwinkle describes him, the amputee is a "poor soul" who, after his surgery, "comes to himself, sick, faint, and wandering; full of strange pains and confused visions, of disagreeable sensations and sights" (69). This description is part of an emphasis on amputation in the text. When Periwinkle first arrives at the hospital, for example, she focuses on the "legless, armless" wounded (22) and her initiation into hospital life involves witnessing the "irrepressible tremor of [the] tortured bodies" of patients awaiting amputation without ether (29); later, at the moment of John's death, "there was no sound in the room but the drip of water, from a stump or two" (44). During Periwinkle's own convalescence, she sits sewing at her window and watches convalescents "going in parties to be fitted to artificial limbs" (55). Finally, she notes that while nurses are not "obliged to witness amputations," she herself "witnessed several operations; for the height of my ambition was to go to the front after a battle, and . . . the sooner I inured myself to trying sights, the more useful I should be" (69–70). Throughout the text, Periwinkle seems irresistibly drawn to the "trying sight" of the amputee, whose sufferings not only structure her work as a nurse but engage her experiences as a patient.

A focus on amputation is inevitable in any account of Civil War nursing, since amputation was the strategy most readily available to doctors coping with bullet-wounds and infection. In linking the physical sufferings of the amputee with his mental condition, moreover, Alcott follows contemporary medical writers systematically exploring such neurological phenomena as "the phantom limb," most famously the Civil War doctor and novelist Silas Weir Mitchell.[12] Alcott's account is distinctive, however, in that she not only relocates injury from bodies to minds but also implicitly connects the gender of the amputee with that of the nurse. In the metaphorical resonance between the "confused visions" of the amputee and Periwinkle, the narrative provides the nurse with the closest possible access to a form of wartime injury which, as a civilian, she is definitionally denied. Amputation, that which typically makes the soldier less than a man, is here used symbolically to make the nurse something more—or at least something other—than a woman. Even as she metaphorically feminizes the male soldier, Alcott also offers a metonymic displacement of war injury from bodies to minds and from men to women. In Alcott's Civil War hospital, the line of demarcation between the sexes is as much under pressure as the integrity of body and psyche.

What is at stake in these multiple forms of cross-gender identification, in which men act like women and women like men? In *Hospital Sketches,* such metaphoric crossovers are intimately linked to Alcott's own psychic conflicts as woman and as writer and to the larger self-divisions of nineteenth-century female subjectivity to which her writings testify. As recent feminist scholarship on Alcott suggests, the sunny public reputation of this writer as "children's friend" was sharply at odds with her childhood struggles against the constraints of Victorian gender norms, the intellectual world of midcentury Concord, and the obligations of an eccentric family. Daughter of educator and reformer Bronson Alcott, raised in the heady intellectual milieu of midcentury Concord, Louisa May Alcott was encouraged in her literary aspirations to a degree unusual for women in Victorian America. Yet as in the case of Phelps, that encouragement was qualified in a variety of ways. Since Bronson and Abba May Alcott closely monitored their four daughters' development, Louisa's work had to satisfy strict parental standards of philosophical value and moral worth. Moreover, since Bronson was chronically insolvent, her writing had to support the family financially. The larger intellectual world of Concord in which the Alcotts circulated added to this sense of constraint. "To have had Mr. Emerson for an intellectual god all one's life," she once remarked in conversation to a friend, "is to be invested with a chain armor of propriety."[13]

In short, Louisa May Alcott came of age in an environment whose innovations compounded, rather than undercut, the propriety demanded by Victorian gender ideology. It is no surprise that by age twelve, she registers the "chain armor of propriety" in her journal as a homiletic discourse on the necessities of self-denial: "What are the most valuable kinds of self-denial? Appetite, temper. How is self-denial of temper known? If I control my temper, I am respectful and gentle, and every one sees it. What is the result of this self-denial? Every one loves me, and I am happy."[14] Faithfully copied from her daily lessons, these comments were probably read by her father, who had been observing Louisa closely since her infancy, and certainly read by her mother, who left a note for daughter, declaring that "I often peep into your diary, hoping to see some record of more happy days."[15] Even Alcott's private exercise of self-discipline was open to surveillance, in a pedagogy of self-control monitored both internally and externally. Her upbringing accords closely with what Richard Brodhead, following Foucault, terms the "disciplinary intimacy" characteristic of antebellum America, whereby self-imposed restraint lovingly taught by the family became the privileged disciplinary mode for the self; Bronson Alcott was a major advocate of this philosophy.[16] For all the joyful eccentricities of Alcott's early life, she was governed by a self-regulating pedagogy that rewrote the implicitly male credo of Emersonian self-reliance as female self-denial.

Situated against this framework of femininity as psychic self-regulation,

Alcott's work provides insight into the possibilities, metaphoric as well as literal, the Civil War afforded women for rebellion. Alcott's private writings make clear an identification with masculinity that long predated but was profoundly energized and transformed by the war. At fourteen, for example, she wrote in her journal: "I was born with a boy's spirit under my bib and tucker. I *can't wait* [for a time] when I *can work*"; and at twenty-eight she echoed in a letter, "I was born with a boys nature & always had more sympathy for & interest in them than in girls, & have fought my fight for nearly fifteen [years] with a boys spirit under my 'bib & tucker' & a boys wrath when I got 'floored,' so I'm not preaching like a prim spinster but freeing my mind like one of 'our fellows.' "[17] In these quotations, a woman who speaks assertively is immediately suspect—"preaching like a prim spinster"—while maleness, by contrast, signifies a way of working and speaking freely, as much a style as an identity. Long before the war begins, Alcott identifies agency with masculinity, in a culture in which the best way to imagine being a person is to envision being a man.

When war arrives, it offers Alcott a particular psychic charge, since it makes available the possibility of masculine freedom through the alibi of patriotic duty. "War declared with the South," she writes in her journal, "I've often longed to see a war, and now I have my wish. I long to be a man; but as I can't fight, I will content myself with working for those who can."[18] Alcott's first war work was sewing soldiers' uniforms while at home. In her journal, this activity metaphorically reaches toward both soldiering and writing: "[B]etween blue flannel jackets for 'our boys' and dainty slips for [niece and nephew] Louisa Caroline or John B., Jr. . . . I reel off my 'thrilling' tales, and mess up my work in a queer but interesting way."[19] The imagery of "blue jackets" and "dainty slips" is literary as well as sartorial, suggesting both items of clothing and "slips" of paper for her "queer but interesting" gothic thrillers. The masculine cloth jacket of the Union soldier alternates with the more feminine "slip," as the rhetoric of masculinity both covers up and gives shape to Alcott's own rebellious desires. Shortly thereafter, Alcott gets her own chance to enter the world of boys in blue jackets: "Thirty years old. Decided to go to Washington as a nurse. . . . Help needed, and I love nursing, and *must* let out my pent-up energy in some new way."[20] Departing, she declares, "I set forth . . . feeling as if I was the son of the house going to war."[21] Metaphorically turning from thirty-year-old "prim spinster" to "son of the house," Alcott grows up in wartime by growing down to her favorite state, that of boyhood. The war, in short, marks Alcott's coming-of-age as a man.

Tribulation Periwinkle's soldier persona in *Hospital Sketches*, then, is first of all a matter of masculine agency. The text's cross-gender identifications serve as part of Alcott's ongoing linkage, at once literal and metaphorical, between war and female self-representation. What Alcott's private writings further suggest is the figurative importance of *civil* war to female identity, for they chart a war against feminine civility energized by the Civil War itself. We may begin to gauge the connection between external Civil War and internal civil war in her texts by tracing the path of one of her favorite adjectives, "topsy-turvy." In a letter to her father on the occasion of their shared birthday, Alcott writes:

> *I* was a crass crying brown baby. . . . I fell with a crash into girlhood & continued . . . tumbling from one year to another till strengthened by such violent exercise the topsey turvey girl shot up into a topsey turvey woman who now twenty three years after sits big brown & brave . . .[22]

Here is Concord at the start of the war:

> [T]he town is in a high state of topsey turveyness . . . when quiet Concord does get stirred up it is a sight to behold. . . Are you going to have a dab at the saucy Southerners? I long to fly at some body & free my mind on several points . . .[23]

And here is Alcott's home life as she prepares to leave for Washington:

> Father [is] keeping his topsy turvy family in order. . . . I am getting ready to go to Washington as an army nurse . . . if I was only a boy I'd march off tomorrow.[24]

In these quotations, the rhetoric of masculine identification forms part of a general language of inversion, one in which both the private Alcott and the public sphere constitute worlds turned upside down. "Topsy-turvy" moves from an ambiguous index of Alcott's own rebelliousness to an approving gloss on the freeing dislocations caused by Civil War. Together, these passages posit civil war as a condition of unruliness in which nation ("those saucy Southerners"), town ("stirred up" Concord), and family (not "in order") are so disrupted that they mirror Alcott's own chronic rebelliousness.

These passages also lead, inescapably, back to the Topsy of *Uncle Tom's Cabin*. Like Topsy, topsy-turvy Louisa is a "brown baby" who "crash[ed] into girlhood." The comparison suggests the inseparability of race from Alcott's self-representation. Raised in a fervently abolitionist family that regularly met with antislavery leaders and hosted John Brown's family, Alcott longed after her Washington experience to "go South & help the blacks as I am no longer allowed to nurse the whites. The former seems the greater work." Her writings of the 1860s, as Sarah Elbert has shown, consistently reflect her commitment to emancipation.²⁵ Apart from her explicit antislavery politics, Alcott's letters also suggest an implicit metaphorical identification between herself as a disorderly woman and free African-Americans. The "brown baby" letter continues: "as the brown baby fought through its small trials so the brown woman will fight thro her big ones & come out I hope queen of herself tho not of the world." As in the case of Stowe, the fantasy of "help[ing] the blacks" is inseparable from white women's self-representation, as objects of civility as well as civilizing agents. If Topsy obliquely symbolizes Stowe's own incivilities, here the image of the fighting "brown baby" openly organizes the disciplinary struggles of the adult "brown woman."²⁶

Alcott's self-representation as "brown" rather than black is also important, for it suggests a liminal position in which her whiteness is energized by, rather than wholly transformed into, blackness. In an 1861 letter to her friend Alf Whitman, she described her photographic image in mixed-race terms: "I will have a 'picter' taken in for my Dolphus & as I always take [i.e. photograph] very dark & hunched up you will be gratified with an image of a stout mulatto lady with a crooked nose, sleepy eyes & a tempestuous gown."²⁷ In these lines to "my Dolphus," Alcott's image of herself as "very dark" joins a series of deviations from normative white femininity, including "stout" and "hunched up" body, "crooked nose," "sleepy eyes," and "tempestuous gown." As "mulatto lady," Alcott symbolically positions herself between white lady and "blackest of her race" Topsy. The photographic medium serves as a precise metaphor for this image, as a black surface against which the outlines of whiteness are projected and developed. Incorporating the legacy of Stowe, Alcott's writings use the image of unruly blackness as a feature of her self-representation in an attempt to escape the constraints of white femininity.

Alcott's topsy-turvyness implicitly involves inversions of sexuality as well as gender and race. She declared in an interview, for example, that "I am more than half-persuaded that I am a man's soul, put by some freak of nature into a woman's body . . . because I have fallen in love in my life with so many pretty girls, and never once the least little bit with any man."²⁸ Bringing together masculine identification with female object-choice, this passage is startlingly proleptic of the sexological language of the "invert," only just emerging by the end of Alcott's lifetime, which pathologized the lesbian as a "man's soul trapped in a woman's body."²⁹ Such codifications were prescriptive rather than descriptive, and Alcott's biographers provide little conclusive evidence that she was what would come to be known as lesbian. But her comment suggests at minimum her swerve away from the accoutrements of heterosexuality—husband, children, household—that normatively accompanied Victorian womanhood. Thirty and unmarried when she went to Washington, Alcott was topsy-turvy—or, to use another of her favorite adjectives, "queer"—by virtue of being a permanent spinster as well as a "boyish" girl.[30]

These multiple modes of inversion take new form, literal and symbolic, in Alcott's representations of her Civil War nursing experiences. In a letter to her mentor, Union nurse Hannah Stevenson, Alcott noted the "all pervading bewilderment [that] fell upon me the first few days" at the hospital: "Everything here strikes me as very odd & shiftless both within and without, people, manners customs & ways of living, but I like to watch it all & am very glad I came."[31] *Hospital Sketches* more fully dramatizes Alcott's carnivalesque enjoyment of her "odd" experience, by transforming topsy-turvyness into a condition symbolic of the Civil War. This transformation begins with the journey of "topsy-turvy Trib" to Washington, a journey which relocates inversion from psychic to social domains. On the train, she watches as encamped soldiers "threw up their caps and cut capers as we passed" (18); when she arrives, she observes that "Pennsylvania Avenue . . . made me feel as if I'd crossed the water and landed somewhere in Carnival time" (18). As Mary Cappello has shown, Alcott's descriptions of Washington are awash in accounts of pigs, dirt, and other boundary-dissolving expressions of the carnivalesque.[32] Her fictional name for the hospital, Hurly-burly House, is a synonym for inversion, and she herself fosters in her patients "the jolliest state of mind their condition allowed" (32). Such inversions are ongoing, for when the men return to the battlefield, "the rooms fall into an indescribable state of topsy-turvyness" (68). A disorderly psyche writ large, Hurly-burly House offers a symbolic extension of, as well as a literal outlet for, Alcott's own rebellions against normative femininity.

Hospital Sketches also adapts the topsy-turvy racial dynamics of Alcott's earlier writings to the political setting of the Civil War. In her letter to Stevenson, Alcott wrote that "My ward is the lower one & I perade [*sic*] that region like a stout brown ghost from six in the morning till nine at night haunted & haunting."[33] In *Hospital Sketches*, the image of the "stout brown ghost" who haunts the lower regions of the hospital has disappeared, but another moment in the text aligns Periwinkle with the racial dynamism of the ongoing war. On New Year's Eve, in this case the night before the enactment of the Emancipation Proclamation (31 December 1862), Nurse Periwinkle is sick in bed, but not too sick to make a connection with a group of African-American men outside her window:

> As the bells rung midnight, I electrified my room-mate by dancing out of bed, throwing up the window, and flapping my handkerchief, with a feeble cheer, in answer to the shout of a group of colored men in the street below. All night they tooted and trampled, fired crackers, sung "Glory, Hallelujah" . . . (59)

Literally and symbolically on the eve of racial freedom, this moment is also a would-be proclamation of emancipation for Alcott herself. The carnivalesque social world below destabilizes her in her room above, as her own dancing and flapping respond to the freedom of singing African-American men below. In Alcott's metaphorical appropriation of racial difference, both she and the men below become slaves freed from masters. Like Stowe's representation of Topsy, the image reveals more about whiteness than about blackness. Alcott constructs African-American characters as a site of psychic release, a screen on which she can project her own unruly desires while safely displacing them elsewhere.[34]

If *Hospital Sketches* resituates Alcott's internal revolt on a national stage, so too does it give new metaphoric resonance to an ongoing vocabulary of madness. In the New Year's Eve moment as elsewhere in her writings, she is never so much herself as when she is sick, an equation that predates the war but takes on new meaning from it. "I was so excited I pitched about like a mad woman," Alcott writes in an 1856 letter after attending an abolitionist event.[35] Six years later, she notes in her first journal account of her nursing experience, "Am brought home nearly dead and have a fever," to which she later added, "which I enjoy very much, at least the crazy part."[36] In this addendum, the delirium caused by typhoid fever, like the earlier excitement of being a "mad woman," serves a liberatory function, providing a rare psychic respite from self-abnegation. Alcott's second journal account of her illness elaborates "the crazy part" more fully:

> A mob at Baltimore breaking down the door to get me; being hung for a witch, burned, stoned & otherwise maltreated were some of my fancies. Also being tempted to join Dr W. & two of the nurses in worshipping the Devil. Also tending millions of sick men who never died or got well.[37]

These images contrast the horrors of daily nursing, a Sisyphean exercise in frustration, with the temptations of Devil-worship and the lure of the witch—that quintessential emblem of unruly femininity. In this realization of topsy-turvyness as the dream-work of the unconscious, Alcott transforms the activity of nursing into a full internal revolt against female civility.

In *Hospital Sketches*, the illness of the soldier-nurse extends the journal's language of hallucination to its metaphorical limits. In fictionalizing the trajectory from "motherliness" to madness, *Hospital Sketches* also masculinizes Periwinkle's fever, aligning it so closely with the illness of male soldiers that the sufferings of John and his fellow soldiers seem to serve as direct preparation for her own delirium. As *Hospital Sketches* crafts a new home, Hurly-burly House, for Alcott's domestic unrest, so too does the text translate her antebellum war fervor into actual war fever. In this translation, her illness gains new value, constructed as a soldier's battle service rather than essentialized as female hysteria. While *Hospital Sketches* grants new narrative power to this hallucination, however, it also curtails that power. The suffering daughter is awakened from fever by the arrival of her father to fetch her safely home: "[W]hen he said, 'Come home,' I answered, 'Yes, father'; and so ended my career as an army nurse" (60).

Yet if the narrative of *Hospital Sketches* records the self-censoring victory of civility over the inversions of war, the existence of the text itself points in a different direction: toward the war's productive effect upon her self-representation as an author. Writing to Annie Adams Fields in 1863, Alcott described the origin of some poems she had sent to Fields's husband, James T. Fields, at the *Atlantic:* "[T]hey jingled into my sleepy brain during a night watch beside the bed of a one-legged lad dying of wound fever in the Hospital last Dec; were forgotten till father found them in my papers [and] read them like a partial parent as he is, to neighbor Hawthorne."[38] While this narrative reprises the theme of paternal surveillance in *Hospital Sketches,* Alcott's combination of father with fever also suggests the war's role in having "jingled" her literary voice. In another letter to a friend, she declared that "'Hospital Sketches' still continues a great joke to me, & a sort of perpetual surprise-party, for to this day I cannot see why people like a few extracts from topsey turvey letters written on inverted tin kettles."[39] Like the language of fever, the imagery of inversion also fueled Alcott's self-representation as author. With her sketches cast as "topsey turvey letters written on inverted tin kettles," Alcott's construction of writing, like her representation of illness and madness, bears an intimate relation to the rhetoric of civil war.

As with her self-conception as "son of the house" and "mad woman," Alcott's representation of writing as rebellion predates her war experience. Throughout her journals and letters, Alcott describes the experience of writing as that of being in a "vortex" which frees her from regular duty, as in this 1860 letter to her sister:

> You ask what I am writing. Well, two books half done, nine stories simmering, and stacks of fairy stories moulding on the shelf. I can't do much, as I have no

time to get into a real good vortex. It unfits me for work, worries Ma to see me look pale, eat nothing, and ply by night. These extinguishers keep genius from burning as I could wish . . .[40]

The feverish implications of such "burning" efforts emerge more clearly in a journal entry about a stint of writing which "was very pleasant and queer while it lasted; but after three weeks of it I found that my mind was too rampant for my body, as my head was dizzy, legs shaky, and no sleep would come."[41] Here, writing is akin to a bout of illness, in which both mind and body are disordered and the former overwhelms the latter. With her mind "too rampant" for her body, Alcott constructs writing as a case of topsy-turvy brain fever. This is also the symptomatic presentation of Periwinkle's illness, but *Hospital Sketches* implicitly valorizes the act of authorship by aligning writing fever with war fever. In her account of Periwinkle's dizzy head and shaky legs, Alcott implicitly legitimates the act of writing by conjoining her personal literary desires with the patriotism of the suffering nurse.

Hospital Sketches authorizes Alcott's authorship through the metaphor of soldiering in another way—namely, by linking her writing to the injuries of male soldiers in battle. One of her hospital activities is to help her patients write their letters to loved ones back home; the wounded soldier produces the writing nurse. In her journal, she describes this activity as something "I like to do for they put in such odd things & express thier [*sic*] ideas so comically I have great fun interiorally while [remaining] as grave as possible exteriorally."[42] This description emphasizes the comic pleasures of reading the letters, as Alcott finds "great fun" in the split between internal and external selves. In *Hospital Sketches,* Alcott subdues the "great fun" of this activity, but she increases its importance:

> [H]aving got the bodies of my boys into something like order, the next task was to minister to their minds, by writing letters to the anxious souls at home. . . . The letters dictated to me, and revised by me . . . would have made an excellent chapter for some future history of the war . . . nearly all giving lively accounts of the battle, and ending with a somewhat sudden plunge from patriotism to provender, desiring "Marm," "Mary Ann," or "Aunt Peters," to send along some pies, pickles, sweet stuff, and apples . . . (29–30)

The account implicitly traces a double trajectory between soldier and nurse: the boys "plunge" from military to domestic description in their letters, while the female nurse ascends from domesticity to the world of war by her very participation in nursing. Significantly revising the letters dictated to her, the nurse momentarily becomes a soldier; in the blurring between dictation and revision, the letters sent are her own "writing." On a larger scale, Alcott realizes the fantasy of writing "some future history of the war" in *Hospital Sketches* itself. In publishing this volume, Alcott writes her own soldier's letter home.

More painfully, *Hospital Sketches* also affiliates Alcott's writing with the legacy of soldiering: its bodily wounds and scars. As Kathleen Diffley has shown, the imagery of scarring is prominent in Civil War fiction by men. For example, the story "Hopeful Tackett—His Mark," by one "Richard Wolcott, 10th Illinois," centers on a soldier's pride in the stump left by his amputated leg:

> Occasionally, when he is resting, he will tenderly embrace his stump of a leg, gently patting and stroking it, and talking to it as to a pet. If a stranger is in the shop, he will hold it out admiringly and ask:
> "Do you know what I call that? I call that 'Hopeful Tackett—His Mark.'" And it is a mark—a mark of distinction—a badge of honor, worn by many a brave fellow who has gone forth, borne and upheld a love for the dear old flag, to fight, to suffer, to die if need be, for . . . [it is] won by unflinching nerve and unyielding muscle; won as a badge of the proudest distinction an American can reach.

As this passage suggests, the stump is not only the defining feature of authentic war experience but also, like Wolcott's own regimental affiliation, a literary "mark" or signature. A beloved object worthy of patting and stroking, the soldier's stump is the foundation of his authorial voice. Women are definitionally excluded from this vision, since they can never gain the battlefield "mark of distinction," let alone honor it as a compensatory phallic "pet." As if enacting Lacan's famous formulation that women "lack lack," stories like "Hopeful Tackett—His Mark" suggest that women lack not only the potential for masculine authority in wartime but also the very opportunity to experience emasculation.[43]

Alcott's representation of her illness implicitly intervenes in this exclusionary terrain, wherein, in John Limon's phrase, "as a daughter, she cannot assume the compensatory postures of wounded literary sons."[44] As a healthy war nurse, she can align herself with wounded soldiers only as their caretaker; in her letter to Hannah Stevenson, Alcott apologizes, "This is a very hasty scribble but half a dozen stumps are waiting to be met & my head is full of little duties to be punctually performed."[45] If Alcott's meeting with "stumps" brings her writing to a halt, however, then her own illness brought her closer to the "mark" of the wounded soldier. Apologizing to Alf Whitman for a delay in writing, she narrates:

> My only excuse is I've been to Washington a nursin in the army, got typhoid fever & came bundling home to rave, & ramp, & get my head shaved & almost retire into the tombs in consequence, not to mention picking up again, & appearing before the eyes of my grateful country in a wig & no particular flesh on my bones, also the writing some Hospital Sketches & when folks said put em in a book, doing the same & being drove wild with proof, & printers, & such matters . . .[46]

This passage characteristically unites different forms of mental disorder with humor, combining the "rave" of typhoid fever with the "wild" pressures of publication. Yet one section more seriously brings the effects of wartime service back to Alcott's body: "get my head shaved & almost retire into the tombs in consequence." One of the many physical effects of her typhoid fever, Alcott's baldness is a striking metaphor for the impact of the war on her: a symbol for self-exposure, it specifically makes visible her skewed relation to conventional femininity. In a letter to a woman friend, she remarked, "I would advise all *young* ladies of thirty to shave their brows, pass a few months in the deepest seclusion & then find themselves back in their teens, as far as appearance goes, both a convenient & artistic arrangement."[47]

In *Hospital Sketches,* this wry image of teenage self-scrutiny undergoes an important transformation. In the story of Tribulation Periwinkle's illness, Alcott makes baldness manly, since it is metaphorically akin to the language of male war injury: "I take some satisfaction in the thought that, if I could not lay my head on the altar of my country, I have [laid] my hair" (61). If Alcott is a soldier returning from Washington, then her hair is her own amputated limb. Appearing, like a wounded soldier, before the eyes of a "grateful country," she wears the wig as a temporary prosthesis for the missing part. Once the "son of the house" off to war, she is now "back in her teens" with the battle scar of baldness.

The imagery of the wig is, finally, intimately linked to her writing, since it serves as a crowning metaphor for the gender ambiguities of *Hospital Sketches* itself. Hair and head are extensions of one another, as she notes in her journal: "Felt badly about losing my one beauty. Never mind, it might have been my head & a wig outside is better than a loss of wits inside."[48] In the parallel between wig and wits, Alcott's fake hair is a physical covering for the outside of her head as her writing is a textual cover for its inside. In both cases, the covering aims at the creation of an appropriate appearance—the dutiful daughter, the "motherly" nurse—only to show up askew. Turning the woman nurse into the author-soldier, Alcott writes a book in which a brief, metaphoric departure from femininity has the hallucinatory yet profound impact of a fever dream. As the literary embodiment of her psychic scars, *Hospital Sketches* ultimately offers the promise of masculine agency as woman's phantom limb.

In aligning her fever with that of the soldier, then, Alcott provides a commentary on the transformative importance of the Civil War to self-representation. Of the two cross-gender images underpinning *Hospital Sketches*—the masculinized nurse and the feminized soldier—the former is particularly significant in relation to Alcott's self-conception as writer, for it constitutes an ingenious point of access to the language of masculine agency. From inversion and illness to madness and writing, Alcott's various languages of rebellion gather metaphorical as well as literal force from her relation to the Civil War. In this context, her metaphoric battle scars constitute a strategic redefinition of female subjectivity, one that reframes female inadequacy as male wounding. Femininity is here aligned with weakness and suffering, but that suffering is coded masculine; women return to the domestic sphere, but that sphere is redefined and honored as that of a convalescent "veteran." Most important, female authorship is newly validated as political duty and battle legacy. To put it another way, Alcott's war writings suggest that in a nineteenth-century culture that defined female subjectivity as scarring self-denial, femininity might inevitably be a wound, but at least the terms of such wounding could be altered and valorized. Alcott, I suggest, rewrites the woman writer's quest for a room of one's own into the double-edged desire—at once rebellious and self-regulating—for a wound of one's own.

III

In *Hospital Sketches,* the Civil War functions as a metaphor for Alcott's struggles as ambivalent Concord daughter and as emerging woman writer. Yet we can also trace this metaphorical relation between warring body politic and topsy-turvy individual body in reverse. For if the Civil War symbolically affects Alcott's own psyche, so too does her representation of individual bodies intervene in contemporary constructions of embodied nationhood. These interventions make allegorical use of Alcott's other figure of cross-gendered identification: the feminized soldier. Along with the masculinized nurse, the feminized soldier serves as a point of departure for Alcott's allegorical reinventions of the nation at war and in peace.

To understand these reinventions, we must first move from the intimate literary domain of Alcott's journals to the public sphere of national political discourse in the 1860s and from the body of the individual soldier to that of the nation as a whole. During the Civil War, a variety of discourses aligned the injured soldier with the injured nation. For example, as Lisa Herschbach has shown, the rhetoric of the rapidly emerging artificial-limb industry, centered in the North, equated prosthetic reconstruction of the soldier's damaged body with national reunion.[49] Less concretely, the metaphor of the injured body politic pervaded the writings of Union politicians, a rhetorical strategy that served to naturalize at least three sets of Northern political needs. Most immediately, the language of injury functioned to condemn secession. As Henry Bellows, a Boston minister who became president of the Sanitary Commission, wrote in a popular 1863 pamphlet, "[A] desperate enemy is stabbing at the heart of the nation, the capital, and clutching at the nation's throat, the Mississippi river."[50] Promoting the integrity of the Union, such images also played a powerful role in the "inner civil war" among Northern intellectuals. For Bellows as for other Northerners, metaphors of an imperiled national body supported an authoritarian approach to reestablishing a democratic nation. Wendell Phillips, for example, used this imagery to argue for a strong Northern government: "The use of surgeons is, that when lancets are needed somebody may know how to use them, and save life. . . . [T]he Government may safely be trusted, in a great emergency, with despotic power, without fear of harm, or of wrecking the state."[51] Finally, in abolitionist rhetoric, the most profound disease of the body politic was not national disunion or Northern disloyalty but slavery. Henry Ward Beecher, for example, warned that "Like an ulcer, this evil eats deeper every day."[52] Often represented as a cancer within the body politic, slavery metaphorically required amputation for the survival of the nation. As Lincoln declared, "[T]he moment came when I felt slavery must die that the nation might live!"[53]

As these examples suggest, the image of the injured body politic had its necessary complement in the figure of the government as a judiciously knife-wielding surgeon. Bellows suggested the full affective reach of the role of the surgeon-amputator: "[T]he nation is in a struggle of life and death, and the Government is the physician alone responsible for applying the remedies for its recovery."[54] The privileged actor in this drama was its principal surgeon, Lincoln, who frequently used the language of surgery to describe his approach to the war:

> I have sometimes used the illustration . . . of a man with a diseased limb, and his surgeon. So long as there is a chance of the patient's restoration, the surgeon is solemnly bound to try to save both life *and* limb; but when the crisis comes, and the limb must be sacrificed as the only chance of saving the life, no honest man will hesitate.[55]

The country's principal surgeon, Lincoln also served as sacred metaphorical incorporation of the nation itself, in an extension of the tradition of the "king's two bodies." As Bellows declared: "The head of a nation *is* a sacred person, representing, for the time he holds his office, the most valuable and solemn rights and duties of a people."[56] Lincoln's synecdochic power took a final turn in the wake of his assassination, when he became not only the nation's sacred leader, but also its most heroic patient-martyr. The body politic, its limbs gangrenous from slavery and fractured by secession, would be cured not by the God-like surgery of Lincoln but by his Christ-like sacrifice.[57]

With such rhetoric in mind, we can return to Alcott's *Hospital Sketches*, for in Alcott's implicitly symbolic narrative as in the explicitly metaphorical prose of Bellows, Phillips, and Lincoln, the suffering of the male body can be read allegorically as the crisis of the warring nation. In *Hospital Sketches*, the body of the soldier is as radically disarticulated as that of the nation, as in the case of a wounded man who speaks jocularly of soldiers' lost limbs: "Lord! what a scramble there'll be for arms and legs, when we old boys come out of our graves, on the Judgment Day: wonder if we shall get our own again? If we do, my leg will have to tramp from Fredericksburg, my arm from here, I suppose, and meet my body, wherever it may be" (25). While this passage comically maps male appendages onto geographic regions, the sufferings of the martyred John may be interpreted more seriously as a metaphorical gloss on the ailing union: "For hours he suffered dumbly, without a moment's respite, or a moment's murmuring; his limbs grew cold, his face damp, his lips white, and, again and again, he tore the covering off his breast, as if the lightest weight added to his agony" (44). If this focus on injury is, as I argued above, a displaced account of Alcott's internal conflicts about gender, it is also a part of the inner civil war among Northerners writing about the nation. In Alcott's allegorical narrative as in more explicitly political rhetoric, bodies signify as nations and the agonies of individual suffering echo the political exigencies of civil war.

The 1869 edition of the text, *Hospital Sketches and Camp and Fireside Stories*, provides further hints of the iconographic significance of John's suffering. Reprinting *Hospital Sketches* along with eight short stories (four of them about the Civil War), this edition also changed the text slightly. In keeping with the postwar emphasis on sectional reconciliation, Alcott noted in her journal that she was "[S]oftening all allusions to rebs. . . . Anything to suit customers"; in the new text, for example, "I could hate" a particular Confederate soldier became "I could dislike him."[58] Tempering sectional hostility in the wake of war, the new edition also included two illustrations, which suggest the symbolic significance of both John and Periwinkle in a reunified nation. The fron-

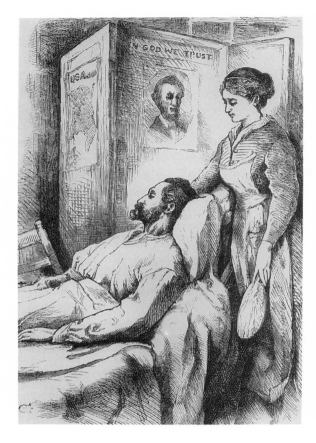

FIGURE 6.
Frontispiece from *Hospital Sketches and Camp and Fireside Stories*, 1869

tispiece for the volume is an illustration of John with Periwinkle, captioned "The manliest man among my forty" (figure 6). Behind these two figures are two illustrations on the wall: Abraham Lincoln, over whose head is the caption "In God We Trust," and a map of the reunified United States of America.

Together, the elements of this illustration effect a series of metonymic connections from Periwinkle to John, from John to the sanctified Lincoln ("In God We Trust"), and from Lincoln to the nation ("USA," which only became a singular noun—that is, a unified body—as a result of the war). Lincoln is the key figure in this tableau, since his power is a synecdoche for the nation, while his assassination echoes the martyr's death of John. This linkage between feminized soldier and fallen president capitalizes on a strand of cultural mythology already in place for Lincoln, whereby the president was described approvingly as feminine. While works like *The Royal Ape* equated Lincoln's feminization with his emasculation, other commentators praised the president for his feminine traits. In the words of contemporaries, for example, he was a man "of almost child-like sweetness" and "womanly tenderness," while William Herndon described him going to market wearing a shawl, children in tow.[59] Similarly, for Louisa May Alcott, Lincoln's femininity was a highly desirable trait, tempering his masculine authority with the compassion and martyrdom of Christ, likewise often represented in feminized terms.[60] Read as a mid-war text, then, John's story indirectly links soldier and nation; read as a retrospective commentary on the war, his story more explicitly unites his martyrdom with that of Lincoln and Christ. Firmly located in a pantheon of feminized male heroes, John carries allegorical weight that extends from soldier to savior to nation.

If Alcott shares with political commentators a rhetoric of national injury, however, she differs from them in her account of cure. *Hospital Sketches* provides a narrative of national embodiment in which male leadership is disorderly at every level: in the operating room of the surgeon-amputator, in the larger social institution of the hospital, and in the national government itself. In this critique, the language of inversion that we have already examined is of central importance, but its valences are reversed. Rather than providing a liberatory discourse for white female subjectivity, topsy-turvyness now appears dystopically as a failure of nationhood.

Most obviously, *Hospital Sketches* has harsh words for surgeons. In particular, Periwinkle objects to one Doctor P., a doctor who has "a somewhat trying habit of regarding a man and his wound as separate institutions" (70), and who

seemed to regard a dilapidated body very much as I should have regarded a damaged garment; and, turning up his cuffs, [began] cutting, sawing, patching and piecing, with the enthusiasm of an accomplished surgical seamstress. . . . The more intricate the wound, the better he liked it. A poor private, with both legs off, and shot through the lungs, possessed more attractions for him than a dozen generals, slightly scratched . . . and had any one appeared in small pieces, requesting to be put together again, he would have considered it a special dispensation. (29)

Here is another gender crossover, but one played for grotesquerie: described in domestic imagery as "an accomplished surgical seamstress," Dr. P. is criticized for his equation of bodies with damaged garments. Similarly, his preference for the private over the general is an index of his fanatical interest in dismembered bodies, rather than a praiseworthy inversion of social hierarchy. "[I]n a state of bliss over a complicated amputation," Dr. P. "works away, with his head upside down" (52). Like his head, Dr. P's sense of responsibility is "upside down," in an account that offers an inverted burlesque of the sacred surgeon-healer described by Bellows and embodied by Lincoln.

If medical authority in *Hospital Sketches* appears grossly inadequate to the demands of the injured bodies in its care, hospital administration fares no better. At Hurly-burly House,

> disorder, discomfort, bad management, and no visible head, reduced things to a condition which I despair of describing. The circumlocution fashion prevailed, forms and fusses tormented our souls, and unnecessary strictness in one place was counterbalanced by unpardonable laxity in another. (51)

This passage offers a veritable frenzy of institutional inversion: disorder, imbalance, circumlocution, and an unbalanced bodily economy in which there is "no visible head." Like the nation sick from war and slavery, the hospital is a poorly regulated body that cannot survive its injuries. "Hurly-burly House," Periwinkle declares without regret at the end, "has ceased to exist as a hospital; so let it rest, with all its sins upon its head" (73).

Finally, the national government is similarly uncontrolled, as Periwinkle discovers when she visits the Senate,

> hoping to hear and see if this large machine was run any better than some small ones I knew of. I was too late, and found the Speaker's chair occupied by a colored gentleman of ten; while two others were . . . having a hot debate on the cornball question, as they gathered the waste paper strewn about the floor into bags; and several white members played leap-frog over the desks, a much wholesomer relaxation than some of the older Senators indulge in, I fancy. (53)

In the "large machine" as in the "small one," the language of unruliness runs riot: waste covers the floor and "leap-frog" is the game of the day. This passage is written for comic effect, but the congruence of its imagery with Alcott's more serious account of hospital administration is revealing. In this version of the "world turned upside down," body and body politic alike suffer from their leaders, who range from sadistic surgeon to absent hospital "head" to missing senators. The ten-year-old "colored gentleman," meanwhile, represents another of Alcott's versions of Topsy but in a pejorative mode. While the language of "brownness" energizes Alcott's self-representation as topsy-turvy, the "colored gentleman" has a less salutary effect on the nation. When such a figure is in "the Speaker's Chair" of Congress, the result is chaos rather than carnival.

What, then, would Periwinkle—and Alcott—prefer instead? *Hospital*

Sketches offers a few glimpses of a very different kind of hospital: at the start, for example, members of Periwinkle's family invent roles for themselves in a "model hospital" upon hearing that she is to be a nurse (4). Later, Periwinkle marvels at the impeccable administration of Armory House, the hospital where she had originally hoped to serve. In an ideal hospital, like Armory House, Periwinkle would be in charge, not only caring for male soldiers but also governing race relations in the hospital. The only other illustration in the second edition of *Hospital Sketches* glosses a revealing moment in the text, when Periwinkle rebukes a white nurse from Virginia who refuses to pick up a black child in the kitchen. Seizing the child, Periwinkle lectures the white nurse on abolitionism; the caption for the accompanying image reads "One hand stirred gruel for sick America, and the other hugged baby Africa" (59) (figure 7). If the frontispiece to *Hospital Sketches* puts Periwinkle in the national picture, this illustration foregrounds her as a leader, literally highlighted against a black background. The black child, rather than providing a liberatory model of misbehavior, functions as a figure to be civilized. In this recasting of Topsy, the two-handed Nurse Periwinkle is an empathetic Miss Ophelia, eager to touch the black child in her midst. The image as a whole offers an allegorical fantasy of white maternal leadership in which Periwinkle leads both "sick America" and "baby Africa."[61]

Periwinkle cannot realize this model of white women's power within the confines of Hurly-burly House, where male leadership still holds sway. In a headless hospital where nurses can only be foot soldiers, she must remain silent in the face of hospital mismanagement: "I feel like a boiling tea-kettle, with the lid ready to fly off and damage somebody" (51). In relation to Dr. P., this domestic language of self-policing is even more overt, as she assumes a divided attitude of external masochism and internal sadism: "I obeyed [Dr. P.], cherishing the while a strong desire to insinuate a few of his own disagreeable knives and scissors into him, and see how he liked it. A very disrespectable and ridiculous fancy, of course" (71). In contrast to her letter-writing for soldiers, wherein the split between interior and exterior selves affords Alcott "great fun," here Alcott's self-splitting is a painful feature of her self-discipline. In *Hospital Sketches*, Alcott suggests that as a female citizen in a male republic, she has no choice but to be patient with surgeons.[62]

In her subsequent Civil War fiction, however, she gets to play doctor, offering several related versions of a revitalized body politic. Alcott's fiction repeatedly returns to the figures of the Civil War soldier and nurse. These figures appear, directly or obliquely, in four stories collected in the 1869 edition of *Hospital Sketches and Camp and Fireside Stories*—"My Contraband" (originally published in 1863 as "The Brothers"), "Nelly's Hospital" (1864), "A Hospital

FIGURE 7.
Illustration from *Hospital
Sketches and Camp and Fireside
Stories*, 1869

Christmas" (1864), "Love and Loyalty" (1864), "The Blue and the Gray"
(1868)—as well as in the novels *Little Women* (1868–69), *Work* (1873), and *Jo's
Boys* (1886). In particular, "My Contraband" and "A Hospital Christmas" begin
to shift the terms of Civil War representation from male injury to female
healing, while *Little Women* and its sequels realize Alcott's vision of a rejuvenated and regendered postwar body politic.

    Like *Hospital Sketches*, "My Contraband" is a story narrated by a nurse in
an army hospital who tends to an injured Union soldier. As with John, this
soldier is an admirable figure, "five-and-twenty at least, strong-limbed and
manly," who dies a heroic death.[63] In this story, however, the soldier, named
Robert, is a mixed-race former slave whose master was his father, whose white

half-brother is also a patient in the same hospital, and whose formal designation in wartime, like that of other slaves now in the North, is that of
Union "contraband." Robert's mixed-race status is central to Alcott's model
of the warring nation, for his body itself literalizes conflict and division.
Robert's back is covered with the scars of slavery: "[H]e tore the shirt from
neck to waist, and on his strong, brown shoulders showed me furrows deeply
ploughed, wounds which, though healed, were stronger than any in that
house" (85). With his torso bifurcated into scarred zones, so too is his wounded
face split into two: "Part of his black hair had been shorn away, and one eye
was nearly closed; pain so distorted, and the cruel sabre-cut so marred that
portion of his face, that, when I saw it, I felt as if a fine medal had been
suddenly reversed" (77). Robert's divided face aligns with his conflicting racial
allegiances: "[It] belonged to neither race; and the pride of one and the help-
lessness of the other, kept him hovering alone in the twilight a great sin has
brought to overshadow the whole land" (78). His wound also aligns him with
his white half-brother, "a Reb . . . crazy with typhoid" (74). Ordinarily "wounds
and fevers should not be together" (77), but when Robert is mistakenly placed
in the same ward with the other man, wound and fever, along with Union
and Confederate, combine. With Robert, then, Alcott symbolically locates the
injured nation, divided regionally, racially, and fraternally, in the figure of her
injured mixed-race hero.

The key to the recovery of this suffering body is the leadership of Nurse
Faith Dane. The first line of the story introduces the melancholy Dane as
efficient seamstress: "Doctor Franck came in as I sat sewing up the rents in
an old shirt, that Tom might go tidily to his grave" (74). Recalling Alcott's
earlier description of Dr. P. as "accomplished surgical seamstress," this beginning aligns Dane with the role of doctor as well as nurse. As the surgeon
reunifies torn bodies, so too does Dane intervene therapeutically in Robert's
story. The turning point of "My Contraband" comes when the nurse prevents
Robert from killing his half-brother. In this scene, Dane awakens to see Robert leaning over his half-brother's bed, "very pale, his mouth grim . . . even
the wounded [eye] was open now, all the more sinister for the deep scar above
and below" (81–82). In this gothic moment, the contrast between pale skin and
dark scar brings the allegory of national struggle into view, with the opening of
Robert's wounded eye suggesting the awakening of violence. In response, the
nurse asserts her own leadership, dissuading Robert from murder by reminding
him of his lost wife:

Thank Heaven for the immortality of love! for when all other means of salvation
failed, a spark of this vital fire softened the man's iron will, until a woman's hand

could bend it. He let me take from him the key, let me draw him gently away, and lead him to the solitude which was now the most healing balm I could bestow. (87–88)

The moment presents "woman's hand" as an omnipotent psychological force, capable of bending "man's iron will." Chastened, Robert later has "the docile look of a repentant child," who has internalized his lesson: "I thank yer, Missis, fer hinderin' me" (88).

Dane's authority in this episode is inseparable from the power of nurse over patient, parent over child, and—crucial to each of these registers—of white over black. Robert's race not only anchors his emblematic national status but abets the fantasy of female leadership that infuses the story. Mixed-race Robert is led by white Nurse Dane, a relationship that continues when he becomes a soldier; enlisting with the Massachusetts 54th Regiment of black soldiers, he declares to her, "I'll fight fer yer till I'm killed" (89). In the last section of the story, Robert participates in the regiment's famous assault on Fort Wagner, where he improbably meets his half-brother in the Confederate army, kills him, and is himself fatally injured. Nurse Dane's authority remains paramount in the national setting of Fort Wagner: when she visits him on his deathbed, she learns that he has taken her last name. The slaveholding connotations of this final act are reinforced by the story's title. The phrase "my contraband" emphatically signals a proprietary relationship, in which the slave claimed as "contraband" status by the Union army becomes the emotional, if not economic, property of the authoritative white nurse.[64]

Yet even as the story's racial dynamics energize Alcott's fantasy of white female authority, they also complicate that fantasy. Unlike John in *Hospital Sketches*, Robert is an object of erotic attraction for Nurse Dane. While the doctor urges her toward his white half-brother with the comment, "you've had the fever, you like queer patients" (74), she herself feels "decidedly more interest in the black man than in the white" (75):

> I had seen many contrabands, but never one so attractive as this. . . . [His profile] possessed all the attributes of comeliness belonging to his mixed-race. He was more quadroon than mulatto, with Saxon features, Spanish complexion darkened by exposure, color in lips and cheek, waving hair, and an eye full of the passionate melancholy . . . (75–76)

Throughout Alcott's writing, the adjective "Spanish" signifies eroticism, and here Robert's comeliness is so great that his eye of "passionate melancholy" threatens to shift the story onto the unstable terrain of interracial romance.

Instead, Alcott immediately shifts focus to Robert's scars, the sight of which changes Nurse Dane's impressions of him: "Not only did the manhood seem to die out of him, but the comeliness that first attracted me . . . though I went in to offer comfort as a friend, I merely gave an order as a mistress" (76–77). This image of the white "mistress" giving "an order" to a black man stabilizes and displaces a less controlled dynamic, that of Nurse Dane's interracial desire for Robert.

Similarly, the translation of Robert's violent impulses into his bravery as a soldier controls the specter of armed black violence within the structured confines of the army. In the earlier attack on his brother, his violence is vengeful and potentially limitless: "I'm lettin' him go too easy; there's no pain in this; we a'n't even yet" (85). Yet this same aggression is sanctioned in the name of national struggle, for Robert later attacks his half-brother "as if he was Jeff, Beauregard, an' Lee, all in one" (92). Robert's death in battle, like the earlier dying out of Dane's desire for him, represents a contained resolution to a potentially explosive form of wartime emotion. The Civil War is the story's catalyst for inventing white women's authority, but Alcott also requires the formal confines of the war to keep passion—erotic and murderous—from excessive expression. As Alcott begins to imagine a nation reconstructed by women, racial difference at once undergirds her narrative fantasy and threatens to undermine it.

In her other Civil War fiction, Alcott retreats from these instabilities by creating wartime scenarios in which lines of racial hierarchy, and white female authority, are more firmly drawn. For example, an 1863 Civil War story written for children, "Nelly's Hospital," recasts the roles of white nurse and black soldier in explicitly fantastic terms. An injured Union soldier inspires his young sister, Nelly, to invent her own Union hospital: "I've been thinking that it would be very pleasant to have a little hospital all my own, and be a nurse in it." Modeling her enterprise on the relief efforts of the Sanitary Commission, Nelly treats animals, birds, and insects; she also cares for her convalescent brother, and both her real and imagined nursing efforts become "an example and a rebuke for others" in the neighborhood. Teaching disciplined selflessness in wartime, the story thus promotes the image of the Union nurse as omnipotent leader. "Nurse Nelly" exercises total control over her patients, including one fly whom she frees from a spider's web: "Nelly had heard much about contrabands . . . so, when she freed the poor black fly, she played he was her contraband . . . [She] bade him rest and recover from his fright, remembering that he was at liberty to fly away whenever he liked, because she had no wish to make a slave of him." While Nelly has "no wish to make a slave" of the anthropomorphized fly, the moment establishes her as master of "her contraband," empowered to enslave or free him as she likes. Translating racial hierarchy into child's play, "Nelly's Hospital" turns the white nurse into a wartime Prospero, magician-ruler of all she surveys.[65]

Relocating this figure of white female authority to a world of human patients, "A Hospital Christmas" (1864) describes the Christmas celebrations of a wartime hospital ward populated primarily by white men and managed by a white doctor and nurse. Like Doctor B. of *Hospital Sketches*, Doctor Bangs in this story is "not a sanguine or conciliatory individual; many cares and crosses caused him to regard the world as one large hospital, and his fellow-beings all more or less dangerously wounded patients in it. He . . . seemed to think that the sooner people quitted it the happier for them."[66] Like John in the earlier work, "Big Ben" in this story is a heroic white man who blurs gender categories: "Patient, strong, and tender, he seemed to combine many of the best traits of both man and woman" (325). And as in "My Contraband," the true leader in this hospital setting is an authoritative white woman, Nurse Hale. The story turns on her presence in the ward on Christmas Day, when she transforms the patients from a fretful and impatient crew into a unified group of Christmas celebrants.

If "A Hospital Christmas" extends the thematics of *Hospital Sketches* and "My Contraband," however, it does so in ways that crucially transform the earlier texts. Big Ben is not a patient but an ex-patient who serves as a ward attendant, a shift from the role of patient to caregiver that signals Alcott's larger concern in the story with how a hospital ward as a whole is to be effectively managed. Miss Hale is more administrator than nurse, and her actions bespeak a wider scope of influence than that of Nurses Periwinkle or Dane. Reversing the disorder of "Hurly-burly House," she equitably distributes gifts, food, and favors. It is as if Alcott fictionally invents her own Sanitary Commission, with Nurse Hale regulating the flow of goods and services in her world as the national organization regularized the conditions of food, medicine, and hygiene for soldiers during the war. Alcott's Nurse Hale, moreover, sanitizes psychic as well as physical interiors. She teaches all her "boys" temperamental control; to one patient, "surly Sam" (318), she cautions, "Better lose both arms than cheerfulness and self-control" (335). Throughout "A Hospital Christmas," Alcott proposes a systematic model of female governance in which men are not only led by female authority but are taught to internalize female virtues of sympathy, sacrifice, and self-restraint.

The effects of this feminizing pedagogy are national as well as individual. "A hospital ward," the narrator remarks, "is often a small republic, beautifully governed by pity, patience, and mutual sympathy which lessens mutual suffering" (325). In this "small republic," the articulation of American identity emerges out of domestic order; after Christmas dinner, "being true Americans, the ruling passion found vent in the usual 'Fellow-citizens!' and allusions to the 'Star-Spangled Banner'" (338–39). Yet if this dinner-table of "true Americans" represents the triumph of domesticity, it also represents a narrower social vision than the mixed-race tableau Alcott invokes at Fort Wagner. The only black man in the ward is Barney, who is known as "the colored incapable" and who attempts to hang a Christmas ornament only to find that "the whole thing tumbled down about his ears" (320). Negating the potential for revolution embodied in Robert Dane, Barney is definitionally incapable, and his tumbling is comic rather than violent. Compared with "My Contraband," the reconstructed nation of "A Hospital Christmas" both contracts the field of racial representation and expands the transformative possibilities of feminization.

In making the "republic" into a "home-like" place, Alcott begins to emphasize the image of the national "household" over that of the injured body politic. Intertwined metaphors of injury and domesticity suffuse her Civil War fiction: in *Hospital Sketches,* Dr. P. is a bad surgeon and a bad housekeeper; in "A Hospital Christmas," the goal of Christmas is both a rejuvenated patient and a happy home. Yet for Alcott, the imagery of national housekeeping is intrinsically more congenial for women than that of nursing. In "My Contraband," Nurse Dane must answer to Dr. Franck, and in "A Hospital Christmas," Miss Hale is subject to the censure of the doctor, who demands that she sit in the chair "with your hands folded for twenty minutes; the clock will then strike nine, and you will go straight up to your bed" (342). In the world of the household, by contrast, white women hold sway, as Alcott's later fiction suggests. Continuing the project of national regeneration begun in the earlier stories, *Little Women* and its sequels effect a full-scale shift from Civil War hospitals to homes. This shift is not unique to Alcott; as Kathleen Diffley has shown, a generation of writers reconstructed the nation which had become not so much a house divided as a "house invaded" by wartime.[67] Of particular interest in Alcott's national allegory is that, in moving from hospitals to homes, she moves in emphasis from male injury to female governance. *Little Women* and its sequels offer Alcott's most sustained and influential version of a reconstructed body politic, one that is effectively controlled by female virtues, even—or especially—when evacuated of female bodies.

Its first half set during the Civil War, *Little Women* is a war novel, though it is seldom defined as such by critics.[68] In particular, the story of the March sisters, like Alcott's earlier writing, interprets war through the figure of the suffering Civil War soldier. There are at least three injured soldiers in *Little Women,* beginning with the patriarch of the March family, a chaplain in the

Union army who falls dangerously ill and recovers at a hospital in Washington. Yet Mr. March is a peripheral character in the narrative, and his war service is presented in terms of its distance from the rest of the family. Far more visible and important to the narrative is Beth, whose illness dominates the novel twice, from her initial bout with scarlet fever to her lingering death twenty-two chapters and several years later. Beth's illness is linked with the female domestic sphere—she contracts scarlet fever from tending a sick baby—but its representation is invested with the narrative energy Alcott had previously given to the wounds of soldiers, and her symptoms are akin to those of the feverish patients of *Hospital Sketches:* "[S]he did not know the familiar faces round her, but addressed them by wrong names, and called imploringly for her mother."[69] Her death is described in the terms of Christian martyrdom Alcott had previously used for the soldier-hero John: "[T]he natural rebellion over, the old peace returned" (415) and "in the dark hour before the dawn, on the bosom where she had drawn her first breath, she quietly drew her last" (419). As with John, her death is available for an allegorical reading, particularly as it coincides with the end of the "rebellion" and the return of "old peace." In Beth's illness, Alcott combines the conventions of the war novel with the narrative frame of domestic fiction, translating the pathos of the dying male soldier into that of the dying little sister.[70]

But there is another, more overtly military figure in the text. Jo March, the novel's heroine, is also its regretful soldier-manqué: "I can't get over my disappointment in not being a boy, and it's worse than ever now, for I'm dying to go and fight with papa" (3), she declares at the outset, and shortly thereafter she laments, "Don't I wish I could go as a drummer, a *vivan*—what's its name? or a nurse, so I could be near him and help him" (8). These adjunct military roles—drummer, nurse, and "vivandière," or female provider of regimental goods and support—are unavailable to her, but she gets her chance to participate in the war metaphorically, when she has her hair cut off for the cause: "I felt queer when I saw the dear old hair laid out on the table, and felt only the short, rough ends on my head. It almost seemed as if I'd an arm or a leg off" (163). This is haircutting as amputation, in a reprise of Alcott's—and Periwinkle's—alignment between a woman giving up her hair and a soldier losing a limb in battle. The moment further reroutes the representation of male injury in the novel, moving not only from sick fathers to sick daughters, but also from dying daughters to live ones. From her initial focus on the soldier as a feminized man, Alcott has come full circle to the model of soldier as masculinized woman.

Like the novel's truest soldier, its ablest surgeon-leader is a woman. Marmee is Beth's most valued nurse, but more important, she is the household's best manager, teaching her daughters practical lessons in domestic economy and moral lessons about "the sweetness of self-denial and self-control" (82). Unlike the administrators of Hurly-burly House, Marmee is able to bring order out of chaos, as when, after the girls have made themselves irritable during a week of leisure, she gently lectures them on the value of industry: "Work is wholesome, and there is plenty for everyone; it keeps us from *ennui* and mischief . . . I am quite satisfied with the experiment, and fancy that we shall not have to repeat it; only don't go to the other extreme, and delve like slaves" (117–18). While Marmee's words offer lessons in individual female self-abnegation, they also articulate a more expansive social vision of a self-regulating body politic. Neither a topsy-turvy Hurly-burly House nor a nation relying on "slaves," the all-female March household of the first half of the novel provides an exemplary model for the wartime nation, its metaphoric frame now shifted from the locus of the body to that of the household.

Set during the postwar years, the second half of *Little Women* provides an allegorical inventory of the types of national household that may emerge once the "house divided" has been restored. If Marmee is the incumbent president of the March republic, then her daughters are her successors, and the households they establish constitute experimental models for the nation recovering from domestic war. Meg, the first to marry, is too insular in her concerns and too dependent on John Brooke to interest Alcott as a symbol of political authority. Her domesticity competes with the public sphere, as when her husband attempts to read the newspaper: "Demi's colic got into the shipping list, and Daisy's fall affected the price of stocks,—for Mrs. Brooke was only interested in domestic news" (389). If Meg is too domestic, Amy is too foreign, both in her European travels and in her marriage to the wealthy Laurie, which establishes her as an aristocrat rather than a truly democratic American. Neither Meg nor Amy can fulfill the mandate whereby "In America," as the narrator remarks, "girls early sign a declaration of independence, and enjoy their freedom with republican zest" (388).

In this equation of the American girl with American government, it is Jo, of course, who is the truest representative of "republican zest"—a legacy of both the earlier "declaration of independence" and the more recently completed Civil War. Jo offers the best hope for leading postwar America, as exemplified in the household of boys she establishes in the novel's final chapter, after marrying Professor Bhaer: "Think what luxury; Plumfield my own, and a wilderness of boys to enjoy it with me!" (483). Ending with a celebration of Marmee's sixtieth birthday, the novel consolidates its election of Jo as new leader, surrounding her with boys, including her own two sons. Ensconced at Plumfield, Jo has now assumed her mother's role; the household of daughters has become a "wilderness of boys." In this new world, Jo's own topsy-turvyness is displaced onto the "topsy-turvy heads" of boys (483), including her own sons "tumbling on the grass beside her" (490). As upright leader of this world of "topsy-turvy" men, she will govern Alcott's reconstructed America.

What kind of body politic does Alcott construct in Plumfield? Plumfield brings to fruition Nurse Periwinkle's hope for a better-managed Hurly-burly House, executed according to her own internal Sanitary Commission. Plumfield is a well-run hospital for the male psyche, centered on a therapeutic search for "the good spot which exists in the heart of the naughtiest, sauciest, most tantalizing little ragamuffin" (485). The key to this world is its homelike status, its domestic construction as an extended family over which Jo holds moral sway. Turning from patient to doctor, Jo fulfills the thwarted legacy of Tribulation Periwinkle. Like Periwinkle, Jo voices a desire for masculine authority from the start: "I'm the man of the family now papa is away" (5). Unlike Periwinkle, however, Jo gets the opportunity to exercise this desire in her own realm of social power; she combines the compassion of Nurse P. with the authority of Dr. P. Now called Mother Bhaer, Jo redefines the leader as matriarch. Motherhood is, however, reconceived of as a strategy rather than an identity; it is significant, for example, that Jo takes on the position of metaphorical mother to the boys of Plumfield *before* she has her own sons. This is a postwar world in which hospital has become home, health is moral rather than physical, and leadership consists of mothering as well as doctoring the nation.

In this world, moreover, feminization takes on a new meaning, at once less visible and more fundamental than in *Hospital Sketches*. Unlike John of *Hospital Sketches*, the boys of Plumfield seem unambiguously male. Yet feminization is essential to Plumfield, since the moral lessons that Jo will teach her "boys" are ones that she herself has learned in the household of "little women" with her sisters and Marmee. These little men are feminized into adulthood, not so much by their literal exposure to the authoritative Mother Bhaer as by their psychic imitation of female self-control. The teaching of self-control that is Plumfield's ultimate goal—"the most rampant ragamuffin was conquered in the end" (485)—makes Jo's boys into self-regulating subjects: that is, psychic little women. As Richard Brodhead notes, Plumfield offers the "disciplinary intimacy" of Alcott's childhood writ large.[71] Now conceived of from the perspective of parent rather than child, self-mastery offers a pedagogic mode of national regeneration. By the end of *Little Women*, Alcott is training the male citizenry of the postwar nation by making a country of little women.

This process will continue in the book's sequel, *Little Men* (1871) and in Alcott's last novel, *Jo's Boys* (1886). *Little Men* is virtually obsessed with the inculcation of male self-discipline as supervised by women; as Mother Bhaer remarks, "[O]ne of my favorite fancies is to look at my family as a small world, to watch the progress of my little men, and, lately, to see how well the influence of my little women works upon them."[72] *Jo's Boys* reemphasizes the symbolic importance of the Civil War to this "small world." Alcott's last novel is haunted by narratives of Civil War injury, most obviously in its extended description of a play performed by the inhabitants of Plumfield, which features an injured Civil War soldier, "a gaunt, wild-eyed man" whose hospital-bed reunion with his mother is the drama's dramatic climax.[73] As the theatricality of this example suggests, in a novel written and set twenty years after the war, the Civil War has become attenuated into an historical pageant rather than a contemporary reference-point. Nonetheless, the war functions as a significant frame for two of the novel's major characters, who reprise the symbolic positions of injured soldier and wartime surgeon. In her characterization of Plumfield residents Dan and Nan, Alcott carries the rhetoric of the feminized body politic to two complementary conclusions.

A loosely structured account of the citizens of Plumfield as adults in their twenties, *Jo's Boys* is particularly concerned with the fate of Dan, Jo's "most interesting boy" (287), and another "manly" man: "At twenty-five he was very tall, with sinewy limbs, a keen, dark face, and the alert look of one whose senses are all alive" (54). Dan's "dark face" is aligned with various forms of racial "otherness": Jo assumes him to have "Indian blood" (53), his Plumfield nickname is "the Spaniard" (76), and he plays Othello in a Plumfield tableau vivant (83). As the term "Spaniard" suggests, Dan is presented as a figure of erotic attraction throughout, recalling Robert Dane in "My Contraband." Dan is also the most adventurous of Jo's boys, a man who has lived in the West with Indians and wants to return west to be the founder of a utopian town he names "Dansville." Compelling as he is, however, Dan is also wild-tempered and undisciplined, full of "wayward impulses, strong passions, and the lawless nature born in him" (66). "Mother Bhaer" muses that "We can't change his nature,—only help it to develop in the right direction," for "her colt was not thoroughly broken yet" (66). Dan is, in short, the perfect subject for Alcott's pedagogic project whereby little men "tame themselves" by becoming little women, and the hypothetical "Dansville," a body politic *tabula rasa*, offers an appropriate testing-ground for the social world a man of Plumfield might produce.

As in earlier texts, Dan's training centers on Civil War injury, now an experience that must be engaged metaphorically. Heading west, Dan kills a man while defending a male friend and is sent to jail. While despondent in prison at Christmas, he hears a woman deliver an inspirational speech about "two soldiers in a hospital during the late war." In this parable, the more patient of these two patients recovers, leading the speaker to conclude:

> This is a hospital for soldiers wounded in life's battle; here are sick souls, weak wills, insane passions, blind consciences . . . There is hope and help for everyone . . . penitence and submission must come before the cure is possible. Pay the forfeit manfully . . . The scar will remain, but it is better for a man to lose both arms than his soul. (186)

The last sentence reprises Alcott's "A Hospital Christmas" as self-consciously metaphorical sermon, complete with the comparison between amputation and self-control. With Dan now recast as another of Alcott's injured soldiers, the rest of his story is dominated by accounts of battle and injury. No sooner has he left prison than he is horribly injured while effecting a rescue; recovered, he returns to the West to perform missionary work among Indians, where he eventually dies the death of a martyred soldier: "Dan never married, but lived, bravely and usefully, among his chosen people till he was shot defending them" (316). Dying a soldier's death, Dan fulfills the heroic promise of Civil War injury. Like John of *Hospital Sketches* and Robert of "My Contraband," he has tamed his "manhood" with the feminizing force of Christianity, now extended in imperialist sweep westward across the nation.

Yet as fully as Alcott engages and extends the image of the injured Civil War soldier in Dan, she also exhausts it. The residents of Plumfield are horrified to learn that Dan is a murderer, and his second trip west functions as exile. As with Robert Dane, Dan's "dark" eroticism is too explosive for the text; he can unite neither with Teddy, Jo's beloved son, nor with his "little Desdemona" (83), Amy's blonde daughter Bess. Alcott's "Othello" has no place in her disciplined and whitened body politic. Bereft of Plumfield, neither does he invent Dansville.

Where Dan fails, however, Nan succeeds. "Naughty Nan" is Dan's symbolic twin, the "tomboy" to his "firebrand" and, like him, a point of identification for Alcott herself. But where Dan ends badly, Nan's adult life is a triumph: she becomes a doctor. Nan is one of a number of "New Women" doctors in fiction of the 1880s, including novels by William Dean Howells, Elizabeth Stuart Phelps, and Sarah Orne Jewett.[74] In the context of Alcott's earlier fiction, Nan represents an idealized version of the Civil War surgeon. Mixing medical zeal with compassion, Nan plans to be the doctor of Dansville: "[D]octors are exceptions to all rules. There won't be much sickness in Dansville . . . But accidents will be frequent . . . That will just suit me. I long for broken bones, surgery is *so* interesting" (60). While Dansville never materializes, she fulfills the work of doctoring among women, becoming "a busy, cheerful, independent spinster, [who] dedicated her life to her suffering sisters and their children, in which true woman's work she found abiding happiness" (315–16). Relocated from the male terrain of soldiers to the homefront, Nan is Alcott's ultimate army doctor, the surgeon to "suffering sisters."

As Nan is Alcott's ultimate surgeon, she is also her final female soldier, now engaged in political battles for women. *Hospital Sketches* had hinted at the struggle for suffrage, with Tribulation Periwinkle declaring at the outset, as she leaves for Washington, "I'm a woman's rights woman" (9). Alcott's novel *Work*, begun in the 1860s and published in 1873, further articulates feminist political goals, concluding with the formation of a women's reform group led by a woman whose husband—yet again—has died from injuries sustained as a soldier in the Civil War.[75] In *Jo's Boys*, women's political struggles are a significant feature of the Plumfield world from the start, with these struggles framed by the language of the Civil War. Nan describes suffrage as the moment "when we take the field," warning the men of Plumfield not to be "one of those who wait till the battle is won, and then beat the drums and share the glory" (94). Meg's son Demi responds to the cry for women's equality with "Still shouting the battle cry of freedom? . . . Up with your flag! I'll stand by and lend a hand if you want it" (91). Civility is still at issue in this version of civil war; after a debate about women's abilities, the elder Mr. March asks, "'What started this civil war?' . . . with a gentle emphasis on the adjective, which caused the combatants to calm their ardor a little" (30). Political representation is still a long way away for women: like Tribulation Periwinkle observing chaotic Congress, Nan reports that "I went to a suffrage debate in the Legislature last winter; and of all the feeble, vulgar twaddle I ever heard, that was the worst; and those men were *our* representatives. . . . I want an intelligent man to represent *me*, if I can't do it myself, not a fool (92). Women may have only farcical political representation, but Nan's confidently uncivil language suggests that they may control their literary representation. The Civil War has entered a new era, its metaphorical connotations newly energized and enlisted in support of feminism.

For Alcott, then, feminization encompasses a variety of imaginative possibilities whereby traditional gender boundaries are breached in the service of the nation. Feminization involves a radical reworking of the relation between men and women, such that men not only come under the influence of women, but also internalize the disciplinary mode of self-mastery that characterizes the female psyche. Women, meanwhile, take on increasingly central roles within the body politic, but their social authority derives more from the deliberate deployment of conventionally female behaviors such as mothering than it does from an essentialized femininity. At its broadest reaches, feminization becomes feminism, metaphorically updated into a civil war over suffrage. Turning boys and girls alike into little women, feminization transforms the nation into a body healed from slavery and a household restored from the disorder of war. In a sustained contribution to the political and literary culture of Civil War America, Alcott reconstructs the body politic in the shape of a woman.

IV

In the fiction of Louisa May Alcott, the Civil War functions as both historical ground and literary figure. On the one hand, the multiple fevers of war provide an overarching metaphor for the topsy-turvyness Alcott experiences as woman and as writer. On the other hand, the civil wars Alcott sketches within her fictional plots symbolically reconstruct the nation itself, intervening in the process by which public understanding of the war had been shaped by corporeal and domestic metaphors from the start. In the work of Alcott, nation and individual are linked by a reversible metaphor, wherein the warring body politic symbolically fashions the white woman's psyche, and that psyche allegorically reconstructs the fractured nation. This reversible metaphor suggests both the centrality of the Civil War to Alcott and her importance to constructions of the war and its aftermath.

These two narratives are themselves related. As with Stowe, Alcott's representations of women in nineteenth-century American culture show how the white female psyche is excessively disciplined. Bringing Stowe's vision into the war itself, she shows how that psyche finds a measure of resistance in the carnivalesque disruptions of Civil War. Her reconstruction of the male-led nation, by contrast, suggests that the Civil War body politic is too topsy-turvy and that it requires for its rehabilitation a full dose of discipline. In this movement between discipline and carnival, gender is the key explanatory term, at once cause and effect. For what animates *Hospital Sketches,* and indeed all of Alcott's writings, is the project of finding female authority in a nation whose public realms of power—political, military, medical—are definitionally male. Her fictional solution to this problem is to recombine masculine and feminine qualities in both male and female bodies, thereby reconfiguring relations of power between the sexes. In *Little Women* and its sequels, Alcott energizes female discipline with male freedom and tempers male agency with female restraint. The result is a utopian world, Plumfield, that reinvents the masculine nation in two ways: by subjecting its citizens to female governance and by modeling their individual development on the disciplined female self.

Yet Alcott, like Stowe, constrains as well as enlarges possibilities for women. First, *Little Women*'s utopia is a fantasy centered on whiteness. As "My Contraband" suggests, Alcott is not uninterested in representing black characters, but the challenges such characters pose to her model of feminization are too great, and the bulk of her later fiction relegates black characters to the margins. Plumfield's residents include a "merry little quadroon" (486), but are otherwise apparently all white. To the extent that black characters enter into Alcott's fictional worlds, they function as metaphors of misrule in the service of white characters' freedoms. From the leap-frogging "colored gentleman of ten," from the "colored incapable" to the "merry little quadroon," black figures remain a symbolic source of inversion. Like Alcott's own self-representation as topsy-turvy, her fiction preserves the dynamics of racial metaphor in Stowe, with these metaphors now operating more overtly in the service of white female authority. Alcott's fictional nation serves more to revitalize white women than to admit black bodies, male or female, into the national body politic.

Second, even within the white world of Alcott's feminized utopia, there are severe limits upon female freedom. If Alcott's writings offer a fictional analogue to the Sanitary Commission, providing relief for the injured nation, they do so only by sanitizing female rebellion. Paradoxically, Alcott strips her white female protagonists of the carnivalesque possibilities that would seem to provide them a measure of mobility. While *Little Women*'s heroine is a character of great vitality, the adult Mother Bhaer who ends the novel is very different from her younger self, Jo March. Topsy-turvy at the start of the novel, Jo must forcibly tame herself, in a psychic struggle that is coterminous with national crisis: "If I was a boy," she complains to Laurie, "we'd run away together [to the war], and have a capital time; but as I'm a miserable girl, I must be proper, and stop at home" (213). Following her own civil war, Jo's postwar years bring a self-reconstruction centered on self-restraint. Married and self-censoring, the later woman seems to leave the earlier one behind, just as the convalescent Tribulation Periwinkle abandons her hallucinatory freedom. From Trib's daughterly recovery to Jo's matronly reconstruction, Alcott's women conclude their inner civil wars with a marked victory of civility over conflict.

Such internal divisions within Alcott's texts suggest, as well, the difficulties of employing both carnivalesque and disciplinary modes of self-reinvention. Alcott's strategies of national feminization use female discipline to great effect, but they also reveal a central paradox in her work. Ironically, it is easier for the boys of Plumfield to act like exemplary girls than it is for girls to be like girls. The first project moderates masculine excesses with feminine restraint, but the latter redoubles female discipline upon an already circumscribed self.

This harsh lesson has, in turn, an important corollary in women's role as disciplinary agents. Not only is it easier for boys to learn the pedagogy of self-restraint; it is easier for little women to instruct little men than it is for women to instruct themselves.

So too for Alcott herself, for whom the topsy-turvy disorder of the entire nation is more manageable than is the strain of cabin fever in Concord. As Jo concedes, "keeping her temper at home was a much harder task than facing a rebel or two down South" (9). The sufferings of the nation may be resolved through recourse to a fictional world of little women, while the woman writer must continue to encode and concede her own anger and ambition. For Alcott, finally, the Civil War may be successfully negotiated through literature, but there is no easy resolution in her fiction to the factions at war within women.

Black Woman, White House

Race and Redress in Elizabeth Keckley's *Behind the Scenes*

I

For African-Americans, the Civil War was first and foremost about ending slavery, a goal whose achievement was centered on access to military service. The fight to end slavery was inseparable from the fight to fight in the Union army, which resisted the arming of black men until midway through the war. The literal result of these dual civil wars was the military service of nearly two hundred thousand black men; their wider cultural impact was the provisional admission of black men to the American body politic. The black soldier became newly, albeit briefly, visible in the popular press, while black male writers emphasized his heroism in a variety of genres. William Wells Brown, for example, updated his 1853 novel *Clotel* with new closing chapters on the war, in which he noted the "noble daring" of black soldiers, and he documented their achievements at length in *The Negro in the American Rebellion: His Heroism and His Fidelity*.[1] "[F]rom the first," remembered Frederick Douglass, who tirelessly commemorated black soldiers, "I reproached the North that they fought the rebels with only one hand, when they might strike effectually with two—that they fought with their soft white hand, while they kept their black iron hand chained and helpless behind them."[2] Once black men became soldiers, the nation could be reembodied in an improved, biracial form. As Douglass's optimistic rhetoric suggests, the "iron hand" of the black man was narrating new versions of the nation, born from the masculine—and masculinizing—body of the black Civil War soldier.[3]

African-American women were at once welcomed into and excluded from this new rhetoric. Black women experienced the Civil War in profoundly different ways. Jacqueline Jones cites three examples of this diversity: a seventy-year-old woman who escaped from slavery along with her twenty-two children and grandchildren; a woman whose plantation was so isolated that she continued in servitude until the 1880s; and a woman who stayed at a plantation even after she was freed mid-war, because it afforded security for herself and her children. For slave women, Jones argues, the possibilities of freedom were often gauged in the context of the risk to family members: "Amid the dislocation of Civil War . . . black women's priorities and obligations coalesced into a single purpose: to escape from the oppression of slavery while keeping their families intact."[4] Many black women, free and enslaved, also participated in the war effort directly, as cooks, laundresses, soldiers, scouts, and spies; in addition to the celebrated Harriet Tubman, their numbers included Susie King Taylor, who served as cook and laundress with the Massachusetts 54th Regiment, and Mary Elizabeth Bowser, who spied for the Union army while working as a servant in the Confederate White House of Jefferson Davis. Many black women also participated in relief work for freed slaves, most famously Sojourner Truth and Harriet Jacobs, who worked in contraband relief camps, and Charlotte Forten, who taught freed slaves on the Sea Islands in the "Port Royal" emancipation project. Whether fleeing from slavery or serving in the war effort, black women participated actively in the racial and regional conflicts of the Civil War.[5]

Like their male counterparts, black women writers joined in celebrating the new visibility of black soldiers. In the *Weekly Anglo-African,* for example, Sattira Douglas urged, "Now is offered the only opportunity that will be extended, during the present generation, for colored men to strike the blow that will at once relieve them of northern prejudice and southern slavery."[6] Mary Ann Shadd Cary, an established antislavery journalist and editor, recruited black soldiers, while Sarah Parker Remond lectured on and wrote about their heroism. Such writers actively developed the rhetoric of black male heroism. "Ask yourself," exhorted Remond of her white readers, "whether future history will not pronounce the black man, morally, not only your equal, but your superior."[7]

Yet Frederick Douglass's deprecation of the "soft white hand" of the white soldier also suggests the potential difficulty for black women writers in negotiating the masculine rhetoric of the body politic. Despite Douglass's own long-standing commitment to black women's rights, his rhetoric promotes two races but only one gender; imagining biracial hands of the male body, his metaphors recognize femininity only in its negative form, as feminization. Meanwhile, the "soft white hand" of the white woman writer, as the writings of Stowe and Alcott suggest, privileged feminization, but at the expense of African-Americans. More generally, the rhetoric of domesticity that white women drew on refused entry for black women or relegated them to the role of "domestics" within domestic spaces.

On the one hand, then, black women writers faced a racial discourse whose language for power, as in the culture as a whole, was that of masculinity; on the other hand, they confronted a feminized model of nationhood aligned with whiteness. In this dichotomy, Civil War rhetoric presented another version of the familiar refrain, "All the men are black, and all the women are white." Moreover, to the extent that black women were culturally embodied, the rhetoric of their embodiment, as shown in the imagery associated with Topsy, moved in pejorative directions, toward masculinization and hypersexualization. Overembodied in racist white culture, black women writers entered into national discourse from a position of rhetorical disembodiment. In contrast to the two-fisted Douglass, the hand of the black woman writer in the Civil War era was positioned as yet another phantom limb.[8]

These issues inflect the Civil War texts of black women from the 1860s, the era of the war and its initial aftermath. This group includes the journalism of Mary Ann Shadd Cary, the journals of Charlotte Forten, the letters of Harriet Jacobs, the dictated autobiography of Mattie Jackson, the memoirs of Elizabeth Keckley, the oratory of Sarah Parker Remond, the biographical writing of Frances Rollin, the biographies written about and influenced by Harriet Tubman and Sojourner Truth, and the early writings—particularly oratory, letters, and fiction—of Frances Ellen Watkins Harper.[9] While these works form a diverse group, some common themes unite them. First, as in the case of white women writers, black women writers exploit the metaphor of civil war to explore the reciprocal relation between the constructed nation and the created self. The Civil War frames internal conflicts in their texts, while the fracture of national identity creates an avenue of entry into national discourses that would otherwise exclude them. However, African-American women writers foreground racism as an axis of Civil War struggle and do so in ways that significantly transform the meaning of gender. Rather than rebelling against middle-class civility, like Alcott, some African-American women writers struggle to claim its prerogatives. Similarly, the metaphor of civil war provides a new symbolic frame for an ongoing story in African-American writing, male and female: the quest for literary as well as political self-representation. In a racist culture that denied not only civility but literary voice to African-Americans except under the most mediated of terms, issues of authentication and authorship constitute a particular battleground in black women's Civil War texts. In these and other issues, black women's texts are often openly at war with those of white women. For black women writers excluded from national discourse by virtue of both race and gender, "civil wars" involve battling not only the dominant national culture but also alternative iconographies— including those constructed by white women and African-American men— that would exclude them as well.

A preliminary examination of two black women's Civil War texts, those of Mattie Jackson and Frances Rollin, will introduce the range of strategies and arguments involved in this body of writing. First, in the autobiography of Mattie Jackson, the Civil War is represented as both a public conflict among soldiers and a private struggle within the slaveholding household, a struggle in which white authority disintegrates as black women claim freedom. Dictated to her stepmother and published in 1866 when she was twenty, Jackson's forty-page narrative focuses in depth on the war years, during which she struggled against her master and mistress in Missouri, was sold to another owner, and escaped from slavery via the Underground Railroad to Indianapolis; there, at war's end, Jackson viewed Lincoln's body on its posthumous journey to burial at Springfield. The remainder of the text focuses on Jackson's postwar reunion with her mother and other family members, her experience of freedom in Massachusetts, and her return trip to Missouri, where she encountered her former master and mistress.[10]

In Jackson's account of the war, sectional conflict both parallels and transforms racial struggle within the domestic sphere. When Jackson's master informs his wife of the strength of Union forces occupying nearby land, for example,

> She was much astonished, and cast her eye around to us for fear we might hear her. Her suspicion was correct; there was not a word passed that escaped our listening ears. My mother and myself could read enough to make out the news in the papers. The Union soldiers took much delight in tossing the paper over the fence to us. It aggravated my mistress very much. My mother used to sit up nights and read to keep posted about the war. (13)

Bringing the external military world into the household, this description also offers war news as the ammunition for a battle between white mistress and black slaves. Allied with Union soldiers through the paper that passes between them, Jackson and her mother constitute an enemy army within the household. Aggravating their mistress, they initiate what Tera W. Hunter characterizes as the "war of nerves" between slaves and their soon-to-be ex-masters during the Civil War.[11]

To wage this war of nerves, Jackson's mother deploys a variety of tactics of resistance against her white masters, creating conflict within the household and support for the war without. These tactics include strategic silences, as when her mistress, Mrs. Lewis, announces that " '[H]er children should never be on an equal footing with a Nigger. She had rather see them dead.' As my mother made no reply to her remarks, she stopped talking" (14). Resisting through silence, Jackson's mother also preserves her own private space within the household:

> On one occasion Mr. Lewis searched my mother's room and found a picture of President Lincoln, cut from a newspaper, hanging in my mother's room. He asked her what she was doing with old Lincoln's picture. She replied it was there because she liked it. He then knocked her down three times and sent her to the trader's yard for a month as punishment. (14)

In this example, the mother's transgressions are multiple, involving her support for Lincoln, her enshrining of his image, and her spoken response when queried about it. Like silence, understatement—"she liked it"—acts as a form of civil disobedience, which so enrages Lewis that he responds with violence.

As the Civil War progresses, the Jacksons' resistance grows, while white power implodes. After the successful Union capture of New Orleans, Jackson recalls, "The days of sadness for mistress were days of joy for us. We shouted and laughed to the tops of our voices. My mistress was more enraged than ever—nothing pleased her" (15). Like her mother, Jackson frustrates white authority:

> [My mistress], in a terrible range [*sic*], declared I should be punished that night. I did not know the cause, neither did she. She went immediately and selected a switch [and awaited] the return of her husband at night for him to whip me. As I was not pleased with the idea of a whipping I bent the switch in the shape of W, which was the first letter of his name, and . . . walked away . . . (15)

In the face of white rage—which grows ever more frustrated as the South comes under siege—Jackson disables the tool of her punishment. Switching the switch, she renders her master impotent by turning his very name against him.

The master's tools do not, in this case, dismantle the master's house: three weeks later, Jackson is beaten by Mr. Lewis at the initiative of his wife. Yet even in this moment of severe punishment, Jackson weakens her abusers' power, summoning both official and unofficial means of resistance. By refusing to change her clothes, Jackson bears witness to her master's brutality: "The blood ran over my clothing, which gave me a frightful appearance. Mr. Lewis then ordered me to change my clothing immediately. As I did not obey he became more enraged" (16). She then calls on the official protection of Union soldiers, who harbor her only briefly before returning her to the Lewises; forced to resume her slave status, she defiantly retains the legacy of past brutality, for "when I went I wore the same stained clothing as when I was so severely punished" (16). The resistance signified by the stained clothing resurfaces, finally, in a subsequent episode when Union authorities punish Lewis for mistreating Jackson: "The General immediately arrested Mr. L. and gave him one hundred lashes with the cow-hide, so that they might identify him by a scarred back, as well as his slaves. My mother had the pleasure of washing his stained clothes" (18). Intertwining clothes-washing with whipping, this episode vindicates the resistant strategies of Jackson and her mother and situates Mr. Lewis in the position of beaten slave.

The text's dynamics of reversal culminate as the war ends. In 1863, Jackson escapes from a second master: "I landed on free soil for the first time in my life . . . I was now under my own control . . . It appeared as though I had emerged into a new world, or had never lived in the old one before" (28). The "new world" does not so much erase as invert the old one, for the text closes with a series of power reversals. When Jackson and her mother return to Missouri after the war, they encounter their former owners in new postures:

> [Mr. Lewis] was so surprised that before he was aware of it he dropped a bow. My mother met Mrs. Lewis, her old mistress, with a large basket on her arm, trudging to market. It appeared she had lived to see the day when her children had to wait upon themselves, and she likewise. . . . When I was [Lewis's] slave I was obliged to keep away every fly from the table, and not allow one to light on a person. They are now compelled to brush their own flies and dress themselves and children. (37)

The involuntary bow literalizes the lowered position of the defeated slaveowner, while the details of the Lewises' self-service emphasize that they must now perform for themselves the labor previously exacted from slaves. The inversions of slavery are even starker for Mr. Lewis's brother, a slaveowner well known for torturing his slaves, who is harshly punished by former comrades:

> For pretending Unionism they placed him on a table and threatened to dissect him alive if he did not tell them where he kept his gold . . . [T]hey changed his position by turning him upside down, and . . . letting him dash his head against the floor until his skull was fractured, after which he lingered awhile and finally died. (38)

In this world literally turned upside down by emancipation, the defeated slaveowner not only bows down but is up-ended, and not only whipped but crushed to death.

In a final extension of this imagery of inversion, Jackson concludes her narrative with a confession that she personally redistributed slaveowners' wealth. She remembers her own theft of twenty-five dollars from my master's pocket as preparation for her escape from slavery:

> After I was safe and had learned to write, I sent him a nice letter, thanking him for the kindness his pocket bestowed to me in time of need. I have never received any answer to it.
>
> When I complete my education . . . I shall endeavor to publish further details of our history in another volume from my own pen. (38)

The deadpan tone of this description extends the rhetorical modes of resistance, including silence and understatement, that Jackson and her mother employ throughout the war. The closing sentences of her autobiography, meanwhile, link resistance through theft with the production of texts, from the letter written to the slaveowner to Jackson's autobiography itself. Like the newspaper filled with war news, the clandestine portrait of Lincoln, and the clothing illustrated with stains of abuse, Jackson's memoirs themselves bear ingenious witness to the dual struggles of the war years. From covert resistance to overt inversion, her text charts a Civil War against slavery in which the formal battles of male soldiers frame and energize the struggles of female slaves against masters.

While Mattie Jackson's autobiography effects its strategic reversals outside of the rhetoric of black male heroism, the writings of Frances Rollin suggest the opportunities and constraints afforded black women writing from within that rhetoric. Born to a prominent free black family in Charleston and educated in Philadelphia, Rollin was a committed supporter of both African-American rights and woman suffrage. At age twenty, she met Martin Delany, leading black activist, novelist, and physician. Delany commissioned her to write his biography, which was published in 1868 as *Life and Public Services of Martin R. Delany* under the name Frank A. Rollin. Rollin subsequently returned to Charleston, where she taught in schools for freedmen and, with her sisters, ran a prominent salon for the city's elite. She married an African-American lawyer and politician, William J. Whipper, and moved with him to Washington; the marriage failed, and after he returned to South Carolina, she remained in Washington, raising their children and working in various clerk positions in the government. Her other literary efforts included occasional articles written in Washington and a diary she kept in Boston while writing the Delany biography, which was passed down to her great-granddaughter, Carole Ione. In 1991, Ione published a family memoir that paid eloquent homage to her great-grandmother.[12]

Together, Rollin's two texts—the Delany biography and her own diary—chart her involvement in a range of civil wars, individual and national, centered on expanding the rhetoric of nationalism to include a black woman's literary voice. The actual Civil War is crucial to this voice. Fourteen of the Delany biography's thirty-six chapters are devoted to Delany's Civil War achievements, as the first African-American officer in the war and a major recruiter of black soldiers. Like other histories of black soldiers, the text uses the war to demonstrate that "A race before persecuted, slandered, and brutalized . . . have scattered the false theories of their enemies, and proved in every way their claim and identity to American citizenship in its every particular."[13] As Rollin's point of entry into national discourse, the biography also provided her with a personal coming-of-age. Rollin's representation of the Civil War soldier is a step forward for both African-American citizenship and her own authorial self.

Yet this literary project also constrained Rollin's voice. Telling someone else's life story, Rollin was limited by Delany's own copious instructions, the advice of her white publisher, and the counsel of her friend Richard Greener, the first black graduate of Harvard. She wrote in her diary about Greener: "Mr. Richard Greener has gone over some of it with me, but he is cynical and apt to discourage instead of acting otherwise. He lives in a grand intellectual sphere and is accustomed to only perfection" (455). The male censure implicit in Greener's critique is literalized in the male pseudonym under which she published the text. According to her great-granddaughter, Rollin was known to friends and family as Frank. However, the pseudonym appears to have been chosen as a necessary concession to an audience that would find a woman's authorship of a biography of a black male hero less credible.[14] If the authorial persona of "Frank" brought Rollin more authority, it also suggested the limitations of a cultural discourse in which the only language for power was masculinity. In Rollin's text, masculinity is both an assumed form of power and an imposed erasure, the "frank" assertion of her authorial signature and that signature's own negation.

This contrast in turn suggests the disjuncture between Rollin's two literary forms, the private diary and the public biography. As with the more famous journals of her friend Charlotte Forten, Rollin's private writings offer a black woman intellectual's unpublished responses to very public features of the Civil War era. Forten recorded her experience teaching freed slaves during the war, while Rollin, a less direct part of the war effort, represented her life while writing the Delany biography. Both women register symbolic as well as literal civil wars, with Forten struggling to situate herself in relation to both Southern ex-slaves and Northern white abolitionists, and occupying what Carla L. Peterson terms "a lonely middle term between these two extremes . . . gazed at by each as radically Other."[15] Rollin's diary registers her own civil wars within the black and white cultural elite of postwar New England. In contrast to her necessarily self-effacing narrative persona in the Delany biography, the voice of her diary is distinctively acerbic. Wholly admiring of Delany in the biography, for example, she expresses irritation at him in the diary. After he stops supporting the project financially, she reports, "not a dollar sent to me again. I was provoked" (460). The diary form also allows for the assertion of ambition: "I pray for success" (458), she writes in one entry, and declares more forthrightly in another, "I am resolved to take some step forward to promote my success in Literature" (459). Both "provoked" and "resolved," she charts a spectrum of emotions that exceed the narrow boundaries of black female civility.

Rollin's diary also charts her own internal fractures, psychic and corporeal, during this period of intense literary production. While writing the Delany biography, she struggled financially—"Feeling very depressed, no money" (461)—and supported herself by sewing and working as a secretary for the Massachusetts Secretary of State. Both activities constrained her literary efforts. Sewing, for Rollin, represented the negation of writing: "Went out to sew today. I thought when I began literature that ended, but find it otherwise" (460). Her secretarial work brought her closer to writing, but in a subordinate role: "Went to the State House this morning. Mr. Warner got me to blot for him while he signed. In afternoon chills and fever" (460). She performs clerical tasks, while her employer composes letters of importance; the subsequent breakdown of her own body into "chills and fever" seems to translate the strain of this hierarchy into corporeal form. Like Rollin's "depressed" psyche, her feverish body registers the strain of her subordinate position as secretary to the Secretary. The language of her diary suggests the stresses Rollin encountered in entering into public discourse through a role in which she only blots what others write and sign.

More redemptively, Rollin's diary also registers the resistant force of her own writing against the exclusions of political discourse. On 22 February 1868, she writes in her diary, "Washington['s] Birthday. If things continue as they are, there will be but little country to celebrate it. For myself I am no enthusiast over Patriotic Celebrations as I am counted out of the body Politic. I wrote very satisfactorily today."[16] As a comment on the racial struggles of Reconstruction, this remark succinctly highlights dominant conceptions of national identity. Consolidated through ritual, the official nation links its identity to a Founding Father, George Washington, whose birthday she does not share. Yet even as she is eliminated from national rhetoric by virtue of both race and gender, Rollin notes her pleasure in writing "very satisfactorily." In an implicit civil war between the limitations of national discourse and the production of her own counternarratives—from her biography and diary to her committed activist career—Rollin's writing wars against being "counted out of the body Politic."

Together, Jackson's strategic wartime reversals and Rollin's warring texts introduce the rhetorical strategies of Elizabeth Keckley's *Behind the Scenes; or, Thirty Years a Slave, and Four Years in the White House.* Keckley's memoir details her years as a slave, her training as a seamstress, her successful purchase of freedom for herself and her son, her tenure as designer and dressmaker to Mary Todd Lincoln during the Civil War, and her participation in a postwar controversy involving Mrs. Lincoln's extravagant wardrobe. The text has traditionally been discussed primarily for its biographical information about Abraham and Mary Todd Lincoln. What scholarly analysis Keckley's narrative has received in its own right focuses on its account of slavery, which occupies only the first three chapters. Such interpretations situate *Behind the Scenes* in the context of the nineteenth-century slave narrative and, more specifically, within what Frances Smith Foster, one of the text's major interpreters, calls African-American "autobiography after emancipation."[17] I would like to interpret *Behind the Scenes,* however, as a Civil War story, on a continuum with other black women's texts of the Civil War era. Like Mattie Jackson and Frances Rollin, Keckley writes a text structured by internal wars over race, gender and nation, redesigning the iconography of the Civil War nation.

First, *Behind the Scenes* frames the internal conflicts of Keckley's story through the symbolism of the Civil War. The setting of Keckley's war years, the Lincoln White House, provides a symbolic point of departure for the construction of her literary voice, while the war provides an organizing rhetorical frame for conflicts of race and gender within her text. More ambiguously, the Civil War also provides a shaping image for the liminal zones of Keckley's text, that of the "border state." As a Civil War story, *Behind the Scenes* occupies "border states" between anger and accommodation, history and fiction, and authorial authentication and absence.

Second, Keckley's story is not only shaped by the rhetoric of the Civil War but, in turn, reshapes national iconography. Unlike allegories that give fictional characters political resonance, *Behind the Scenes* begins with real-life icons and revises their political meaning. The center of this revision is Keckley's representation of clothing, which offers her an authoritative point of entry into commenting on such public figures as Abraham Lincoln and Jefferson Davis.

If African-American male writers could fight with one hand and write with the other, *Behind the Scenes* suggests a two-fisted combination of writing and dressmaking. Combining her needle and her pen, Keckley at once rips apart national discourse and sews up her own political authority.

Finally, Keckley's most complex civil war, at once a private vindication and a political intervention, is her battle with Mary Todd Lincoln. Keckley wages this battle, again centered on clothing, in such coded rhetorical forms that condemnation passes for tribute—a strategy that a vicious parody of the text, *Behind the Seams*, inadvertently confirms. In its antagonism toward Mary Todd Lincoln, moreover, Keckley's text reverses the coordinates of racial projection in a writer like Alcott, wherein a white woman uses black figures to revitalize white femininity. By contrast, in a literary culture that often mediated black women's voices through those of white women, Keckley's account of Mary Todd Lincoln undresses a white woman to reclothe a black female speaker. In *Behind the Scenes*, dress is a means of redress, through which Elizabeth Keckley refashions both herself and the Civil War body politic.

II

Elizabeth Keckley's lived experience during the Civil War involved unusual access to power. An elite "modiste" in Washington, she became dressmaker and designer to Mary Todd Lincoln. She spent significant amounts of time in the White House with the Lincoln family, spoke frequently with the president and was privy to political discussions. Keckley also participated in the African-American war effort in both personal and political ways. Early in the war, she lost her only child, George, in combat; shortly thereafter, she helped to found an organization for freed slaves, the Contraband Relief Fund. By the end of the war, she had become a respected figure among black activists as well as an intimate of the president and his family (figure 8). In *Behind the Scenes*, these Civil War events are symbolically as well as factually central to the text as a whole. The setting of the Civil War White House provides a metaphoric point of departure for the establishment of Keckley's literary voice, while the bifurcations of the war serve as a symbolic template for the internal "civil wars" and "border states" within her text as a whole.

In Keckley's memoir, the White House is as much a space of imaginative fantasy as it is a literal setting. Built in 1792, the building was first referred to as the "White House" in the 1810s and officially given that name a century later by Theodore Roosevelt. The structure has always been a densely symbolic realm, serving both as a residence for the president and a metonym for national

FIGURE 8.
Elizabeth Keckley, 1860s
(Prints and Photographs
Division, Moorland-Spingarn
Research Center, Howard
University)

authority ("The White House said today"). In these dual functions—executive mansion and Executive Branch—the building has been both a male and female realm, uniting the feminized sphere of domestic life managed by the First Lady with the masculine arena of governmental decision-making presided over by the president. So too does the White House represent the racial hierarchies of dominant domestic ideology in material form. First whitewashed in 1798, the building's exterior whiteness has also been an inadvertent signifier of the racial identity of all of its presidential inhabitants to date. Within one physical setting converge two versions of gender politics, those of male leader and First Lady, as well as the racial whitewashing that structures national discourse as a whole.[18]

During the Civil War, the White House was also a militarized zone, serving as the headquarters for the President in his capacity as Commander-in-Chief of the Union army. In the memoir *Inside the White House in War Times*,

William Stoddard, one of Lincoln's secretaries, emphasized the national importance of spaces like Lincoln's office, "the nerve centre of the Republic." By contrast, the living quarters of the White House were ostensibly apolitical, feminized domains over which "Mrs. Lincoln is absolute mistress." Yet as Stoddard notes, the boundary between these two kinds of space inevitably blurred. In Lincoln's office, for example, a yell might come "from the forces belonging to quite another seat of war. Tad has been trying to make a war-map of Willie."[19] If the play of Lincoln's sons domesticated the war room, then the politics of the Civil War inevitably informed Mary Todd Lincoln's side of business as well. Although Stoddard loyally defends her, the First Lady's huge expenditures to renovate the entire house, including the private quarters and so-called "Lincoln bed," were highly politicized projects. Her extravagance was seen as insufficient patriotism, and used, along with her Southern background, to attack her. In these and other ways, the exigencies of the Civil War era prompted a further erosion of the already ambiguous boundaries between the public and private zones of the president's home. In the era of the national "house divided," the White House was at once symbolic extension of the Union army and metaphorical battleground of the Civil War.[20]

In *Behind the Scenes,* Keckley uses the ambiguities of this setting to establish the authority of her own voice. Nominally a member of the White House only in its feminized sphere, she stakes symbolic claim to its masculine military connotations as well. One of her few descriptions of the war, for example, begins, "Mr. Lincoln returned to Washington in November, and again duty called me to the White House."[21] Syntactically and thematically, the opening of the passage aligns Keckley with Lincoln, as parallel figures equally pulled to important locations by the needs of service. Similarly, Keckley first begins to work for Mary Todd Lincoln just as Lincoln takes office; seamstress and president are inaugurated at the same time (80). When Keckley's own son dies in the Civil War, she mentions this event only in direct connection with the death of the Lincolns' son Willie (105). In each of these examples, Keckley not only remarks her literal proximity to the Lincolns but uses that proximity to symbolic effect. By the time she is elected president of the Contraband Relief Fund and embarks on a fundraising tour "armed with credentials" (114), she has assumed symbolic as well as literal presidential functions of her own. "In the White House," as her subtitle announces, Keckley imagines herself among the Lincolns not as employee or even as confidante, but as wartime leader. Her narrative constructs an altered landscape in which an African-American woman is not only resident but president in the White House.[22]

If the White House metaphorically authorizes Keckley's voice, then the rhetoric of civil war shapes the story she tells. Her account of being "called to the White House" continues:

> The war was now in progress, and every day brought stirring news from the front— the front, where the Gray opposed the Blue . . . where brother forgot a mother's early blessing and sought the life-blood of brother, and friend raised the deadly knife against friend. Oh, the front, with its stirring battle-scenes! Oh, the front, with its ghastly heaps of dead! The life of the nation was at stake; and when the land was full of sorrow, there could not be much gayety at the capital. The days passed quietly with me. (91–92)

This description accumulates dichotomies, joining the conventional divisions of Gray against Blue, brother against brother, and friend against friend with the implicit contrasts between live nation and dead soldier and between stirring battle front and subdued home front. While Keckley positions herself outside these conflicts, related images of internal division organize her text. The book's opening chapters, for example, focus on her struggles against white men, from the master who first whipped her to the white man who fathered her child, of whom she writes, "[H]e persecuted me for four years, and I— I—became a mother" (39). These stories of personal struggle draw metaphoric force from the rhetoric of national fracture: both individual and nation suffer domestic crisis. Keckley occupies her own "house divided," with the national battle over slavery mirrored in her struggles against these men. As the four-year national struggle ultimately produces a reunified polity, moreover, so too does her four-year persecution by this man end with a child. In complementary resolutions to domestic struggles, both country and Keckley end their battles by giving birth to a new body.

While Keckley's struggles against white men exemplify conflicts over both gender and race, her text also represents internecine conflicts along each of these axes. Conflict between women crosses lines of race, as when Keckley battles with her white mistresses. Such battles include covert class tensions as well as overt racial hierarchies, as in the case of one mistress who "imagined that I regarded her with contemptuous feelings because she was of poor parentage" (31). Conversely, the text also charts intraracial "battles of the sexes," including Keckley's dissatisfaction with her husband, about whom she says simply, "Mr. Keckley . . . proved dissipated, and a burden instead of a helpmate" (50). Here as elsewhere, *Behind the Scenes* emphasizes internal fracture, narrating a series of domestic battles symbolically structured by the crisis of the Civil War itself.

In the battles I have sketched so far, the conflict between antagonists appears clear-cut. Yet Keckley's struggles are briefly and elliptically rendered; it is not clear, for example, what happened in her marriage, or what degree of coercion was involved in her relationship to her son's father.[23] In general, as Rafia Zafar argues, Keckley's voice is reticent and "rhetorically veiled."[24] In such ambiguities, Keckley's narrative intersects with another important feature of the Civil War: the rhetoric of the "border state." This term referred to those states of the Upper South that contained both pro- and antisecession sentiment. Four border states—Missouri, Kentucky, Maryland, and Delaware—ultimately stayed with the Union, while adjacent Southern states harbored considerable Union support; so divided was Virginia that it split into two states over secession and contained numerous Union sympathizers within its pro-Confederate portion.[25] In both her upbringing and employment, Keckley is literally involved with border states. Born in Virginia, she lived in North Carolina, Missouri, and Maryland before coming to Washington. Before the war, she worked briefly for Jefferson and Varina Davis and seriously considered an offer to head south with them before the South seceded.

In *Behind the Scenes,* such literal encounters with both sides of the Civil War border give metaphorical shape to the ambiguities of Keckley's position, including liminalities of color and class. Keckley's "light complexion" (60) not only marks her biracial origin (her father was her first master, Colonel Burwell) but also suggests racial alignments outside of the black/white binary altogether. According to contemporaries, "She was so much out of the ordinary in looks and dress, that people would turn and wonder what nationality she belonged to" and one "thought she was an Indian."[26] Her son George is so light-skinned that he successfully enlists in the Union army as white, under his white father's last name. Mother and son both embody ambiguous racial border states, which appear so uncertain that they may be transmuted into questions of "nationality" in the first generation or visually erased, in the next, through passing.

Keckley's skin color is closely related to her class position as a free black woman with her own trade and her own shop, known as "Madam Elizabeth" and consistently described by contemporaries as "a woman of refinement and culture."[27] Keckley's "refinement" is at once a set of behavioral norms, bodily self-management, and professional independence; she is both civilizing agent and object of civility. Yet this status is fragile, since Keckley is employee as well as employer, and her status as refined "modiste" rides on the satisfaction of her wealthy, exacting, and impatient white female clients. Her livelihood depends on women like "Mrs. Gen. McLean," who imperiously demands a dress made immediately and declares, "Now don't say no again. I tell you that you must make the dress" (79). Independent of slavery but dependent on her clients, she occupies a zone of hard-won yet tenuous privilege.

Vulnerably positioned within the elite, Keckley's self-proclaimed separation from nonelite African-Americans is also tenuous. Wartime Washington, filled with newly freed slaves, was an unstable space, racially and politically. In Alcott's *Hospital Sketches,* I have suggested, the dancing of freedmen provides a celebratory framework for the white heroine's own incivility. By contrast, in *Behind the Scenes,* Keckley separates herself, in class and sensibility, from the world of recent ex-slaves in Washington, for whom "dependence had become a part of their second nature, and independence brought with it the cares and vexations of poverty" (140). The world of ex-slaves is one of unrefined excess: "The colored people are fond of domestic life, and with them domestication means happy children, a fat pig, a dozen or more chickens, and a garden" (142–43). Despite her own separation from this world, the geographic and symbolic distance between Keckley and such "colored people" is small. Her imagery of uncontained expansion—pigs, fatness, children, chickens—suggests the difficulties, internal as well as external, in stabilizing the boundary separating refinement from its opposite. Keckley's elite civility is contingent not only on maintaining her separation from ex-slaves but on monitoring the internal psychic border between civilizer and civilizee.[28]

Liminal in relation to color and class, Keckley's most pronounced "border state" is her apparent ambivalence toward slavery. Early in the text, she fiercely condemns slavery, but later she literally embraces her former owners; her Northern friends, she laments, do not understand "how warm is the attachment between master and slave" (242). William L. Andrews has analyzed such attitudes as a constructed accommodationism designed, in postwar slave narratives, to effect a reunion between regions and races in which the African-American protagonist is the authoritative agent of reconciliation.[29] Psychologizing this accommodationist project, Jennifer Fleischner argues that Keckley's attitudes toward reunion represent an attempt to mourn the profoundly painful losses of her life and function as part of her book's "strategies of unconscious repression or deliberate suppression, substitutions, splitting, and inversions that seem intended to mask some of the anger and sorrow associated with her experiences of racism and slavery."[30] Aligning these historical frames with the text's wartime focus, we can also see Keckley's oscillation between condemnation and apology—and the psychic "splittings" that characterize her narrative as a whole—as a literary version of the Civil War "border state."

Keckley herself suggestively brings this context into play when, early in the text, she describes a formative moment at age seven when she first witnessed a slave being sold, after which his mother was whipped for grieving. From this experience she generalizes that slaves were often forced to appear cheerful to avoid punishment: "Alas! the sunny face of the slave is not always an indication of sunshine in the heart" (29); such cruelty, she notes, was a feature of

"Slavery in the Border States forty years ago" (29). Concluding the chapter, she then remarks that "Slavery had its dark side as well as its bright side" (30). In these two pages, her language moves from one form of dichotomy (happy face versus sad emotion), to another ("dark" versus "bright" sides of slavery). It is difficult to determine whether her concluding allusion to the "bright" side of slavery is sincere or whether, as seems more likely, it marks Keckley's own ironic dualism, akin to the falsely "sunny" faces of slaves. In this indeterminacy—an ambiguity about an ambivalence—Keckley's unreadable attitudes toward slavery occupy their own inner border state, midway between apologia and exposé.

The language of border states also provides an ironic metacommentary on the structure, reception, and authorship of Keckley's text. *Behind the Scenes* conforms to no one genre, moving among war memoir, presidential biography, domestic novel, and slave narrative. These genres, moreover, are themselves internally split. As Rollin's *Life and Public Services of Martin R. Delany* suggests, biography inevitably includes traces of autobiography, while the slave narrative in the mid-nineteenth century, as William Andrews has argued, operated as "novelized autobiography," mixing a professedly factual narrative with protofictional literary elements like invented dialogue.[31] James Olney, stressing the text's affiliation with novelistic forms ranging from sentimental to war fiction, concludes that *Behind the Scenes* "occupies a mixed middle ground between history and fiction."[32] Fictionality was also a charge leveled against the text. Marketed by its publisher for its sensational qualities, *Behind the Scenes* was then excoriated and challenged for its account of the Lincolns. In a racist culture, this challenge was rooted in the customary suspicion that charged any African-American writing—let alone presidential biography—as inauthentic.[33] In its reception as well as its contents, *Behind the Scenes* was on the border between history and fiction.

Finally, Keckley's authorship of the text occupies yet another liminal zone. Her sole authorship of the text has long been considered a fiction. Frances Rollin, for example, was unimpressed by Keckley and wrote in her diary that *Behind the Scenes* "is well written but not by Mrs. K that's clear" (459).[34] Historians have proposed various candidates for true authorship of the text, with at least one claiming that there was "no such person at all" as Elizabeth Keckley.[35] In 1942, John Washington argued that Keckley had written *Behind the Scenes* with the assistance of white abolitionist and publisher James Redpath.[36] The nature of Redpath's involvement, if indeed he served as the collaborator, is still unknown. Recent accounts describe Keckley's text as "ghostwritten."[37]

Like accusations of inauthenticity, the assertion of authorial collaboration, and more specifically of dependence on white authors, was a frequent response to African-American writing. In Keckley's case, the possibility of shared authorship situates *Behind the Scenes* in yet another Civil War border zone, wherein the hierarchy of white publisher and black author is ambiguously encoded in the text itself.[38] The critical commonplace about *Behind the Scenes*—the idea of the "ghostwritten" text—leaves Keckley in an uncertain state between authorship and absence. In a continuum of struggles over self-representation, this battle over authorship is closely related to ambiguities of authentication: on the one side, the claims of fact (history, a true biography, a real author); on the other, the falseness of fiction (novel, an exaggerated story, a ghost author). On the "mixed middle ground" of *Behind the Scenes*, this Civil War is not over. The ghost of an unknown author continues to haunt Elizabeth Keckley's literary battlefields.

III

The Civil War provides a metaphorical framework for Keckley's story, as a model for the internal conflicts and ambiguities that structure her text. Reversing this metaphor, we can see how Keckley intervenes in national discourse to offer her own commentary on the larger Civil War. While traditional allegories infuse fictional characters with political resonance, Keckley takes figures already in public discourse and privatizes them, using her personal access to national figures to recast their meaning. The metaphoric vehicle for this recasting, I suggest, is Keckley's representation of clothing, which functions throughout her text as an elaborate metaphor for representing individual and national identity. Throughout her memoir, Keckley uses the design, production, display, and ownership of clothing to refashion both self and nation.

As historians have shown, clothing was a central issue in black women's experience before, during, and after the Civil War. Although Frances Rollin, raised in an elite family, complained about her work as a seamstress, sewing was an important form of paid employment for free black women. For many slave women, clothing could be a meaningful arena of resistance to a dehumanizing system. Slave women, for example, often dyed cloth and made clothes for themselves and others, creating distinctive forms of dress and other modes of adornment; another use of cloth, quiltmaking, constituted a developed form of both political protest and artistic expression. The Civil War prompted new opportunities for the creative use of clothing by African-American women. Emancipation was sometimes symbolized in new forms of dress, as reported by a number of resentful former slaveholders. Belle Kearney, for example, reported that freed African-American women "bought brilliant-hued stuffs and had them made with most bizarre effects."[39] Inverting slavery's norms even more directly, some freed women wore their former mistresses' clothing. Myrta Lockett Avary recalled such reversals with horror:

> Mrs. Postell Geddings was in the kitchen getting Dr. Geddings' supper, while her maid, in her best silk gown, sat in the parlour and entertained Yankee officers . . . A Columbia lady saw in Sherman's motley train an old negress arrayed in her mistress' antiquated, ante-bellum finery . . . [Another woman] saw her negro man walking behind the Yankee Army with her husband's suit of clothes done up in a red silk handkerchief and slung on a stick over his shoulder. Her two mulatto nurse-girls laid down their charges, attired themselves in her best apparel and went; her seamstress stopped sewing, jumped on a horse behind a [Yankee] soldier who invited her, and away she rode.[40]

In these examples, the authority of ex-slaves to wear, take, or refuse to make their ex-masters' clothing is inseparable from both black freedom and Yankee victory. Long after emancipation, black women continued to use clothing as a directed form of both political and cultural expression. The origin, manufacture, cost, color, cut, and display of clothing were all significant features of black women's self-representation, as constituted both in opposition to white ex-masters and in affirmative relation to communities of free African-Americans.[41]

The memoirs of Keckley, an accomplished seamstress, dress designer, and quilter, similarly foreground the importance of clothing. As a slave, she begins taking in outside sewing and is so successful that her earnings support her owners: "[I]n a short time I had acquired something of a reputation as a seamstress and dress-maker . . . With my needle I kept bread in the mouths of seventeen persons for two years and five months" (45). When her supporters lend her money to buy herself and her son out of slavery, Keckley repays this loan with earnings from dressmaking. Keckley's subsequent career as fashion "modiste" was hardly typical of the more modest lives of most black seamstresses: as the celebrated "Madam Elizabeth" designing dresses for the elite of Washington, she employed as many as twenty workers. Nor did she literally participate in the kinds of clothing reversals prompted by emancipation for Southern slaves. Yet *Behind the Scenes* nonetheless shares in the larger symbolic affiliations among clothing, emancipation, and self-fashioning. Like the seamstress who stopped sewing and rode away with the Yankees, Keckley's control over clothing is the foundation of her journey into freedom.[42]

In *Behind the Scenes*, Keckley uses clothing not only to narrate her own story but also to comment in several ways on the national disruptions of the Civil War. First, clothing allows Keckley to position herself as an authoritative commentator on the relation of freed slaves to the wartime nation. Clothing and national symbolism intertwine in her account of a nameless ex-slave, "a good old, simple-minded woman, fresh from a life of servitude" (140–41), who mistakenly thinks that "Mr. and Mrs. Lincoln were the government" (141) and who claims that they are taking insufficient care of her:

> "I is been here eight months, and Missus Lingom an't even give me one shife. . . . My old missus us't gib me two shifes eber year."
>
> I could not restrain a laugh at the grave manner in which this good old woman entered her protest. Her idea of freedom was two or more old shifts every year. Northern readers may not fully recognize the pith of the joke. On the Southern plantation, the mistress, according to established custom, every year made a present of certain under-garments to her slaves, which articles were always anxiously looked forward to, and thankfully received. The old woman had been in the habit of receiving annually two shifts from her mistress, and she thought the wife of the President of the United States very mean for overlooking this established custom of the plantation. (141–42)

In this anecdote, Keckley uses clothing to show how the nameless ex-slave misunderstands her new world. In her false assumption that she would be given underwear by Mary Todd Lincoln, the old woman is doubly naked, literally denied her expected clothing and metaphorically stripped of the familiar customs of her world. Keckley's laughter underscores the other woman's ignorance, compounding it with ridicule. Despite Keckley's own committed efforts on behalf of the Contraband Relief Fund, this moment mocks the ex-slave who is unable to understand the fashions of the body politic.

The particular item of clothing involved in this misapprehension, the "shift," is also significant. "Shiftlessness" was a common racist stereotype about slaves. In George Aiken's theatrical adaptation of *Uncle Tom's Cabin*, for example, Topsy's initial appearance prompts Miss Ophelia to a flood of observations about her shiftlessness: "Good gracious! What a heathenish, shiftless looking object . . . She's dreadful dirty and shiftless! . . . How shiftless!"[43] Keckley's ridicule comes close to reproducing this stereotype, as she conflates the woman's literal lack of shifts with the alleged "shiftlessness" of those ex-slaves who "fretted and pined like children" (140). By contrast, Keckley presents herself as anything but shiftless, in several senses of the term. Industrious and successful, she herself has direct access to "Missus Lingom." The intimacy that the ex-slave falsely assumes she shares with Mary Todd Lincoln actually belongs to Keckley, for whom "Mr. and Mrs. Lincoln were the government" after all. Moreover, rather than receiving cast-off clothes from the First Lady, Keckley designs and makes Mary Todd Lincoln's clothes. The anecdote uses clothing symbolically not only to distance Keckley by class from recently freed slaves but also to register her own proximity to and power over the making of national symbols.[44]

Keckley rewrites her relation to national political power more explicitly in her representation of the clothing worn by Abraham Lincoln. To align herself with the president, she tracks the circulation of several densely symbolic items worn by Lincoln at key moments. Before the election of 1864, for example, she tells Mary Todd Lincoln, "I should like for you to make me a present of the right-hand glove that the President wears at the first public reception after his second inaugural" (153–54). Mary Todd Lincoln agrees, the president is re-elected, and when Keckley sees Lincoln just before the reception, she notes, "I went up to him, proffering my hand with words of congratulation. He grasped my outstretched hand warmly, and held it while he spoke: 'Thank you'" (156). Keckley is only the first of many to shake Lincoln's hand at the ball: his well-wishers include Frederick Douglass, whom Keckley herself greets and then urges to "shake the President by the hand" (159), whereupon "Mr. Lincoln pressed his hand warmly" (159). All told, "The President's hand was well shaken, and the next day, on visiting Mrs. Lincoln, I received the soiled glove that Mr. Lincoln had worn on his right hand that night" (158). That glove, Keckley notes with satisfaction, is "now in my possession, bearing the marks of the thousands of hands that grasped the honest hand of Mr. Lincoln on that eventful night" (154–55).

This vignette uses Lincoln's glove to create a circuit of power stretching from the president to Frederick Douglass to Keckley herself. Descriptions of shaking Abraham Lincoln's hand were common in writing by and about African-Americans of the Civil War era. Frances Rollin's biography of Martin Delany, for example, foregrounded the president's handshake: in Delany's words, "On entering the executive chamber . . . a generous grasp and shake of the hand brought me to a seat in front of him." Frederick Douglass equated the extended hand of the president with his acceptance: "As I approached and was introduced to him he arose and extended his hand, and bade me welcome. I at once felt myself in the presence of an honest man."[45] As in these accounts, Keckley invests the image of meeting the president with symbolic significance. In a culture that equated the president's body with that of the nation, meeting Lincoln signals her direct access to the prerogatives, white and male, of citizenship.

Keckley's vignette, moreover, offers a rhetorical extension of this trope of presidential hand-shaking, through her focus on Lincoln's glove. She inserts herself into the orbit of presidential authority not only by shaking Lincoln's hand but also by serving as the conduit between Douglass and Lincoln and, most fundamentally, by asserting her ownership of the glove. The glove itself is an overdetermined item that signifies Lincoln's authority but also, by virtue of its overuse and "soiling," his democratic impulses; intimately fitted to Lincoln's body but easily detachable from it, it becomes a mobile extension of Lincoln himself.[46] In her narration of this object, then, Keckley symbolically suggests her own authority: not only the "right-hand woman" to Mary Todd Lincoln, she is here "hand-in-glove" with the President of the United States.

The sartorial circuit between Lincoln and Keckley established at his second inauguration is further consolidated in *Behind the Scenes* by her account of the president's assassination. After Lincoln is shot, Mary Todd Lincoln sends for Keckley, who is given access to the corpse. "They made room for me, and, approaching the body, I lifted the white cloth from the white face of the man that I had worshipped as an idol—looked upon as a demi-god" (190). The legacy of this emotional moment is her possession of the items Lincoln wore at his death: "The cloak, stained with the President's blood, was given to me, as also was the bonnet worn on the same memorable night. Afterwards I received the comb and brush that Mr. Lincoln used during his residence at the White House. With this same comb and brush I had often combed his head" (202). The subsequent history of these items is one of further circulation, as controlled by Keckley: "The cloak, bonnet, comb, and brush, the glove worn at the first reception after the second inaugural, and Mr. Lincoln's over-shoes, also given to me, I have since donated for the benefit of Wilberforce University, a colored college near Xenia, Ohio, destroyed by fire on the night that the President was murdered" (203).

This description again highlights the intimate relation of Keckley to the president, through her possession of both Lincoln's outer garments and his toiletries. In the language of the body politic, the head, like the hand, was another overdetermined body part. Douglass, for example, characterized the president as "the head man of a great nation," while Frances Titus commented of Sojourner Truth that "From the head of the nation she sought that authority which would enable her to take part in the awful drama which was enacting in this Republic."[47] Keckley redoubled the importance of this rhetoric, for she was popularly known for her access to Lincoln's head. One newspaper article, for example, declared that "President Lincoln himself preferred not to make a public appearance unless 'Madame Keckley'. . . had first tamed his unruly hair."[48] The gift of Lincoln's toiletries in the wake of his death underscores the symbolic terms of this access. Literally affiliated with Lincoln's head, she retains her ongoing proximity to the head of the body politic as well.

The timing of this moment—immediately after Lincoln's death—is also of crucial symbolic importance. After his death, Lincoln's body lay in state at the White House and was subsequently exhibited for public viewing at many stops en route from Washington to Springfield, Illinois. This ritual of public display both sanctified the martyred president and elevated his viewing audience, uniting them as members of the Lincolns' national "family" mourning his death.[49] For newly emancipated African-Americans, access to Lincoln's dead body served as a vital test of their membership in this family. In her autobiography, for example, Mattie Jackson records at length the importance of seeing the president's body:

> On the Saturday after the assassination of the President there was a meeting held on the Common, and a vote taken to have the President's body brought through Indianapolis, for the people to see his dear dead face. The vote was taken by raising the hands, and when the question was put in favor of it a thousand black hands were extended in the air, seemingly higher and more visible than all the rest. . . . The body was placed in the centre of the hall of the State House, and we marched by in fours . . . The death of the President was like an electric shock to my soul. I could not feel convinced of his death until I gazed upon his remains, and heard the last roll of the muffled drum and the farewell boom of the cannon. (30)

This account represents the viewing of Lincoln's body as an event of both collective and individual importance. The "thousand black hands extended in the air, seemingly higher and more visible than all the rest," testify to the visible authority of African-Americans, whose collective strength can summon the body of the president. Jackson's own viewing of Lincoln is "an electric shock," a catalytic moment of witness whose sadness is intermixed with the celebration of new freedom and the power of her spectatorship.

Extending such accounts, Keckley's moment with the dead president testifies to her power. According to Melba Joyce Boyd, African-Americans were initially not allowed to view Lincoln's body, a policy changed in response to the protests of Frances Harper.[50] As she describes it in *Behind the Scenes*, Keckley's intimacy with the Lincoln family short-circuits such exclusions: even before Lincoln's funeral, her access to the president provides her with a privileged preview of his body. The racial coordinates of Keckley's description also suggest the collective dimensions of this moment. Regarding the Christ-like

Lincoln, Keckley first emphasizes a double whiteness of cloth and skin. By the end of the passage, however, this emphasis on whiteness has become a focus on blackness, in the form of Wilberforce, the "colored college." Her closing clause suggests that the assassination of Lincoln is mirrored by the arson against Wilberforce University, extending the alignment between Lincoln and Keckley to his association with an entire African-American community. And as the crime against Lincoln also wounds Wilberforce, so too is the aftermath of these events a kind of sartorial resurrection for both entities. Through the money raised by the exhibition of Lincoln's artifacts, the death of the white president helps the "colored college" to rise again.[51]

If Keckley's account of Lincoln simultaneously elevates herself along with the president, her representation of Jefferson Davis's clothing is more divided. Having worked as a seamstress for the Davises in pre-war Washington, Keckley narrates the story of a dressing-gown she made for the Confederate leader, a garment which "was worn, I have not the shadow of a doubt, by Mr. Davis during the stormy years that he was the President of the Confederate States" (69). As with her account of Lincoln, Keckley emphasizes her access to a figure of national political stature via a story about his clothing; also as with Lincoln, Keckley professes a strong liking for this president. Davis "always appeared to me," she writes, "as a thoughtful, considerate man in the domestic circle" (69). In this case, Keckley's access to a presidential "domestic circle" is even more certain than what she will have with Lincoln, since the clothing that connects her with the Confederate president is something she has herself produced.

Even as she appears to present a seamless connection between liking Davis and sewing for him, however, Keckley offers a very different account of the Confederate president a few pages later:

> In the winter of 1865 I was in Chicago, and one day visited the great charity fair held for the benefit of the families of those soldiers who were killed or wounded during the war. In one part of the building was a wax figure of Jefferson Davis, wearing over his other garments the dress in which it was reported that he was captured. There was always a great crowd around this figure, and I was naturally attracted towards it. I worked my way toward this figure, and in examining the dress made the pleasing discovery that it was one of the chintz wrappers that I had made for Mrs. Davis, a short time before she departed from Washington for the South. When it was announced that I recognized the dress as one that I had made for the wife of the late Confederate President there was great cheering and excitement, and I at once became an object of the deepest curiosity. Great crowds followed me, and in order to escape from the embarrassing situation I left the building. (74–75)

This account is one of many in the postwar period that represented Jefferson Davis as attempting unsuccessfully to flee the Union army while dressed in his wife's clothing. Dozens of Northern political cartoons and songs showed Davis cross-dressed as the "Belle of Richmond." Cartoons punned on his capture with such captions as "Jeff's Last Shift," the end of "petticoat government," and—in images that showed him being carried upside down by Union officers—as "the head of the Confederacy on a new base."[52]

Such imagery was the precise Northern counterpart of the transvestite fantasies of a work like *The Royal Ape*, in which the cross-dressing of Northerners signaled their defeat. The cross-dressed Davis, as Nina Silber argues, was part of a larger pejorative postwar characterization of the South as emasculated by loss.[53] Like the Northern white cartoonists, songwriters, and journalists developing the "Belle of Richmond" imagery, Keckley uses the imagery of feminization to humiliate Davis. No longer wearing the gown of Confederate leadership—another version of "shiftlessness"—Davis is now wrapped in the feminized chintz of disgrace, dummied into wax and preserved in prose. In her account, she implicitly humiliates him not once but three times: by making the very dress that is his reputed downfall; by staging her confirmation of the dress for an appreciative audience; and by including the story in her memoir. Despite her professed admiration for Davis, the image of the cross-dressed ex-president functions implicitly to rip apart the legacy of the Confederacy.

In the context of African-American writing about the Civil War, moreover, this anecdote suggests an attack on slavery as well as the Confederacy. Burlesques of Davis were common in African-American writing about the war. In Harriet Tubman's dictated description of the famous rescue of slaves near the Combahee River, for example, she mentions one woman who boarded the Union boat with "two pigs, a white one an' a black one; we took 'em all on board . . . [and named] de black pig Jefferson Davis." As a metaphor for Davis's impotence at this moment of black resistance, the image at once blackens the Confederate leader and turns him into a pig.[54] In a more sustained example of such imagery, William Wells Brown burlesqued Davis and honored freed slaves through his representation of Davis's Southern estate. Brown's *The Negro in the American Rebellion* includes an entire chapter, entitled "Fourth-of-July Celebration at the Home of Jeff. Davis," detailing the celebration of the national holiday by a group of freed slaves visiting Davis's now-vacant Mississippi home. Satiric reversals structure the chapter throughout. "[T]his site," introduces Brown, "from being the home of traitors and oppressors of the poor, has become a sort of earthly paradise for colored refugees. There they flock in large numbers . . . The rich men of the Southern Confederacy [are] now homeless wanderers." In this world turned upside down, the domestic space originally built as "a temple of slavery by the great chief" has been desecrated, its back door marked "exit traitor." For the freed slaves now present, eating and drinking in carnivalesque celebration, "There was an abundance of all that could be desired." Occupying Davis's domestic space, ex-slaves also lay claim to the national ritual of Independence Day, reciting the Declaration of Independence and singing "The Star-Spangled Banner."[55]

Like Tubman and Brown, Keckley invests the ridicule of Davis with racial significance. Davis's dress as a woman not only emasculates him but reverses the sexual associations between slavery and clothing forged in her youth. In Keckley's most extended account of the violence she endured as a slave, she describes how a white man, the village schoolteacher, demanded that she disrobe as preparation for whipping: "Recollect, I was eighteen years of age, was a woman fully developed, and yet this man coolly bade me take down my dress." This man eventually succeeds in "tearing my dress from my back" and viciously whips her (33–34). As in other slave narratives, the sexualized connotations of whipping are clear, and here the ripping of clothing suggests both preparation for and symbol of sexual violation.[56] In this context, Keckley's anecdote about Jefferson Davis redresses the dynamics of that earlier experience. In postwar America, it is the slaveholder, not the slave, whose state of undress brings humiliation.

Conversely, it is the female ex-slave, not the male slaveholder, who shapes the political discourse surrounding slavery. As with her own account of Lincoln, Keckley's relation to Davis's clothing underscores her own role in the making of political iconography. The scene highlights Keckley's own power, placing her at the center of a drama of authentication in which she plays a starring role. After making known her recognition of the dress, Keckley apparently signed a notarized statement attesting to having made the dress worn by Davis; the statement was printed in the newspaper, and ten thousand people then entered a lottery to win the garment.[57] She does not include this denouement in *Behind the Scenes,* but her account of being cheered and followed by crowds makes clear her own celebrity.

While Keckley professes embarrassment at her own role in this story, the story nonetheless suggests her pleasure at her authority in this moment, as does another anecdote in *Behind the Scenes.* After the war, Keckley visits the Garland family, her former owners. During this visit, "It did not take me long to discover that I was an object of great curiosity in the neighborhood. My association with Mrs. Lincoln, and my attachment for the Garlands, whose slave I had once been, clothed me with romantic interest" (253–54). Here Keckley is again the "object of great curiosity," but the experience is more obviously positive, as Keckley registers the clear pleasure of being "clothed" with interest. The verb, of course, is not accidental. In a text that consistently associates revenge with dress, pleasure is linked metaphorically to the acquisition and display of clothing. Here as elsewhere, the sartorial circuitry of *Behind the Scenes* allows Elizabeth Keckley both to dress down her enemies and dress up herself.

IV

Feminist critics have shown that American women's writing consistently links the needle with the pen, aligning literary production with quilting, embroidery, dressmaking, and other forms of clothmaking.[58] *Behind the Scenes* also conjoins needle and pen but less in a model of domestic artisanship than in a militarized mode of political critique. Keckley's needle is a weapon, not unlike the guns of the Civil War itself. Connections between female needles and male guns were made elsewhere in Civil War culture; for example, Henry Bellows, praising the women of the Sanitary Commission, had likened them to an "Army, whose bayonets were glittering needles."[59] Wielding her own bayonets of "glittering needles," Keckley symbolically comments on the wartime emancipation of slaves, the legacy of Abraham Lincoln, and the meaning of Confederate defeat. In each case, her commentary turns on items of clothing—shifts, gloves, dresses—whose meaning she invests with political resonance. Privatizing national icons, Keckley also publicizes herself. Whether celebrating her targets or condemning them, her accounts of clothing valorize her own symbolic authority in the Civil War nation.

Keckley most fully develops these strategies in her account of her relationship with Mary Todd Lincoln, a relationship that forms the heart of the memoir. Demonized in Southern works like *The Royal Ape,* Mary Todd Lincoln was also very unpopular in the North, condemned for her alleged extravagance, vulgarity, temper, and egotism. Her reputation reached its nadir in 1867, when she attempted unsuccessfully to sell off a large portion of her wardrobe. Writing *Behind the Scenes* in the volatile wake of this scandal, Keckley positions her memoir carefully. At the outset, she professes dedication to her former employer, declaring in the preface that "she should be judged more kindly than she has been" (xiv). Yet the preface to *Behind the Scenes* also suggests that the narrative to follow will not be entirely benevolent: "The veil of mystery must be drawn aside; the origin of a fact must be brought to light with the naked fact itself. . . . I have written nothing that can place Mrs. Lincoln in a worse light before the world than the light in which she now stands" (xiv). In this ambiguous passage, Keckley's tone is one of neutral truth-telling, but her metaphors suggest a more ominous project. On the next page, this idea returns more directly: "I have written with the utmost frankness in regard to her—have exposed her faults as well as given her credit for honest motives" (xv). As *Behind the Scenes* begins, then, Keckley's goal is to draw aside the "veil" covering Mary Todd Lincoln, leaving her "naked" and "exposed"—in short, to undress the former First Lady.

We can interpret this impulse in several ways, most immediately as Keckley's pragmatic need to balance intimacy with distance in her account of the public figure whose fame made her own success possible but whose infamy threatened her too. Yet in a narrative so "rhetorically veiled," to return to Rafia Zafar's phrase, Keckley's language also registers less neutrally. Her imagery of "unveiling" echoes that of the slave narrative, recalling, in particular, Lydia Maria Child's introduction to Harriet Jacobs's *Incidents in the Life of a Slave Girl:* "This peculiar phase of Slavery has generally been kept veiled; but the public ought to be made acquainted with its monstrous features, and I willingly take the responsibility of presenting them with the veil withdrawn."[60] Adapting the language of the slave narrative, Keckley turns it against Mary Todd Lincoln. As Jennifer Fleischner argues, in Keckley's descriptions of the First Lady, a "narrative inversion takes place, in which the 'mistress' comes to be cast in the role of the black slave as Other."[61]

This inversion takes place in the context of Keckley's accounts of her slave mistresses. Keckley's first mistress is a horrific figure, responsible for her vicious whippings. Remembering that "She whom I called mistress seemed to be desirous to wreak vengeance on me" (32), she describes her whippings as the fulfillment of her mistress's wishes: "Mr. Bingham had pledged himself to Mrs. Burwell to subdue what he called my 'stubborn pride'" (36). In apparent contrast, Keckley professes love for another former mistress, Ann Garland, and her daughters, describing them as "those who claimed my first duty and my first love" (241). Yet even in this positive phrase, the enslavement connoted by "first duty" clouds the romance of "first love," and during her happy reunion with the Garlands, the vector of power is clearly one-way. When Ann Garland inquires, "Do you always feel kindly towards me, Lizzie?" Keckley responds with obliquely devastating effect: "I have but one unkind thought, and that is, that you did not give me the advantages of a good education" (257). Characteristically, Keckley hints at her resentment through the metaphorics of clothing. She and Garland together reminisce about Keckley's aunt, who was once given a silk dress by her mistress, and then returned it to her upon request: "[The mistress] made her appearance at the social gathering, duly arrayed in the silk that her maid had worn to church on the preceding Sunday. We laughed over the incident" (256). While their laughter is ostensibly shared, this anecdote also lays bare the hierarchy of mistress and slave, since the story of the aunt gains its humor only through reversal, in the absurd image of a slave giving clothing to a mistress. Like the earlier moment in the text when Keckley laughs at the idea of the First Lady giving clothing to an ex-slave, this image of humor is edged with hostility. In this anecdote, the joke is on the white woman who both owns and mocks slaves.[62]

In *Behind the Scenes*, Mary Todd Lincoln picks up symbolically where Ann Garland leaves off, reprising the spirit if not the letter of the slavemistress. In reconstructing Mary Todd Lincoln, it is difficult to determine how she actually behaved, in relation to Keckley or anyone else. The public vilification of Mary Todd Lincoln was undoubtedly fueled by the same cultural biases against assertive women that continue to circumscribe the role of "First Lady." The contradictory expectations for this role called for both self-effacement and spectacle, mandating democratic accessibility along with aristocratic elegance; these were tests that Mary Todd Lincoln, who arrived in Washington unused to elite society and fascinated by money, was destined to fail. During the war, Mary Todd Lincoln's transgressions against appropriate standards of femininity were compounded by public suspicion over her border-state Kentucky origins and the fact that some of her family fought for the Confederacy. Initially judged with approval as a "Republican queen," she was later seen as a latter-day Marie Antoinette who, at worst, actively supported the Confederacy and, at best, went shopping while others suffered. Such condemnations relied at least in part on assumptions about female duplicity during wartime; there was little public sense, for example, of her grief at the death of her Confederate brother Robert in the war. A recent, sympathetic biography suggests that Mary Todd Lincoln was more victim than victimizer, suffering illnesses, family crises, and insecurities that we might also term the First Lady's inner civil wars.[63]

Whatever Mary Todd Lincoln's own internal conflicts, however, she was indisputably Keckley's employer, her boss if not also bossy. "[F]or as long as I remained with Mrs. Lincoln," Keckley remarks at one point, "I do not recollect ever having seen her with a needle in her hand" (225). Ostensibly neutral in tone, this statement sharply points out the hierarchical structure of their relationship, wherein Keckley and her staff prepare dresses for Mary Todd Lincoln, and Mary Todd Lincoln never picks up a needle. Photographs of Lincoln bear witness to this hierarchy, featuring the fantastically elaborate dresses that were the product of Keckley's creative design and exhausting labor (figure 9). Mary Todd Lincoln apparently naturalized this inequality as "best friendship"—"Lizabeth," she declares, "I love you as my best friend" (210)—but Keckley herself, I suggest, did not. Despite Lincoln's many statements of affection for Keckley, such affection always took place in a doubly hierarchical

FIGURE 9. Mary Todd Lincoln, photograph by Mathew Brady, 1861 (Library of Congress)

context: an unequal class relation in which an employee served and an employer commanded, and an unequal race relation in which a black woman attended to a white woman who had been raised in a household that included female slaves.[64]

In *Behind the Scenes,* Keckley gets her revenge on Mary Todd Lincoln, leveling an attack that functions on several levels. Most immediately, Keckley's account of Mary Todd Lincoln is a critique of the control white women may exert over black women, in ostensibly free Northern settings as well as clearly coercive Southern ones. Given Mary Todd Lincoln's role as First Lady, this critique also has a national dimension. Mary Todd Lincoln is at once private individual, emblem of white womanhood, and demonized national symbol. In undressing her, Keckley enters into each of these realms, offering an account poised between national allegory and personal vindication. The wartime context for this attack further energizes Keckley's aggression, embedding internecine White House struggles within the "house divided" of the nation. Cloaked in false civility, *Behind the Scenes* articulates Elizabeth Keckley's civil war with Mary Todd Lincoln.

As with Keckley's critique of Jefferson Davis, the weapon of this war is the language of clothing. Her overt tone is one of unimpeachable civility, but that tone is a cover for uncivil critique. Through indirect rhetorical strategies of juxtaposition, understatement, and silence, she uses the language of dress both to demote Mary Todd Lincoln and to promote her own power. When Mary Todd Lincoln first interviews Keckley, for example, she warns her, " 'I cannot afford to be extravagant . . . [I]f you will work cheap, you shall have plenty to do. I can't afford to pay big prices, so I frankly tell you so in the beginning' " (85). Since Keckley later reports in full the details of Mary Todd Lincoln's extravagant expenditures, this admonition rings false, and its inclusion serves implicitly to expose Mrs. Lincoln's hypocrisy. Indirect condemnation also emerges in her account of the first dress she sewed for Mary Todd Lincoln. As Keckley narrates this episode, when she arrives to fit Mary Lincoln in the dress, her new employer responds angrily: "But you are not in time, Mrs. Keckley; you have bitterly disappointed me. I have no time now to dress, and what is more, I will not dress, and go down-stairs" (87). The rest of this episode, however, vindicates Keckley's behavior: the other women present confirm that Mary Todd Lincoln has ample time, Keckley finishes dressing her, and the outfit is a success. Keckley provides no further commentary, but her silence, combined with the approval of the other women, stands as an implicit critique of Mary Todd Lincoln.

Elsewhere, Keckley not only disguises her condemnation of the First Lady but displaces her exposure of Mary Todd Lincoln onto an account of the other woman's self-exposure. Here is her description of Abraham Lincoln's response to one of his wife's dresses, which included a long train in back and a low décolletage:

"Whew! Our cat has a long tail tonight . . .

Mother, it is my opinion, if some of that tail was nearer the head, it would be in better style;" and he glanced at her bare arms and neck. She had a beautiful neck and arm, and low dresses were becoming to her. She turned away with a look of offended dignity . . . (101)

Keckley's account nominally defends Mary Todd Lincoln, but since Abraham Lincoln functions as a godlike figure in the text, the anecdote is at his wife's expense. This displacement of criticism onto another voice also occurs when Keckley reprints a newspaper article excoriating Mary Todd Lincoln: "'The peculiarity of [Mary Todd Lincoln's] dresses is that the most of them are cut low-necked—a taste which some ladies attribute to Mrs. Lincoln's appreciation of her own bust'" (304–5). Here Mary Todd Lincoln is not only tasteless but narcissistic and, in the image of the exposed breast, sexually indecent. The same article also describes Keckley as Mary Todd Lincoln's "bosom friend" (308), an ironic phrase in this context. Throughout *Behind the Scenes*, Keckley turns the other woman's own naked bosom against her.

As with her unwrapping of Jefferson Davis, Keckley's critique of Mary Todd Lincoln also elevates her own position. Like Mary Todd Lincoln, Keckley rapidly attains celebrity: "As soon as it was known that I was the modiste of Mrs. Lincoln, parties crowded around and affected friendship for me, hoping to induce me to betray the secrets of the domestic circle" (92). Mary Todd Lincoln, however, is condemned for her excesses, while Keckley is the emblem of refinement and elegance, widely praised. Early in the text, Keckley describes Mary Todd Lincoln in regal terms—"No queen . . . could have comported herself with more calmness and dignity than did the wife of the President" (89)—but she herself more fully embodies the virtues of the "Republican Queen." One contemporary, for example, wrote that "[E]very eye would turn to see [Keckley] because of her queenly walk, and to admire the beautiful and fitting way that she was gowned; refined and rich, but not gaudy."[65] Implicitly aligned with the president, Keckley symbolically offers herself as the text's truly deserving First Lady as well.

Keckley's most elaborate project of unveiling Mary Todd Lincoln emerges in her account of what came to be known as the "Old Clothes Scandal." In September 1867, Mary Todd Lincoln traveled in disguise to New York City, accompanied by Keckley, to attempt to pay off debts by selling a portion of her huge wardrobe. Quickly identified by the clothing dealer with whom she tried to broker her wardrobe discreetly, Lincoln then held a public exhibition and auction of her clothes. The exhibition was a financial failure and a public-relations disaster, further compounded when Lincoln's backers initiated an unsuccessful tour of her wardrobe in Rhode Island. Throughout the scandal, the contemptuous press condemned Mary Todd Lincoln as a pathetic spendthrift, desecrator of her husband's name, and "mercenary prostitute."[66]

Keckley's account of the Old Clothes Scandal in *Behind the Scenes* fully exploits its connotations of exposure. "Mrs. Lincoln wore a heavy veil so as to more effectually conceal her face," Keckley notes, remarking neutrally that "an accident would have exposed us to public gaze, and of course the masquerade would have been at an end" (288–89). Yet her own account contributes to this public gaze, defacing Mary Todd Lincoln as she unveils her. By recounting the whole scandal in full detail—complete with lists of clothing and financial information—Keckley authenticates the public spectacle already made of Mary Todd Lincoln. Her narrative aims to praise her former employer but ends up burying her.

At the same time that Keckley's account of the scandal strips Mary Todd Lincoln, she represents herself as a highly sympathetic figure, in this case a loyal ally now reduced to poverty. "Mrs. Lincoln's venture proved so disastrous," she notes, "that she was unable to reward me for my services, and I was compelled to take in sewing to pay for my daily bread" (326). Professing no anger at this turn of events, she concludes the final chapter of *Behind the Scenes:* "Though poor in worldly goods, I am rich in friendships, and friends are a recompense for all the woes of the darkest pages of life" (330). Given the fully delineated account of scandal that precedes these words, this closing statement seems disingenuous. Friends may be a figurative "recompense" for suffering, but in writing *Behind the Scenes,* Keckley makes her employer pay, controlling literary production as she has earlier controlled sartorial production. The result is a narrative from which the seamstress profits both literally and metaphorically at her former employer's expense.

In a further twist to this project, *Behind the Scenes* ends with an appendix that reprints, without her permission, some twenty-four of Mary Todd Lincoln's confidential letters written to Elizabeth Keckley during and after the Old Clothes Scandal. It is unclear whether Keckley willingly added these letters, or if, as seems likely, a collaborator like James Redpath included them against her wishes for their commercial value.[67] Whatever the impulse behind their inclusion, however, the presence of the letters confirms the critique of Mary Todd Lincoln undertaken by the preceding narrative of *Behind the Scenes.* As a continuation of the story Keckley tells all along, the appendix functions as her final and most aggressive exposure of Mary Todd Lincoln against her will.

The First Lady's own words serve as Keckley's primary weapon in this assault, with the other woman's words, as well as her clothes, put nakedly on display. Lincoln consistently links text and dress in her letters, writing Keckley, for example, that "You would not recognize me now. The glass shows me a pale, wretched, haggard face, and my dresses are like bags on me" (334). A pathetic figure, she also makes constant demands for her clothes: "I sometimes wish myself out of this world of sorrow and care. I fear my fine articles at B.'s are getting pulled to pieces and soiled. I do not wish you to leave N.Y. without having the finest articles packed up and returned to me" (347). In both passages, Mary Todd Lincoln aligns her haggard psyche with her ragged wardrobe, a juxtaposition of internal and external states in which she exposes herself as both vain and impotent.

As these letters condemn Mary Todd Lincoln, they once again assert Elizabeth Keckley's own authority. As the appendix continues, Lincoln expresses increasing frustration with Keckley: "I am greatly disappointed," she writes, "having only received one letter from you since we parted" (336), and then "I cannot understand your silence" (339). Keckley's silence implicitly gives her control over the other woman, as does her unexplained delay in sending Lincoln some clothing she desperately wants. "I am positively suffering for a decent dress. . . . Do send my black merino dress to me very soon; I must dress better in the future" (363). Two weeks later, Lincoln turns the same dress into an index of the other woman's ability to make her suffer: "I am literally suffering for my black dress. Will you send it to me when you receive this?" (369). Like the "war of nerves" waged by slaves against their mistresses, Keckley's silence is a tactic designed to disempower Lincoln.

If Keckley's silence frustrates, then her actions drive the other woman crazy with rage:

> Your letter announcing that my clothes were to be paraded in Europe—those I gave you—has almost turned me wild. . . . How little did I suppose you would do *such a thing;* you cannot imagine how much my overwhelming sorrows would be increased. May kind Heaven turn your heart, and have you write that *this* exhibition must not be attempted. . . . Why are you so silent? (364–66)

Keckley's voice intervenes at this point in the text, for what follows is a letter she had written to the founder of Wilberforce University, in which she explains that she had donated the clothes there (the European exhibition was later canceled). Drawing the reader into her epistolary confidence, Keckley's letter exonerates her from Lincoln's charge. Since the letter is not intended for Mary Todd Lincoln, the other woman remains ignorant of Keckley's explanation, appearing isolated and hysterical.

Lincoln's last letter to Keckley concludes with an entreaty trailing into an ellipsis: "Do get my things safely returned to me. . . ." (371). *Behind the Scenes* thus ends with Mary Todd Lincoln's voice, but in closing with this unanswered request, it more powerfully gives the last word to Keckley herself. The aggression that Keckley elsewhere accomplishes through understatement and juxtaposition, she here effects through silence, in the refusal to respond to Lincoln's pleas or otherwise to provide closure. The final impression is not only of Mary Todd Lincoln's pitiful dependence on Elizabeth Keckley but of the power that dependence gives to Keckley. Winning this war of nerves, Keckley's narrative leaves Mary Todd Lincoln symbolically naked and the seamstress herself holding the needle.

So outraged was Mary Todd Lincoln at this portrait that she immediately broke off all contact with her "dearest friend," subsequently referring to Keckley contemptuously only as "*the colored* historian"; her son Robert Lincoln was so furious that he attempted to take all copies of *Behind the Scenes* out of circulation.[68] Mary Todd Lincoln's final years were isolated and unhappy, reaching their nadir when Robert put her on trial for insanity.[69] Keckley, meanwhile, lost many of her friends because of the public condemnation of her book as scandalous. Briefly a teacher at Wilberforce University, she later became an inmate of the Home for Destitute Women and Children (an organization she had helped to found) until her death in 1907. The declining fortunes of both women suggest an ironic parallel across differences of race and class. Despite Lincoln's vastly greater power—and, conversely, despite Keckley's superior "refinement"—both women were condemned for their violations of civility.

This similarity is delineated with shocking venom in a work published in 1868 entitled *Behind the Seams; by A Nigger Woman Who Took in Work from Mrs. Lincoln and Mrs. Davis.* This twenty-three page text, copyrighted to one "Daniel Ottolengul," is, as its title implies, a racist parody of Keckley's memoir.[70] The parody reproduces each of the major events in Keckley's book but distorts them violently. The racism of *Behind the Seams* is exemplified in its repeated use of the word "nigger," which hammers throughout the narrative with toxic force, as in the story of "Kickley" being given Abraham Lincoln's glove from his Second Inauguration: "She promised me the dirty glove, gave it to me when the time came, and I have it now. The glove was even dirtier than I had hoped it would be, for it had the honor of being grasped by the paw of Frederick Douglass, nigger" (15). The racism of the text, here and throughout, offers further evidence of the cultural resistance prompted by Keckley's narration of her achievements. Parody may be an aggressive genre, and here the aggression is a protest against the very idea of African-American authorship and against the existence of an African-American elite that might stretch from Keckley to Douglass. The parodist cannot grant the status of author to Keckley, substituting "Betsey Kickley, her mark," for the writer's signature.

Yet parody is a complex genre, enacting not only an attack on a target but an ambivalent dependence on and an admiration of the original source text.[71] *Behind the Seams* illustrates such dependence, for even as its existence demon-

strates the racist resistance to Keckley, the parody's narrative strategies ironically intersect with Keckley's own. With imitative precision, the parodist needles Keckley precisely as Keckley herself had attacked Mary Todd Lincoln.
The result of this mimicry is that while the parody aims to nullify Keckley's
text, it ultimately confirms the techniques of *Behind the Scenes.*

Like Keckley, the narrator of *Behind the Seams* sets up an equation between
dressmaking and bookwriting, a goal forecast in the title and outlined in the
preface: "I am going to try an experiment and see if I can't make more money
by writing a book than by taking in sewing." "Kickley" aligns writing with
wearing as well as making clothes, having decided that "if I could find a publisher who would engineer my book, I'd try the thing on as I used to do with
Mrs. Lincoln's dresses." The finished product, the scandalous book, is equal
to the scandalous dress: "As a *modiste,* I have always succeeded in dressing my
bosom friend to her satisfaction, and now I modestly assert that in this work
she is 'dressed up' better than ever. It is a kind of low neck and short sleeve
affair, like the dresses Mrs. Lincoln prefers, and if it shows a little too much
I cannot help it." Far more overtly than Elizabeth Keckley herself, the parodist
equates literary and sartorial strategies. While Keckley offers only indirect critique, the parodist introduces from the outset a project of exposure in which
both Mary Todd Lincoln's dresses and her biography will "[show] a little too
much."

Outlining Keckley's metaphors, the parodist also exaggerates her disingenuous tone. "[A]lthough I was a slave for thirty years," "Kickley" writes in the
preface, "I do not blame the Southern people, nor hold them responsible. I
only blame the God of nature and the fathers who framed the Constitution
of the United States." This is Keckley's refusal to indict slaveowners, but it
is exaggerated to the point of absurdity. Similarly, "Kickley"'s treatment of
slaveowners brings out the critique implicit in Keckley: "Heaven bless this
good Southern lady. I love her, and I love the South for her sake; and so I
shall not be ungrateful, and I never shall write a book full of no-such-things
about the Southern people, and how they used to whip us poor slaves only
for exercise, like Bangham did, as I have before related" (9). The parodist not
only captures the combination of nostalgia and critique in Keckley's text but
also, in exaggerating both modes, tips the balance between them. The end of
the passage is so disingenuous that it undermines the first half, as Keckley's
own graphic accounts of slavery more implicitly condemn her professions of
nostalgia.

As the parody highlights Keckley's disingenuousness, so too does it emphasize her ambivalence toward Mary Todd Lincoln. *Behind the Seams* includes
many of Keckley's anecdotes about Mary Todd Lincoln but with just enough

changes to bring out their damning effect. Relating Abraham Lincoln's response to his wife's décolletage, for example, Keckley subtly suggests the president's displeasure; "Kickley" has him declaring "that if some of the cat's tail was nearer to the cat's head the dress would not be so low" (12). The new context of the parody gives such anecdotes maximum scandalous impact: "I almost feel ashamed of myself when I . . . reflect that in order to make my book pay, both myself and the publisher, I shall be compelled, at times, to draw the long bow a little, even in speaking of my dear, bosom friend, Mrs. Lincoln" (13). The parody also exaggerates the language of Mary Todd Lincoln's letters just enough so that they are unambiguously self-condemning: "I was thinking all the time of you," writes Mary Todd Lincoln in "Kickley"'s version, "also, of number One" (21). Such passages openly assert what Keckley only indirectly reveals: the egotism of Mary Todd Lincoln.

In hyperbolizing Keckley's strategies, moreover, the parodist turns them back on Keckley herself. Like Mary Todd Lincoln, "Kickley" is narcissistic throughout, describing herself as a "great authoress" (4), recounting "the airs I put upon myself" (9), and characterizing another woman as "one of the loveliest ladies that I ever met, not even excepting myself" (11). Explaining her success as a seamstress, she narrates, "I began to sew, and I did more than so-so . . . Thus it was that I became a *modiste,* though I could hardly be called modest any longer" (7). The puns in this passage effect its satiric points, equating sewing with profit and dressmaking with immodesty. These links among narcissism, impropriety, and clothing are the same ones that Elizabeth Keckley's narrative forges in relation to Mary Todd Lincoln. Like Mary Todd Lincoln's dresses, "Kickley"'s own clothing is a "low neck and short sleeve affair." What *Behind the Scenes* does to Mary Todd Lincoln, *Behind the Seams* does to Keckley herself.

The parody also extends this attack significantly, by describing both Lincoln and "Kickley" in language that approaches pornography. Reviewers had condemned *Behind the Scenes* as "grossly and shamelessly indecent," language whose sexual implications the parodist literalizes in its descriptions of female bodies.[72] Keckley, for example, had invoked Mary Todd Lincoln as her "bosom friend"; the parodist uses this phrase many times, as both "Kickley"'s and Lincoln's terms for each other.[73] Given the parody's emphasis on female self-exposure throughout, the effect of this repetition is not only to highlight Keckley's betrayal of Lincoln but also to raise the question of the actual bosoms literally "behind the seams" of the women's low-cut dresses. This is a question that "Kickley" highlights throughout the text, in comments like "I was eighteen years old and was a fine looking nigger girl and well developed" (6). The language of the parody turns "Kickley" into a version of the lascivious Jezebel stereotype, as "bosom" and "nigger," the parody's most frequently repeated words, combine. Yet this racist logic operates precisely by borrowing the terms of Keckley's own attack on Mary Todd Lincoln in order to turn them back on Keckley herself.

The conclusion of *Behind the Seams* brings money back into this circuit: "I write books and I take in sewing. I write in the night, and sew in the day. Publishers and ladies please take notice. Terms moderate" (23). Given the implications of impropriety that permeate the parody, the presentation of writing as a nighttime activity is sexually suggestive. Creating low-cut texts for paid circulation, "Kickley" implicitly represents the black woman author as a prostitute and the publisher as her pimp. Such metaphors deploy both racist stereotypes of black women's sexuality and the longstanding misogynist association between the woman writer and the prostitute.[74] In this confluence of racism and misogyny, the parody converges a final time with the narrative strategies of its target. *Behind the Scenes* had unveiled the actions that led to Mary Todd Lincoln's condemnation as "mercenary prostitute"; *Behind the Seams* constructs "Kickley"'s literary efforts as symbolic prostitution. In its concluding emphasis on the Old Clothes Scandal, Keckley's own text provides the very model for parody that *Behind the Seams* exploits.

Even as it attempts to negate Keckley with "Kickley," then, *Behind the Seams* offers an ironic testament to the success of Keckley's own rhetorical tools. Like Keckley herself, the parodist sets up a sustained equation between text and dress that allows criticism to pass as tribute. This comparison in no way negates the force of the parody's racism, nor of its misogyny that reduces both women to grotesquerie. It does, however, suggest a mutually revealing relationship between the text and its parody. The convergence between the two texts reveals the parodist's dependence on Keckley's own text, which sets the precise terms of discourse that would negate it. *Behind the Seams* aims at the annihilation of its target, but *Behind the Scenes* emerges from this attack with redoubled strength, for the parody makes clear just how ingeniously Keckley's text encodes aggression. Expressing hostility without sacrificing civility, Keckley costumes attack in the language of self-effacing tribute. As a defense of Mary Todd Lincoln, *Behind the Scenes* is already a parody.

v

In *Behind the Scenes*, Elizabeth Keckley fashions a Civil War of her own design. The bifurcations and ambiguities of the war symbolically frame Keckley's self-narration, which situates her in a set of social, psychic, and literary "border states." Framed by the war, Keckley also reframes it, intervening in Civil War rhetoric through her representation of clothing. Sewing, for Keckley, is simultaneously a form of fighting and a mode of writing that allows her to enter into national iconography by privatizing and inverting its terms. The text itself becomes Keckley's final garment, sewn from the remnants of other stories—including Mary Todd Lincoln's own words—and exhibited through publication. Displayed for a reading audience, the book then takes its place alongside the series of sartorial spectacles charted within the narrative itself, following the unhanded glove of Abraham Lincoln, the cross-dressed dress of Jefferson Davis, and above all, the defrocked frocks of Mary Todd Lincoln. By the end of *Behind the Scenes,* as the parody inadvertently confirms, Mary Todd Lincoln's vulgar excesses are fully on display, while Keckley is both First Lady and President of her own text.

In this civil war, the sharpest conflicts are ultimately between African-American and white women, an antipathy that contrasts sharply with the war narratives that white writers like Alcott present. Both Keckley and Alcott narrate inner civil wars in relation to public conflict, and both organize their stories of nationhood through evocative metaphors—respectively, injured and undressed bodies—that bring women symbolically closer to centers of power. But the two writers also diverge profoundly. Alcott's utopia is centered on white women, presuming a communion between black and white people while maintaining racial hierarchies. Keckley's text purports to endorse such interracial communion but more covertly refuses it throughout. For Alcott, blackness serves as a symbol of and outlet for topsy-turvyness; for Keckley, the white woman is the figure of uncontrolled excess, as Mary Todd Lincoln becomes the grotesque double to Keckley herself. Related to this contrast, the organizing national metaphors of the two writers work in opposite ways. Both women use sharp implements to reconstruct the body politic, but Alcott's surgical needles aim to heal, while Keckley's sewing needles puncture. Accordingly, Alcott's texts progress toward therapeutic closure—in national if not individual terms—while Keckley rips apart the seams of both sisterhood and nationhood. At the end of *Behind the Scenes* lies not the feminized, whitened utopia of Plumfield and literary celebrity for its author, but a world of differences between women and a culture hostile to the very act of African-American authorship.

As *Behind the Scenes* illuminates the sharp divisions between black and white women's Civil War texts, it both contributes to and challenges critical paradigms for African-American Civil War commentary. The editor of a twentieth-century anthology of African-American writing on the war remarks that "All of these writers were engaged . . . in redressment, in placing the story of black men and women in its fullness on view against a chorus of disparagement and calumny."[75] *Behind the Scenes,* I have argued, literalizes the idea of "redressment," fully exploiting the metaphorics of dress in its narration of the Civil War years. In so doing, Keckley becomes what Mary Todd Lincoln accused her of being, a "colored historian," putting black experience at the center of the war years. Like other African-American women authors of the Civil War era, she wars with the hierarchies of race, gender, and nation that would otherwise silence black women's voices. Along with Mattie Jackson and Frances Rollin, among others, Keckley uses literary strategies—juxtaposition, silence, irony, reversal—that both reflect and create a world inverted by emancipation.

At the same time, Keckley's account of African-American war experience is far more complex than simply "placing the story of black men and women in its fullness on view." For example, although Keckley's relief work brought her into contact with a variety of African-Americans, there are few black men in her version of the war. Her representation of black women, meanwhile, is sharply divided along class lines, and she offers no developed portraits of other black women, elite or nonelite. The version of "redressment" offered in *Behind the Scenes* is idiosyncratic and uneven, and the text occupies an ambiguous relation to the very tradition—African-American women's Civil War writing—in which it would seem most welcome.

Ultimately, *Behind the Scenes* suggests the difficulties of constituting such a tradition in unitary terms. Hortense Spillers has theorized black women's literary history in terms of contradictions, breaks, and ruptures, which constitute not a coherent literary tradition but "a matrix of literary *discontinuities.*" Black women's writing, in this model, "not only redefines tradition, but also disarms it by suggesting that the term itself is a critical fable."[76] *Behind the Scenes* is a similarly discontinuous text, cautioning against the construction of a singular black women's countercanon—or any female countercanon—of Civil War writing. What Spillers characterizes as the "disarmament" of tradition is, in this context, a fitting term for a text that so fully intermixes military and sartorial imagery. Positioned against literary and national traditions, Keckley is, as ever, a warring presence, and her needling combinations of text and textile remain at once cutting and disarming.

FOUR

Confederate Counterfeit

The Case of the Cross-Dressed Civil War Soldier

I

In Elizabeth Keckley's carefully tailored Civil War narrative, dress reveals as much as it conceals, all seams are cut on the bias, and every garment has something up its sleeves. For another group of women of the Civil War era, the link between fabric and fabrication was even more pressing. The image of the cross-dressed woman soldier appears in a surprisingly large number of Civil War texts, consistently cited in journalism, memoirs, and fiction about the war from the 1860s onward.[1] While images of women soldiers emerged during earlier wars, they proliferated dramatically in the Civil War and after. In an 1879 survey of "female warriors" throughout history, British writer Ellen Clayton declared that "If we may believe Transatlantic newspapers, the Civil War in America was more productive of female warriors than almost any conflict since the days of the Amazons."[2] In her war memoir, Mary Livermore suggested that at least four hundred women actually cross-dressed during the war, adding that "Some startling histories of these military women were current in the gossip of army life; and extravagant and unreal as were many of the narrations, one always felt that they had a foundation in fact."[3] More common on the Union side than on the Confederate, these women capitalized on their resemblance to the image of the soldier as a beardless, adolescent boy and adopted soldiers' uniforms with varying degrees of success. Verifiable cross-dressing experiences ranged from those of Jennie Hodgers, who masqueraded as a Union soldier through three years of combat and continued passing as a man until 1911; to Elizabeth Compton, who reenlisted in different regiments each time she was discovered, seven in all; to an unnamed woman recruit in Rochester whose masquerade ended much earlier, when she "was discovered by her trying to put her pants on over her head."[4] The experience of these women forms a vital part of such fields as the histories of women, gender, sexuality, and war—as well, of course, as the history of cross-dressing itself.[5]

My concern here is less with the documentary recovery of the lives of women soldiers than with the symbolic significance of stories about them. Accounts of women Civil War soldiers are examples of a nineteenth-century genre that Kathleen De Grave has characterized as the "confidence woman" narrative, a form that reflects an ongoing American fascination with stories of passing, disguise, counterfeit, and tricksterism.[6] Within this capacious literary genealogy, Civil War cross-dressing narratives suggest the particular symbolic opportunities the war afforded for the representation of female boundary-crossing. As Livermore's reference to "extravagant and unreal narration" suggests, the woman soldier functioned as a figure of rhetorical excess, violating the literary boundaries of identifiable fact along with the social limits of appropriate femininity. The Civil War, I suggest, is at once catalyst and alibi for these violations, authorizing stories of female adventure that exceed their patriotic frame. The civil wars that emerge from these texts are less internal struggles against civility, as in the writings of Alcott and Keckley, than flagrant violations of it. Overtly defying the disciplinary imperatives of civility, these texts are dominated by boundary-crossing performances and masquerades.

The most famous account of a Union woman soldier, *Nurse and Spy in the Union Army* (1864) by S. Emma E. Edmonds, introduces the symbolic complexities of narratives of Civil War cross-dressing. In *Nurse and Spy,* Edmonds describes her experiences as a field nurse for Michigan soldiers at the front and her subsequent work as a spy, for which she disguised herself as a black male slave, an Irish female peddler, a black female slave, a white Confederate soldier, and finally a white Confederate male civilian. Published during the Civil War, *Nurse and Spy* concludes with Edmonds's honorable discharge after falling ill. The book sold more than 175,000 copies; Edmonds contributed her profits to relief organizations. In the 1880s, she successfully applied for a pension for her military service and was formally inducted into the Grand Army of the Republic.[7]

Edmonds's story offers a representation of the extraordinary mobility possible for white women within the context of wartime espionage. Her first disguise as a male contraband, for example, extends and complicates the language of masculine fantasy central to writers like Alcott.[8] In a section entitled "I Turn Contraband," she describes her assumption of this disguise: "I went to a barber and had my hair sheared close to my head. Next came the coloring process—head, face, neck, hands and arms were colored black as any African, and then, to complete my contraband costume, I required a wig of real negro wool" (107). As in Alcott's writing, haircutting is a significant symbolic act, but here it allows for the actual performance of masculinity rather than the muted fantasy of a battle scar. Edmonds's memoirs were first published under the title "Unsexed," a word that succinctly captures the extent to which she not only assumes masculinity but abandons femininity.[9]

At the same time, "unsexing" is inseparable from racial masquerade, with Edmonds's new "wig of real negro wool" specifying "negro" masculinity. As Werner Sollors has shown, the theme of racial passing emerges in early nineteenth century American literature and is in full force by the Civil War period. Representations of passing often incorporate cross-dressing, as in the slave narrative *Running a Thousand Miles for Freedom* (1860), in which Ellen Craft, a light-skinned slave, disguises herself as her husband's white male master, and in *Uncle Tom's Cabin,* in which Eliza Harris cross-dresses and presents herself as a white man.[10] In these examples, black people pass for white to escape from slavery, but passing narratives also portrayed white people darkening their skin. Part of this latter tradition, Edmonds's racial disguise also extends the racial dynamics of a story like Alcott's "My Contraband." In both works, the figure of the contraband is part of a fantasy of white female power, but while Alcott exerts only symbolic control over this figure, Edmonds actually becomes him. The ensuing account of espionage is detached from its actual political context. Had she been truly "contraband," Edmonds would have faced a return to slavery, but in *Nurse and Spy,* "turn[ing] contraband" signals not danger but adventure. The episode suggests the importance of racial disguise as another fantasy of freedom in Civil War narratives about white women.[11]

Edmonds's second disguise, that of an Irish woman peddler, further expands the racial and sexual dimensions of her masquerade. During the Civil War, many Irish men served in the Union army, but most did not support emancipation; Irish immigrants were prominent in the racist violence of the 1863 New York City Draft Riots. As Noel Ignatiev has shown, such racism was as much a reaction against perceived affinities between African-Americans and Irish-Americans as a register of differences between them. The Irish in America were frequently vilified as "niggers turned inside out," while blacks were sometimes known as "smoked Irish." Anti-black racism was one means by which the Irish in America severed these equations and gained access to the prerogatives of whiteness.[12]

Edmonds's description of her Irish disguise provides an ironic commentary on this tense history. When she decides "to abandon the African relation, and assume that of the Hibernian" (147), Irishness functions as a form of costume congruent with blackness:

I found a number of articles which assisted me much in assuming a more perfect disguise. There was mustard, pepper, an old pair of green spectacles, and a bottle of red ink. . . . [W]ith the ink I painted a red line around my eyes, and after giving my pale complexion a deep tinge with some ochre which I found in a closet, I put on my green glasses and my Irish hood.

. . . I took from my basket the black pepper and sprinkled a little of it on my pocket handkerchief, which I applied to my eyes. The effect was all I could have desired, for taking a view of my prepossessing countenance in a small mirror which I always carried with me, I perceived that my eyes had a fine tender expression, which added very much to the beauty of their red borders. (162–64)

Edmonds's green glasses and "Irish hood" provide ethnic costume akin to her contraband wig, while the pepper, ink, and ochre "tinge" reprise the "coloring process" of her first disguise. In addition to equating blackness and Irishness, the passage also suggests the extent to which this new disguise alters conventions for female behavior. The mirror, ordinarily an emblem of female self-regulation, reflects Edmonds's self-admiration back as she happily views her artificially reddened eyes. By fighting against the Confederacy, Edmonds gets to wage her own war against female civility.

Taken at face value, then, *Nurse and Spy* shows how the demands of war authorized both mobility and mutability for white women, turning gender, race, and ethnicity into made-up costumes. The language of duty sanctions these movements throughout: Edmonds's publisher introduces the text by praising her "purest motives and most praiseworthy patriotism" (6), while Edmonds closes *Nurse and Spy* with a heartfelt wish for "peace which is no counterfeit" (384). Yet "counterfeit" gets the last word in her text in more ways than one, since for all that *Nurse and Spy* reveals about the female masquerade in the Civil War, there is much that it also disguises. What *Nurse and Spy* conceals is that when Edmonds first enlisted in the Union army, she was already cross-dressing, passing as a man she named "Franklin Thompson." When Edmonds became a spy, her army comrades witnessed "Thompson," whom they assumed to be male, temporarily assuming the costumes of "contraband" and Irishwoman. Edmonds deserted from the army rather than have "Thompson" be discovered; she publicly revealed her own female identity only when she applied for her pension. While she apparently revised her story to include her cross-dressing, the revision was never published and was subsequently lost. Her memoir as it stands is thus a form of textual counterfeit, as much a disguise for its protagonist as the inks, wigs, and accents Edmonds adopts within her story.[13]

Reinterpreted in light of Edmonds's long-term masquerade as "Thompson," *Nurse and Spy* is an extended study of omissions, ironies, and double-bluffs. Edmonds sometimes deliberately misleads, as when she declares that "Col. R.'s wife [and] Mrs. B. and myself were, I think, the only three females who reached Fairfax that night" (33). This comment obscures the persona of "Franklin Thompson," while other remarks make sense only with knowledge of "his" existence, as when she leaves the army: "I procured female attire, and laid aside forever (perhaps) my military uniform; but I had become so accustomed to it that I parted with it with much reluctance" (360). Most often, her narrative slyly avoids the question of her gender presentation entirely. Upon enlisting, for example, Edmonds remarks that "I could only thank God that I was free and could go forward and work, and was not obliged to stay home and weep" (20–21). Edmonds's relief at not having to "stay home and weep" is intelligible as a female nurse's rejection of domestic life, but it takes on ironic force given that her freedom to "go forward and work" is actually based on her male costume. So too does her meditation on her war years extend beyond nostalgia: "I look back now upon my hospital labors as being the most important and interesting in my life's history" (364). This comment offers a veiled appreciation not only of Edmonds's declared "labors" but also of the freedom afforded her by adopting the uniform of "Franklin Thompson" from the start.

One extraordinary episode in *Nurse and Spy* both courts and displaces the exposure of "Thompson." Edmonds encounters a soldier after the battle of Antietam:

> In passing among the wounded . . . my attention was attracted by the pale, sweet face of a youthful soldier who was severely wounded in the neck . . . I stooped down and asked him if there was anything he would like done for him. The soldier turned a pair of beautiful, clear, intelligent eyes upon me, and then, as if satisfied with the scrutiny, . . . said faintly, "Yes, yes" . . . Something in the tone and voice made me look more closely at the face of the speaker, and that look satisfied me that my suspicion was well founded. . . . The little trembling hand beckoned me closer, and I knelt down beside him and bent my head until it touched the golden locks on the pale brow before me; I listened with breathless attention . . .
>
> "I am not what I seem, but am a female. I enlisted from the purest motives, and have remained undiscovered and unsuspected. . . . I wish you to bury me with your own hands, that none may know after my death that I am other than my appearance indicates." . . .
>
> I assured her that she might place implicit confidence in me . . . (270–72)

Improbable as an actual event, this encounter between the two women offers a covert symbolic meditation on Edmonds's own experience "passing among the wounded." In this moment of mutual identification, the cross-dressed soldier not only recognizes Edmonds as a kindred cross-dresser but provides a mirror-image to describe Edmonds herself. Edmonds's account of the other woman reveals her own "looks"—idealized as "sweet face," "golden locks," purest motives—to an astute reader.

Imperfectly concealing the existence of "Franklin Thompson," the text also hints at Edmonds's motives for inventing him. Writing to Congress in support of her pension, Edmonds's colleagues accommodated the startling news of "Franklin Thompson"'s true identity with testimonials to her "care, kindness, and self-sacrificing devotion" and "pure morals and Christian character."[14] In a later interview, Edmonds described "Thompson" in similar terms: "I had no other motive in enlisting than love to God, and love for suffering humanity. . . . I went with no other ambition than to nurse the sick and care for the wounded. I had inherited from my mother a rare gift of nursing."[15] *Nurse and Spy* itself, however, alludes to a set of motives very different from maternal piety and self-sacrifice:

> I am naturally fond of adventure, a little ambitious and a good deal romantic, and this together with my devotion to the Federal cause . . . made me forget the unpleasant items, and not only endure, but really enjoy, the privations connected with my perilous positions. Perhaps a spirit of adventure was important—but *patriotism* was the grand secret of my success. (121)

Ostensibly describing only her contraband costume, Edmonds's account refers as well to her larger masquerade as Thompson. Under the cloak of patriotism, adventure and ambition emerge, albeit briefly, as motivations for her cross-dressing.

A fuller biography of Edmonds reveals the extent to which *Nurse and Spy* uses the Civil War as literary camouflage for her impulse to cross-dress. In later interviews, Edmonds recalled a difficult childhood growing up in Nova Scotia with a tyrannical father: "In our family the women were not sheltered but enslaved."[16] Her turning point, she remembered, came when she read *Fanny Campbell, the Female Pirate Captain* (1844), a story of cross-dressing set during the American Revolution, in which a heroine disguises herself as a sea-captain to rescue an imprisoned lover; after the rescue, she remains cross-dressed for other adventures, with her husband serving as her first mate. When reading *Fanny Campbell*, Edmonds recalls,

> All the latent energy of my nature was aroused, and each exploit of the heroine thrilled me to my finger tips. I went home that night with the problem of my life

solved. I felt equal to the emergency. I was emancipated, and could never be a slave again.

When I read where "Fanny" cut off her brown curls and donned the blue jacket, and stepped into the freedom and glorious independence of masculinity, I threw up my old straw hat and shouted, as I have since heard McClellan's soldiers do, when he rode past the troops on a march. . . .[17]

Seeking escape from metaphorical "enslavement," Edmonds describes cross-dressing as a conduit to "the freedom and glorious independence of masculinity." The American Civil War enters into this account as belated analogy, rather than patriotic catalyst, for her own "emancipation."

In fulfillment of the promise of *Fanny Campbell,* Edmonds's first cross-dressing episode long preceded the war. After running away from home to avoid an arranged marriage, she began cross-dressing and, passing as a man, became a successful traveling Bible salesman. She later recalled: "The publishing company told me that they had employed agents for 30 years, and they never had employed one that could outsell me. I made money, dressed well, owned and drove a fine horse and buggy . . . [and] took my lady friends out riding occasionally and had a nice time generally."[18] The same firm for whom she sold Bibles would later publish *Nurse and Spy.* Two contrasting texts, then, metaphorically frame *Nurse and Spy:* the Bible, the signifier of God's authentic word, and *Fanny Campbell,* a story of female counterfeit. Read against this literary genealogy, Edmonds's memoirs are both adventure-story sequel and Biblical burlesque. Disguising the "glorious independence of masculinity" with the languages of patriotism and piety, Edmonds writes a memoir of cross-dressing in which the Civil War is a cover story for her own rebellious desires.

Edmonds's comment that she "took my lady friends out riding" suggests one further dimension of masquerade in *Nurse and Spy.* "Franklin Thompson"'s skill as salesmen was inextricable from his "success" with women, or as Edmonds described another stint as salesman: "I stopped at first-class houses, lived well, dressed well . . . and came near marrying a pretty little girl who was bound that I should not leave Nova Scotia without her."[19] Such descriptions suggestively introduce the prospect of same-sex romance, with the soldier's uniform enabling affairs between Edmonds and her "lady friends." In this context, we may reread the encounter between Edmonds and the other cross-dressed soldier in *Nurse and Spy* as a fantasy of intimacy between women. The golden-haired soldier is not only a figure of identification for Edmonds but also an object of her desire. In its intimations of same-sex intimacy, *Nurse and Spy* once again engages in double disguise. As the war dresses Edmonds's adventures in the cloak of patriotism, so too do her revealed boundary-crossings themselves cover over another story: the sustained adoption of male dress for the pleasures of masculine agency and romance with women. Cross-dressing, in short, is at once theme and technique in *Nurse and Spy*, as Edmonds layers one story of counterfeit over the dress of another.

An even more extravagant narration of counterfeit informs the memoirs of Edmonds's Confederate counterpart. *The Woman in Battle* (1876) purports to be the autobiography of Loreta Velazquez, a Cuban-born woman who describes her extended masquerade as a Confederate officer and spy during the war. Along with *Nurse and Spy*, *The Woman in Battle* is the most well-known Civil War cross-dressing memoir, although, in contrast to Edmonds, Velazquez's exploits have long been condemned as scandalous and her text itself dismissed as fiction.[20] I turn now to *The Woman in Battle*, taking the charge of "fiction" as a point of departure for literary analysis rather than as cause for historical censure. Interpreted as fiction, *The Woman in Battle* serves as a productive site for inquiry into the symbolic meanings of Civil War masquerade. Cross-dressing serves in this text as a metaphorical point of exchange for intersections between individual bodies and the national body politic. As both fantasy and nightmare of boundary-crossing, *The Woman in Battle* forges a series of connections linking a nation divided between regions and races and an individual oscillating among sexes and sexualities.

These metaphoric connections flow in two directions. In the first half of the chapter, I argue that the Civil War symbolically energizes the cross-dressing plot of *The Woman in Battle* in several ways. The language of regional rebellion authorizes Velazquez's initial plot of gender reversal, and the rhetoric of Confederate espionage energizes her authority over the performance of both masculinity and femininity. At the same time, the regional flux of the Civil War also frames a less controlled presentation of gender and sexuality in the text. As the war progresses, Velazquez's story turns masculinity and femininity into a series of metaphoric "border states," while pride of narrative place goes to a series of protolesbian seduction narratives.

In the second half of the chapter, I argue that these metaphoric connections between individual and region also operate in reverse. Reading Velazquez through the lens of her harshest critic, Confederate General Jubal Early, I argue that her story threatens multiple mythologies of the postwar white South. Inadvertently burlesquing the iconography of the "Lost Cause," Velazquez destabilizes anxious Southern constructions of whiteness, along with those of masculinity and heterosexuality. By the end of *The Woman in Battle*, the legacy of Confederate defeat is one of carnivalesque flux, in which Velazquez's postwar adventures in South America and the American West, as well as her own Cuban origins, disrupt racial, regional, and national, as well as sexual, boundaries. From the phantasmatic possibilities of a "lesbian confederacy" to the cultural myths of the postwar Lost Cause, *The Woman in Battle* affirms the instabilities of identity, both individual and regional, in the Confederate and Reconstruction South.

II

The Woman in Battle presents itself as the first-person story of Loreta Janeta Velazquez, a Cuban-born, Confederate woman whose Civil War experience, by her own account, encompassed an astonishing range of activities. The book's subtitle gives some sense of its scope:

> A Narrative of the Exploits, Adventures, and Travels of Madame Loreta Janeta Velazquez, otherwise known as Lieutenant Harry T. Buford, Confederate States Army. In which is given Full Descriptions of the numerous Battles in which she participated as a Confederate Officer; of her Perilous Performances as a Spy, as a Bearer of Despatches, as a Secret-Service Agent, and as a Blockade-Runner; of her Adventures Behind the Scenes at Washington, including the Bond Swindle; of her Career as a Bounty and Substitute Broker in New York; of her Travels in Europe and South America; her Mining Adventures on the Pacific Slope; her Residence among the Mormons; her Love Affairs, Courtships, Marriages, &c., &c.[21]

As the length of this subtitle suggests, the book's overall size (six hundred pages, fifty-two chapters) is massive; its structure ("&c., &c."), episodic; and its tone ("Exploits, Adventures, and Travels"), sensational. Edited by a Union navy veteran, C. J. Worthington, the book narrates Velazquez's adventures while disguised as an officer of her own invention, Lieutenant Harry T. Buford (figures 10 and 11). As Buford, Velazquez fights in a number of early battles, including Bull Run, Fort Donelson, and Shiloh, and is wounded twice, escaping detection the first time but not the second. After her unmasking, she becomes a spy and engages in a dizzying round of disguises in both North and South, including those of a Confederate male private, a Confederate woman, a Union woman fleeing from the Confederacy, a Spanish widow spying for the Union army, a Northern war widow, and a Spanish-speaking servant girl in the North. *The Woman in Battle* frames these activities with additional material about Velazquez's life, from her childhood to her postwar travels and business ventures in Europe, South America, the Caribbean, and the Ameri-

MADAM VELASQUEZ IN FEMALE ATTIRE.

FIGURE 10.
Frontispiece from *The Woman in Battle*, 1876: Loreta Velazquez as Loreta Velazquez

can West. In the course of this account, Velazquez also marries four times and gives birth to several children; the final chapter remarks the birth of her only surviving child, a boy. Both editor and author assure readers of Velazquez's authenticity and propriety. Worthington introduces her story as "the only authentic account of the career of a Confederate heroine" (13), while Velazquez concludes with a self-deprecating appeal to her readers: "I did what I thought to be right; and, while anxious for the good opinion of all honorable and right-thinking people, a consciousness of the purity of my motives will be an ample protection against the censure of those who may be disposed to be censorious" (606).

Such appeals to the "honorable and right-thinking" public, however, have been dramatically at odds with the book's reception. Unlike the celebrated Emma Edmonds, Loreta Velazquez was censured from the start on the dual grounds of sexual impropriety and textual inauthenticity. In 1878, a Confederate General, Jubal Early, argued in an eleven-page letter to a Southern congressman that the Velazquez was "no true type of a Southern woman," and her book was filled with inaccuracies, improbabilities, impossibilities, suspicious omissions, and many statements that are "simply incredible."[22] Subsequent discussions continue to link sex and text; as one censorious history of Southern women put it: "The only person impressed with the valor and worth of Loreta Janeta Velazquez was that woman herself. . . . [T]he stories of her adventures have an air of the tawdry and the unreal."[23] More recent discussions of the work center on this issue of authenticity, concluding that Velazquez's career, in its range and successes, is simply in excess of verisimilitude. The book appears so resistant to any definitive pronouncements on its accuracy that even an apparently authentic piece of evidence, a nineteenth-century letter written in support of Velazquez, was later revealed to have been written by a forger.[24] Like Elizabeth Keckley's *Behind the Scenes*, *The Woman in Battle* told a story

FIGURE II.
Illustration from *The Woman in Battle*, 1876: Loreta Velazquez as Lt. Harry T. Buford

so scandalous that it was condemned as false. The reception of *The Woman in Battle* explicitly aligned two forms of counterfeit: gender indeterminacy and historical inauthenticity.[25]

In these condemnations, moreover, what emerges in the absence of authenticity is the presence of the literary. Early writes: "[T]he book . . . cannot be a truthful narrative of the adventures of any person. If intended as a work of fiction, then it is one which ought not to be patronized by Southern men or women, for it is a libel on both." In a less hostile echo of this same opposition, a leading Civil War historian declared: "If Madame Velasquez's account be true, her career was indeed a phenomenal one; if it be false, she deserves high rating as a fictionist."[26] Further questions of fictionality arise from the book's composition. Velazquez wrote the book a decade after the war, and she herself concedes, "The loss of my notes has compelled me to rely entirely upon my memory; and memory is apt to be very treacherous" (5). As with Elizabeth Keckley's memoirs, the ambiguous interventions of her editor introduce an additional level of uncertainty to the text. Worthington notes, "[I]t was left entirely to the judgment of the editor what to omit or what to insert" (11). Although he claims that "corrections and additions have been made after consultation with the author, and with her entire approbation" (11), the details of Worthington's changes remain unknown. In its production as well as its reception, Velazquez's story is divided between fact and fiction.

This opposition between truth and fiction is a stagnant one if it focuses on the issue of the book's empirical truth-value, but what happens if we embrace rather than repudiate the label of fiction for this text? Velazquez herself invokes fictional frames of reference for her story. Of her courtship with her second husband, for example, she notes that "It was like a romance, and it was in the scenes of a romance . . . that I alone could find any similitude to it" (319). "Romance" is one fictional reference point, but the word "adventures" is a better clue, for Velazquez is consistently motivated, as she puts it, by an "insatiable love for adventure" (133). *The Woman in Battle* is an adventure story, a genre that took various forms in the late 1870s, from Civil War fiction to the stories of Horatio Alger and Mark Twain.[27] More specifically, with its episodic structure, its protagonist on the road, and its breathless movement from one adventure to the next, *The Woman in Battle* loosely conforms to the conventions of a particular kind of adventure story: the picaresque novel. As Cathy N. Davidson has shown, early nineteenth-century American versions of the picaresque both excluded and invited women. The genre was so inseparable from the figure of the male adventurer that women could enter it only by masquerade; yet once they did so, they had extraordinary mobility. In a subgenre of "female picaresques," women enjoyed a precarious but extravagant life of freedom by cross-dressing.[28] Like these earlier works, *The Woman in Battle* twins mobility of literary form—the episodic novel of repetitive vignettes—with mobility of character so great that gender is in constant flux.

Reading *The Woman in Battle* as a picaresque novel, we can interpret its presentation of cross-dressing as a literary fantasy prompted by the real-life transformations of Southern white women during wartime. In the South, the needs of the Confederacy authorized a variety of activities for white women, including sewing flags and uniforms, raising money for the militia, forming relief societies, nursing, and teaching. The war years also brought Southern white women into the public sphere, in angry mass gatherings including bread riots. Some women participated in the military effort itself, as cooks, nurses, and camp-followers, and also, in smaller numbers, as spies, scouts, and soldiers. Confederate women wrote about the Civil War in great numbers and with unprecedented boldness, describing a war wherein boundaries between battlefront and homefront, and masculine and feminine spheres, had eroded significantly. In Augusta Jane Evans's novel *Macaria* (1864), for example, "the Promethean spark of patriotic devotion" inspires one young lady to disguise herself and pass through enemy lines with an important letter for General Beauregard hidden in her hair. In a less hair-splitting form of boundary-crossing, the novel's two heroines become artists and teachers for the Confederacy. One determines to create "the first offering of Southern Art" for the new Confederate republic, while the other resolves to open a school for the "numbers of women in the Confederacy [who] will be thrown entirely upon their own resources for maintenance."[29] The enormous popularity of *Macaria* among Southerners suggests the extent to which the war had authorized literary fantasies as well as literal experiences of expanded authority for white women.[30]

Cross-dressing was one such important fantasy. While only a small number of women actually adopted men's clothing to fight in the army, cross-dressing was a prominent desire among many white Confederate women struggling to escape from gender constraints. As Drew Gilpin Faust shows, many Southern white women expressed the desire to be a man, freed, as Sarah Morgan wrote, from "her misfortune in being clothed in petticoats."[31] *The Woman in Battle* is a sustained meditation on the meaning of this desire, offering a narrative in which war so transforms the ideology of separate spheres that gender masquerade can be pursued in the name of Confederate nationalism. Velazquez's cross-dressing evidences, if not the actual realization of power for Confederate women during wartime, then the war's catalytic role in giving voice to the fantasy of such power. Authorized by the Confederacy, Velazquez's masquer-

ade far outstrips it. Cross-dressing in her text moves from the controlled performance of both masculinity and femininity into a more blurred narrative of
gender indeterminacy and same-sex eroticism.

The opening chapters of *The Woman in Battle* establish the framework for
this extravagant narrative, aligning new constructions of individual and national identity. Like Edmonds's identity as "Franklin Thompson," Velazquez's
cross-dressing precedes the needs of wartime patriotism. The book dutifully
begins with a survey of "women who had the courage to fight like men—ay,
better than most men—for a great cause, for friends, and for father-land"
(37); within this tradition, Velazquez's heroine is Joan of Arc, "a great-hearted
patriot" (37).[32] Yet as Worthington notes in his Introduction, *The Woman in
Battle* is distinguished by Velazquez's "frank egotism" (7), and this quality suffuses her own motives for cross-dressing from the start. Velazquez admires
Joan of Arc for her fame, not her patriotism: "I longed for an opportunity to
become another such as she. . . . I was fond of imagining myself as the hero
of most stupendous adventures. I wished that I was a man, such a man as
Columbus or Captain Cook, and could discover new worlds, or explore unknown regions of the earth" (42). Like Edmonds imagining herself "emancipated" as a female sea-captain, Velazquez's desires suggest a cultural equation
between the agency of masculinity and the imperial authority of the male "ex-
plorer."

Compared with Edmonds, Velazquez's "frank egotism" generates a much
franker account of her cross-dressing. While Edmonds erases the birth of
"Franklin Thompson," Velazquez openly celebrates the pleasures of her first
moments of cross-dressing:

> I was especially haunted with the idea of being a man. . . . [I]t was frequently my
> habit, after all in the house had retired to bed at night, to dress myself in my cousin's
> clothes, and to promenade by the hour before the mirror, practising the gait of a
> man, and admiring the figure I made in masculine raiment. I wished that I could
> only change places with my brother Josea. If I could have done so I would . . .
> have marked out for myself a military career, and have disported myself in the gay
> uniform of an officer. (42)

Characterized in gothic terms as a "haunted" nighttime activity, cross-dressing
functions primarily as an illicit form of self-admiration. Edmonds's quiet pleasure in her Irish costume expands here to the pleasures of promenading by
the hour and "admiring the figure I made." As Kathleen De Grave notes,
"Confidence women, or at least the mythic figures they self-created, first and
foremost had confidence in themselves."[33] In the fantasy of changing places

with her brother, Velazquez makes clear her true desire: a heroine's romance with her own image.

Introducing cross-dressing in advance of the Civil War, *The Woman in Battle* also frames "America" as a volatile entity before sectional conflict begins. Like the Canadian Emma Edmonds, Loreta Velazquez is not native to the United States. In the opening chapter, she narrates her family's border-crossing history, which encompasses Spain and Spanish America as well as the shifting boundaries of North and South America. Her family descends from one Don Diego Velazquez, whose name is honored "in Spain and in the Spanish dominions on this side of the Atlantic" (39); her mother is the daughter of a French naval officer and a woman from the United States, and her father was born in Cartagena, educated in Europe, and appointed to a diplomatic position in Cuba. Velazquez herself was born in Cuba, raised in Texas (then part of Mexico), taken to the Caribbean, and sent to New Orleans. Just outside the boundaries of the United States in her youth and within them in her adulthood, she constructs herself as an American speaking to others: "[M]y adopted country people will have to decide for themselves whether the writing of it was worth the while or not" (6). As the book begins, then, Velazquez's story of shifting identity and adopted masculinity emerges from her mobile family history and "adopted" country.

Velazquez begins to align conflicts of national and individual identity in her account of the Mexican War. Her father, owner of property in contested territory, supports Mexico; when the United States seizes control of Mexican territory, he becomes a bitter opponent of the United States government and moves his family to Cuba. This battle over what constitutes the borders of "America" is conjoined with sexual struggles, when Velazquez elopes with her first husband, a United States citizen, to her father's disapproval:

> When I met [my father] for the first time after my marriage, he turned his cheek to me, saying, "You can never impress a kiss on my lips after a union with my country's enemy,"—from which I concluded that it was not so much my marriage without his consent, as my alliance with an American soldier that imbittered him. (50)

The father's accusation—a version of "sleeping with the enemy"—combines national and sexual transgressions, with the marital union of Velazquez and her husband literalizing what is for him the blasphemous geographic union of disputed areas of Mexico with the United States. The father's condemnation is both an explicit invocation of paternal authority and an implicit rejection of his own half-American wife. Conversely, to Velazquez, her marriage

represents a filial rebellion that metaphorically echoes, even as it literally contradicts, the terms of her father's own fight against the American government.
In this battle between Velazquez and her father, social and sexual struggles
begin to converge.[34]

The commencement of the Civil War further intertwines national and familial conflicts. As the war begins, Velazquez, an adopted Southerner, pas-
sionately supports the Confederacy, while her husband, William, is reluctant
to leave the Union: "When my husband's State determined to secede, I
brought all my influence to bear to induce him to resign his commission in
the United States army. . . . I was resolved to forsake him if he raised his
sword against the South" (50–51). With Velazquez's antagonist shifted from
father to husband, this passage realigns national fracture with marital antagonism. The antagonism worsens when Velazquez contemplates cross-dressing,
and her husband attempts to dissuade her: "I pretended to be satisfied with
his arguments, but was, nevertheless, resolved more firmly than ever" (56).
Her commitment to the Confederacy outstrips his authority: "My desire was
to serve with him, if possible; but if this could not be done, I intended to play
my part in the war in my own way, without his assistance" (70–71). Ultimately,
the South's regional secession from the North brings about a decisive marital
separation, since her husband dies almost immediately after he assumes his
military commission. Through this relay of rebellions, Southern secession
from the national union both prompts and symbolizes Velazquez's secession
from her marital union. In a double divorce, Loreta retains her maiden
name—indeed, we never even learn William's surname—while the rebellious
South sheds the name, as it were, of "Mrs. America."

As the rebellion of the Confederacy authorizes Velazquez's marital rebellion, so too does it allow for the realization of her cross-dressing fantasies.
When war arrives, "I felt that now the great opportunity of my life had arrived,
and my mind was busy night and day in planning schemes for making my
name famous above any of the great heroines of history, not even excepting
my favorite, Joan of Arc" (51). The conduit to this opportunity is the uniform of
the soldier, the paramount signifier of Confederate identity: "[My husband's]
hardest struggle had been to throw off the [United States] uniform he had
so long worn . . . I cannot tell how proud and delighted I felt when he attired
himself in his elegant new gray uniform" (52). What Velazquez really wants
is that elegant uniform for herself: "As I surveyed myself in the mirror I was
immensely pleased with the figure I cut, and fancied that I made quite as good
looking a man as my husband" (53). New clothing is accompanied by other
changes. As in Edmonds and Alcott, haircutting is the signifier of new possibility: "The only regret I had in making up my disguise, was the necessity of

parting with my long and luxuriant hair. This gave me a real pang; but there was no help for it, and I submitted with as good grace as I could muster" (63). From her nighttime identification with her brother's image to her impersonation of her husband, she can now enter the light of day as a short-haired, cross-dressed man.

Velazquez's descriptions of her inaugural episodes of disguise suggest the particular significance of the Confederacy, as a self-determined new nation, for narratives of female adventure. Just as the South gains new power by separating itself from the rest of the country, so too does the process of what Velazquez calls "unsexing myself" (62) open up new opportunities for her. These two developments are conjoined when she first wears the costume of her alter ego in public and then makes a toast at a saloon: "Gentlemen, here's to the success of our young Confederacy" (54). As the Confederacy acquires the artifacts of new identity—*The Woman in Battle* includes illustrations of Confederate stamps, insignia, and currency—so too does Buford develop what she calls her masculine "apparatus":

> [I had a tailor] make for me half a dozen fine wire net shields. These I wore next to my skin, and they proved very satisfactory in concealing my true form, and in giving me something of the shape of a man. . . . Over the shields I wore an undershirt of silk or lisle thread, which fitted close, and which was held in place by straps across the chest and shoulders, similar to the shoulder-braces sometimes worn by men. . . . These undershirts could be rolled up into the small compass of a collarbox. Around the waist of each of the undershirts was a band, with eyelet-holes arranged for the purpose of making the waistbands of my pantaloons stand out to the proper number of inches. (58)

With her apparatus "[standing] out to the proper number of inches," both Buford and the Confederacy are newly potent phallic entities. As the Confederacy takes on new political, economic, and social form, Buford learns "to act, talk, and almost to think as a man" (58). Her new name, "Lieutenant H. T. Buford, C. S. A.," testifies both to the christening of her masculine disguise and the naming of the Confederate States of America.

As the birth of the Confederacy gives birth to Buford, so too do its military battles afford "him" a symbolic coming-of-age. Velazquez's study of military documents prepares her to assume the duties of masculinity as well as those of the militia: "[I] prepared a lot of recruiting papers on the model of some genuine ones . . . and procured a manual of tactics, and before the day was over, was pretty nearly ready to commence active operations" (68). When Velazquez puts this training to work, the early battles of the Civil War both symbolize and provide a setting for her gender disguise. The first battle of Bull Run—Velazquez uses this name for the engagement the South often called Manassas—is both a key early victory for the South and a triumph of bull-running for her impersonated masculinity. Resolved to prove that "I was as good a man as any one of them" (100), she reports afterward with satisfaction that "[N]o man on the field that day fought with more energy or determination than the woman who figured as Lieutenant Harry T. Buford" (105). At another Confederate victory in Virginia, the Battle of Ball's Bluff, "[W]hen we did finally succeed in routing the enemy, I experienced a sense of satisfaction and relief that was overwhelming" (120–21). Velazquez's pleasures sound as much erotic as patriotic, with her own "satisfaction and relief" framed by Confederate pleasure at defeating the Union army. On the suggestively named battleground of "Ball's Bluff," as at "Bull Run," both Velazquez and the Confederacy symbolically prove their manhood.

When Velazquez becomes a Confederate spy, her geographic movements between regions provide a metaphorical gloss on her oscillation between genders. This alignment is implicit from early in the narrative, when her debut performance as Buford involves her masquerading as an expert on the Yankees, "just returned from the North" (67); since she has in fact just come from the state of femininity, her words provisionally align gender and geography. Velazquez's espionage literalizes this connection between femininity and the Yankees. For her initial espionage foray in Union territory, Velazquez returns to female dress, or as she puts it, "Here, in the enemy's country . . . I passed for exactly what I was" (136), since "it would be safer . . . for me to attempt no disguise, but to figure as myself" (137). Returning to the South, she resumes her male uniform and takes on an assignment as military conductor, whose duty it is to "examine passes" (149). Later, as a full-fledged spy planning to leave New Orleans, she declares, "I had made a goodly number of trips in different directions, sometimes with passes and sometimes without, and consequently knew exactly how to proceed" (265). The language of "passes" and "passing" central to wartime espionage captures the highly constructed presentation of gender in the text. With her "different directions" pointing toward male and female as well as North and South, Velazquez is passing between sexes as well as regions.

The result of this "passing" is a strategic redefinition of femininity along with masculinity. *The Woman in Battle* situates masculinity in the realm of performance from the start, with Velazquez proclaiming her "ability to play the part I had assumed" (64), rejoicing in her "masculine *début*" (68), and "resolving to play the man right manfully" (74). When Velazquez becomes a spy, her descriptions also position femininity as a form of theatrical imperson-

ation. In a section entitled "I Determine to Figure Again as a Woman," Velazquez decides to return to New Orleans

> not inelegantly attired in the appropriate garments of my sex—garments that I had
> not worn for so long that they felt strangely unfamiliar, although I was not alto-
> gether displeased at having a fair opportunity to figure once more as a woman, if
> only for variety sake. (234)

Estranging her femininity into something "unfamiliar," Velazquez turns it
from a form of weakness into a source of power: "As a woman, and especially
as a woman who had facilities for appearing as a representative of either sex,
I knew that I would be able to observe the enemy's movements, and ferret out
their plans in a signally advantageous manner" (234–35). As the text progresses,
Velazquez becomes not only spy but double agent, masquerading as a Union
woman spy while working for the Confederacy. The rhetoric of counterespio-
nage, or what Velazquez calls "playing a double game" (392), again glosses her
gender performances. In particular, what she terms her shift from "battles and
sieges" to "stratagems and wiles" (391) emphasizes the performance of femininity in wartime. Like other women who worked as Confederate spies, such as
Belle Boyd, Velazquez presents femininity as an ideal cover for espionage:
"[W]omen . . . are really quicker witted and more wide awake than men; they
more easily deceive other people . . . [A]s a rule, for an enterprise that requires
real *finesse,* a woman will be likely to accomplish far more than a man" (364).
Trading on the common cultural equation of women with duplicity, Velazquez
performs femininity to her advantage. Within an "unsexed" world in which
female dress itself feels "strangely unfamiliar," Velazquez turns femininity into
masquerade.[35]

Velazquez's "double agency" in gender terms also activates her sexual authority. While dressed as a pro-Union woman, Velazquez frequently outwits
Northern officials. These political deceptions are implicitly framed as sexual
seductions, as when she fools two Union officers in New Orleans: "[I] invited
them to call upon me, and soon managed to establish such friendly relations
with them that, through their influence, I gained access to headquarters" (242).
The most sustained example of such seductive deception is her relationship
with Colonel Lafayette C. Baker, head of the United States Secret Service.
After she tells him one set of lies, for example, "Baker fell into the trap just
as innocently as if he had been a young man from the country, instead of the
chief detective officer of a great government" (422–23). Velazquez reflects on
this seduction with smug triumph: "I am sorry he is not alive now, that he
might be able to read this narrative, and so learn how completely he was taken

in, and by a woman, too. He was a smart man, but not smart enough for all occasions" (400). Velazquez's "intimate relations" with Baker, as with other men, combine heterosexual seduction with gender masquerade.

Yet in the course of Velazquez's narrative, her absolute control over masquerade becomes a more mobile and uncontrollable blur of "border states." In Elizabeth Keckley's memoir, I have suggested, the Civil War border state is an implicit metaphoric frame for ambiguities of class, race, and the internal tensions of civility. In Velazquez's case, moving through the war's borders quite literally undoes her gender costume. In one espionage adventure, she crawls back to Confederate lines so bedraggled that she "was not by any means so masculine in appearance as I had been at one time" (308). Earlier, her mustache comes loose while she is dining with a family, and she responds so strongly that the loosened part seems more phallic than facial: "I fancied that it was loose and was about to fall off. Here was a terrible situation, and I cannot undertake to describe what I felt. To say that I was frightened, scarcely gives an idea of the cold chills that ran down my back" (77). At this moment of metaphorical castration, the failure of the mustache localizes, even as it displaces upward, the detachability inherent in Velazquez's out-of-order male underwear. Later, when she is arrested in Lynchburg, she loses another phallic element of her costume: "I was again arrested on the charge of being a woman in disguise. My sword was taken from me, and I was otherwise treated with a good deal more rudeness than I thought there was any occasion for" (284). Unmanned within her adopted South, Velazquez finds that both gender disguise and regional affiliation are under assault. If her participation in the Civil War at first appears clear-cut, it increasingly involves unstable battles within as well as between regions and sexes.

This gender confusion in *The Woman in Battle* corresponds, in turn, to a blurring of the lines of heterosexual seduction. Although the overt sexual narrative of this text privileges marriage—Velazquez weds four times—her husbands have an extraordinarily enervated presence in her life and text. Her first husband, William, dies early and ingloriously in the war, when he "undertook to explain the use of the carbine to one of the sergeants, and the weapon exploded in his hands" (87). Her second husband, Captain de Caulp, sickens immediately after their marriage and dies, in the course of a chapter entitled "Again a Wife and Again a Widow." Her third husband, whom she meets while preparing for a postwar trip to South America, rates only three paragraphs of initial discussion; six pages later, she reports succinctly, he was "taken ill with the black vomit and [died]" (545). Finally, she accounts for her fourth husband, an unnamed "gentleman who paid me attention," in only two sentences (585). Despite the many husbands in the text, then, their impact is in inverse proportion to their quantity. It is as though heterosexual relations, like masculinity, have so tenuous an ideological hold in this text that they must be rehearsed repeatedly. The performance of what Adrienne Rich named "compulsory heterosexuality" is so lackluster in this text that its very visibility only serves to call its existence into question.[36]

In contrast to this uncompelling portrait of heterosexuality, *The Woman in Battle* repeatedly hints at same-sex possibilities, both male and female. For male soldiers, the homosocial world of the military afforded new opportunities for the expression and representation of homoerotic desire. Whitman's paeans to wounded soldiers are the best-known literary version of this desire, but other evidence appears in such sources as military records of sailors court-martialed for sodomy and in erotic letters between officers.[37] More speculatively, accounts of cross-dressed soldiers suggest that such women appealed to their male colleagues in ways that complicated the boundaries between same-sex and heterosexual desire. One male soldier, for example, described a drunken evening during which his regiment "enlisted a new recruit on the way at Eastport. The boys all took a notion to him. On examination he proved to have a Cunt so he was discharged. I was sorry for it, for I wanted him for a Bedfellow."[38] In this account, the new recruit appeals in his guise as young boy, not as young girl. While the speaker does not overtly eroticize his feelings, his laconic response to the recruit's departure leaves open the possibility that the young man might appeal as a "Bedfellow" for sexual reasons.

The Woman in Battle offers similar instances of sexual ambiguity, with military masquerade providing a symbolic frame for the representation of male homoeroticism. In Velazquez's account, Lt. Buford is a figure of exceptional appeal, "an uncommonly good-looking fellow, when dressed in my best uniform" (38). She repeatedly describes Buford as a "dandy," a man with an excessive interest in clothes, and while this term did not necessarily connote male homosexuality, Velazquez's account suggests that the spectacle of the "uncommonly good-looking" Buford appeals to men as well as women.[39] This possibility infuses her narration of her courtship with her second husband, Capt. Thomas de Caulp. To the extent that Velazquez mentions de Caulp, it is with constant reference to the fact that his love for her as a woman overlaps with his affection for Lt. Buford. De Caulp "little suspected . . . that the woman to whom his heart and hand were pledged was by his side as he led his men into that bloody fray" (206); Velazquez, for her part, "almost dreaded to reveal to him that the little dandified lieutenant, who had volunteered to fight in his company at Shiloh, and the woman to whom he was bound by an engagement of marriage, were the same" (316). Although Velazquez eventually unmasks herself, the wedding that follows retains the influence of the "dandified lieutenant." "[T]he main thing," Velazquez remembers, was "that I should be dressed as a woman when the ceremony took place, for fear of creating too much of a sensation, and, perhaps, of making the clergyman feel unpleasant should I appear before him, hanging on the captain's arm, in my uniform" (335). In this description, the normalizing ritual of heterosexual marriage coexists with the possibility, as much exciting "sensation" as unsavory threat, of two men marrying each other.

While *The Woman in Battle* provides brief glimpses of male homoeroticism, the romances on which the text lavishes its most overt, abundant, and enthusiastic narrative attention are those between figures who, beneath their costumes, are both women. The romances between women that Edmonds expels from her text are a central feature of Velazquez's story. From the moment she first cross-dresses, Velazquez causes—as a chapter subhead terms it—"A Sensation Among the Women" (73). Throughout her narrative, as Jubal Early himself noted, "[T]he women, especially the young and pretty ones, are ever ready to throw themselves into the arms of the dashing 'Lieutenant Harry T. Buford', and surrender, without waiting to be asked, all that is dear to a woman of virtue."[40] Virtually every time Velazquez comes in contact with women, they fall in love with her. Reflecting on one such woman, whom she had tried unsuccessfully to match up with a male friend, she remarks, "I scarcely knew whether to be amused or disgusted at the perversity of Fate, which made me such an irresistible lady-killer" (194–95).

How are we to read the role of the female "lady-killer" in this text? Like men, nineteenth-century women may have found the Civil War battlefield a liberatory arena for the expression of same-sex desire, in a period just before the sexological codification of the category of lesbian. The war memoirs of General Philip Sheridan, for example, included the story of two inseparable male soldiers who were exposed as women, one "coarse and masculine" and the other "a rather prepossessing young woman": "How the two got acquainted I never learned, and though they had joined the army independently of each other, yet an intimacy had sprung up between them." Sheridan's memoirs do not specify the terms of this "intimacy," but his account strongly suggests that these two women constituted a sexual couple.[41] As historians of sexuality have expanded the scope of lesbian experience to include such cross-dressing stories, cultural critics have also enlarged the definition of a lesbian text. Lesbian possibilities may emerge in the interstices of ostensibly heterosexual narratives, through ambiguous characters, relationships, and episodes, as well as in the text's relation to readers. Stories of cross-dressing make such possibilities particularly available, as they generate same-sex romances with the potential to overflow their overtly heterosexual frames. Situating Velazquez's text in these enlarged genealogies of lesbian history and culture, we can see *The Woman in Battle* as a text in which the literary as well as literal resonances of Civil War cross-dressing contribute to the representation of lesbian possibility.[42]

In Velazquez's narrative, same-sex possibilities first emerge from the exigencies of her military persona. On her first day in disguise as Buford, she travels to Arkansas to raise a battalion of soldiers. While staying with a family there, she becomes increasingly aware of the family's sixteen-year-old daughter Sadie:

> The idea of having a mild little flirtation with this fair flower of the Arkansas forest rather grew upon me as I noticed the impression I was making upon her susceptible imagination. I had some curiosity to know how love-making went from the masculine standpoint, and thought that the present would be a good opportunity to gain some valuable experience in that line; for it occurred to me that if I was to figure successfully in the *rôle* of a dashing young Confederate officer, it would be necessary for me to learn how to make myself immensely agreeable to the ladies. (75)

Introducing her "curiosity to know how love-making went from the masculine standpoint," Velazquez quickly frames the idea of romance as a necessity of her military disguise. Over the next few days, she simultaneously charms Sadie—"the heart which beat under that yellow calico dress was in a great state of excitement" (76)—and assembles her battalion of young men, who "yielded without making any trouble about it" (84). By the time she departs four days later, her seductions of both lady and army are complete. Aligning Velazquez's duties as military leader with her charms as seducer, this episode inaugurates protolesbian plots of same-sex seduction under the cover of military need.

When Velazquez commences actual battle, her prowess as a soldier is inseparable from her success as a lover:

> After the battle of Bull Run I . . . swaggered about in fine style, sporting my uniform for the admiration of the ladies, and making myself agreeable to them in a manner that excited the envy of the men, and raised me immensely in my own esteem; for I began to pride myself as much upon being a successful lady's man as upon being a valiant soldier. (109)

In a context of exaggerated masculinity on the battlefield, Velazquez's military success authorizes her after-hours romances. As the soldier's uniform allows for the realization of her midnight fantasies of power, it also gives expression to the pleasures of "love-making from the masculine standpoint." Like her initial assumption of male dress, her accelerating identity as "lady's man" outstrips its ostensible justifications.

Velazquez's accelerating identity as "lady's man" results in a series of romances, each of which, like the story of Sadie, is framed by seduction and departure. The story of "Miss E." of Leesburg, Virginia, provides an exemplary case of this plot. Dressed as Buford, Velazquez happily engages in "winning the regards of the members of my own sex" (110) and meets "Miss E.," who falls in love with "him." To prevent her from becoming too attached, he shows her a photograph of a woman whom he falsely claims is his fiancée, and breaks her heart. "So ended my Leesburg flirtation," Velazquez writes, "and a desire to avoid meeting Miss E. again, at least until she had time to recover her equanimity . . . induced me to leave the town as soon as possible" (114). "It afforded me some amusements," Velazquez reflects, "to carry on a bit of a flirtation with a nice girl; and I was very much tempted to entertain myself in this manner, without reflecting very deeply as to the consequences. I am very willing to admit that I ought not to have acted as I did" (111). In this prototypical plot of seduction and betrayal, remorse only thinly veils the pleasurable "amusements" of the lady's man.

These dynamics of female seduction in turn characterize Velazquez's relationship with groups of women, both within and outside of the text. At one point, she describes the public mayhem that ensues when she is arrested in Richmond "on the charge of being a woman a disguise, and supposably [*sic*] a Federal spy" (278). Velazquez purports to be irritated by "the gaze of the impertinently curious people, who watched my every motion" (287), but what her account more powerfully suggests is her pleasure at seduction on a grand scale:

> [E]verybody—the women in particular—evinced the most eager desire to see the heroine of innumerable bloody conflicts. . . . While it was generally believed I was a woman . . . my visitors were none of them quite sure which sex I belonged to, and all their efforts were directed to solving the mystery. (284)

Here, Velazquez effects a kind of striptease with "the women in particular" as audience. Ostensibly the confined object of their gaze, she wields power over her viewers, her public "readers," as their active seducer. To her actual female readers as well, Velazquez is a powerful seducer: "My error in allowing myself to indulge in flirtations with my own sex, arose from thoughtlessness . . . I am sure my readers will forgive me, as I hope the young ladies, whom I induced to indulge false expectations, will, when the publication of this narrative makes known to the world the whole truth about the identity of Lieutenant Harry T. Buford, C.S.A." (111). Here and throughout, Velazquez's text transforms the Confederacy into a confederacy of female bodies, one that extends from author to protagonist to secondary characters to female readers.

This protolesbian confederacy serves to expand traditional accounts of relations between women in nineteenth-century America. A founding discussion of this topic presents the period as a "female world of love and ritual," in which women's bonds of friendship shaded over into love, affection, and emotional passion, if not necessarily sexual contact per se. More recent lesbian theory has reinvestigated this model, along with those of "romantic friendship" between women and of a "lesbian continuum," for a variety of reasons, including the need to bring into view the physicality of lesbian sexuality, the dynamics of power between women, and the pleasures, erotic and political, of butch-femme practices. *The Woman in Battle* can be read as proleptically contributing to these reinvestigations, for the text constructs desire between women as inextricable from masquerade, performance, and the power dynamics of seduction. In particular, Velazquez's self-representation as "lady's man" foreshadows the figure of the butch lesbian. Like the "coarse and masculine" woman in the memoirs of Philip Sheridan, Velazquez is an early representation of this figure, whose presentation of masculinity has been a central feature of twentieth-century lesbian culture. Expanding the narration of Confederate nationalism to include protolesbian plots, Velazquez's text also offers an early corrective to a model of lesbianism that might translate nineteenth-century desire between women into a domesticated version of domestic feminism.[43]

Before leaving this account of the book's protolesbian Civil War story, however, we should note the severe constraints Velazquez places on such an apparently mobile textual fantasy. The positionalities of same-sex seduction are neither completely pleasurable nor completely mobile in this text. Velazquez is comfortable only in the role of *desiring* seducer, and she intensely dislikes women who assert their desire for her. Of one female pursuer, for example, she declares, "The courting was pretty much all on her side," and she is decidedly unhappy with the result: "[T]o tell the truth, I was not particularly pleased with the decidedly unfeminine advances that were made towards me" (88); of another woman, she writes, "I was a little bit disgusted with her very evident desire to capture me" (92). The only acceptable agent of desire in this text is Velazquez herself in her disguise *as a man*, experiencing "love-making . . . from the masculine standpoint." Even though the text translates the gender "male" into the positionality of "masculinity," it still requires that position to act as the catalyst for desire—even when the two participants in a narrative of seduction are both women.

Moreover, if the text opens some spaces for reconfigurations of lesbian sexuality, it closes off others. We can chart this closure by a scene late in the book when Velazquez is literally in bed with another woman. Traveling in the American West after the war, she occupies a carriage with a "disagreeable" woman (577) and is repelled by her profanity, smoking, and drunkenness. That night, forced to share a bed with her, she reports: "[I] did not obtain much satisfaction from my couch, for, independently of its unpleasant human occupant, it was fairly alive with vermin." In the morning, she adds, "From under her pillow she took a belt containing a formidable-looking knife and a six-shooter, which she buckled around her waist . . . Soon, to my infinite relief, this delectable creature was gone" (580–81). Here is Velazquez in bed with another woman, and her response is revulsion, followed by sarcasm. Velazquez's horrified recoil suggests that she views the woman not as an object of desire but as a grotesque reflection, complete with phallic knife and gun, of her own "butch" identity. This moment stands as an end point on a larger spectrum of Velazquez's ambivalence toward other women, such as those with whom she must spend an evening while in disguise: "The society of these girls was no pleasure to me whatever, especially as I had things of much more importance to think of than their love affairs" (447). As if in a reversal of the lesbian continuum, Velazquez, too, has a spectrum of attitudes toward women, but hers is marked by antipathy rather than affection. What is entirely absent from the text—and what, by contrast, fuels the lesbian continuum model—is any sense of her interest in "the society of these girls." In short, *The Woman in Battle* firmly expels any conception of sisterhood from its pro-tolesbian plot.

Consistent with these attitudes, Velazquez is not only antiwoman but antifeminist. *The Woman in Battle* stands in stark contrast to contemporary novels of domestic feminism like Alcott's *Work* (1873), which extend sisterly bonds between women into feminist activism. Velazquez's one mention of feminism, in a section entitled "A Woman's Advantages and Disadvantages," is negative:

> A woman labors under some disadvantages in an attempt to fight her own way in the world, and at the same time, from the mere fact that she is a woman, she can often do things that a man cannot. I have no hesitation in saying that I wish I had been created a man instead of a woman. This is what is the matter with nearly all the women who go about complaining of the wrongs of our sex. But being a woman, I was bent on making the best of it . . . (130)

The passage is muddled, both conceding the "disadvantages" of being female and reducing feminists to women who "go about complaining." We might account for such conservatism as a Southerner's perception of feminism as primarily a Northern movement or as an individualist "bootstrap" rejection of the political struggles of others.[44] Both reasons underscore a similar point: that Velazquez's pleasure in seducing individual women corresponds to her antipathy toward any possible feminist body politic. Her most radical notions about gender and sexuality remain at the level of fantasy, divorced from the emerging social formations—feminism and lesbianism—to which their structuring terms might seem to belong.

What can we conclude from this paradox? That the bonds of womanhood chafe rather than unite in this text is not, of course, a determining pronouncement about the political immutabilities of a rhetoric of seduction between women. Quite the reverse: the hostility to women in Velazquez's text is, at least in part, a result of nineteenth-century social constraints that might make "the ladies," confined to a round of domestic duties, seem less appealing companions than male adventurers. What the story of the "lady's man" does suggest, however, is the importance of metaphors in constructing bodies and the relations between them. As a symbolic frame, the Civil War makes possible Velazquez's self-representation as soldier, spy, and seducer. Birthed by the new Confederate nation, Velazquez is a literary "double agent" in a culture that would normally accord her little agency at all.

III

I have been tracing the ways in which *The Woman in Battle* maps the outlines of national Civil War onto a set of "civil wars" surrounding Loreta Velazquez. The Civil War provides not only setting but symbol for the cross-dressing plot of *The Woman in Battle*, intersecting with the book's narratives of gender insurrection and of same-sex seduction. Yet as the war gives new form to Velazquez's adventures, so too does *The Woman in Battle* metaphorically engage the regional identity of the wartime and postwar white South. Despite Velazquez's dedication to the Confederacy, the cross-dressing plot of *The Woman in Battle* inadvertently enacts the consequences of white Southern feminization. Paradoxically, Velazquez's story threatens even as it celebrates the memory of the Confederacy, disturbing configurations of gender, sexuality, and race in the postwar South.

The immediate results of the Civil War for white Southerners included the formal end of the slave labor system, the destruction of the Confederacy as a political entity, the devastation of the physical landscape of the South, and the death of a generation of young men. This loss of manhood was symbolic as well as literal; as one Mississippi man described the defeated South, " 'his Comb was cut,' or as you say his manhood was emasculated."[44] In response, many white Southerners commemorated the Confederacy in the variety of writings, illustrations, songs, rituals, statuary, household artifacts and other cultural texts collectively known as the ideology of the "Lost Cause." Emerging in the 1860s, Lost Cause imagery praised the valor of the Confederacy and particularly its men. The iconic celebration of Confederate masculinity extended from Confederate Memorial Day tributes to the common soldier to the sanctification of the hero of the Lost Cause, Robert E. Lee.[45]

White women were indispensable to the creation of this imagery, both literally and metaphorically. Active creators of postwar groups like the Ladies Memorial Associations, they also served crucial symbolic functions. As one man noted shortly after the war: "[T]he remnants of survivors [were] subjugated to every influence from without, which can be malignantly devised to sap the foundation of their manhood, and degrade them into fit material for slaves. If our women do not sustain them, they will sink."[46] To rejuvenate Southern manhood, white women were to function as iconic repositories of the tragic glory of the Confederacy. Female imagery included the representation of women as devoted Confederate wives, selfless mothers, or patriotic daughters. More abstractly, Lost Cause ideology also allegorized feminine figures to represent the wartime South as a whole.[47]

This iconographic continuum, created by women as well as men, had multiple ideological implications. Images of pure white womanhood, an important weapon in the racist postwar assault on African-American men, served as a rallying-cry for accusations of interracial rape. Such images also circumscribed appropriate behavior for white women; while Northerners mocked Confederate women as uncontrolled in their aggression, Lost Cause imagery reinvigorated Southern masculinity by keeping white women in their proper place. Stabilizing race and gender hierarchies, this imagery as a whole was an essential part of what Susan Jeffords, analyzing American responses to defeat in Vietnam, terms "remasculinization." Like texts about Vietnam, Lost Cause proponents reimagined wartime defeat in ways that rejuvenated individual and national masculinity.[48] While Lost Cause ideology ostensibly reconstructed only the past, its implications for more militant adherents were a resurgence of Confederate nationalism in the future. Reimagining a war in which white Southern aspirations were so closely linked to the metaphorical achievement of "manhood," diehard Confederate followers mythologized the promise—at once regional, racial, and sexual—that the white male South would "rise again."

The Woman in Battle is unswerving in its retroactive embrace of the Confederacy. "[N]o man or woman in the whole Confederacy," Velazquez asserts, "was inspired by a more ardent devotion to the cause than myself, or had greater faith in its ultimate success" (161). Some Southern readers re-responded warmly to Velazquez's story as a celebration of the Confederate South; forty Southern congressmen publicly endorsed *The Woman in Battle*, and Confederate General James Longstreet wrote a letter verifying a part of her story.[49] Yet despite Velazquez's support of the Confederacy, the picaresque narrative of *The Woman in Battle* troubles the restorative iconography of the postwar white South. We may begin to gauge this contradiction by returning to a less positive contemporary response: the vehement critique written by Confederate General Jubal Early.

Early's biography exemplifies a militant posture of "unreconstructed" post-war devotion to the Confederacy. He refused to accept the terms of Confederate defeat, fleeing the United States for Canada and Mexico; when he reluctantly returned, he devoted himself to the memory of the Confederacy, writing a history of the war, continuing to defend slavery and secession, and serving as president of the Southern Historical Society. One colleague remembered him in 1890, at age 73, as "bitter and violent as an adder. He has no use for the government or the northern people. Boasts of his being unreconstructed." Early was so loyal to the Confederacy that he wore gray suits for the rest of his life.[50]

In 1878, after she learned that he planned a public attack on her book, Velazquez wrote to Early:

> Now General, if you have any suggestions to make please let me hear from you, for my Book and Correspondence with the Press is my entire support of my self and little Son. (My health is failing,) and my whole soul's devotion is the Education of him who is to live after I have passed away. . . . [M]y labors and devotion this winter has been to him and the prosperity of our Glorious Sunny south. No one man or a section of men can deter me from my duty to her (May god Bless her and her people). . . . [A]ll I now ask from you is Justice to my *child*. I live for him and him alone.[51]

Velazquez draws on common rhetoric in this passage. As in many wars, narratives of maternal sacrifice were essential to the ideological construction of the Confederacy. After the war, maternal imagery continued to play an important symbolic role, particularly in relation to Southern rituals of mourning in which the death of a son or husband was seen to represent the loss of the Confederacy as a whole. Sharing in this imagery, Velazquez's plea works to reconfirm her underlying allegiance to feminine norms. Like the struggling South hoping to support "her people," Velazquez only wants to provide for her child: "I live for him and him alone." Literally dedicated to the Confederate army, her book registers her devotion to South and to son.

This appeal, however, came too late for Early:

> Madame Velasquez herself is no true type of a Southern woman, and the women she describes are not fair specimens of the pure devoted women who followed with their prayers the armies of the Confederate States through all their struggles and trials. . . . I have no disposition to injure the alleged author of that book, and still less to deprive her of the means of training and educating her child; but I cherish most devotedly the character and fame of the Confederate armies, and of the people of the South, especially of the women of the South, and when a book affecting all these is [sought?] to be [palmed?] on the public as true, and bears on its face the evidence of its want of authenticity, then I have the right to speak my opinion and will speak it, whether the author be man or woman.[52]

While Early concedes that "I have no disposition to . . . deprive her of the means of training and educating her child," he will not accept Velazquez's appeal to motherhood. What supersedes this appeal is her story's defamation of the "character and fame of the Confederate armies, and of the people of the South," and in particular her fraudulent depiction of those "pure devoted women who followed with their prayers the armies of the Confederate States." Velazquez's adventures contradict the gender mythologies of the postwar South, in which white women are meant to follow and pray, their passive purity serving as the iconic ballast for Confederate glory. More specifically, Early's rhetoric suggests that Velazquez's transgressions involve both textual and sexual counterfeit. In his eyes, the book itself is a large-scale counterfeit operation in which a story that "bears on its face the evidence of its want of authenticity" is passed off on the public as a true self-representation. The inauthentic "face" of the book, in turn, mirrors that of Velazquez. *The Woman in Battle* must be stopped "whether the author be man or woman," an ambiguous phrase that may mean "even though the author is a woman," or "even though I am uncertain that the author is really female." In Early's anxious eyes, Velazquez is so false a woman that she remains in the realm of masculinity a decade after removing her uniform.

Condemning Velazquez for her resemblance to masculinity, Early also implies her proximity to prostitution. During the Civil War, prostitution flourished as part of the military economy; Washington was particularly well known as a center of prostitution during the war, supporting dozens of brothels and more than five thousand prostitutes. Prostitution was also a key symbolic feature of sectional antagonism. General Sherman allegedly boasted that "he could buy the chastity of any Southern woman for a few pounds of coffee," while General Benjamin Butler's infamous "woman order" during the Union occupation of New Orleans condemned any Southern woman who appeared in public as a prostitute.[53] This association between female misbehavior and prostitution extended to cross-dressing: women soldiers, if caught, were frequently assumed to be prostitutes. During the war, Jubal Early himself severely punished two women who were discovered cross-dressing as soldiers. Their captain condemned them as prostitutes, and Early had them sent to prison.[54] A decade later, his response to Velazquez reprises the terms of this condemnation. In Early's attack on *The Woman in Battle*, cross-dressing and prostitution function as two complementary anxieties about female counterfeit.

Ironically and inadvertently, Velazquez's narrative confirms these dual anxieties. While she declares at the start that she emerged from military life "with my womanly reputation unblemished by even a suspicion of impropriety" (38), her account of counterfeiting in wartime Washington prefigures the terms of Early's condemnation. During the war, Washington was a center for counterfeit operations in which government officials reproduced false versions of Union and Confederate currency. These operations had particularly disastrous consequences for the Confederate dollar, already massively overproduced; weakened by inflation and counterfeit, the Confederate dollar was almost worthless by the end of the war.[55] In *The Woman in Battle*, Velazquez is a direct participant in Confederate counterfeiting, conveying money, securities, and electrotype plates among different cities. Her selfless motive, she asserts, was "promoting the interest of the Confederacy" (458), and she elsewhere insists that "my actions as a secret agent of the Confederate government are not to be put in comparison with those of the . . . counterfeiters" (389). Yet Velazquez's entire narrative implicitly aligns duplicitous women and false currency. Just as her counterfeiting literally contributes to the declining value of the Confederate dollar, her impersonation of Buford symbolically burlesques Confederate iconography. Velazquez's purpose may be "embarrassing the Federal government" (468), but the joke is on the Confederacy. Her cross-dressing provides an inadvertent reminder that both the literal currency of the Confederacy and its symbolic currency—the pure Southern white woman—may be without foundation.

Aligning counterfeiting with cross-dressing, Velazquez's account of criminality in the Treasury Department also intertwines the circulation of inauthentic money with prostitution. Treasury Department officials allegedly engaged in drinking and carousing with their female employees. These activities were widely recounted in the press, including accounts of women who recounted sexual improprieties, among them two who recalled cross-dressing at their employers' request.[56] Reporting in detail on these "gross immoralities in the treasury department," Velazquez notes with horror the carousing of well-paid "abandoned women," including those taken "to the Canterbury saloon in male attire" (477). Women are linked with counterfeiting as well as cross-dressing, as in the case of one official's mistress who "conveyed the electrotype duplicates of the plates to parties outside, and performed other services of a similar character, for which she was paid handsomely" (480). Velazquez predictably distances herself from these women, yet her own work as "go-between" (483) echoes the structure of prostitution. Circulating between men and cities, Velazquez is false "sexual type," at once cross-dresser and prostitute. So strong is Early's subsequent revulsion from her that she seems to function as a kind of Medusa's head, incarnating anxieties about both political and sexual instability.[57] More specifically, her masquerade suggests the horrors of a world in which women are like Confederate dollars, "unsecured," as one historian puts it, "with anything of intrinsic value."[58] For Lost Cause adherents like Early, Velazquez's text raises a disturbing question: what is the Confederacy worth, if its white women—as well as its dollars—are worthless?

As Velazquez destabilizes the currency of Southern femininity, so too does she disturb the symbolic economy of masculinity in the postwar white South. If Velazquez is the quintessential painted woman, then her alter ego, Lt. Harry Buford—who is such false coin that his very gender is unreal—is the ultimate confidence man. Indeed, in a conflation of the traditional roles of nineteenth-century duplicity, Buford is a painted man literally put together by a confidence woman.[59] Foregrounding false masculinity more fully, Velazquez follows her account of counterfeiting with descriptions of the fraudulent wartime practices of bounty-jumping, in which men enlisted, deserted, and reenlisted elsewhere for profit, and substitute-brokering, in which wealthy men purchased substitutes to fight in their place.[60] Velazquez predictably deplores these practices, contrasting "the whole-souled enthusiasm of the Southern people with the disposition shown by so many prominent adherents of the Northern cause, to let anybody and everybody who could be purchased or beguiled do their fighting for them" (491). Yet bounty-jumping and substitute-brokering are forms of male fraud different only in degree from Velazquez's own invention of Lieutenant Buford. Like bounty-jumpers, she too evades her own designated role in wartime; as in substitute-brokering, she too represents herself with an alternate male body. Her own false recruiting documents are scarcely different from the "bogus enlistment papers" used by substitute brokers, "each one of which was supposed to represent an able-bodied man" (489). As wartime prostitution involves the circulation of female bodies in ways that mimics Velazquez's own, it also prompts an invention of male identities that echoes the falseness of her own "Lt. Buford."

Reprising the evasions of the bounty-jumper and substitute-broker, Velazquez has disastrous repercussions for the allegorical "manhood" of the Confederacy as a whole. Since Velazquez's text twins Buford and the Confederacy as newly born "men," then when Buford suffers, so too does the Confederacy metaphorically decline. Even in the optimistic early days of the war, Velazquez's falling mustache hints at the potential transience of Southern phallic authority. This potential for decline emerges overtly after Confederate defeat at Shiloh, when "the success of the Confederate cause was more remote, and more uncertain, than ever. It made me gnash my teeth with impotent fury" (218). After another defeat, when Velazquez is wounded, "all my manliness oozed out" and her "sex was discovered (225)." As she moves closer to abandoning her disguise, the South moves closer to defeat: off to Havana for a blockade-running project, Velazquez confesses that "My health was not so robust as it had been" (244), while "things were in a bad way in many respects in the beleaguered Confederacy" (246). When she finally resumes female dress, the disappearance of her masculine persona quells some gender anxieties, but given the South's loss in the war, it raises others. If Velazquez is insufficiently passive while dressed as a woman, the very action that quells her transgressions against femininity—the abandonment of male costume—is what threatens her "masculinity" most directly. Shedding Buford's uniform, Velazquez returns to her "proper" gender, but she also literalizes the rhetoric of Confederate feminization, wherein losing a war means becoming a woman.

The metaphorical inseparability of Velazquez and the Confederacy not only emphasizes the South's loss of "manhood" through military defeat, but also raises the question of whether that manhood—like Velazquez's "Lt. Buford"—had ever existed at all. For Southerners, the memory of Confederate valor in the war served to counter two sets of Northern images of a feminized South: the antebellum image of the weak, indecisive "Southern Hamlet" as well as the postwar figure of the emasculated soldier.[61] Symbolically speaking, Southerners used the memory of the Civil War not only to make a man out of the boyish South, but to prove that the region was a boy and not a girl in the first place. But since Velazquez *is* a girl in the first place, she inadvertently affirms this disavowed characterization. Despite her own passionate support of the Confederacy, her very adoption of its gendered rhetoric not only feminizes the tenuously "masculine" South, but returns it to its initial condition—like her own—of femininity. "So many men have weak and feminine voices," she declares in her initial account of her apparatus, "that, provided the clothing is properly constructed and put on right, and the disguise in other respects is well arranged, a woman with even a very high voice need have very little to fear on that score" (58). The line between masculinity and femininity erodes in two directions here, demoting men to the realm of "weak and feminine voices" as cross-dressed women ascend to masculinity. Undermining Velazquez's pro-Confederate motives, this hydraulic model of gender relations precisely enacts the plea of Southern men that "if our women do not sustain them, they will sink." To put it another way, it is not that Velazquez contradicts the Southern desire for a myth of masculinization, but that she occupies this myth so literally that she brings its defensive underpinnings clearly into view. Literalizing a gender iconography that is supposed to remain only metaphorical, Velazquez unmans the masculinity of the Confederacy.

So too does *The Woman in Battle* hint at the specifically sexual dimensions of Confederate loss. When the Confederate army, aided by Buford, is triumphant, its representation is that of victorious rapist. Describing the optimistic beginning of the battle of Shiloh, Velazquez announces proudly, "We took possession of their camp . . . almost without resistance" (203). Conversely, when the South loses the war, its sexual relation to the North is that of potential female rape victim, as when the strength of the Union army "compelled the Confederates . . . to think about the means of resisting invasion" (108). The relation of Velazquez to her Northern editor reinforces the heterosexual dynamics of Confederate defeat. As Northerners secured political control over the South, Worthington has editorial control over Velazquez's text: "It has been necessary . . . while expanding in some places, to make large excisions in others . . . The excisions, therefore, have carefully been made" (11). Yet the gender valences of such military "invasions" and textual "incisions" are not entirely clear. For if the South symbolically emerges from the war as a woman, it also assumes a posture of defeat as a feminized man; the North takes on yet more masculinity through its victory in the war. Hence the South risks being "raped" by the remasculinized North both heterosexually and homosexually. In a process of cultural feminization that addresses two sides of the male body, what the Confederacy faces in remembering its defeat is, symbolically speaking, both losing its phallic potency and being raped from behind.

Velazquez's text does not, to be sure, speak explicitly about the South as a victim of male rape. But the text nonetheless raises this figurative possibility in displaced form, through a strand of imagery that constructs Southern military aggression as anal penetration. In a chapter entitled in part "Preparations for an Attack on the Federal Rear," Velazquez discusses a plan for the Confederate army to liberate a prisoners' camp by entering Federal lines through Canada; the idea is "to make such a diversion in the Federal rear as would compel the withdrawal of a large force from the front" (441). Yet this plan fails because one Confederate soldier is captured by the Union army and, to Velazquez's disgust, confesses everything about the plan. After this, "The failure of the contemplated raid in the rear . . . put an end to all expectations," and "there was nothing to be done but to fight the thing out to the bitter end" (432). Since the eventual conclusion to this fight is Southern defeat, the story provides a metaphoric circuit whereby an original plan to raid the Northern "rear" results, instead, in the South's own metaphorical violation by the North—its "bitter end." In his introduction, Worthington defends the Confederacy: "[T]hey were justified . . . in doing all in their power to defeat their enemies . . . by demoralizing them by insidious attacks in the rear" (8). Yet his remarks, for all that they overtly name Southern military prowess, inadvertently highlight its converse, since their context is a postwar vantage point from which the defeated Confederacy exists only in hindsight. In this reversible imagery of anal rape and raid, as with the narrative of phallic potency and castration, Velazquez's cross-dressed body exposes the compensatory faultlines of Confederate symbolism by virtue of inhabiting that symbolism too fully. Vanishing at a moment's notice from her persona as Buford, Velazquez literalizes a model of regional masculinity that is so permeable to assault—both "front" and "rear"—as to disappear entirely.

In this context, the story of the cross-dressed Jefferson Davis takes on new resonance. We have already seen this story cited in Elizabeth Keckley's *Behind the Scenes,* where it functions as part of a critique of slavery and a celebration of Keckley's own authority. Not surprisingly, the pro-Confederate Velazquez does not refer to the image of the cross-dressed Davis.[62] Yet her own cross-dressing implicitly literalizes and extends the transvestite terms of his humiliation as they had been developed in "Belle of Richmond" imagery. An image such as "Jeff's Last Skedaddle" (figure 12), for example, equates femininity with failure in ways that prefigure the imagery of Velazquez. Subtitled "How Jeff in His Extremity Put His Navel Affairs and Ram-parts Under Petticoat Protection," the image foregrounds a cross-dressed Davis fleeing from Union soldiers. Davis's dress signals his failed masculinity, while the woman who stands at the image's center announces that he is now part of the world of women: "please Gentlemen don't disturb the Privacy of Ladies before they have time to dress." Velazquez's narrative takes this announcement even further, not only aligning Davis with "Ladies" but also, in her creation of Buford, reducing masculinity to the status of an epiphenomenal uniform. Not only are male bodies hiding under female dress; now there are female bodies beneath male costumes. The trail from the leader recostumed in female dress to the lieutenant unmasked as a woman is one marked by a descent into feminization, whereby Confederate manhood not only erodes but disappears.

The iconography of the "Belle of Richmond" also suggests the sexual ambi-

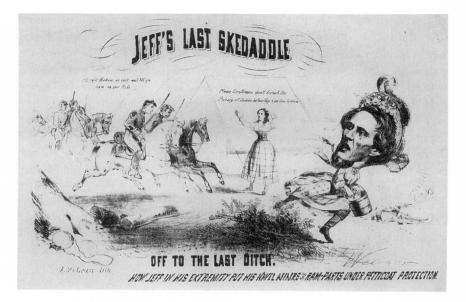

FIGURE 12. "Jeff's Last Skedaddle," cartoon by A. McLean, 1865 (Rare Book, Manuscript, and Special Collections Library, Duke University)

guities at stake in Confederate feminization. As Nina Silber argues, images of Davis as a woman symbolize the South's implicit vulnerability to heterosexual rape. Davis finds himself, as many captions presented him, an "unprotected female," open to Northern male assault.[63] Yet male cross-dressing in the Civil War era also invoked the realm of homosexual possibility. One account of an 1864 ball staged by Massachusetts soldiers, for example, featured young soldiers cross-dressed as prostitutes, about whom an observer wrote to his wife, "We had some little Drummer boys dressed up and I'll bet you could not tell them from girls if you did not know them . . . some of them looked almost good enough to *lay* with and I guess some of them did get laid with."[64] In a more anxious mode, cartoons such as "Jeff's Last Skedaddle" also suggest the same-sex possibilities of the image of Davis in drag, with the pun on Davis's "ram-parts" highlighting the *maleness* of the body at risk. Another cartoon, "Finding the Last Ditch" (figure 13), explicitly showcases another body part. In this image, a Union soldier prepares to hurl Davis downward; the Devil lurks below to the right, while a freed slave rejoices at left. The prominent of Davis's backside in this cartoon suggests the specific part of the male body most vulnerable to sexual assault: his anus. Doubly metaphoric, Jeff's "ram-parts" are both the phallus he could lose and the anal bulwark he can no longer defend.

FIGURE 13. "Finding the Last Ditch," cartoon by Burgoo Zac, 1865 (Library of Congress)

Another Civil War text, a pornographic song called "Jeff Davis' Dream," confirms the salience of this anatomical imagery in characterizations of Davis's defeat. Describing Davis and his wife in bed one night, this song initially equates his phallic potency with Confederate military prowess: "With his cock as hard as crystal. / "Swab", he cried, "Swab out the gun, / And give old Lincoln thunder—." As the song progresses, however, its focus shifts from Davis's phallus to his anus:

> He let a fart, and then he spent—
> Says Jeffrey's wife, "I'm co- co- coming."
>
> "Fine, fine," cried Jeff, "the gun is clean,"
> He strained enough to split—
> And throwing his arms around his dear
> He strained again and shit.
>
> "Oh, oh," cried Jeff, "I'm shot, I'm shot,
> "My leg is bleeding— bleeding—
> "Help, help, come here to this spot,
> "Oh, death is slowly feeding.
>
> "Oh, would that I were loyal now
> "I hear old Abe coming,
> "He'll hang me, he will, I vow,
> "Yes, yes, I hear him drumming."

In these lyrics, phallic ejaculation brings involuntary anal excretion, first flatulence and then defecation. The loss of anal control is constructed as a political allegory, signaling vulnerability to Lincoln's army. As the song concludes, Davis joins his wife in flight: "Oh, my wife please take my trembling hand / And we will both secede."[65] This song predates the end of the war, but its overall trajectory foreshadows the "Belle of Richmond" imagery, with phallic potency undermined by anal vulnerability. If Lincoln's head, as we have already seen, served Northerners as reverential synecdoche for the president, then "Jeff Davis's Dream" and the "Belle of Richmond" iconography together suggest that Davis's anus was the consistent anatomical site for burlesque of the disgraced Confederate leader.

While these images are specific to Davis, their larger implication is that for the male Confederacy, defeat brings not only an attack against femininity but also an implicitly homosexual "raid on the rear." In expressing such anxieties, the cultural work of the "Belle of Richmond" imagery, like that of "Jeff Davis' Dream," is to act as a hinge, at once literal and metaphoric, between two mutually dependent and similarly vulnerable regions: the male body politic that suffers military humiliation and the male body that faces physical conquests such as phallic castration and anal rape. The depiction of Jefferson Davis as cross-dressed suggests the intrinsic difficulties of mobilizing narratives of masculine potency in the service of national power, when masculinity is itself such a vulnerable fiction. Similarly, despite her professed dedication to Davis and the Confederacy, Velazquez's text devalues Confederate masculinity precisely by making its vulnerability so visible. Her story of wartime cross-dressing illuminates a series of cultural fears that move in two figurative directions: metaphorically, between bodies and costumes; and metonymically, from counterfeit women to counterfeit men, from femininity to feminization, and from gender inversion to homosexual invasion. The result is a text that up-ends rather than buttresses Southern claims to masculinity and indeed seems to render the metaphorical gendering of the Confederacy as a whole a "lost cause." Velazquez's masquerade inadvertently exposes the contradictions of a symbolic system that demands the maintenance of femininity as a contrast to Confederate masculinity but is so unable to sustain this contrast that femininity invades and usurps the domain of the masculine itself.

Burlesquing the sexual faultlines of Lost Cause ideology, Velazquez debases that ideology's foundation: racial hierarchy in the postwar South. African-Americans, I suggested in the last chapter, joyously responded to emancipation with practices and images of inversion that at once elevated freed slaves and brought former masters low—literally so, in Mattie Jackson's descriptions of her former masters turned upside down. For many Southern whites, by contrast, emancipation was a double source of horror, linked to defeat by both Yankees and newly freed slaves. Reversing the imagery of a work like *The Royal Ape,* cultural constructions of the postwar white South suggested that it was symbolically blackened as well as feminized by defeat. The man who worries about being "[degraded] into fit material for slaves" articulates this possibility of racial reversal, as do caricatures of Jefferson Davis. In "Finding the Last Ditch," the figure of an unchained black man in the lower left functions as the necessary complement, at once cause and effect, of Davis's disempowerment. Other images literalized white fears about black power by darkening Davis's white skin. For example, an illustration for an 1864 anti-Confederate song, entitled "Jeff Wants to Get Away," showed Davis so eager to escape the war that he pleads "Black me" to a fellow secessionist, who begins to paint his face with blacking.[66] Images of Davis's flight from the Yankees extended this equation between defeat and blackface, as in a Northern cartoon of Davis fleeing via the Underground Railroad (figure 14). Entitled "The End of Jeff Davis," this image aligns the sexual anxieties of the cross-dressed "Belle

FIGURE 14.
"The End of Jeff Davis," cartoon, ca. 1865 (Rare Book, Manuscript, and Special Collections Library, Duke University)

of Richmond"—the fear of rear-end assault by the Yankees—with the racial fear of being blackened by defeat.

Published in 1876, *The Woman in Battle* inadvertently highlights the anxious construction of Southern whiteness in Reconstruction. Many Southern whites caricatured Reconstruction as a nightmare of so-called "Negro rule," in which freed slaves, abetted by the federal government, tyrannically ruled over ex-Confederates.[67] Velazquez's comments about the Reconstruction South typify these racist beliefs: "The men of intellect, and the true representatives of Southern interests, were disfranchised and impoverished, while the management of affairs was in the hands of ignorant negroes, just relieved from slavery, and white 'carpet-baggers'" (535). When she visits Venezuela as a member of an emigration group, she concludes that "the negroes, Indians, and half-breeds seem to be incapable of doing anything to advance their own condition, or to promote the interests of the country" (552). In Trinidad, "the majority of the people were negroes or half-breeds, whose habitations were disgustingly dirty and squalid" (558). To complete this circuit of racist denunciation, she finds on her return to the South that "the freedmen and carpet-baggers were having things their own way throughout the length and breadth of the late Confederacy" (570).

Yet if such comments are typical of Reconstruction-era invective, their accompanying narrative of cross-dressing is not. Southern whites resistant to "Negro rule" looked toward a future restoration of white power, and they rapidly dismantled black achievements after the formal end of Reconstruction in 1877. In *The Woman in Battle,* however, white disenfranchisement points not toward future redress but toward anxious undress. From the start, Velazquez's condemnation of black figures is linked to anxieties about maintaining her masculine disguise. When she first dresses as Buford, a visit to a "negro barber" (63) threatens to expose her. Dissuading him with difficulty from shaving her, she remarks that "The negro took the hint, but grinned a little as he put away the shaving apparatus, at which I was almost inclined to believe that he had suspicions with regard to me" (64). This description offers a condensed image of white anxiety about black power: the specter of a black man grinning as he holds a razor to the throat of a white man. Velazquez's cross-dressing literalizes this anxiety still further, featuring a white man so feminized by his fear that he is actually a woman.

Velazquez reprises these racial dynamics in her relationship with an African-American man, Bob, whom she calls her "darkey" and treats as her slave: "I told him that if he ran off and left me, I would kill him if I ever caught him again; which threat had its desired effect, for he stuck to me through thick and thin" (96). Her inclusion of this character ostensibly appeases white anxiety, like other stories of faithful black "body servants" in the Confederate army.[68] Yet Bob's presence in *The Woman in Battle* destabilizes white authority. With the success of her disguise contingent on his aid, Velazquez needs Bob to "stick to" her for her costume of masculinity to stick as well. Buford's unproven masculinity contrasts with his military skill, for Bob is "a better soldier than some of the white men who thought themselves immensely his superiors" (121–22). While Velazquez professes herself proud of "the darkey's pluck and enthusiasm" (122), her condescension coexists with the uneasy possibility of his authority. Despite her command to Bob to stand by her, he in fact deserts, going "plump into the Federal camp" (218). His abandonment suggests, in microcosm, the failure of the Confederacy to maintain racial hierarchies while attempting to reverse regional ones.

Although Bob later returns loyally to Velazquez—an unlikely scenario—Velazquez's anxiety about white emasculation and black power continues in other ways. Crossing into enemy territory on an espionage mission, she is sick, uncertain, and anxiously dependent on a black man to lead the way: "I took care to keep him in front of me all the time, and had my hand constantly on the pistol . . . which I was resolved to use upon my colored companion in case he should be inclined to act treacherously" (354). Like the image of the black man poised to cut the white man's throat, this moment positions Velazquez as vulnerable to African-American power. Attempting to assert her own independence, Velazquez instead finds herself vulnerable to yet another raid from behind.

Another moment in the text literalizes Velazquez's vulnerable dependence on African-Americans still further. Early in the text, as part of her disguise, Velazquez acquires "a solution with which to stain my face, in order to make it look tanned" (68). This image of tanning suggests that white masculinity requires a degree of physical coloration, darker than "pure" white but not so dark as to seem "black," to assert its own potency. When the Confederacy suffers reverses, this coloring process is also reversed. After an espionage episode, Velazquez returns from Union territory with her skin in disrepair: "I had no mustache, and having become somewhat bleached, was not by any means so masculine in appearance as I had been at one time" (308). Tanned skin and mustache, the conjoined signifiers of her masculinity, have eroded together. This image of disempowerment suggests that anxieties about the loss of white power may move in two directions, toward "too much" as well as "too little" whiteness. In this moment at least, the declining Confederacy suffers both a blackening and a bleaching of whiteness.[69]

Velazquez's account of her postwar activities expands these anxieties about whiteness into a broader setting, bringing together descriptions of white impotence with an unusually revealing narrative of masculinity under siege. Her emigration trip to Venezuela, like other Confederate ventures in Mexico, Honduras, and Brazil, represents a defensive attempt to recover from defeat at home with imperialism abroad. As one proponent of emigration wrote, "[W]e cannot look upon this country as *ours* any longer. Our best men are disfranchised, Negroes are put into power, [and] the vilest scum of society is to be allowed to hold office."[70] Another proponent urged expatriation for "manly motives," suggesting more explicitly that such trips represented attempts at white Southern remasculinization.[71] In Velazquez's version of this rhetoric, Venezuela "appeared to [the emigrants] like a second Garden of Eden . . . with no free negroes or carpet-baggers to intrude upon them" (539). This project fails, in part due to corrupt leadership, but more significantly because of racial disillusionment: "A good many of the emigrants . . . seemed to think that if the negroes were of as much importance as they seemed to be in Venezuela, it would have been just as well to have remained at home and fought the battle for supremacy with the free negroes and carpet-baggers on familiar ground" (543). As with Velazquez's story of Bob's authority, the proximity of the Venezuela failure to cross-dressing inadvertently aligns expatriation with feminization. The project of Southern emigration provides not an escape from feminization but a further advance into it.

Like her descriptions of Venezuela, Velazquez's comments about her Cuban origins link ambiguities of gender with the changing social boundaries of the Americas. Velazquez's self-proclaimed status as Cuban aligns the question of Confederate rebellion with issues of territorial control and rebellion in nearby regions. In her narrative, Cuba and the Confederacy are similarly enslaved by tyrannical powers. Visiting Havana during the war, she declares:

> I begrudged that this fair island should be the dependence of a foreign power; for I was, despite my Spanish ancestry, an American, heart and soul, and if there was anything that could have induced me to abandon the cause of the Southern Confederacy, it would have been an attempt on the part of the Cubans to have liberated themselves from the Spanish yoke.
>
> . . . [I] more than half resolved that should the Cubans strike a blow for independence, I would join my fortunes to theirs, and serve their cause with the same assiduity that I was now serving that of the Confederacy. (248)

Velazquez's support for Cuban independence is historically affiliated with the larger movements of ex-Confederates. Later in the century, Cuba would take on triumphant symbolic associations for Southern adherents of the Lost Cause, with participation in the Spanish-American War providing another opportunity for Southern remasculinization. In 1876, however, when Velazquez publishes her book, both the lost Confederacy and contemporary Cuba remain slaveholding regions symbolically enslaved to tyrannical powers. Developing the comparison between her Cuban and Confederate affinities, Velazquez inadvertently expands the frontiers of male feminization from the South to the Americas as whole.[72]

Moreover, since Velazquez is immigrant as well as emigrant, her Cuban origins represent a second form of challenge to Confederate integrity. While her Cubanness is partially aligned with the Confederacy, it is also affiliated with a potentially destabilizing "otherness." As Cuban, Velazquez occupies a zone aligned with blackness, both literally—Cuba also contained many dark-skinned slaves—and metaphorically. Light-skinned African-Americans were often linked with Cubans: Frances Harper, for example, was sometimes described as a "Cuban belle," while Octavia Albert's *The House of Bondage* includes a description of a woman slave who "was of a fine oily brunette complexion. She might easily have passed for Cuban."[73] Potentially twinned with blackness, Velazquez's Cubanness is also a form of linguistic disguise. At several points in *The Woman in Battle*, she uses her fluency in Spanish as an occasion for masquerade, as when she travels in Europe after the war and at first pretends not to understand two men speaking Spanish: "I smiled and thanked him in his native tongue. It was most amusing to see the expression of horror that overspread his countenance as he heard me" (521). With her foreign surname, her Cuban origins, and her fluency in Spanish, Velazquez's self-professed status as cross-dressing Cuban combines unruly femininity with the threats of racial and national difference.

The last three chapters of *The Woman in Battle* further extend Velazquez's ambiguous relation to the Americas, recounting her travels in the western United States, including Utah, Nevada, Colorado, New Mexico, and Texas. These descriptions are historically cognate with other representations of the West in this period, as is Velazquez's interest in the region as a whole; like Venezuelan emigration and the Spanish-American War, the West offered yet another opportunity for the remasculinization of ex-Confederate soldiers, who journeyed there in great numbers.[74] Yet as with her descriptions of Venezuela and Cuba, Velazquez's account of the West inadvertently burlesques Confederate remasculinization. Her descriptions consistently align an unruly West with her own unruly femininity. This equation is sometimes direct, as when she expresses sympathy for Indians ("I had much more respect for these savages than I had for the ruffianly white men who were dispossessing them of their country" [580–81]). More metaphorically, her account implicitly expands her own individual criminality to a regional scale. The West is a terrain of "lawlessness" (599), filled with swindlers, speculators, and desperadoes, including one "big negro" armed with six-shooters (599). Transgressions against femininity saturate the region, from Julesburg, a town of gamblers and drinkers where "The women were, if anything, worse than the men" (576), to Salt Lake City, where she meets polygamous Mormons. These male swindlers of the West mirror Velazquez's own counterfeit writ large, while the women of Julesburg and elsewhere elevate her gender violations to the scale of municipal custom. As her portrait of the West inadvertently suggests, Velazquez's story sets in motion a carnivalesque American social space in which the remaking of identity, individual and national, constantly violates new boundaries.

Returning to the comments of Jubal Early one last time, we can see the convergence of these anxieties about ethnicity and nation with criticism of gender impropriety. To Early, Velazquez is unsettling not only because she seems foreign, but also, ironically, because her very foreignness—like her masculinity—may be yet another masquerade. Near the beginning of his letter of protest, Early declares his belief that "Madame Velasquez [*sic*] is not of Spanish birth or origin, but is an American and probably from the North," an assessment that refights the Civil War by imagining Velazquez as a Northerner. Later, he elaborates:

> [T]he solecisms in grammar contained in her letter do not result from the broken English of a foreigner, but are the blunders of an American whose education is imperfect. Her appearance and voice are those of an American woman, and has no resemblance to those of a cultivated Spanish lady. If she is really Spanish in origin, then her associations with camp life have thoroughly Americanized her.[75]

Velazquez is not "really Spanish in origin," or if so she is "thoroughly Americanized"; her speech is not that of a "cultivated Spanish lady" but the result of "imperfect" education. These uncertainties both blur the boundary between not-American and American and reverse the traditional narrative by which an immigrant moves from a condition of original ethnicity to one of self-made "Americanness." In Velazquez's case, ethnic otherness may be donned as well as discarded. In an extension of the American ethos of self-reinvention, the making of an American—like the making of masculinity—is a process open to disguise and reversal. Velazquez literalizes the implicit uncertainties of the "self-made man," effecting a vision of masculinity literally self-made by a woman, of Southernness constructed by a Northerner, and of Spanishness mimicked by an American.

In the multifaceted conflict between Loreta Velazquez and Jubal Early, the battles of the Civil War are refought on the terrain of Confederate metaphor. *The Woman in Battle* debases the value of Confederate iconography by literalizing its terms, turning Confederate masculinity into femininity, femininity into fakery, and sexual prowess into vulnerability to assault. These instabilities of gender and sexuality in turn threaten the narratives of racial hierarchy on which both Velazquez and Early rely. *The Woman in Battle* ultimately reveals that the ex-slave—and the racial "other" more broadly conceived—stand alongside the white woman as the South's Medusa. In ethnic as well as racial terms, Velazquez's text points the way toward Southern life after the Confederacy as a carnivalesque social field occupied by figures Northern and Southern, American and un-American, black and white. More unstably still, her text suggests that in a world filled with figures like those of the "Cuban" Velazquez, these dichotomies are themselves inadequate to capture alternative and ambiguous identities. In this eruption of "otherness," gender masquerade is both its own form of revolt and a protean symbol for myriad forms of misrule. In the wake of a lost war, the figure of the cross-dressed Confederate soldier at once upends feminine civility and turns the world of the white South topsy-turvy.

In *The Woman in Battle*, then, Civil War cross-dressing forges a range of reciprocal connections among bodies regional and individual. As the war alters the postwar memorialization of the Confederacy, so too does it symbolically transform Velazquez's story of cross-dressing into a picaresque, protolesbian adventure story. Flowing in two directions, the metaphorics of masquerade are politically unstable. In Velazquez's text, radical notions of gender do not affiliate with radical gender politics, any more than a conservative use of gender symbolism, as in the writings of Jubal Early, necessarily secures reactionary ideals. For Early, the masculine body politic of the postwar South is all too easily literalized in the form of a woman. Similarly, in the protolesbian world of *The Woman in Battle*, capacious fantasies of gender mobility translate into hostility toward other women. Even in this fictionalized world of female pleni- tude, it turns out that ladies lack, and when women unite, they cannot seem to secede. So too for the Confederacy, whose failed rebellion in fact translates, in this text at least, into an unsuccessful campaign in fiction. For in the losing metaphors of the Lost Cause, even the stories created in defense of the Con- federacy open its boundaries to penetration.

FIVE

"Army of Civilizers"

Frances Harper's Warring Fictions

I

When Frances Ellen Watkins Harper published *Iola Leroy; or, Shadows Uplifted,* the first novel about African-American experience in the Civil War, in 1892, she intervened in a struggle over the memory of the war that was reaching new levels of political urgency. For African-Americans, the 1890s were a period of severe racial retrenchment, shaped by both the official segregation of Jim Crow laws and unofficial forms of anti-black violence such as lynching. Directly contributing to contemporary racism, the ideology of the Lost Cause gained even greater visibility in this period. New organizations like the United Daughters of the Confederacy sponsored Confederate rituals and monuments, novelists like Thomas Dixon celebrated the Confederacy in their popular novels, and white Southerners capitalized on the Spanish-American War as an opportunity to reprise Confederate glory. Nor were racist reframings of the Civil War limited to the white South. By the 1880s, Northern representations of the war downplayed the role of slavery and highlighted the positive qualities of white Southerners, approaches that framed sectional reconciliation as a reunion among compatible white people. African-American participation in the conflict, treated with ambivalence by white Northerners from the start, faded from view. Like the openly reactionary nostalgia of white Southerners, the historical amnesia of white Northerners functioned not only to whitewash the memory of the Civil War but also to thwart contemporary African-American struggles for survival and equality.[1]

In response to this assault, many African-American writers, male and female, strategically revived the memory of the Civil War in terms that challenged both Northern and Southern white representations. Frederick Douglass, as David W. Blight has shown, systematically memorialized the war in his last writings; W. E. B. Du Bois, who would dominate the next generation of black intellectuals, launched his oratorical career with an 1890 Harvard commencement speech on the legacy of Jefferson Davis.[2] Like their male counterparts, black women writers turned repeatedly to the legacy of the war, in oratory, poetry, fiction, essay, memoir, and biography from the 1890s through the turn of the century. Their works addressing the Civil War include the group biography of ex-slaves compiled by Octavia Victoria Rogers Albert, *The House of Bondage; or Charlotte Brooks and Other Slaves* (1890); memoirs by Annie L. Burton (*Memories of Childhood's Slavery Days* [1909]), Kate Drumgoold (*A Slave Girl's Story* [1898]), and especially Susie King Taylor (*Reminiscences of My Life in Camp* [1902]); poetry by Josephine Delphine Henderson Heard, Lizelia Augusta Jenkins Moorer, Effie Waller Smith, Clara Ann Thompson, and Priscilla Jane Thompson; fiction by Pauline Hopkins; and writing across several decades and genres by Frances Ellen Watkins Harper.[3]

Born free in the slave state of Maryland in 1825, Frances Ellen Watkins was already established as a writer and antislavery activist when the war began. In 1860, she married Fenton Harper, a widower with three children, and during the Civil War, she lived with Harper on a farm in Ohio, gave birth to their daughter, Mary, was widowed in 1864, and struggled to support the family following her husband's death. Despite her domestic obligations, she remained politically active during the war years. "Mrs. Harper," William Still remembered in his 1872 tribute to her, "took the deepest interest in the war, and looked with extreme anxiety for the results; and she never lost an opportunity to write, speak, or serve the cause in any way that she thought would best promote the freedom of the slave."[4] For several decades afterward, Harper pursued the legacy of the Civil War in her oratory, correspondence, essays, poetry, and fiction. The war is a central presence in her novella *Minnie's Sacrifice* (1869); in poems such as "An Appeal to the American People" (1871), "Words for the Hour" (1871), "President Lincoln's Proclamation of Freedom" (1871), the "Aunt Chloe" sequence (1872), "A Story of the Rebellion" (1894), "Then and Now" (1894), and "Home, Sweet Home" (1895); and in speeches over three decades, from "The Mission of the War" (1864), to "Duty to Dependent Races" (1891). When she was sixty-seven, a veteran activist for suffrage and temperance as well as African-American rights, Harper returned to the Civil War as the setting for her first and only full-length novel, *Iola Leroy* (1892).[5]

Iola Leroy is the story of a woman, the novel's eponymous heroine, who is raised as a privileged white daughter of the antebellum South and who discovers, on the eve of the Civil War, that she is of mixed-race ancestry and is then sold into slavery. Rescued by the Union army, she reunites with her family when the war is over. In the last generation, a variety of scholars, prompted by the growth of black feminist criticism, have made clear the importance of the novel and its narrative strategies. In an influential interpretation of *Iola Leroy*, for example, Hazel V. Carby argues that Iola's journey from orphaned youth to family-filled adulthood both recalls the mid-nineteenth-century domestic novel and recasts its plot in the context of the black family. Iola's triumphant claim of family at novel's end serves, Carby argues, as the vehicle for Harper's observations on the black diaspora and the emerging postwar role of black intellectuals. Similarly, Claudia Tate suggests that the novel's focus on domestic concerns such as marriage and family marks *Iola Leroy* as one of many black women's texts in this era that offer "domestic allegories of political desire."[6]

We may take the politics of domesticity in another direction by viewing *Iola Leroy* as a domestic novel about a domestic war. In this chapter, I analyze *Iola Leroy* as a Civil War novel, situating it within the contexts of contemporary African-American commentaries about the war, Harper's own body of Civil War writing, and constructions of the war in racist cultural discourse of the era. I first identify prominent themes in turn-of-the-century African-American women's Civil War writing. Like texts by black women that emerged immediately after the war, this body of work consistently counters both the racism that would discount black wartime participation and the sexism that would erase women from war stories entirely. In the later period, representations of the Civil War texts take on new self-consciousness, as retrospective interventions into a culture that increasingly understood the conflict through the lenses of competing fictions and commemorations. In particular, the nonfiction writings of Susie King Taylor and Octavia Albert reshape the conventions of war narrative in significant ways, foregrounding maternal figures within their stories and offering matrilineal storytelling as a model for the memorialization of the war.

Turning to *Iola Leroy*, I argue that the novel both expands on these revisionist strategies and revises Harper's own earlier writings on the war. Exploiting the possibilities of the novel, Harper honors black heroism while recasting the war's gender politics. With the figure of the black mother at the thematic and narrative center of her text, Harper embeds the Civil War in a trajectory of maternal quest and reunion.

Within this trajectory, I then argue, Harper explores the metaphoric meanings of the Civil War as an internal conflict. Engaging and interleaving a variety of antinomies—black/white, male/female, North/South—*Iola Leroy* employs the idea of "civil war" as a frame for the construction of black female subjectivity. As she maps the Civil War onto her heroine's individual struggles, so too does Harper intervene in turn-of-the-century fictions that aligned the "rape" of the South with the racist mythology of the black rapist. Reading Harper's novel against D. W. Griffith's racist film epic *The Birth of a Nation* (1915), I suggest that *Iola Leroy* operates as a recoloring of national allegory. Her plots act as a counternarrative to both white Southern constructions of the war as a regional rape and ostensibly more sympathetic white Northern narratives of the war as a regional romance.

Finally, I argue that *Iola Leroy* offers a double-edged commentary on another form of civil war: the dynamics of civility in African-American women's writing of this era. Harper's novel shows the radical potential of civility, as a discourse linking bodily self-mastery with the transformation of a racist body politic. Yet as contemporary black etiquette books and one of Harper's earlier novellas, *Trial and Triumph,* also suggest, civility's emphasis on self-regulation constrained as well as enlarged possibilities for black women activists. So too in *Iola Leroy,* a novel in which civility at once provides the vocabulary for a new body politic and silences voices of female rebellion.

II

For many black male writers at the end of the nineteenth century, the importance of the Civil War continued to center on the heroism of the black soldier. Frederick Douglass, for example, focused his memories of the war on "men, young men and strong [going] to the front."[7] George Washington Williams and Joseph T. Wilson comprehensively recounted the achievements of black Civil War soldiers in *A History of the Negro Troops in the War of the Rebellion* (1888) and *The Black Phalanx* (1890).[8] In such works, masculinity constituted the central language of African-American achievement, and military battles were the vocabulary of that language. Black men's representations of the Civil War conformed to what Patricia Morton has analyzed as the primary project of black historiography in this period, that of "restoring black men to a man's world."[9]

Black men were by no means univocal, however, in their memorializations of the black Civil War soldier. Less redemptively and more ironically, for example, Paul Lawrence Dunbar circumscribed the black soldier in the deforming context of white racism in his Civil War novel *The Fanatics* (1901). Although this work focuses on white residents of an Ohio border town, its characters significantly include a black man known as "Nigger Ed." Introduced as a grotesque figure, ridiculed as both "town crier and town drunkard," Ed is transformed by his experience assisting white men in a Union regiment.[10]

After marching off to war "very stern, dignified and erect" (53), he returns newly masculinized:

> Among those who came back, proud and happy, none was more noticeable than "Nigger Ed." The sight of camps, the hurry of men and the press of a real responsibility had evoked a subtle change in the negro . . . he capered no more in the public square for the delectation of the crowd that despised him. He walked with a more stately step and the people greeted him in more serious tones, as if his association with their soldiers . . . had brought him nearer to the manhood which they still refused to recognize in him. (122)

"Nearer to . . . manhood," Ed has now risen above the minstrel-like performances of his prewar self. By the end of *The Fanatics,* he has become a respected figure in the town: "There were men who had seen that black man on bloody fields . . . and these could not speak of him without tears in their eyes . . . And so they give him a place for life and everything he wanted, and from being despised he was much petted and spoiled, for they were all fanatics" (311–12). For Dunbar, whose father had served in the Union army, the "black man on bloody fields" is transformed by the Civil War in his own eyes and in the teary vision of others.

Yet this transformation is deceptive, since in a world of "fanatics," Ed's new status as beloved "pet" differs in degree but not in kind from his earlier position as reviled "black buffoon" (53). Dunbar was often accused of reinforcing racist stereotypes in his dialect writing, and in this novel, his characterization of Ed consistently reduces him to the status of "a child who has tried to be good and been misunderstood" (182). Inhabiting the terrain of stereotype, however, Dunbar also ironizes it. His interest is less in redeeming black manhood than in condemning the white society that constructs Ed as a disempowered spectacle, whether "buffoon" or "pet." Thus at one town meeting, Ed remains silent, but his presence encourages an anti-Union speaker: "The unhappy advent of the negro had put a power into the words of a man who otherwise would have been impotent" (180). He serves to unite white men otherwise fiercely divided, for "Both sides hated him and his people. He was like a shuttlecock. He was a reproach to one and an insult to the other" (181). As black "shuttlecock," Ed empowers white men otherwise "impotent," which is to say that his manhood is inevitably distorted by the anxieties of white men about their own masculinity. In Dunbar's corrosively ironic vision, the Civil War alone cannot undo the racist system within which the representation, if not the experience, of black "manhood" took place.

If Dunbar's novel begins to suggest the complexity of Civil War memory for black men, then for black women writers, the task of coming "nearer to . . . manhood" was even more challenging, since they were definitionally excluded from a discourse of emancipation predicated on masculinity. The end of the century was a period of tremendous activism for black women, who led campaigns against lynching and for racial uplift and developed new organizations such as the National Association of Colored Women. Concentrated literary production accompanied these initiatives; in 1892 alone appeared Harper's *Iola Leroy*, Ida B. Wells-Barnett's *Southern Horrors: Lynch Law in All Its Phases*, and Anna Julia Cooper's *A Voice from the South*. In their activism and writing, black women supported black men, but they also contested, implicitly or explicitly, the masculine bias of much black male discourse. Their contestations ranged from the moderate rhetoric of *The Work of the Afro-American Woman* by "Mrs. N. F. Mossell," which offered a tribute to black women's achievements as aided by black men who, "in most instances, have been generous"; to the more radical rhetoric of *A Voice from the South*, a manifesto for black women who were, in Cooper's famous phrase, "confronted by both a woman question and a race problem." "[S]o long as woman sat with bandaged eyes and manacled hands," wrote Cooper in her critique of sexism, "the world of thought moved in its orbit like the revolutions of the moon; with one face (the man's face) always out, so that the spectator could not distinguish whether it was disc or sphere."[11]

In their representations of the Civil War as in their discussions of contemporary issues, black women writers accordingly changed the "orbit" of war narrative so that eclipsed female faces could appear. Like their male contemporaries, some women centered their accounts of the war on the heroism of black soldiers. Lizelia Moorer, for example, juxtaposed the Civil War soldier with contemporary struggles in her volume of poems, *Prejudice Unveiled, and Other Poems* (1907). In "Loyalty to the Flag," she declares: "O, how brave the Negro soldiers when the Civil war was fought! / Shall they fight such noble battles in the nation's cause for naught?"[12] This tribute to men is immediately followed by "Negro Heroines," a poem that celebrates black women nurses in the Spanish-American War. In the preface to the volume, Moorer inserts a female voice into war narrative more directly, aligning herself—as Elizabeth Keckley had done—with Abraham Lincoln: "Like Lincoln, when he was filled with sympathy for the slave, I resolved at my first opportunity to deal the hydra-headed monster, prejudice, a blow."[13] Enlarging the possibilities for military heroism, Moorer represents "Negro heroines" as warriors and herself as "like Lincoln."

Black women who had directly participated in military activities transformed the genre of the memoir as a whole with their stories. Susie King Taylor's memoir *Reminiscences of My Life in Camp* (1902) narrates her experience within the Union army during her teens, where she first worked as paid cook and laundress and then taught reading and writing to soldiers. As the war went on, she "learned to handle a musket very well while in the regiment, and could shoot straight and often hit the target. . . . I thought this great fun."[14] After the war, she helped to organize a relief organization in Boston. Her war story thus encompassed a range of activities, from the male preserve of gun-shooting to the all-women postwar "Relief Corps." Near the end of her account, she laments that there are "many people who do not know what some of the colored women did during the war. . . . These things should be kept in history before the people" (141–42).

In offering a record of these experiences, Taylor's narrative also suggests the ways in which black women's Civil War stories reshaped the gendered contours of war narrative. Her first chapter, "A Brief Sketch of My Ancestors," begins: "My great-great-grandmother was 120 years old when she died. She had seven children, and five of her boys were in the Revolutionary War" (25). Following this intertwined genealogy of women and wars, Taylor moves on to her great-grandmother, a noted midwife and "the mother of twenty-four children, twenty-three being girls" (25), and then to her grandmother, a free woman who lived by selling food, doing laundry, and taking care of some "bachelors' rooms" (27). The second chapter expands this web of matrilineal relations to include the topic of literacy, as Taylor's grandmother orchestrates her education by sending her to two women teachers. Taylor, in turn, passes on her skills by writing "passes for my grandmother, for all colored persons, free or slaves, were compelled to have a pass" (31).

Taylor's two opening chapters, then, frame the text such that when war does appear, it is against the background of a black matrilineal legacy and a female tradition of literacy. Taylor's work as a laundress for male soldiers recalls her grandmother's work; her teaching evokes the lessons her own grandmother sponsored so that she might read. Her great-great-grandmother's household, that of a woman with five sons off to the American Revolution, echoes in this description of the gratitude of Union soldiers toward Taylor: "[Y]ou took an interest in us boys ever since we have been here, and we are very grateful for all you do for us" (67). Finally, the relief activities that close the war are balanced by the opening matrix of women that includes her midwife-grandmother and her dozens of girls. It is as though the war itself were one event on a continuum of mothering, repeated in a range of activities over generations.

While Taylor's account inserts the Civil War into a continuous lineage of

mothers, other black women align the war with plots of maternal loss. Both
Kate Drumgoold and Annie L. Burton were children during the war, and
both open their memoirs with accounts of their early years that intertwine
military conflict and maternal absence. In *A Slave Girl's Story,* Drumgoold
recalls that "My dear mother was sold at the beginning of the war. . . . The
money that my mother was sold for was to keep the rich man from going to
the field of battle, as he sent a poor white man in his stead." Connecting the
arrival of the war with the departure of her mother, Drumgoold's comment
remarks a double conversion of bodies into commodities, wherein the sale of
the slave mother enables the purchase of a substitute soldier by her white
master. The fall of the slaveholding Confederacy, by contrast, makes possible
the return of Drumgoold's mother, a reunion she describes in ecstatic terms:
"I would that the whole world could have seen the joy of a mother and her
two girls on that heaven-made day—a mother returning back to her own once
more, a mother that we did not know that we should ever see her face on this
earth more."[15]

In Annie L. Burton's *Memories of Childhood's Slavery Days,* by contrast, the
war paradoxically allows for a "happy, care-free childhood," since "Neither
master nor mistress . . . had time to bestow a thought upon us, for the great
Civil War was raging." Yet Burton's "happy" account of the war is also organized by a story of maternal separation, one that involves two women: "My
mother and my mistress," who "were children together, and grew up to be
mothers together." During the war, Burton's mother flees the plantation after
a whipping, and the white mistress claims possession of Burton and her siblings, even after the Emancipation Proclamation is issued: "Mistress suggested
that the slaves should not be told of their freedom . . . [She] said she could
keep my mother's three children." Finally, her mother returns to rescue her,
securing her freedom by threatening to go "to the Yankee headquarters to find
out if it were really true that all the negroes had been made free."[16] As Burton's
false white "mother" rejects the formal dictates of the war, her true black
mother embraces them. In the narratives of both Burton and Drumgoold, the
public developments of the Civil War—from Confederate conscription to the
Emancipation Proclamation—not only parallel but enable trajectories of maternal loss and reunion.

This maternal emphasis is common to other genres of African-American
writing, male and female. In Hortense Spillers's words, "the 'romance' of
African-American fiction is a tale of origins that brings together once again
children lost, stolen, or strayed from their mothers."[17] African-American
women's writing is strongly marked by this family romance, frequently focus-

ing on both the search of mothers for children and that of daughters for mothers.[18] Within the subgenre of black women's Civil War writing, I suggest, such maternal thematics have particular significance. The maternal plots that structure these stories offer supplementary and alternative paradigms to traditional war narratives that center on black male heroism. Maternal paradigms operate in earlier black women's writings about the war, like the memoirs of Mattie Jackson, but they take on additional significance in this second generation of war writing. As the war is increasingly represented through reconstructed memory and invented fiction—this is the era of *The Red Badge of Courage*—mother–child plots provide a model for the transmission and reception of black women's war stories. In contrast to male writers who frame the war as a story that passes from father to son, black women's Civil War texts from this era construct a matrilineal context for both the experience of the war and the telling of stories about it.

This interplay between military and maternal Civil War narratives emerges in multivalent form in Octavia Albert's *The House of Bondage; or Charlotte Brooks and Other Slaves* (1890). *The House of Bondage,* a loosely structured group biography of former slaves, was based on interviews conducted by Albert in the late 1870s and 1880s when she was living in the South with her minister husband. The interviews were published posthumously, first serially in the *South-western Christian Advocate* and then in book form. While Albert did not intend her interviews for book publication, *The House of Bondage* can nonetheless be read as a coherent full-length narrative. Frances Smith Foster, for example, interprets *The House of Bondage* as a powerful intervention into the literature of slavery, positioning Albert between Harriet Beecher Stowe and Thomas Nelson Page. Foster suggests that Albert implicitly revises Stowe, granting slave figures more agency, and openly combats Page, a premier shaper of racist plantation nostalgia.[19] As it contests these fictional models for the representation of antebellum slavery, so too, I suggest, does *The House of Bondage* intervene in cultural constructions of the Civil War. *The House of Bondage* offers a book-length negotiation of the war's legacy, in which Albert places patrilineal and matrilineal experiences of the war in literal and metaphorical conversation with one another.

At several points in *The House of Bondage,* black men narrate their experiences of the Civil War, which range from active military service to less formal battles with the Confederacy. The longest of these stories is that of Colonel Douglass Wilson, "a colored man of considerable prominence, not only in Louisiana, but in the nation" (129). In a chapter entitled "A Colored Soldier" he recounts in detail his experiences in Civil War battle, including the famous battle of Port Hudson, in which black regiments heroically seized a Louisiana port. Paying tribute to the valor of black soldiers, Wilson frames questions of social equality, as well as military service, in all-male terms:

> When it was proposed to make a soldier out of [the Negro], why, they said, "He can't fight." But what was the universal verdict at the close of every battle? Why, he fought like a demon. After the war they said, "O, he can't learn!" But what mean these laurels that he is getting at Yale, Cornell, Dartmouth, and other colleges over white competitors? (133)

This account offers a seamless transition from one all-male sphere of struggle, the battlefield, to another, the Ivy League university. This focus on men continues in a story about violence against black children in postwar Louisiana:

> Big white boys and half-grown men used to pelt them with stones and run them down with open knives, both to and from school. Sometimes they came home bruised, stabbed, beaten half to death, and sometimes quite dead. My own son himself was often thus beaten. He has on his forehead to-day a scar over his right eye which sadly tells the story of his trying experience in those days in his efforts to get an education. I was wounded in the war, trying to get my freedom, and he over the eye, trying to get an education. So we both call our scars marks of honor. (140–41)

This reminiscence combines the schoolroom and the battlefield as zones of violence, with the quest for education an extension of military engagements. In Wilson's genealogy of struggle, the soldier-father becomes the scholar-son, while a battle scar is the ultimate mark of male experience.

Yet in giving voice to Wilson, Octavia Albert also interrupts his patrilineal story. Throughout *The House of Bondage,* as Foster stresses, Albert's narrator "initiates, controls, and interprets the testimonies of her informants."[20] Wilson's story, for example, emerges from Albert's opinionated prompting: "I know your story would delight almost any one. Don't keep all the good things to yourself; tell us about them sometime" (130). Albert's questions to Wilson also structure the contents of his story, as she directs him to speak about such issues as the rise of the Ku Klux Klan and the prospects for racial equality. Finally, her closing comment to him reminds the reader of her own place in the story of the war: "I declare, colonel, I would not miss this interview I have had with you for a great deal. I was so young when the war broke out that I had no personal knowledge of many of the things that you have told me, and I assure you that you have interested me with their recital" (143). At once listener and speaker, Albert frames Wilson's story within her own authoritative voice.

Albert also counterposes Wilson's account with women's stories of combat. The first eight chapters of *The House of Bondage* are devoted to an ex-slave whom Albert calls "Aunt Charlotte," the source of the book's subtitle. Recounting her "sad life of bondage in the cane-fields of Louisiana" (2), Aunt Charlotte repeatedly focuses on the experience of slave women, particularly mothers. Her own story begins with a double maternal deprivation: separated from her mother, she was also forced to leave her newborn infant during the day to work in the cane-fields. Another woman, Nellie, escaped to find her children and was recaptured: "Aunt Jane told me Nellie was almost white, and had pretty, long, straight hair. When they got her back they made her wear men's pants for one year. They made her work in the field that way" (20). This account of cross-dressing is a stark contrast to that of Loreta Velazquez. Male clothing here signifies not a fantasy of freedom but a punishment for desiring it, and Nellie's pants constitute a violent denial of femininity and a restoration of the racial hierarchies that her "almost white skin" threatens. In keeping with her maternal focus, Aunt Charlotte's heroine is also a mother-figure, a slave named Aunt Jane Lee whose prayers and song "made me think of my old Virginia home and my mother" (9). Aunt Jane's forced departure functions as yet another mother–child rupture, but it also catalyzes the emergence of Aunt Charlotte's own voice: "We all cried when she left us. We felt lost, because we had nobody to lead us in our little [religious] meetings. After a while I begun to lead" (19). Throughout *The House of Bondage*, Aunt Charlotte constructs slavery as a war against black mothers, in which the loss of children is a female form of battle scar and the recreation of maternal bonds is the strongest weapon of female resistance.

When the Civil War itself enters Aunt Charlotte's story, it continues an ongoing battle rather than initiating a new one:

> La, child! when the Yankees came out here our eyes began to open, and we have been climbing ever since . . . When the war was going on I heard they was fighting for us. I tell you, when it was going on I did not cease to pray. We done the praying and the Yankees done the fighting, and God heard our prayers 'way down here in these cane-fields. Many times I have bowed down between the cane-rows, when the cane was high, so nobody could see me, and would pray in the time of the war! (56)

Engaging in her own form of fighting through prayer, Aunt Charlotte extends the matrilineal legacy of Aunt Jane. While Wilson's story began with the Civil

War, Charlotte's story ends with it. Taken together, their accounts constitute a continuous narrative of combat, in which the male soldiers of the Civil War take up, but do not supersede, the battles already engaged in by black women.

As Albert's editorial voice intervenes in Wilson's war story, so too does she insert herself in Aunt Charlotte's memoir. Her comments construct the speaker–editor relation as part of a warmly familial conversation between women: "I must confess to you," she remarks to Aunt Charlotte, "that I have enjoyed your conversation very much. I have concluded to write the story of your life in the cane-fields of Louisiana, and I desire to write it in your own words, as near as possible" (27). Albert's interest in Aunt Charlotte's story shapes the conclusion of the book as well. The last chapter of *The House of Bondage* is her account of an 1884 exposition at which she witnesses the reunion between one of the speakers, a young black clergyman, and his long-lost mother—who turns out to be none other than Aunt Charlotte's beloved Aunt Jane. Albert's pleasure in this moment is distinctly familial: "I almost felt that I was one of the family, too, for Aunt Charlotte had told me so many things about Aunt Jane Lee . . . I could not restrain my tears nor my joy" (160). As Aunt Charlotte's story opens the book, this reunion closes it, with Wilson's narrative, among other stories, circumscribed within a female frame. In *The House of Bondage,* final word goes to a mother-and-child reunion in which Albert herself is symbolic participant.

Like Susie King Taylor, then, Octavia Albert simultaneously inserts female heroism into a male combat narrative and genders this portrait by reframing fighting—and its later narration—as mothering. While Taylor's memoirs were not published until ten years after *Iola Leroy,* it is quite possible that Harper, a tireless campaigner for black rights, was aware of her participation in the war; Harper would almost certainly have known of *The House of Bondage,* which was a modest popular success in its serial and book forms. More generally, *Iola Leroy* explores the thematic concerns of contemporaries like Taylor and Albert within a declared fictional framework. Interweaving maternal and military narratives, Harper's novel builds upon the broader cultural discourse of black women's writing about the Civil War and consolidates her own long-standing interest in the war in new form.

III

Iola Leroy opens in the midst of the Civil War, on a North Carolina plantation in which a close-knit slave community eagerly awaits news of the Union army. Initial chapters focus on the experience of black soldiers and of Iola Leroy, a light-skinned slave serving as a Union nurse. The action then shifts back in time to the story of Eugene Leroy, a white Southerner who falls in love with, frees, educates, and marries a slave named Marie, to the horror of white Southern society. After Eugene dies suddenly, his cousin seizes his property and sells Marie Leroy and her children, who were unaware of their biracial origins, into slavery. Here the action returns to the present, as Iola rejects the attentions of a white Northern doctor, the war ends, and she searches for her family. United with them in the North, Iola marries a fellow activist, and they return to the South. The novel concludes with the major characters resolutely involved in initiatives of racial uplift.

From the beginning, the Civil War is an important presence, literal and symbolic, in *Iola Leroy*. The opening words of the novel slyly introduce the war as both historical ground and literary figure: "Good mornin', Bob; how's butter dis mornin'?" asks one slave, while another answers, "Fresh; just as fresh as fresh can be."[21] As Harper's narrator explains, these words are part of a wartime code:

> During the dark days of the Rebellion . . . some of the shrewder slaves, coming in contact with their masters and overhearing their conversations, invented a phraseology to convey in the most unsuspected manner news to each other from the battle-field. . . . In conveying tidings of the war, if they wished to announce a victory of the Union army, they said the butter was fresh, or that the fish and eggs were in good condition. If defeat befell them, then the butter and other produce were rancid or stale. (8–9)

Like other African-American accounts of the war, Harper emphasizes black agency, representing slaves as manipulators of the marketplace rather than as commodities within it. As a self-consciously literary beginning to a novel, moreover, this moment presents war news as a set of coded fictions. Harper introduces her novel as an "invented phraseology," both produced and consumed in new ways by an African-American audience.[22]

Central to this new war story, for Harper as for her contemporaries, is the heroism of black soldiers. During the Civil War, Harper had optimistically exulted that "Once the slave was a despised and trampled on pariah; now he has become a useful ally to the American government.[23] By the 1890s, however, her optimism was tempered by new waves of racist violence, and she turned to the memory of the war as an urgent reminder that Northern armies "did not get their final victories . . . till they clasped hands with the negro . . . I claim for the negro protection in every right with which the government has invested him."[24] As part of this claim, Harper offers three characters in *Iola*

Leroy who exemplify different features of black male heroism in wartime. For Robert Johnson, raised as a slave, the war offers a new arena in which to fight for freedom. "It would have been madness and folly for him to have attempted an insurrection against slavery" before the war (35), but now he "waited eagerly and hopefully his chance to join the Union army; and was ready and willing to do anything required of him by which he could earn his freedom and prove his manhood" (36). Robert promptly becomes "lieutenant of a colored company" (43).[25] To Harry Leroy, Iola's brother, enlistment is a test of his racial allegiances. Raised as white and light enough to pass, Harry decides that "I am a colored man, and unless I can be assigned to a colored regiment I am not willing to enter the army" (127). Finally, Harper devotes considerable attention to the story of a slave, Tom Anderson, "a man of herculean strength and remarkable courage" (40), who becomes an indispensable Union army scout, then dies when he opens himself to Confederate fire in order to free a grounded boat filled with Union soldiers. Together, the stories of Harry, Robert, and Tom chart inseparable commitments to blackness and manhood as well as to the Union cause.

The story of Tom is also significant for the context, at once homosocial and feminized, in which Harper embeds it. Tom's death is modeled on an actual Civil War anecdote, which Harper repeated throughout her writings as an exemplary story of black valor.[26] Here, she recounts his death in the voice of another soldier, who reports that "Tom took in the whole situation, and said, 'Some one must get us out of this. I mought's well be him as any. You are soldiers and can fight. If they kill me, it is nuthin'" (52–53). Enshrining Tom's death as an act of devotion between men, she then reprises that devotion in the reaction of Tom's friend Robert: "Robert followed his friend into the hospital, tenderly and carefully helped to lay him down, and remained awhile, gazing in silent grief upon the sufferer" (53). When Tom worsens, "Robert entered the room, and seating himself quietly by Tom's bedside, read the death signs in his face. 'Good-bye, Robert,' said Tom, 'meet me in de kingdom'" (55). As with John's death in *Hospital Sketches,* the language creates a homosocial world of tenderness between men. Also as with Alcott, this homosociality occurs within a larger context of male feminization. Before he himself is wounded, Tom cares for others, as the soldier reports: "[W]hen he brought in that wounded scout, he couldn't have been more tender if he had been a woman. How gratefully the poor fellow looked in Tom's face as he laid him down so carefully and staunched the blood which had been spurting out of him" (50–51). Like Alcott's "manly" John, the hero of *Hospital Sketches,* Harper's Tom is all the more masculine for his proximity to feminine traits.

Here, too, the heroic soldier is inseparable from the nurse who cares for him. Iola Leroy is not only Tom's deathbed nurse but the source of inspiration for his wartime heroism: "[H]e loved Iola. And he never thought he could do too much for the soldiers who had rescued her and were bringing deliverance to his race" (40). Injured, he is comforted by her: "He recognized her when restored to consciousness, and her presence was balm to his wounds" (53). As he fades, "she wiped the death damps from his dusky brow, and imprinted upon it a farewell kiss" (54–55). With Iola's touch "imprinted" upon dying soldiers, Harper imprints the figure of the nurse upon an episode of male heroism. As Alcott's Tribulation Periwinkle nurses her "boys," turning the war setting into a domestic space, so too does Iola feminize the Civil War.

Yet feminization in *Iola Leroy* operates in a very different context than in *Hospital Sketches*. While both Alcott and Harper feminize male soldiers to bring them within a domestic orbit, Harper's feminized men may also function to counter racist stereotypes of black men as violently hypermasculine.[27] The racial context for feminization also alters the image of the Civil War nurse in *Iola Leroy*. Alcott's nurse enters into the hospital from the security of an established domestic space; the home front is a sphere that she already inhabits and whose boundaries she wishes to expand. Iola, by contrast, has been denied secure domesticity, as she states: "Instead of coming into this hospital a self-sacrificing woman, laying her every gift and advantage upon the altar of her country, I came as a rescued slave, glad to find a refuge from a fate more cruel than death" (113). Rather than simply stepping into the role of white nurse, Iola finds in the hospital both a "refuge" from slavery and an arena for struggle against it. Her nursing efforts in turn align, across class, with the war work of other black women in the novel, such as Aunt Linda, who sells food to Union soldiers as they come through the South, and an unnamed woman who works as a laundress and spy. With these characters, Harper revises both white women's stories of feminization and black men's stories of male heroism.

Like her contemporaries, moreover, Harper plots the war specifically in relation to black mothers. Harper had experimented with this alignment in her serialized novella *Minnie's Sacrifice* (1869). The earlier story features parallel plots of two light-skinned characters, Louis and Minnie, both born of slave mothers and white fathers and raised in the North as white. As the Civil War begins, they meet, fall in love, learn separately of their true racial origins and choose to identify as black; married, they return after war's end to the South, where Minnie is killed by the Ku Klux Klan. The parallel turning-points of *Minnie's Sacrifice*, its dual revelations of blackness, are both characterized in terms of new maternal identifications. Minnie reunites with her mother after the older woman is brought North by Union soldiers: "I have found you, at last, my dear, darling, long-lost child. Minnie, is this you, and have I found

you at last?"[28] Louis's mother is dead, but he effects a symbolic switch from
one maternal legacy to another. Initially committed to Confederate politics,
he "feels a sense of honor in defending the South. She is his mother, she says,
and that man is an ingrate who will not stand by his mother and defend her
when she is in peril" (36). Informed of his true origins after the war begins,
however, he chooses to stand by his literal black mother rather than the metaphorically maternal white South: "I can never raise my hand against my mother's race" (60). For both characters, the Civil War is inseparable from black
motherhood, with the war literally relocating one mother near her child and
symbolically bringing another into existence.

In *Iola Leroy,* Harper deepens this conjunction between the Civil War and
mothers, embedding the war in a matrix of maternal stories. Before the war
begins, Iola identifies hostility to slavery with her mother: "I know mamma
don't like slavery very much. . . . My father does not think as she does" (98).
The war enters Iola's life simultaneously with her father's death and her mother's disappearance; its presence in her life, as in the childhoods of Burton and
Drumgoold, parallels her quest for reunion with her mother. Nursing Tom,
she thinks, "You are the best friend I have had since I was torn from my
mother" (54). When the white Dr. Gresham proposes marriage to her in the
midst of their war experience, he frames it as a maternal recovery: "What is
to hinder you from sharing my Northern home, from having my mother to
be your mother?" (116). Her response underscores the importance of mothers:
"Oh, you do not know how hungry my heart is for my mother!" (117). The
end of the war brings the realization of this desire, as Iola announces "I am
on my way South seeking for my mother, and I shall not give up until I find
her" (168). When she and her mother are at last reunited, "Marie rushed forward, clasped Iola in her arms and sobbed out her joy in broken words" (195).

Maternal search defines not only Iola's experience of war but that of the
men who fight it. The soldiers in the novel are often portrayed in relation to
their mothers. One character named Ben, for example, longs to join the army,
but his greater devotion is to his mother: "My mother . . . is the only thing
that keeps me from going. If it had not been for her, I would have gone long
ago. She's all I've got, an' I'm all she's got . . . while I love freedom more than
a child loves its mother's milk, I've made up my mind to stay on the plantation"
(30–31). For other soldiers, participating in the war is a way of claiming both
freedom and "mother's milk." Debating whether to run off to war, Robert
asserts early in the novel, "I ain't got nothing 'gainst my ole Miss, except she
sold my mother from me. And a boy ain't nothin' without his mother" (17–
18). When he wakes up after being wounded, he assumes Iola is his mother

rather than recognizing her as his niece. Meanwhile, Harry has joined a black regiment because it is the one most likely to reunite him with his mother; wounded, he wakes up to find a nurse bending over him, and shouts "Mamma; oh, mamma! have I found you at last?" (191). The active search for mothers unites the novel's male and female characters and its middle-class and folk cultures, functioning as an organized framework for the novel as a whole. Lost and found, the black mother serves as a metaphor for the familial dislocations of slavery and for the struggles of the war. Accordingly, Iola's own goals for the Reconstruction era emphasize—as she titles a speech after the war—"The Education of Mothers." It is only when mothers have been found that Reconstruction can truly begin.

As a historical novel of the Civil War, then, Harper's text executes a series of generic maneuvers that crosscut race and gender, extending the interests of her contemporaries and her own earlier writings in new fictional form. In a novel that consistently thematizes the need to rewrite the war story, Harper recasts both white and black male narratives of combat, making black women central actors in the war. The figure of the black nurse also transforms white versions of feminization. Iola's feminizing efforts are a directed form of racial struggle, while in a narrative that links fighting with mothering, nursing is a crucial hinge between both realms. Throughout the story, mothering is the lens through which Harper filters her wartime plot. An elusive figure, the figure of the black mother turns the war into a maternal quest for women, a familial quest for the slave community as a whole, and an opportunity to rewrite the fictional forms of war narrative with a black female signature.

IV

Reshaping the Civil War as a story about mothers, *Iola Leroy* is also a narrative of embattled daughters. Iola Leroy's quest for her mother is only one of her many struggles given metaphorical shape, I suggest, from the Civil War. Exploring the symbolic possibilities of internal conflict, national and individual, Harper situates Iola at the center of a variety of "civil wars"—from interracial rape to intraracial marriage—that parallel and intersect the declared conflict of North and South.

Harper had already begun to explore the metaphoric conjunction between the conflicts of the Civil War and individual struggles over identity in *Minnie's Sacrifice*. In the earlier text, the revelation of Louis's·mixed-race background catalyzes not only a new declaration of maternal loyalty but a sustained inner conflict over regional loyalties. Initially, Louis enlists enthusiastically in the Confederate army, but his new knowledge of his origins prompts a crisis over regional as well as racial allegiances:

> [If] he belonged to the race he would not join its oppressors. And yet his whole sympathy had been so completely with them, that he felt that he had no feeling in common with the North.
>
> And as to the colored people, of course it never entered his mind to join their ranks, and ally himself to them; he had always regarded them as inferior . . . (61)

Lodged in a liminal zone between armies, Louis decides that "he would face the perils of re-capture rather than the contempt of his own soul" (61), and he deserts from his Confederate regiment, "guiding himself northward at night by the light of the stars and a little pocket compass" (62). This clandestine nighttime journey northward resonates with accounts of slave escapes, inaugurating an affiliation between Louis and African-Americans that the remainder of his journey openly develops. Representing himself as a Union soldier, Louis is assisted en route by sympathetic slaves, and for the first time, he appreciates black commitments to freedom. He is particularly moved by one "colored man," who helps him to evade bloodhounds on his trail by "[cutting] his own feet so that the blood from them might deepen the scent on one track, and throw them off from Louis's path" (64). While the success of this gesture literally depends on the difference between the two men's blood, its symbolic significance lies in the assertion of common blood between them. In this symbolic joining of the unnamed "colored man" and the light-skinned mulatto, a literal journey out of the Confederacy enables a symbolic departure from whiteness.

Accordingly, Louis's arrival in the North cements his dual commitments to the Union army and blackness. Crossing the boundary to Union territory, he enters a zone of symbolic freedom: "[A]t last Louis got beyond the borders of the Confederacy, and stood once more on free soil, appreciating that section as he had never done before" (65). Geography and identity intertwine, as Louis's literal boundary-crossing signal his new eagerness "to benefit that race to whom he felt he owed his life, and with whom he was connected by lineage" (65). Inspired by the events at Fort Wagner, he enlists in the Union army, and while Harper does not specify whether he joins a black regiment, his military service clearly involves contact with black heroism: "Hitherto Louis had known the race by their tenderness and compassion, but the war gave him an opportunity to become acquainted with men brave to do, brave to dare, and brave to die" (67). By the end of the war, Louis is unswerving in his identification with struggles for black freedom, the "cause he had learned to love" (68). In *Minnie's Sacrifice,* then, Harper presents the Civil War as both symbol and catalyst for struggles over individual identity. The national conflict at once mirrors Louis's own racial crisis and stimulates him to cross over the borders of his own racial background.

In *Iola Leroy,* Frances Harper resituates this metaphoric alignment between national and individual "civil wars" on issues central to African-American women. Primary among these is the vulnerability of black women to rape from white men, an issue that stands, Darlene Clark Hine has suggested, at the heart of black women's self-presentation at the turn of the century.[29] In *Iola Leroy,* the violent outer limits of "civil wars" are marked by the threat of inter-racial rape. Iola's experience of the Civil War begins with her descent into slavery, an experience that immediately catapults her into her own battle against rape. She is introduced as a woman "held in durance vile by her reckless and selfish master, who had tried in vain to drag her down to his own low level of sin and shame" (38–39). Tom's description a few pages later makes clear that Iola is actively battling her white master's sexual advances:

"One day when he com'd down to breakfas', he chucked her under de chin, an' tried to put his arm roun' her waist. But she jis' frew it off like a chunk ob fire. She looked like a snake had bit her. Her eyes fairly spit fire. Her face got red ez blood, an' den she turned so pale I thought she war gwine to faint, but she didn't, an' I yered her say, 'I'll die fust.'" (41)

This passage is congruent with the language of battle: the master strikes a blow; she ignites like "fire" and throws it off; she heroically declares that she would "die fust," as though she were a soldier preparing for death. Like Octavia Albert's Aunt Charlotte, Iola's struggles situate slavery as an antebellum war zone for women. As the Confederate and Union armies do battle, Iola and her white master engage in their own war, no less ferocious for being outside the perimeters of official combat.

If interracial rape marks the endpoint on this spectrum of civil wars, Harper suggests that interracial marriages in a context of slavery mark a potential conflict only slightly less oppressive. Iola's parents, Marie and Eugene, join together voluntarily in an interracial union, in which there is no suggestion of rape. When they first marry, Marie is overjoyed: "Instead of being a lonely slave girl, with the fatal dower of beauty, liable to be bought and sold, exchanged and bartered, she was to be the wife of a wealthy planter; a man in whose honor she could confide, and on whose love she could lean" (74–75). Yet the contrast between slave and wife is not absolute, since Marie's willingness to "lean" blindly on Eugene is ultimately disastrous. After his death, she is at the mercy of his cousin, and she learns too late that the slave system exercises an all-powerful hold on black women, even though they may hope to insulate themselves from it. Marie's story illustrates the risks for women of not doing active battle with the slave system. This attitude is exemplified in the indifference of her response to the declared war: "'A civil war?' exclaimed Marie, with an air of astonishment. 'A civil war about what?'" (87).

The result of this marriage, Iola appears, in the words of Tom Anderson, "putty. Beautiful long hair comes way down her back; putty blue eyes, an' jis' ez white ez anybody's in dis place" (38). Like Louis in *Minnie's Sacrifice*, Iola's mixed-race status represents a symbolic civil war over racial identity. As a woman, moreover, she is also at the center of conflicts over gender, with her light-skinned appearance—the symbolic "putty" of femininity—occasioning crises of definition among white observers. The white Dr. Gresham remarks in puzzlement to his superior that he saw her kiss the dying Tom Anderson:

> She is one of the most refined and lady-like women I ever saw. . . . Her accent is slightly Southern, but her manner is Northern. . . . Without being the least gloomy, her face at times is pervaded by an air of inexpressible sadness . . . I cannot understand how a Southern lady, whose education and manners stamp her as a woman of fine culture and good breeding, could consent to occupy the position she so faithfully holds. It is a mystery I cannot solve. (57)

This passage situates Iola at the center of conflicts of region and class as well as race. To Gresham, Iola's apparent whiteness is reinforced by her "refined and lady-like status," an elite class affiliation in turn consolidated by her regional affinity with the "Southern lady." Yet Iola's willingness to touch black bodies and to undertake the unrefined physical duties of a nurse contradicts these signifiers of identity. At this moment, Iola's conflicted biregionalism— the contradiction between her "Northern manner" and "Southern accent"— symbolically brings into view the "civil wars" between blackness and whiteness that the reader, unlike Gresham, already knows to be in place.

When Gresham learns the reason for Iola's mysterious contradictions, his response generates new forms of internal conflict for both characters. Gresham at first recoils from Iola, then resolves his inner struggle: "All the manhood and chivalry of his nature arose in her behalf, and he was ready to lay on the altar of her heart his first grand and overmastering love" (110). His subsequent marriage proposal prompts Iola's own psychic struggle: "[S]he fought with her own heart and repressed its rising love. . . . Iola, after a continuous strain upon her nervous system for months, began to suffer from general debility and nervous depression" (111–12). With the rise of Gresham's "manhood," Iola goes into decline, and she seems destined for tragedy. Her symptoms invoke the stereotypical trajectory of the "tragic mulatta," whose racial liminality dooms her to isolation and death.[30]

Yet Harper recasts the terms of the tragic mulatta plot. Iola's refusal of Gresham constitutes a strategic use of what Ann duCille terms the "coupling convention" in black women's fiction, wherein marriage—unrecognized during slavery and a major right of emancipation—functions as a powerful symbol through which to explore questions of female subjectivity and racial identity.[31] When Iola refuses Gresham, she turns away from a life of racial assimilation, if not actual passing, that marriage to Gresham would involve. Instead, she explains to him, "I intend spending my future among the colored people of the South" (234). Iola's rejection of Gresham also leaves behind the gender inequality that his model of marriage would represent. When Gresham implores, "Consent to be mine, as nothing else on earth is mine" (112), his invitation combines the claims of patriarchal authority with those of slavery. In contrast to her mother, who had looked for a man "on whom she could lean," Iola refuses this model of marriage. Turning down an "overmastering" love, she chooses instead to be her own master.

While Gresham's unacceptable proposal reprises the rhetoric of the white master, Harper is also concerned to suggest that gender conflict is not simply confined to relations between white men and black women: it is its own axis of struggle, circulating within white and black communities. The war frames gender struggles both between white characters, and—more important for the novel's focus—within black partnerships. The folk community of the novel most overtly enacts such dynamics. Uncle Daniel says of women that "I sometimes think de wuss you treats dem de better dey likes you" (20); after the war's end, Aunt Linda describes a conflict with her husband John in which he "didn't want to let on his wife knowed more dan he did, an' dat he war ruled ober by a woman" (155). Iola, for her part, undergoes a transformation from the "gentle ministrations" of wartime nursing (40) to an assertive mode during Reconstruction that privileges female independence: "I have a theory that every woman ought to know how to earn her own living" (205).

As the Civil War prompts civil wars within Iola, so too does national Reconstruction represent the reconstruction of her subjectivity as an adult woman. Iola further consolidates her commitment to the black community in her friendship with Lucille Delany, to whom, as sister-in-law, she is eventually literal kin. Lucille, who is "grand, brave, intellectual, and religious" (242), is also unambiguously dark-skinned. In allying herself with Lucille, Iola distances herself as far as possible from the white Southern lady, a figure to whom she is otherwise linked in a lineage extending from her mother—a plantation mistress, albeit a reluctant one—to the "ole Miss" who separated Robert from his mother, and to a woman identified as "ole Gundover's wife," in Uncle Daniel's words "de meanest woman dat I eber did see" (27). Iola's wartime turn away from this role echoes indirectly in Aunt Linda's description of the war itself: "I wanted ter re'lize I war free, an' I couldn't, tell I got out er de sight and soun' ob ole Miss" (154). Like Aunt Linda, Iola's war is signaled by her successful flight away from "de sight and soun' ob ole Miss."

Iola's eventual marriage to Dr. Frank Latimer, who is also mixed-race and middle-class, consolidates her new identity. In contrast to Gresham's imagery of love as property, Latimer woos Iola with the lines "To prove myself thy lover / I'd face a world in arms," and she responds, "And prove a good soldier . . . when there is no battle to fight" (269). While these military metaphors are cliches of love poetry, they also mark this marriage as an amicable fight— a truly civil war—between equal partners. From the grim days when she fought with her white master, through her refusal of the "overmastering" Gresham, Iola has entered a new era in which mastery has no place. In her marriage to Latimer, she emerges victorious over the conflicts that would divide her from freedom, equality, and community.

v

The Civil War, I have argued, functions in *Iola Leroy* as a capacious metaphor for struggles about individual identity, framing the internecine conflicts of race and gender—from interracial rape to intraracial marriage—that characterize Iola's story. The novel's historical cognates intimately shape its fictional plots, an intimacy enhanced by the characters' very names. As critics have noted, "Iola" was well known as the journalistic pen name of Ida B. Wells-Barnett, whose name unmistakably symbolized political radicalism. To an attuned black audience, the names of *Iola Leroy* were richly connotative, poised between biography and fiction.[32] I have suggested that the novel's most prominent proper noun—Civil War—similarly flows beyond its referential borders, transforming its characters and plots.

This flow moves in two directions, for Harper's plots of individual identity also offer a direct intervention into national politics. By the time Harper wrote *Iola Leroy,* Civil War stories were an increasingly important feature of contemporary political discourse about race. The longstanding narrative of the Civil War as the "rape" of the South now combined with the racist mythology of black men as potential violators of white womanhood. Overtly targeting black men, this racist mythology also attacked white and black women, subduing white women as passive icons of Southern femininity and demonizing black women as the hypersexual complement to black male aggression.[33] This ideology crystallized in the novels of Thomas Dixon, which were themselves, as suggested earlier, a response to the Northern "invasion" of Harriet Beecher Stowe. While Dixon focused exclusively on the Reconstruction era, D. W. Griffith's film *The Birth of a Nation* (1915) pushed the novelist's plots back to the Civil War itself. *Birth of a Nation* follows *Iola Leroy* by more than two decades, but it merits brief examination here, for it remains the most fully elaborated, starkly realized, and popularly successful example of racist turn-of-the-century representations of the Civil War. Read against *Birth of a Nation*, *Iola Leroy* not only suggests the way the Civil War could serve as a metaphor for black women writers in this era but also comments critically on this metaphoric transfer in reverse.

Civil War films flourished in the early nineteen teens, the fiftieth anniversary of the conflict. Before making *Birth of a Nation*, Griffith had already explored the Civil War in numerous films, including two, *The House with Closed Shutters* (1910) and *Swords and Hearts* (1911), that reprised the theme of Confederate cross-dressing in its most dystopian mode. These films, Susan Courtney has argued, offer anxious elaborations of white male impotence, in which white women are forced to assume the masculinity that cowardly Confederate men lack.[34] In *Birth of a Nation*, however, Griffith represented the Civil War in ways that stabilized gender boundaries along with racial ones. *Birth of a Nation* chronicles the war and early years of Reconstruction through a focus on two families, the Northern Stonemans and Southern Camerons. When the war begins, both families send boys to fight while the women remain at home. The film constructs the war as a regional rape of the South: one title, for example, bemoans the "torch of war against the breast of Atlanta." The second half of *Birth of a Nation* realigns this motif of rape in racial terms. Griffith imagines the rise of the black rapist as the inevitable consequence of emancipation and celebrates the founding of the Ku Klux Klan, "the organization that saved the South from anarchy." The narrative moves from literal rape threats against specific women—particularly young Flora Cameron, who kills herself rather than be raped by the mulatto Gus—to a metaphoric rape sequence in which black men struggle to enter a cabin, inside of which white men and women cower fearfully. Arriving just in time to rescue the whites, the Klan acts as savior. The Klan's triumph at the moment of this second "rape" remasculinizes the white South, which is now able to win the war it had lost once before.[35]

Both Griffith's film and Dixon's novels were repeatedly attacked by African-Americans of the era. The film *The Birth of a Race* (1918), for example, began as an attempt by black activists to revise *Birth of a Nation;* while this project was compromised by the constraints of white Hollywood, Oscar Micheaux would independently make a body of films that comprehensively countered the racist vision of Griffith.[36] Direct literary protests against Dixon and Griffith flourished. Gertrude Dorsey-Browne's 1901 serialized novella "A Case of Measure for Measure," for example, directly cited "Mr. Dixon" and "such unhealthy compositions as . . . 'The Clansman' " in the course of its ingenious plot, in which racist whites "black up" for a costume ball and then, literally stained by their racist fantasies, cannot remove their coloration; the makers of the staining dye, an African-American couple, are the story's shrewd and triumphant heroes.[37] Carrie Williams Clifford's poems "A Reply to Thos. Dixon" (1911) and "The Birth of a Nation" (1922) offered angry retorts to Dixon and Griffith; "Birth," for example, closed with the threat that "your acts soon or late, / Will reap a bounteous harvest,—hate for hate."[38] Less directly, black women at the turn of the century contested the racist discourses that Dixon and Griffith reflected and fostered. Ida B. Wells-Barnett, for example, attacked lynching by constructing an alternative discourse of masculinity in which white men who participated in or did not protest lynching demonstrated a failure of manhood, while black men represented the apotheosis of true masculinity.[39]

Like Wells-Barnett's journalistic "Iola," Frances Harper's fictional Iola constructed a counternarrative to the racist imagery later articulated by Dixon and adapted by Griffith. Like *Birth of a Nation, Iola Leroy* intertwines war, race, and rape, but Harper posits precisely opposite conjunctions of these terms. In Griffith's film, rape is metaphorically perpetrated on the white South during the Civil War and on white women after it; black women are represented by the character of Lydia, the hypersexual and hysterical mulatta mistress of a pro-black Northern senator. Harper, by contrast, represents rape as a literal structure of oppression perpetrated against black women in the antebellum South. For Iola, the arrival of the Union army signals the North's decision to take up institutionally the battle that she has already been fighting against rape: "The last man in whose clutches I found myself was mean, brutal, and cruel. I was in his power when the Union army came into C——" (196). Rather than effecting a metaphorical "rape" of the white South, the Civil War exposes the white South's literal rape of black women.

Harper also combats the other half of this equation—the supposed black rapist of the Reconstruction South—by contrasting the image of the antebellum white rapist with that of the novel's black men, for whom the war years bring an opportunity to forge a positive masculinity. Her narrator emphasizes that wartime heroism did not involve unsanctioned violence: although "fragile women and helpless children were left on the plantations," the slaves "refrained from violence" (9). Like Wells-Barnett, Harper frames black manhood as heroic, a heroism that carries over into the Reconstruction era, when Robert wants "the young folks to keep their brains clear, and their right arms strong, to fight the battles of life manfully" (170). Later, Dr. Latimer hears about a young black man fired for refusing to strew flowers before Jefferson Davis and reasserts the importance of having "our boys . . . grow up manly citizens, and not cringing sycophants" (242). Latimer's comment suggests that the nonviolent restraint of black men has its own limits, stopping short of feminized "cringing" before an icon of the slave South. In *Iola Leroy*, the Civil War offers a doubly-bounded education in black masculinity, graduating "manly citizens" who neither attack white women nor honor racist white men.

Reconstruction, in this context, does appear as a new war, but it is continuous with the values of the Civil War, not—as in the cultural account that Griffith helped to crystallize—an antagonistic reenactment of it. After the war, Gresham describes the arrival of "numbers of excellent and superior women . . . from the North to engage as teachers of the freed people" (145); these women are "a new army that had come with an invasion of ideas" (146). Harry also "joined the new army of Northern teachers" (192), and Iola "found a place in the great army of bread-winners" (211). In contrast to Griffith's armylike Klan, which stands as antagonist to the outcome of the earlier Civil War, Harper presents a "great army" whose struggles continue not one but two earlier wars: the antebellum struggles of resistance to slavery and the official battles of the Civil War itself.

As Harper inverts the Southern strategy of using rape plots for racist and misogynist ends, her marriage plots also rework white Northern visions of the war as a regional romance. Conventionally, in such plots, the wooer was white, Northern, and male; the wooed, white, Southern, and female. The Northern victory at the end of the war symbolized happy marriage, with the marital union standing in for the newly forged reunion of the nation.[40] *Iola Leroy* initially offers such a plot: the marriage proposal of Dr. Gresham, a Northerner, to the Southern Iola. While Iola's rejection of Gresham functions to revise the "tragic mulatta" plot of doomed interracial love, this refusal also recasts national allegory. For with its white Northern husband and light-skinned Southern wife, the Leroy/Gresham marriage would come close to replicating the whiteness of Northern marriage plots. Rejecting this plot, Harper instead foregrounds two black couples: Iola and Latimer, and Harry and Lucille. These unions, moreover, confound any straightforward regional alignments. Iola and Harry are Southerners who travel North and return

South, while Latimer and Lucille are Northerners who go South; both couples ultimately return to North Carolina. In these geographic circulations, Harper's couples reclaim both North and South as territory available to black people in fiction as in fact. Recoloring national allegory, she continues the project of "present[ing] the negro," as she elsewhere declared, "not as a mere dependent asking for Northern sympathy or Southern compassion, but as a member of the body politic who has a claim upon the nation for justice."[41]

Both couples, moreover, feature black women who remain relatively auton-omous rather than ceding to male authority. Indeed, the very center of the reconstructed nation will be, in Reverend Eustace's words, a "union of women with the warmest hearts and clearest brains" (254). The phrase "union of women" suggests the extent to which Harper resists the conventional gender dynamics, as well as the whiteness, of regional metaphor. Romances of sec-tional reconciliation were traditionally vested in the "male" term ("North" or "husband"), which then subsumed its "female" term ("South" or "wife"). In *Iola Leroy*, by contrast, women not only remain unsubordinated within the marital and national union: they form its core "union of women." As it explic-itly challenges racist Southern formulations like those of Dixon and Griffith, the novel carefully rewrites the race and gender terms of ostensibly more sym-pathetic Northern Civil War discourse as well.

At the end of *Iola Leroy*, Harper self-reflexively thematizes this project of rewriting national allegory. In *Minnie's Sacrifice*, Harper's heroine declares that "the South will never be rightly conquered until another army should take the field, and that must be an army of civilizers; the army of the pen, and not the sword. . . . [A]s soon as she possibly could she intended to join that great army" (68). Minnie dies shortly thereafter, but in *Iola Leroy*, Harper's female protagonist prepares to "join that great army," and Iola is poised, near the novel's end, to become a writer. Encouraging her, Latimer declares that "out of the race must come its own thinkers and writers . . . it seems to be almost impossible for a white man to put himself completely in our place" (263). Iola laughingly promises that "[W]hen I write a book I shall take you for the hero of my story," whereupon he responds, "Why, what have I done . . . that you should impale me on your pen?" (263).

This exchange brings the novel's multiple "civil war" plots to fruition, mili-tarizing literary representation as a sphere of both national and personal con-flict. In national terms, Iola's future writing stands to effect a literary version of the Civil War, fulfilling the logic wherein an "army of the pen" would "rightly [conquer]" the South. This exchange also legitimates the woman writer. In Latimer's query about being "impale[d]" on Iola's pen, he symboli-cally, if anxiously, grants her symbolic leadership. As a commentary on Harper herself, the moment provisionally promises the black woman writer the power to command "the army of the pen," emerging from her own civil wars victorious.

VI

War-formation and self-formation, then, stand in a dialectical relation in *Iola Leroy*. In a reciprocal use of metaphor, *Iola Leroy* simultaneously employs the war as a metaphor for identity and offers a novelistic plot of individual identity that metaphorically restages the war itself. For all the battles that Harper wins, however, there are also some internal struggles that *Iola Leroy* evades or suppresses. Harper concentrates only on the later years of the Civil War, evading the era of overt white opposition to black enlistment. She also sidesteps the ongoing issue of programmatic racism within the Union army and among its white supporters—the same supporters who might comprise part of the audience for *Iola Leroy*. A white audience, no doubt, wanted reminders of the successful integration of the army, not of that army's exclusion of and hostility toward black soldiers. While the novel deliberately addresses a black audience as well, that address takes particular didactic form: as William Still's original introduction to the novel declares, "Doubtless the thousands of colored Sunday-schools in the South, in casting about for an interesting, moral storybook . . . will not be content to be without *Iola Leroy*" (3). As "moral storybook," the novel's vision of black advancement is centered on a heroine who, in Deborah E. McDowell's words, "comes to resemble a human being less and less and a saint more and more."[42] With a saintly heroine and a sanitized army, the novel constructs a civil Civil War indeed.

These circumscriptions, I suggest, point toward a final, underlying civil war within the novel: its struggles within a turn-of-the-century discourse of black female civility. I argued earlier that Anna Julia Cooper's articulation of civility in *A Voice from the South* serves as a powerful corrective to the racism that relegated black women to the role of uncivilized "Topsy." More generally, civility served black women writers in this era as a powerful language through which to articulate political demands. While civility applied to both black men and women, its relevance for women was redoubled in a culture that thwarted their access to more public expressions of citizenship, such as suffrage. As Ann duCille and Claudia Tate have shown, civility often functions in black women's writings as a pivot between ostensibly private concerns and the public sphere. DuCille focuses on the role of marriage as the "calling card" of civility, while Tate emphasizes the close ties between black women and another mechanism of civility: etiquette. At the turn of the century, as uplift ideology spread, etiquette manuals for African-Americans proliferated. Citing the popularity of books such as *Golden Thoughts on Chastity and Procreation* (1903), Tate argues that the language of etiquette provided black women access to issues of gender and racial equality.[43]

Yet if civility profited black women as a powerful language for political reform, it also exacted high costs. As Kevin K. Gaines notes, racial uplift ideology relied on both psychological and social forms of internal repression, with a focus on middle-class respectability often producing feelings of shame and anger that were displaced onto other African-Americans.[44] For black women, the potentially repressive dynamics of racial uplift conjoined exacting standards for appropriate racial behavior with those of acceptable femininity. These standards of black civility were taught by other women and internalized. Mary Church Terrell, for example, recalled a childhood incident when, after being mistreated by a racist train conductor, she tearfully explained the event to her mother in terms of her own behavior:

> I assured [my mother] I had been careful to do everything she told me to do. For instance, my hands were clean and so was my face. I hadn't mussed my hair; it was brushed back and was perfectly smooth. . . . I hadn't soiled my dress a single bit. I was sitting up "straight and proper" . . . I wasn't talking loud. In short, I assured my mother I was "behaving like a little lady," as she told me to do.[45]

Terrell's recollection suggests the painful consequences of civility for black girls, as a mode whose aim of black uplift in the face of racism results instead in rigorous self-policing between and within women. The self-consuming consequences of these disciplinary imperatives emerge with startling clarity in the 1891 conduct manual entitled *Don't. A Book for Girls*, which articulates a dizzying number of rules for young black women to teach themselves.

Written by Robert Benjamin, a prominent black attorney in California, *Don't* promises its intended audience an all-important role in racial uplift: "GIRLS this little book is addressed to you; the future destiny of the race is in your hand."[46] Yet Benjamin's hand-off to girls consists of numerous behavioral injunctions against unacceptable words, deeds, and thoughts, each introduced with the capitalized imperative DON'T. So thorough is his catalogue that femininity seems to consist entirely in self-negation, from "DON'T talk about yourself or your affairs" (47) to "DON'T anticipate too much; disappointment is not pleasant" (7). As this latter warning suggests, the greatest threat to girls is their capacity for desire of any kind: "Vague unrest and formless needs will disturb your inner life. Your safety lies in discerning the danger and watching

against it with determined and sleepless vigilance" (7). Advising girls to police
their own unconscious, Benjamin further reinforces these relentless imperatives through his consistent address to the book's readers. Self-reflexive injunctions scattered throughout the book caution, "DON'T expect to find in this
little book anything except a few practical hints of every day concern to yourself" (7), "DON'T be impatient, I am coming to the point" (12), and, in a
preemptive strike against a resisting reader, "DON'T say that these *don'ts* are
not spoken to you in the kindest manner" (51). The project of racial uplift that
is Benjamin's ostensible aim seems virtually eclipsed by his model of repressing
the female self. By the end of *DON'T*, it is difficult to see how girls will change
the "destiny of the race" when they have been rendered—and are henceforth
expected to render themselves—so thoroughly speechless.

   DON'T appears to occupy a different ideological universe from *Iola Leroy*, whose sixty-seven-year-old author was far removed from Benjamin's intended audience of girls and whose narrative advocates self-assertion throughout. So thoroughly did Harper's career as public speaker transgress the dicta
of female "don'ts" that her audiences could not reconcile her words with her
body: "I don't know but that you would laugh," she wrote to William Still in
1871 in a now well-known passage, "if you were to hear some of the remarks
which my lectures call forth: 'She is a man,' again 'She is not colored, she is
painted.'"[47] Yet Harper's career also registers her strategic uses of civility. Carla
L. Peterson has suggested that in order to counter attacks on her public speaking, Harper developed an oratorical style that emphasized modesty and chaste
femininity, consciously manipulating female civility for radical political ends.[48]
And in an 1898 essay, Harper extolled the virtues of a key feature of civility:
politeness. In terms nearly identical to Anna Julia Cooper's praise of manners,
Harper suggests that "true politeness has a mission everywhere": "The truly
polite woman has no snub in her voice nor scorn upon her lips for those who
occupy a lower social grade than herself." Performing civility in her own public
persona, Harper here exhorted black women to be civilizing agents for others.[49]

   More ambiguously, however, Harper's writing also suggests the implications of civility as a discourse of self-restraint whose terms could thwart as
well as legitimate political claims. In the 1893 speech "Woman's Political Future," for example, she prophesies that "[I]n the political future of our nation
woman will not have done what she could if she does not endeavor to have
our republic stand foremost among the nations of the earth, wearing sobriety
as a crown and righteousness as a garment and a girdle."[50] This rhetoric offers
a two-tiered promise of female authority, with Harper's allegorical invocation
of a female America buttressed by her literal address to women activists who
will realize this vision. Like Stowe's vision of Topsy becoming an African

missionary, the image projects imperial expansion, with America standing "foremost among the nations of the earth." However, Harper's female republic is authorized by a "girdle" of "righteousness," a metaphor that symbolically restrains her figurative female body. Like Anna Julia Cooper, Harper critiques the racist legacy of a figure like Topsy but also reproduces its internal contradictions. In this moment at least, America assumes the radical rhetorical form of a black female speaker, but she is able to stand as a statue of liberty only by corseting herself.

The shaping force of the female girdle emerges more fully in *Trial and Triumph* (1888–89), another of Harper's serialized novellas. *Trial and Triumph* is the coming-of-age story of Annette Harcourt, an African-American girl raised by her grandmother, Susan Harcourt, after the death of Annette's abandoned mother. *Trial and Triumph* can be interpreted as a narrative of female self-civilizing that at once prepares for the more ambitious *Iola Leroy* and offers important insights into what Iola Leroy, in winning her own civil wars, will also lose.

From the start, *Trial and Triumph* characterizes Annette as a problem child whose problem is her excessive will. "Oh, that child! She is the very torment of my life," laments her grandmother in the novella's opening lines, "She is the most mischievous and hard-headed child I ever saw."[51] Though Susan has successfully raised five children to accomplished self-sufficiency—one son is a doctor; her daughters are seamstresses—her granddaughter's "hard head" resists all her attempts at discipline: "I hardly know what to do with her. I've scolded and scolded till my tongue is tired [and] whipping don't seem to do her a bit of good" (180). Annette remains impenitent, and when Susan asks, "[W]hat makes you behave so bad?" she responds, "I don't know, grandma, I 'specs I did it for the devil. The preacher said the devil makes people do bad things" (183). Annette's recitation of her preacher's words bespeaks a general talent for mockery and mimicry, with Susan admonishing "I want you to behave yourself and don't roll up your eyes at [a neighbor] and giggle at her and make ugly speeches" (195). With her catalogue of inversions, Annette suggests a strategic revision of the character of Topsy in the context of racial uplift. Whereas Stowe's character is a racist projection of white women's fantasies, Annette functions as a reflection of conflicts over civility among black communities and within black women themselves.[52]

As Annette grows, her incivility expands. Two years pass and Annette, now fifteen, becomes a figure of community ridicule; as one unfriendly townswoman gossips, "They all say that she is very odd and queer and often goes out into the street as if she never saw a looking glass. . . . Why, Annette just makes herself a perfect laughingstock" (230). This language recalls Alcott as well as Stowe: like Jo of *Little Women*, Annette is "odd and queer," but with the stakes of female misbehavior dramatically heightened in an African-American context. To her own community, Annette's unruliness threatens to reinforce racist stereotypes, shaped by minstrelsy, of black people as "laughingstocks." Annette is now also an avid poet, an activity that her grandmother describes as yet another form of transgressive behavior: "She's got too many airs for a girl in her condition. She talks about writing a book, and she is always trying to make up what she calls poetry. I expect that she will go crazy some of these days" (228). Never looking at looking-glasses yet putting on "airs," Annette's self-management is poorly calibrated in two directions. She is at once insufficiently self-aware and too self-absorbed.

Having developed Annette so fully as an emblem of misbehavior, the narrative's project is to turn her right-side up. She blossoms under the maternal support of a mentor, Mrs. Lasette, whose own even temper becomes a source of mirror-like identification: "Oh Mrs. Lasette," admires Annette, "you are too sweet for anything. I wish I was like you" (218). School also begins to influence Annette, and after another year, she has become "very much changed in her conduct and character" (240). When she is chosen to deliver her commencement speech, the event highlights her new self:

> Simply attired in a dress which Mrs. Lasette thought fitted for the occasion, Annette took her seat quietly on the platform and calmly waited till her turn came. Her subject was announced: "The Mission of the Negro." It was a remarkable production for a girl her age. . . . Men grew thoughtful and attentive, women tender and sympathetic as they heard this member of a once despised people, recount the trials and triumphs of her race, and the hopes that gathered around their future. (240–42)

At this moment, Annette is "fitted for the occasion" in more ways than one, as she successfully channels both her "odd" public behavior and her excessive literary ambitions into public speaking. The project of racial uplift organizes her unruliness in acceptable form, at once propelling her forward into larger political struggles and holding her in place so that she "calmly [waits] her turn." Trained by other women, she now pleases both her censorious grandmother and her warmly maternal mentor. The first of the novella's turning points, the moment represents the "trials and triumphs" not only of Annette's race but also of her reshaped psyche.

If political commitment represents one civilizing force for Annette, then personal renunciation is the other. After a slide into unhappiness, Annette finds emotional reprieve in the form of the "wealthy, handsome, and intelli-

gent" Clarence Luzerne (271), who is drawn to her despite her lingering reputation as "a spitfire" (270). Just as the two are preparing to marry, a first wife
mysteriously surfaces, suffering from "nervous prostration and brain fever"
(276). In this revision of *Jane Eyre*, the first wife recovers to tell a complicated
story of self-arranged disappearance; declaring that "I have sinned; it is right
that I should suffer" (279), she willingly cedes Clarence to Annette. Yet Annette renounces her beloved: "This, Clarence, is the saddest trial of my life
. . . But Clarence, the great end of life is not the attainment of happiness but
the performance of duty and the development of character. The great question
is not what is pleasant but what is right" (280). The moment is Annette's
second turning point, again occasioned by the renunciatory pedagogy of other
women. Trained by one female mentor, Mrs. Lasette, she now follows the
self-abnegating example of the first Mrs. Luzerne.

Like the earlier moment, too, this renunciation focuses on the project of
racial uplift. Annette seeks inspiration in religion and relief work, finding
"opportunity among the freedmen to be a friend and sister to those whose
advantages had been less than hers" (282). In return, she is universally beloved, appreciated in particular for her ability—like that of Alcott's "Mother
Bhaer"—to tame young men: "Before she came my boy was just as wild as a
colt, but now he is jist as stiddy as a judge" (284). At her thirty-first birthday
she stands "Happy and smiling, like one who had passed through suffering
into peace" (284). This is not, however, the very end. Like *Jane Eyre*, *Trial
and Triumph* concludes in marriage, with the widowed Luzerne proposing to
Annette on the novella's final page:

> [H]e had come not to separate her from her cherished life work, but to help her
> in uplifting and helping those among whom her lot was cast as a holy benediction,
> and so after years of trial and pain, their souls had met at last, strengthened by
> duty . . . and fitted for life's highest and holiest truths. (285)

This rhetoric ingeniously politicizes the conclusion of *Jane Eyre*, so that marriage functions not as the private fulfillment of romance but as the declaration
of shared public commitment to racial struggle. Yet in characterizing Annette's
marriage in terms of political selflessness, Harper also cements the disciplinary
project of civilizing her heroine. "Fitted for the occasion" of her first speech,
she is now "fitted for life's highest and holiest truths," an echo that underscores
the corseting impulse implicit even in Annette's most triumphant moments.

In *Trial and Triumph*, then, the internal dynamics of civility both enable
and constrain the novel's radical political vision. As with the earlier movement
from trial into triumph, Annette's final movement from suffering into peace

represents a significant moment of political reform, both among freedpeople and within herself. Her temperamental transformation banishes racist cultural stereotypes associated with both comedy and anger: on the one hand, a minstrel tradition—filtered through Stowe—that renders happy black girls "Topsies"; and on the other hand, a stereotype of black female hypersexuality that links the "spitfire" to the "hot" Jezebel. Yet the genuinely rebellious impulses of the unrestrained child and the creative poet have also disappeared along with the "spitfire" of Annette's young adulthood. This disappearance recalls the transformation of Alcott's undisciplined Jo March into the disciplinary Mother Bhaer, now situated within the collective context of racial uplift. The black heroine's self-mastery is the foundation of Harper's triumphant model of community transformation, but that self-mastery—inculcated and reinforced by other women—necessarily vanquishes the rebellious impulses, angry and comic, that define her earlier self.

In *Iola Leroy*, Iola's civility is similarly double-edged, producing an expansive political vision even as it is produced by implicit psychic contraction. In the novel's final description of Iola, she, like Annette, appears to be at peace:

> Soon after Iola had settled in C——— she quietly took her place in the Sunday-school as a teacher, and in the church as a helper . . . In lowly homes and windowless cabins her visits are always welcome. Little children love her. Old age turns to her for comfort, young girls for guidance, and mothers for counsel. Her life is full of blessedness. (278–79)

Happily ensconced as teacher and helper, Iola will now reproduce her own values of piety and education among others. Part of Harper's ideal "army of civilizers," she is an integral soldier in the war for racial uplift, both agent and object of civility. Yet like the black woman wearing a "girdle" of righteousness among the nations of the earth, Iola's new role is constricting as well as expansive. Extending uplift to "lowly homes," she serves as imperial missionary, but as "helper" working "quietly," she also limits her personal ambitions. This subordinate role speaks partly to the intractability of a patriarchal culture in which men have greater access to the public sphere; in the next paragraph, by contrast, her husband is "more than a successful doctor; he is a true patriot and a good citizen" (279). But Iola's status as "helper" also reflects her own choice of a circumscribed role within the range of opportunities Harper elsewhere outlines for black women. For example, Harper does not characterize Iola in this last description as either a public speaker, a role she occupies earlier in the novel, or as a writer, the project she discusses with Latimer. The avid literary desires of the earlier Annette—desires fulfilled by Harper herself—

are not even present in order to be restrained. While Harper clearly imagines Iola's activities as important, she nonetheless leaves her heroine in a domestic world that represents, relative to the rest of her story, domesticated ambitions.

Similarly, Iola's "quiet" temperament at the novel's close is a far cry from the reader's first glimpse of her as combative and rebellious—like Annette, a "reg'lar spitfire" (38). This Iola is an angry figure; conversely, moving further back into her life story, Harper represents her childhood temperament as comic. When she reunites with her brother Harry and their mother after the war, Harry is shocked to see how much she has changed:

> "And I," said Harry, "can hardly realize that you are our own Iola, whom I recognized as sister a half dozen years ago."
> "Am I so changed?" asked Iola, as a sigh escaped her lips.
> "Why, Iola," said Harry, "you used to be the most harum-scarum girl I ever knew—laughing, dancing, and singing from morning until night."
> "Yes, I remember," said Iola. "It all comes back to me like a dream. . . . I have passed through a fiery ordeal of suffering since then. But it is useless . . . to brood over the past." (195)

"Harum-scarum," Iola's earlier self is described here as carnivalesque, filled with uninhibited expressions of pleasure. While her happy youth sharply contrasts with the horror of her enslavement, the emotions that characterize these two periods—comedy and anger—share a common intensity. By contrast, her later self is far more sedate, her closing "blessedness," like that of Annette, neither comic nor angry. As with the transformation of Annette, this modulation performs important cultural work, banishing the racist legacies of "Topsy" and "Jezebel." Yet in combatting these images, Harper also moderates and modulates Iola, circumscribing her within the regulated emotional world of female civility.

In this psychic war, two forms of internal repression enable Iola's movement away from her earlier self. First, in declaring that "it is useless . . . to brood over the past," Iola displaces her rebellious self to the realm of childhood. This developmental narrative echoes that of *Trial and Triumph*, except that here the displacement is not only temporal but racial, since in childhood Iola knew herself as white. She retroactively aligns merriment with the other false beliefs of her racist white childhood, remembering to Latimer, "I was thinking of the bright, joyous days of my girlhood, when I defended slavery . . . I would not change the Iola of then for the Iola of now" (273). This comment implicitly recasts Iola's childhood pleasures as those of a spoiled Southern white girl.[53] Harper's racial reversal also recalls Anna Julia Cooper's allegorical version of the Civil War, which caricatured the slaveholding South as an obnoxiously strong-willed white girl. Like Cooper, Harper constructs a model of black female civility in which it is the Southern white girl rather than her black counterpart who is the repository of excessive will and desire.

Second, if Iola repudiates her "harum-scarum" behavior by aligning it with her earlier "white" self, then the novel as a whole displaces expressions of excess from its middle-class characters to its black "folk." Describing the arrival of the Union army, for example, Aunt Linda remarks that "[W]e jis' broke loose. Jake turned somersets . . . When he goes down ter git de letters he cuts up all kines ob shines and capers" (11). Turning "somersets" in defiance of their masters, the novel's folk characters invert established orthodoxies throughout, including those of their middle-class black friends as well as their white ex-masters. At the novel's end, for example, Aunt Linda still refuses to learn to read, even though literacy is the sacred touchstone of uplift: "'Oh, yer can't git dat book froo my head, no way you fix it'" (276). While Aunt Linda remains a beloved and venerated figure, this refusal inevitably diminishes her as a model for racial uplift in comparison with the novel's literate middle-class characters. Thus as Iola moves her transgressive pleasures backward toward her white childhood, the novel as a whole also pushes inversion socially "downward" toward the black folk. The body politic of the novel's social world and the psyche of its protagonist converge as realms in which images of inversion—whether "somersets" or "harum-scarum" behavior—are displaced and discredited. As with *Trial and Triumph*, the result is a work whose capacious political vision is founded on both the rebellious energies of its female protagonist and the disciplinary project of their erasure.

In identifying *Iola Leroy*'s affinity with the disciplinary discourse of etiquette books like *Don't*, however, I do not intend thereby to dismiss it, as Houston A. Baker does, as simply "a courtesy book" and "bright Victorian morality in whiteface."[54] Rather, I wish to suggest that the novel's genuine radicalism is inseparable from its internal dynamics of psychic struggle, dynamics that reflect the contradictions of a contemporary discourse of civility predicated on self-restraint. Iola's own triumphant claims to race and gender equality are dependent on, and in turn help to constitute, her interior war over civility. As in *Trial and Triumph*, political advancement is centered on the triumph of a black heroine, but that triumph requires that the heroine—like the reunited nation—be purged of earlier rebellion.

VII

In what little textual evidence remains of Frances Harper's own experience of the Civil War, one anecdote provides a suggestive final emblem of the trials and triumphs that suffuse her Civil War fiction. For Harper, who described herself in the late 1850s as "an old maid,"⁵⁵ the war years brought marriage at age thirty-five, motherhood and stepmotherhood, housework on a struggling farm, and a partial retreat from public activities. Harper remained largely silent about the challenges of combining these activities; her surviving speeches from the era focus, unsurprisingly, on "the great topic of the day—the war."⁵⁶ The death of her husband in 1864, however, created severe hardships which she openly related in an 1866 lecture:

> [M]y husband died in debt, and before he had been in his grave three months, the administrator had swept the milk-crocks and wash tubs from my hands. . . . what could I do, when they had swept all away? *They left me one thing—and that was a looking-glass!* Had I died instead of my husband, how different would have been the result! . . . [N]o administrator would have gone into his house, broken up his home . . . and taken away his means of support.
>   . . . I say, then, that justice is not fulfilled so long as woman is unequal before the law.⁵⁷ [emphasis added]

The symbolic implications of the "looking-glass" reverberate in this passage in several contrasting directions. Harper offers the mirror as literal evidence for the lack of resources accorded black women in a patriarchal and racist culture. Within the discourse of civility as I have been tracing it, the mirror is also a mechanism of self-surveillance from which rebellious women flee. Harper's Annette, who "goes out into the street as if she never saw a looking glass," offers a fantasy of such flight, albeit one quickly circumscribed. It is difficult to know how closely Annette Harcourt and Frances Harper correspond, but *Trial and Triumph*, Frances Smith Foster suggests, may be Harper's most autobiographical novel.⁵⁸

However, the looking-glass in this passage is also, implicitly, a generative emblem of self-scrutiny. In *The Woman in Battle*, Loreta Velazquez's night-time parades before the mirror prompt her picaresque adventures. Velazquez's unabashed celebration of rebellion, her own and that of the Confederacy, is a far cry from the rhetoric of *Iola Leroy;* indeed, Velazquez represents a version of the spoiled Southern white lady whom Harper deplores. But Harper's own mirror was nonetheless productive, literally and symbolically. With this speech, she converted her experience with the mirror into literary capital; more literally, she rebuilt her finances from the nadir of postwar debt into a half-century of self-sufficiency. With her successful career as lecturer, activist, and writer, Harper ventured through the looking-glasses of civility even as her literary heroines struggled within them.

The image of the Civil War looking-glass also returns us to Robert Penn Warren's characterization, in *The Legacy of the Civil War*, of civil wars as double mirrors, which reflect conflicts within societies at war and within the individuals affected by them. If civil wars are like mirrors, then in Frances Harper's writing as I have traced it, the mirror and the civil war not only align but converge, as mutually revealing realms of internecine self-scrutiny. In *Iola Leroy*, the nation is indeed a mirror, one whose reflections are so distorted by racism that its lens must be remade. Harper creates a new mirror of the Civil War, in which the bodies of African-Americans, previously erased or disfigured, dramatically reappear. Her black heroine, civilized and civilizing, is triumphant maker and holder of this mirror.

As the nation at war is like a mirror, so too, for Harper, is the mirror like a warring nation. Imposing self-surveillance, the mirror fractures the woman it reflects into rebellious and restrained selves. The resulting process of self-discipline, necessarily dynamic, is not, however, necessarily complete. In Iola's reminiscences about her "harum-scarum" childhood, memories of her earlier self hover, in the repressed excess of the unconscious, "like a dream." As she reminisces with her mother and brother, the sigh of regret that "[escapes] her lips" is like steam escaping from her psychic engine. These traces of psychological exhaust trail behind *Iola Leroy*, while its heroine propels her reconstituted community triumphantly into the future. As the Civil War itself would be repeatedly reenacted in cultural form, the battle over civility remains, in Harper's novel as in the culture at large, to be fought again and again.

SIX

The Rhett and the Black

Sex and Race in *Gone With the Wind*

I

When the most influential Civil War novel of the twentieth century was being
made into a film, *The New Yorker* subtitled its two-page cartoon "preview" of
the result "Gone with the Birth of a Nation; or, Gold Diggers of 1860."[1] As
this title suggests, the racist nostalgia of D. W. Griffith resurfaces, updated
but intact, in Margaret Mitchell's 1936 novel *Gone With the Wind.* Like Griffith, Mitchell glorifies Southern slaveholders, her elegy for the lost Confederacy emphasized rather than undermined by her portraits of "good" loyal slaves.
From Mammy's "monkey's face" to "the black apes" of postwar Atlanta, the
novel's black characters are defined by their dehumanization.[2] *Gone With the
Wind*'s filmmakers made some changes to the story, but the 1939 result was
so offensive to black spectators that Malcolm X, for one, remembered that
"when Butterfly McQueen went into her act [as Prissy], I felt like crawling
under the rug."[3] The terms of the film's consumption also reprised its racist
inheritance from Griffith. The young Martin Luther King, Jr., first saw the
film when he appeared as one of a group of black children dressed in so-called
"pickaninny" costume on stage for the entertainment of the all-white audience
during the segregated Atlanta premiere of the film.[4] The distance from Griffith's white actors in blackface to this humiliating scene was a chronological
quarter-century but only an ideological minute.[5]

Directly continuing the project of *The Birth of a Nation*, *Gone With the
Wind* bore a more ambiguous relation to another of its predecessors: Harriet
Beecher Stowe's *Uncle Tom's Cabin.* Like Thomas Dixon, Mitchell accompanied her revivification of the Confederacy with an assault on Stowe. In *Gone
With the Wind,* her narrator condemns "smug and condescending" Northerners
for "accepting *Uncle Tom's Cabin* as revelation second only to the Bible" (662);
the author wrote to a fan in Germany, "It makes me very happy to know that

Gone With the Wind is helping refute the impression of the South which people abroad gained from Mrs. Stowe's book."[6] Yet the two novels clearly share thematic terrain on what Leslie Fiedler terms the "inadvertent epic" of American popular culture centered on race, sex, and the Civil War.[7] Like *Uncle Tom's Cabin, Gone With the Wind* not only achieved phenomenal success in its initial form but also generated myriad literary, theatrical, cinematic, and commodity redactions, which continue unabated.

Today, for example, a *Gone With the Wind* fan may buy a dizzying array of commemorative products, both new and original to the era of the novel. In Atlanta, the home of *Gone With the Wind* memorabilia, she may visit "The Road to Tara," a museum wholly devoted to Mitchell, and "Inn Scarlett's Footsteps," a bed-and-breakfast where bedrooms are named for characters in the story. She may journey between these venues via the "Gone With the Wind One Day Tour Package," during which customers "Enjoy the display of GWTW dolls and dream of an 18 inch waist," and, having arrived at the Inn, "choose a hoop skirt, open that parasol and enjoy an old fashioned southern BBQ" with hosts costumed as Scarlett and Rhett. At the 1996 Atlanta Olympics, a Scarlett O'Hara impersonator named Melly Meadows was steadily booked for up to five hundred dollars an hour. From the topsy-turvy doll birthed by *Uncle Tom's Cabin* to the plastic and living dolls of *Gone With the Wind,* a lineage of commodification connects the texts of Stowe and Mitchell as profitable "gold diggers" for their respective eras.[8]

Not coincidentally, the phenomenal popularity of both texts—like the images of the gold digger and the doll—is intimately connected with their relation to women, as authors, characters, and consumers. Like *Uncle Tom's Cabin, Gone With the Wind* is a novel by a woman that represents political crises through upheavals in domestic order, focuses on female protagonists, and is indelibly linked with female readers and viewers. As with *Uncle Tom's Cabin,* moreover, the critical reception of *Gone With the Wind* has been shaped by male anxieties about these associations with women. From the start, *Gone With the Wind*'s male critics both reflected and fostered what Andreas Huyssen has characterized as high culture's projection of hysterical femininity onto mass culture.[9] In its initial reception, Mitchell's novel provoked jeremiads against the successful female author that intertwined the specters of popularity and feminization.

Influential critic Bernard De Voto, for example, was so incensed by the novel that he attacked it three times, first dismissing it in an article entitled "Writing for Money," then disparaging it in a survey of Civil Way fiction, and finally condemning it in an editorial as a book whose sentiments were "commonplace and frequently cheap."[10] Like writers who attacked *Uncle Tom's*

Cabin through assaults on Stowe, these comments linked the circulation of Mitchell's novel in the marketplace with the suggestion of the author's own uncontrolled femininity. In the case of Mitchell, such dismissals focused on her commercial success, in a pattern whereby, as Jane Tompkins summarizes, critics attempted "to strip [*Gone With the Wind*'s] power of its authority by denigrating its object—the popular audience; its rewards—hard cash; and its source—a woman writer."[11] At issue in the reception of *Gone With the Wind* was the impotence of the male writer who had not achieved comparable success. As another critic complained, "[W]hy should we practice five-finger exercises with the English language when a young woman sells a million copies of her first novel[?]"[12] With the serious writing hand presumably connected only to the male body, Margaret Mitchell was fingered from the start as either mercenary hack or unambitious ingenue—fingered, in short, as either gold digger or doll.

Condemned for its feminized popularity, *Gone With the Wind* was specifically expelled from the emerging canon of Civil War fiction. In "Fiction Fights the Civil War," for example, De Voto disparaged Mitchell as a war novelist:

> [*Gone With the Wind*] documents very well the daily life of a society at war and under reconstruction, but its ideas are rudimentary, its author has no eye and no feeling for human character, and its page by page reliance on all the formulas of sentimental romance and all the effects of melodrama is offensive.[13]

Excoriating the eyeless author, De Voto dismisses her novel as a formulaic exercise in romance and melodrama, two feminized genres equated with a lack of literary value. By contrast, De Voto privileged *The Red Badge of Courage*—"an isolated masterpiece" in its era—and *Marching On*, a 1927 novel by James Boyd, although the latter's "weakness is the use of a romantic love story . . . The romantic convention cheapens its context."[14] In De Voto's scale of value, highest praise went to the man who stood alone—as a soldier unprotected in battle, a fictional character unencumbered by "cheap" romance, a novel unpurchased by readers, and an author "isolated" from his literary contemporaries. These criteria not only slighted Mitchell but seem designed to exclude her, as if her "offensive" prompted his defensive canon-formation. As De Voto's response suggests, *Gone With the Wind* was not only denigrated by critics but actively catalyzed the construction of a Civil War canon whose terms devalued women.

Subsequent Civil War criticism reaffirmed Mitchell's place in this scale of value, as suggested in the contrast between the critical fates of *Gone With the Wind* and another novel of sex, race, and romance in the Civil War South.

William Faulkner's *Absalom, Absalom!* was published four months after *Gone With the Wind*, and like Mitchell, Faulkner received mixed reviews; one critic scorned his "unreadable and uncommunicative prose."[15] *Absalom, Absalom!* was also a major commercial failure next to *Gone With the Wind*, leading Faulkner to comment, "I seem to be so out of touch with the Kotex Age here."[16] Faulkner's own reputation has since climbed to a secure place in the canon, while his assessment of Mitchell as the menstrual effluvia at the bottom of the literary body politic has been vindicated. In *The Unwritten War*, for example, Daniel Aaron devoted two half-sentences to Mitchell and a full concluding chapter to Faulkner, musing that "Surely the clues to [the war's] meaning are less likely to be found in . . . historical novels like *Gone With the Wind* (that blend of solid journalism, dogged research, and personal fantasizing) than in Faulkner's novels or in Robert Penn Warren's passionate yet disinterested reflections."[17] Like De Voto, Aaron erected male triumph on the remains of female trash, carefully distinguishing the "passionate yet disinterested reflections" of men from the parenthetical "personal fantasizing" of women. Within the academy, Faulkner and Crane have indisputably trumped Mitchell. As a representative emblem of Civil War fiction—and of American literature as a whole—better a red badge than a Kotex.

As feminist critics have reversed critical neglect of *Uncle Tom's Cabin*, so too have they brought new attention to *Gone With the Wind*, albeit on a much smaller scale. Like recent approaches to *Uncle Tom's Cabin*, critics of *Gone With the Wind* have focused on its relation to women, restoring Mitchell to a literary genealogy of Southern women writers, interpreting her heroine at length, and analyzing rather than dismissing her female fans. Helen Taylor, for example, takes the concept of "personal fantasizing" seriously, in a reader-response study that respectfully considers the pleasures afforded by *Gone With the Wind* to its female fans. In her analysis, *Gone With the Wind*'s romance with the reader is inseparable from its romance plot, whose lack of resolution, Taylor suggests, demands that readers invent their own endings for Scarlett's story.[18] More generally, as feminist analyses of the soap opera, the Harlequin Romance, and the "woman's film" suggest, understanding *Gone With the Wind* means taking seriously the serialized, repeating, or otherwise self-sustaining forms of popular culture addressed to women. Like these cultural forms, *Gone With the Wind* offers endlessly renewable fantasies to its women consumers, fantasies that are literalized in the very setting of Inn Scarlett's Footsteps. Combining two powerful ideals in popular culture addressed to women, the Inn embodies the eternal promise of both romance and domesticity—otherwise known as "bed" and "breakfast."[19]

However, the female fantasies at work in *Gone With the Wind* are inseparable from the story's racism, and responses to the novel and film are sharply segregated by race. Helen Taylor's survey respondents, primarily British, are almost all white, and their responses downplay racial issues in the novel. For those readers and viewers to whom the novel's primary romance is with slavery, however, *Gone With the Wind*'s racism is preeminent. In Octavia E. Butler's science fiction novel *Kindred,* for example, an African-American woman traveling between the 1970s and the antebellum South tries to read *Gone With the Wind* but finds that "its version of happy darkies in tender loving bondage was more than I could stand."[20] Alice Walker's short story, "A Letter of the Times, or Should This Sado-Masochism Be Saved?" extends this critique of the story's racism, positioning *Gone With the Wind*'s popularity among white women as a source of black women's pain. Written in the form of a letter from a black woman, Susan Marie, to an estranged white friend, Lucy, this story begins with the narrator's shock at seeing Lucy at a costume ball: "Such a fine idea, our ball: Come as the feminist you most admire! But I did not know you most admired Scarlett O'Hara and so I was, for a moment, taken aback." Later, she returns to her response as one of profound anger: "[O]nce seeing you dressed as Scarlett, I could not see you. I did not *dare* see you . . . For if I had seen you, Lucy, I'm sure I would have struck you."[21] While Walker's narrator ends with a gesture of reconciliation toward Lucy, her story underscores the impossibility of situating *Gone With the Wind* within a racially undifferentiated framework of female fans. In the long tradition of African-American critique of *Gone With the Wind* to which Walker and Butler belong, one woman's feminist costume is another's unredressed fantasy of slavery.[22]

Yet if analyses of the novel that celebrate Scarlett whitewash the story's racism, then interpretations of *Gone With the Wind* that focus on its depiction of black characters leave untouched its central romance plot. While *Gone With the Wind* is clearly racist in its depiction of black people, analysis of the text's racial formations should not stop there. As recent interpretations of the novel have suggested, images of blackness may also inflect Mitchell's characterization of her white protagonists, a possibility that Joel Williamson poses as the question "How Black Was Rhett Butler?" and Diane Roberts as "How White Is Scarlett?"[23] Other critics have begun to reassess *Gone With the Wind* seriously as a Civil War text, showing that the novel's background of regional conflict is inseparable from its romance foreground.[24] Collectively, these recent approaches suggest that in order to understand the workings of this extraordinarily influential text, critics need to attend not only to its representations of gender, race, and war, but also to the instabilities within these categories and the conflicted relations among them.

Pursuing such an analysis, I argue that whiteness, masculinity, and heterosexuality are internally divided and entwined categories in Mitchell's novel. Whiteness in *Gone With the Wind* is constituted not only by its external contrast to black characters but also and more powerfully by its internal absorption of black traits. At the same time as it separates blackness from black bodies, *Gone With the Wind* simultaneously decouples masculinity from men and eroticism from heterosexuality. The Civil War is both setting and symbol for these volatilities, with the war at once attenuated by Mitchell's seventy-year distance from it and freshly energized by the uses to which she puts it. Like Loreta Velazquez's story, *Gone With the Wind* is a Civil War novel in which Confederate rebellion propels its heroine toward masculinity and the overt abandonment of civility. The racial anxieties that undergird Velazquez's story also structure *Gone With the Wind*, albeit in different ways and to different ends. In *Gone With the Wind*, I suggest, the most significant representation of racial conflict is hidden in plain sight, in a metaphorically interracial romance between the novel's two white protagonists. At stake in this covert civil war is Mitchell's central investment: finding a new language for white women's agency through the mutable racist vocabularies of the Confederate South. Toward this end, *Gone With the Wind*'s romance plot both manages the racial conflicts elsewhere muted in the novel and vivifies a pornographic narrative of white female sexual desire.

More specifically, in what follows, I argue, first, that several features of Mitchell's biography provide a fresh framework for assessing her literary project in *Gone With the Wind*. Mitchell's well-known interest in Civil War history coexisted with her interests in cross-dressing, "vamping," and sexually explicit prose. Together, these interests suggest a literary sensibility shaped by cultural discourses that moved graphically, if asymmetrically, across sexual and racial boundaries. In writing *Gone With the Wind*, Margaret Mitchell was influenced as much by the mobilities of disguise and pornography as by the history of the Confederate body politic.

Turning to the novel, I then claim that Mitchell feminizes and "queers" one male protagonist, Ashley Wilkes, even as she masculinizes her female heroine, Scarlett O'Hara. *Gone With the Wind* is indeed a "girl book," but the girls show up in some unexpected places in the text. These migrations are metaphorically shaped by the Confederate South, whose postwar anxieties about race and gender Mitchell resituates. Dramatizing regional emasculation through Ashley, Mitchell reembodies Southern masculinity in the form of her white heroine.

A complementary form of Confederate remasculinization emerges in the character of Rhett Butler. I argue that Mitchell symbolically darkens her hero, situating Rhett against contemporary images of nonwhite masculinity that range from demonic representations of the mythic black rapist to valorized images of screen idol Rudolph Valentino. The figure of "brown" Rhett mediates among racial anxieties about both exhausted whiteness and rapaciousness blackness. In the relationship between Rhett and Scarlett, moreover, Mitchell symbolically constructs an interracial couple. Energizing sexual fantasies and containing racial anxieties, their romance constitutes the novel's most intimate and complex civil conflict. The story's famous scene of marital rape at once brings this inner civil war to a controlled climax and cannot fully contain it.

This lack of containment extends, as well, to the postnovel life of Mitchell's story. In the final section of the chapter, I analyze three African-American challenges to *Gone With the Wind:* the on- and off-screen negotiations of the film's black actors; the panoramic literary reconstruction of Margaret Walker's novel *Jubilee;* and the photographic imagery of a recent comic parody of the text. Recalling both the directed political critique of Frances Harper and the covert symbolic reversals of Elizabeth Keckley, these African-American responses to *Gone With the Wind* suggest that the racial faultlines of Mitchell's text, while deeply entrenched, are also open to interventions that turn the story topsy-turvy.

II

Margaret Mitchell's official biography is short: born into a prominent Atlanta family in 1900, she attended Smith College briefly; returned to Atlanta, made her debut, and worked for several years as a journalist; married unhappily, divorced, and remarried; wrote *Gone With the Wind,* which was an immediate, enormous success; and spent the next ten years as a beloved Atlanta celebrity until being run over by a taxi in 1949. I will focus here, however, on three unofficial aspects of Margaret Mitchell: her interest in cross-dressing, her adventures as a sexual "vamp," and her enthusiasm for sexology and pornography. Together with her more well-known passion for Civil War history, these issues provide an important context for rethinking gender and sexuality in *Gone With the Wind* as dispersed phenomena, at once cross-gendered, cross-racial, and homoerotic.

In Mitchell's memories of her childhood, the history of the Civil War is inseparable from her immersion in both Confederate fantasy and masculine ritual. As Mitchell later remembered in interviews, she learned a history so partisan that she believed the Confederacy had won the war:

When I was a child I had to hear a lot about the Civil War on Sunday afternoons
. . . . I heard everything in the world except that the Confederates lost the war.
When I was 10 years old, it was a violent shock to learn that General Lee had been
defeated. I didn't believe it when I first heard it and I was indignant. I still find it
hard to believe, so strong are childhood impressions.[25]

Shaped by the ongoing fantasy of Confederate victory, Mitchell's attachment
to the Civil War was also filtered through male camaraderie. At age six, she
recalled, she would accompany groups of ex-Confederate soldiers, along with
one woman:

[T]he day seldom passed that they didn't have a heated argument about the Civil
War. And the day seldom passed when the young lady who accompanied us didn't
turn her horse and race for home. She realized, even if I didn't, that the company
of quarrelsome old gentlemen was no place for a lady. . . . I didn't [go home], for
at the age of six I was not concerned about being a lady. Besides I was too fascinated
by the way the veterans shouted at each other.[26]

Mitchell positions her child self in a male world that was "no place for a lady,"
the only female witness remaining after an adult woman decides to "race for
home." In this moment of parallel fantasies, childhood frees Mitchell from
femininity, while the veterans' rituals stave off Confederate defeat.

Other gender crossovers, literal and metaphorical, pervaded Mitchell's childhood. When Margaret was a child, her brother Stephens Mitchell noted, her
dress caught fire and their mother, an ardent suffragist, decided to alter her
clothing accordingly: "Thereafter until she was old enough to go to school
her mother dressed her in pants, as if she were a little boy. The neighbors
called her 'Jimmy.'"[27] She joined the boys' baseball team and learned to swear
and shoot.[28] A passionate fan of theatre, she performed male roles in school
productions and especially in neighborhood theatricals, which she also wrote
and directed. While her interest in the Civil War brought Mitchell into a world
of men, cross-dressing allowed her to inhabit as well as to witness the performance of masculinity.

Mitchell's intertwined interests in masculinity and the Confederacy re-
appeared throughout her childhood; one of her earliest attempts at fiction, for
example, was a Civil War story about male soldiers.[29] Cross-dressing and the
Confederacy converged most overtly, however, in her fierce attachment to the
work of Thomas Dixon. Dixon wrote Mitchell an effusive fan letter in 1936,
to which she responded that "I was practically raised on your books, and love

them very much," and described her childhood adaptation of one of his novels
into a neighborhood play:

> When I was eleven years old I decided that I would dramatize your book "The
> Traitor"—and dramatize it I did in six acts. I played the part of Steve because none
> of the little boys in the neighborhood would lower themselves to play a part where
> they had to "kiss any little ol' girl." The clansmen were recruited from the small-
> fry of the neighborhood, their ages ranging from five to eight.[30]

Correcting this memory, Mitchell's most thorough biographer, Darden Asbury Pyron, attests that the "clansmen" were almost certainly all played by
girls. In dramatizing *The Traitor*, Mitchell had organized and starred in a full-
scale cross-dressed pageant centered on the memory of the Confederacy and
its glorification in the Ku Klux Klan.[31]

Mitchell's Dixon theatricals encapsulate the complexity of her cross-
dressing, which simultaneously engaged issues of gender, race, and sexuality.
First, as with Loreta Velazquez's masquerade, Mitchell's Confederate cross-
dressing afforded her access to the world of masculinity. Staging as well as
starring in Dixon's novels, she produced fantasies in which little girls got to
act like men. *Klans*men, that is: the agency of masculinity is here *white* masculinity, and the freedom to cross gender boundaries, as in the case of Velazquez,
is secured through the upholding of racial ones. Since Dixon's Klansmen were
white men wearing white robes, this is whiteness as constructed spectacle,
with Mitchell performing a version of white masculinity that was itself staged
through performance. These theatricals also involved a second form of racial
performance, in which white girls adopted blackface to portray Dixon's black
characters. Like other twentieth-century examples of what Susan Gubar terms
"racechanges," such events updated minstrelsy traditions into new forms of
cross-racial performance.[32] A friend remembered one such occasion in which
"[Mitchell's] parents objected to her blacking her face so she wore a Halloween
blackface mask."[33] As with Mitchell's portrayals of Klansmen, this image presents racial identity at a double remove: blackness is represented by a Halloween mask of blackface, or a mask of a masquerade. Yet these constructions of
blackness and whiteness were not symmetrical in the racially hierarchical world
in which Mitchell was raised. Her parents' prohibition on the wearing of actual
blackface suggests their greater anxiety behind her coming so close to blackness.

Finally, Mitchell's comment to Dixon that she was the only one willing to
"kiss any little ol' girl" suggests the implications for sexuality of her cross-
dressing. Her masculinity in these performances was cemented through the
role of the male seducer, a figure she also revived in her theatrical adaptation

of *Birth of a Nation*. A neighbor remembered the actors in this production "drawing straws to determine whose turn it was *this* time to make the noble leap off the six-foot-high-cliff and be seduced, usually as I recall, by one Margaret Mitchell in the role of the Little Colonel."[34] This account is a startling revision of the actual role of the Little Colonel: in Griffith's film, he mourns rather than seduces the cliff-jumping girl, who is in fact his sister. If the account is accurate, then it suggests that her persona as male seducer infused her fraternal as well as romantic roles—or rather, that it brought to the surface the incestuous undertones of sibling relations in *Birth of a Nation* itself. Collapsing fraternal and romantic relations, Mitchell's performances also recall the blurring of sexual boundaries occasioned by *The Woman in Battle*. Both Mitchell and Velazquez intervene in heterosexual scenarios from the perspective of the authoritative male. However, while Velazquez's text produces protolesbian romances, Mitchell's interest in the figure of the male seducer swerves away from lesbian possibility. As Mitchell's earliest fiction suggests, this figure afforded a way for her to imagine occupying a position of authority in her heterosexual relationships with men.

In a recently recovered 1917 novella called *Lost Laysen*, for example, Mitchell tells a story of romance and adventure through the first-person voice of a male narrator named Bill Duncan. At sea in the South Pacific aboard a ship called the "Caliban," Duncan falls in love with an American woman, Courtenay, who is also pursued by the novel's villain, Juan Mardo. When Mardo tries to assault Courtenay, Duncan stabs him; ultimately, Mardo and Courtenay die, with Courtenay using a dagger given to her by Duncan to kill herself rather than be raped. As this outline suggests, the male narrator of *Lost Laysen* offers the woman writer a figure for heroic male identification in a story that replaces the figure of male seducer with that of male rapist. This replacement is inseparable from the story's pervasive racism. Juan Mardo is denigrated as both "that Spaniard" and "a dog of a Jap," and his crimes occur on a ship named for the ultimate untamed man and populated by "Japs, Chinks, Kanakas and half breeds."[35]

Yet even as *Lost Laysen* demonizes Juan Mardo, it also suggests that the figure of the "savage" man was titillating as well as repulsive to Mitchell. As Gail Bederman has shown, in early twentieth century America, social constructions of masculinity underwent a dramatic shift, with the nineteenth-century ideal of " 'the white man's' civilized self-mastery" giving way to interest in " 'the natural man's' primitive masculinity." Characters such as Tarzan, who first appeared in 1912, signaled the force of this new image, which was inseparable from stories of interracial rape.[36] In *Lost Laysen*, the narrator is one such new man. Assimilating to the customs of the *Caliban*, Bill Duncan finds that he is not quite white: "I was forgetting that I was a white man and turning yellow" (67). Duncan is also uncontrollably savage, as Courtenay perceives: "I felt her cool hands slide over my shoulder with its hard packs of muscle and down my arm. I looked up into her eyes then and I caught a fleeting glance of pure terror in them . . . I realize now that it was my pure brute strength that she feared" (83). The eroticized Duncan unsettles the boundaries between white and "yellow," rescuer and rapist. In her early fiction as in her theatrical performances, Mitchell's imagination was engaged by "brute" men who functioned for her as figures of both masculine identification and heterosexual desire.

Such men reemerged, in her late teens and early twenties, as actual suitors in Mitchell's career as a "baby-faced l'il vamp." The vamp, as popularized by the actress Theda Bara, was a heartless "bad girl" who combined the force of New Womanhood with predatory sexuality.[37] The complexities of Mitchell's construction of this role emerge in her letters to Allan Edee, a former beau. In one letter to Edee, for example, she described her approach to men as "finding out how far I could play a man without getting into trouble," a formulation that equates vamping with theatrical performance.[38] Having assumed the role of the man who kisses reluctant girls, Mitchell now assumed an equally constructed persona: the girl who is reluctant to be kissed. Her phrase for this activity, "play a man," ostensibly refers to manipulating him—playing him for a fool—but it also evokes the idea portraying a man. At stake in both definitions is the seizure of sexual agency, a quality normally accorded only to men, and one to which Mitchell gains access by both identifying with and desiring masculinity. In the idea of "playing a man," she shifts from stimulating masculinity through cross-dressing to stimulating it through vamping.

Like Mitchell's Civil War theatricals, her vamping continued an association with the mythologies of Confederate masculinity. In a letter to Edee, for example, she offered a glowing account of a local reunion of Confederate Veterans:

> Al, the reunions were glorious and the vets were such fun! I could have cried during the last parade, tho, for "those fast-thinning grey ranks" looked so pitifully brave alongside the Camp Gordon men; they seemed to forget that '61 was passed when they swapped lies with the overseas men about the "fights they'd fit" at Bull Run and Gettysburg. Every deb in town jazzed around with her car full of vets or with one on each arm, showing them a good time.[39]

Mitchell represents Confederate veterans as comic objects for vamping. The "overseas" and "Camp Gordon" men, who are World War I soldiers, pick up symbolically where the older men leave off, as serious objects for seduction. Mitchell had a serious beau who was killed in the war, and as a student at Smith College in 1917–18, she was known for her large collection of photographs of young soldiers. She also continued to entertain her classmates with Civil War battle stories; her roommate remembered that "She felt about Robert E. Lee pretty much as if he was the current film idol."[40] Idolizing the Confederate soldier in both his idealized and aging forms, she proceeded to vamp his heir, the World War I soldier.

Seducing the soldier rather than cross-dressing as him, Mitchell implicitly sustained the dynamics of racial crossover from her earlier theatrical performances. Mitchell's social world and beliefs remained rigidly divided along racial lines; she apparently disliked Smith College in part because of her inability to accept black classmates.[41] Yet her self-representation continued to rely on symbolic departures from whiteness, moving away from the wearing of blackface toward the staging of ethnic exoticism. The figure of the vamp was itself inseparable from images of European decadence—the "dark" female vampire—and, moving further east and south, from a pervasive discourse of orientalism. Margaret Mitchell celebrated the foreignness of the vamp when she staged a scandalous performance of the "Apache dance" at a 1921 Atlanta debutante ball. Popularized by Rudolph Valentino in the film *Four Horsemen of the Apocalypse,* the Apache dance enacted a violent relationship between an Indian "brave" and his "maiden." With a dance instructor friend, Mitchell rehearsed so enthusiastically that "They threw one another around like rag dolls." To Mitchell's delight, their final performance outraged Atlanta high society, with one woman querying in horror, "[D]id you see how he *kissed* her?"[42] As this response suggests, the moment again framed Mitchell as the star and producer of an outrageous kiss. As with Mitchell's adventures in cross-dressing and vamping, the Apache dance was a fantasy of her own making, enabled by a temporary abdication of whiteness.

While Mitchell celebrated this scandal, her letters also suggest the dangers of vamping. She welcomed, indeed expected, the seductive kiss as a sign of her sexual prowess. Yet she could not always control its outcome, as she wrote to her sister-in-law: "I used to have an elegant time in my youth . . . by giving a life like imitation of a modern young woman whose blistering passions were only held in check by an iron control. It frequently succeeded so well that all thoughts of seduction were tabled and rape became more to the point."[43] Her letters to Edee repeatedly detail courtships in which real-life "primitive masculinity" became coercive. One relationship with a suitor she nicknamed the "cave man," for example, ended with him "so unmanageable, I was glad to get him out of town."[44] The denouement of an evening with

"A. B." was so bad that she would describe it only to her best friend, Courtenay Ross:

> Court, when you've liked and trusted a man, it is no pleasant sight to see him lose his head and go wild. . . . I never had such a hectic time in my life before I got him out. It's the last time A. B. ever comes here. I felt absolutely dirtied up everywhere he touched me . . . I looked for all the world like "Act I, Scene II. Why Girls Leave Home!"[45]

After Edee somehow got hold of this letter, he criticized her behavior, to which she angrily retorted, "You don't believe me when I tell you I've drawn a line that men can't pass except by force."[46] Force was a feature of her first marriage to Berrien K. "Red" Upshaw, an unstable alcoholic who apparently beat her. In a grim outcome to the project of balancing seduction and self-defense, Mitchell kept a pistol by her bedside to protect herself from her husband.[47]

If Mitchell's lived experiences suggests the difficulties of sustaining authority over "cave men," then her emerging role as fiction writer afforded her a more utopian domain for the imagination of sexuality. Her letters are themselves self-consciously literary exercises, with her evening with A. B. theatrically reshaped as "Act I, Scene II. Why Girls Leave Home!" And while her account of feeling "dirtied up" clearly condemns A. B., an earlier description in the same letter moves him into a more ambiguous realm:

> Ever know a man who makes you acutely conscious that your dress is too low? That's A.B. I suddenly began to loathe him. I took sidelong glances at him, noting his sensual mouth and closely cropped moustache and meeting his assured, faintly sneering eyes. I hated him.[48]

The effect of such a description is to shift the grounds of agency. As a factual account of being "dirtied," Mitchell's letter presents her as victim of her own vamping. But as a fictional shaping of this experience, this passage recuperates A. B.'s brutality as "sensual" seduction and recasts Mitchell's apparent loss of control as her own desire to be "dirtied." Moving toward the terrain of fiction, Mitchell's epistolary voice functions as a theatrical space—akin to the neighborhood stage and the dance floor—in which she could construct male aggression as female-authored fantasy.

Reframing her sexual experiences in epistolary form, Mitchell explored related issues in her fictional efforts of this era. In a letter to Edee, Mitchell discusses her difficulty writing the climactic kiss of a short story: "I can't write that kiss! How the devil *would* he kiss her, anyway? I have had him run the whole scale of emotions, poor man, from cavemannish roughness to dispassionate coolness, but nothing seems right." Struggling with "cavemannish roughness" in fiction as in her own life, Mitchell later clarified that her real difficulty lay elsewhere.

> You see, Al, this story is written from the viewpoint of a girl's diary, and that makes it difficult to describe the kiss. I don't believe anyone ever has truthfully portrayed a girl's mental processes during a love scene—or just exactly what she thought and felt when kissed. It seems almost a betrayal of one's sex to write such things!

The fundamental problem is not the male kiss but the female response, or "a girl's mental processes during a love scene." So great is the prohibition on this project that she abandons it: "I do see vast possibilities for 'hot stuff' in that passage . . . But just now, I can't write such a kiss from a girl's viewpoint. I could do it beautifully from the masculine angle." The fantasy of "[doing] it beautifully from the masculine angle" reprises the idea of cross-dressing, turning the dangerous ambiguities of real-life vamping into the pleasurable possibilities of writing fiction over which she has complete control. This fantasy allows Mitchell to construct herself as a sexual agent, in a culture that either denies this role entirely to women or punishes its expression with violence.[49]

While Mitchell at twenty had few models in legitimate fiction for such fantasies, she was already encountering, and would shortly immerse herself in, an array of sexually explicit prose. The details of Mitchell's enthusiasm for pornography emerge most fully in her correspondence with another friend, Harvey Smith, to whom she wrote, after a trip to New York, that "[Y]ou'd have been the only person, man or woman, of my acquaintance who would have enjoyed haunting dirty book shops (I'll send you the address)."[50] In his later annotations to her letters, Smith identified her favorite pornographic novels as *Fanny Hill, The Perfumed Garden,* and *Aphrodite.*[51] Along with literary pornography, Mitchell avidly read sexology, including the works of Havelock Ellis, Kraft-Ebbing, and William Stekel. She also shared this literary passion in conversation. By twenty-five, Mitchell had divorced and remarried, and she and her second husband, John Marsh, were part of a group of friends who, in the words of another biographer, "reveled in their new-found freedom to express sexual matters. And they discussed everything from Freudian case studies to erotic literature to dirty jokes and limericks."[52] As Harvey Smith remembered, they called themselves the "sex worshippers."[53]

Mitchell's career as a "sex worshipper" is crucial for understanding her literary imagination, for her preferred texts, both pornographic and sexological, addressed precisely the question of female sexual agency that concerned her in her own life and writing. The well-known eighteenth-century novel *Fanny Hill*, for example, graphically delineates the "memoirs of a woman of pleasure," from the opening encounter of the female protagonist with a fellow chambermaid to her closing night with a male lover. Yet even as graphic sexual encounters suffuse the novel, its coy first-person voice also sustains Mitchell's own prohibitions on female agency. Throughout the novel, Fanny presents herself as the naive innocent who falls into sexual activity rather than sexual initiator: "I was determin'd not to be behind-hand with her, and returned her the kiss and embrace, with all the fervour that perfect innocence knew." Her story ends with a disingenuous appeal to virtue: "If I have painted Vice in all its gayest colours . . . it has been solely in order to make the worthier, the solemner sacrifice of it, to Virtue."[54] Written by a man for male readers, *Fanny Hill* achieves its pornographic effect by heightening, rather than eliminating, the gap between the performance of female innocence and the experience of a "woman of pleasure." Reading this male fantasy, Mitchell encountered a novel whose voyeuristic strategy was to exploit rather than to resolve her own difficulty in representing "a girl's mental processes during a love scene."

By contrast, the two authors whose works Mitchell owned more of than any other, James Branch Cabell and Havelock Ellis, evaded this problem by focusing on male protagonists. Selected works by these authors returned Mitchell to the firmer ground of "playing a man," providing stories whose male adventurers moved beyond heterosexuality and across racial boundaries in successful pursuit of sexual pleasure. James Branch Cabell, a prolific writer from an elite Virginia family, was best known as the author of the scandalous *Jurgen* (1919), a comic novel briefly suppressed by the New York courts upon its publication.[55] *Jurgen* details the sexual adventures of a pawnbroker who passes into a fantasy world populated by personages from classical, Judeo-Christian, and medieval mythologies. Its primary narrative is one of unbounded masculine heterosexuality, in which Jurgen is the seducer of many willing women; Guenevere, for example, "came delightfully perfumed, in her night gown, and in nothing else . . . He remembered always the feel of that warm and slender and yielding body."[56] As Jurgen's adventures progress, he finds women who are not only "yielding" but predatory, particularly when he marries a vampire named Florimel, who "[spends] her time seducing and murdering young men . . . Jurgen felt, in his illogical masculine way, that her vocation was not wholly nice" (285–86). As the coy tone of this passage suggests, Jurgen remains a comic faux-naif throughout the story. A kind of male Fanny Hill, he experiences the pleasures of experience while maintaining the performance of innocence.

Jurgen also locates its protagonist within suggestive same-sex scenarios. In a chapter entitled "The Brown Man with Queer Feet," Jurgen comes upon Pan, described as "a sun-browned brawny fellow" (132), who takes him into the heart of the forest:

> "You will presently forget that which you are about to see, or at worst you will tell pleasant lies about it, particularly to yourself."
> "I do not know about that," says Jurgen, "but I am willing to taste any drink once. What are you about to show me?"
> The brown man answered, "All."
> So it was near evening when they came out of the glen. It was dark now, for a storm had risen. The brown man was smiling, and Jurgen was in a flutter. (133)

Withholding the details of "All," Cabell connotatively frames this encounter between Jurgen and Pan as one of homosexual seduction. Pan is also notable for his "brown" skin, whose coloration is a crucial feature of his sexual authority. The "brown man" beckons the way to an exotic sexual world, while Jurgen's faux-naivete allows him to experience the pleasures of seduction across gender—without compromising either his reputed innocence, on the one hand, or his heterosexuality, on the other.[57]

If *Jurgen* slyly intimates a world of pansexual masculinity, a far more explicit account delighted Mitchell from within the interstices of sexology. Harvey Smith recalled that "[Mitchell's] ideal man, she said, was right out of Havelock Ellis, a swashbuckling British army officer in India who would perform any sexual act with anyone—or so it seemed with anything!"[58] The officer in question appears in an appendix to Ellis's multivolume *Studies in the Psychology of Sex*, first published in 1903. One of many lengthy sexual biographies included in this series, the officer's story is a long, remarkably matter-of-fact first-person account of his sexual experiences with, respectively, his sister's underwear, a donkey, himself, a series of schoolboys, a horse, many women, an army officer, and several melons. He travels constantly, and his encounters with women alone comprise "English, French, German, Italian, Spanish-American, American, Bengali, Punjabi, Kashmiri, Kaffir, Singhalese, Tamil, Burmese, Malay, Japanese, Chinese, Greek, and Pole."[59]

As this outline suggests, Ellis's officer is a hyperbolic figure of sexual agency. He incarnates the sexual protagonist as unembarrassed and self-aware agent rather than coy innocent like Fanny Hill or Jurgen. In his story, the possibilities of seduction expand to a dauntingly wide array of object-choice, beyond either heterosexuality or homosexuality, from mares to melons. As his list of nationalities suggests, his picaresque narrative also conjoins sexual freedom with mobility across geographic, racial, and ethnic borders. Implementing the implicit cross-racial dynamics of *Jurgen,* Ellis's experiences confirm what Joseph A. Boone terms the "homoerotics of orientalism," wherein an imagined nonwhite East offers the setting for sexual adventure. The officer is manifestly Mitchell's ideal, but his adventures also suggest that he serves her as a figure of identification as well as desire. Ellis's version of "playing a man" results in a fantasy of sexual omnipotence, in which temporary contact with racial "otherness" allows a white person to experience—or at least to narrate—a temporary walk on the wild side.[60]

A reader of sexually explicit prose, Mitchell emerges in this period as a writer of it as well. Another letter to Harvey Smith embodies this possibility:

> While on the subject of obscene things, John [Marsh] and I were at supper in a tea room not long ago when a man who I think was Mr. Straiton Hard came in. John had always wanted to see what a man with a name like that really looked like, so I got out a pencil and my library card . . . and wrote "Your dreams have come true! Straight and hard over there!" John looked at me and was eddified [*sic*] and I put up the card and forgot about it. The next day, I was at the library and the boy on the desk was that black haired boy who always reminds me of you. . . . I handed in my books and shoved my card over, as usual and he took the usual cursory glance at it and then froze. . . . [H]e raised his black eyes and gave me a look, dearie, *such* a look! "I shall be dust when I forget!" And then I saw my card. Great God, I got out of the libe without even my books checked and lurked, scarlet, in the odorous ladies rest room till he went off duty and I could get one of the ladies to check them for me. . . . [H]e must think I am so smitten with his swarthy charms that I took a very bold way of notifying him of my state.[61]

This anecdote hyperbolically fulfills the project of "playing a man" in the invented figure of "Mr. Straiton Hard." As Mitchell narrates it, this is a story that links sexual virility to not one but four men—"Mr. Hard" himself, Mitchell's husband, Harvey Smith, and the unwitting librarian. Like the stories of Cabell and Ellis, her account raises same-sex possibilities for men, in the enigmatic suggestion that John Marsh "had always wanted to see what a man with a name like that would look like." In its covert homoerotic dimensions as well as its overt heterosexual framework, the story of "Mr. Straiton Hard" situates Mitchell's ideal of pansexual masculinity in a pornographic story of her own devising.

Mitchell's own behavior in this story, meanwhile, conjoins the roles of vamp, ingenue, and writer. Mitchell the vamp makes an outrageous sexual joke, while Mitchell the ingenue waits in the library's bathroom to evade further embarrassment. The connection between these two roles is the blush, which at once signals her innocence and aligns her with the outrageous "scarlet woman."[62] The "swarthy charms" of the librarian, meanwhile, form a dark background against which her "scarlet" transgressions appear in high relief. Set off against male swarthiness, the "scarlet" Mitchell is not only literary vamp, but vamp as writer. Encoding several levels of fiction-writing, her story originates in a dirty joke written on a library card—itself the conduit for literary circulation—and then shaped into a literary vignette and further "published" in letter form to Smith. The setting in which Mitchell lurks offers a precise architectural metaphor for her writing activities. Recalling Faulkner's dismissal of Mitchell as an emblem of "the Kotex Age," the "odorous ladies rest room" is the perfect liminal space for the woman who writes as well as reads dirty books.

In the course of her career as "sex worshipper," then, Margaret Mitchell read, discussed, and began to write imaginative fantasies involving multiple sexual possibilities. Several themes link her interest in sexually explicit prose with her earlier activities. First, as cross-dressed actor, vamp, and "sex worshipper," Mitchell consistently explored ways to expand conventional restrictions on female sexual agency, restrictions that would divide vamp from virgin and male seducer from female seducee. Second, like her early blackface and orientalist costumes, the pornographic narratives she favored consistently enacted sexual adventure in racialized contexts. Sex and race are interdependent but asymmetrical domains for experimentation in Mitchell's biography. Her sexual adventures consistently include journeys into racial "otherness," but those journeys take place in a hierarchical world that privileges white protagonists and readers. In Mitchell's biography, finally, fantasies of the Civil War continued to infuse the otherwise modern cultural contexts in which she came of age. As a child who rode with ex-soldiers, a teenager who portrayed Dixon's war heroes, and a vamp who "jazzed around" with veterans, Mitchell absorbed mythologies of Confederate glory congruent with her favorite pornographic texts. Like the aging veterans who reimagined themselves as winners, Cabell's Jurgen and Ellis's army officer are eternally virile and ever victorious. Riding amongst Confederates and reading about conquests, Mitchell similarly ventured into "no place for a lady." In response, she began to invent her own versions of the "ideal man," from the recuperated "A. B." to the celebrated "Mr. Straiton Hard."

These were not, however, her only literary versions of "playing a man." The decade of Mitchell's immersion in pornography was also the period in which she began researching and drafting the novel that would become *Gone With the Wind.*[63] Written by a woman drawn to both Confederate history and sexual fantasy, Mitchell's novel is equally the legacy of the Lost Cause and the "vamp de luxe," of Thomas Dixon and Havelock Ellis, and of "Mr. Straiton Hard" and the "scarlet" woman who created him.

III

In *Gone With the Wind,* Margaret Mitchell resituated her project of "playing a man" on the capacious symbolic ground of Confederate struggle. Like acting, vamping, and "sex worshipping," the story of the Confederacy afforded Mitchell a narrative space for the reconsideration of gender and sexuality. Masculinizing Scarlett and "queering" Ashley, she uses the Confederacy as a symbolic catalyst for the rise of her "scarlet" woman. As in Mitchell's biography, moreover, this rise is inseparable from racism and racial ambiguity, aligned in this case along a continuum of black, white, and Irish-American relations. As Ashley exhausts Confederate potency, Scarlet both loses and regains Southern whiteness.

From the start, *Gone With the Wind* promotes the assertive performance of femininity: "Scarlett O'Hara was not beautiful, but men seldom realized it when caught by her charm as the Tarleton twins were" (5). In a sharply dichotomized world that offers romance as the only leverage for female authority, Scarlett must use her "charms" as Mitchell used her "innocent tricks," vamping men while preserving her virtue. "I'm tired of acting like I don't eat more than a bird . . . and I'm tired of pretending I don't know anything" (81), she complains of her constant masquerade. But Scarlett's response to masquerade is more often pleasure, as when she famously devises a dress out of green curtains: "How pretty she looked! . . . It was so nice to know that she looked pretty and provocative, and she impulsively bent forward and kissed her reflection in the mirror and then laughed at her own foolishness" (557). Combining virgin and vamp, Scarlett's self-admiring reflection is the triumph of a literally made-up femininity. Throughout *Gone With the Wind,* Scarlett O'Hara epitomizes a denaturalized femininity achieved through settings, costume, and make-up: femininity, in short, as a function of theatrical design.

Yet in portraying femininity, Scarlett also "plays a man," simulating as well as stimulating masculinity. The catalyst for this simulation is the Civil War, on whose eve the book begins, and whose disruptions turn Southern life "topsy-turvy" (131). Scarlett initially professes indifference to the war, but she is transformed when Atlanta burns and she returns to a ruined home:

"Tara stretched before her, negroes gone, acres desolate, barns ruined, like a body bleeding under her eyes, like her own body, slowly bleeding" (412). Rather than accept Tara as metaphorical rape victim, she becomes its brutal protector: "Scarlett reigned supreme at Tara now, and like others suddenly elevated to authority, all the bullying instincts in her nature rose to the surface" (425). Scarlett's natural "bullying" is inseparable from her assumption of masculinity, a transformation that culminates in her murder of a Yankee soldier:

> Quickly and noiselessly, she ran . . . down the stairs, steadying herself on the banisters with one hand and holding the pistol close to her thigh in the folds of her skirt . . .
> Like lightning, she shoved her weapon over the banisters and into the startled bearded face. Before he could even fumble at his belt, she pulled the trigger . . .
> Yes, he was dead. She had killed a man. (433)

Resisting what is clearly, in the soldier's belt-fumble, the beginning of a rape, Scarlett refuses to be victimized like the bleeding body of Tara. Instead, she assumes the phallic authority of the gun, "close to her thigh in the folds of her skirt." Killing a man requires becoming one, in a rite of passage for which the Civil War is both setting and excuse.

In postwar Atlanta, Scarlett's masculinity rises. Her activities as a millowner continue her wartime seizure of male authority: "[D]uring the lean months at Tara she had done a man's work and done it well . . . With the idea that she was as capable as a man came a sudden rush of pride and a violent longing to prove it, to make money for herself as men made money" (611). In the male business world, "[H]er reactions were all masculine. Despite her pink cheeks and dimples and pretty smiles, she talked and acted like a man" (630). Scarlett's "pink cheeks" would normally render her innocent, but they also link her with the redness of the prostitute Belle Watling, "a tall handsome woman with a bold face and a mass of red hair, too red to be true . . . 'Good Heavens!' thought Scarlett . . . 'That must be a bad woman!'" (149). Redness also moves Scarlett toward masculinity, affiliating her with the masculine, red-headed Bea Tarleton, who "bullied her grown sons and laid her riding crop on their backs" (9). Redness and masculinity conjoin, too, in Scarlett's inheritance of the temperament of her "high-colored" father (32). Throughout the novel, Scarlett is her father's daughter, from his opening treatment of her "in a man-to-man manner" (33) to her memory of him in postwar Atlanta, when "She knew with conscious pride in her own smartness that she was the equal of any of [her competitors]. She was Gerald's own daughter" (653). Like Mitchell's epistolary self-portrait as "scarlet," the blushing woman goes in multiple directions, toward vamp as well as virgin, and toward masculinity as well as femininity. In her affiliations with Belle, Bea, and Gerald, Scarlett gets to be both "bad woman" and brute man.[64]

Scarlett's masculinization in the context of war recalls Loreta Velazquez's Confederate cross-dressing, and indeed Mitchell, in her journalism for the *Atlanta Journal*, wrote a profile of a Confederate cross-dresser. In an article on women in Georgia history, she featured "Private Bill Thompson," a.k.a. "Mrs. Lucy Mathilda Kenny," who "was large, masculine in appearance, a fine rifle shot, and absolutely fearless . . . This 'daughter of the Confederacy' was animated by no less brave spirit than the Maid of Orleans herself."[65] Yet for all her affinities with Kenny's "Private Bill"—and with Velazquez's "Lt. Buford"—Scarlett does not literally impersonate men. In another article for the *Atlanta Journal*, a profile of a distinguished woman doctor, Mitchell expressly condemned "this day of men-aping women."[66] Rather, Scarlett's "bullying" is cross-dressing as mobile fantasy, akin to Mitchell's childhood theatricals and the mutable erotics of her favorite works of sexually explicit prose. In Scarlett, Mitchell found the perfect framework for combining fantasies of female transgression with mythologies of Confederate glory. In her version of white femininity, the best alibi for the assumption of male authority is Confederate self-defense, and in her revivification of the Confederacy, the best soldier for the South is a woman.

By contrast, the truly feminine figure in *Gone With the Wind* is not Scarlett O'Hara but Ashley Wilkes. Ashley may be "a young girl's dream of the Perfect Knight" (213), but he is more like a young girl himself, and his gentility and decorum qualify him far more fully than Scarlett for the role of Southern lady. Ashley himself makes this comparison when he says to his wife, "We are alike, Melanie, loving the same quiet things, and I saw before us a long stretch of uneventful years in which to read, hear music and dream" (211). His idealized femininity is captured brilliantly in *Mad* magazine's parody of the novel, "Groan With the Wind," which ends with Rhett running off with "someone who's been waiting for me for years, someone who's loving and warm and kind." That someone is Ashley—or as *Mad* calls him, "Ashtray."[67]

As this parody suggests, in fleeing from masculinity, Ashley also leaves heterosexuality behind. Mitchell originally intended to call Scarlett "Pansy," but it is Ashley who occupies the space of the "pansy" in this novel, since he is represented throughout the novel as effete and "queer." Here, for example, is Scarlett's father, Gerald O'Hara, warning her about Ashley:

"[W]hen I say queer, it's not crazy I'm meaning. . . . I don't mean that Ashley would run off with another woman, if you were his wife, or beat you. You'd be happier if he did, for at least you'd be understanding that. But he's queer in other ways, and there's no understanding him at all . . . [D]o you understand his folderol about books and poetry and music and oil paintings and such foolishness?"

"Oh, Pa," cried Scarlett impatiently, "if I married him, I'd change all that!" (37)

As George Chauncey has shown, the term "queer," along with "pansy," was already associated with homosexuality in the 1930s, and in this passage, "queer" clearly carries a sexual connotation.[68] Gerald associates Ashley's improper aesthetic interests with his inadequacy as husband, and Scarlett responds with anger at this "slur of effeminacy flung on Ashley" (38). After the war, when Ashley is "a man livin' at Tara on a woman's charity" (686), his queerness registers as impotence. As he tells Scarlett, in the face of her authority, "I saw myself less than a man—much less, indeed, than a woman" (718). It is no accident that Ashley is introduced wearing "the head of a Medusa in cameo on his cravat pin" (27). Ashley's image, like that of the Medusa, so consistently embodies castration that he plunges into effeminacy, impotence, and a nether region beneath gender altogether.

The imagery of Ashley as impotent "queer," which saturates the novel, is further reinforced by the casting of Leslie Howard to play this role in the film. The women whom Helen Taylor surveyed characterized Howard's Ashley as "wet, weak, wimpish, wishy-washy, spineless, insipid, boring, a ninny, indecisive, a failure, a moral coward, too good, ineffectual, timid, dishonest, pathetic, defeatist [and] a sop."[69] To an American audience, moreover, Howard's obvious Britishness—the actor made little attempt to conceal his accent—would recall stereotypes of the effeminate British esthete. The casting of Howard as "smooth, anemic, intellectual Ashley," as *Time* magazine put it, confirmed the equation of the male esthete with effeminacy and the association of both with Britishness.[70] Howard's Ashley is not a universally unappealing figure; some women may share Scarlett's own initial attraction to the character and to the model of the aristocratic British aesthete that he embodies—a model embodied elsewhere in, for example, his fictional contemporary, Dorothy L. Sayers's Lord Peter Wimsey.[71] Yet in the novel and film, Ashley is a diminished figure next to Scarlett. In contrast to the red-blooded, pink-skinned Scarlett, who energizes femininity with phallic power, Ashley downgrades white masculinity into impotent anemia.

Ashley is, moreover, not alone in this plunge, for *Gone With the Wind* represents the majority of its white male characters as pansies, sissies, and queers.

Charles Hamilton, Scarlett's first husband, is "a pretty, flushed boy" (128) raised by an old maid, Miss Pitty, who made him "a damn sissy" (159). Her second husband, Frank Kennedy, is described as an "an old maid in britches" (98). As Rhett tells Scarlett, "You seem to think [men] are like old ladies past the change of life" (886). Mitchell's disdain for these men is continuous with her literary sensibility as I have traced it, for what Ashley, Frank, and Charles all lack is the signature of Cabell's Jurgen, Ellis's army officer, and her own "Mr. Straiton Hard": male potency. In comparison with Ellis's confidently pansexual army officer, the problem with *Gone With the Wind*'s men is not that they are "queer," but that they are not sexually potent, whether with women or men.

As with Scarlett's ascension to masculinity, the fate of these white men is inseparable from the fall of the white Confederacy. Mitchell specifically links the weakness of the Confederate body politic with the imagined impotence of male bodies; wartime newspapers in Atlanta, for example, advertise "restoratives for lost manhood" (233). After the war, defeat registers as sexual victimization: "The Yankees had the South prostrate and they intended to keep it so . . . [T]hose who had once ruled were now more helpless than their former slaves had ever been" (644). Like "sissy" Charles and "old maid" Frank, Ashley represents the impotence of the white South, whose men are now rendered not only feminine but sexually "prostrate." In this version of postwar inversion, as in cartoons of a cross-dressed Jefferson Davis, the Confederate body politic faces the prospect of same-sex as well as heterosexual violation. Rather than warding off the prospect of violation, Ashley suggests that Southerners might as well "swallow our pride as best we can, submit gracefully and get the whole thing over with as easily as possible" (751).

Ashley's loss of heterosexual virility to the point of "graceful" submission is, in turn, inseparable from the exhaustion of his whiteness to the point of cadaverous pallor. The film throws Howard's excessive whiteness into high relief; the actor recalled that "I had my hair bleached and had to use a grayish-white makeup on my face to get a natural pale skin tone."[72] These adjustments to the needs of technicolor are also an inadvertent gloss on Ashley's color as a constructed extra-white, rather than a "natural pale." His name, like his make-up, a signifier of paleness, Ashley—or "Ashtray"—offers only the burned-out cinders of whiteness. Ashley's pallid skin literalizes the idea of Confederate death in the presence of emancipated black vitality. The racial coordinates of his impotence reprise what Richard Dyer has theorized as the complementary relation between cinematic whiteness and blackness: "If blacks have more 'life' than whites, then it must follow that whites have more 'death' than blacks."[73] Ashley's alignment between bleaching and feminization also recalls Velazquez's "Lt. Buford," who loses his tan while the white South is under assault. In a metaphoric overlay between gender and race, Ashley's feminization reflects his failed whiteness, while his excess paleness also connotes his failed masculinity.

In this context, Scarlett's postwar achievements offer a compensatory resurgence of whiteness as well as a strategic seizure of the prerogatives of masculinity. Confederate defeat potentially feminizes white men, but it also threatens to blacken white women. During the war, Scarlett implicitly loses whiteness along with wealth, an equation she starkly articulates in conversation with a neighbor: "'Me? Pick cotton?' cried Scarlett aghast, as if Grandma had been suggesting some repulsive crime. 'Like a field hand?'" (441). After a fire at Tara, Scarlett tells Melanie, "You look like a nigger," while Melanie responds, "You look like the end man in a minstrel show" (462). This invocation of minstrelsy evokes Mitchell's own theatrical performances but with their valences reversed. Like the image of the defeated Jefferson Davis as a runaway slave, this moment of blackface symbolizes the involuntary loss of white power rather than the voluntary play of racial masquerade.

Conversely, Scarlett's heightened masculinity in the postwar era—like Margaret Mitchell's own performance of white-robed Klansmen—represents a reassertion of racial boundaries through a transgression against gender norms. Scarlett's business dealings with Yankees do not please the women of the Old Guard, to whom "The Lost Cause was stronger, dearer now in their hearts than it had ever been at the height of its glory. It was a fetish now" (866). But her success as masculine entrepreneur is nonetheless the fulfillment of the phallic "fetish" of the Lost Cause. While Ashley and his peers are too impotent to reinvigorate white masculinity, Scarlett is "Southerner enough to believe that both Tara and the South would rise again out of the red fields" (450). Her redness aligned with the "red fields" of the slaveowner, Scarlett is herself a "restorative for lost manhood."

Scarlett's commitment to whiteness is also inseparable from her Irishness, the inheritance of her father. The story of Gerald O'Hara, sketched in the novel's opening pages, is that of a man whose American whiteness is implicitly wrested from pejorative associations between Irishness and blackness. Having left Ireland at twenty-one to escape persecution by the British, Gerald is a "self-made man" (44) who consciously affiliates himself with the white South upon arrival in America. While the Irish in America were frequently equated with blacks, Gerald strategically uses his ethnicity to ingratiate himself with slaveholders: "[T]here was a brisk and restless vitality about the young Irishman . . . that set him apart from these indolent gentlefolk of semi-tropical weather and malarial marshes" (47). The turning point in Gerald's assimilation comes when he wins his black valet, Pork, in a poker game: "[T]he possession of his first slave . . . was the first step upward toward his heart's desire. Gerald wanted to be a slave owner and a landed gentleman" (48). He completes his social ascent through his marriage to Ellen Robillard, whose aristocratic French background moves him even closer to whiteness. From Gerald, Scarlett inherits a hard-won form of whiteness crafted by marrying up and mastering slaves.

The Civil War both threatens and strengthens this project of Irish self-whitening. For Irish-Americans, who participated in both Union and Confederate armies, the Civil War offered an opportunity to help advance their claims to Americanness. Mitchell, herself part Irish, was well aware of this history, writing admiringly to a fan of "the part the Irish played in the building up of our Southern section and in the Civil War . . . our Southern Irish became more Southern than the Southerners. When the trouble in the 'sixties began they went out with the Confederate troops and did great deeds for their new land."[74] In *Gone With the Wind*, Gerald does not embody such Irish-Confederate heroism, since the inversions of the war destroy him: "In [his] face . . . there was none of the virility, the restless vitality of Gerald . . . He was only a little old man and broken" (398). Breaking Gerald's virility, the war also threatens his claims to American whiteness, reducing him to the status of slave rather than master. Similarly, Scarlett's temporary "blackening" during the war ominously threatens to return to the pejorative equation between blackness and Irishness that her father had initially escaped.

Yet Scarlett, as a second-generation Irish-Confederate, rejects this equation, reasserting her claims to the white South. Her commitment to revivifying Tara upholds her father's opening prophecy that " 'Twill come to you, this love of land. There's no getting away from it, if you're Irish" (39). In postwar Atlanta, the Irish-American daughter identifies with the city itself: "[S]he and Atlanta were exactly the same age . . . [Atlanta was] as headstrong and impetuous as herself" (140). Deepening her father's assimilation to the white South, Scarlett stakes her claim to its new urban centers as well as its slaveowning plantations. Her red-cheeked Irishness is part of her moneyed whiteness, differentiated in class terms, as Jim Cullen notes, from both "rednecks" and "white trash."[75] As the too-white Ashley declines, the new-white Scarlett rises, a contrast ironically redoubled in the film. Although both Leslie Howard and Vivien Leigh were English, their performances nonetheless constructed Howard's recognizably "English" persona in contrast to Leigh's presumptively "Irish" vitality. In film as well as novel, Scarlett's postwar triumph is not only a remasculinization of Southern whiteness but also a rewhitening of American Irishness.[76]

In the story of Scarlett and Ashley, then, Mitchell disperses femininity and masculinity across a series of racial and sexual borders. Between them, Scarlett and Ashley occupy metaphorical terrain criss-crossed by the terms of masculine and feminine, masculinized and emasculated, whitened and blackened, "Irish" and "English," heterosexual and "queer." In the contrasting trajectories of Ashley's fall and Scarlett's rise, Mitchell pursues her project of "playing a man" within the highly partisan historical space of the Civil War. This historical setting catalyzes the triumph of a heroine cross-dressed in male authority, but Scarlett's success, in turn, transforms the conventional narrative of Confederate loss. In Mitchell's version of the "fetish" of the Lost Cause, Confederate men remain unrecuperated, but Confederate women carry on their ideals. Surpassing Loreta Velazquez, who unsuccessfully flees southward and westward in search of a new Confederate Eden, Scarlett triumphantly reconstitutes whiteness and manhood at home.

IV

In its mythologies of Southern resurgence, *Gone With the Wind* belongs to a genre of racist apologia for slavery that Catherine Clinton, in another context, has termed "Confederate porn."[77] Yet for all the volatility that Scarlett and Ashley enact, neither character, alone or together, realizes the promise of erotic pleasure so important to Mitchell. If this is porn, where is the sex? The answer is, of course, embodied in the novel's other male protagonist, Rhett Butler. Rhett, I suggest, is a liminal figure who is literally white but symbolically poised between black and brown colorations and who is masculine in a way that also incorporates forms of feminization. Like Scarlett, his character operates on two levels of fantasy, offering both a figure for gender identification—another version of "playing a man"—and a racial model of remasculinized Confederate whiteness. In this section, I focus on the racial ambiguities of Rhett himself; in the next section, I analyze Rhett and Scarlett as a symbolically interracial couple. Together, these interpretations show the centrality of race to the novel's romance "foreground" as well as its Civil War and Reconstruction "background."

With Rhett Butler's first appearance in *Gone With the Wind*, he provides the novel's missing erotic center:

[Scarlett's] eyes fell on a stranger, standing alone in the hall, staring at her in a cool impertinent way that brought her up sharply with a mingled feeling of feminine pleasure that she had attracted a man and an embarrassed sensation that her dress was too low in the bosom. He looked quite old, at least thirty-five. He was a tall man and powerfully built. Scarlett thought she had never seen a man with such wide shoulders, so heavy with muscles, almost too heavy for gentility. When her eye caught his, he smiled, showing animal-white teeth below a close-clipped black mustache. He was dark of face, swarthy as a pirate, and his eyes were as bold and black as any pirate's appraising a galleon to be scuttled or a maiden to be ravished. . . . She did not know who he could be, but there was undeniably a look of good blood in his dark face. It showed in the thin hawk nose over the full red lips, the high forehead and the wide-set eyes. (98–99)

As both gazer and object of Scarlett's gaze, Rhett recalls the sneering, handsome A. B., "a man who makes you acutely conscious that your dress is too low," now transplanted to the Civil War era. Mitchell later wrote that she had taken his features from nineteenth-century daguerreotypes and that she "had a bet up that either [Augusta Jane Evans's] St. Elmo or [Charlotte Brontë's] Mr. Rochester would be Rhett's comparison."[78] In her own account of Rhett, Mitchell framed him as a reprinting of both historical and literary type.

Yet Rhett Butler's "dark" face and "animal-white teeth" have quite specific relationships to the racial world in which his creator came of age. The black man of Margaret Mitchell's Atlanta was a demonized figure: the mythic rapist of the American racist imaginary. As discussed previously, this figure made its way into Mitchell's world through the black villains of Thomas Dixon. More locally, this racist imagery was prominent in the Atlanta race riots of 1906, in which thousands of whites gathered for several nights in angry mobs to hunt down supposed black rapists; the rioters came within a mile of the Mitchell household. In *Gone With the Wind*, the mythology of the black rapist is a featured element of Mitchell's dystopian portrait of Southern life after Confederate defeat, when freed slaves threaten Scarlett: "The negroes she passed turned insolent grins at her and laughed among themselves as she hurried by . . . How dared they laugh, the black apes! How dared they grin at her, Scarlett O'Hara of Tara! She'd like to have them all whipped until the blood ran down their backs" (579).

Overtly vilified in Scarlett's racist reaction, the figure of the black rapist is also present in a far more ambiguous manner elsewhere in *Gone With the Wind*, for his iconography, as Joel Williamson suggests, vivifies the character of Rhett Butler. Mitchell makes reference, for example, to Rhett's "swarthy face" (204), "brown chest" (846) and "black head" (953). These adjectival forms of blackness are closely linked to putative traits of African-American or African masculinity: "He came up the walk with the springy stride of a savage and his fine head was carried like a pagan prince" (371). Rhett's "stride of a savage" bespeaks his general deviousness at outwitting the world around him; his behavior, Williamson suggests, marks him metaphorically as a kind of "hipster-trickster," a black man who is "independent, cocky, and insufferably yet subtly insolent."[79] The key to this insolence is Rhett's sexual aggression: his "impertinent stare" and "animal"-like smile are twins to the "insolent grins" of "black apes." Rhett's "cockiness" is both explicitly sexual and implicitly dark and, within that "darkness," both explicitly insolent and implicitly black.

While close to black, however, Rhett's coloration also shades into a spectrum of other racial possibilities. The range of "exotic" masculinities that shaped Mitchell's imagination included the "yellow brown" figures of *Lost Laysen* and the "Indian" figures of the Apache dance. Joining this spectrum, Rhett Butler has a "lithe Indian-like gait" (179), a designation linked explicitly to blackness in the character of Dilcey, one of the O'Hara slaves: "Indian blood was plain in her features, overbalancing the negroid characteristics. The red color of her skin . . . showed the mixture of two races" (65). Rhett's closest affiliation with exotic masculinity, however, is with a major cultural icon of Mitchell's era: Rudolph Valentino. Popularizer of the "Apache dance," Valentino's image was that of both "Latin lover" and "Arab sheik," and references to the actor in both guises saturate Margaret Mitchell's journalism of the early 1920s. In an article on romance in Atlanta, for example, her debutante sources cite their ideal as "a man of the Rudolph Valentino type." In another piece, she compared him with Ramon Navarro and other "Latin Lovers." Most important, Mitchell interviewed Valentino in person when he visited Atlanta in 1923, declaring that "Visions of white clad sheiks, fascinating caballeros from the Argentine, slim toreadors, floated before my eyes."[80]

In *Gone With the Wind*, Rhett Butler unmistakably inherits the imagery of Valentino, as constructed in the culture at large and by Mitchell herself. Mitchell's opening account of Rhett—"he smiled, showing animal-white teeth . . . He was dark of face, swarthy as a pirate"—is a direct reprise of her description of Valentino: "His face was swarthy, so brown that white teeth flashed in startling contrast to his skin." Like Valentino, Rhett combines physical "swarthiness" with proprietary sexual aggression. The Sheik's signature line in the 1921 film was, "When an Arab sees a woman, he takes her"; in Rhett's case, "It was the bold way his eyes looked out of his swarthy face with a displeasing air of insolence, as if all women were his property to be enjoyed in his own good time" (220). If Rhett Butler, as one critic notes, behaves like the "son of the Sheik," this genealogy is sustained and comprehensive.[81]

Rhett's similarity to Valentino does not contradict his construction as black "savage," but the connotations of ethnic brownness significantly recast those of racial blackness. As Miriam Hansen has shown, pejorative caricatures of

Valentino turned his brownness into blackness, setting up "a color continuum between the 'olive-skinned idol' and descendants of African Americans."[82] In *Gone With the Wind*, Mitchell travels this color continuum in reverse, for her construction of Rhett as black yet brown "lightens" the absolute racial contrast signified by blackness with the more ambiguous connotations of ethnicity. The effect of this lightening is to recuperate Rhett as an acceptable object of white women's desire. Valentino's exoticized masculinity was associated not only with the millions of women who constituted his main constituency of fans but also, in the case of *The Sheik*, with another female-authored fantasy. Based on the 1921 novel by white Englishwoman Edith Hull, *The Sheik* is a white woman's fantasy of male brutality redeemed, with the sheik rehabilitated from rapist to lover and the female abductee thrilling to her capture. The film softens Hull's overt rape plot into a near-rape and concludes with the Sheik's death but still unites the couple in mutual love. In drawing from the cult of Valentino, Mitchell appropriated a discourse of racial fantasy with more capacious boundaries for use by the white woman novelist. The black man could not be approvingly rendered as an object of white female fantasy; the "brown" man could.

Mitchell's journalistic treatment of Valentino again brings this contrast into view. Her articles about Valentino center on his sexual appeal for women, an appeal she both satirizes and confirms. Her tongue-in-cheek interview begins: "Rodolph Valentino casts his fascination over femininity of every class . . . A glance from his dark eyes gives them a thrill and the privilege of standing near him is apparently something to be fought for." In person, she finds him shorter, stockier, and older than he appears on film, but despite her cynicism, she responds involuntarily to him:

> "Allow me," breathed a husky voice in my ear, and as masterfully as ever he sheiked Agnes Ayres, he picked me up in his arms and lifted me through the window!
> . . . I scrambled to my feet, all aglow, wondering whether I had better register deep emotion, thrills, or say "Sir, how dare you!" I ended by registering a world-beating blush.

Even as Mitchell mocks Valentino's appeal, she performs a scenario of feminine abandonment before him. Thrilled despite herself to be "sheiked," Mitchell is literally swept off her feet and, blushing, turned scarlet by Valentino.

As white woman's object of desire, Rhett inherits from the Sheik not only his racial exoticism but his dual status as both savage and aristocrat. In his novelistic and cinematic incarnations, the Sheik is revealed at story's end as an elite Westerner in origin: "He is not an Arab. His father was an Englishman, his mother a Spaniard." The Sheik's underlying whiteness stabilizes his savage brownness, a combination that also, as Gail Bederman argues, aligns him with his fictional contemporary, Tarzan, the child of English aristocrats raised in the African jungle.[83] In *Gone With the Wind,* Rhett recapitulates this duality; as a Charleston aristocrat, his "swarthy" vitality is balanced with the "look of good blood in his dark face." For Rhett as for the Sheik and Tarzan, "dark face" and "good blood" have reciprocal effects. Rhett's darkness rejuvenates his potentially tired white "blood," while that blood infuses and defuses his skin color; as close as Rhett comes to being "black," his metaphorical blackness is made possible by his literal whiteness. Rhett's brown skin is a dual racial signifier, on the one hand invoking an even more dangerous blackness and on the other hand summoning a reassuring whiteness.

This racial positioning has specific meaning in the historical setting of the Civil War and postwar South. In his iconographic similarity to black men, Rhett both summons up and siphons off the danger of the "black apes" Mitchell otherwise demonizes. His function as defuser of racial anxiety is complementary with that of the novel's "good" black men, loyal servants like Big Sam, who saves Scarlett from assault, and Pork, who so thoroughly endorses slavery that when Gerald dies, his "black face [is] as forlorn as a lost and masterless hound" (713). If the novel's black servants provisionally subsume the imagery of the black rapist within the figure of the loyal slave, then Rhett more fully domesticates that imagery in another register: by absorbing it within the figure of the white hero.

Tempering the racial anxiety posed by black men, so too does Rhett "darken" whiteness, stabilizing the uneven ground of white Confederate masculinity evacuated by Ashley. Rhett represents "pure" masculinity, as when he visits Scarlett in Atlanta: "When he came to call, his complete masculinity made Aunt Pitty's well-bred and ladylike house seem small, pale and a trifle fusty" (219). Rhett's "complete masculinity" also anchors his greater access to heterosexuality, a contrast again echoed in the film's casting of Clark Gable, who had a well-developed Hollywood persona as virile heterosexual, at once polished "king" and savage lover. The casting of Gable as Rhett resecured the grounds of heterosexuality from a threatened fall into effeminacy, a process precisely reduplicated when the actor helped fire the film's first director, gay "woman's film" director George Cukor, for the more overtly macho Victor Fleming.[84]

More of a "real man" than Ashley, Rhett is also the better Confederate. For while Ashley's early partisanship fades to impotent nostalgia, Rhett's initial cynicism rises to effective commitment. Joining the army while Atlanta burns, he expresses a patriotism all the truer for being illogical: "I shall never understand or forgive myself for this idiocy. I am annoyed to find that so much quixoticism still lingers in me. But our fair Southland needs every man" (383). Paradoxically, Rhett's turn toward the "fair" Confederacy is enabled by his racial darkness, the catalyst for his virility. While Ashley's impotence is embodied in his surplus whiteness, Rhett's masculinity is exuded in his surplus brownness.

Rhett does not, however, wholly leave behind the connotations of "queer" femininity that surround Ashley: "[Rhett] was foppishly groomed, the clothes of a dandy on a body that was powerful and latently dangerous in its lazy grace" (179). A fop and a dandy in his own relation to fashion, Rhett gossips about it endlessly with Scarlett: "Had he been less obviously masculine, his ability to recall details of dresses, bonnets, and coiffures would have been put down as the rankest effeminacy" (225). These descriptions again evoke Valentino, whose critics used his image as a dandy to slur him.[85] In *Gone With the Wind,* by contrast, Rhett's femininity further consolidates his heterosexuality. Saved from "rankest effeminacy" by his "obvious" masculinity, Rhett retains his virility not by subduing femininity but by absorbing it within masculinity.[86] Rhett's incorporation of femininity also functions as a tempering force to his racial ambiguity. Aligned with the world of fashionable white women, his femininity is implicitly "white," and as such it counterbalances his "dark" masculinity. If darkness energizes Rhett's white "blood," then femininity keeps his savagery within recognizable limits. In Mitchell's construction of Rhett, darkness and femininity are complementary mechanisms—fuel and brakes— for a vehicle of white masculinity that cannot move forward without them.

"Both the Sheik and Tarzan," James Baldwin noted in his discussion of Hollywood film, "are white men who look and act like black men—act like black men, that is, according to the white imagination which has created them: one can eat one's cake without having it, or one can have one's cake without eating it."[87] Rhett Butler, I have suggested, is another such creation: a white character who is drawn from fantasies of black masculinity, as mediated through the "brown" skins of Arab sheik and Latin lover. The "white imagination" at work in Rhett's case is that of a woman, Margaret Mitchell, whose investments in reviving white masculinity were at once personal and historical. Eating the cake of blackness without having to have it, she conjured her own ideal man within the historical space of the Confederacy. The novel's Confederate setting at once makes Rhett's "brownness" possible and is destabilized by him. For as with Mitchell's creation of Scarlett, the ironic implication of her pro-Confederate fantasy is that white Southern masculinity is so exhausted that it requires rebuilding from an outside source. Between Rhett and Scarlett, the best Confederate men in *Gone With the Wind* are, respectively, brown and female.

v

Scarlett and Rhett, then, are complementary figures of white remasculinization who embody Mitchell's own dual-sided fantasies about "playing a man" as well as her version of Confederate mythology. A figure of identification for Mitchell, Rhett Butler is also her object of sexual desire. The romance between Rhett and Scarlett that forms the core of the novel functions as a complicated arena of white fantasy about interracial relationships. The relationship of Scarlett and Rhett is the novel's most important civil war, one that realizes its two major investments: restabilizing the racial anxieties of an idealized Confederate world and authorizing a narrative of white female pleasure.

I have already suggested that images of interracial sex, coercive and voluntary, consistently engaged Mitchell's literary imagination. Her favorite texts imagined a thin line between rape and seduction in racially charged contexts, from the interracial threats of *Birth of a Nation* to Jurgen's adventures with the "queer brown man" and those of the white women "sheiked" by Valentino. Experimenting with such scenarios in *Lost Laysen*, Mitchell returned to them in the 1920s. During this time, she drafted a novella called *'Ropa Carmagin*, whose manuscript she destroyed, but whose plot probably involved a white heroine who falls in loves with a mulatto man.[88] Together, these stories suggest her sustained interest in sexual encounters between white-skinned people, especially women, and dark-skinned people, especially men. In *Gone With the Wind*, Mitchell imagined another such encounter, as set in a historical moment that both transforms and is transformed by this symbolically interracial plot.

As Martha Hodes has shown, the cultural construction of sexual relations between white women and black men in the South changed dramatically during the nineteenth century, from an early period of relative toleration to increasing politicization of and violence toward such liaisons. The Civil War was the historical pivot for this transition, with black emancipation catalyzing a new demonization of interracial sex.[89] The Civil War was also the moment when the term "miscegenation" was invented, in a 1864 satirical pamphlet written to smear Lincoln's reelection campaign with the suggestion that the Republican Party advocated "the blending of the races." Presented as if it were a vigorous endorsement of this "blending," the pamphlet failed to affect the campaign, but it helped to shape contemporary white racist anxieties about interracial contact, as well as to provide a new vocabulary for describing it.[90]

Two features of this pamphlet provide a suggestive context for understanding *Gone With the Wind*. First, the authors interpreted the Civil War as "a war for the negro. Not simply for his personal rights or his freedom—it is a war if you please, of amalgamation, so called—a war looking, as its final fruit, to the blending of white and black" (18). In this recasting of the war, the axis of struggle was not sectional fragmentation but racial "amalgamation." Among the forms of "amalgamation" the authors feared were liaisons between black men and Irish women, a fear that adapted existing prejudices about the supposed affinities between blackness and Irishness. Second, the authors located a key element of "amalgamation" in the desires of white women, particularly Southerners, for black men: "The mothers and daughters of the aristocratic slaveholders are thrilled with a strange delight by daily contact with their dusky male servitors. . . . It is idle for the Southern woman to deny it; she loves the black man" (42–43). Deliberately inflammatory, such language symbolically framed miscegenation as the key to both the national Civil War and to white women's internal war over their sexual desires. The outrage this scenario promised was double, in the specter of black men freed from slavery and united with uncontrolled white women acting on their sexual fantasies. At its moment of textual origin, the rhetoric of miscegenation turned not on fears of interracial rape coerced by black men, but on the fear beneath this fear: consensual interracial sex initiated by white women.

While it is unlikely that Margaret Mitchell read this pamphlet, she implicitly reprises its rhetoric, for *Gone With the Wind*, I suggest, frames the Civil War as a the desires of a white woman, both Irish and Southern, for a "dark" man. This desire was not, of course, openly discussable. Early twentieth-century American culture censured interracial sexuality in myriad ways, from the murderous violence of the Ku Klux Klan, which underwent a significant revival in the 1920s, to the film censorship of the Hays Office, whose Production Code mandated from the 1930s onward that "Miscegenation (sex relation between the white and black races) is forbidden."[91] Predictably, *Gone With the Wind*'s references to sex between black men and white women[92] are racist and pejorative, as in Scarlett's encounter with an unnamed man in postwar Atlanta:

> The negro was beside her, so close that she could smell the rank odor of him as he tried to drag her over the buggy side. With her one free hand she fought madly . . . Then the black hand fumbled between her breasts, and terror and revulsion such as she had never known came over her and she screamed like an insane woman. (780)

The sexual connotations of this passage are unmistakable: to Scarlett this is the mythic black rapist at work, and "terror and revulsion" are her only possible responses.[93] The idea that a white woman might desire contact with a black man is unmentionable except as generalized insult, when Scarlett is condemned by Atlantans for doing business with carpetbaggers: "Scarlett had cast her lot with the enemy and, whatever her birth and family connections, she was now in the category of a turncoat, a nigger lover, a traitor, a Republican— and a Scallawag" (864). A synonym for "turncoat" and "traitor," the "nigger lover" appears here in female form, in a version of "sleeping with the enemy" that casts a white woman's regional transgressions in the form of interracial sex.

Yet *Gone With the Wind* nonetheless elaborates the possibility of the white woman who is "nigger lover" in more salutary form. For example, the successful, long-term cohabitation of Aunt Pittypat and her black coachman, Uncle Peter, is suggestively close.[94] As Charles Hamilton informs Scarlett, Pittypat and her household are utterly reliant on Peter:

> She is the most helpless soul—just like a sweet grown-up child, and Uncle Peter treats her that way. To save her life, she couldn't make up her mind about anything, so Peter makes it up for her. He was the one who decided I should have a larger allowance . . . he insisted that I should go to Harvard . . . And he decided when Melly was old enough to put up her hair and go to parties. He tells Aunt Pitty when it's too cold or too wet for her to go calling and when she should wear a shawl. . . . He's the smartest old darky I've ever seen and about the most devoted. The only trouble with him is that he owns the three of us, body and soul, and he knows it. (143)

In this mystification of the actual property relations of slavery, Peter is represented as the family's master rather than their slave. Within this account of Peter's ostensible authority, he has an ambiguously intimate relation, at once parental and marital, to Pittypat. The desexualized pairing of "grown-up child" and "devoted old darky" recalls that of Stowe's Little Eva and Uncle Tom, and, within Mitchell's own era, that of Shirley Temple and Bill "Bojangles" Robinson, whose cinematic partnership began in the early 1930s in Civil War films like *The Little Colonel* and *The Littlest Rebel*. As James Snead and Ann duCille have argued, dance sequences between Temple and Robinson both invoked and disavowed interracial sexuality. As Temple's later reminiscences about her relationship with Robinson confirm, the two presented an image of inseparable intimacy: "Whenever we walked together it was hand in hand, and I was always his 'darlin'."[95] In *Gone With the Wind*, Pittypat and Peter

constitute another such pairing, whose benign outward appearance domesticates, but also makes visible, their status as an interracial couple.

If Pittypat and Peter constitute an overtly interracial but desexualized duo,
then Scarlett and Rhett, conversely, are an overtly sexual but covertly racialized
pair. Rhett's "brownness" is an integral feature of his erotic bond with Scarlett,
both the catalyst of his gaze upon her and an object of her own gaze upon
him. Mitchell consistently embeds Rhett's gaze in the imagery of brownness,
from his introductory look—"He was dark of face . . . and his eyes were as
bold and black as any pirate's appraising . . . a maiden to be ravished" (98)—
through a late-night encounter in which "his eyes [were] amused in his swarthy
face. He took in her dishabille in one glance that seemed to penetrate through
her wrapper" (204), and still more directly, to a moment when "His white
teeth gleamed startlingly against his brown face and his bold eyes raked her"
(612). In each case, Rhett's erotic invitation to Scarlett is so inseparable from
his coloring that the sexual promise of his scrutiny seems to emerge directly
out of the brownness of his face.

As the romance between Rhett and Scarlett develops, Mitchell combines
interracial imagery with the language of gothic romance. If Rhett, as Mitchell
herself noted, is Mr. Rochester, then he is Mr. Rochester darkened—or more
accurately, further darkened, since Brontë's Rochester already has "a dark face,
with stern features and a heavy brow."[96] In Rhett, Mitchell resituates the psychological "darkness" of the brooding, inscrutable gothic lover in covertly racialized terms. Borrowing the gothic hero, she also employs the genre's metaphors of mastery and enslavement. Thus Rhett warns Scarlett, "I'm riding you
with a slack rein, my pet, but don't forget that I'm riding with curb and spurs
just the same" (850); later, she implores, "I belong to you" (881). Here and
elsewhere in the novel, the gothic representation of love as sadomasochism—
and in particular, the genre's depiction of female love as eroticized masochism—converges with the history of American slavery. Octavia Butler's description of *Gone With the Wind*—"happy darkies in tender loving bondage"—
suggests that slavery and sadomasochism already converge elsewhere in the
novel. Butler condemns Mitchell for suggesting that slaves voluntarily embraced their servitude. In a racist mystification of the history of slavery, Mitchell downplays the actual sadism of white masters toward slaves and foregrounds instead the supposed masochism of slaves. The romance of Scarlett
and Rhett, I suggest, represents another mystified convergence of race and
"tender loving bondage," but one that centers on its putatively white characters
rather than its black ones. In a central romance so saturated with images of
blackness, Scarlett's desire to "belong" to Rhett—along with his "curb and
spurs"—cannot be understood in isolation from the racial history that surrounds them.[97]

In this racialization of gothic romance, race and gender function as both metaphoric languages for and literal spheres of power relations. With Rhett framed as Scarlett's "brown" lover, Mitchell gives voice to and contains the racist fear that black men might come to control a postslavery world. On the one hand, Rhett's mastery over Scarlett seems to give a black person authority over a white person. As Peter psychologically "owns" Pittypat, Rhett's possession of Scarlett literalizes through the language of romantic enslavement the white anxiety that "The negroes were on top" (639). On the other hand, by imagining a black man "on top" in this way, Mitchell effectively martials all the potential for racial conflict elsewhere suppressed in the novel into the privatized sphere of heterosexual romance. This sphere then tilts in favor of its white protagonist: as Pittypat literally owns Peter, so too does Scarlett sexually captivate Rhett. As Scarlett's devoted lover, Rhett is further restrained by his own self-control: "The most exciting thing about him was that even in his outbursts of passion . . . he seemed always to be holding himself under restraint, always riding his emotions with a curb bit" (843). Rhett's "curb" over Scarlett is here applied to himself, a metaphor that, in racial terms, turns him into his own slave. He exercises control over his anger, while the novel as a whole regulates its racial anxieties through its romance plot. With the black man in thrall to the white woman and "riding" himself, Mitchell domesticates the explosive possibilities of slaves without masters into the domestic drama of lovers mastering each other and themselves.

Yet if gender serves in *Gone With the Wind* as a metaphoric structure for organizing race relations, so too does race function in the novel as a language for articulating fantasies and anxieties about gender. Again, this language assumes bivalent form. On the one hand, Mitchell presents Rhett as "brown" master to Scarlett's white slave in an inversion of racial order that deepens gender hierarchies. Berating Scarlett for her activities as millowner, Rhett laments that "It's all Frank's fault for not beating you with a buggy whip" (821). The threat of whipping is here a punishment for Scarlett's aspirations to male power, a punishment upon which he makes good when they marry: "There's never going to be any doubt in anybody's mind about who wears the pants in the Butler family" (850). Rhett's assertion is one of racial as well as sexual mastery, an equivalence set in motion much earlier in the novel, at the Confederate charity ball. On this occasion, men bid for dances with women, a ritual which Melanie describes as "a little like a slave auction" (190) and which culminates in Rhett paying "one hundred and fifty dollars—in gold" (191) for Scarlett. Having "bought" Scarlett at this earlier moment, Rhett's later courtship formalizes enslavement with marriage. While she and Melanie earlier compare themselves to "field hands," she is now Rhett's "house slave." In an overlay of racial and gender metaphors, Rhett both refeminizes Scarlett and reblackens her.

On the other hand, the interracial cognates of this moment also have a more liberatory function for Scarlett, for they help to animate her sexual desires. As with Mitchell's own "vamping," female sexuality is meditated through male sexuality. Rhett's desire initiates Scarlett's, as when they are on the road to Atlanta: "He was kissing her now and his mustache tickled her mouth, kissing her with slow, hot lips that were so leisurely as though he had the whole night before him. Never had [kisses] made her go hot and cold and shakey like this" (384). Later, when he proposes marriage:

> His insistent mouth was parting her shaking lips, sending wild tremors along her nerves, evoking from her sensations she had never known she was capable of feeling . . . she was kissing him back . . .
>   His mouth was on hers again and she surrendered without a struggle, too weak even to turn her head, without even the desire to turn it . . . If he would only stop—if he would never stop. (826–27)

With such descriptions, Mitchell continues the project she had begun in the letters about the "caveman" and A. B.: the conversion of frightening male aggression into pleasurable literary fantasy. Rhett forces Scarlett's mouth open, but the motivation for this penetration is love rather than violence, and its result is the realization of female pleasure. Scarlett's "surrender" is a voluntary capitulation to the force of her own desire, which she cannot openly acknowledge without becoming the openly scarlet woman, Belle Watling. Through this indirect route, Mitchell resolves the problem of representing "a girl's mental processes during a love scene" without "betrayal of one's sex." Under the alibi of "surrender," Mitchell tames fears about male violence and gives voice to fantasies of female pleasure.

These fantasies are, again, inseparable from metaphors of racial enslavement. Like his probing gaze, Rhett's "insistent mouth" is fueled by his brownness, and Scarlett's "wild tremors" are animated through contact with his "dark" sexuality. Scarlett at this moment is sexually enslaved by her "brown" master, in an inversion of racial hierarchies deepened by the city Rhett chooses for their honeymoon, New Orleans.[98] Traditionally associated with racial mixing and sexual decadence, New Orleans appears in Mitchell's novel as a site of postwar racial inversion: "New Orleans was such a strange, glamorous place and Scarlett enjoyed it with the pleasure of a pardoned life prisoner. The Carpetbaggers were looting the town . . . and a negro sat in the lieutenant governor's chair. But the New Orleans Rhett showed her was the gayest place she had ever seen" (839). The pleasures of New Orleans are enhanced for Scarlett by its black man "on top," as Scarlett's own sensations are awakened by her "brown" master. As Rhett's love-slave, Scarlett inhabits a doubly subservient posture—explicitly sexual, implicitly racial—whose constraints are a racially reinforced cover beneath which she can experience pleasure.

Scarlett's romance with Rhett, then, produces a series of contradictory effects. His metaphorical brownness is racially both explosive and controllable and sexually both chastening and liberatory. Two of these possibilities—racial containment and sexual transgression—are dominant in the story and mutually sustaining. As Rhett's brownness animates Scarlett's desire, the very expression of that desire further domesticates his racial difference into a contained narrative form. These metaphoric overlays culminate in *Gone With the Wind*'s famous marital rape scene, when a drunken Rhett, enraged at the possibility that Scarlett still loves Ashley, declares that "this is one night when there are only going to be two in my bed":

> Up the stairs, he went in the utter darkness, up, up, and she was wild with fear. He was a mad stranger and this was a black darkness she did not know, darker than death. . . . [H]e stopped suddenly on the landing and, turning her swiftly in his arms, bent over and kissed her with a savagery and a completeness that wiped out everything from her mind but the dark into which she was sinking and the lips on hers. . . . He was muttering things she did not hear, his lips were evoking feelings never felt before. She was darkness and he was darkness and there had never been anything before this time, only darkness and his lips upon her. She tried to speak and his mouth was over hers again. Suddenly she had a wild thrill such as she had never known; joy, fear, madness, excitement, surrender to arms that were too strong, lips too bruising, fate that moved too fast. For the first time in her life she had met someone, something stronger than she, someone she could neither bully nor break, someone who was bullying and breaking her . . . [T]hey were going up, up into the darkness again, a darkness that was soft and swirling and all enveloping. (929)

In both cinematic and literary versions, a significant break follows this moment. The film script initially called for a scene of struggle in the bedroom, but head Production Code censor Joseph Breen protested; in the end, the filmmakers cut directly to a shot of Scarlett humming in bed the next morning.[99] The novel, after a break on the page, offers her morning-after meditations in more detail:

> She went crimson at the memory . . . The man who had carried her up the dark stairs was a stranger of whose existence she had not dreamed. . . . He had humbled her, hurt her, used her brutally through a wild mad night and she had gloried in it . . . Oh, she should be ashamed . . . But, stronger than shame, was the memory of rapture, of the ecstasy of surrender. (930)

More than a half-century after its appearance, this sequence remains controversial, in a debate that turns, as the *New York Times* put it, on the question of "Rough Sex or Rape? Feminists Give a Damn."[100]

Before assessing this ostensible dichotomy between "rough sex or rape," however, it is essential to begin with the centrality of racial metaphor to the scene. Scarlett's arousal is here inextricable from Mitchell's imagery of "utter darkness," "black darkness," "savagery," and "bullying and breaking."[101] Like Mitchell's depictions of the "dark" Rhett, this language is racially overdetermined within the novel and in the larger culture in which it appeared. The racist image of the black rapist particularized in earlier films like *Birth of a Nation* was widely dispersed across 1930s culture. This image was directly invoked in the wave of lynchings resurgent in the South in this decade, while its cinematic representations ranged more diffusely from the image of the brutish Frankenstein monster ravishing the ultra-blond heroine on her wedding night to that of the violent King Kong molesting blond white Fay Wray—a film whose sets literally went up in flames as kindling for the burning of Atlanta scene in *Gone With the Wind*. In *Gone With the Wind* as in *King Kong* and *Frankenstein,* the "dark" man who ravishes the light woman enacts an overdetermined script, illegible outside of cultural anxieties and fantasies about interracial sexuality.[102]

Interpreted within an interracial context, this scene is a representation of *both* "rough sex" and "rape," in a deliberate blurring of categories that has both racial and sexual implications. First, as a fantasy about race relations, the scene further contains and resolves the white anxieties about black power circulating through the novel. Juxtaposed with the earlier assault by the unnamed black man, Rhett's "bullying and breaking" reprises the fear of interracial rape as a fantasy of interracial "rough sex." In contrast to the unbounded terror produced by the earlier figure, this assault by a "stranger of whose existence she had not dreamed" results in ecstasy. Indeed, the very congruence between these two encounters retroactively reframes the earlier episode as a prelude to this more significant moment. As Leslie Fiedler puts it, Mitchell comes close to implying that interracial rape arises "not out of the lustful obsession with white female flesh that presumably afflicts all black men, but in part at least out of the troubled erotic dreams (cued half by fear, half by wish) of Southern white women."[103] In Scarlett's recuperation of rape as "rapture," Mitchell subdues the fear of the black rapist by enfolding him within the narrative climax of ostensibly white romance.

While Mitchell's blurring of rape as "rough sex" intervenes in her racial narrative, the scene's racial imagery also affects its narrative of female sexuality. The misogyny of the scene is starkly signaled by Rhett's behavior in the moment before he carries Scarlett up the stairs: "I'll put my hands, so, on each side of your head and I'll smash your skull between them like a walnut" (926). Prefaced by this murderous impulse, Rhett's sexual "bruising" is followed by Scarlett's celebration, in a processing of male violence—from murder to rape to enjoyment—that suggests Scarlett "really wanted" to be raped. To the extent that the sequence reinforces this misogynist lesson, its misogyny is strengthened by its interracial implications. As she thrills to her abuse, Scarlett's desire for debasement is redoubled by the specter of interracial violence that surrounds this moment.

Yet the language of sexual "surrender," here as earlier, also has a very different purpose, serving as a conduit for the textual management of male violence and the expression of female sexual pleasure. As a strategy for countering male aggression, Mitchell's transformation of rape into "rough sex" echoes that of other romance novels in which, as Tania Modleski notes, "Male brutality comes to be seen as a manifestation not of contempt, but of love."[104] Mitchell's fullest transformation of male brutality, this is also her ultimate fantasy of female pleasure; while Rhett's earlier kisses initiated Scarlett's "tremors," his more brutal assault now produces ecstasy. Interracial metaphors redouble this project of redeeming male violence into female pleasure. Like the Englishwoman "sheiked" in the distant desert, Scarlett's ecstasy violates racial as well as sexual taboos. The connotations of interracial rape in this scene provide a double screen for allowing Scarlett to experience desire without seeming to desire it.

As this scene brings the erotic promise of "brown" Rhett to its fullest expression, it also registers Scarlett's pleasure as a metaphoric change in her own racial identification: "She was darkness and he was darkness. . . . [T]hey were going up, up into the darkness again, a darkness that was soft and swirling and all enveloping." In Scarlett's recognition of the "dark into which she was sinking," it is as if the potency of the "dark" Rhett is contagious, and what starts as a scene between white hero and white heroine has become not only an interracial bond but also a dual excursion into blackness. The moment extends the novel's linkage between sexuality and race across gender, blackening women as well as men, with two effects. As with Rhett's incorporation of the imagery of "black apes," Scarlett's "blackening" absorbs outside external challenges to her whiteness. Once reduced by poverty to the status of "end man in a minstrel show," Scarlett is now a rich white lady whose "darkness" is safely internalized.

Neutralized as a social threat, Scarlett's incorporated blackness then becomes a catalyst for white woman's pleasure. As a voluntary rather than coerced participant in the novel's "minstrel show," Scarlett is free to appropriate the pleasurable rebellion with which she associates blackness. These associations, I have suggested, were consistently Mitchell's own, from her blackface performances onward, and they resurfaced, during the filming of the novel, in a moment of proprietary identification with the character of Prissy. Inquiring about the casting of this role, Mitchell declared that "I have been especially interested in who would play this little varmint, possibly because this is the only part I myself would like to play."[105] Mitchell's interest in playing the role of "the little varmint," in turn, reprises the relationship between Stowe and Topsy. Prissy updates Topsy's self-proclaimed ignorance and wickedness into the infamous confession, "Ah don't know nuthin' 'bout birthin' babies . . . Ah don't know huccome Ah tell sech a lie!"[106] Scarlett punishes Prissy for this Topsy-like lie, but the rest of her story suggests a profound identification with blackness. In *Gone With the Wind*'s climactic moment, the white woman's implicit racial "darkness," coupled with her explicit subjugation, is the foundation of her sexual ecstasy.

Darkness, but also redness: "She went crimson at the memory." This blush completes the circuitry of reds that follow Scarlett throughout the novel, including her associations with the "scarlet woman" Belle, the red-headed Bea Tarleton, her "high-colored" Irish father, and the "red fields" of Tara. As Diane Roberts argues, Scarlett's associations with the earthiness of Tara move her closer toward the imagery of blackness. Red and black trigger each other, or as Roberts puts it, Mitchell's "erotically-charged colours—red, black, and white—never stabilize. In Rhett's 'blackness' lies his attraction and in Scarlett's 'redness' lies her freedom."[107] These color configurations, as I have suggested, more broadly suffuse Mitchell's imagination of heterosexuality. As Mitchell the letter-writer turns "scarlet" before the swarthy librarian—and as Mitchell the journalist blushes before the swarthy Valentino—so too does Scarlett experience herself as "crimson" when she is with the swarthy Rhett. As red and black refer inexorably to each other, so too do these colors function as metonymic neighbors on an intricate color scale that includes Indianness and Irishness. The legacy of "high-colored" Irish Gerald, Tara is "savage red"; Rhett is similarly "savage" and "Indian-like" but also "swarthy," "brown," "dark" and "black"; and Dilcey, combining both colors, is a mixture of "red" Indian and "negroid" blackness. In the metaphoric relays of *Gone With the Wind*, red and black are ultimately not so much antonyms as appositives. While Rhett opens the way toward brownness, it is finally Scarlett herself who is the novel's savage.

In Rhett and Scarlett, then, Mitchell invents a romantic couple whose racial instabilities function both to energize white sexual fantasy and to control white racial anxiety. In Mitchell's version of a Civil War novel, both the Confederacy and the female vamp rise again, through white protagonists who are symbolically cross-dressed and blackened. The novel's war and romance plots, both crisscrossed by race, are finally asymmetrical: Scarlett's sexual awakening, begun while Atlanta burns, supersedes and surpasses Confederate defeat and its aftermath. For the white Confederacy, the result of the war is surrender, first to the Yankees and then to the "negroes on top." In Scarlett's romance with Rhett, however, unconditional "surrender" to the "brown" hero marks a victory for the white woman's pleasure. In her conversion of Confederate mythology into pornography, Mitchell attempts to translate the "rape of the South" from an image of white men's emasculation into the source of a white woman's ecstasy.

VI

In her 1949 memoir, *Killers of the Dream*, Lillian Smith, a writer contemporary with Margaret Mitchell, summarized the cultural prohibitions under which she and other white Southern women of her generation had been raised. "By the time we were five years old," she wrote, "we had learned, without hearing the words, that masturbation is wrong and segregation is right, and each had become a dread taboo that must never be broken."[108] *Gone With the Wind*, I have argued, situates itself in relation to precisely the same prohibitions: the first, a taboo upon female sexuality that kept desire, masturbatory and otherwise, at bay; the second, an absolute boundary between races that kept the body politic in strictly quarantined zones. Mitchell's solution to these complementary erotic and racial segregations was to costume her hero, and ultimately her heroine, in metaphorical blackness, in an interracial drama performed on the historical stage of the Civil War. Within this drama, she animated female sexuality not by overturning gender or racial hierarchies but by deepening them, redeeming "dark" male violence into white female pleasure.

Mitchell's narrative strategies were circumscribed by her era, but even so, other white women writers in the 1920s and 1930 responded to racial and sexual prohibitions in radically different ways. At the furthest remove of gentility from Mitchell, for example, the openly and authoritatively sexual Mae West wrote a novel that overtly explored interracial sex.[109] Closer to home, white Southerners such as Virginia Durr, Katharine Du Pre Lumpkin, and Lillian Smith contested the racist Confederate nostalgia on which they had been raised. Lillian Smith's career represents a particularly direct contrast to that of Mitchell. A lesbian who lived and worked with her partner, Paula Snelling, for many years, she became a radical activist and a leader in the fight against racial discrimination. Not surprisingly, Smith and Mitchell, who met each other, were enemies. Smith wrote a negative review of *Gone With the Wind*, and Mitchell, a virulent anticommunist, kept notes on the other woman's left-wing writings in what she called her "Red files."[110] Smith's alleged "redness" and Mitchell's Scarlett constituted two opposing ways of countering the fictions of white femininity in the twentieth-century South. Smith's project was to reveal those fictions as fictions; Mitchell, by contrast, fought fiction with more fiction. Shifting but not overturning the worlds of Dixon and Griffith, she used racist fantasies as a foundation for white female pleasure.

While some white women like Smith offered alternatives to Mitchell, African-Americans have systematically challenged *Gone With the Wind*'s configurations of race and sex. Three examples suggest the range of strategies at work in these challenges. First, black resistance, covert and overt, shaped the filming of *Gone With the Wind*. Adapting Mitchell's novel, producer David O. Selznick authorized the removal of references to the Ku Klux Klan, the word "nigger," and the black man's assault on Scarlett (in the film, her attacker is white). These alterations were motivated not only by Selznick's self-proclaimed liberalism—he insisted that "we have to be awfully careful that the Negroes come out decidedly on the right side of the ledger"—but also by his fear of black protest. Black organizations like the NAACP were, in the end, relatively inactive during production, but the film's black actors overtly and covertly resisted the conditions under which they labored. Butterfly McQueen, for example, stopped action on the set until Vivien Leigh apologized to her for slapping her too hard during the filming of one scene. More directly, a group of black actors demanded and won desegregation of set bathroom facilities.[111]

Within the film itself, this struggle is visible in Hattie McDaniel's performance as Mammy. As in the novel, the film's conception of this role is a racist fantasy, in which a desexualized black woman is the selflessly devoted laboring surrogate "mother" for a privileged white lady; the casting process duplicated this racism, with one white woman auditioning in blackface, and Eleanor Roosevelt recommending that her black maid, Elizabeth McDuffie, be cast in the role.[112] Experienced actress Hattie McDaniel, however, was so successful in the role that she became the first black actor to receive an Academy Award, thereby catalyzing a small but significant measure of new respect for African-American actors. Within the film, moreover, McDaniel's performance represented an important intervention into the racism of Mitchell's novel. As Hazel V. Carby argues, the struggles between Mammy and Scarlett are conflicts over the appropriate limits of the behavior of the black woman as well as the white woman. When Mammy succeeds, early in the film, in persuading Scarlett to eat before the Wilkes' ball, her victory registers "not only the fictional triumph of 'Mammy' over the willful mistress but the triumph of McDaniel as an actress over the limitations of her role."[113] Mitchell's novel enslaved Mammy within white literary fantasy, but McDaniel's performance, in animating that fantasy, also opened its limitations to scrutiny.

Vivifying the racial conflicts at stake in the role of "Mammy," McDaniel also disrupts the film's visual flow. The actress dominates many of the scenes in which she appears, becoming, as Donald Bogle puts it, an "all-seeing, all-hearing, all-knowing commentator and observer. She remarks. She annotates. She makes asides. She always opinionizes."[114] So skillful are these annotations and asides that Mammy functions as a figure of excess, an excess physically encoded as stereotype in her large body, but ideologically enacted in relation to the film's racism as well. Mammy's chastisement of white characters, for example, is intended condescendingly to function as comic aside, as when she admonishes Rhett that "It ain't fittin'" for him to have Bonnie ride horses astride. The actress, however, infuses this moment with such authority that she dislodges its ideological "fit." Repeated twice, her admonition spills over the allotted time frame for black commentary, as her face, highlighted in extended close-up, refuses to remain part of the film's background. These refusals, like McDaniel's Academy Award, had only a limited effect on the world outside the film: excluded from *Gone With the Wind*'s segregated Atlanta premiere, she was henceforth stereotyped within "Mammy" roles. Yet within the racist confines of what Thomas Cripps terms "antebellum Hollywood," Hattie McDaniel nonetheless negotiated a measure of power.[115] As her corset-tightening of Scarlett makes visible, behind the white woman, the black woman is forced to labor, but in her own performance, McDaniel is pulling the strings.

While McDaniel's performance intervened interstitially in *Gone With the Wind*'s racism, other black artists offered a second form of challenge in their creation of full-scale alternatives to it. As with *Birth of a Nation*, new stories were difficult to realize within the hierarchical structures of Hollywood; Langston Hughes, for example, was hired to co-write an alternative to *Gone With the Wind*, but the resulting film, *Way Down South*, bore little resemblance to his initial script.[116] Black writers, however, published numerous fictional challenges to *Gone With the Wind*, of which I have already cited Octavia Butler's *Kindred* and Alice Walker's "A Letter of the Times."[117] Within this lineage, Margaret Walker's *Jubilee* (1966) offers a particularly self-conscious, sustained, and complex reconstruction of the racial dynamics of *Gone With the Wind*. *Jubilee* is a panoramic novel of slavery, the Civil War, and Reconstruction set in the rural South, centered on African-American experience over a roughly thirty-five year span, and focused on the character of Vyry Ware, a black woman born into slavery on a Georgia plantation whose white master is her father. Two years old at the start of the novel, Vyry grows to young womanhood in slavery, becoming the plantation cook, marrying a free black man with whom she has two children, and unsuccessfully attempting to escape to join her departing husband. During the Civil War, she remains on the plantation as its white slaveowners die, then marries a second man, Innis Brown. After the war ends, she and Innis struggle to support a new home, in Georgia and in rural Alabama, where Vyry becomes a midwife. Given the chance to reunite with the returned Ware, Vyry chooses to remain with Brown at the novel's close. Begun in the 1930s and completed in the 1960s, *Jubilee* was the result of enormous amounts of scholarly research and personal dedication. Walker based the character of Vyry on her own great-grandmother.[118]

As Margaret Walker's own later writings make clear, she specifically wanted *Jubilee* to rewrite *Gone With the Wind*. In a later essay, she targeted Mitchell's novel as the epitome of a literary tradition in which "slavery is romanticized and glorified and the Old South is given mythical qualities which in fact it never possessed."[119] Produced in relation to *Gone With the Wind*, *Jubilee* was consumed accordingly, albeit in ways that assimilated Walker to the terms set by Mitchell; *Jubilee*'s paperback jacket advertises it as "The 1,000,000 copy bestseller with all the sweep and grandeur of *Gone with the Wind*! . . . A heroine to rival Scarlett O'Hara."[120] Asked whether *Jubilee* was "the Black *Gone With the Wind*," Walker responded equivocally, "I am sometimes amused at the comparison, though there are a number of things alike. I was writing about the backwoods of Georgia, and so was she. I was writing about the same period." Her critique, she elaborated, lay in Mitchell's inaccurate representation of poor whites, her "turgid expository passages," and especially her "romantic nostalgia": "I am not a romanticist in *Jubilee*. It is a realistic book." Summarizing the relationship between the two works, she declared: "In some respects I suppose we could compare superficially the two Margarets—Margaret Mitchell and Margaret Walker. But she was coming out of the front door, and I was coming out of the back door."[121]

Despite her understandable reluctance to be subsumed within Mitchell's legacy, Walker's closing architectural metaphor precisely captures the sustained focal contrast between "the two Margarets" on their shared literary field of the nineteenth-century South. In *Gone With the Wind*'s "Big House" of slavery, Mitchell sees black people only when they enter the living space of whites, but Walker's *Jubilee* follows slaves to their own cabins and describes the richly self-sustaining folk culture visible to her there. For both authors, the "Big House" of antebellum slavery becomes the "house divided" of national war, but while Mitchell's characters fight to preserve peaceful Southern homes,

Walker's characters actively fight for emancipation from domestic spaces already dominated by violence. And after the war, when Mitchell converts the symbolic house divided into the rebuilt plantation and the thriving lumbermill, Walker focuses on the continued quest of African-Americans to find a home of their own, safe from Klan torches. In the novel's final moments, Vyry, like Scarlett, returns to the "red-clay hills" of Georgia (416), but that land represents black progress rather than white retrenchment. While *Gone With the Wind* fortifies plantation myth anew, *Jubilee* moves back door to front, and then rebuilds the architecture of black experience from the ground up.

Within this alternative historical space, Walker reconstructs what she condemned as "the demeaning role of Black women" in *Gone With the Wind*.[122] Vyry, as critics have noted, is not so much "a heroine to rival Scarlett O'Hara" as a demystification of Mitchell's "Mammy."[123] While McDaniel's performance provisionally resists this stereotype, Walker's novel overtly attacks the image of the black woman laboring happily for white slaveowners. Black women are at the center of *Jubilee,* and violent assault, sexual and otherwise, perpetrated by white women as well as men, is an anchoring feature of their experience. The novel begins with the death of Vyry's mother at age twenty-nine in childbirth, the result of her sixteenth pregnancy by the white master who "had wanted Hetta, so his father gave her to him, and he had satisfied his lust with her" (8). Vyry is tortured by her white mistress, "Big Missy," and brutally whipped after her escape attempt at her father's orders. After the whipping, on her chest, "one of the lashes had left a loose flap of flesh like a tuck in a dress. It healed that way" (145); in the novel's final chapter, Randall Ware and Innis Brown stand "horrified before the sight of her terribly scarred back" (406). Testifying to Vyry's suffering, this moment also commemorates her survival within an ongoing context of family and community. Vyry's double-sided scarring constitutes a corporeal reembodiment of the black woman given neither "front" nor "back" in Mitchell's history.

Directly rewriting the historical ground of *Gone With the Wind, Jubilee* also implicitly literalizes its metaphors of racial border-crossing. In Mitchell's novel, white women momentarily and pleasurably identify with blackness. In *Jubilee,* however, racial cross-identifications are the permanent, painful result of slavery. Vyry and the master's white daughter, Lillian, are half-sisters, who "could pass for twins—same sandy hair, same gray-blue eyes, same milk-white skin" (13). Vyry's "milk-white skin" elicits constant abuse from Big Missy, to whom it is the enraging sign of her husband's infidelity; later, Vyry encounters racist invective among whites who assume that she too is white. When Vyry and Innis are treated with respect by white shopkeepers in a new town, they realize belatedly that, in Innis's words, "They not only thought you was a white

woman, they figgered I'm your nigger" (277). Vyry is ultimately able to pass
to her own advantage, befriending white people and then educating them
about their racism. Yet her forays into "whiteness," unlike Mitchell's fantasies
of "blackness," are demeaning rather than liberatory. Interpellated involuntarily into a culture that can see a woman with white skin only as a slaveowner,
Vyry experiences her ability to pass through racial boundaries as an education
in racism.

As the image of Vyry and Innis as mistress and slave suggests, Walker also
reorients the interracial metaphors of *Gone With the Wind*'s central romance.
Both of Vyry's marriages present the outward appearance of a white woman
with a black man, replacing the image of white Scarlett and "brown" Rhett
with that of "milk-white" Vyry and her two black husbands. While Innis is
a pragmatic choice for Vyry, Walker represents Randall Ware, her first husband, as a figure of erotic appeal in language that invokes Rhett Butler. Randall
enters the story when, as a free blacksmith, he visits the plantation to work.
Meeting Vyry, he flirts unsuccessfully with her; after she rejects him, he lectures:

> "Miss Stuck-up, with your ass on your shoulder. If you would marriage with me,
> I'd buy your freedom!" With that he turned to one side, looked her full in the eye,
> tossed back his massive black head, sparked his eyes, flashed his pearl-white teeth,
> and jingled the coins in his pocket. The word "freedom" caught her up short, and
> giving him a quick questioning glance she sized him up from head to toe. He had
> the strong, hard, muscular body that went with his trade and his shoulders were
> as big as a barrel. Black as a spade and stockily built, he looked like a powerful
> giant. There was just enough animal magnetism in him to trouble Vyry . . . (74)

Here are the same erotic signifiers—"hard, muscular body," "black head,"
"pearl-white teeth," and "animal magnetism"—that characterize Rhett, along
with the same air of insouciant mastery. Two traits, however, signal Walker's
recasting of the "brown" Rhett: Randall is not metaphorically but literally
black, and his arrival represents not metaphoric subjection but literal freedom.
As a free black man in antebellum Georgia, Randall appeals to Vyry because
his blackness connotes emancipation, not enslavement: "She could not get the
black face of the free man out of her mind . . . She tried to imagine what it
meant to be free . . . All day long she thought of nothing but Randall Ware
and freedom" (78–79).

As their relationship develops, Vyry predictably embraces Randall, but that
embrace recasts Scarlett's "surrender" to Rhett. Randall, like Rhett, initiates
their first kiss: "Instantly, without speaking, his arms went around her and he

kissed her hard on the mouth. When she pushed him away and pulled free of his arms she was trembling violently, and her heart beat so fiercely that for a moment she could not speak" (82). As in *Gone With the Wind*, the sexual relationship that follows overcomes Vyry's resistance:

> She lay often in the arms of Randall Ware after that first time of shock. She could not remember . . . how many times . . . nor could she speak in knowing ways of the hot young blood of passion that flowed between them, fumbling and simmering like a fever in her flesh. She ceased to struggle against him, for she was certain when he was near there would be no frightening dreams in the night to shake her awake. (107)

Like Scarlett, Vyry ceases to struggle against the husband who protects her from nightmares. Yet these scenarios have different consequences. In *Gone With the Wind*, Rhett's sexual mastery reinforces his claims upon Scarlett, as the one "who wears the pants in the Butler family." In *Jubilee*, the "hot blood of passion" leads to Vyry's escape attempt, inspired by Randall, in which she wears "men's clothes, a pair of britches and a coat, and a man's old cap" (138). This disguise, reminiscent of Ellen Craft's cross-dressing in the slave narrative *Running a Thousand Miles for Freedom*, implicitly reverses the relation between marriage and female emancipation established in *Gone With the Wind*. While Rhett's status as husband cements his pants-wearing authority, Randall's influence on Vyry pushes her toward both cross-dressing and freedom.

More generally, the two plots of sexual struggle have opposite relationships to racial conflict. Vyry's response to the whipping that follows her capture is represented through metaphors of darkness:

> Everything went black; she was caught up in the blackness of a storm. . . . she kept sinking down in the fire and fighting the blackness until every light went out like a candle and she fainted.
> . . . [A]ll her flesh looked black. She was as black as a man's hat and she was black like that all over (144).

The language of this moment, as John Limon notes, deeroticizes Scarlett's moment of immersion into "a black darkness she did not know."[124] Where Mitchell, in the marital rape scene, deanchors blackness from black people and turns it into white fantasy, Walker moves in this passage from metaphor ("the blackness of a storm") into literally wounded black flesh. Walker does not abandon figurative language entirely, since she aligns Vyry's skin with "a man's hat," but her simile emphasizes racial violence rather than evacuating it. Sex, violence, and blackness, conflated within *Gone With the Wind*'s privatized white romance, are here carefully separated and situated to lead toward rather than away from large-scale racial conflict. As the last scene of the novel's antebellum section, Vyry's whipping is the connective tissue, narrative and ideological, to the novel's Civil War middle. While Scarlett retrospectively goes "crimson at the memory" of her night with Rhett, *Jubilee* advances unflinchingly from the "blood of passion" toward the wounds of whipping and finally to the liberatory violence of the Civil War battlefield.

Even as the romance of Randall and Vyry recasts the racial metaphors of *Gone With the Wind*, however, their relationship also sets in place new mystifications of blackness. When Randall returns in the novel's closing chapters, he and Vyry argue about race relations. Vyry justifies her work as midwife to white people, declaring that "White folks needs what black folks got just as much as black folks needs what white folks is got, and we's all got to stay here mongst each other and git along" (402). In response, Randall condemns Vyry's politics as the result of her "blood": "I still say you've got white man's blood in you. That's the way he made the black slave docile and a good nigger in the first place . . . You got his color and his blood and you got his religion, too, so your mind is divided between black and white" (402). The differing colorations of "Black as a spade" Randall and "milky-white" Vyry here become a contrast in political ideology, one that both invokes 1960s debates about black political strategy and revives the metaphoric differentiations of *Gone With the Wind* as well. Randall sees Vyry as less "black" than he, along a political axis in which he represents a pure-blooded black nationalism to her adulterated accommodationist views.[125]

While Walker does not necessarily endorse Randall's politics, the contrast between Randall and Vyry also establishes a gender dichotomy in which the black hero possesses an articulate and educated political sensibility and the black heroine, while admirable, speaks very little and operates finally as mute symbol: "Peasant and slave, unlettered and untutored, she was nevertheless the best true example of the motherhood of her race, an ever present assurance that nothing could destroy a people whose sons had come from her loins" (407). Monumentalized as unlettered mother of sons, Vyry chooses the man who has helped her raise her children over the man who awakens her own eroticism. *Jubilee* brilliantly reconstructs both the historical ground and metaphoric figuration of Mitchell's story, but it also suggests the continuing difficulty—within African-American as well as white women's texts, and in 1966 as well as 1936—of representing female agency with pleasure and without renunciation.

Hattie McDaniel's cinematic performance intervenes in *Gone With the Wind* from within; Margaret Walker's literary narrative reconstructs an alternative story from without. A third form of African-American challenge to Mitchell's racial legacy operates through the destabilizing terms, at once faithful and mocking, of comic parody. As a pervasive cultural icon, *Gone With the Wind* has been a frequent target for parody, including two I have already mentioned: *The New Yorker*'s "Gone With the Birth of Nation" and *Mad*'s "Groan With the Wind."[126] Such parodies tend to center on the exaggerated performance of gender. Not surprisingly, Scarlett O'Hara is also a common figure for male drag, a form of performance that captures perfectly the character's combination of hyperbolic femininity and symbolic masculinity. From cartoons to drag, *Gone With the Wind*'s most effective parodies are those which expand on key themes already implicit in Mitchell's original novel: the cross-identified performance of gender and the accompanying disruption of heterosexuality. Yet the humor of these reinventions cannot be divorced from the text's racism. As the racist parody of Elizabeth Keckley's *Behind the Scenes* confirms, parody is not an intrinsically progressive genre. Redactions of *Gone With the Wind* that maintain its original hierarchies between white protagonists and black servants challenge some boundaries, but they implicitly shore up others. As in Mitchell's original novel, such parodies reinvent gender by ratifying whiteness.

A recent parody of *Gone With the Wind*, however, begins to suggest the genre's potential to destabilize the racial fantasies on which the text is based. "Scarlett 'n the Hood," a ten-page set of captioned illustrations published in the magazine *Vanity Fair* in 1995, reimagines *Gone With the Wind* with black protagonists and cross-dressed white slaves. Conceived of by black fashion editor André Leon Talley, this parody began as Talley's response to what he perceived as the egregious emphasis on whiteness in that season's fashion shows: "I said at some show in Europe, 'Is this the Aryan collection?'" Turning to *Gone With the Wind* as a version of "Aryan" sensibility, he collaborated with fashion designer Karl Lagerfeld to create "a historical comment in the 90s that you rarely see in a magazine."[127] In a series of fashion industry in-jokes, they posed well-known designers and models as characters from the story, in photographs accompanied by a short article—an imagined monologue about fashion by Scarlett—along with captions that identify the fashions worn and characters portrayed in each image.[128]

The results provisionally challenge the construction of race in the original story. Like *Jubilee*, these illustrations imagine a Civil War story with a black hero and heroine, but unlike Walker's serious narrative, these illustrations op-

In the image, the following text appears:

SCARLETT 'N THE HOOD

Yo, Rhett! Ghosting for the ultimate
southern belle: LAURA JACOBS recounts
her fashion breakthroughs—
remember those fabulous curtains?—
while KARL LAGERFELD and
ANDRÉ LEON TALLEY summon
the spirit of a thoroughly
modern Tara

THE YANKEES
ARE COMING!

*Our fin de siècle Scarlett,
Naomi Campbell, wears
"Valentine," a silk-dupioni gala
suit by Gianfranco Ferré
for Christian Dior Haute Couture,
spring-summer 1995. Meanwhile,
Rhett Butler—Charles Corm is
an evening shirt by Charvet
and Vivienne Westwood tweaking
trousers—accepts a last kiss
before the first shot.*

FIGURE 15. Scarlett and Rhett, from "Scarlett 'n the Hood," *Vanity Fair*, 1995

erate via comic mimicry. The opening image features Rhett holding Scarlett in precise reenactment of the staircase embrace in the film (figure 15). In this repetition with a difference, the photograph makes visible the racism of a Hollywood that, today scarcely less than in 1939, is unable to structure and foreground black actors as protagonists of epic romance. Recoloring Scarlett and Rhett, these photographs also estrange the conventional subservience of the film's black slaves. In an image that reprises the corset-tightening scene of the film, fashion designer Gianfranco Ferré is dressed as Mammy, his large white body encased in white clothes, his eyes looking into the camera (figure 16). Ferré's outsized whiteness defamiliarizes the conventional coloring of the role, while his direct gaze acknowledges its fictionality. A figure of exaggerated theatricality, he extends the ideological excess already introduced into the character of Mammy by Hattie McDaniel.

As ironic quotations of *Gone With the Wind,* these images also queer the text in several ways. One caption announces that "Anything goes today: boys in tattersall skirts, girls in Grandpa's waistcoat, men in bed linens," and the cross-dressing poses of Mammy and Prissy suggest that "anything goes" in

17-INCH WAIST

Scarlett braces herself
while "Mammy"
Ferré (whose turban is an
Hermès silk square)
adjusts his grass-
green taffeta gala dress,
for Christian Dior
Haute Couture, spring-
summer 1996. Tulle
gloves are by Chanel
Haute Couture, spring-
summer 1996.

FIGURE 16. Scarlett and Mammy, from "Scarlett 'n the Hood," *Vanity Fair*, 1995

the direction of gay male camp. In an image depicting Mammy and Rhett celebrating the birth of Bonnie, for example, Ferré, as Mammy, offers a frankly appreciative glance at Rhett—a look that literalizes the interracial fantasies of Mitchell's own text in the register of homoerotic male desire. Another image shows a pair of "house servants," played by female models in male dress, ostensibly "[making] off with the silver during the burning of Atlanta" (figure 17). This image, newly invented rather than mimicked, flirts with the spectacle of the two women as a young couple, extending the novel's camp same-sex fantasies from male to female homoerotic realms. Like the cross-dressed, cross-race servants stealing the silver, the parody as a whole loots Tara in imaginative ways, offering a protean cultural fantasy that not only plays with gender and sexuality—as in Mitchell's original novel—but also puts parody in the service of inverting racial hierarchy.

Of course, such images operate within a severely compromised context: a magazine with a history of racist representations, known less for antiracist parody than for reverential profiles of rich white people. The cover of the issue in which "Scarlett 'n the Hood" appeared is a group photograph of American athletes competing in the then-upcoming Atlanta Olympics, an image in which five white hopefuls are positioned around and above a lone black male weightlifter. The cover image offers a stark reminder of the racist context in which the parody appears, wherein whiteness is featured front and center, and token black figures are relegated to the marginalized and overdetermined role of political "weightlifters." Yet "Scarlett 'n the Hood" nonetheless begins to suggest the power of parody to overturn rather than whitewash the racism of *Gone With the Wind*. Together with the interventions of McDaniel and Walker, the parody offers strategies for the ideological interruption of a work whose racial fantasies are at once rigidly hierarchical and internally in flux. Like other African-American texts under examination in this study, such interruptions turn the conventional racial dynamics of the Civil War story—as imagined by white women as well as men—topsy-turvy.

Both oppositional and adulatory, reinventions of *Gone With the Wind* at the end of the twentieth century appear in a much franker culture than that of the 1930s. Guarding against such frankness, when the Margaret Mitchell Estate authorized a sequel to *Gone With the Wind* in the late 1980s, it enjoined any new writer "against the presentation of explicit sex scenes, homosexuality, or miscegenation."[129] This injunction was reissued to the prospective writer of a second sequel, Pat Conroy, who responded: "I told them that if they insisted on that . . . I'd write the novel with this first sentence: 'After they made love, Rhett turned to Ashley Wilkes and said, "Ashley, have I ever told you that my grandmother was black?"'"[130] Conroy's calculated outrageousness

FROM ATLANTA TO
APPOMATTOX

House servants
Shalom Harlow and
Amber Valletta
make off with the silver
during the burning of
Atlanta, dressed nattily
in men's wear
by Gianni Versace,
fall 1996, with
white evening shirts
by Charvet.

FIGURE 17. "House Servants," from "Scarlett 'n the Hood," *Vanity Fair,* 1995 provides an ironic commentary on the original *Gone With the Wind* itself, for what he proposes to do is, I have argued, what Mitchell had already done. In the racial and sexual fantasies of *Gone With the Wind*, Mitchell represented, in dispersed and displaced form, each of the taboo topics later named by her literary executors. The continuing popularity of *Gone With the Wind* in novelistic, cinematic, and touristic versions is testimony to the intractability of a culture that she both fought and ratified. For Scarlett, "tomorrow is another day," but rather than looking toward the future, her story is a reminder of the ongoing burdens of the past. The "Lost Cause" of *Gone With the Wind* is finally not that of Confederate victory, but of imagining female pleasure with undisguised authority and without racist mystification. Visible through *Gone With the Wind* are the war wounds—as raw today as in 1936—of a culture in which female sexuality can only be imagined under the heaviest of covers and in which representing blackness still means seeing red.

Afterword

The Civil War has been over for a long time, but its battles continue to be fought afresh, in some surprising ways. I conclude this study with three examples of the war's ongoing engagements: a novel, an essay, and a lawsuit. All are authored by women; all resonate with earlier texts, offering "civil wars" over gender, race, sexuality, region, nation, and civility itself; and all provide evidence of the continuing connections among women, the Civil War and fiction—no matter what their genre.

Consider, first, the case of Lauren Cook Burgess, a white North Carolina university administrator whose lawsuit against the United States Department of Interior was widely reported in the early 1990s. Like her husband, Fred Burgess, Burgess is an avid Civil War reenactor, one of at least forty thousand people who enjoy recreating the battles, encampments, and military and civilian life of the war era. Unlike Fred, however, Lauren Cook Burgess was banned from participating in these events because she was discovered attempting to impersonate a male soldier in the 21st Georgia Infantry, one of three volunteer organizations to which she belongs. Although her disguise was convincing on other occasions, Burgess was unmasked during a reenactment at the Antietam Battlefield Park in August 1989. Ordered to remove her uniform or to leave the park, she refused; when her protests met with a hostile response, she filed a sex discrimination suit against the National Park Service, which oversees this site. In March 1993, she won her suit. In the wake of her victory, the number of cross-dressing women reenactors has steadily grown, and Burgess herself has become a prominent historian of Civil War women soldiers.[1]

The case of Lauren Cook Burgess was hotly contested among Civil War reenactors, who are primarily middle-class, white, and male, and who "bitterly debated," as one journalist acerbically wrote, "whether middle-aged men with beer bellies had more right than Burgess to portray an 18-year-old Rebel soldier."[2] The Park Service asserted that her uniform, which was that of a fife player, was inappropriate because it was inaccurate; the superintendent of the Antietam Battlefield Park insisted that no cross-dressed women soldiers were present at Antietam, explaining that "If you're going to portray anything here . . . you have to portray an accurate picture." This group of opponents held that historical authenticity, rather than gender per se, was the problem. As one man put it, "her lack of authenticity happens to be caused by her gender." But another male commentator revealed that "There was no hedging about why she wasn't allowed to participate. . . . [It was] because she was a woman." To Lauren Cook Burgess herself, the issue was sex discrimination, and she believed her own abilities to be not only sufficient but superior: "I think I do a far better job than a lot of the men out there." She also argued for the authenticity of her participation, presenting evidence in her defense that cross-dressed soldiers were actually present at the battle of Antietam. The judge vindicated both of Burgess's claims, declaring that her exclusion constituted "discrimination against women" and that she herself "takes historical accuracy seriously." This judgment has encouraged subsequent women reenactors, although their presence continues to provoke strong resistance.[3]

Burgess's story and its aftermath seem at first to suggest a particularly contemporary version of the Civil War, one in which both sides mobilize the overlapping claims of "gender" and "authenticity" in late-twentieth-century ways. As a translation of cross-dressing into the terms of gender equity, Burgess's lawsuit employed the mechanisms of legal redress made possible by feminist activism of the last three decades. Her victory overturns the separate spheres of the Civil War reenactment, whose usual roles for women—nurse, seamstress, soldier's wife—implicitly ward off contemporary feminism with a return to the nineteenth century.[4] Illustrating the perils of sex discrimination, Burgess's story also registers the problem of discriminating between the sexes, and her masquerade offers cross-dressing as the cultural destabilization, rather than the legal consolidation, of gender categories. In this context, media coverage of Burgess is part of a late-twentieth-century interest in cross-dressing, which pervades both popular culture and academic discourse and includes the emergence of transgender identity politics.[5] Her story appears to animate theoretical models of the performativity of gender, as advanced by Judith Butler and others.[6] Burgess's masquerade involves repeated performances that are not only acts but *re*enactments and that reinforce the idea of gender as a belated imitation rather than a stable original. In terms of both gender politics and gender theory, then, the story of Lauren Cook Burgess would seem to offer feminist cultural critics that rare thing: a case of life imitating not only art but theory.

If Burgess's imposture seems to offer an exemplary case of gender as an inauthentic copy, so too does it suggest, in contemporary terms, that history is itself a series of imitations. History in the reenactment world is secured by authenticity, the ostensible antonym and antidote to fiction; self-termed "hardcore" reenactors proudly eschew twentieth-century hygiene, food, and equipment. Yet "authenticity" is a slippery term in this context, since a Civil War reenactment is by definition a belated, partial, and decontextualized version of an earlier event. What authenticity actually means is adherence to a model of history wherein wounds are make-believe, battlefields have been sanitized as tourist sites, and actors play roles that are only as permanent as their costumes. Even these costumes may be switched at will, as in the reenactment practice of "galvanizing," whereby individual reenactors change uniforms from one event to the next. When the superintendent at Antietam asserts that "you have to portray an accurate picture," the terms "portrayal" and "picture" inadvertently highlight the inevitable fictionality of historical representation. Instead of looking backward toward historical authenticity, the reenactors seem to operate in the fictive, deracinated, and self-reflexive contemporary realm of the postmodern.[7]

In Lauren Cook Burgess's masquerade, then, the ostensible conflict between "gender" and "historical authenticity," which begins to collapse within the arguments of both sides, is ultimately self-canceling. In this world of performances, both gender and history are finally "inauthentic" imitations, subject to cross-dressing and galvanizing. Yet if this story seems quintessentially postmodern, its terms also echo, with startling precision, the controversy surrounding Loreta Velazquez. What emerges in this comparison is not simply that Burgess, like Velazquez, is a scandalous figure but that the terms of scandal are so similar. Like Velazquez, Burgess brings the figure of an unruly woman into a world of men. As with Velazquez's arrest, Burgess's exposure extends the threat of unruly femininity to its most dangerous form: male feminization. In her vision of performing maleness to excess, to *out*man becomes, by implication, to *un*man. Both scandals also involve accusations of fictionality, with Velazquez's memoir denounced as inaccurate and Burgess's costume condemned as inauthentic. As in the response to Velazquez, gender indeterminacy and historical inauthenticity are not simply analogous anxieties for Burgess's critics but interdependent ones. As the fictive quality of the reenactment helps to call Burgess's gender into question, so does her gender masquerade unsettle the historical foundations of the reenactment. In equal measure, her gender is caused by her inauthenticity, and "her inauthenticity happens to be caused by her gender."

As Velazquez's story brings the scandal of Burgess into sharper focus, it also makes visible a form of "inauthenticity" not as immediately apparent in the contemporary case: that of heterosexuality. The sexual instabilities that Loreta Velazquez's story accomplishes through its literary form are evoked iconographically in the media coverage of Lauren Cook Burgess. For example, the photograph accompanying a 1991 *New York Times* story about Burgess is sexually suggestive in two ways (figure 18). While the original caption identifies the man in the image as her husband, Fred Burgess, Lauren Cook Burgess's visual image disrupts her verbal status as wife. With the hand of Fred Burgess resting on the costumed body of a soldier boy, the image offers implications of male homoeroticism, since it brings together the theatricality of camp with the homosocial domain of the military encampment. This domain is as much a feature of the reenactment world as of its real-life counterpart; in the practice called "spooning," for example, male reenactors sleep pressed up sideways against each other.[8] Meanwhile, if we focus only on the figure of Lauren Cook Burgess, the photograph is sexually suggestive in another direction, less homo-erotic male "spooning" than seductive female swooning. Reading the photo-graph against the grain, we can see the insouciance of her look and posture as offering a parodic version of the figure of the butch lesbian.[9] Burgess's re-fusal to be a female camp-follower in the male world of the military makes her image available as a figure of camp, both gay male and lesbian. Independent of her own lived sexuality, Burgess's image operates with its own camp force, so that same-sex possibilities may emerge—as in the seduction stories of Loreta Velazquez—in the relation between text and reader.

In her Confederate affiliation, too, Burgess's story echoes that of Velazquez. While reenactments faithfully recreate both sides of the war, they are often characterized by a particular investment in the Confederacy, especially at events held in Southern venues. These events often feature highly partisan books like *The South Was Right* and *Southern By the Grace of God* and bumper stickers such as "Unreconstructed," "Southern Nationalism—Always in Style," and "Don't Blame Us, We Voted for Jefferson Davis." So great is the enthusi-asm for reenacting the Confederacy that some events in Southern venues must enforce galvanizing to ensure enough Union-clad participants.[10] One context for this Confederate emphasis is a larger contemporary resurgence of Confed-erate commemoration in the South, whose forms include groups such as the new "Southern League," the renewed "Sons of Confederate Veterans," cam-paigns in support of the Confederate flag, and the growth of "neo-Confeder-ate" thought.[11]

Nostalgia is about the future as well as the past, and as with nineteenth-century narratives of the Lost Cause, these backward-looking initiatives reimagine future Confederate resurgence. Reenactments function as recon-

FIGURE 18.
Lauren Cook Burgess (*left*)
and Fred Burgess, 1991
(AP/Wide World Photos)

structive fantasies in which fictive Confederates can return to the moment of the war as one of eternal possibility. In reenacting the war, however, Confederate nostalgists are not simply contradicting their defeat in the tradition of declared inventions like Mackinlay Kantor's historical fantasy *If the South Had Won the Civil War* (1961).[12] Rather, Confederate reenactors plunge voluntarily into their legacy of loss and reimagine its terms, so that no matter who won the actual battle, Confederates win the ritual. At the start of every battle, Confederate soldiers are bound for glory; at the end, even if actual Confederates were defeated, today's reenactors can get up and walk away. In another attempt to make the South "rise again," reenactments promise the possibility of Confederate remasculinization.

Like Loreta Velazquez's made-up Lt. Buford, Lauren Cook Burgess's fictive Confederate soldier both corroborates and ironizes this exercise. Burgess is a self-made Confederate: although she grew up hearing stories of a relative who fought for the Union, she lives in the South, is a member of Confederate regiments, displays Confederate flags in her home, and was married in a Confederate-style wedding ceremony.[13] Whatever her own political allegiances, her enthusiastic embrace of its iconography promotes Confederate revival. Her construction of Confederate identity implicitly participates in the female twist upon remasculinization, whereby Southern white women become the region's masculine heroes. Burgess's literal uniform vivifies such literary versions of this project as *The Woman in Battle* and *Gone With the Wind*, as well as more recent works like Rita Mae Brown's historical novel *High Hearts* (1986), in which a white Southern woman cross-dresses to join her husband in the Confederate army and fights more heroically than he.[14] Yet as with Velazquez, Burgess's story also challenges this project of remasculinization. For like the exposure of Velazquez, the unmasking of Burgess threatens to reveal that the metaphoric manhood of the Confederacy is without foundation.

Similarly, the racial coordinates of the Confederate world in which Burgess participates reprise those of *The Woman in Battle*. Confederate nostalgia has frequently swelled in moments of racist backlash, from the emergence of Lost Cause imagery in the wake of the war, through the success of Thomas Dixon in the era of lynching and Jim Crow, to the promotion of the Confederate flag in the 1950s and 1960s, when its iconography was deployed in direct opposition to the Civil Rights Movement.[15] Contemporary neo-Confederate culture is similarly inseparable from anti-black racism in both its historical revisionism and its contemporary politics. First, as a version of Civil War history, Confederate nostalgia promotes a revisionist narrative that minimizes slavery. *Southern By the Grace of God*, for example, declares that "in the mild form of slavery practiced in the South [slaves] would more fittingly have been called servants."[16] So mild was slavery, goes this distorted narrative, that many African-Americans chose to fight for the South. Like Loreta Velazquez emphasizing the loyalty of her black "servant," revisionist reenactors wishfully overinflate the number of Civil War "Black Confederates."[17]

With slavery minimized, Confederate nostalgists can represent themselves as the "slaves" of perceived Northern aggression, from the battlefields of the war to those of contemporary cultural politics. For example, the Heritage Preservation Association promotes itself as follows:

> Southern heritage is a part of American heritage but "civil rights" groups want to remove ALL Confederate symbols from public property. Join HPA today and help us fight political correctness and cultural bigotry against the South.
> HPA is a nonprofit, national membership organization that utilizes educational,

legal and political resources to protect Southern symbols, Southern culture, and Southern civil rights.[18]

"Civil rights" appears first in quotation marks, in a mockery of the Civil Rights movement and its legacy; by the end of the passage, however, the term has been relegitimated, with no quotation marks, as the property of the white South suffering its own form of "bigotry." Similarly, phrases like "Confederate Americans Have Rights Too," which surface within the reenactment world, simultaneously mock and appropriate identity politics discourse. In this revision of both past and present, the federal government and African-Americans are perceived as conjoined, all-powerful enemies. These irredeemably racist ideas are congruent with other paranoid narratives of white martyrdom. Confederate iconography is embraced by a range of right-wing groups, from the Ku Klux Klan to neo-Nazis.[19]

This ideology of racist backlash is by no means embraced by the majority of Confederate reenactors. Most Confederate enthusiasts adamantly separate their activities from racism, as exemplified in the common slogan "Heritage Not Hate." Declared motives for reenacting the Confederacy center on the pleasures of adopting the "underdog" role and of understanding a transformative historical moment. Journalist Tony Horwitz suggests that participation in Civil War rituals may provide "a badge of citizenship," particularly for immigrants or others newly claiming their identity as Americans.[20]

Independent of the politics of individual reenactors, however, the collective impact of an admiring reanimation of the Confederacy is the renewal of racism. It is important to note that this renewal is not unique to the South but is available to participants and spectators from any region. As *The Birth of a Nation* captivated white audiences everywhere, so too can anyone involved in reenactments become a galvanized Confederate. Indeed, the racist impact of Confederate iconography is all the more powerful for the way it appears to localize racial questions to the American South. White Southerners have long resented such localizations, which turn their region into the national scapegoat in discussions of racism. As Robert Penn Warren famously formulated, white Northerners emerged from the Civil War with a "Treasury of Virtue," granted "a plenary indulgence, for all sins past, present, and future, freely given by the hand of history."[21] For the white Northerner—or any non-Southerner—participating in or witnessing Civil War reenactments, the "treasury of virtue" may pay a double dividend. The iconography of the Confederacy potentially promotes white remasculinization through the performance of Southernness while displacing racism at home.

Nor does a focus on the iconography of the Union counteract the possible reactionary effects of reenactments. As long as these rituals commemorate the war primarily as a set of conflicts among white people, they obscure the centrality of African-Americans to the causes, battles, and aftermath of the war. For all the fetishistic commitment to historical authenticity among reenactors, their rituals mystify the meaning and legacy of the war for race relations. This mystification also informs Ken Burns's television series on the Civil War, whose final episode frames the war's legacy as one of shared experiences among white men North and South.[22] Decades ago, John Hope Franklin criticized the first major wave of Civil War reenactments, held during the war's centennial, for their similar failure to address issues of race and slavery. The unresolved status of freed slaves in postwar America, he argued, is the war's truest and least confronted legacy, and that lack of confrontation has served "to haunt every Civil War observance from Appomattox to 1961 and . . . to make such observances false as well as iniquitous."[23] His critique still holds today.

Now as always, however, Civil War culture is a contested domain. In the tradition of antiracist writers like Lillian Smith, some Southern whites continue to demythologize the Confederacy, as in Allan Gurganus's novel *Oldest Living Confederate Widow Tells All* (1989).[24] Within the reenactment world, a growing group of black participants, catalyzed by the film *Glory* (1990), challenges mainstream Civil War history.[25] Black reenactors belong to the larger genealogy of revisionist African-American Civil War commentary I have been tracing, whose contemporary forms include novels as well. Alex Haley's *Roots* (1976), for example, touches on the Civil War in its concluding chapters, while Ernest Gaines's *The Autobiography of Miss Jane Pittman* (1971) opens with the war. Ishmael Reed's *Flight to Canada* (1976) skewers the war era through anachronistic satire, and Wesley Brown's *Darktown Strutters* (1994) embeds it within a fictional narrative of nineteenth-century black stage performers.[26]

Contemporary black women novelists have more commonly focused on the antebellum era, although novels such as J. California Cooper's *Family* (1991) and *The Wake of the Wind* (1998) include the war years.[27] What John Hope Franklin calls the "haunt[ing]" conjunction of African-Americans and the Civil War emerges most dramatically, however, in Toni Morrison's novel *Beloved* (1987). If the war itself, as John Limon has noted, has a curiously marginal presence in a novel that oscillates between 1855 and 1873, that margin is nonetheless a defining one.[28] The ghost of Beloved first appears during the Civil War, prompting Howard and Buglar to enlist as soldiers—"they rather be around killing men than killing women"—and inaugurating Sethe's own battles with the daughter she has murdered.[29] We might interpret the conflicts of reunification and division that are set in motion by Beloved as the novel's version of the Civil War—a war waged between these two "killing women" and within Sethe herself.

While Toni Morrison, like Lauren Cook Burgess, returns to nineteenth-century Civil War settings, other women carry the resonances of the Civil War into contemporary narratives. Two identically entitled texts, Rosellen Brown's novel *Civil Wars* (1984) and June Jordan's essay "Civil Wars" (1980), move further away from the moment of the Civil War but retain and transform its metaphoric legacies. Brown's *Civil Wars* focuses on a white woman, Jessie Carll, living with her husband and children in Jackson, Mississippi, after the waning of the Civil Rights Movement that brought her South from New York in the 1960s. In the Jackson of 1979, the Carlls are the only white family in a once-integrated neighborhood whose black residents increasingly pressure them to leave. Meanwhile, Jessie, raised in a New York Jewish Communist family, struggles with her marriage to a white Southerner, Teddy, who clings to his memories of the Movement. The plot centers on the transformation of the Carlls after they adopt O'Neill and Helen, the orphaned son and daughter of Teddy's bigoted sister. While Jessie attempts to keep this expanded family intact, Teddy begins an affair with an admiring young editor, and Helen documents her growing alienation and racism in her diary. *Civil Wars* culminates in an apocalyptic rainstorm, in which the Carlls lose their new home and Helen tries to kill herself, and after which Jessie tentatively decides to leave Teddy and return to New York with the children. As this summary suggests, the novel establishes a variety of "civil wars," a phrase that Brown—a white novelist and poet who worked in Mississippi in the 1960s—describes as "an absolute title for me. It represents every conceivable rift between intimates that I can imagine . . . every cross purpose at which friends and family can move."[30] More broadly, this work features "civil wars" between and among North and South, black and white, men and women, past and present, public history and private life, and idealism and disillusionment.

Beneath these strata of internecine conflict, the Civil War is the novel's original ground. Brown characterizes the Civil Rights Movement that motivated Jessie to come South as an explicit reprise of the earlier war: "Half the campuses in the country had committed their able-bodied students, like villages their soldiers, to the second Civil War."[31] Fought as a second Civil War, the Civil Rights movement should be duly memorialized, as O'Neill reports to his sister: "Teddy says there are these places where people actually got killed and stuff, and we can go visit them, he says they ought to make them just like the Civil War monuments with markers and everything. So people will always remember" (280). Teddy himself is a living monument to both wars. His Civil Rights speeches are anthologized "as an example of Southern white eloquence, second only to black eloquence in the recent history of persuasion" (26), while he enthralls his children with "Civil War history which could almost make them cry" (34). This connection between childhood and the war replicates Teddy's own: "When he was about nine, he had found two Civil War bullets on the lawn under an oleander bush, shining at its roots . . . [Jessie] would bet there wasn't a child in this state who missed that experience—it was like a confirmation" (17). Like other white Southerners, Teddy's coming-of-age is inseparable from the "confirmation" experience the Civil War affords the region as a whole.

Underpinning the novel's representation of Civil Rights, the Civil War painfully shapes the psyches of its adult protagonists. Teddy is the novel's confident voice of historical memory, but he is also its scarred embodiment. Early in the novel, Jessie describes him as "Teddy Carll the Confederate child growing up to be a moral Yankee with those hard little bullets lodged in his flesh somewhere, surrounded by the scar tissue of his reform" (18). The scars of Teddy's internal bifurcation between "Confederate" and "Yankee" take literal form in his face, which is damaged from an earlier episode when racists ran his car off the road and is "forever tortured by scarring" (22). Other zones of Teddy's body register his memories of growing up in the segregated South: "Sometimes his chest constricted at his memories, he told her he could feel a band of numbness circling front to back as if his heart were all scar tissue" (94). Multiply scarred, Teddy is the embodiment of a white body politic trying to secede from its own racist history. This attempt is unsuccessful, for Teddy's only weapon, as Jessie describes him, is the memory of his past glory. After he awes the young editor with stories of the Movement, Jessie condemns him as "a goddamn necrophiliac" (363); when he conducts a misguided political protest, she reflects that "He had chosen an impossible campaign so that he could hang his flag of surrender" (363). Lodged between the necrophilia of remembering victory and the masochism of embracing defeat, Teddy ironically emerges as another version of a Lost Cause myth-maker. Despite his commitment to transforming the South, he—like the Confederate apologists whose politics he would despise—cannot move beyond the twitching scars of his own past.

Jessie too struggles with internal division in an era when, as she wryly acknowledges, "the days of Earnest White Girls for Integration were over" (19). Like Teddy, Jessie is scarred; contemplating divorce, she despairs, "Somewhere there must be other scarred old veterans—a union organizer? An antiwar campaigner? Anybody with scars; she would have to hope he was not a pile of smothered ashes" (366). Yet her scars are different, defined not by self-consuming internal divisions but by the alienations of exile: "She was, she thought, without having crossed a national boundary, an expatriate" (18). For Jessie, expatriation involves internal alienation as well as geographic isolation. Repulsed by a group of conservative Southern women, she thinks, "She was a traitor to female solidarity. Well, how many ways could one divide oneself? The women who threw stones at small black children, were they women before they were racists, were they allies first, or deadly foes?" (227). Jessie also suffers from the territorialities of a marriage in which Teddy's "annexation of her independence made it hard for others to know her" (244). Even her closest friendship, with an African-American lawyer named Andréa, reaches its limits during a discussion of the Black Power movement, when Andréa gleefully criticizes Teddy to her, and "Jessie, divided, did not smile back" (369). Jessie's expatriation is psychic as well as regional, in a novel in which, as Brown describes, "No one . . . is living with the same sense of place as anyone else, even when they stand with shoulders touching."[32]

Yet if Jessie cannot escape displacement and division, she can at least confront her own civil wars, as two passages late in the novel suggest. Alone on New Year's Eve, she stares at the kitchen clock, an inheritance from Teddy's family, for whom, she surmises, "it had ticked on evenly through the Civil War" (353). She realizes that "There was public time—at a sufficient distance it was called history—and there was private time that beat like a small hot heart inside the body of that history. All those fluttering failing hearts, trying only to sustain one body at a time. You couldn't escape the public part, you were in it and it in you" (353). The relationship between public and private time is one of mutual coexistence, with Brown's corporeal imagery that of hearts rather than scars. The Civil War is symbolically central to this language, as represented in the domestic image of the kitchen clock, whose ticking is another form of heartbeat. Similarly, in the novel's closing scene, after the flood, the war is an essential reference point: "Electric as a lure across the water, the stripes of the rebel flag bobbed just at the corner of her eye" (419). The mechanical Civil War clock resurfaces as an electrical Rebel flag, offering "a lure" to another meditation on past and present: "All she could hear was the intimate lick and suckle of the instant, which was deepening around her. She would walk in it a good deal longer before it became the past" (419). Like the earlier passage about time, these closing lines of the novel feature the living body, with the "small hot heart" joined by the "lick and suckle" of the instant. These images of corporeal vitality do not erase the novel's metaphors of scarring, but they do redirect them. If the novel ends with Jessie contemplating her own form of secession—divorce from Teddy—then this civil war will at least carry her forward rather than back into the past.

While Rosellen Brown's *Civil Wars* takes the Confederate iconography of contemporary Mississippi as its point of origin, June Jordan's "Civil Wars" returns to the civil war with which I introduced this study: the divided domain of civility. A prominent poet, essayist, and activist, Jordan is one of many African-American commentators on civility, but her approach contrasts dramatically with the nineteenth-century celebrations of civility found in writers like Anna Julia Cooper and from the contemporary promotion of civility by the legal scholar Stephen Carter. In the context of renewed public interest in the topic, Carter's *Civility: Manners, Morals, and the Etiquette of Democracy* (1998) offers a jeremiad about the "collapse of civility in America" and sketches a manifesto for its revival, in which civility, he suggests approvingly, "teaches us to discipline our desires for the sake of others."[33] By contrast, Jordan's 1980 essay is a critique of civility in the context of radical political activism. "Civil Wars" is the closing selection in a 1981 anthology of the same title, whose essays range from topics such as Black Studies and Black English to discussions of gender and sexuality. Although the Civil War is nowhere named directly in this collection, it serves implicitly as its governing metaphor. Analyzing her shared allegiances to "the Black Movement, the Third World Movement, and the Women's Movement," for example, Jordan decries "a magnitude of internecine, unfortunate, and basically untenable conflicts of analysis."[34] In the essay "Civil Wars," Jordan moves from this metaphor of "internecine" conflicts to an attack on the civil wars caused by civility itself.

"Civil Wars" begins with an account of an unnamed political meeting in which "Everybody's on best behavior: politely taking turns, preparing to vote or write letters. The problem is the yearning courtesies, the underlying patience, the honcho upfront and the followers who face him, or her. . . . Look at the meaning of the manners of the scene!"[35] The "meaning of manners," for Jordan, is both repression and oppression, as rooted in the events of her own childhood: "In the context of tragedy, all polite behavior is a form of self-denial. I can remember being eight years old and there was my mother warning me to watch *the tone of my voice* in the middle of a violent fight between my father and myself" (179). Moving outward from this story, she condemns the large-scale consequences of civility:

> Deceit, surrender, and concealment: these are not virtues.
>   . . . The courtesies of order, of ruly forms pursued from a heart of rage or terror or grief defame the truth of every human crisis. . . .
>   But the lobby for polite behavior is fairly inescapable. Most often, the people who can least afford to further efface and deny the truth of what they experience, the people whose very existence is most endangered and, therefore, most in need

of vigilantly truthful affirmation, these are the people—the poor and the children—who are punished most severely for departures from the civilities that grease oppression. (180)

Civility, in this account, is a dangerous fiction, which effaces emotion and polices politics. In response, Jordan calls for the violent abolition of civility: "Violation invites, and teaches, violence. Less than that, less than a scream or a fist, less than the absolute cessation of normal events in the lock of absolute duress is a lie" (180). Yet Jordan concludes this opening account of civility with her own complicity: "Nonetheless, I am a liar. I am frequently polite. I go to meetings and sit, properly, in one chair. I write letters to Washington. It's been a long while since I actually hit anybody at all" (180). The silenced daughter has become the self-silencing woman. In this self-mocking self-description, Jordan offers both her ironic compact with civility's fictions and an incipient rebellion against them.

Against this divided critique of civility, Jordan outlines the central plot of the essay: her sustained fight with a close friend, white scholar Frances Fox Piven. In response to an essay Jordan has written on Black-Jewish relations, Piven, who is Jewish, accuses her of anti-Semitism; conversely, Jordan feels that Piven is homophobic:

> "Oh, Gay Rights," she said. "No," I said, "Civil Rights."
> Well, about this we disagreed, and seriously. Of course, that had been an area of silence between us for many years: "Gay Rights," or my loving a woman, these were subjects excluded from the compass of her radical humanitarian concern. (181)

This conflict pivots on the question of silence:

> It seemed to me that my silence . . . and my continuing self-denial around the "issue" of my bisexuality was what had kept the friendship alive. Without my collaboration, without my self-censorship, the disagreements between us seemed irreconcilable.
> . . . I had chosen to keep silent and to politely slide by, or omit, references to these explosive spaces between us. But now that such silence was broken, and after our fight, I felt I had to make a choice I had never expected to make. And so I did. I chose complete silence. (182)

Several forms of "civil war" are in play at this moment. The overt arena of dissent is that of sexuality. Inseparable from the "explosive spaces" between the two women over this issue is Jordan's own war with civility. Her "continuing self-censorship" moves the axis of conflict from between the two women to within Jordan, with her silence the evidence of defeat.

Jordan concludes the essay, however, with a breakthrough. Energized by contemporary black protest in Miami—"At a minimum we have the power to stop cooperating with our enemies . . . to stop the courtesies and to let the feelings be real" (187)—she is prompted by her son to read Piven's book, *Poor People's Movements: How They Succeed, Why They Fail.* Afterwards, she is inspired to contact the other woman, but pauses. The essay concludes:

> But I hesitated. I thought again about all the other things that we would not talk about and all the arguments that would persist between us, and my feeling was, "What the hell; friendship is not a tragedy; we can be polite."
> And so I called her up, to talk. (188)

This moment revalues the previously discredited modes of politeness and civility, not only revising the idea that "all polite behavior is a form of self-denial" but also recasting her painful earlier image of civility between women as a mother's policing of her daughter. Here, by contrast, civility is the foundation of connection between women, deployed without coercion and across division. The outcome of the effort is unclear: Jordan does not specify whether her politics of sexuality—more fully articulated in her subsequent writing[36]—remained in the closeted category of "things that we would not talk about," formed an openly voiced persisting argument, or, more redemptively, became a commitment supported by Piven. The essay's ambiguous ending does suggest, however, that the only possibility of moving forward is through the previously discredited route of civility. By the end of "Civil Wars," civility remains a fiction, but it may also be a necessary one.

From the male battle reenactment to the embattled female friendship, these contemporary examples of women's civil wars provide less self-divided conclusions than those offered by the original "Earnest White Girls," to borrow Rosellen Brown's phrase, with whom I began this study: Harriet Beecher Stowe and Louisa May Alcott. Alcott's topsy-turvy female protagonist finds relief only in imposing discipline on others; Stowe's white female characters displace incivility onto Topsy. By contrast, Burgess wins her lawsuit, Brown's Jessie prepares to move, and Jordan's "I" makes her call. An emblem of the contrast between earlier and later texts is provided in *Civil Wars,* when Brown includes an image of what is unmistakably a topsy-turvy doll: "one of those [dolls] that turns over, this way it is blonde and white and when you flip its skirts it is colored but both have the exact same face sewed on in different colors" (343). The voice here is that of Helen, the racist child, writing in her diary; the setting is the house of Andréa and her white husband Tommy. The passage both recalls *Uncle Tom's Cabin* and transforms it, with Brown situating the white girl's racism within an interracial venue and alongside the more self-aware and antiracist narrative of Jessie. In Jordan's "Civil Wars," the topsy-turvy doll has been even more fully dismembered. Jordan concludes with her black and white female protagonists facing each other, in conflict but in conversation. While the civil war between the two women continues, at least one of its combatants has renegotiated the rules of engagement.

Yet if these current stories conclude the "civil wars" of earlier texts more victoriously, they nonetheless reenact their psychic scars and political contradictions. By the end of "Civil Wars," Jordan has redefined civility to redeem a female friendship, but she has not escaped its psychic pressures. Whatever the outcome of Jordan's closing phone call, her attack upon civility is also a struggle within it, and the cease-fire between women with which the essay concludes does not evade civility's constraining frame. In the case of Lauren Cook Burgess, the racist connotations of the Confederacy radically undermine the feminist yield of a contemporary story of Civil War cross-dressing. Even a high-camp appropriation of the image presented by Burgess cannot escape the associations of her costume with a history of determined efforts against black freedom. Now as in the nineteenth century, women's "civil wars" encompass multiple conflicts and point in contrary directions, both repressive and liberatory. The civility that silences some women provides the vocabulary with which others can speak. In these conflicts of metaphor against itself, the Civil War continues to be fought, today no less than a hundred and thirty years ago. Still expatriates in the nation of the male war story, women continue to shape its outcome, fighting in the many ongoing battles—at once internecine and uncivil—among warring fictions.

Notes

INTRODUCTION

1. Henry Ward Beecher, "Against a Compromise of Principle" (1860), reprinted in *"God Ordained This War": Sermons on the Sectional Crisis, 1830–1865,* edited by David B. Chesebrough (Columbia: University of South Carolina Press, 1991), p. 71; Abraham Lincoln, address at Gettysburg, Pennsylvania, 19 November 1863, in *Abraham Lincoln: Speeches and Writings, 1859–1865,* edited by Don E. Fehrenbacher (New York: Library of America, 1989), p. 536. On birth imagery in the Gettysburg Address, see James Hurt, "All the Living and the Dead: Lincoln's Imagery," *American Literature* 52:3 (November 1980): 376–80; Stephanie A. Smith, *Conceived by Liberty: Maternal Figures and Nineteenth-Century American Literature* (Ithaca: Cornell University Press, 1994); Priscilla Wald, *Constituting Americans: Cultural Anxiety and Narrative Form* (Durham: Duke University Press, 1995); and Garry Wills, *Lincoln at Gettysburg: The Words That Remade America* (New York: Simon and Schuster, 1992). On Lincoln and paternal imagery, see George B. Forgie, *Patricide in the House Divided: A Psychological Interpretation of Lincoln and His Age* (New York: W. W. Norton, 1979); on paternal imagery in antebellum America, see Russ Castronovo, *Fathering the Nation: American Genealogies of Slavery and Freedom* (Berkeley: University of California Press, 1995); and on masculinity and American national identity, see Dana D. Nelson, *National Manhood: Capitalist Citizenship and the Imagined Fraternity of White Men* (Durham: Duke University Press, 1998).

2. David Lundberg, "The American Literature of War: The Civil War, World War I, and World War II," *American Quarterly* 36 (bibliography 1984): 376, 373.

3. The two classic surveys of Civil War literature are Daniel Aaron, *The Unwritten War: American Writers and the Civil War* (1973; rpt. Madison: University of Wisconsin Press, 1987), and Edmund Wilson, *Patriotic Gore: Studies in the Literature of the American Civil War* (1962; rpt. Boston: Northeastern University Press, 1984). Important recent analyses of this literature include Jim Cullen, *The Civil War in Popular Culture: A Reusable Past* (Washington: Smithsonian Institution Press, 1995); Kathleen Diffley, "The Roots of Tara: Making War Civil," *American Quarterly* 36 (bibliography 1984):

359–72; Diffley, *"Where My Heart Is Turning Ever": Civil War Stories and Constitutional Reform, 1861–1876* (Athens: University of Georgia Press, 1992); Gregory Eiselein, *Literature and Humanitarian Reform in the Civil War Era* (Bloomington: Indiana University Press, 1996); John Limon, *Writing After War: American War Fiction from Realism to Postmodernism* (New York: Oxford University Press, 1994); Jane Ellen Schultz, "Women at the Front: Gender and Genre in the Literature of the American Civil War," Ph.D. diss., University of Michigan, 1988; and Timothy Sweet, *Traces of War: Poetry, Photography, and the Crisis of the Union* (Baltimore: Johns Hopkins University Press, 1990). Other useful works are David Kaser, *Books and Libraries in Camp and Battle: The Civil War Experience* (Westport, CT: Greenwood Press, 1984); Robert A. Lively, *Fiction Fights the Civil War: An Unfinished Chapter in the Literary History of the American People* (Chapel Hill: University of North Carolina Press, 1957); Albert J. Menendez, *Civil War Novels: An Annotated Bibliography* (New York: Garland Press, 1986); and Rebecca Washington Smith, *The Civil War and Its Aftermath in American Fiction, 1861–1899* (Chicago: University of Chicago Libraries Private Edition, 1937). For a recent anthology of Civil War writing, see Louis P. Masur, ed., *"The Real War Will Never Get in the Books": Selections from Writers During the Civil War* (New York: Oxford University Press, 1993); for an anthology of commentary on Civil War fiction, see David Madden and Peggy Bach, eds., *Classics of Civil War Fiction* (Jackson: University of Mississippi Press, 1991). The most important archive of Civil War fiction is the Reverend Richard H. Wilmer, Jr., Collection of Civil War Novels at the University of North Carolina at Chapel Hill.

4. This concept is foregrounded, for example, in the title of LeeAnn Whites's study, *The Civil War as a Crisis in Gender: Augusta, Georgia, 1860–1890* (Athens: University of Georgia Press, 1995). For an overview of new scholarship on gender and the Civil War, see Drew Gilpin Faust, "'Ours as Well as That of the Men': Women and Gender in the Civil War," in *Writing the Civil War: The Quest to Understand*, edited by James M. McPherson and William J. Cooper, Jr. (Columbia: University of South Carolina Press, 1998), pp. 228–40. For an important anthology of new scholarship, see Catherine Clinton and Nina Silber, eds., *Divided Houses: Gender and the Civil War* (New York: Oxford University Press, 1992). More citations are given below and in subsequent chapters.

5. For discussion of Crane that emphasizes the consistent belatedness of his lived experience in relation to his literary subject matter, see Christopher Benfey, *The Double Life of Stephen Crane* (New York: Alfred A. Knopf, 1992).

6. Aaron, *Unwritten War*, p. 328.

7. Wilson, *Patriotic Gore*, p. xiii.

8. For an anthology of African-American writing on the war, see Richard A. Long, ed., *Black Writers and the American Civil War* (Secaucus, NJ: Blue and Grey Press, 1988). Citations to individual authors and other relevant texts are given in chapters 3 and 5.

9. Mary Chesnut is praised in Wilson, *Patriotic Gore*, p. 279, and Aaron, *Unwritten War*, p. 259; for a more recent assessment of her diaries, see Drew Gilpin Faust, "In Search of the Real Mary Chesnut," in *Southern Stories: Slaveholders in Peace and War*

(Columbia: University of Missouri Press, 1992), pp. 141–47. On "Marion Harland" [Mary Virginia Hawes Terhune], see Elizabeth Moss, *Domestic Novelists in the Old South: Defenders of Southern Culture* (Baton Rouge: Louisiana State University Press, 1992), pp. 194–221. On Johnston, Glasgow, King, and Chopin, see Anne Goodwyn Jones, *Tomorrow Is Another Day: The Woman Writer in the South, 1859–1936* (Baton Rouge: Louisiana State University Press, 1981); on Chopin and the Civil War, see also Christopher Benfey, *Degas in New Orleans* (New York: Alfred A. Knopf, 1997), pp. 231–38, 245–52. Southern interest in the historical romance is analyzed by George Dekker, *The American Historical Romance* (Cambridge: Cambridge University Press, 1987), pp. 272–333. On the publishing industry in the Confederate South, see Elisabeth Muhlenfeld, *The History of Southern Literature,* edited by Louis D. Rubin, Jr., et al. (Baton Rouge: Louisiana State University Press, 1985), pp. 178–87. For further citations to Southern women's writing, see chapter 4.

10. Alcott and Phelps are discussed in chapter 2. On Dickinson, see Shira Wolosky, *Emily Dickinson: A Voice of War* (New Haven: Yale University Press, 1984). On Howe, see Mary H. Grant, *Private Woman, Public Person: An Account of the Life of Julia Ward Howe from 1819 to 1868* (Brooklyn: Carlson, 1994). On Child, see *A Romance of the Republic,* introduction by Dana D. Nelson (1867; rpt. Louisville: University of Kentucky Press, 1997); for discussion of Child and the Civil War, see Carolyn Karcher, *The First Woman in the Republic: A Cultural Biography of Lydia Maria Child* (Durham: Duke University Press, 1994), pp. 443–86. On Davis, see "John Lamar" (1862) and "David Gaunt" (1862), both reprinted in *A Rebecca Harding Davis Reader,* edited by Jean Pfaelzer (Pittsburgh: University of Pittsburgh Press, 1995), and *Waiting for the Verdict,* edited by Donald Dingledine (1867; rpt. Albany: NCUP, 1995). Civil War fiction by Northern and Southern white women is anthologized in *Civil War Women: The Civil War Seen Through Women's Eyes in Stories by Louisa May Alcott, Kate Chopin, Eudora Welty, and Other Great Women Writers,* edited by Frank McSherry, Jr., Charles G. Waugh, and Martin Greenberg (New York: Touchstone/Simon and Schuster, 1988), and *Civil War Women II: Stories by Women about Women,* edited by Martin H. Greenberg, Charles G. Waugh, and Frank D. McSherry, Jr. (Little Rock: August House, 1997).

11. Lively, *Fiction Fights the Civil War,* p. 46. See also Lawrence Thompson, "The Civil War in Fiction," *Civil War History* 2:1 (March 1956), who terms this writing "the feminine school" and emphasizes its "crudity" (84); and, less pejoratively, Jan Cohn, "The Civil War in Magazine Fiction of the 1860s," *Journal of Popular Culture* 4 (1970): "Generally, the fiction about the war is written by women before 1865, and only after the war had ended did male writers begin to invade the market" (379). For an overview of wartime best-sellers, see James D. Hart, *The Popular Book: A History of America's Literary Taste* (1950; rpt. Berkeley: University of California Press, 1961), pp. 113–18. For an overview of women's writing during the war, see Mary Elizabeth Massey, *Women in the Civil War,* introduction by Jean V. Berlin (1966; rpt. Lincoln: University of Nebraska Press, 1994), pp. 175–96.

12. This series is discussed in Kaser, *Books and Libraries in Camp and Battle,* pp. 94–95.

13. For discussion of this novel, see Drew Gilpin Faust, Introduction to Augusta Jane Evans, *Macaria; or, Altars of Sacrifice* (1864; rpt. Baton Rouge: Louisiana State University Press, 1992), pp. xiii–xxvi, and Moss, *Domestic Novelists in the Old South*, pp. 171–94. On the burning of *Macaria*, see Kaser, *Books and Libraries in Camp and Battle*, p. 36.

14. I discuss this quotation at length in chapter 1; its original source is Annie Adams Fields, *Life and Letters of Harriet Beecher Stowe* (Boston: Houghton Mifflin, 1897 [1898]), p. 269.

15. For introductions to the extensive scholarship on women and war, see the following anthologies: Miriam Cooke and Angela Woollacott, eds., *Gendering War Talk* (Princeton: Princeton University Press, 1993); Helen M. Cooper, Adrienne Auslander Munich, and Susan Merrill Squier, eds., *Arms and the Woman: War, Gender, and Literary Representation* (Chapel Hill: University of North Carolina Press, 1989); Lois Ann Lorentzen and Jennifer Turpin, eds., *The Women and War Reader* (New York: New York University Press, 1998); and Margaret Randolph Higonnet et al., eds., *Behind the Lines: Gender and the Two World Wars* (New Haven: Yale University Press, 1987). For an excellent study of women's writing in relation to another American war, see Susan Schweik, *A Gulf So Deeply Cut: American Women Writers and the Second World War* (Madison: University of Wisconsin Press, 1991).

16. A few representative texts: The Civil War is infrequently discussed in such pioneering studies of Northern women's writing as Nina Baym, *Woman's Fiction: A Guide to Novels by and about Women in America, 1820–1870* (Ithaca: Cornell University Press, 1978); Mary Kelley, *Private Woman, Public Stage: Literary Domesticity in Nineteenth-Century America* (New York: Oxford University Press, 1984); and Jane Tompkins, *Sensational Designs: The Cultural Work of American Fiction, 1790–1860* (New York: Oxford University Press, 1985), as well as more recent works by Gillian Brown, *Domestic Individualism: Imagining Self in Nineteenth-Century America* (Berkeley: University of California Press, 1990); Susan K. Harris, *Nineteenth-Century American Women's Novels: Interpretative Strategies* (Cambridge: Cambridge University Press, 1990); and Shirley Samuels, ed., *The Culture of Sentiment: Race, Gender, and Sentimentality in Nineteenth-Century America* (New York: Oxford University Press, 1992). The war has only a trace presence in such important studies of African-American women's writing as Hazel V. Carby, *Reconstructing Womanhood: The Emergence of the Afro-American Woman Novelist* (New York: Oxford University Press, 1987); Deborah E. McDowell, *"The Changing Same": Black Women's Literature, Criticism, and Theory* (Bloomington: Indiana University Press, 1995); and Claudia Tate, *Domestic Allegories of Political Desire: The Black Heroine's Text at the Turn of the Century* (New York: Oxford University Press, 1992). The war appears more often in literary analyses of white Southern women's writing, such as Moss, *Domestic Novelists in the Old South*, and Jones, *Tomorrow Is Another Day*.

17. *Frank Leslie's Illustrated Newspaper*, 10 October 1863, quoted in Massey, *Women in the Civil War*, p. 175.

18. For discussion of gender anxieties in postwar literary culture, see Elizabeth

Ammons, "Gender and Fiction," in *The Columbia History of the American Novel*, edited by Emory Elliott (New York: Columbia University Press, 1991), pp. 267–84; Joan D. Hedrick, *Harriet Beecher Stowe: A Life* (New York: Oxford University Press, 1994), pp. ix–x; and Kenneth W. Warren, *Black and White Strangers: Race and American Literary Realism* (Chicago: University of Chicago Press, 1993), pp. 89–108. For divergent analyses of the reception of antebellum women's fiction, see Nina Baym, "The Rise of The Woman Author," in *The Columbia Literary History of the United States*, edited by Emory Elliott (New York: Columbia University Press, 1988), pp. 289–305; Ann Douglas, *The Feminization of American Culture* (New York: Alfred A. Knopf, 1977); David Leverenz, *Manhood and the American Renaissance* (Ithaca: Cornell University Press, 1989); Lora Romero, *Home Fronts: Domesticity and Its Critics in the Antebellum United States* (Durham: Duke University Press, 1997); and Tompkins, *Sensational Designs*. On the centrality of the jeremiad form in American culture, see Sacvan Bercovitch, *The American Jeremiad* (Madison: University of Wisconsin Press, 1978).

19. Aaron, for example, calls *Miss Ravenel* "the best novel about the War to be written by a veteran or, for that matter, by anyone" (*Unwritten War*, 165), and Stephen Becker praises De Forest as "the first American to write realistically and grimly of war from first-hand experience" ("On John William De Forest's *Miss Ravenel's Conversion from Secession to Loyalty*," in *Classics of Civil War Fiction*, 28). For a recent analysis of *Miss Ravenel*, see Limon, *Writing After War*, pp. 59–83.

20. William Dean Howells, "The Stamp of Verity," *Atlantic Monthly* (July 1867), reprinted in William Dean Howells, *"Criticism and Fiction" and Other Essays*, edited by Clara Marburg Kirk and Rudolf Kirk (New York: New York University Press, 1959), p. 110.

21. Nina Baym, "Melodramas of Beset Manhood: How Theories of American Literature Exclude Women Authors," in *Feminism and American Literary History: Essays* (New Brunswick: Rutgers University Press, 1992), pp. 3–18.

22. Quoted in Wilson, *Patriotic Gore*, p. 697.

23. William Dean Howells, *Heroines in Fiction* (1901), quoted in Wilson, *Patriotic Gore*, p. 698.

24. Stephen Crane, *The Red Badge of Courage* (New York: W. W. Norton, 1976), p. 109; all subsequent quotations are from this edition and cited parenthetically in the text. For discussion of this passage, see Howard Horsford, "'He Was a Man,'" in *New Essays on "The Red Badge of Courage,"* edited by Lee Clark Mitchell (Cambridge: Cambridge University Press, 1986), pp. 109–50.

25. Amy Kaplan, "The Spectacle of War in Crane's Revision of History," in *New Essays on "The Red Badge of Courage,"* p. 100.

26. John Carlos Rowe also cites the "negro teamster" in "Race and Imperialism in Stephen Crane: A Monstrous Case," a paper delivered at the Colloquium for the Study of American Culture, Huntington Library, San Marino, CA, March 1997. Ralph Ellison notes that "for all the complex use of the symbolic connotations of blackness, only one Negro, a dancing teamster, appears throughout the novel" ("Stephen Crane

and the Mainstream of American Fiction," in *Shadow and Act* [New York: Signet, 1964], p. 81).

27. "Maternalized engulfment" is Mark Seltzer's term, in *Bodies and Machines* (New York: Routledge, 1992), p. 112.

28. I adapt the term "remasculinized" from Susan Jeffords, *The Remasculinization of America: Gender and the Vietnam War* (Bloomington: Indiana University Press, 1989). I discuss her use of this term and its applications elsewhere in Civil War culture in chapter 4.

29. "Opposed to the Name Rebellion," *Confederate Veteran* 2:7 (July 1894): 199.

30. Quoted in Edmond S. Meany, *Name of the American War of 1861–1865* (Seattle, 1910), p. 4.

31. See Gaines M. Foster, *Ghosts of the Confederacy: Defeat, the Lost Cause, and the Emergence of the New South, 1865 to 1913* (New York: Oxford University Press, 1987), pp. 117–19, and James I. Robertson, Jr., entry on "Names of the War," in *Encyclopedia of the Confederacy*, edited by Richard N. Current (New York: Simon and Schuster, 1993), vol. 1, pp. 316–17.

32. On women's leadership in the name-change campaign, see Catherine Clinton, *Tara Revisited: Women, War, and the Plantation Legend* (New York: Abbeville, 1995), p. 183.

33. *Oxford English Dictionary*, 2d ed., s.v. "civil."

34. John Kasson, *Rudeness and Civility: Manners in Nineteenth-Century Urban America* (New York: Hill and Wang, 1990); also relevant are Richard L. Bushman, *The Refinement of America: Persons, Houses, Cities* (New York: Vintage, 1992), and Kenneth Cmiel, *Democratic Eloquence: The Fight Over Popular Speech in Nineteenth-Century America* (New York: William Morrow, 1990). On the more general emergence of these terms, see Norbert Elias, *The Civilizing Process*, 2 vols., translated by Edmund Jephcott (Oxford: Basil Blackwell, 1978, 1982), and Raymond Williams, "Civilization," in *Keywords: A Vocabulary of Culture and Society* (New York: Oxford University Press, 1976), pp. 48–50.

35. Mark Twain, *The Adventures of Huckleberry Finn* (Berkeley: University of California Press, 1985), p. 362.

36. These examples are all cited in Kasson, *Rudeness and Civility*, pp. 163, 161, 161, taken respectively from *Social Customs* (1881), *Young Lady's Own Book* (1833), and *Miss Leslie's Behaviour Book* (1859). Kasson analyzes the importance of mirrors to the maintenance of civility on pp. 165–77. For a relevant examination of female "moodiness," see Nancy Schnog, "Changing Emotions: Moods and the Nineteenth-Century American Woman Writer," in *Inventing the Psychological: Toward a Cultural History of Emotional Life in America*, edited by Joel Pfister and Nancy Schnog (New Haven: Yale University Press, 1997), pp. 84–103.

37. On Wood, see Kasson, *Rudeness and Civility*, p. 54, and Leon F. Litwack, *Trouble in Mind: Black Southerners in the Age of Jim Crow* (New York: Alfred A. Knopf, 1998), p. 81. On antebellum attitudes toward "civilizing" African-Americans, see

George M. Fredrickson, *The Black Image in the White Mind: The Debate on Afro-American Character and Destiny, 1817–1914* (New York: Harper and Row, 1971), pp. 53–58. On civilizing imperatives in racial uplift discourse, see Kevin K. Gaines, *Uplifting the Race: Black Leadership, Politics, and Culture in the Twentieth Century* (Chapel Hill: University of North Carolina Press, 1996).

38. R[obert] C[harles] O['Hara] Benjamin, *Don't. A Book for Girls* (San Francisco: Valleau and Peterson, 1891), pp. 9–10. I discuss *Don't*, Wells-Barnett, and other black women's uses of civility in this period in chapter 5.

39. Mary A. Livermore, *My Story of the War*, with an introduction by Nina Silber (1887; rpt. New York: Da Capo, 1995), p. 9.

40. Quoted in Wendy Hamand Venet, *Neither Ballots Nor Bullets: Women Abolitionists and the Civil War* (Charlottesville: University Press of Virginia, 1991), p. 135; Venet discusses the League on pp. 94–122. On "republican motherhood," see Linda K. Kerber, *Women of the Republic: Intellect and Ideology in Revolutionary America* (New York: W. W. Norton, 1980).

41. On women's participation in the Draft Riots, see Mary P. Ryan, *Women in Public: Between Banners and Ballots, 1825–1880* (Baltimore: Johns Hopkins University Press, 1990), pp. 148–52. The "inner civil war" is the influential formulation of George M. Fredrickson, *The Inner Civil War: Northern Intellectuals and the Crisis of the Union* (New York: Harper and Row, 1965); a recent return to this material is Anne C. Rose, *Victorian America and the Civil War* (New York: Cambridge University Press, 1992).

42. On white women in Civil War New Orleans, see Drew Gilpin Faust, *Mothers of Invention: Women of the Slaveholding South in the American Civil War* (Chapel Hill: University of North Carolina Press, 1996), pp. 207–14; George Rable, "'Missing in Action': Women of the Confederacy," in *Divided Houses*, pp. 137–46; and Ryan, *Women in Public*, pp. 137–45. On bread riots, see Victoria E. Bynum, *Unruly Women: The Politics of Social and Sexual Control in the Old South* (Chapel Hill: University of North Carolina Press, 1992), pp. 125–29; and George Rable, *Civil Wars: Women and the Crisis of Southern Nationalism* (Urbana: University of Illinois Press), pp. 108–11.

43. Tubman describes the Combahee River raid in a dictated letter of 30 June 1863 to friends in Boston, reprinted in *The Black Abolitionist Papers*, edited by C. Peter Ripley (Chapel Hill: University of North Carolina Press, 1992), vol. 5, pp. 220–22. Her war experience is also dictated and discussed in Sarah Bradford, *Harriet Tubman: The Moses of Her People* (1881; rpt. Bedford, MA: Applewood Books, 1993). On Tubman and the war, see also Earl Conrad, *Harriet Tubman* (1943; rpt. New York: Paul Eriksson, 1969), pp. 149–87; Ella Forbes, *African American Women During the Civil War* (New York: Garland, 1998), pp. 37–40; Darlene Clark Hine and Kathleen Thompson, *A Shining Thread of Hope: The History of Black Women in America* (New York: Broadway Books, 1998), pp. 132–33; and Lyde Cullen Sizer, "Acting Her Part: Narratives of Union Women Spies," in *Divided Houses*, pp. 127–33.

44. Quoted in Venet, *Neither Ballots Nor Bullets*, p. 1.

45. I discuss the role of Southern white women in shaping Confederate memory

in chapter 4. On Southern white women's antipathy to feminism, see Rable, *Civil Wars*, pp. 285–88; and Marjorie Spruill Wheeler, "Divided Legacy: The Civil War, Tradition, and 'the Woman Question,'" in *A Woman's War: Southern Women, Civil War, and the Confederate Legacy*, edited by Edward D. C. Campbell, Jr., and Kym S. Rice (Richmond: Museum of the Confederacy/Charlottesville: University Press of Virginia, 1996), pp. 165–91.

46. See Nina Baym, *American Women Writers and the Work of History, 1790–1860* (New Brunswick: Rutgers University Press, 1995), pp. 152–86. For discussion of American historical fiction in this period, see Dekker, *American Historical Romance;* the most influential formulation of the genre is György Lukács, *The Historical Novel*, translated by Hannah and Stanley Mitchell (London: Merlin Press, 1962).

47. Margaret R. Higonnet, "Civil Wars and Sexual Territories," in *Arms and the Woman*, pp. 80, 81.

48. Robert Penn Warren, *The Legacy of the Civil War* (New York: Random House, 1961), pp. 83–84.

49. For an overview of this imagery, see Jenijoy La Belle, *Herself Beheld: The Literature of the Looking-Glass* (Ithaca: Cornell University Press, 1988).

50. See Diffley, "The Roots of Tara: Making War Civil," and *"Where My Heart Is Turning Ever,"* esp. pp. xlvi–xlvii.

51. I owe the formulation of the "ironic iconic" to Tom Herron, "City of Brotherly Love: Dis/imagining Community in *Philadelphia."* Paper delivered at the conference on "Film/Culture/History," University of Aberdeen, Scotland, August 1996. The phrases "foundational fictions," "invented traditions," and "imagined communities" draw respectively from Doris Sommer, *Foundational Fictions: The National Romances of Latin America* (Berkeley: University of California Press, 1991); Eric Hobsbawm and Terence Ranger, eds., *The Invention of Tradition* (New York: Cambridge University Press, 1983); and Benedict Anderson, *Imagined Communities: Reflections on the Origin and Spread of Nationalism* (London: Verso, 1983).

52. Willie Lee Rose, "Race and Region in American Historical Fiction: Four Episodes in Popular Culture," in *Region, Race, and Reconstruction: Essays in Honor of C. Vann Woodward*, edited by J. Morgan Kousser and James McPherson (New York: Oxford University Press, 1982), p. 114.

53. Leslie A. Fiedler, *The Inadvertent Epic: From "Uncle Tom's Cabin" to "Roots"* (New York: Simon and Schuster, 1979), p. 17.

54. Two definitions are in order here. First, while I will use this word without quotation marks, I understand "race" in American culture to be a social construction, defined in scientifically and politically illegitimate ways, whose effects nonetheless take very material forms. I use race rather than "race" for ease of analysis but do not want to reify the term's fictitious definitional underpinnings. Second, while my primary focus in analyzing race is on representations of white people and African-Americans, I do not intend for the black/white racial binary to subsume or displace other racial, ethnic, and cultural issues raised by the Civil War and its literatures; a larger study of multiethnic and multilingual Civil War literature remains to be done. However, one

of my aims is to show how the black/white cultural binary in the war era can itself only be understood in relation to shifting definitions of white ethnicity. For a discussion of defining race in quotation marks, see Dana D. Nelson, *The Word in Black and White: Reading "Race" in American Literature, 1638–1867* (New York: Oxford University Press, 1992), pp. vii–x; on the American history of this concept, see Thomas F. Gossett, *Race: The History of an Idea in America* (1963; rpt. New York: Oxford University Press, 1997).

55. Toni Morrison, *Playing in the Dark: Whiteness and the Literary Imagination* (New York: Vintage, 1992), p. 17. Other formulations of "whiteness" that I have found useful include Richard Dyer, *White* (London: Routledge, 1997); Ruth Frankenberg, *White Women, Race Matters: The Social Construction of Whiteness* (Minneapolis: University of Minnesota Press, 1993); George Lipsitz, *The Possessive Investment in Whiteness: How White People Profit from Identity Politics* (Philadelphia: Temple University Press, 1998); and David R. Roediger, *The Wages of Whiteness: Race and the Making of the American Working Class* (London: Verso, 1991). For an overview of new scholarship on whiteness, see Shelley Fisher Fishkin, "Interrogating 'Whiteness,' Complicating 'Blackness': Remapping American Culture," *American Quarterly* 47:3 (September 1995): 428–66; for a discussion of the politics of studying whiteness, see Dyer, *White*, pp. 8–14.

CHAPTER ONE

1. Elizabeth Ammons, "Stowe's Dream of the Mother-Savior: *Uncle Tom's Cabin* and American Women Writers Before the 1920s," in *New Essays on "Uncle Tom's Cabin,"* edited by Eric J. Sundquist (Cambridge: Cambridge University Press, 1986), p. 155. Helen Gray Cone, "Woman in Literature" (1891), reprinted in *Uncle Tom's Cabin: A Norton Critical Edition*, edited by Elizabeth Ammons (New York: W. W. Norton, 1994) [hereafter cited as *Norton Uncle Tom's Cabin*], p. 490; for discussion of Cone, see Ammons, *Conflicting Stories: American Women's Writing at the Turn into the Twentieth Century* (New York: Oxford University Press, 1992), pp. 12, 17–18, 26–27. There is no single guide to women writers' citations of Stowe, but the most comprehensive account of her influence is Thomas F. Gossett, *"Uncle Tom's Cabin" and American Culture* (Dallas: Southern Methodist University Press, 1985). See also Harry Birdoff, *The World's Greatest Hit: Uncle Tom's Cabin* (New York: S. F. Vanni, 1947), and Stephen A. Hirsch, "Uncle Tomitudes: The Popular Response to *Uncle Tom's Cabin*," *Studies in the American Renaissance*, edited by Joel Myerson (Boston: Twayne, 1978), pp. 303–30.

2. Florence J. O'Connor, *The Heroine of the Confederacy; or, Truth and Justice* (London, 1864), pp. 19, 31. For an overview of this text, see Maureen Murphy, "Florence J. O'Connor," *American Women Writers*, edited by Lina Mainiero (New York: Frederick Ungar, 1981), pp. 292–93.

3. *Mary Chesnut's Civil War*, edited by C. Vann Woodward (New Haven: Yale

University Press, 1981), pp. 298, 347. Other references to Stowe or *Uncle Tom's Cabin* appear in the diaries on pp. 153, 163, 168, 245, 307, 381, 428, 583, 599, 606–7, 642, 730, and 806.

4. Annie Adams Fields, ed., *Life and Letters of Harriet Beecher Stowe* (Boston: Houghton, Mifflin, 1897 [1898]), pp. 268–69. Gossett remarks this delay in *"Uncle Tom's Cabin" and American Culture*, p. 344.

5. Quoted in Joan D. Hedrick, *Harriet Beecher Stowe: A Biography* (New York: Oxford University Press, 1994), p. 306.

6. Ibid., p. 304.

7. Harriet Beecher Stowe, letter to James T. Fields, 27 October 1863, reprinted in James C. Austin, *Fields of "The Atlantic Monthly": Letters to an Editor, 1861–1870* (San Marino, CA: Huntington Library, 1953), p. 275.

8. On Stowe's experience of the Civil War, see Gossett, *"Uncle Tom's Cabin" and American Culture*, pp. 309–20; Wendy F. Hamand, "'No Voice From England': Mrs. Stowe, Mr. Lincoln, and the British in the Civil War," *New England Quarterly* 61:1 (March 1988): 3–24; Hedrick, *Harriet Beecher Stowe*, pp. 299–325; Patricia R. Hill, "Writing Out the War: Harriet Beecher Stowe's Averted Gaze," in *Divided Houses: Gender and the Civil War*, edited by Catherine Clinton and Nina Silber (New York: Oxford University Press, 1992), pp. 260–78; and Forrest Wilson, *Crusader in Crinoline: The Life of Harriet Beecher Stowe* (Philadelphia: J. B. Lippincott, 1941), pp. 460–505.

9. Catharine Beecher, *True Remedy for the Wrongs of Woman* (1851), quoted in Jeanne Boydston, Mary Kelley, and Anne Margolis, eds., *The Limits of Sisterhood: The Beecher Sisters on Women's Rights and Woman's Sphere* (Chapel Hill: University of North Carolina Press, 1988), p. 139; on Beecher, see also Kathryn Kish Sklar, *Catharine Beecher: A Study in American Domesticity* (New York: W. W. Norton, 1973). On domestic ideology, see Gillian Brown, *Domestic Individualism: Imagining Self in Nineteenth-Century America* (Berkeley: University of California Press, 1990); Lora Romero, *Home Fronts: Domesticity and Its Critics in the Antebellum United States* (Durham: Duke University Press, 1997); and Mary P. Ryan, *The Empire of the Mother: American Writing about Domesticity, 1830–1860* (New York: Haworth Press, 1982).

10. A founding analysis of the ethos of "feminization" is Ann Douglas, *The Feminization of American Culture* (New York: Alfred A. Knopf, 1976), which views this ethos pejoratively. For an influential critique of Douglas, see Jane Tompkins, *Sensational Designs: The Cultural Work of American Fiction, 1790–1860* (New York: Oxford University Press, 1985); for a reassessment of the Douglas/Tompkins debate, see Laura Wexler, "Tender Violence: Literary Eavesdropping, Domestic Fiction, and Educational Reform," in *The Culture of Sentiment: Race, Gender, and Sentimentality in Nineteenth-Century America*, edited by Shirley Samuels (New York: Oxford University Press, 1992), pp. 9–15.

11. Quoted in Hedrick, *Harriet Beecher Stowe*, pp. 55–56.

12. Abraham Lincoln, speech delivered at the Republican State Convention in Springfield, Illinois, 16 June 1858, now known as the "House Divided Speech"; reprinted in *Abraham Lincoln: Speeches and Writings, 1832–1858*, edited by Don E. Fehren-

bacher (New York: Library of America, 1989), p. 431. For analyses of the house metaphors in this speech, see David Herbert Donald, *Lincoln* (New York: Simon and Schuster, 1995), pp. 206–9; Priscilla Wald, *Constituting Americans: Cultural Anxiety and Narrative Form* (Durham: Duke University Press, 1995), pp. 54–57; and Garry Wills, *Lincoln at Gettysburg: The Words That Remade America* (New York: Simon and Schuster, 1992), pp. 112–13.

13. Abraham Lincoln, speech at New Haven, Connecticut, 6 March 1860, in *Abraham Lincoln: Speeches and Writings, 1859–1865*, edited by Don E. Fehrenbacher (New York: Library of America, 1989), p. 132.

14. On Lincoln's use of metaphor throughout his career, see George B. Forgie, *Patricide in the House Divided: A Psychological Interpretation of Lincoln and His Age* (New York: W. W. Norton, 1979), pp. 243–81, and James M. McPherson, "How Lincoln Won the War With Metaphors," in *Abraham Lincoln and the Second American Revolution* (New York: Oxford University Press, 1990), pp. 93–112.

15. Quoted in Gossett, *"Uncle Tom's Cabin" and American Culture,* p. 167.

16. Ibid., p. 169.

17. See Carlton Mabee, "Sojourner Truth and President Lincoln," *New England Quarterly* 61:4 (December 1988): 519–29, and Nell Irvin Painter, *Sojourner Truth: A Life, A Symbol* (New York: W. W. Norton, 1996), pp. 203–7.

18. Harriet Beecher Stowe, "The Libyan Sibyl" (1863), in [Olive Gilbert and Frances W. Titus], *Narrative of Sojourner Truth, a Bondswoman of Olden Time: With a History of Her Labors and Correspondence Drawn from Her "Book of Life,"* introduction by Jeffrey C. Stewart (1878; rpt. New York: Oxford University Press, 1991), pp. 161, 151.

19. See Hill, "Writing Out the War." For other analyses of "The Libyan Sibyl," see Painter, *Sojourner Truth,* pp. 151–63, and Jean Fagan Yellin, *Women and Sisters: The Antislavery Feminists in American Culture* (New Haven: Yale University Press, 1989), pp. 81–87. On "romantic racialism," see George M. Fredrickson, *The Black Image in the White Mind: The Debate on Afro-American Character and Destiny, 1817–1914* (New York: Harper and Row, 1971), pp. 97–129.

20. Carla L. Peterson, *"Doers of the Word": African-American Women Speakers and Writers in the North (1830–1880)* (New York: Oxford University Press, 1995), pp. 39–45. For a congruent interpretation of the 1850 *Narrative of Sojourner Truth* as a "facilitated autobiography," see Jean M. Humez, "Reading *The Narrative of Sojourner Truth* as a Collaborative Text," *Frontiers* 16:1 (1996): 29–52.

21. *Narrative of Sojourner Truth,* pp. 140–41.

22. See Scot M. Guenter, *The American Flag, 1777–1924: Cultural Shifts from Creation to Codification* (Cranbury, NJ: Associated University Presses, 1990), pp. 66–87.

23. This critical framework was established by Tompkins, *Sensational Designs,* pp. 123–46; Ammons, "Stowe's Dream of the Mother-Savior"; and Ammons, "Heroines in *Uncle Tom's Cabin,*" in *Critical Essays on Harriet Beecher Stowe,* edited by Ammons (Boston: G. K. Hall, 1980), pp. 152–65. Recent discussions of these arguments include Brown, *Domestic Individualism,* pp. 13–60; David Leverenz, *Manhood and the*

American Renaissance (Ithaca: Cornell University Press, 1989), pp. 190–204; and Cynthia Griffin Wolff, "Masculinity in *Uncle Tom's Cabin*," *American Quarterly* 47:4 (December 1995): 595–618.

24. Hortense Spillers, "Changing the Letter: The Yokes, the Jokes of Discourse, or, Mrs. Stowe, Mr. Reed," in *Slavery and the Literary Imagination,* edited by Deborah E. McDowell and Arnold Rampersad (Baltimore: Johns Hopkins University Press, 1989), p. 35.

25. *The Provincial Freeman* (1852), quoted in Gossett, *"Uncle Tom's Cabin" and American Culture,* p. 172. On black responses to the novel, see also Robert S. Levine, *Martin Delany, Frederick Douglass, and the Politics of Representative Identity* (Chapel Hill: University of North Carolina Press, 1997), pp. 58–98; Robert B. Stepto, "Sharing the Thunder: The Literary Exchanges of Harriet Beecher Stowe, Henry Bibb, and Frederick Douglass," in *New Essays on "Uncle Tom's Cabin,"* pp. 135–53; Richard Yarborough, "Strategies of Black Characterization in *Uncle Tom's Cabin* and the Early Afro-American Novel," in *New Essays on "Uncle Tom's Cabin,"* pp. 45–84; and Jean Fagan Yellin, Introduction to *Uncle Tom's Cabin* (New York: Oxford University Press, 1998), pp. xx–xxvi.

26. Classic critiques of racial representation in *Uncle Tom's Cabin* are James Baldwin, "Everybody's Protest Novel," in *Notes of a Native Son* (Boston: Beacon Press, 1955), pp. 13–23; and J. C. Furnas, *Goodbye to Uncle Tom* (New York: William Sloane, 1956). More recent discussions include Brown, *Domestic Individualism,* pp. 38–60; P. Gabrielle Foreman, "'This Promiscuous Housekeeping': Death, Transgression, and Homoeroticism in *Uncle Tom's Cabin,*" *Representations* 43 (Summer 1993): 51–72; and Spillers, "Changing the Letter." On Stowe's response to revolution, see Larry J. Reynolds, *European Revolutions and the American Literary Renaissance* (New Haven: Yale University Press, 1988), pp. 52–53, 153–57.

27. Toni Morrison, *Playing in the Dark: Whiteness and the Literary Imagination* (New York: Vintage, 1992), p. 17.

28. Harriet Beecher Stowe, *Uncle Tom's Cabin,* introduction by Ann Douglas (Harmondsworth: Penguin, 1981), p. 104. All subsequent quotations are from this edition and cited parenthetically in the text.

29. For analyses of Cassy and the novel's gothic plots, see Sandra M. Gilbert and Susan Gubar, *The Madwoman in the Attic: The Woman Writer and the Nineteenth-Century Literary Imagination* (New Haven: Yale University Press, 1979), pp. 532–35; Karen Halttunen, "Gothic Imagination and Social Reform: The Haunted Houses of Lyman Beecher, Henry Ward Beecher, and Harriet Beecher Stowe," in *New Essays on "Uncle Tom's Cabin,"* pp. 107–34; Diane Roberts, *The Myth of Aunt Jemima: Representations of Race and Region* (London: Routledge, 1994), pp. 23–54; and Stephanie A. Smith, *Conceived by Liberty: Maternal Figures and Nineteenth-Century American Literature* (Ithaca: Cornell University Press, 1994), pp. 95–105.

30. On Dinah's kitchen, see Brown, *Domestic Individualism,* pp. 13–24, and Lynn Wardley, "Relic, Fetish, Femmage: The Aesthetics of Sentiment in the Work of Stowe," in *Culture of Sentiment,* pp. 203–20.

31. Patricia A. Turner, *Ceramic Uncles and Celluloid Mammies: Black Images and Their Influence on Culture* (New York: Anchor, 1994), p. 13. Stowe herself described Topsy as "representative of that class of children who have grown up under slavery—quick, active, subtle and ingenious, apparently utterly devoid of principle and conscience" (*The Key to "Uncle Tom's Cabin"* [Boston, 1853], p. 91). E. Bruce Kirkham suggests that the source for the character was a freed slave to whom Stowe gave religious instruction (*The Building of Uncle Tom's Cabin* [Knoxville: University of Tennessee Press, 1977], p. 127). Brief discussions of Topsy may be found in Rachel Bowlby, "Breakfast in America—*Uncle Tom*'s Cultural Histories," in *Nation and Narration,* edited by Homi K. Bhabha (London: Routledge, 1990), pp. 199–202; Leonard Cassuto, *The Inhuman Race: The Racial Grotesque in American Literature and Culture* (New York: Columbia University Press, 1997), pp. 149–52; Gossett, *"Uncle Tom's Cabin" and American Culture,* pp. 132–37; Saidiya V. Hartman, *Scenes of Subjection: Terror, Slavery, and Self-Making in Nineteenth-Century America* (New York: Oxford University Press, 1997), pp. 25–29; W. T. Lhamon, Jr., *Raising Cain: Blackface Performance from Jim Crow to Hip Hop* (Cambridge: Harvard University Press, 1998), pp. 140–46; Arnold Weinstein, *Nobody's Home: Speech, Self, and Place in American Fiction from Hawthorne to DeLillo* (New York: Oxford University Press, 1993), pp. 57–60; and Yarborough, "Strategies of Black Characterization in *Uncle Tom's Cabin,*" pp. 47–50.

32. Peter Stallybrass and Allon White, *The Politics and Poetics of Transgression* (Ithaca: Cornell University Press, 1986); the quotation is on pp. 5–6.

33. See respectively Peter Oliver, *Peter Oliver's Origin and Progress of the American Rebellion: A Tory View,* edited by Douglass Adair and John A. Schutz (Stanford: Stanford University Press, 1961), pp. 120–21, and John Adams, *The Diary and Autobiography of John Adams,* edited by L. H. Butterfield (Cambridge: Harvard University Press, 1961), vol. 2, p. 259. I am indebted to Alfred F. Young for these citations. For an influential account of earlier uses of inversion metaphors, see Christopher Hill, *The World Turned Upside Down: Radical Ideas During the English Revolution* (Harmondsworth: Penguin, 1975).

34. *Uncle Tom's Cabin* also includes inversion imagery centered on the Revolutionary era: in Tom's cabin hangs a portrait of George Washington in blackface. For discussion of the portrait, see Christina Zwarg, "Fathering and Blackface in *Uncle Tom's Cabin,*" in *Norton Uncle Tom's Cabin,* pp. 568–84.

35. Br'er Rabbit and other animal trickster stories were in circulation throughout slave culture long before Harris added the "Uncle Remus" frame tale; for discussion of the subversive potential of the animal trickster, see Lawrence W. Levine, *Black Culture and Black Consciousness: Afro-American Folk Thought from Slavery to Freedom* (New York: Oxford University Press, 1977), pp. 102–21, and John W. Roberts, *From Trickster to Badman: The Black Folk Hero in Slavery and Freedom* (Philadelphia: University of Pennsylvania Press, 1989), pp. 17–64. Carla L. Peterson observes that Frado "like Stowe's Topsy . . . is depicted as 'a wild, frolicky thing' . . . in whom black readers might well have recognized a figure of resistance" (*"Doers of the Word,"* p. 167). For

other connections between *Our Nig* and *Uncle Tom's Cabin*, see Ammons, "Stowe's Dream of the Mother-Savior," pp. 181–85.

36. Quoted in Birdoff, *The World's Greatest Hit*, p. 163.

37. Anonymous [Charles Briggs], "Uncle Tomitudes," *Putnam's Monthly* (1853), reprinted in *Critical Essays on Harriet Beecher Stowe*, p. 40.

38. Robert Alexander, *I Ain't Yo' Uncle: The New Jack Revisionist "Uncle Tom's Cabin"* (1990); the play is discussed in Turner, *Ceramic Uncles and Celluloid Mammies*, pp. 86–88.

39. Mary Russo, *Female Grotesques: Risk, Excess and Modernity* (New York: Routledge, 1994). For discussion of the comic dimensions of the female grotesque, see Kathleen Rowe, *The Unruly Woman: Gender and the Genres of Laughter* (Austin: University of Texas Press, 1995). For a conceptualization of the grotesque in racial terms, see Cassuto, *The Inhuman Race*.

40. Hedrick, *Harriet Beecher Stowe*, p. 201.

41. Romero, *Home Fronts*, pp. 70–88.

42. Lhamon, *Raising Cain*, pp. 97–99; on Harry, see also Smith, *Conceived by Liberty*, pp. 176–81.

43. [Unknown author], letter to Edward Beecher, 4 February 1819, quoted in Hedrick, *Harriet Beecher Stowe*, p. 404.

44. Quoted in ibid., pp. 110, 210.

45. Quoted in Gossett, *"Uncle Tom's Cabin" and American Culture*, p. 352.

46. For a relevant discussion of contemporary relations between black women "domestics" and their white women employers, see Judith Rollins, *Between Women: Domestics and Their Employers* (Philadelphia: Temple University Press, 1985).

47. See Julia Stern, "Spanish Masquerade and the Drama of Racial Identity in *Uncle Tom's Cabin*," in *Passing and the Fictions of Identity*, edited by Elaine K. Ginsberg (Durham: Duke University Press, 1996), pp. 103–30.

48. Roberts, *Myth of Aunt Jemima*, p. 27.

49. On Topsy's links to minstrelsy, see Lhamon, *Raising Cain*, pp. 140–46, and Eric Lott, *Love and Theft: Blackface Minstrelsy and the American Working Class* (New York: Oxford University Press, 1995), pp. 217–18. On the stage history of *Uncle Tom's Cabin*, see also Birdoff, *World's Greatest Hit*; Gossett, *"Uncle Tom's Cabin" and American Culture*; Hartman, *Scenes of Subjection*, pp. 25–29; Vera Jiji, ed., *Showcasing American Drama: George L. Aiken/Harriet B. Stowe* (Brooklyn: Humanities Institute/Brooklyn College, 1983); Bruce A. McConachie, "Out of the Kitchen and Into the Marketplace: Normalizing *Uncle Tom's Cabin* for the Antebellum Stage," *Journal of American Drama and Theatre* 3 (1991): 5–28; Laurence Senelick, *The Age and Stage of George L. Fox, 1825–1877* (Hanover, NH: University Press of New England, 1988); Robert C. Toll, *Blacking Up: The Minstrel Show in Nineteenth-Century America* (New York: Oxford University Press, 1974), esp. pp. 88–97; and Hannah Page Wheeler Andrews, "Theme and Variations: *Uncle Tom's Cabin* as Book, Play, and Film," Ph.D. diss., University of North Carolina, 1979.

50. Lott, *Love and Theft*, p. 18. See also Lott, "White Like Me: Racial Cross-

Dressing and the Construction of American Whiteness," in *Cultures of United States Imperialism,* edited by Amy Kaplan and Donald E. Pease (Durham: Duke University Press, 1993), pp. 474–95.

51. For discussion of these changes, see McConachie, "Out of the Kitchen and Into the Marketplace," pp. 10–12.

52. See Birdoff, *World's Greatest Hit,* pp. 42–43, and Senelick, *Age and Stage of George L. Fox,* p. 59.

53. Patricia Morton, *Disfigured Images: The Historical Assault on Afro-American Women* (Westport, CT: Greenwood Press, 1991), p. 31. Discussions of the alignment between slave women and masculinity include bell hooks, *Ain't I a Woman: Black Women and Feminism* (Boston: South End Press, 1981), pp. 22–23, and Painter, *Sojourner Truth,* pp. 138–42.

54. George L. Aiken and George C. Howard, *Uncle Tom's Cabin* (1852), edited by Thomas Riis (New York: Garland, 1994), p. 26. All subsequent quotations are from this edition and cited parenthetically in the text; since line numbers are not given, quotations are identified by page number.

55. On the promiscuous sexuality associated with actresses, see Faye E. Dudden, *Women in the American Theatre: Actresses and Audiences, 1790–1870* (New Haven: Yale University Press, 1994), esp. pp. 21–23. On the stereotype of the black woman as hypersexual "Jezebel," see Deborah Gray White, *Ar'n't I a Woman? Female Slaves in the Plantation South* (New York: W. W. Norton, 1985), pp. 27–61. On stereotypes of black women as both masculine and hypersexual, see Peterson, *"Doers of the Word,"* pp. 19–22.

56. Birdoff, *World's Greatest Hit,* p. 202.

57. Ibid., pp. 162–63.

58. Quoted in Gossett, *"Uncle Tom's Cabin" and American Culture,* p. 266.

59. Turner, *Ceramic Uncles and Celluloid Mammies,* p. 14. I am grateful to Patricia Turner for further information about this doll.

60. According to the catalogue for the exhibition "Ethnic Notions," "The Topsy-Turvy doll originated during slavery. The black child played with the white doll in imitation of black women who cared for white children; when the master or his family were present, the skirt was reversed and the child played with a black doll" (Robbin Henderson et al., *Ethnic Notions: Black Images in the White Mind* [Berkeley: Berkeley Art Center Association, 1982], p. 74). See also Doris Y. Wilkinson, "The Toy Menagerie: Early Images of Blacks in Toys, Games, and Dolls," in *Images of Blacks in American Culture: A Reference Guide to Information Sources,* edited by Jessie Carney Smith (Westport, CT: Greenwood Press, 1988), p. 283. Numerous illustrations of the doll appear in Douglas Congdon-Martin, *Images in Black: 150 Years of Black Collectibles* (West Chester, PA: Schiffer Publishing Co., 1990), pp. 28–31.

61. Karen Sánchez-Eppler, *Touching Liberty: Abolition, Feminism, and the Politics of the Body* (Berkeley: University of California Press, 1993), p. 133; see also Shirley Samuels, "The Identity of Slavery," in *Culture of Sentiment,* p. 157.

62. On *Topsy and Eva,* see Birdoff, *World's Greatest Hit,* pp. 382–84, 401–2; on the

Howard family productions, see Birdoff, pp. 27–59, and Senelick, *Age and Stage of George L. Fox*, pp. 59–70. On Eva and Topsy imagery, see also Robert M. MacGregor, "The Eva and Topsy Dichotomy in Advertising," in *Images of the Child*, edited by Harry Eiss (Bowling Green, OH: Bowling Green State University Popular Press, 1994), pp. 287–306.

63. On the sexualization of Little Eva and Uncle Tom, see Foreman, "'This Promiscuous Housekeeping,'" pp. 51–52; Roberts, *Myth of Aunt Jemima*, pp. 37–38; and Spillers, "Changing the Letter," pp. 42–46. On the sexualization of Little Eva, see also Leslie A. Fiedler, *Love and Death in the American Novel* (1960; rev. ed. New York: Dell, 1966), pp. 259–65.

64. O'Connor, *The Heroine of the Confederacy*, p. 31. For discussions of orientalism in the novel, see Roberts, *Myth of Aunt Jemima*, pp. 29–38, and Spillers, "Changing the Letter," pp. 25–28. For other readings of this passage, see Lhamon, *Raising Cain*, pp. 144–45, and Weinstein, *Nobody's Home*, pp. 59–60.

65. *Pictures and Stories from Uncle Tom's Cabin* (Boston: John P. Jewett and Co., 1853), n.p. (cover). "Topsy at the Looking Glass" appears on pp. 22–24 and is reprinted in *Collected Poems of Harriet Beecher Stowe*, edited by John Michael Moran, Jr. (Hartford: Transcendental Books, 1967), poem 69, n.p.

66. Bowlby, "Breakfast in America," p. 200.

67. Henry Ward Beecher, "Against a Compromise of Principle" (1860), reprinted in *"God Ordained This War": Sermons on the Sectional Crisis, 1830–1865*, edited by David B. Chesebrough (Columbia: University of South Carolina Press, 1991), p. 68. On the relation of domesticity to imperial expansion, see Amy Kaplan, "Manifest Domesticity," *American Literature* 70:3 (September 1998): 581–606.

68. On Stowe's positive attitude toward the South, see Anne Rowe, *The Enchanted Country: Northern Writers in the South, 1865–1910* (Baton Rouge: Louisiana State University Press, 1978), pp. 1–21.

69. On filial rebellion and the American Revolution, see Jay Fliegelman, *Prodigals and Pilgrims: The American Revolution Against Patriarchal Authority, 1750–1800* (Cambridge: Cambridge University Press, 1982), and Michael Kammen, *A Season of Youth: The American Revolution and the Historical Imagination* (Ithaca: Cornell University Press, 1978). On paternal metaphors in antebellum America, see Forgie, *Patricide in the House Divided*, and Russ Castronovo, *Fathering the Nation: American Genealogies of Slavery and Freedom* (Berkeley: University of California Press, 1995).

70. On the symbolic blackening and feminization of the South, see Anne Norton, *Antebellum Americas: A Reading of Antebellum Political Culture* (Chicago: University of Chicago Press, 1986), pp. 132–99, and Carolyn Porter, "Social Discourse and Nonfictional Prose," in *The Columbia Literary History of the United States*, edited by Emory Elliott (New York: Columbia University Press, 1988), pp. 351–57. On abolitionist iconography, see Yellin, *Women and Sisters*. On white nationalism in the antebellum era, see Fredrickson, *Black Image in the White Mind*, pp. 130–64.

71. On Northern gender iconography, see Mary P. Ryan, *Women in Public: From Banners to Ballots, 1825–1860* (Baltimore: Johns Hopkins University Press, 1990),

pp. 42–49, and Shirley Samuels, "Miscegenated America: The Civil War," *American Literary History* 9:3 (Fall 1997): 482–501. Northern images of Liberty and Columbia are reproduced in Bernard F. Reilly, Jr., *American Political Prints, 1766–1876: A Catalogue of the Collections in the Library of Congress* (Boston: G. K. Hall, 1991), pp. 467 and passim. On Southern gender iconography, see Drew Gilpin Faust, "Altars of Sacrifice: Confederate Women and the Narratives of War" and "Race, Gender, and Confederate Nationalism: William D. Washington's 'Burial of Latané,'" both in *Southern Stories: Slaveholders in Peace and War* (Columbia: University of Missouri Press, 1992), pp. 113–40, 148–59; on "The Burial of Latané," see also Mark E. Neely, Jr., Harold Holzer, and Gabor S. Boritt, *The Confederate Image: Prints of the Lost Cause* (Chapel Hill: University of North Carolina Press, 1987), pp. ix–xiv. On the importance of liberty to both sides, see James M. McPherson, *For Cause and Comrades: Why Men Fought in the Civil War* (New York: Oxford University Press, 1997), pp. 104–16. On Confederate uses of the French Revolution, see Faust, *The Creation of Confederate Nationalism: Ideology and Identity in the Civil War South* (Baton Rouge: Louisiana State University Press, 1988), pp. 11–14. For an overview of female iconography in the United States, see Martha Banta, *Imaging American Women: Ideas and Ideals in Cultural History* (New York: Columbia University Press, 1987); for discussion of France, see Maurice Agulhon, *Marianne Into Battle: Republican Imagery and Symbolism in France, 1789–1880*, translated by Janet Lloyd (Cambridge: University of Cambridge Press, 1981); and for a survey of female iconography, see Marina Warner, *Monuments and Maidens: The Allegory of the Female Form* (New York: Atheneum, 1985).

72. On postwar gender metaphors, see Kathleen Diffley, *"Where My Heart Is Turning Ever": Civil War Stories and Constitutional Reform, 1861–1876* (Athens: University of Georgia Press, 1992), and Nina Silber, *The Romance of Reunion: Northerners and the South, 1865–1900* (Chapel Hill: University of North Carolina Press, 1993), which revises Paul H. Buck, *The Road to Reunion, 1865–1900* (1937; rpt. New York: Vintage, 1959).

73. Wendell Phillips, "The War for the Union; A Lecture," in *Union Pamphlets of the Civil War*, vol. 1, edited by Frank Freidel (1862; rpt. Cambridge: Harvard University Press, 1967), pp. 299, 314–15, 318.

74. The founding analysis of male homosociality is Eve Kosofsky Sedgwick, *Between Men: English Literature and Male Homosocial Desire* (New York: Columbia University Press, 1985). For a variety of perspectives on the relation between national and sexual identities, see Andrew Parker et al., eds., *Nationalisms and Sexualities* (New York: Routledge, 1992).

75. Lincoln's "African" origins were implied in such titles as *Abraham Africanus* (1862), cited in John R. Rhodehamel and Thomas F. Schwartz, *"The Last Best Hope on Earth": Abraham Lincoln and the Promise of America* (San Marino, CA: Huntington Library, 1993), p. 62. Lincoln is represented as Othello in the lithograph "Behind the Scenes" (1864), reprinted in Reilly, *American Political Prints*, pp. 536–38; a newspaper description of him as "the conscientious actor who, when he played Othello, insisted on *blacking himself all over*," is quoted in Forrest G. Wood, *Black Scare: The Racist Response to Emancipation and Reconstruction* (Berkeley: University of California Press,

1968), p. 74. Adalbert Volck, "Beneath the Veil," is reproduced in Rufus Rockwell Wilson, *Lincoln in Caricature* (New York: Horizon Press, 1953), pp. 180–81, and the artist's career is analyzed in Neely, Holzer, and Boritt, *Confederate Image*, pp. 44–54. For analyses of Lincoln imagery in the Civil War era, see also Martin Abbott, "President Lincoln in Confederate Caricature," *Illinois Historical Journal* 51:3 (Autumn 1958): 306–19; Michael Davis, *The Image of Lincoln in the South* (Knoxville: University of Tennessee Press, 1971), pp. 62–104; Harold Holzer, "Confederate Caricature of Abraham Lincoln," *Illinois Historical Journal* 80:1 (Spring 1987): 23–36; Harold Holzer, Gabor S. Boritt, and Mark E. Neely, Jr., *The Lincoln Image: Abraham Lincoln and The Popular Print* (New York: Scribner's, 1984); and Albert Shaw, *Abraham Lincoln: A Cartoon History*, 2 vols. (New York: Review of Reviews Corporation, 1930).

76. Anonymous [William Russell Smith], *The Royal Ape: A Dramatic Poem* (Richmond: West and Johnston, 1863). All subsequent quotations are from this edition and cited parenthetically in the text; since line numbers are not given, quotations are identified by page number. For brief discussions of *The Royal Ape*, see Davis, *Image of Lincoln in the South*, p. 71, and Richard Barksdale Harwell's Introduction to *King Linkum the First: A Musical Burletta* (1863; rpt. Atlanta: Emory University Library, 1947), p. 7.

77. On Mary Todd Lincoln's negative reputation, see Jean H. Baker, *Mary Todd Lincoln: A Biography* (New York: W. W. Norton, 1987). I discuss this issue at length in chapter 3.

78. Joan Scott, "Gender: A Useful Category of Historical Analysis," in *Gender and the Politics of History* (New York: Columbia University Press, 1988), p. 49.

79. For an important analysis of national rhetoric in terms of the "family romance," see Lynn Hunt, *The Family Romance of the French Revolution* (Berkeley: University of California Press, 1992). For an influential theorization of the figure of the "woman on top," see Natalie Zemon Davis, "Women on Top," in *Society and Culture in Early Modern France* (Stanford: Stanford University Press, 1975), pp. 124–51. For an elaboration of the subversive potential of this figure, see Rowe, *Unruly Woman*.

80. George F. Holmes, review of *Uncle Tom's Cabin*, *Southern Literary Messenger* 18 (October 1852), reprinted in *Norton Uncle Tom's Cabin*, p. 468; *New Orleans Crescent*, 5 January 1854, quoted in Gossett, *"Uncle Tom's Cabin" and American Culture*, p. 190; William Gilmore Simms, review of *A Key to "Uncle Tom's Cabin," Southern Quarterly Review* n.s. 7 (July 1853), quoted in Gossett, *"Uncle Tom's Cabin" and American Culture*, p. 190.

81. McCord's review is reprinted in *Louisa S. McCord: Selected Writings*, edited by Richard C. Lounsbury (Charlottesville: University Press of Virginia, 1997), pp. 83–118; the anonymous letter-writer is quoted in Gossett, *"Uncle Tom's Cabin" and American Culture*, p. 191.

82. Roberts, *Myth of Aunt Jemima*, p. 61.

83. *New Orleans Crescent* quoted in Gossett, *"Uncle Tom's Cabin" and American Culture*, p. 190. Volck's "Worship of the North" is reproduced and discussed in Holzer, "Confederate Caricature of Abraham Lincoln," pp. 33–34.

84. Holmes review, in *Norton Uncle Tom's Cabin*, p. 469.

85. Lott, *Love and Theft*, pp. 211–33, esp. 222–23.

86. Samuels, "Miscegenated America," p. 483; see also Catherine Clinton, *Tara Revisited: Women, War and the Plantation Legend* (New York: Abbeville Press, 1995), p. 47. This image is one of a series of antisecessionist images entitled "Strong's Dime Caricatures," documented in Reilly, *American Political Prints*, p. 463.

87. "Miss Columbia Calls Her Unruly School to Order" (1860), reproduced in Shaw, *Abraham Lincoln*, vol. 1, p. 249; "Stephen Finding His Mother" (1860) is reproduced and discussed in Reilly, *American Political Prints*, p. 446.

88. See JoAnn Menezes, "The Birthing of the American Flag and the Invention of an American Founding Mother in the Image of Betsy Ross," in *Narratives of Nostalgia, Gender, and Nationalism*, edited by Jean Pickering and Suzanne Kehde (New York: New York University Press, 1997), pp. 74–87.

89. Speech by Sarah P. Remond, 14 September 1859, reprinted in *The Black Abolitionist Papers*, edited by C. Peter Ripley (Chapel Hill: University of North Carolina Press, 1985), vol. 1, pp. 458, 459–60; the only record of this speech is the newspaper account, which alternately quotes and paraphrases Remond. For discussion of Remond's lecture tour, see Peterson, *"Doers of the Word,"* pp. 135–45; for an overview of her career, see Ruth Bogin, "Sarah Parker Remond: Black Abolitionist from Salem," in *Black Women in American History*, edited by Darlene Clark Hine (Brooklyn: Carlson, 1990), vol. 1, pp. 120–50.

90. On Helper, see James M. McPherson, *Battle Cry of Freedom: The Civil War Era* (New York: Oxford University Press, 1988), pp. 198–200. On Green, see *Black Abolitionist Papers*, vol. 1, p. 461.

91. Gossett, *"Uncle Tom's Cabin" and American Culture*, pp. 370–71.

92. Michael Rogin, *Blackface, White Noise: Jewish Immigrants in the Hollywood Melting Pot* (Berkeley: University of California Press, 1996), p. 42.

93. Gossett, *"Uncle Tom's Cabin" and American Culture*, pp. 382–83.

94. I located this image in a motion picture herald for an unnamed film version of *Uncle Tom's Cabin*, possibly the 1903 production directed by Edwin S. Porter. A very similar image is reproduced in Gossett, *"Uncle Tom's Cabin" and American Culture*, and identified as "The cover of a 12-page pamphlet advertising a Davis Company theatrical production of *Uncle Tom's Cabin*, probably in the 1890s" (photographic insert, n.p.).

95. The unnamed Confederate woman is quoted in Laura F. Edwards, *Gendered Strife and Confusion: The Political Culture of Reconstruction* (Urbana: University of Illinois Press, 1997), p. 112; William Middleton is quoted in Walter J. Fraser, Jr., *Charleston! Charleston! The History of a Southern City* (Columbia: University of South Carolina Press, 1989), p. 275.

96. Myrta Lockett Avary, *Dixie After the War* (1906; rpt. New York: Negro Universities Press, 1969), p. 182.

97. Thomas Dixon, *The Leopard's Spots* (New York: Doubleday, 1902), p. 442; all subsequent quotations are from this edition and cited parenthetically in the text. For discussion of this novel, see Sandra Gunning, *Race, Rape, and Lynching: The Red Record*

of American Literature, 1890–1912 (New York: Oxford University Press, 1996), pp. 19–47, and Joel Williamson, *The Crucible of Race: Black-White Relations in the American South Since Emancipation* (New York: Oxford University Press, 1984), pp. 140–79. On Dixon's relation to Stowe, see Raymond Allen Cook, *Fire From the Flint: The Amazing Careers of Thomas Dixon* (Winston-Salem, NC: John F. Blair, 1968), pp. 105–6; Thomas P. Riggio, "*Uncle Tom* Reconstructed: A Neglected Chapter in the History of a Book," *American Quarterly* 28:1 (Spring 1976): 56–70; and Kenneth W. Warren, *Black and White Strangers: Race and American Literary Realism* (Chicago: University of Chicago Press, 1993), pp. 102–6.

98. On the rehabilitation of Lincoln's image in the postwar South, see Davis, *Image of Lincoln in the South*, pp. 135–70, and Merrill D. Peterson, *Lincoln in American Memory* (New York: Oxford University Press, 1994), pp. 38–50.

99. Harper's early poetic tributes to Stowe are "To Mrs. Harriet Beecher Stowe," "Eliza Harris," and "Eva's Farewell," reprinted in *A Brighter Coming Day: A Frances Ellen Watkins Harper Reader*, edited by Frances Smith Foster (New York: Feminist Press, 1990), pp. 57, 60–62, 75–76.

100. Mary Church Terrell, *A Colored Woman in a White World*, introduction by Nellie Y. McKay (1940; rpt. Boston: G. K. Hall, 1996), p. 282; Terrell's tribute to Stowe is *Harriet Beecher Stowe: An Appreciation* (Washington, 1911). See also Eloise Bibb, "Eliza in *Uncle Tom's Cabin*," in *Poems* (Boston, 1895), pp. 14–19, reprinted in *Collected Black Women's Poetry*, vol. 4, edited by Joan R. Sherman (New York: Oxford University Press, 1988); Andasia Kimbrough Bruce, *Uncle Tom's Cabin of Today* (1906; rpt. Freeport, NY: Books for Libraries Press, 1972); Olivia Ward Bush-Banks, "To the Memory of Harriet Beecher Stowe," in *The Collected Works of Olivia Ward Bush-Banks*, edited by Bernice F. Guillaume (New York: Oxford University Press, 1991), pp. 153–54; H. Cordelia Ray, "Greeting to Mrs. Harriet Beecher Stowe, on her Eighty-Fifth Birthday," in *Poems* (New York, 1910), pp. 164–66, reprinted in *Collected Black Women's Poetry*, vol. 3, edited by Joan R. Sherman (New York: Oxford University Press, 1988); and Katherine Davis Chapman Tillman, "Afro-American Women and Their Work," *A. M. E. Church Review* (1895), and "Clancy Street," *A. M. E. Church Review* (1898), both reprinted in *The Works of Katherine Davis Chapman Tillman*, edited by Claudia Tate (New York: Oxford University Press, 1991), pp. 76, 256–57.

101. On Albert and Stowe, see Francis Smith Foster, Introduction to Octavia Victoria Rogers Albert, *The House of Bondage* (1890; rpt. New York: Oxford University Press, 1988), pp. xxxvii–xxxix. Ammons discusses the relation of *Uncle Tom's Cabin* to several black women's texts in "Stowe's Dream of a Mother-Savior," pp. 179–88.

102. Tillman, "Afro-American Women and Their Work," p. 76.

103. Susie King Taylor, *A Black Woman's Civil War Memoirs: Reminiscences of My Life in Camp with the 33rd U. S. Colored Troops, late 1st South Carolina Volunteers*, edited by Patricia W. Romero (1902; rpt. New York: Markus Wiener, 1988), pp. 139–40. For discussion of this text, see Anthony Barthelemy, Introduction to *Collected Black Women's Narratives* (New York: Oxford University Press, 1988), pp. xxix–xlvii; Joanne M. Braxton, *Black Women Writing Autobiography: A Tradition Within a Tradition* (Phila-

delphia: Temple University Press, 1989), pp. 43–49; Ella Forbes, *African American Women During the Civil War* (New York: Garland, 1998), pp. viii–ix and passim; Darlene Clark Hine and Kathleen Thompson, *A Shining Thread of Hope: The History of Black Women in America* (New York: Broadway Books, 1998), pp. 130–32; and Emmy E. Werner, *Reluctant Witnesses: Children's Voices from the Civil War* (New York: Westview Press, 1998), pp. 41–44.

104. Anna Julia Cooper, *A Voice from the South*, edited by Mary Helen Washington (1892; rpt. New York: Oxford University Press, 1988), p. ii. All subsequent quotations are from this edition and cited parenthetically in the text. Discussions of *A Voice from the South* include Hazel V. Carby, *Reconstructing Womanhood: The Emergence of the Afro-American Woman Novelist* (New York: Oxford University Press, 1987), pp. 97–108, and Kevin K. Gaines, *Uplifting the Race: Black Leadership, Politics, and Culture in the Twentieth Century* (Chapel Hill: University of North Carolina Press, 1996), pp. 128–51.

105. Warren also notes Cooper's critique of Stowe in this passage (*Black and White Strangers*, p. 72).

106. On connections between racial uplift and imperialism, see Kevin Gaines, "Black Americans' Racial Uplift Ideology as 'Civilizing Mission': Pauline E. Hopkins on Race and Imperialism," in *Cultures of United States Imperialism*, pp. 433–55.

CHAPTER TWO

1. Elizabeth Stuart Phelps, *Chapters from a Life* (Boston, 1896), p. 98.

2. Elizabeth Stuart Phelps, *The Gates Ajar*, edited by Helen Sootin Smith (1868; rpt. Cambridge: Harvard University Press, 1964), pp. 13, 14, 149.

3. On Phelps and Stowe, see Elizabeth Ammons, "Stowe's Dream of the Mother-Savior: *Uncle Tom's Cabin* and American Women Writers Before the 1920s," in *New Essays on "Uncle Tom's Cabin,"* edited by Eric J. Sundquist (New York: Cambridge University Press, 1986), pp. 172–73. On *The Gates Ajar*, see Lisa A. Long, "'The Corporeity of Heaven': Rehabilitating the Civil War Body in *The Gates Ajar*," *American Literature* 9:4 (December 1997): 781–811, and Nancy Schnog, "'The Comfort of My Fancying': Loss and Recuperation in *The Gates Ajar*," *Arizona Quarterly* 49:1 (Spring 1993): 21–47. On Phelps's other Civil War writings, see Carol Farley Kessler, *Elizabeth Stuart Phelps* (Boston: Twayne, 1982), and Timothy Morris, "'A Glorious Solution': Gender, Families, Relationships, and the Civil War Story," *Arizona Quarterly* 51:1 (Spring 1995): 61–79.

4. Alcott included *Uncle Tom's Cabin* in an 1852 list of "the best" novels, "books I like," in *The Journals of Louisa May Alcott*, edited by Joel Myerson, Daniel Shealy, and Madeleine Stern (Boston: Little, Brown, 1989) [hereafter cited as *Journals*], pp. 67–68. Sarah Elbert, *A Hunger for Home: Louisa May Alcott's Place in American Culture* (New Brunswick: Rutgers University Press, 1987), p. 147; Ammons, "Stowe's Dream of the Mother-Savior," p. 172; James Baldwin, "Everybody's Protest Novel," in *Notes*

of a Native Son (Boston: Beacon Press, 1955), p. 14; J. C. Furnas, *Goodbye to Uncle Tom* (New York: William Sloane, 1956), p. 40.

5. Jane E. Schultz, "The Inhospitable Hospital: Gender and Professionalism in Civil War Medicine," *Signs* 17:2 (Winter 1992): 363–92, and *Women at the Front: Female Hospital Workers in Civil War America* (Chapel Hill: University of North Carolina Press, forthcoming). On Clara Barton, see Stephen B. Oates, *A Woman of Valor: Clara Barton and the Civil War* (New York: Free Press, 1994). On Mary Livermore, see Nina Silber, Introduction to Livermore, *My Story of the War* (1887; rpt. New York: Da Capo, 1995), pp. v–xii; on women and the Sanitary Commission, see Jeanie Attie, *Patriotic Toil: Northern Women and the American Civil War* (Ithaca: Cornell University Press, 1998). Other recent discussions of Civil War nursing include Marilyn Mayer Culpepper, *Trials and Triumphs: The Women of the American Civil War* (East Lansing: Michigan State University Press, 1991), pp. 315–53; Elizabeth D. Leonard, *Yankee Women: Gender Battles in the Civil War* (New York: W. W. Norton, 1994), pp. 3–49; and Kristie Ross, "Arranging a Doll's House: Refined Women as Union Nurses," in *Divided Houses: Gender and the Civil War,* edited by Catherine Clinton and Nina Silber (New York: Oxford University Press, 1992), pp. 97–113.

6. In the 1860s, in addition to *Hospital Sketches,* Alcott published the novels *Moods* and *Little Women* and more than fifty short works of fiction and journalism, including war stories, gothic thrillers, fantasy tales, and essays on contemporary political issues. On Alcott's career in this decade, see Richard H. Brodhead, *Cultures of Letters: Scenes of Reading and Writing in Nineteenth-Century America* (Chicago: University of Chicago Press, 1993), pp. 69–106. For discussion of *Hospital Sketches,* see Mary Cappello, "'Looking About Me With All My Eyes': Censored Viewing, Carnival, and Louisa May Alcott's *Hospital Sketches,*" *Arizona Quarterly* 50:3 (Autumn 1994): 59–88; Robert Leigh Davis, *Whitman and the Romance of Medicine* (Berkeley: University of California Press, 1997), pp. 52–59; Gregory Eiselein, *Literature and Humanitarian Reform in the Civil War Era* (Bloomington: Indiana University Press, 1996), pp. 98–101; Elbert, *A Hunger for Home,* pp. 164–68; Bessie Z. Jones, Introduction to *Hospital Sketches* (Cambridge: Harvard University Press, 1960), pp. vii–xliv; and Jane E. Schultz, "Embattled Care: Narrative Authority in Louisa May Alcott's *Hospital Sketches,*" *Legacy* 9:2 (1992): 104–18.

7. See Elaine Showalter, ed., *Alternative Alcott* (New Brunswick: Rutgers University Press, 1988), which reprints both *Hospital Sketches* and "Behind a Mask." For feminist reassessments of Alcott's career, see Showalter's Introduction to this anthology, pp. ix–xliii; Elbert, *A Hunger for Home;* Elizabeth Lennox Keyser, *Whispers in the Dark: The Fiction of Louisa May Alcott* (Knoxville: University of Tennessee Press, 1993); and Madeleine Stern, Introduction to *Louisa May Alcott: Selected Fiction,* edited by Daniel Shealy, Madeleine B. Stern, and Joel Myerson (Boston: Little, Brown, 1990), pp. xi–xlvi. Alcott's thrillers were first rediscovered by Leona Rostenberg and Madeleine Stern, as recounted in Rostenberg, "Some Anonymous and Pseudonymous Thrillers of Louisa May Alcott," in *Critical Essays on Louisa May Alcott,* edited by Madeleine B. Stern (Boston: G. K. Hall, 1984), pp. 43–50, and are reprinted in Made-

leine Stern, ed., *Louisa May Alcott Unmasked: Collected Thrillers* (Boston: Northeastern University Press, 1995). Analyses of the thrillers include Lynette Carpenter, " 'Did They Never See Anyone Angry Before?': The Sexual Politics of Self-Control in Alcott's 'A Whisper in the Dark,' " *Legacy* 3:2 (Fall 1986): 31–41; Ann Douglas, "Mysteries of Louisa May Alcott," in *Critical Essays on Louisa May Alcott*, pp. 231–40; Elbert, *A Hunger for Home*, pp. 169–85; Judith Fetterley, "Impersonating 'Little Women': The Radicalism of Alcott's *Behind a Mask*," *Women's Studies* 10 (1983): 1–14; and Keyser, *Whispers in the Dark*, pp. 3–13, 32–57. On Alcott's interest in theater, see also Karen Haltunnen, "The Domestic Drama of Louisa May Alcott," *Feminist Studies* 10:2 (Summer 1984): 233–54, and Lynne Vallone, *Disciplines of Virtue: Girls' Culture in the Eighteenth and Nineteenth Centuries* (New Haven: Yale University Press, 1995), pp. 106–34.

8. Louisa May Alcott, *Hospital Sketches*, in *Alternative Alcott*, pp. 43, 46. All subsequent quotations are from this edition and cited parenthetically in the text.

9. Walt Whitman, "The Wound-Dresser," in *Walt Whitman: Complete Poetry and Collected Prose*, edited by Justin Kaplan (New York: Library of America, 1982), p. 445. For discussion of the homoerotics of Whitman's poetry, see Michael Moon, *Disseminating Whitman: Revision and Corporeality in "Leaves of Grass"* (Cambridge: Harvard University Press, 1991), pp. 171–222; for comparison between Whitman and Alcott, see Davis, *Whitman and the Romance of Medicine*, p. 60; and for an overview of contemporary scholarship on Whitman, see Betsy Erkkila and Jay Grossman, eds., *Breaking Bounds: Whitman and American Cultural Studies* (New York: Oxford University Press, 1996).

10. Schultz, "Embattled Care," p. 106.

11. See Diane Price Herndl, *Invalid Women: Figuring Feminine Illness in American Fiction and Culture, 1840–1940* (Chapel Hill: University of North Carolina Press, 1993).

12. On amputation in the war, see Stewart Brooks, *Civil War Medicine: Care and Comfort of the Wounded* (Springfield, IL: Charles C. Thomas, 1966), pp. 90–105; on neurological imagery in nineteenth-century America, see Joan Burbick, *Healing the Republic: The Language of Health and the Culture of Nationalism in Nineteenth-Century America* (Cambridge: Cambridge University Press, 1994), pp. 225–61. On Mitchell, see note 43 below.

13. LaSalle Corbell Pickett, *Reminiscences of People I Have Known*, reprinted in *Critical Essays on Louisa May Alcott*, p. 42.

14. Alcott, journal entry, January 1845, *Journals*, p. 56.

15. Ibid., p. 55.

16. See Brodhead, *Cultures of Letters;* "disciplinary intimacy" is defined on pp. 17–18 and linked to Louisa May Alcott on pp. 72–74.

17. Alcott, journal entry, October 1856, *Journals*, p. 79; Alcott, letter to Alfred Whitman, 2 March 1860, in *The Selected Letters of Louisa May Alcott*, edited by Joel Myerson, Daniel Shealy, and Madeleine Stern (Boston: Little, Brown, 1987) [hereafter cited as *Letters*], pp. 51–52.

18. Alcott, journal entry, April 1861, *Journals*, p. 105.

19. Ibid., September, October 1862, p. 109.

20. Ibid., November 1862, p. 110.

21. Ibid., December 1862, p. 110.

22. Alcott, letter to Amos Bronson Alcott, 28 November 1855, *Letters*, p. 14.

23. Alcott, letter to Alfred Whitman, 19 May 1861, *Letters*, pp. 64–65.

24. Alcott, letter to Mrs. Joseph Chatfield Alcox, early December 1862, *Letters*, p. 80.

25. Alcott, letter to Thomas Wentworth Higginson, 12 November 1863, *Letters*, p. 96. On Alcott's racial politics, see Sarah Elbert, Introduction to *Louisa May Alcott on Race, Sex, and Slavery*, edited by Elbert (Boston: Northeastern University Press, 1997), pp. ix–lx. On women abolitionists in this period, see Wendy Hamand Venet, *Neither Ballots Nor Bullets: Women Abolitionists and the Civil War* (Charlottesville: University Press of Virginia, 1991).

26. Davis, *Whitman and the Romance of Medicine*, also suggests a connection between Alcott and Topsy (59). For a different interpretation of the "brown baby" letter, see Martha Saxton: "The significance of 'brown' came from Bronson's deranged and harmful theory of complexions that blond, blue-eyed people, like himself, were god-like, whereas dark-haired, dark-eyed people, like his wife and Louisa, were, as Emerson paraphrased him, 'a reminder of brutish nature'" (*Louisa May: A Modern Biography of Louisa May Alcott* [Boston: Houghton Mifflin, 1977], p. 205). On Bronson's beliefs about "brown" skin, see also Elbert, Introduction to *Louisa May Alcott on Race, Sex, and Slavery*, pp. xv–xvi.

27. Alcott, letter to Alfred Whitman, 4 August 1861, *Letters*, p. 67. See also another letter from Alcott to Whitman: "My only excuse [for a delay in writing] is that when publishers once get hold of a body they give that body no peace and keep them at work like 'negro mulatto slaves' all day & every day, & are never satisfied. James Redpath is my present overseer & a sweet time I have of it, but as money is rather a necessity of life & he hands it over with a charming ease I cleave unto him, & devote my energies to the earning of filthy lucre" (2 January 1864, *Letters*, pp. 99–100).

28. Interview with Louise Chandler Moulton, in *Our Famous Women* (Hartford, 1884), p. 49; quoted in Showalter, Introduction to *Alternative Alcott*, p. xx.

29. The first American usages of "inversion" were in the 1870s. For discussion of the development of this language, see George Chauncey, Jr., "From Sexual Inversion to Homosexuality: Medicine and the Changing Conceptualization of Female Deviance," *Salmagundi* 58–59 (1982–83): 114–46.

30. For another interpretation of Alcott in relation to heterodox sexuality, see Michael Warner, "Written on the Bodice: Louisa May Alcott Unbound," *Voice Literary Supplement* 133 (March 1995): 10–11.

31. Alcott, letter to Hannah Stevenson, 26 December 1862, in *Massachusetts Historical Society Miscellany* 65 (Fall 1996): 4.

32. Cappello, "'Looking About Me With All My Eyes,'" esp. p. 60.

33. Alcott, letter to Hannah Stevenson, p. 4.

34. For congruent discussion of racial politics in Alcott's representation of wartime Washington, see Cappello, "'Looking About Me With All My Eyes,'" pp. 74–79.

35. Alcott, letter to Anna Alcott, 6 November 1856, *Letters*, p. 22. Alcott's full description of the event suggests its sexual connotations: "I was so excited I pitched about like a mad woman, shouted, waved, hung onto fences, rushed thro crowds, & swarmed about in a state [of] rapterous insanity till it was all over & then I went home hoarse and worn out."

36. Alcott, journal entry, "Notes and Memoranda" section for 1862, *Journals*, pp. 111, 112. She added "which I enjoy very much, at least the crazy part" at an unspecified later date. This description was followed by a more extensive account of her Washington experience in the journal entry for January 1863, pp. 113–17.

37. Alcott, journal entry, January 1863, *Journals*, p. 117. For analyses of the dreams, see Elbert, *A Hunger for Home*, pp. 156–58; Saxton, *Louisa May*, pp. 257–58; and Showalter, Introduction to *Alternative Alcott*, pp. xix–xx.

38. Alcott, letter to Annie Adams Fields, 24 June 1863, *Letters*, p. 84.

39. Alcott, letter to Mary Elizabeth Waterman, 6 November 1863, *Letters*, p. 95.

40. Alcott, letter to Anna Alcott Pratt, ca. August 1860, *Letters*, p. 59.

41. Alcott, journal entry, February 1861, *Journals*, p. 104.

42. Ibid., January 1863, p. 114.

43. Richard Wolcott, "Hopeful Tackett—His Mark," *Continental Monthly* 2:2 (September 1862): 264. Diffley situates this story within the larger "adventure of national initiation," a literary genre whose terms and plots privileged men. See *"Where My Heart Is Turning Ever": Civil War Stories and Constitutional Reform, 1861–1876* (Athens: University of Georgia Press, 1992), pp. 124–49; "Hopeful Tackett" is discussed on pp. 128–29. A more complex example is S. Weir Mitchell's "The Case of George Dedlow," which posits amputation as the mark of the soldier in a radically different mode. In this mercilessly bleak story, a soldier who has lost both arms and legs in the war experiences himself as "a useless torso, more like some strange larval creature than anything of human shape"; the story closes with a phantom limb fantasy in which Dedlow briefly believes that his legs have returned, only to collapse again. Mitchell's story is as dystopian as Wolcott's is utopian, but they share a fetishistic focus on the stump as a phallic extension of male war experience. See Mitchell, "The Case of George Dedlow," *Atlantic Monthly* 18: 105 (July 1866): 5. For discussion of this story, see Lisa Herschbach, "'True Clinical Fictions': Medical and Literary Narratives from the Civil War Hospital," *Culture, Medicine and Psychiatry* 19:2 (June 1995): 183–205; Debra Journet, "Phantom Limbs and 'Body-Ego': S. Weir Mitchell's 'George Dedlo,'" *Mosaic* 23:1 (Winter 1990): 87–99; and Long, "'The Corporeity of Heaven.'"

44. John Limon, *Writing After War: American War Fiction from Realism to Postmodernism* (New York: Oxford University Press, 1994), p. 188.

45. Alcott, letter to Hannah Stevenson, p. 4.

46. Alcott, letter to Alfred Whitman, September 1863, *Letters*, pp. 91–92.

47. Alcott, letter to Mary Elizabeth Waterman, 6 November 1863, *Letters*, p. 95.

48. Alcott, journal entry, February 1863, *Journals*, p. 117.

49. Lisa Herschbach, "Prosthetic Reconstructions: Making the Industry, Re-

Making the Body, Modelling the Nation," *History Workshop Journal* 44 (Autumn 1997): 22–57.

50. Henry Whitney Bellows, "Unconditional Loyalty" (1863), in *Union Pamphlets of the Civil War, 1861–1865*, edited by Frank Freidel (Cambridge: Harvard University Press, 1967), vol. 1, p. 515.

51. Wendell Phillips, "The War for the Union; A Lecture" (1862), in *Union Pamphlets of the Civil War*, vol. 1, p. 312.

52. Henry Ward Beecher, "Against a Compromise of Principle" (1860), reprinted in *"God Ordained This War": Sermons on the Sectional Crisis, 1830–1865*, edited by David B. Chesebrough (Columbia: University of South Carolina Press, 1991), p. 81.

53. Lincoln's comment is recounted by F. B. Carpenter in *Six Months at the White House with Abraham Lincoln* (New York, 1866), p. 76. For discussion of this metaphor in context, see James M. McPherson, "How Lincoln Won the War with Metaphors," in *Abraham Lincoln and the Second American Revolution* (New York: Oxford University Press, 1990), pp. 93–112. For an overview of Northern tropes of the Civil War body politic, see Timothy Sweet, *Traces of War: Poetry, Photography, and the Crisis of the Union* (Baltimore: Johns Hopkins University Press, 1990), esp. pp. 16–24.

54. Bellows, "Unconditional Loyalty," p. 515.

55. Carpenter, *Six Months at the White House*, pp. 76–77.

56. Bellows, "Unconditional Loyalty," p. 513.

57. For discussion of Lincoln as a sacrificial body, see Michael Rogin, "The King's Two Bodies: Lincoln, Wilson, Nixon, and Presidential Sacrifice," in *Ronald Reagan, the Movie, and Other Episodes in Political Demonology* (Berkeley: University of California Press, 1987), pp. 81–114.

58. Alcott, journal entry, 1 February 1868, *Journals*, p. 164. The "hate" phrase is in *Hospital Sketches*, p. 26.

59. Quoted in George B. Forgie, *Patricide in the House Divided: A Psychological Interpretation of Lincoln and His Age* (New York: W. W. Norton, 1979), p. 255.

60. On feminized images of Christ in nineteenth-century America, see Ann Douglas, *The Feminization of American Culture* (New York: Alfred A. Knopf, 1977), pp. 124–30.

61. For a relevant discussion of racial hierarchy in photographs of white women abolitionists and African-American children, see Karen Sánchez-Eppler, *Touching Liberty: Abolition, Feminism, and the Politics of the Body* (Berkeley: University of California Press, 1993), pp. 6–7.

62. For analyses of conflicts between nurses and doctors in Civil War hospitals, see Leonard, *Yankee Women*, pp. 20–41; and Schultz, "Inhospitable Hospital."

63. Alcott, "My Contraband," in *Alternative Alcott*, p. 76. All subsequent quotations are from this edition and cited parenthetically in the text. Discussions of this story include Jan Cohn, "The Negro Character in Northern Magazine Fiction of the 1860s," *New England Quarterly* 43 (December 1970): 572–92; Davis, *Whitman and the Romance of Medicine*, pp. 59–60; Diffley, *"Where My Heart Is Turning Ever,"* pp. 34–39; Mary

Dougherty, "Contraband Desire," paper presented at the annual convention of the Modern Language Association, Chicago, December 1995; Elbert, Introduction to *Louisa May Alcott on Race, Sex, and Slavery*, pp. xl–xliv; and Abigail Hamblen, "Louisa May Alcott and the Racial Question," in *Critical Essays on Louisa May Alcott*, pp. 30–40.

64. "The Brothers," as the story was entitled when it was first published in *The Atlantic Monthly*, was the choice of editor James T. Fields. "My Contraband" was always Alcott's preference, and after the story was published, she referred to it in a letter to James Redpath as "the 'Contraband' (or 'Brothers' as he [Fields] insists on naming it" (letter to James Redpath, 29 September 1863, *Letters*, p. 94). When the story was reprinted in *Hospital Sketches and Camp and Fireside Stories*, it was retitled "My Contraband." On the politics of the term "contraband," see Ella Forbes, *African American Women During the Civil War* (New York: Garland, 1998), pp. 9–10, and Thavolia Glymph, "'This Species of Property': Female Slave Contrabands in the Civil War," in *A Woman's War: Southern Women, Civil War, and the Confederate Legacy*, edited by Edward D. C. Campbell, Jr., and Kym S. Rice (Richmond: Museum of the Confederacy/Charlottesville: University Press of Virginia, 1996), pp. 55–58.

65. Alcott, "Nelly's Hospital" (1863), in *Louisa May Alcott on Race, Sex, and Slavery*, pp. 29, 39, 35. On children's Civil War literature, see James Marten, *The Children's Civil War* (Chapel Hill: University of North Carolina Press, 1998), pp. 31–67. Another Civil War story from this era, "An Hour" (1864), approaches racial struggle more directly, focusing on a possible slave revolt on an isolated island off the coast of Louisiana in the middle of the war. Like other Alcott stories, this story turns on a woman's unusual authority—in this case, that of a mixed-race slave named Milly, who informs her white master, Gabriel, of the coming revolt, demanding "Who is the mistress now?" (in *Louisa May Alcott on Race, Sex, and Slavery*, p. 53). And as in "My Contraband," interracial desire surfaces, here represented in the mutual attraction of Milly and Gabriel. Yet the story swerves away from both slave mutiny and interracial romance. Milly and Gabriel do not unite, and "An Hour" climaxes instead with Gabriel's decision to free the slaves, an act that prompts the spectacle of "the freedmen . . . clinging to his garments, kissing his feet and pouring blessings on his head" (p. 68). The story concludes with the arrival of the Union army, further containing any threat that the slaves might revolt on their own. Like "My Contraband" and "Nelly's Hospital," "An Hour" is energized by the racial struggles of the Civil War, but the story domesticates both its female body and body politic into contained form. For discussion of this story, see Elbert, *A Hunger for Home*, pp. 158–60, and Elbert, Introduction to *Louisa May Alcott on Race, Sex, and Slavery*, pp. xlix–liii.

66. Alcott, "A Hospital Christmas," in *Hospital Sketches and Camp and Fireside Stories*, p. 339. All subsequent quotations are from this edition and cited parenthetically in the text. For discussion of this story, see Eiselein, *Literature and Humanitarian Reform in the Civil War Era*, p. 101.

67. Diffley, *"Where My Heart Is Turning Ever,"* pp. 14–15.

68. Notable exceptions are Limon, *Writing After War,* pp. 183–88, and Judith Fetterley, *"Little Women:* Alcott's Civil War," *Feminist Studies* 5:2 (Summer 1979): 369–83. For an overview of critical commentary on *Little Women,* see Ann B. Murphy, "The Borders of Ethical, Erotic, and Artistic Possibilities in *Little Women,*" *Signs* 15:3 (Spring 1990): 562–85; for discussion of readers' responses to the text, see Barbara Sicherman, "Reading *Little Women:* The Many Lives of a Text," in *U.S. History as Women's History,* edited by Linda K. Kerber, Alice Kessler-Harris, and Kathryn Kish Sklar (Chapel Hill: University of North Carolina Press, 1995), pp. 245–66.

69. Alcott, *Little Women,* edited by Elaine Showalter (New York: Penguin, 1989), p. 183. All subsequent quotations are from this edition and cited parenthetically in the text.

70. For discussion of Mr. March, see James D. Wallace, "Where the Absent Father Went: Alcott's *Work,*" in *Refiguring the Father: New Feminist Readings of Patriarchy,* edited by Patricia Yaeger and Beth Kowaleski-Wallace (Carbondale: Southern Illinois University Press, 1989), pp. 259–74, and Lynda Zwinger, *Daughters, Fathers, and the Novel: The Sentimental Romance of Heterosexuality* (Madison: University of Wisconsin Press, 1991), pp. 46–75. Limon also links Beth to the Civil War (*Writing After War,* p. 185).

71. Brodhead, *Cultures of Letters,* pp. 70–72. On Plumfield, see also Nina Auerbach, *Communities of Women: An Idea in Fiction* (Cambridge: Harvard University Press, 1978), pp. 69–73, and Elbert, *A Hunger for Home,* pp. 231–36.

72. Alcott, *Little Men* (1871; rpt. Boston: Little, Brown, 1994), p. 329. For analysis of this novel's disciplinary project, see also Michael Moon, "Nineteenth-Century Discourses on Childhood Gender Training: The Case of Louisa May Alcott's *Little Men* and *Jo's Boys,*" in *Queer Representations: Reading Lives, Reading Cultures,* edited by Martin Duberman (New York: New York University Press, 1997), pp. 209–15.

73. Alcott, *Jo's Boys* (1886; rpt. Boston: Little, Brown, 1994), p. 212. All subsequent quotations are from this edition and cited parenthetically in the text. The novel is discussed in Auerbach, *Communities of Women,* pp. 71–73; Elbert, *A Hunger for Home,* pp. 277–81; and Moon, "Nineteenth-Century Discourses on Gender Training," pp. 211–15.

74. On these doctors, see Marcia Jacobson, "Popular Fiction and Henry James's *The Bostonians,*" *Modern Philology* 73 (1976): 266–68, and Michael Sartisky, Afterword to Elizabeth Stuart Phelps, *Doctor Zay* (1882; rpt. New York: Feminist Press, 1987), pp. 299–305.

75. For discussion of *Work,* see Barbara Bardes and Suzanne Gossett, *Declarations of Independence: Women and Political Power in Nineteenth-Century American Fiction* (New Brunswick: Rutgers University Press, 1990), pp. 100–103; Glenn Hendler, "The Limits of Sympathy: Louisa May Alcott and the Sentimental Novel," *American Literary History* 3:4 (Winter 1991): 685–706; and Margaret Higonnet, "Civil Wars and Sexual Territories," in *Arms and the Woman: War, Gender, and Literary Representation,* edited by Helen M. Cooper, Adrienne Auslander Munich, and Susan Merrill Squier (Chapel Hill: University of North Carolina Press, 1989), pp. 87–89.

CHAPTER THREE

1. William Wells Brown, *Clotelle; or, The Colored Heroine* (1867; rpt. Miami: Mnemosyne, 1969), p. 105, and Brown, *The Negro in the American Rebellion: His Heroism and His Fidelity* (1867, 1880; rpt. Miami: Mnemosyne, 1969).

2. Frederick Douglass, *Life and Times of Frederick Douglass,* introduction by Rayford W. Logan (1892; rpt. New York: Collier, 1962), p. 336. For a comprehensive exploration of the effect of the war on Douglass, see David W. Blight, *Frederick Douglass' Civil War: Keeping Faith in Jubilee* (Baton Rouge: Louisiana State University Press, 1989).

3. Additional Civil War writings by black men may be found in Ira Berlin et al., eds., *Freedom: A Documentary History of Emancipation, 1861–67* (Cambridge: Cambridge University Press, 1982–93), 4 vols.; Richard A. Long, ed., *Black Writers and the American Civil War* (Secaucus, NJ: Blue and Grey Press, 1988); James M. McPherson, *The Negro's Civil War* (New York: Vintage, 1967); C. Peter Ripley, ed., *The Black Abolitionist Papers,* 5 vols. (Chapel Hill: University of North Carolina Press, 1985–92), and the microfilm edition of this collection, edited by C. Peter Ripley et al. (1981), reels 13–16. Reprinted collections of letters by black soldiers include James Henry Gooding, *On the Altar of Freedom: A Black Soldier's Civil War Letters from the Front,* edited by Virginia Matzke Adams (Amherst: University of Massachusetts Press, 1991); Edwin S. Redkey, ed., *A Grand Army of Black Men: Letters from African-American Soldiers in the Union Army, 1861–1865* (Cambridge: Cambridge University Press, 1992); and Daniel Yacovone, ed., *A Voice of Thunder: The Civil War Letters of George E. Stephens* (Urbana: University of Illinois Press, 1997). For analyses of the experience and representation of black Civil War soldiers, see David W. Blight and Brooks D. Simpson, eds., *Union and Emancipation: Essays on Politics and Race in the Civil War Era* (Kent, OH: Kent State University Press, 1997); Jim Cullen, "'I's a Man Now': Gender and African American Men," in *Divided Houses: Gender and the Civil War,* edited by Catherine Clinton and Nina Silber (New York: Oxford University Press, 1992), pp. 76–91; Joseph T. Glatthaar, *Forged in Battle: The Civil War Alliance of Black Soldiers and White Officers* (New York: Free Press, 1990); Randall C. Jimerson, *The Private Civil War: Popular Thought During the Sectional Conflict* (Baton Rouge: Louisiana State University Press, 1988), pp. 86–123; Sydney Kaplan, "The Black Soldier of the Civil War in Literature and Art," in *American Studies in Black and White: Selected Essays, 1949–89,* edited by Allan D. Austin (Amherst: University of Massachusetts Press, 1991), pp. 101–23; Leon F. Litwack, *Been in the Storm So Long: The Aftermath of Slavery* (New York: Alfred A. Knopf, 1979), pp. 64–103; and Kirk Savage, *Standing Soldiers, Kneeling Slaves: Race, War, and Monument in Nineteenth-Century America* (Princeton: Princeton University Press, 1997), pp. 180–207.

4. Jacqueline Jones, *Labor of Love, Labor of Sorrow: Black Women, Work, and the Family from Slavery to the Present* (New York: Vintage, 1986), pp. 47, 51.

5. For discussions of black women in the Civil War, see Victoria E. Bynum, *Unruly Women: The Politics of Social and Sexual Control in the Old South* (Chapel Hill: Univer-

sity of North Carolina Press, 1992), pp. 111–29; Bynum, "Misshapen Identity: Memory, Folklore, and the Legend of Rachel Knight," in *Discovering the Women in Slavery: Emancipating Perspectives on the American Past*, edited by Patricia Morton (Athens: University of Georgia Press, 1996), pp. 29–46; Catherine Clinton, "Civil War and Reconstruction," in *Black Women in America: An Historical Encyclopedia*, vol. 1, edited by Darlene Clark Hine (Brooklyn: Carlson, 1993), pp. 241–49; Drew Gilpin Faust, Thavolia Glymph, and George C. Rable, "A Woman's War: Southern Women in the Civil War," in *A Woman's War: Southern Women, Civil War, and the Confederate Legacy*, edited by Edward D. C. Campbell, Jr., and Kym S. Rice (Richmond: Museum of the Confederacy/Charlottesville: University Press of Virginia, 1996), pp. 1–27; Ella Forbes, *African American Women During the Civil War* (New York: Garland, 1998); Noralee Frankel, "The Southern Side of *Glory:* Mississippi African-American Women During the Civil War," in *"We Specialize in the Wholly Impossible": A Reader in Black Women's History*, edited by Darlene Clark Hine, Wilma King, and Linda Reed (Brooklyn: Carlson, 1995), pp. 335–41; Thavolia Glymph, "'This Species of Property': Female Slave Contrabands in the Civil War," in *A Woman's War*, pp. 55–71; Darlene Clark Hine and Kathleen Thompson, *A Shining Thread of Hope: The History of Black Women in America* (New York: Broadway Books, 1998), pp. 125–46; Tera W. Hunter, *To 'Joy My Freedom: Southern Black Women's Lives and Labors After the Civil War* (Cambridge: Harvard University Press, 1997), pp. 4–20; and Jones, *Labor of Love, Labor of Sorrow*, 1985), pp. 44–51.

6. Sattira A. Douglas, letter to Robert Hamilton, 9 June 1863, in *Black Abolitionist Papers*, vol. 5, p. 212.

7. Sarah Parker Remond, *The Negroes and Anglo-Africans as Freedmen and Soldiers* (London, 1864), p. 5, in *Black Abolitionist Papers, 1830–1865*, microfilm edition, reel 15, no. 0171. On Shadd Cary and the Civil War, see Jane Rhodes, *Mary Ann Shadd Cary: The Black Press and Protest in the Nineteenth Century* (Bloomington: Indiana University Press, 1998), pp. 135–62.

8. For the classic articulation of this exclusionary dichotomy, see *All the Women Are White, All the Blacks Are Men, But Some of Us Are Brave: Black Women's Studies*, edited by Gloria T. Hull, Patricia Bell Scott, and Barbara Smith (Old Westbury, NY: Feminist Press, 1982). On the "overembodiment" of black women, see Lauren Berlant, "National Brands/National Body: *Imitation of Life*," in *Comparative American Identities: Race, Sex, and Nationality in the American Text*, edited by Hortense Spillers (New York: Routledge, 1991), pp. 110–40, and Carla L. Peterson, *"Doers of the Word": African-American Women Speakers and Writers in the North (1830–1880)* (New York: Oxford University Press, 1995), pp. 19–22.

9. I have focused here on authors accessible through the Schomburg Library of Nineteenth-Century Black Women Writers, published by Oxford University Press, and other reprinted sources. Jackson, Rollin, and Keckley are cited in notes below; Tubman and Truth are cited in notes to earlier chapters; and Harper is cited in notes in chapter 5. On Forten, see Charlotte Forten, *The Journals of Charlotte Forten Grimké*, edited by Brenda Stevenson (New York: Oxford University Press, 1988). On Jacobs,

see letters in Dorothy Sterling, ed., *We Are Your Sisters: Black Women in the Nineteenth Century* (New York: W. W. Norton, 1984), 245–48; a scholarly edition of the Jacobs family papers, edited by Jean Fagan Yellin, is forthcoming. Additional Civil War writings by black women may be found in Gerda Lerner, ed., *Black Women in White America: A Documentary History* (New York: Pantheon, 1972); Bert James Loewenberg and Ruth Bogin, eds., *Black Women in Nineteenth Century American Life* (University Park: Penn State University Press, 1976); and Sterling, *We Are Your Sisters*. See also the anthologies cited in note 3 above.

10. The text concludes with a separate essay by Jackson, entitled "Christianity," not directly related to the autobiography. See *The Story of Mattie J. Jackson; Her Parentage—Experience of Eighteen Years in Slavery—Incidents During the War—Her Escape from Slavery,* "written and arranged by Dr. L. S. Thompson, (formerly Mrs. Schuyler) as given by Mattie," in *Six Women's Slave Narratives,* edited by William L. Andrews (1866; rpt. New York: Oxford University Press, 1988); all subsequent quotations are from this edition and cited parenthetically in the text. For discussion of Jackson, see the Introduction by Andrews, pp. xxix–xli, and Emmy E. Werner, *Reluctant Witnesses: Children's Voices from the Civil War* (New York: Westview Press, 1998), pp. 44–46.

11. Hunter, *To 'Joy My Freedom*, p. 5. On tensions among Union soldiers, Confederates, and slaves in the occupied South, see Stephen V. Ash, *When the Yankees Came: Conflict and Chaos in the Occupied South, 1861–1865* (Chapel Hill: University of North Carolina Press, 1995). On the practice of slaves learning war news from their masters, see Peter Bardaglio, "The Children of Jubilee: African American Childhood in Wartime," in *Divided Houses*, pp. 218–19.

12. Carole Ione, *Pride of Family: Four Generations of American Women of Color* (New York: Summit, 1991). The Delany biography is Frank A. [Frances] Rollin, *Life and Public Services of Martin R. Delany* (1868), reprinted in *Two Biographies of African-American Women*, edited by William L. Andrews (New York: Oxford University Press, 1988); the quotation is on p. 8. Rollin's diary is excerpted in *Pride of Family* and in *We Are Your Sisters*, pp. 453–61. Ione includes some fuller individual entries than Sterling, but they are scattered throughout the memoir; Sterling reprints the diary in aggregate form with annotations. I have cited the Sterling version; page numbers appear parenthetically in the text. For discussion of Rollin, see Catherine Clinton, *Civil War Stories* (Athens: University of Georgia Press, 1998), pp. 100–111, and Willard B. Gatewood, Jr., "'The Remarkable Misses Rollin': Black Women in Reconstruction South Carolina," *South Carolina Historical Magazine* 92 (July 1991): 172–88.

13. Rollin, *Life and Public Services of Martin R. Delany*, p. 8. For discussion of this text, see Clinton, *Civil War Stories*, pp. 104–8, and Robert S. Levine, *Martin Delany, Frederick Douglass, and the Politics of Representative Identity* (Chapel Hill: University of North Carolina Press, 1997), pp. 219–23.

14. Ione refers to Rollin as "Frank" throughout, citing it as her family nickname and quoting a letter from Rollin's sister Charlotte addressed to "Frank" (*Pride of Family*, pp. 95, 123–24). Sterling assesses the decision to use "Frank" for the Delany biogra-

phy as follows: "Rollin and her publisher decided that the reading public was not yet ready to accept a book by a black woman" (*We Are Your Sisters,* p. 461).

15. Peterson, *"Doers of the Word,"* p. 192. Other assessments of Forten's journals include Joanne M. Braxton, "A Poet's Retreat: The Diaries of Charlotte Forten Grimké, 1837–1914," in *Wild Women in the Whirlwind: Afra-American Culture and the Contemporary Literary Renaissance,* edited by Joanne M. Braxton and Andrée Nicola McLaughlin (New Brunswick: Rutgers University Press, 1990), pp. 70–88; and Nellie Y. McKay, "The Journals of Charlotte L. Forten-Grimké: 'Les Lieux de Mémoire' in African-American Women's Autobiography," in *History and Memory in African-American Culture,* edited by Geneviève Fabre and Robert O'Meally (New York: Oxford University Press, 1994), pp. 261–71.

16. Rollin, quoted in Ione, *Pride of Family,* p. 109. This entry is reprinted in *We Are Your Sisters* in abridged form (456).

17. Frances Smith Foster, "Autobiography After Emancipation: The Example of Elizabeth Keckley," in *Multicultural Autobiography: American Lives,* edited by James R. Payne (Knoxville: University of Tennessee Press, 1992), pp. 32–63; see also Foster, *Written by Herself: Literary Production by African American Women, 1746–1892* (Bloomington: Indiana University Press, 1993), pp. 117–30. Critical discussions of *Behind the Scenes* include the following: William L. Andrews, "The Changing Moral Discourse of Nineteenth-Century African American Women's Autobiography: Harriet Jacobs and Elizabeth Keckley," in *De/Colonizing the Subject: The Politics of Gender in Women's Autobiography,* edited by Sidonie Smith and Julia Watson (Minneapolis: University of Minnesota Press, 1992), pp. 225–41; Andrews, "Reunion in the Postbellum Slave Narrative: Frederick Douglass and Elizabeth Keckley," *Black American Literature Forum* 23:1 (Spring 1989): 5–16; Joanne M. Braxton, *Black Women Writing Autobiography: A Tradition Within a Tradition* (Philadelphia: Temple University Press, 1989), pp. 40–43; Julia Copeland, "Behind the Signs: An Approach to Reading Keckley's *Behind the Scenes*" (unpub. ms., Bloomington, IN); Kimberley Dillon, "Authorial Bodily Effacement in 'Classic' Nineteenth-Century African-American Autobiographies: Narrative Strategies and Ideological Inheritances," Ph.D. diss., University of California at San Diego, 1996; Lynn Domina, "I Was Re-Elected President: Elizabeth Keckley as Quintessential Patriot in *Behind the Scenes, Or, Thirty Years a Slave and Four Years in the White House,*" in *Women's Life-Writing: Finding Voice/Building Community,* edited by Linda S. Coleman (Bowling Green, OH: Bowling Green State University Popular Press, 1997), pp. 139–51; Jennifer Fleischner, *Mastering Slavery: Memory, Family, and Identity in Women's Slave Narratives* (New York: New York University Press, 1997), pp. 93–132; Minrose C. Gwin, "Green-Eyed Monsters of the Slavocracy: Jealous Mistresses in Two Slave Narratives," in *Conjuring: Black Women, Fiction, and Literary Tradition,* edited by Marjorie Pryse and Hortense J. Spillers (Bloomington: Indiana University Press, 1985), pp. 39–52; Estelle Jelinek, *The Tradition of Women's Autobiography: From Antiquity to the Present* (Boston: Twayne, 1986), pp. 82–84; Jill Wacker, "Elizabeth Keckley, the Badges of Slavery and the Culture of Display," paper delivered at the conference on "Nineteenth-Century American Women Writers in the Twenty-

First Century," Hartford, May 1996; and Rafia Zafar, *We Wear the Mask: African Americans Write American Literature, 1760–1870* (New York: Columbia University Press, 1997), pp. 151–83. The only full-length biography of Keckley is Becky Rutberg, *Mary Lincoln's Dressmaker: Elizabeth Keckley's Remarkable Rise from Slave to White House Confidante* (New York: Walker and Company, 1995), which is written for a young-adult audience. John E. Washington documented Keckley's life in *They Knew Lincoln* (New York: E. P. Dutton, 1942), pp. 205–41. A more recent overview of Keckley's life and text is provided by Frances Smith Foster in a new, limited edition of *Behind the Scenes* (Chicago: R. R. Donnelley and Sons/Lakeside Press, 1998); see Foster, "Historical Introduction," pp. xix–lxxvii.

18. On the history of the White House, see Frank Freidel and William Pencak, eds., *The White House: The First Two Hundred Years* (Boston: Northeastern University Press, 1994).

19. William O. Stoddard, *Inside the White House in War Times* (New York, 1890), pp. 23, 62, 25.

20. On the Lincolns' tenure in the White House, see Jean H. Baker, *Mary Todd Lincoln: A Life* (New York: W. W. Norton, 1987), and Donald, "'This Damned Old House': The Lincolns in the White House," in *The White House*, pp. 53–74.

21. Keckley, *Behind the Scenes. Or, Thirty Years a Slave, and Four Years in the White House*, edited by James Olney (1868; rpt. New York: Oxford University Press, 1988), p. 91. All subsequent quotations are from this edition and cited parenthetically in the text.

22. On Keckley as symbolic national president, see also Domina, "'I Was Re-Elected President.'"

23. For different perspectives on the relationship between Keckley and her master, see Gwin, who argues that "Her half-apologetic account of her own sexual coercion. . . . shows above all a continuing psychological enslavement to the white man" ("Green-Eyed Monsters of the Slavocracy," p. 49); Foster, who notes that "[Keckley] does not claim to have been raped. Indeed, her self-characterization and the abrupt, brief, and vague manner in which she relates the incident suggest otherwise" (*Written by Herself*, p. 120); and Saidiya V. Hartman, who suggests that the elisions in Keckley's account "articulate both the literal absence of rape in the law . . . and the textual crisis engendered by the effort to represent it" (*Scenes of Subjection: Terror, Slavery, and Self-Making in Nineteenth-Century America* [New York: Oxford University Press, 1997]), p. 108.

24. Zafar, *We Wear the Mask*, p. 175.

25. See James M. McPherson, *Battle Cry of Freedom: The Civil War Era* (New York: Ballantine, 1988), pp. 276–307. For a relevant discussion of Civil War "border" fiction, see Kathleen Diffley, "Home from the Theatre of War: The *Southern Magazine* and Recollections of the Civil War," in *Periodical Literature in Nineteenth-Century America*, edited by Kenneth M. Price and Susan Belasco Smith (Charlottesville: University Press of Virginia, 1995), pp. 183–201.

26. Quoted in Washington, *They Knew Lincoln*, pp. 218, 220.

27. Ibid., p. 216.

28. For an overview of racial issues in Washington during this time, see Constance McLaughlin Green, *The Secret City: A History of Race Relations in the Nation's Capital* (Princeton: Princeton University Press, 1967), pp. 55–74.

29. Andrews, "Reunion in the Postbellum Slave Narrative."

30. Fleischner, *Mastering Slavery*, p. 99. On accommodationism in Keckley, see also Foster, *Written by Herself*, pp. 125–26; Olney, Introduction to *Behind the Scenes*, p. xxx; and Zafar, *We Wear the Mask*, p. 175.

31. William L. Andrews, *To Tell a Free Story: The First Century of Afro-American Autobiography, 1760–1865* (Urbana: University of Illinois Press, 1986), pp. 265–91. See also Andrews, "The Novelization of Voice in Early African American Narrative," *PMLA* 105:1 (January 1990): 23–34, and Peterson, *"Doers of the Word,"* pp. 146–75.

32. Olney, Introduction, p. xxvii.

33. The many discussions of this issue include Andrews, *To Tell a Free Story*; Charles T. Davis and Henry Louis Gates Jr., eds., *The Slave's Narrative* (New York: Oxford University Press, 1985); Robert B. Stepto, *From Behind the Veil: A Study of Afro-American Narrative* (Urbana: University of Illinois Press, 1979); and Frances Smith Foster, *Witnessing Slavery: The Development of Antebellum Slave Narratives* (Westport, CT: Greenwood Press, 1979).

34. Rollin was equally unimpressed when she attended a public reading by Keckley, as she noted in her diary: "It was poor to say the least. It is too late in the day for her to attempt it especially without a first class teacher" (*We Are Your Sisters*, p. 460).

35. David Rankin Barbee, quoted in [Anon.], *"Behind the Scenes," Lincoln Lore*, no. 363 (23 March 1936): n.p. This accusation is discussed in Foster, "Historical Introduction," pp. xxiv–xxvi.

36. Washington, *They Knew Lincoln*, pp. 232–39.

37. See, for example, Baker, who calls it a "ghostwritten exposé" (*Mary Todd Lincoln*, p. 212); Justin G. Turner and Linda Levitt Turner, who assert that Keckley wrote by "dictating her reminiscences to a professional writer" and suggest that the most likely candidate is a journalist named Hamilton Busbey (*Mary Todd Lincoln: Her Life and Letters* [New York: Fromm International, 1987], p. 471); and Gerry Van der Heuvel, who writes that "with the help of a couple of newspapermen as ghostwriters, the seamstress published her memoirs" (*Crowns of Thorns and Glory: Mary Todd Lincoln and Varina Howell Davis, The Two First Ladies of the Civil War* [New York: E. P. Dutton, 1988], p. 85.

38. For an analysis that emphasizes the role of Redpath and of Keckley's publishers, G. W. Carleton and Co., see Foster, *Written by Herself*, and "Historical Introduction," pp. lx–lxvii.

39. Quoted in Shane White and Graham White, *Stylin': African American Expressive Culture from Its Beginnings to the Zoot Suit* (Ithaca: Cornell University Press, 1998), p. 127.

40. Myrta Lockett Avary, *Dixie After the War* (1906; rpt. New York: Negro University Press, 1969), pp. 182–83.

41. On African-American women and clothing, see Clinton, "Civil War and Reconstruction," p. 245; Helen Bradley Foster, *"New Raiments of Self": African-American*

Clothing in the Antebellum South (New York: Berg, 1997); Patricia K. Hunt, "The Struggle to Achieve Individual Expression through Clothing and Adornment: African American Women Under and After Slavery," in *Discovering the Women in Slavery*, pp. 227–40; Jones, *Labor of Love, Labor of Sorrow*, pp. 68–71; and White and White, *Stylin'*, esp. pp. 21–25. On African-American women's quiltmaking, see Elsa Barkley Brown, "African-American Women's Quiltmaking: A Framework for Conceptualizing and Teaching African-American Women's History," in *Black Women in America: Social Science Perspectives*, edited by Micheline R. Malson et al. (Chicago: University of Chicago Press, 1988), pp. 9–18; and Elaine Hedges, *Hearts and Hands: The Influence of Women and Quilts on American Society* (San Francisco: Quilt Digest Press, 1987).

42. For information on Keckley's career as seamstress, designer, and "modiste," see Rutberg, *Mary Lincoln's Dressmaker*; on her quiltmaking, see Hedges, *Hearts and Hands*, pp. 45, 76–77. Analyses of *Behind the Scenes* that focus on Keckley as clothing entrepreneur are Dillon, "Authorial Bodily Effacement in 'Classic' Nineteenth-Century African-American Autobiographies," and Wacker, "Elizabeth Keckley, the Badges of Slavery, and the Culture of Display."

43. George L. Aiken and George C. Howard, *Uncle Tom's Cabin*, edited by Thomas Riis (1852; rpt. New York: Garland, 1994), pp. 18, 19.

44. For other interpretations of this anecdote, see Domina, " 'I Was Re-Elected President,' " pp. 143–44, and Fleischner, *Mastering Slavery*, pp. 126–27.

45. Rollin, *Life and Public Services of Martin R. Delany*, p. 166. Douglass, *Life and Times of Frederick Douglass*, p. 347. African-Americans were by no means united in their attitudes toward Lincoln. For example, Harriet Tubman, who preferred the more militant John Brown, resisted meeting the president. She later remembered that she "didn't like Lincoln in those days" but had since changed her mind (Earl Conrad, *Harriet Tubman* [New York: Paul Ericksson, 1943], pp. 183–84).

46. According to David Herbert Donald, Lincoln was uncomfortable with wearing gloves, because his hands were large from years of manual labor (" 'This Damned Old House,' " p. 59).

47. Douglass, *Life and Times of Frederick Douglass*, p. 347; *Narrative of Sojourner Truth*, edited by Jeffrey C. Stewart (1878; rpt. New York: Oxford University Press, 1991), p. 181.

48. Unnamed source, quoted in Marie Garrett, "Elizabeth Keckley" entry in *Notable Black American Women*, edited by Jessie Carney Smith (Detroit: Gale, 1992), p. 618.

49. For examples of African-American responses to Lincoln's assassination, see *Black Abolitionist Papers*, vol. 5, pp. 315–20. On the public display of Lincoln's body, see Gary Laderman, "The Body Politic and the Politics of Two Bodies: Abraham and Mary Todd Lincoln in Death," *Prospects* 22 (1997): 109–32, and Laderman, *The Sacred Remains: American Attitudes Toward Death, 1799–1883* (New Haven: Yale University Press, 1996), pp. 157–63.

50. Melba Joyce Boyd, *Discarded Legacy: Politics and Poetics in the Life of Frances E. W. Harper, 1825–1911* (Detroit: Wayne State University Press, 1994), p. 87.

51. For another interpretation of the glove and cloak incidents, see Fleischner, *Mas-*

tering Slavery, pp. 122–23. On the subsequent fate of the Lincoln items, see Lloyd Ostendorf, "Elizabeth Keckley's Lost Lincoln Relics," *Lincoln Herald* 71:1 (Spring 1969): 14–18.

52. A number of these images are reproduced in Mark E. Neely, Jr., Harold Holzer, and Gabor S. Borritt, *The Confederate Image: Prints of the Lost Cause* (Chapel Hill: University of North Carolina Press, 1987), pp. 79–96. For an assessment of what Davis was actually wearing when captured, see Chester D. Bradley, "Was Jefferson Davis Disguised as a Woman When Captured?" *Journal of Mississippi History* 36:3 (August 1974): 243–68.

53. Nina Silber, *The Romance of Reunion: Northerners and the South, 1865–1900* (Chapel Hill: University of North Carolina Press, 1993), pp. 13–38. Other discussions of this imagery include Neely, Holzer, and Boritt, *Confederate Image,* pp. 79–96; Drew Gilpin Faust, *Mothers of Invention: Women of the Slaveholding South in the American Civil War* (Chapel Hill: University of North Carolina Press, 1996), pp. 228–30; Gaines M. Foster, *Ghosts of the Confederacy: Defeat, the Lost Cause, and the Emergence of the New South, 1865–1913* (New York: Oxford University Press, 1987), pp. 26–28; and Kenneth S. Greenberg, *Honor and Slavery* (Princeton: Princeton University Press, 1998), pp. 25–31.

54. Sarah Bradford, *Harriet Tubman: The Moses of Her People* (1881; rpt. Bedford, MA: Applewood Books, 1993), p. 101.

55. Brown, *Negro in the American Rebellion,* pp. 298–308; the quotations are from 299, 302–3, and 304.

56. The most well-known representation of sexualized whipping is the abuse of Frederick Douglass's Aunt Hester. On this scene, see Deborah E. McDowell, "In the First Place: Making Frederick Douglass and the Afro-American Narrative Tradition," in *African American Autobiography,* edited by William L. Andrews (Englewood Cliffs, NJ: Prentice-Hall, 1983), pp. 36–58; on the representation of violence against slave women, see Hartman, *Scenes of Subjection,* pp. 79–112.

57. See Rutberg, *Mary Lincoln's Dressmaker,* pp. 117–18.

58. See Elaine Hedges, "The Needle or the Pen: The Literary Rediscovery of Women's Textile Work," in *Tradition and the Talents of Women,* edited by Florence Howe (Urbana: University of Illinois Press, 1991), pp. 338–64; Elaine Showalter, "Common Threads," in *Sister's Choice: Tradition and Change in American Women's Writing* (New York: Oxford University Press, 1991), pp. 145–75; and Alice Walker, *In Search of Our Mothers' Gardens* (New York: Harcourt Brace Jovanovich, 1983), pp. 231–43.

59. Henry Bellows, Introduction to L. P. Brockett and Mary C. Vaughan, *Woman's Work in the Civil War: A Record of Heroism, Patriotism and Patience* (Philadelphia, 1867), p. 64.

60. Lydia Maria Child, Introduction to Harriet Jacobs, *Incidents in the Life of a Slave Girl, Written by Herself,* edited by Jean Fagan Yellin (1861; rpt. Cambridge: Harvard University Press, 1987), p. 4. For recent critical perspectives on Jacobs, see *Harriet Jacobs and "Incidents in the Life of a Slave Girl": New Critical Essays,* edited by Deborah M. Garfield and Rafia Zafar (Cambridge: Cambridge University Press, 1996).

61. Fleischner, *Mastering Slavery*, p. 130.

62. For another discussion of this anecdote, see Zafar, *We Wear the Mask*, pp. 179–80; for analysis of the relationship between Keckley and Mrs. Burwell, see Gwin, "Green-Eyed Monsters of the Slavocracy," pp. 48–51; and for discussion of relationships between women slaves and slave mistresses, see Elizabeth Fox-Genovese, *Within the Plantation Household: Black and White Women of the Old South* (Chapel Hill: University of North Carolina Press, 1988).

63. See Baker, who argues that "popular stereotypes of Mary Lincoln are classic instances of a male-ordered history that is no longer acceptable" and that Lincoln was "a victim battered by personal adversity and trapped by destructive conventions of Victorian domesticity" (*Mary Todd Lincoln*, pp. xiv–xv). For comparison between the reputations of Abraham and Mary Todd Lincoln, see Laderman, "The Body Politic and the Politics of Two Bodies." On the history of the role of "First Lady," see Betty Boyd Caroli, *First Ladies* (New York: Oxford University Press, 1987); Caroli cites Mary Todd Lincoln as "Republican Queen" on p. 71.

64. On slaves in Mary Todd Lincoln's household, see Baker, *Mary Todd Lincoln*, pp. 12–18.

65. This was the description of Laura Fisher, a retired Washington school teacher (quoted in Washington, *They Knew Lincoln*, p. 218).

66. *Columbus [Georgia] Sun*, quoted in Baker, *Mary Todd Lincoln*, p. 277; for accounts of the scandal, see Baker, pp. 271–80, and Turner and Turner, *Mary Todd Lincoln*, pp. 429–71.

67. Foster emphasizes the latter (*Written by Herself*, p. 128).

68. See Mary Todd Lincoln, letter to Rhoda White, 2 May 1868, in which she describes Keckley as "*the colored* historian" (Turner and Turner, *Mary Todd Lincoln*, p. 476).

69. See Mark E. Neely, Jr. and R. Gerald McMurtry, *The Insanity File: The Case of Mary Todd Lincoln* (Carbondale, IL: Southern Illinois University Press, 1986).

70. [D. Ottolengul], *Behind the Seams; by a nigger Woman who took in work from Mrs. Lincoln and Mrs. Davis* (New York: National News Company, 1868). I have been unable to obtain more information on the author of the parody or the circumstances of its production. The preface is unpaginated; all subsequent page references are cited parenthetically in the text.

71. For useful discussions of parody, see Linda Hutcheon, *A Theory of Parody: The Teachings of Twentieth-Century Art Forms* (New York: Methuen, 1985), and Margaret A. Rose, *Parody//Meta-Fiction: An Analysis of Parody as a Critical Mirror to the Writing and Reception of Fiction* (London: Croom Helm, 1979).

72. See Foster, "Historical Introduction," lxvii–lxix; the quotation is on p. lxviii.

73. For example: "my bosom friend, Mrs. Abraham Lincoln" (10); "my dear, bosom friend, Mrs. Lincoln" (13); "Your bosom friend, Mary" (18).

74. On the longstanding image of the woman writer as prostitute, see, for example, Catherine Gallagher, *Nobody's Story: The Vanishing Acts of Women Writers in the Marketplace, 1670–1820* (Berkeley: University of California Press, 1994), pp. 1–48.

75. Long, Introduction to *Black Writers and the American Civil War*, p. 12.

76. Hortense J. Spillers, "Cross-Currents, Discontinuities: Black Women's Fiction," in *Conjuring*, p. 251.

CHAPTER FOUR

1. The two best-known accounts of Civil War cross-dressing, discussed below, are S. Emma E. Edmonds, *Nurse and Spy in the Union Army* (Hartford, 1864), and Loreta J. Velazquez, *The Woman in Battle* (Hartford, 1876). Contemporary histories and memoirs of the war that mention cross-dressed soldiers include Linus P. Brockett, *The Camp, the Battle Field, and the Hospital; or, Lights and Shadows of the Great Rebellion* (Chicago, 1866), pp. 67–72; Brockett and Mary C. Vaughan, *Woman's Work in the Civil War: A Record of Heroism, Patriotism and Patience* (Philadelphia, 1867), p. 770; Frazar Kirkland [Richard Miller Devens], *The Pictorial Book of Anecdotes of the Rebellion* (St. Louis, 1889), pp. 170–71, 206, 567, 580, 596–97; Mary A. Livermore, *My Story of the War*, introduction by Nina Silber (1887; rpt. New York: Da Capo, 1995), pp. 113–14, 119–20; Frank Moore, *The Rebellion Record* (New York, 1861), vol. 4, p. 70, vol. 7, p. 87, and vol. 8, pp. 37–38, 53–54; Moore, *Women of the War; Their Heroism and Self-Sacrifice* (Hartford, 1867), pp. 529–32; Albert D. Richardson, *The Secret Service; the Field, the Dungeon, and the Escape* (Hartford, 1865), p. 175; Philip Sheridan, *Personal Memoirs of P. H. Sheridan, General United States Army* (1888), reprinted as *Civil War Memoirs: Philip Sheridan*, introduction by Paul Andrew Hutton (New York: Bantam, 1991), pp. 86–87; and Annie Wittenmyer, *Under the Guns; A Woman's Reminiscences of the Civil War* (Boston, 1895), pp. 17–20. The letters of one woman soldier are collected in *An Uncommon Soldier: The Civil War Letters of Sarah Rosetta Wakeman, alias Pvt. Lyons Wakeman, 153rd Regiment, New York State Volunteers, 1862–1864*, edited by Lauren Cook Burgess (New York: Oxford University Press, 1994). A nineteenth-century ballad about Civil War cross-dressing is Alta Isadore Gould's "Allan Worth: A Story in Two Parts" (1894), reprinted in *Minerva* 14:1 (Spring 1996): 35–50. Novels of Civil War cross-dressing published during or soon after the war include John Esten Cooke, *Hilt to Hilt* (New York, 1868); Edward Edgeville, *Castine* (Raleigh, 1865); Justin Jones [Harry Hazel], *Virginia Graham, the Spy of the Grand Army* (Boston, 1868); Mrs. C. H. Gildersleeve [Rachel Longstreet], *Remy St. Remy; or, The Boy in Blue* (New York, 1866); Madeline Moore, *The Lady Lieutenant* (Philadelphia, 1862), and Mrs. E. D. E. N. Southworth, *Britomarte, the Man-Hater* (Philadelphia, 1868–69). Turn-of-the-century Civil War cross-dressing novels include Joel Chandler Harris, *A Little Union Scout* (New York, 1904); J. Perkins Tracy, *The Heart of Virginia* (New York, 1896); and William Isaac Yopp, *A Dual Role: A Romance of the Civil War* (Dallas, 1902). Twentieth-century novels in which Civil War cross-dressing appears include William Faulkner, *The Unvanquished* (New York: Random House, 1938) and, more recently, Rita Mae Brown, *High Hearts* (New York: Bantam, 1986) and Allan Gurganus, *Oldest Living Confederate Widow Tells All* (New York: Alfred A. Knopf, 1989).

2. Ellen C. Clayton, *Female Warriors. Memorials of Female Valour and Heroism, From the Mythological Ages to the Present Era* (London, 1879), vol. 2, p. 121. On the "female warrior" as an Anglo-American cultural motif, see Dianne Dugaw, *Warrior Women and Popular Balladry, 1650–1850* (Cambridge: Cambridge University Press, 1989); on images of women soldiers in earlier American wars, see Daniel Cohen, *"The Female Marine" and Related Works: Narratives of Cross-Dressing and Urban Vice in America's Early Republic* (Amherst: University of Massachusetts Press, 1997), and Alfred F. Young, *Masquerade: The Life and Times of Deborah Sampson Gannett, Continental Soldier* (New York: Alfred A. Knopf, forthcoming).

3. Livermore, *My Story of the War:* "Some one has stated the number of women soldiers known to the service as little less than four hundred. I cannot vouch for the correctness of this estimate, but I am convinced that a larger number of women disguised themselves and enlisted in the service, for one cause or another, than was dreamed of" (119–20). For discussion of this number, which is probably low, see Elizabeth D. Leonard, *"All the Daring of the Soldier": Women of the Civil War Armies* (New York: W. W. Norton, 1999), chap. 5; I am grateful to the author for sharing this material in manuscript.

4. On Jennie Hodgers, see Leonard, *"All the Daring of a Soldier,"* chap. 5; on Compton and the unnamed Rochester woman, see Richard Hall, *Patriots in Disguise: Women Warriors of the Civil War* (New York: Paragon, 1993), pp. 161, 157.

5. For discussions of Civil War women soldiers, see Linda Grant De Pauw, *Battle Cries and Lullabies: Women in War from Prehistory to the Present* (Norman: University of Oklahoma Press, 1998), pp. 147–56; Hall, *Patriots in Disguise;* Estelle C. Jelinek, "Disguise Autobiographies: Women Masquerading as Men," *Women's Studies International Forum* 10:1 (1987): 53–62; David E. Jones, *Women Warriors: A History* (Washington: Brassey's, 1997), pp. 231–39; Janet E. Kaufman, "'Under the Petticoat Flag': Women Soldiers in the Confederate Army," *Southern Studies* 23:4 (Winter 1984): 363–75; Wendy A. King, *Clad in Uniform: Women Soldiers of the Civil War* (Collingswood, NJ: C. W. Historicals, 1992); C. Kay Larson, "Bonny Yank and Ginny Reb," *Minerva* 8:1 (1990): 33–48; Larson, "Bonny Yank and Ginny Reb Revisited," *Minerva* 10:2 (1992): 35–61; Trudy Carmany Last, "Alta Isadore Gould's 'Allan Worth': An American Revival of the Female Warrior Ballad," *Minerva* 14:1 (Spring 1996): 15–33; Leonard, *"All the Daring of the Soldier";* Mary Elizabeth Massey, *Women in the Civil War* introduction by Jean V. Berlin (1966; rpt. Lincoln: University of Nebraska Press, 1994), pp. 78–85; Jane Ellen Schultz, "Women at the Front: Gender and Genre in the Literature of the American Civil War," Ph.D. diss., University of Michigan, 1988, chap. 5. Lyde Cullen Sizer, "Acting Her Part: Narratives of Union Women Spies," in *Divided Houses: Gender and the Civil War,* edited by Catherine Clinton and Nina Silber (New York: Oxford University Press, 1992), pp. 114–33; and Julie Wheelwright, *Amazons and Military Maids: Women Who Dressed as Men in Pursuit of Life, Liberty and Happiness* (London: Pandora, 1989).

6. Kathleen De Grave, *Swindler, Spy, Rebel: The Confidence Woman in Nineteenth-Century America* (Columbia: University of Missouri Press, 1995). For an introduction to the literary expressions of these themes in nineteenth-century America, see Elaine

K. Ginsberg, ed., *Passing and the Fictions of Identity* (Durham: Duke University Press, 1996); for an investigation of the figure of the "female trickster," see Lori Landay, *Madcaps, Screwballs, and Con Women: The Female Trickster in American Culture* (Philadelphia: University of Pennsylvania Press, 1998); and for an overview of cross-dressing, see Marjorie Garber, *Vested Interests: Cross-Dressing and Cultural Anxiety* (New York: Routledge, 1992).

    7. S. Emma E. Edmonds, *Nurse and Spy in the Union Army* (Hartford: W. S. Williams and Co., 1865); all subsequent quotations are from this edition and cited parenthetically in the text (a reprint of this edition of *Nurse and Spy* is forthcoming in 1999, edited by Elizabeth D. Leonard, from Northern Illinois University Press). For discussion of Edmonds and *Nurse and Spy,* see Sylvia G. L. Dannett, *She Rode With the Generals* (New York: Thomas Nelson and Sons, 1960); Robert Leigh Davis, *Whitman and the Romance of Medicine* (Berkeley: University of California Press, 1997), pp. 49–53; De Grave, *Swindler, Spy, Rebel,* pp. 108–44; Hall, *Patriots in Disguise,* pp. 46–97; Betty Fladeland, "Alias Franklin Thompson," *Michigan History* 42 (December 1958): 435–62; Pat Lammers and Amy Boyce, "Alias Franklin Thompson: A Female in the Ranks," *Civil War Times Illustrated* 22:9 (January 1984): 24–30; Leonard, *"All the Daring of the Soldier,"* chaps. 5 and 7; Diane Montgomery, "Biographical Note on Sarah Edmonds, Alias Franklin Thompson," *Minerva* 14:2 (Summer 1996): 48–66; Schultz, "Women at the Front"; Sizer, "Acting Her Part," pp. 122–27; and Wheelwright, *Amazons and Military Maids,* pp. 21–24 and passim.

    8. Robert Leigh Davis argues that Edmonds directly mimics Alcott (*Whitman and the Romance of Medicine,* pp. 52–53).

    9. S. Emma E. Edmonds, *Unsexed; or, the Female Soldier: The Thrilling Adventures, Experiences and Escapes of a Woman, as Nurse, Spy and Scout, in Hospitals, Camps and Battle-Fields* (Philadelphia: Philadelphia Publishing Co., 1864). The title was changed to *Nurse and Spy* in editions published in 1865 and after.

    10. Werner Sollors, *Neither Black Nor White Yet Both: Thematic Explorations of Interracial Literature* (New York: Oxford University Press, 1997), pp. 246–84. See also Garber, *Vested Interests,* pp. 267–303, and Ellen M. Weinauer, "'A Most Respectable Gentleman': Passing, Possession, and Transgression in *Running a Thousand Miles for Freedom,*" in *Passing and the Fictions of Identity,* pp. 37–56.

    11. On Edmonds's contraband disguise, see Sizer, "'Acting Her Part,'" in *Divided Houses,* pp. 123–25. Narratives of cross-dressed Civil War soldiers overwhelmingly feature white women, although evidence suggests that at least two black women disguised themselves as soldiers; see De Pauw, *Battle Cries and Lullabies,* pp. 13–64, and Ella Forbes, *African American Women During the Civil War* (New York: Garland, 1998), p. 41.

    12. Noel Ignatiev, *How the Irish Became White* (New York: Routledge, 1995), p. 41. On black-Irish relations, see also David R. Roediger, *The Wages of Whiteness: Race and the Making of the American Working Class* (London: Verso, 1991), pp. 133–63; on Irish-Americans in the Civil War, see William L. Burton, *Melting Pot Soldiers: The Union's Ethnic Regiments* (Ames: Iowa State University Press, 1988), pp. 112–54; and

on Irish-Americans in the Draft Riots, see Iver Bernstein, *The New York City Draft Riots: Their Significance in American Society and Politics in the Age of the Civil War* (New York: Oxford University Press, 1990).

13. For an authoritative assessment of Edmonds's actual Civil War career, see Leonard, *"All the Daring of the Soldier,"* chap. 5.

14. Both quoted in Hall, *Patriots in Disguise,* p. 94. Hall continues this tradition by dedicating his book to Edmonds, "whose character I found to be admirable, without qualification" (p. v).

15. Ibid., p. 81.

16. Ibid., p. 75.

17. Ibid., p. 76. On Edmonds's attachment to this text, see Wheelwright, *Amazons and Military Maids,* pp. 21–22; for discussion of *Fanny Campbell,* see Leonard, *"All the Daring of the Soldier,"* chap. 7.

18. Quoted in Hall, *Patriots in Disguise,* 77.

19. Ibid., p. 79.

20. For detailed comparison between the two texts, see De Grave, *Swindler, Spy, Rebel,* and Schultz, "Women at the Front."

21. Loreta J. Velazquez, *The Woman in Battle* (Richmond: Dustin, Gilman and Co., 1876; rpt. New York: Arno Press, 1972). The same text was later reprinted in 1890 under the less sensational title, *Story of the Civil War or, The Exploits, Adventures and Travels of Mrs. L. J. Velasquez* (New York: Worthington Co., 1890). All subsequent quotations are from the 1876 edition and cited parenthetically in the text.

22. Jubal Early, letter to W. F. Slemons, 22 May 1878; hereafter cited as Early, letter to Slemons. Early apparently never sent this letter to Slemons but included it in another letter about Velazquez, written to John Randolph Tucker, a Virginia Congressman. In Tucker Family Papers, Collection #2605, Southern Historical Collection, Wilson Library, University of North Carolina at Chapel Hill; all quotations from this collection used by permission.

23. Francis Butler Simkins and James Welch Patton, *The Women of the Confederacy* (Richmond: Garrett and Massie, 1936), p. 81.

24. Sylvia D. Hoffert, "Loretta Velazquez, Questionable Heroine," *Civil War Times Illustrated* 17:3 (June 1978): 31.

25. Discussions of Velazquez may be found in De Grave, *Swindler, Spy, Rebel,* pp. 108–44; Hall, *Patriots in Disguise,* pp. 107–53; Hoffert, "Loretta Velazquez, Questionable Heroine"; Jones, *Women Warriors,* pp. 233–37; Kaufman, "'Under the Petticoat Flag,'" pp. 367–74; Leonard, *"All the Daring of the Soldier,"* chap. 7; Massey, *Women in the Civil War,* pp. 82–84; Schultz, "Women at the Front," chap. 5; and Wheelwright, *Amazons and Military Maids,* p. 26 and passim.

26. Early, letter to Slemons. Bell Irvin Wiley, *The Life of Johnny Reb: The Common Soldier of the Confederacy* (Indianapolis: Bobbs-Merrill, 1943), p. 335.

27. On the adventure story as an important genre of Civil War fiction, see Kathleen Diffley, *"Where My Heart Is Turning Ever": Civil War Stories and Constitutional Reform, 1861–1876* (Athens: University of Georgia Press, 1992), pp. 124–49.

28. Cathy N. Davidson, *Revolution and the Word: The Rise of the Novel in America* (New York: Oxford University Press, 1986), pp. 179–92.

29. Augusta Jane Evans, *Macaria; or, Altars of Sacrifice*, introduction by Drew Gilpin Faust (1864; rpt. Baton Rouge: Louisiana State University Press, 1992), pp. 332, 409, 410. For discussion of this novel, see the Introduction by Faust, pp. xiii–xxvi, and Elizabeth Moss, *Domestic Novelists in the Old South: Defenders of Southern Culture* (Baton Rouge: Louisiana State University Press, 1992), pp. 171–94.

30. For discussions of Southern white women in the Civil War, see Elizabeth Baer, "Ambivalence, Anger, and Silence: The Civil War Diary of Lucy Buck," in *Inscribing the Daily: Critical Essays on Women's Diaries*, edited by Suzanne L. Bunkers and Cynthia A. Huft (Amherst: University of Massachusetts Press, 1996), pp. 207–19; Carol Bleser and Frederick M. Heath, "The Clays of Alabama: The Impact of the Civil War on a Southern Marriage," in *In Joy and In Sorrow: Women, Family, and Marriage in the Victorian South*, edited by Carol Bleser (New York: Oxford University Press, 1991), pp. 135–53; Victoria E. Bynum, *Unruly Women: The Politics of Social and Sexual Control in the Old South* (Chapel Hill: University of North Carolina Press, 1992); Edward D. C. Campbell, Jr., and Kym S. Rice, eds., *A Woman's War: Southern Women, Civil War, and the Confederate Legacy* (Richmond: Museum of the Confederacy/Charlottesville: University Press of Virginia, 1996); Catherine Clinton, *Tara Revisited: Women, War, and the Plantation Legend* (New York: Abbeville, 1995); Drew Gilpin Faust, *Southern Stories: Slaveholders in Peace and War* (Columbia: University of Missouri Press, 1992), esp. pp. 113–40; Faust, *Mothers of Invention: Women of the Slaveholding South in the American Civil War* (Chapel Hill: University of North Carolina Press, 1996); Patricia Morton, ed., *Discovering the Women in Slavery: Emancipating Perspectives on the American Past* (Athens: University of Georgia Press, 1996); George Rable, *Civil Wars: Women and the Crisis of Southern Nationalism* (Urbana: University of Illinois Press, 1989); Jane E. Schultz, "Mute Fury: Southern Women's Diaries of Sherman's March to the Sea, 1864–1865," in *Arms and the Woman*, edited by Helen M. Cooper, Adrienne Auslander Munich, and Susan Merrill Squier (Chapel Hill: University of North Carolina Press, 1989), pp. 59–79; and LeeAnn Whites, *The Civil War as a Crisis in Gender: Augusta, Georgia, 1860–1890* (Athens: University of Georgia Press, 1995).

31. Faust, *Mothers of Invention*, pp. 220–33; Sarah Morgan is quoted on p. 221. Southern women's Civil War diaries, letters, and other writings are anthologized in Joan E. Cashin, ed., *Our Common Affairs: Texts from Women in the Old South* (Baltimore: Johns Hopkins University Press, 1996), pp. 255–304; Katharine M. Jones, ed., *Heroines of Dixie* (1955; rpt. New York: Konecky and Konecky, 1995); and Walter Sullivan, ed., *The War the Women Lived: Female Voices from the Confederate South* (Nashville: J. S. Sanders, 1995).

32. On the importance of this figure, see Marina Warner, *Joan of Arc: The Image of Female Heroism* (London: Weidenfeld and Nicolson, 1981).

33. De Grave, *Swindler, Spy, Rebel*, p. 9.

34. This treatment of the Mexican War runs counter to that of many Confederates, who fought against Mexico in the earlier war. For Velazquez's father, "native" loyalties are with the Mexican side against the invasive tyranny of the United States. In this text, the Mexican War fills the symbolic position that was more commonly occupied for Southerners by the American Revolution: that of an earlier war in which a maligned power justifiably fought for its independence. On the legacy of the American Revolution to Confederate nationalism, see Emory M. Thomas, *The Confederate Nation, 1861–1865* (New York: Harper and Row, 1979), pp. 221–24.

35. On Belle Boyd, see Faust, *Mothers of Invention,* pp. 214–19, and De Grave, *Swindler, Spy, Rebel,* pp. 131–39. On women spies in the Civil War, see Nancy B. Samuelson, "Employment of Female Spies in the American Civil War," *Minerva* 7: 3–4 (1989): 57–66; Penny Colman, *Spies: Women in the Civil War* (Cincinnati: Betterway, 1992); and Sizer, "Acting Her Part," in *Divided Houses.* The literature on femininity as masquerade is substantial: for a founding theorization, see Joan Riviere, "Womanliness as a Masquerade," in *Formations of Fantasy,* edited by Victor Burgin, James Donald, and Cora Kaplan (London: Methuen, 1986), pp. 35–44; for an influential approach to this topic in relation to film, see Mary Ann Doane, "Film and the Masquerade: Theorizing the Female Spectator," in *Femmes Fatales: Feminism, Film Theory, Psychoanalysis* (New York: Routledge, 1991), pp. 17–32; and for discussion of its possibilities in relation to contemporary gender theory, see Judith Butler, *Gender Trouble: Feminism and the Subversion of Identity* (New York: Routledge, 1990), pp. 46–54.

36. See Adrienne Rich, "Compulsory Heterosexuality and Lesbian Existence," in *The Lesbian and Gay Studies Reader,* edited by Henry Abelove, Michèle Aina Barale, and David M. Halperin (New York: Routledge, 1993), pp. 227–54.

37. See Thomas P. Lowry, *The Story the Soldiers Wouldn't Tell: Sex in the Civil War* (Mechanicsburg, PA: Stackpole Books, 1994), pp. 109–18. On midcentury sexual possibilities between men, see John d'Emilio and Estelle Freedman, *Intimate Matters: A History of Sexuality in America* (New York: Harper and Row, 1988), pp. 121–30.

38. Quoted in Lowry, *The Story the Soldiers Wouldn't Tell,* p. 35.

39. On the history of the dandy, see Ellen Moers, *The Dandy: Brummell to Beerbohm* (New York: Viking Press, 1960); on the sexual ambiguities of this figure, see James Eli Adams, *Dandies and Desert Saints: Styles of Victorian Masculinity* (Ithaca: Cornell University Press, 1995). An image of the "Soldier Dandy" in the Civil War is reprinted in Sylvia G. L. Dannett, *A Treasury of Civil War Humor* (New York: Thomas Yoseloff, 1963), p. 158.

40. Early, letter to Slemons.

41. Sheridan, *Civil War Memoirs,* p. 87; Jonathan Katz includes this passage in *Gay American History: Lesbians and Gay Men in the U.S.A.* (New York: Avon, 1976), pp. 345–46. For discussions of nineteenth-century female cross-dressing that emphasize its lesbian possibilities, see d'Emilio and Freedman, *Intimate Matters,* pp. 124–25, and the San Francisco Lesbian and Gay History Project, "'She Even Chewed To-

bacco': A Pictorial History of Passing Women in America," in *Hidden from History: Reclaiming the Gay and Lesbian Past*, edited by Martin Bauml Duberman, Martha Vicinus, and George Chauncey, Jr. (New York: New American Library, 1989), pp. 183–94. For accounts of the emergence of the figure of the lesbian in this era, see George Chauncey, Jr., "From Sexual Inversion to Homosexuality: Medicine and the Changing Conceptualization of Female Deviance," *Salmagundi* 58–59 (1982–83): 114–46, and Martha Vicinus, " 'They Wonder to Which Sex I Belong': The Historical Roots of Modern Lesbian Identity," in *The Lesbian and Gay Studies Reader*, pp. 432–52. Since the term "lesbian" emerged later in the nineteenth century, I will be using "protolesbian" to characterize relations between women in *The Woman in Battle*.

42. For discussions of what constitutes a lesbian text, see Julie Abraham, *Are Girls Necessary? Lesbian Writing and Modern Histories* (New York: Routledge, 1996); Terry Castle, *The Apparitional Lesbian: Female Homosexuality and Modern Culture* (New York: Columbia University Press, 1993); Marilyn Farwell, *Heterosexual Plots and Lesbian Narratives* (New York: New York University Press, 1996); Karla Jay and Joanne Glasgow, eds., *Lesbian Texts and Contexts: Radical Revisions* (New York: New York University Press, 1990); and Biddy Martin, "Lesbian Identity and Autobiographical Difference[s]," in *The Lesbian and Gay Studies Reader*, pp. 274–93. For an anthology that identifies a range of nineteenth-century American women's texts as lesbian, see Susan Koppelman, ed., *"Two Friends" and Other Nineteenth-Century Lesbian Stories by American Women Writers* (New York: Meridian, 1994). On same-sex possibilities in cross-dressing narratives, see Chris Straayer, *Deviant Eyes/Deviant Bodies: Sexual Re-Orientations in Film and Video* (New York: Columbia University Press, 1996), pp. 42–78, and Kristina Straub, "The Guilty Pleasures of Female Theatrical Cross-Dressing and the Autobiography of Charlotte Charke," in *Body Guards: The Cultural Politics of Gender Ambiguity*, edited by Julia Epstein and Kristina Straub (New York: Routledge, 1991), pp. 142–66.

43. On the "female world of love and ritual," see Carroll Smith-Rosenberg, *Disorderly Conduct: Visions of Gender in Victorian America* (New York: Oxford University Press, 1985), pp. 53–76; on "romantic friendship," see Lillian Faderman, *Surpassing the Love of Men: Romantic Friendship and Love between Women from the Renaissance to the Present* (New York: William Morrow, 1981); and on the "lesbian continuum," see Rich, "Compulsory Heterosexuality and Lesbian Existence." Influential critiques of these models include Sue-Ellen Case, "Toward a Butch-Femme Aesthetic," in *The Lesbian and Gay Studies Reader*, pp. 294–306, and Cherríe Moraga and Amber Hollibaugh, "What We're Rollin' Around in Bed With: Sexual Silences in Feminism," in *Powers of Desire: The Politics of Sexuality*, edited by Ann Snitow, Christine Stansell, and Sharon Thompson (New York: Monthly Review Press, 1983), pp. 395–405. On the history and representation of butch lesbians, see Lily Burana, Roxxie, and Linnea Due, eds., *Dagger: On Butch Women* (Pittsburgh: Cleis Press, 1994); Elizabeth Lapovsky Kennedy and Madeline D. Davis, *Boots of Leather, Slippers of Gold: The History of a Lesbian Community* (New York: Routledge, 1993); and Joan Nestle, ed., *The Persistent Desire: A Femme/Butch Reader* (Boston: Alyson, 1992), an anthology whose earliest text articu-

lating what would now be called a butch/femme relationship dates from 1843. For an important recent reconsideration of the figure of the butch lesbian in relation to the larger category of "female masculinity," see Judith Halberstam, *Female Masculinity* (Durham: Duke University Press, 1998).

44. H. Cassidy, letter to O. J. F. Stuart, quoted in Gaines M. Foster, *Ghosts of the Confederacy: Defeat, the Lost Cause, and the Emergence of the New South, 1865–1913* (New York: Oxford University Press, 1987), p. 29.

45. See Foster, *Ghosts of the Confederacy;* Mark E. Neely, Jr., Harold Holzer, and Gabor S. Boritt, *The Confederate Image: Prints of the Lost Cause* (Chapel Hill: University of North Carolina Press, 1987); and Charles Reagan Wilson, *Baptized in Blood: The Religion of the Lost Cause, 1865–1920* (Athens: University of Georgia Press, 1980).

46. Robert L. Dabney, "The Duty of the Hour," quoted in Foster, *Ghosts of the Confederacy,* p. 29.

47. For discussion of women as creators of and symbols in the Lost Cause, see Clinton, *Tara Revisited,* pp. 139–59; John M. Coski and Amy R. Feely, "A Monument to Southern Womanhood: The Founding Generation of the Confederate Museum," in *A Woman's War,* pp. 131–63; Faust, *Southern Stories,* pp. 148–59; Rable, *Civil Wars,* pp. 236–39; and LeeAnn Whites, " 'Stand by Your Man': The Ladies Memorial Association and the Reconstruction of Southern White Manhood," in *Women of the South: A Multicultural Reader,* edited by Christie Anne Farnham (New York: New York University Press, 1997), pp. 133–49.

48. See Susan Jeffords, *The Remasculinization of America: Gender and the Vietnam War* (Bloomington: Indiana University Press, 1989); Jeffords first defines the term on p. xii. On links between Vietnam and the Confederacy, see Owen W. Gilman, Jr., *Vietnam and the Southern Imagination* (Jackson: University Press of Mississippi, 1992).

49. See Wheelwright, *Amazons and Military Maids,* pp. 139–40.

50. See Charles C. Osborne, *Jubal: The Life and Times of General Jubal A. Early, C.S.A., Defender of the Lost Cause* (Chapel Hill: Algonquin, 1992); the quotation is from p. 469.

51. Velazquez, letter to Early, 18 May 1878; Early included a copy of this letter with his letter to Tucker. In Tucker Family Papers, Southern Historical Collection, Wilson Library, The University of North Carolina at Chapel Hill.

52. Early, letter to Slemons.

53. On prostitution in Civil War Washington, see Lowry, *The Story the Soldiers Wouldn't Tell,* pp. 61–69; the boast by Sherman is quoted on p. 31. On Butler, see Faust, *Mothers of Invention,* pp. 202–12, and Mary P. Ryan, *Women in Public: Between Banners and Ballots, 1825–1880* (Baltimore: Johns Hopkins University Press, 1990), pp. 143–45.

54. See Hall, *Patriots in Disguise,* p. 103, and Leonard, *"All the Daring of the Soldier,"* chap. 7.

55. On counterfeit currency, see Ted Schwarz, "Counterfeit Confederate," *Civil War Times Illustrated* 16:2 (May 1977): 34–39; on the Confederate economy, see Douglas B. Ball, *Financial Failure and Confederate Defeat* (Urbana: University of Illinois

Press, 1991), and James F. Morgan, *Graybacks and Gold: Confederate Monetary Policy* (Pensacola, FL: Perdido Bay Press, 1985).

56. These women's stories are included in Lafayette C. Baker, *History of the United States Secret Service* (Philadelphia, 1868), pp. 293–96. For discussion of this scandal, see Charles F. Cooney, "Nothing More . . . than a Whorehouse: The State of the Treasury, 1864," *Civil War Times Illustrated* 21:8 (December 1982): 40–43.

57. See Neil Hertz, "Medusa's Head: Male Hysteria Under Pressure," and Catherine Gallagher, "More About Medusa's Head," both in *Representations* 4 (Fall 1983): 27–54, 55–57.

58. Morgan, *Graybacks and Gold*, p. 9.

59. See Karen Halttunen, *Confidence Men and Painted Women: A Study of Middle-Class Culture in America, 1830–70* (New Haven: Yale University Press, 1982).

60. For discussion of these practices, see Ella Lonn, *Foreigners in the Union Army and Navy* (Baton Rouge: Louisiana State University Press, 1951), pp. 437–78.

61. On the symbolic feminization of the antebellum South, see Anne Norton, *Alternative Americas* (Chicago: University of Chicago Press, 1986), pp. 164–76, and Carolyn Porter, "Social Discourse and Nonfictional Prose," in *The Columbia Literary History of the United States,* edited by Emory Elliott (New York: Columbia University Press, 1988), pp. 354–57. On the "Southern Hamlet," see William R. Taylor, *Cavalier and Yankee: The Old South and American National Character* (New York: Anchor, 1961), pp. 271–78.

62. Velazquez represents Davis as a defender of traditional gender roles. When she meets with him, for example, he is "opposed to permitting me to serve in the army as an officer, attired in male costume" (345).

63. See Nina Silber, *The Romance of Reunion: Northerners and the South, 1865–1900* (Chapel Hill: University of North Carolina Press, 1993), esp. p. 26; other analyses of these images are cited above in chapter 3, note 53.

64. Quoted in Lowry, *The Story the Soldiers Wouldn't Tell,* pp. 112–13. On other instances of male-to-female cross-dressing in the Civil War, see Faust, *Mothers of Invention,* pp. 228–30; Webb Garrison, *More Civil War Curiosities* (Nashville: Rutledge Hill Press, 1995), pp. 87–89; and John D. and Linda C. Pelzer, "The French Lady," *Civil War Times Illustrated* 31:2 (May/June 1992): 28–31, 66–67. The most extraordinary representation of male-to-female Civil War cross-dressing appears decades later, in William Isaac Yopp's *A Dual Role: A Romance of the Civil War.* In this 1902 novel, Hal, a young Confederate soldier, cross-dresses as "Hallie" in order to spy; a Union woman, Kate, falls deeply in love with "Hallie"; and when "Hallie" departs, Kate, in turn, cross-dresses as "Hal" in order to find her lover. These cross-dressing plots conclude asymmetrically: Hal easily resumes male dress, going on to postwar adventures in Texas, while Kate, convinced that she is "Hal," is confined to an insane asylum. The lovers are eventually reunited, in a conclusion that restores normative femininity to Kate and further celebrates the masculinity of Hal. The novel, which merits further discussion, thus brings together emerging discourses of sexual deviance and ongoing cultural mythologies of Confederate remasculinization. (I have located only one commentary on it, in John Zubritsky, Jr., "Gone But

Not Forgotten: The American Civil War in Novels, 1900–1939," Ph.D. diss., George Washington University, 1980, pp. 286–94.)

65. Reprinted in Lowry, *The Story the Soldiers Wouldn't Tell*, pp. 49–50.

66. This image is reproduced in Bernard F. Reilly, Jr., *American Political Prints, 1766–1876* (Boston: G. K. Hall, 1991), pp. 546–47.

67. For a comprehensive overview of the racial politics of Reconstruction, see Eric Foner, *Reconstruction: America's Unfinished Revolution, 1863–1877* (New York: Harper and Row, 1988); for a focus on white anxiety about emancipation, see Forrest Wood, *Black Scare: The Racist Response to Emancipation an Reconstruction* (Berkeley: University of California Press, 1968); and for discussion of gender and race, see Laura F. Edwards, *Gendered Strife and Confusion: The Political Culture of Reconstruction* (Urbana: University of Illinois Press, 1997).

68. See Ervin L. Jordan, Jr., *Black Confederates and Afro-Yankees in Civil War Virginia* (Charlottesville: University Press of Virginia, 1995), pp. 185–200.

69. A similar moment occurs in *Nurse and Spy*, when Edmonds's "contraband" coloring begins to lighten and she is nearly discovered. A black man remarks, "Jim, I'll be darned if that fellow aint turnin' white; if he aint then I'm no nigger" and Edmonds responds, "I took a look at my complexion by means of a small pocket looking-glass which I carried for that very purpose—and sure enough, as the negro had said, I was really turning white. I was only a dark mulatto color now, whereas two days previous I was black as Cloe" (116).

70. W. W. Legaré, quoted in Alfred Jackson Hanna and Kathryn Abbey Hanna, *Confederate Exiles in Venezuela* (Tuscaloosa, AL: Confederate Publishing Co., 1960), p. 14; Velazquez is discussed on pp. 23–24.

71. Ballard S. Dunn, *Brazil, the Home for Southerners* (1866), quoted in Hanna and Hanna, *Confederate Exiles in Venezuela*, p. 18.

72. On the Spanish-American War as an opportunity for Southern remasculinization, see Foster, *Ghosts of the Confederacy*, pp. 145–59, and Silber, *Romance of Reunion*, pp. 178–85.

73. Grace Greenwood describes Harper as "about as colored as some of the Cuban belles I have met with at Saratoga"; quoted in William Still, *The Underground Railroad* (Philadelphia, 1872), p. 779. Octavia V. Rogers Albert, *The House of Bondage, or Charlotte Brooks and Other Slaves*, edited by Frances Smith Foster (1890; rpt. New York: Oxford University Press, 1988), p. 120.

74. On the significance of the West in the wake of the Civil War, see Silber, *Romance of Reunion*, pp. 187–95.

75. Early, letter to Slemons.

CHAPTER FIVE

1. *Iola Leroy* is cited as the first African-American Civil War novel in Bernard Bell, *The Afro-American Novel and Its Traditions* (Amherst: University of Massachusetts

Press, 1987), p. 58. On race and the memory of the Civil War in this period, see David W. Blight, "Quarrel Forgotten or a Revolution Remembered?: Reunion and Race in the Memory of the Civil War, 1875–1913," in *Union and Emancipation: Essays on Politics and Race in the Civil War Era*, edited by Blight and Brooks D. Simpson (Kent, OH: Kent State University Press, 1997), pp. 151–79; Gaines M. Foster, *Ghosts of the Confederacy: Defeat, the Lost Cause, and the Emergence of the New South, 1865 to 1913* (New York: Oxford University Press, 1987); Amy Kaplan, "Nation, Region, and Empire," in *The Columbia History of the American Novel*, edited by Emory Elliott (New York: Columbia University Press, 1991), pp. 240–66; Cecilia Elizabeth O'Leary, "'Blood Brotherhood': The Racialization of Patriotism, 1865–1918," in *Bonds of Affection: Americans Define Their Patriotism*, edited by John Bodnar (Princeton: Princeton University Press, 1996), pp. 53–81; Kirk Savage, *Standing Soldiers, Kneeling Slaves Race, War, and Monument in Nineteenth-Century America* (Princeton: Princeton University Press, 1997); Nina Silber, *The Romance of Reunion: Northerners and the South, 1865–1900* (Chapel Hill: University of North Carolina Press, 1993); Joel Williamson, *The Crucible of Race: Black-White Relations in the American South Since Emancipation* (New York: Oxford University Press, 1984); and Charles Reagan Wilson, *Baptized in Blood: The Religion of the Lost Cause, 1865–1920* (Athens: University of Georgia Press, 1980).

2. See David W. Blight, *Frederick Douglass' Civil War: Keeping Faith in Jubilee* (Baton Rouge: Louisiana State University Press, 1989), pp. 219–39, and Blight, "W. E. B. Du Bois and the Struggle for American Historical Memory," in *History and Memory in African-American Culture*, edited by Geneviève Fabre and Robert O'Meally (New York: Oxford University Press, 1994), pp. 45–71.

3. Citations for Albert, Burton, Drumgoold, Moorer, Taylor, and Harper are given below. On poetry, see Josephine Delphine Henderson Heard, "Decoration Day" and "The National Cemetery, Beaufort, South Carolina," in *Morning Glories* (1890), pp. 43, 103, reprinted in *Collected Black Women's Poetry*, vol. 4, edited by Joan R. Sherman (New York: Oxford University Press, 1988); Effie Waller Smith, "Decoration Day," "Somebody's Father" and "Decoration Day—1899," in *Songs of the Months* (1904), pp. 32–33, 62–63, 97–99, reprinted in *The Collected Works of Effie Waller Smith*, edited by David Deskins (New York: Oxford University Press, 1991); Clara Ann Thompson, "Memorial Day" and "Uncle Rube to the Young People," in *Songs from the Wayside* (1908), pp. 5–6, 49–59, reprinted in *Collected Black Women's Poetry*, vol. 2, edited by Joan R. Sherman (New York: Oxford University Press, 1988); Priscilla Jane Thompson, "The Old Freedman," in *Ethiope Lays* (1900), pp. 49–52, and "The Husband's Return," "Emancipation," and "Uncle Jimmie's Yarn," in *Gleanings of Quiet Hours* (1907), pp. 13–16, 35–36, 91–94, reprinted in *Collected Black Women's Poetry*, vol. 2; and Katherine Davis Chapman Tillman, "A Tribute to Negro Regiments" (1898), reprinted in *The Works of Katherine Davis Chapman Tillman*, edited by Claudia Tate (New York: Oxford University Press, 1991), p. 146. Pauline Hopkins's novel *Hagar's Daughter* (1901–2) addresses the Civil War in at least two ways: it opens on the eve of Confederate secession, and later returns to the war in a crucial episode in which an African-American detective masquerades as a Civil War veteran. See *The Magazine Novels*

of Pauline Hopkins, introduction by Hazel V. Carby (New York: Oxford University Press, 1988).

4. William Still, *The Underground Record* (Philadelphia, 1872), p. 765.

5. Citations for *Minnie's Sacrifice* and *Iola Leroy* are given below. Harper's writings are anthologized in the following: Melba Joyce Boyd, *Discarded Legacy: Politics and Poetics in the Life of Frances E. W. Harper, 1825–1911* (Detroit: Wayne State University Press, 1994); Frances Smith Foster, ed., *A Brighter Coming Day: A Frances Ellen Watkins Harper Reader* (New York: Feminist Press, 1990); and Maryemma Graham, ed., *Complete Poems of Frances E. W. Harper* (New York: Oxford University Press, 1988). Harper's Civil War oratory is also quoted and discussed in Ella Forbes, *African American Women During the Civil War* (New York: Garland, 1998), pp. 199–203; the speech "The Mission of the War" is described in *The Christian Recorder* and *The Liberator*, in *Black Abolitionist Papers, 1830–1865*, microfilm edition, edited by C. Peter Ripley et al. (New York, 1981), reel 15, nos. 0356 and 0790. For overviews of Harper's career, see Boyd, *Discarded Legacy;* Foster, Introduction to *A Brighter Coming Day;* and Bettye Collier-Thomas, "Frances Ellen Watkins Harper: Abolitionist and Feminist Reformer, 1825–1911," in *African American Women and the Vote*, edited by Ann D. Gordon et al. (Amherst: University of Massachusetts Press, 1997), pp. 41–65.

6. Hazel V. Carby, *Reconstructing Womanhood: The Emergence of the Afro-American Woman Novelist* (Oxford: Oxford University Press, 1987), pp. 62–94; Claudia Tate, *Domestic Allegories of Political Desire: The Black Heroine's Text at the Turn of the Century* (New York: Oxford University Press, 1992), pp. 144–49, 169–71. Discussions of *Iola Leroy* also include the following: Elizabeth Ammons, *Conflicting Stories: American Women Writers at the Turn into the Twentieth Century* (New York: Oxford University Press, 1991), pp. 20–33; Lauren Berlant, "The Queen of America Goes to Washington City: Harriet Jacobs, Frances Harper, Anita Hill," in *Subjects and Citizens: Nation, Race and Gender from "Oroonoko" to Anita Hill*, edited by Michael Moon and Cathy N. Davidson (Durham: Duke University Press, 1995), pp. 455–80; Barbara Christian, *Black Feminist Criticism: Perspectives on Black Women Writers* (New York: Pergamon Press, 1985), pp. 165–70; Christian, *Black Women Novelists: The Development of a Tradition, 1892–1976* (Westport, CT: Greenwood Press, 1980), pp. 3–5, 25–31; Ann duCille, *The Coupling Convention: Sex, Text, and Tradition in Black Women's Fiction* (New York: Oxford University Press, 1993), pp. 43–47; Marilyn Elkins, "Reading Beyond the Conventions: A Look at Frances E. W. Harper's *Iola Leroy, or Shadows Uplifted*," *American Literary Realism* 22:2 (Winter 1990): 44–53; John Ernest, *Resistance and Reformation in Nineteenth-Century African-American Literature: Brown, Wilson, Jacobs, Delany, Douglass, and Harper* (Jackson: University Press of Mississippi, 1995), pp. 180–207; P. Gabrielle Foreman, "'Reading Aright': White Slavery, Black Referents, and the Strategy of Histotextuality in *Iola Leroy*," *Yale Journal of Criticism* 10:2 (1997): 327–54; Karla F. C. Holloway, "Economies of Space: Markets and Marketability in *Our Nig* and *Iola Leroy*," in *The (Other) American Traditions: Nineteenth-Century Women Writers*, edited by Joyce W. Warren (New Brunswick: Rutgers University Press, 1993), pp. 126–

40; Lynda Koolish, "Spies in the Enemy's House: Folk Characters as Tricksters in Frances E. W. Harper's *Iola Leroy*," in *Tricksterism in Turn-of-the-Century American Literature: A Multicultural Perspective,* edited by Elizabeth Ammons and Annette White-Parks (Hanover, NH: University Press of New England, 1994), pp. 158–85; Vashti Lewis, "The Near-White Female in Frances Ellen Harper's *Iola Leroy:* Public Image Versus Private Reality," *Phylon* 45:4 (1985): 314–22; Deborah McDowell, *"The Changing Same": Black Women's Literature, Criticism, and Theory* (Bloomington: Indiana University Press, 1995), pp. 34–57; Carla L. Peterson, "'Further Liftings of the Veil': Gender, Class, and Labor in Frances E. W. Harper's *Iola Leroy*," in *Listening to Silences: New Essays in Feminist Criticism,* edited by Elaine Hedges and Shelley Fisher Fishkin (New York: Oxford University Press, 1994), pp. 97–112; and Mary Helen Washington, *Invented Lives: Narratives of Black Women, 1860–1960* (New York: Anchor/Doubleday, 1987), pp. 73–86.

7. Quoted in Blight, *Keeping Faith in Jubilee,* p. 238.

8. For discussion of these works, see John Hope Franklin, *George Washington Williams: A Biography* (1985; rpt. Durham: Duke University Press, 1998), pp. 127–32; both are excerpted in Richard A. Long, ed., *Black Writers and the American Civil War* (Secaucus, NJ: Blue and Grey Press, 1988).

9. Patricia Morton, *Disfigured Images: The Historical Assault on Afro-American Women* (Westport, CT: Greenwood Press, 1991), p. 45.

10. Paul Lawrence Dunbar, *The Fanatics* (1901; rpt. Miami: Mnemosyne, 1969), p. 13. All subsequent quotations are from this edition and cited parenthetically in the text. For discussion of *The Fanatics,* see Addison Gayle, Jr., "Literature as Catharsis: The Novels of Paul Lawrence Dunbar," and Kenny J. Williams, "The Masking of the Novelist," both in *A Singer in the Dawn: Reinterpretations of Paul Lawrence Dunbar,* edited by Jay Martin (New York: Dodd, Mead, 1975), pp. 139–51, 152–207. For a relevant analysis of Dunbar's use of irony elsewhere in his fiction, see Kevin K. Gaines, *Uplifting the Race: Black Leadership, Politics, and Culture in the Twentieth Century* (Chapel Hill: University of North Carolina Press, 1996), pp. 179–93. On Dunbar's other literary responses to the Civil War, see Allen Flint, "Black Response to Colonel Shaw," *Phylon* 45:3 (1984): 210–19.

11. Mrs. N. F. [Gertrude] Mossell, *The Work of the Afro-American Woman,* introduction by Joanne Braxton (1894; rpt. New York: Oxford University Press, 1988), p. 10; Anna Julia Cooper, *A Voice from the South,* edited by Mary Helen Washington (1892; rpt. New York: Oxford University Press, 1988), pp. 134, 56. On black women's activism and writing in this period, see Carby, *Reconstructing Womanhood,* pp. 95–120; Frances Smith Foster, *Written by Herself: Literary Production by African American Women, 1746–1892* (Bloomington: Indiana University Press, 1993), pp. 178–90; Paula Giddings, *When and Where I Enter: The Impact of Black Women on Race and Sex in America* (New York: William Morrow, 1984), pp. 85–117; and Darlene Clark Hine and Kathleen Thompson, *A Shining Thread of Hope: The History of Black Women in America* (New York: Broadway Books, 1998), pp. 165–212.

12. Lizelia Augusta Jenkins Moorer, "Loyalty to the Flag," in *Prejudice Unveiled,*

and Other Poems (1907), p. 69, reprinted in *Collected Black Women's Poetry*, vol. 3, edited by Joan R. Sherman (New York: Oxford University Press, 1988).

13. Moorer, "Negro Heroines," in *Prejudice Unveiled*, pp. 72–75; Moorer, Preface to *Prejudice Unveiled n.p.*

14. Susie King Taylor, *A Black Woman's Civil War Memoirs: Reminiscences of My Life in Camp With the 33rd U.S. Colored Troops, Late 1st South Carolina Volunteers*, edited by Patricia Romero (1902; rpt. New York: Markus Wiener, 1988), p. 61. Criticism of this text is cited in chap. 1, note 103.

15. Kate Drumgoold, *A Slave Girl's Story*, in *Six Women's Slave Narratives*, edited by William L. Andrews (1898; rpt. New York: Oxford University Press, 1988), pp. 4, 6. For discussion of this text, see Jennifer Fleischner, *Mastering Slavery: Memory, Family, and Identity in Women's Slave Narratives* (New York: New York University Press, 1996), pp. 133–53. On slave children's experiences of the Civil War, see Peter Bardaglio, "The Children of Jubilee: African American Childhood in Wartime," in *Divided Houses: Gender and the Civil War*, edited by Catherine Clinton and Nina Silber (New York: Oxford University Press, 1992), pp. 213–29; Wilma King, *Stolen Childhood: Slave Youth in Nineteenth-Century America* (Bloomington: Indiana University Press, 1995), pp. 129–39; James Marten, *The Children's Civil War* (Chapel Hill: University of North Carolina Press, 1998), pp. 125–41; and Emmy E. Werner, *Reluctant Witnesses Children's Voices from the Civil War* (New York: Westview Press, 1998), pp. 39–49.

16. Annie L. Burton, *Memories of Childhood's Slavery Days* (1909), reprinted in *Six Women's Slave Narratives*, pp. 3, 8, 10, 12.

17. Hortense J. Spillers, "'The Permanent Obliquity of an In(pha)llibly Straight': In the Time of the Daughters and Fathers," in *Changing Our Own Words: Essays on Criticism, Theory, and Writing by Black Women*, edited by Cheryl A. Wall (New Brunswick: Rutgers University Press, 1989), p. 148.

18. Fleischner analyzes Spillers' claim in relation to Drumgoold; see *Mastering Slavery*, p. 137. Other discussions of this theme in African-American women's writing include Joanne Braxton, *Black Women Writing Autobiography: A Tradition Within a Tradition* (Philadelphia: Temple University Press, 1989), pp. 18–38, and Marianne Hirsch, *The Mother/Daughter Plot: Narrative, Psychoanalysis, Feminism* (Bloomington: Indiana University Press, 1989), pp. 176–98.

19. Frances Smith Foster, Introduction to Octavia V. Rogers Albert, *The House of Bondage; or, Charlotte Brooks and Other Slaves*, edited by Foster (1890; rpt. New York: Oxford University Press, 1988), pp. xxvii–xliii; all subsequent quotations are from this edition and cited parenthetically in the text. On *The House of Bondage*, see also Foster, *Written by Herself*, pp. 154–77. On Thomas Nelson Page, see Lawrence J. Friedman, *The White Savage: Racial Fantasies in the Postbellum South* (Englewood Cliffs, NJ: Prentice-Hall, 1970), pp. 62–74.

20. Foster, *Written by Herself*, p. 165.

21. Frances Ellen Watkins Harper, *Iola Leroy, or, Shadows Uplifted*, introduction by Frances Smith Foster (1892; rpt. New York: Oxford University Press, 1988), p. 7. All subsequent quotations are from this edition and cited parenthetically in the text.

22. For other discussions of this coded language, see Ernest, *Resistance and Reformation*, pp. 187–88; Holloway, "Economies of Space," pp. 133–34; and Koolish, "Spies in the Enemy's House," pp. 161–62.

23. Harper, letter to William Still, quoted in Still, *Underground Railroad*, p. 766.

24. Harper, "Duty to Dependent Races" (1891), reprinted in Boyd, *Discarded Legacy*, p. 209.

25. For discussion of Robert, see Peterson, "'Further Liftings of the Veil,'" pp. 107–8.

26. In Harper's 1885 essay "A Factor in Human Progress," for example, she retells this anecdote with the conclusion: "Who shall say that the race out of which such men could spring from under the dark shadow of slavery has not within it the elements out of which a great people may yet be produced?" (*A Brighter Coming Day*, pp. 279–80). The anecdote also appears in the 1869 novella *Minnie's Sacrifice* and in an 1895 poem, "A Story of the Rebellion." Ernest also notes Harper's interest in this anecdote (*Resistance and Reformation*, pp. 199–200).

27. For discussion of male feminization in African-American writing of this period, see Donald Gibson, "Chapter One of Booker T. Washington's *Up From Slavery* and the Feminization of the African American Male," in *Representing Black Men*, edited by Marcellus Blount and George P. Cunningham (New York: Routledge, 1996), pp. 95–110; and Morton, *Disfigured Images*, pp. 39–40.

28. Frances Harper, *Minnie's Sacrifice* (1869), reprinted in *Minnie's Sacrifice, Sowing and Reaping, Trial and Triumph: Three Rediscovered Novels by Frances E. W. Harper*, edited by Frances Smith Foster (Boston: Beacon Press, 1994), p. 50. All subsequent quotations are from this edition and cited parenthetically in the text.

29. Darlene Clark Hine, "Rape and the Inner Lives of Black Women in the Middle West: Preliminary Thoughts on the Culture of Dissemblance," in *Unequal Sisters: A Multicultural Reader in U.S. Women's History*, edited by Vicki L. Ruiz and Ellen Carol DuBois (New York: Routledge, 1994), pp. 342–47. On the importance of the theme of rape in *Iola Leroy*, see Ammons, *Conflicting Stories*, pp. 29–33.

30. Analyses of Iola's status as mulatta include Carby, *Reconstructing Womanhood*, pp. 88–91; Lewis, "Near-White Female in Frances Ellen Harper's *Iola Leroy*"; Peterson, "'Further Liftings of the Veil,'" pp. 99–102; and Tate, *Domestic Allegories of Political Desire*, pp. 144–47. For overviews of the figures of the tragic mulatto and mulatta, see Judith R. Berzon, *Neither White Nor Black: The Mulatto Character in American Fiction* (New York: New York University Press, 1978), pp. 99–115, and Werner Sollors, *Neither Black Nor White Yet Both: Thematic Explorations of Interracial Literature* (New York: Oxford University Press, 1997), pp. 220–45.

31. duCille, *Coupling Convention;* the term is defined on p. 13.

32. See Foreman, "'Reading Aright,'" pp. 339–47, and Ernest, *Resistance and Reformation*, pp. 200–202.

33. Discussions of the mythology of interracial rape in this era include Angela Y. Davis, *Women, Race and Class* (New York: Vintage, 1983), pp. 172–201; Sandra Gunning, *Race, Rape, and Lynching: The Red Record of American Literature, 1890–1912* (New York: Oxford University Press, 1996), pp. 3–17; Glenda Elizabeth Gilmore, *Gender*

and Jim Crow: Women and the Politics of White Supremacy in North Carolina, 1896–1920 (Chapel Hill: University of North Carolina Press, 1996), pp. 61–89; Jacqueline Dowd Hall, "'The Mind That Burns In Each Body': Women, Rape, and Racial Violence," in *Powers of Desire: The Politics of Sexuality,* edited by Ann Snitow, Christine Stansell, and Sharon Thompson (New York: Monthly Review Press, 1983), pp. 328–49; Martha Hodes, *White Women, Black Men: Illicit Sex in the Nineteenth-Century South* (New Haven: Yale University Press, 1997), pp. 176–208; and Robyn Wiegman, *American Anatomies: Theorizing Race and Gender* (Durham: Duke University Press, 1995), pp. 95–113.

34. In *The House With Closed Shutters,* for example, a Confederate soldier is so overcome by cowardice that he flees the battlefield for home, whereupon his sister Agnes cross-dresses in his uniform and heroically preserves the Confederate flag in battle. See Susan Christianne Courtney, "Hollywood's Fantasy of Miscegenation," Ph.D. diss., University of California at Berkeley, 1997, chap. 1; I am grateful to Susan Courtney for alerting me to these films. On the popularity of Civil War films in this period, see Eileen Bowser, *The Transformation of Cinema 1907–1915* (New York: Scribner's, 1990), pp. 177–79, and Evelyn Ehrlich, "The Civil War in Early Film: Origin and Development of a Genre," *Southern Quarterly* 19:3–4 (Spring–Summer 1981): 70–82.

35. The literature on this film is extensive within film studies as well as cultural history; I leave unaddressed here its visual complexities as a cinematic text. For an introduction to scholarship on the film, see Robert Lang, ed., *The Birth of a Nation: D. W. Griffith, Director* (New Brunswick: Rutgers University Press, 1994).

36. On *Birth of a Race,* see Thomas Cripps, "The Making of *The Birth of a Race:* The Emerging Politics of Identity in Silent Movies," in *The Birth of Whiteness: Race and the Emergence of U.S. Cinema,* edited by Daniel Bernardi (New Brunswick: Rutgers University Press, 1996), pp. 38–55; on Micheaux and Griffith, see Jane Gaines, *"The Birth of a Nation* and *Within Our Gates:* Two Tales of the American South," in *Dixie Debates: Perspectives on Southern Culture,* edited by Richard H. King and Helen Taylor (London: Pluto Press, 1986), pp. 177–92.

37. Gertrude Dorsey Brown[e], "A Case of Measure for Measure" (1906), reprinted in *Short Fiction by Black Women, 1900–1920,* collected with an introduction by Elizabeth Ammons (New York: Oxford University Press, 1991), p. 383.

38. Carrie Williams Clifford, "A Reply to Thomas Dixon," in *Race Rhymes* (1911), p. 11, and "The Birth of a Nation," in *The Widening Light* (1922), p. 78, both reprinted in *Writings of Carrie Williams Clifford and Carrie Law Morgan Figgs,* introduction by P. Jane Splawn (New York: G. K. Hall, 1997).

39. See Gail Bederman, *Manliness and Civilization: A Cultural History of Gender and Race in the United States, 1880–1917* (Chicago: University of Chicago Press, 1995), pp. 45–76; other discussions of Wells-Barnett include Carby, *Reconstructing Womanhood,* pp. 107–16; Giddings, *When and Where I Enter,* pp. 19–31; Gunning, *Race, Rape, and Lynching,* pp. 81–89; and Hine and Thompson, *A Shining Thread of Hope,* pp. 194–200.

40. For discussion of these marriage plots, see Kathleen Diffley, *"Where My Heart Is Turning Ever": Civil War Stories and Constitutional Reform, 1861–1876* (Athens: Uni-

versity of Georgia Press, 1992), pp. 54–79, and Silber, *Romance of Reunion,* pp. 39–65, 109–22.

41. Harper, "Duty to Dependent Races," p. 208.

42. McDowell, *"The Changing Same,"* p. 40. For discussion of the novel's audiences, see Carby, *Reconstructing Womanhood,* p. 71, and Foster, Introduction to *Iola Leroy,* pp. xxxiv–xxxv.

43. duCille, *Coupling Convention,* p. 30. Tate, *Domestic Allegories of Political Desire,* p. 4; see also pp. 110–11, 196–97.

44. Gaines, *Uplifting the Race,* esp. pp. 5–9.

45. Terrell, *A Colored Woman in a White World,* p. 16; quoted in part and discussed in Hine and Thompson, *A Shining Thread of Hope,* p. 183, and Stephanie J. Shaw, *What a Woman Ought to Be and Do: Black Professional Women Workers During the Jim Crow Era* (Chicago: University of Chicago Press, 1996), p. 22.

46. R[obert] C[harles] O['Hara] Benjamin, *Don't. A Book for Girls* (San Francisco: Valleau and Peterson, 1891), p. 10. All subsequent quotations are from this edition and cited parenthetically in the text. Born in the British West Indies, Benjamin (1855–1900) was also a minister and a newspaper editor. His other books included a biography of Toussaint L'Ouverture and a volume of poetry.

47. Frances Harper, letter to William Still, 20 February 1871, reprinted in Still, *Underground Railroad,* p. 772.

48. Carla L. Peterson, *"Doers of the Word": African-American Women Speakers and Writers in the North (1830–1880)* (New York: Oxford University Press, 1995), pp. 119–35.

49. Harper, "True and False Politeness" (1898), reprinted in *A Brighter Coming Day,* p. 398.

50. Harper, "Woman's Political Future" (1893), reprinted in Boyd, *Discarded Legacy,* p. 223.

51. Frances Harper, *Trial and Triumph* (1888–89), reprinted in *Minnie's Sacrifice, Sowing and Reaping, Trial and Triumph,* p. 179. All subsequent quotations are from this edition and cited parenthetically in the text.

52. The character of Topsy was apparently invoked more directly in a 1915 story by Pauline Hopkins entitled "Topsy Templeton." In this story, of which only a fragment survives, a lively black child named Topsy is adopted by two Northern white women. I am indebted to Lois Brown for this reference.

53. Harper employs this characterization more explicitly in *Minnie's Sacrifice,* in which the narrator condemns a slave mistress for her excessive self-will: "Proud, imperious, and selfish, she knew no law but her own will; no gratification but the enjoyment of her own desires" (21).

54. Houston A. Baker, *Workings of the Spirit: The Poetics of Afro-American Women's Writing* (Chicago: University of Chicago Press, 1991), pp. 32–33.

55. Harper described herself as an "old maid . . . going about the country meddling with the slaveholders' business," in "Letter from Miss Watkins," *Anti-Slavery Bugle,* 23 April 1859 (*Black Abolitionist Papers, 1830–1865,* microfilm edition, reel 11, no. 0698).

56. "Mrs. Frances E. Watkins Harper on the War and the President's Colonization Scheme," *Christian Recorder,* 27 September 1862, in *Black Abolitionist Papers, 1830–1865,* microfilm edition, reel 14, no. 0511.

57. Harper, speech at the National Woman's Rights Convention, reprinted in Boyd, *Discarded Legacy,* p. 114. For discussion of this speech, see Boyd, *Discarded Legacy,* pp. 116–17, and Peterson, *"Doers of the Word,"* pp. 228–29.

58. Foster, Introduction to *Minnie's Sacrifice, Sowing and Reading, Trial and Triumph,* p. xxxiii.

CHAPTER SIX

1. Rea Irvin, "Our Own Previews of Hollywood Attractions: Joan Crawford and Clark Gable in 'Gone With the Birth of a Nation, or The Gold Diggers of 1860,'" *The New Yorker,* 20 February 1937, reprinted in *Margaret Mitchell's "Gone With the Wind" Letters, 1936–1939,* edited by Richard Harwell (New York: Macmillan, 1976) [hereafter cited as *Letters*], illustrations insert, n.p. The film's reviewers frequently praised it through comparison with *Birth of a Nation;* see Edward D. C. Campbell Jr., *The Celluloid South: Hollywood and the Southern Myth* (Knoxville: University of Tennessee Press, 1981), pp. 118, 138.

2. Margaret Mitchell, *Gone With the Wind* (New York: Avon, 1973), pp. 409, 579. All subsequent quotations are from this edition and cited parenthetically in the text.

3. Quoted in Thomas Cripps, "Winds of Change: *Gone With the Wind* and Racism as a National Issue," in *Recasting: "Gone With the Wind" in American Culture,* edited by Darden Asbury Pyron (Miami: University Presses of Florida, 1983), p. 137.

4. This story is cited in Patricia Storace, "Look Away, Dixie Land," *The New York Review of Books,* 19 December 1991, p. 31.

5. On the links between Griffith and Mitchell, see Leslie A. Fiedler, *The Inadvertent Epic: From "Uncle Tom's Cabin" to "Roots"* (New York: Simon and Schuster, 1979), pp. 59–70; Willie Lee Rose, "Race and Region in American Historical Fiction: Four Episodes in Popular Culture," in *Region, Race, and Reconstruction,* edited by J. Morgan Kousser and James McPherson (New York: Oxford University Press, 1982), pp. 113–39; and Gerald Wood, "From *The Clansman* and *Birth of a Nation* to *Gone With the Wind:* The Loss of American Innocence," in *Recasting,* pp. 123–36.

6. Mitchell, letter to Alexander L. May, 22 July 1938, in *Letters,* p. 217.

7. See Fiedler, *Inadvertent Epic,* esp. pp. 61–62.

8. "*Gone With the Wind* One Day Tour Package" advertised on flyer, Summer 1995. On Melly Meadows, see "Belle System," *People,* 29 July 1996, pp. 86–87. For an introduction to the *Gone With the Wind* industry, see Cynthia Marylee Molt, *"Gone With the Wind" on Film: A Complete Reference* (Jefferson, NC: McFarland and Co., 1990); for a guide to *Gone With the Wind*'s mythologized presence in Atlanta, see Don O'Briant, *Looking for Tara: The "Gone With the Wind" Guide to Margaret Mitchell's Atlanta*

(Marietta, GA: Longstreet Press, 1994); and for an analysis of that mythology, see Charles Rutheiser, *Imagineering Atlanta: The Politics of Place in the City of Dreams* (New York: Verso, 1996), pp. 40–46.

9. Andreas Huyssen, "Mass Culture as Woman: Modernism's Other," in *Studies in Entertainment: Critical Approaches to Mass Culture*, edited by Tania Modleski (Bloomington: Indiana University Press, 1986), pp. 188–207.

10. Bernard De Voto, "Writing for Money," *Saturday Review*, 9 October 1937, p. 3; De Voto, "Fiction Fights the Civil War," *Saturday Review*, 18 December 1937, p. 3; De Voto, Editorial, *Saturday Review*, 8 January 1938, p. 8.

11. Jane Tompkins, "'All Alone, Little Lady?'" in *The Uses of Adversity: Failure and Accommodation in Reader Response*, edited by Ellen Spolsky (Lewisburg: Bucknell University Press, 1990), p. 191.

12. I. A. R. Wylie, "As One Writer to Another," *Harper's*, quoted in Richard Dwyer, "The Case of the Cool Reception," in *Recasting*, p. 26.

13. De Voto, "Fiction Fights the Civil War," p. 16. This assessment was not unanimous. The novel won the Pulitzer Prize, and Stephen Vincent Benét, for example, praised Mitchell: "This is war, and the wreck and rebuilding that follows it, told entirely from the woman's angle. We have had other novels about the Civil War by women . . . But I don't know of any other in which the interest is so consistently centered, not upon the armies and the battles . . . but upon that other world of women who heard the storm, waited it out, succumbed to it or rebuilt after it, according to their natures" (*Saturday Review*, 4 July 1936, reprinted in *Gone With the Wind as Book and Film*, edited by Richard Harwell [Columbia: University of South Carolina Press, 1983], p. 19).

14. De Voto, "Fiction Fights the Civil War," p. 16.

15. Quoted in James W. Mathews, "The Civil War of 1936: *Gone With the Wind* and *Absalom! Absalom!*," *Georgia Review* 21 (1967), p. 463.

16. Quoted in Claudia Roth Pierpont, "A Study in Scarlett," *New Yorker*, 31 August 1992, p. 88. On Faulkner and Mitchell, see also Louis Rubin, "Scarlett O'Hara and the Two Quentin Compsons," in *A Gallery of Southerners* (Baton Rouge: Louisiana State University Press, 1982), pp. 26–48. For an overview of the novel's reception, see Darden Asbury Pyron, "Bibliographic Essay," in *Recasting*, pp. 203–24.

17. Daniel Aaron, *The Unwritten War: American Writers and the Civil War* (1973; rpt. Madison: University of Wisconsin Press, 1987), p. 340.

18. Helen Taylor, *Scarlett's Women: "Gone With the Wind" and Its Female Fans* (New Brunswick: Rutgers University Press, 1989); see also Taylor, "Anniversaries, Sequels and Bandwagons: *Gone With the Wind*, 1989–1991," *Women: A Cultural Review* 4:1 (1993): 78–90. For analyses of Scarlett, see also Elizabeth Fox-Genovese, "Scarlett O'Hara: The Southern Lady as New Woman," in *Half Sisters of History: Southern Women and the American Past*, edited by Catherine Clinton (Durham: Duke University Press, 1994), pp. 154–79; Laura Hapke, *Daughters of the Great Depression: Women, Work and Fiction in the American 1930s* (Athens: University of Georgia Press, 1995), pp. 213–18; Harriett Hawkins, "Shared Dreams: Reproducing *Gone With the Wind*," in *Novel*

Images: Literature in Performance, edited by Peter Reynolds (London: Routledge, 1993), pp. 122–38; and Anne Goodwyn Jones, *Tomorrow Is Another Day: The Woman Writer in the South, 1859–1936* (Baton Rouge: Louisiana State University Press, 1981), pp. 313–50. For a reconsideration of *Gone With the Wind* in relation to Southern women's history, see Catherine Clinton, *Tara Revisited: Women, War, and the Plantation Legend* (New York: Abbeville, 1995).

19. For discussion of soap operas, see Tania Modleski, *Loving With a Vengeance: Mass-Produced Fantasies For Women* (New York: Routledge, 1990), pp. 85–109, and Martha Nochimson, *No End to Her: Soap Opera and the Female Subject* (Berkeley: University of California Press, 1992). On Harlequin Romances, see Modleski, *Loving With a Vengeance,* pp. 35–58, and Janice A. Radway, *Reading the Romance: Women, Patriarchy, and Popular Literature* (Chapel Hill: University of North Carolina Press, 1984). On the "woman's film," see Mary Ann Doane, *The Desire to Desire: The Woman's Film of the 1940s* (Bloomington: Indiana University Press, 1987), and Christine Gledhill, ed., *Home Is Where the Heart Is: Studies in Melodrama and the Woman's Film* (London: British Film Institute, 1987).

20. Octavia E. Butler, *Kindred,* introduction by Robert Crossley (1979; rpt. Boston: Beacon Press, 1988), p. 116.

21. Alice Walker, "A Letter of the Times, or Should This Sado-Masochism Be Saved?" in *You Can't Keep a Good Woman Down* (New York: Harcourt Brace Jovanovich, 1981), pp. 118, 122.

22. For an overview of this lineage, see Mary Condé, "Some African-American Fictional Responses to *Gone With the Wind,*" *Yearbook of English Studies* 26 (1996): 208–17. Condé makes the overly broad claim that "Since the novel has been so broadly influential, I think it is fair to assume that all African-American fiction about slavery since its publication in 1936 has contained some measure of response to it even if this is not made explicit" (210).

23. Joel Williamson, "How Black Was Rhett Butler?" in *The Evolution of Southern Culture,* edited by Numan V. Bartley (Athens: University of Georgia Press, 1988), pp. 87–107; Diane Roberts, *The Myth of Aunt Jemima: Representations of Race and Region* (London: Routledge, 1994), pp. 171–81.

24. See John Limon, *Writing After War: American War Fiction from Realism to Postmodernism* (New York: Oxford University Press, 1994), pp. 188–93, and Jim Cullen, *The Civil War in Popular Culture: A Reusable Past* (Washington: Smithsonian Institution Press, 1995), pp. 65–107.

25. Medora Field Perkerson, "Margaret Mitchell Told in Her Only Radio Broadcast How GWTW Was Written," *Atlanta Journal Magazine,* 18 December 1949, p. 25.

26. Ibid., p. 26.

27. Stephens Mitchell, "Margaret Mitchell and Her People," *Atlanta Historical Bulletin,* "Margaret Mitchell Memorial Issue," 9 (May 1950): 15.

28. See Darden Asbury Pyron's chapter on "Jimmy" in *Southern Daughter: The Life of Margaret Mitchell* (New York: Oxford University Press, 1991), pp. 28–52. Pyron is the most comprehensive of the Mitchell biographers, updating Anne Edwards, *Road*

to Tara (New York: Dell, 1983), and Finis Farr, *Margaret Mitchell of Atlanta* (New York: Avon, 1965).

29. The manuscript fragments of this untitled, undated story are assembled as "Through the Eyes of Youth: A Civil War Story," edited by Jane Powers Weldon, *Atlanta Historical Journal* 29 (1985–86): 47–59, and discussed in Pyron, *Southern Daughter,* pp. 51–52.

30. Mitchell, letter to Thomas Dixon, 15 August 1936, in *Letters,* pp. 52–53.

31. Pyron, *Southern Daughter,* pp. 56–57.

32. Susan Gubar, *Racechanges: White Skin, Black Face in American Culture* (New York: Oxford University Press, 1997). For discussion of racial masquerade in Dixon's novels, see Judith Jackson Fossett, "(K)night Riders in (K)night Gowns: The Ku Klux Klan, Race, and Constructions of Masculinity," in *Race Consciousness: African-American Studies for the New Century,* edited by Fossett and Jeffrey A. Tucker (New York: New York University Press, 1997), pp. 35–49.

33. Quoted in Jane Bonner Peacock, Introduction to Margaret Mitchell's *A Dynamo Going to Waste: Letters to Allen Edee, 1919–1921,* edited by Peacock (Atlanta: Peachtree Press, 1985), p. 16.

34. Quoted in Pyron, *Southern Daughter,* p. 56.

35. Margaret Mitchell, *Lost Laysen,* edited by Debra Freer (New York: Scribner, 1996), pp. 83, 80, 72. All subsequent quotations are from this edition and cited parenthetically in the text.

36. Gail Bederman, *Manliness and Civilization: A Cultural History of Gender and Race in the United States, 1880–1917* (Chicago: University of Chicago Press, 1995), pp. 217–39; the quotation is from p. 232.

37. On the figure of the vamp, see Janet Staiger, *Bad Women: Regulating Sexuality in Early American Cinema* (Minneapolis: University of Minnesota Press, 1995), pp. 147–62, and Gaylyn Studlar, "'Out-Salomeing Salome': Dance, the New Woman, and Fan Magazine Orientalism," in *Visions of the East: Orientalism in Film,* edited by Matthew Bernstein and Gaylyn Studlar (New Brunswick: Rutgers University Press, 1997), pp. 99–129. Pyron details Mitchell's career as vamp in *Southern Daughter,* pp. 117–36; "baby-faced l'il vamp" is quoted on p. 120.

38. Mitchell, letter to Allen Edee, 26 March 1920, in *Dynamo,* p. 79.

39. Ibid., 12 October 1919, pp. 38–39.

40. Quoted in Edwards, *Road to Tara,* p. 53.

41. See Pyron, *Southern Daughter,* pp. 84–85.

42. For accounts of this incident, see Pyron, *Southern Daughter,* pp. 107–8, and Peacock, *Dynamo Going to Waste,* pp. 111–12; the quotations are from *Southern Daughter,* p. 107. On the popularity of such dances, see Studlar, "'Out-Salomeing Salome.'"

43. Mitchell, letter to Frances Marsh, ca. 1924–1926, quoted in Pyron, *Southern Daughter,* p. 124.

44. Mitchell, letter to Allan Edee, 13 September 1919, in *Dynamo,* p. 32. Mitchell described the climax to this conflict in her letter of 1 December 1919 to Edee: "[H]e lost his head and . . . picking me up in his arms . . . he proceeded to caveman me in

the old and approved style. Well, I was so sickened and helpless that I began to cry and begged him to put me down, but he wouldn't . . . I was pretty much unnerved by that time . . . So I said I'd marry him if he would only put me down and not kiss me . . . I was on the verge of hysteria, so he left" (*Dynamo,* p. 55).

45. Mitchell, letter to Courtenay Ross, n.d., in *Dynamo,* p. 88.

46. Mitchell, letter to Allan Edee, 26 March 1920, in *Dynamo,* p. 77.

47. On "Red" Upshaw, see Pyron, *Southern Daughter,* pp. 130–36, 192–95.

48. Mitchell, letter to Courtenay Ross, n.d., in *Dynamo,* p. 86.

49. Mitchell, letters to Allan Edee, 13 March 1920, p. 70; 26 March 1920, p. 81; 26 March 1920, p. 83.

50. Mitchell, letter to Harvey Smith, "July 23 or 34, [19]27," Box 1, Margaret Mitchell Collection (Collection #265), Special Collections, Robert W. Woodruff Library, Emory University; all subsequent references to the Harvey Smith letters are from this collection and box and are used by permission.

51. These titles, among others, are listed in his annotation to an undated letter, probably from 1929. For discussion of Mitchell's interest in pornography, see Pyron, *Southern Daughter,* pp. 153–55.

52. Marianne Walker, *Margaret Mitchell and John Marsh: The Love Story Behind "Gone With the Wind"* (Atlanta: Peachtree Press, 1993), p. 134.

53. Smith, annotation to letter of July 1927.

54. John Cleland, *Fanny Hill: Memoirs of a Woman of Pleasure* (New York: Putnam's, 1963), pp. 14, 214. Discussions of voice in the novel include Julia Epstein, "Fanny's Fanny: Epistolarity, Eroticism, and the Transsexual Text," in *Writing the Female Voice: Essays on Epistolary Literature,* edited by Elizabeth C. Goldsmith (Boston: Northeastern University Press, 1989), pp. 135–53, and Gary Gautier, "Fanny's Fantasies: Class, Gender, and the Unreliable Narrator in Cleland's *Memoirs of a Woman of Pleasure,*" *Style* 28:2 (Summer 1994): 133–45.

55. Pyron cites Cabell and Ellis as Mitchell's most-owned authors (*Southern Daughter,* p. 154). For discussion of Cabell, see M. Thomas Inge and Edgar E. MacDonald, eds., *James Branch Cabell: Centennial Essays* (Baton Rouge: Louisiana State University Press, 1983), and Edgar MacDonald, *James Branch Cabell and Richmond-in-Virginia* (Jackson: University Press of Mississippi, 1983).

56. James Branch Cabell, *Jurgen: A Comedy of Justice* (New York: Robert M. McBride, 1928), pp. 101. All subsequent quotations are from this edition and cited parenthetically in the text.

57. Cabell's own relation to such connotations is ambiguous. Although he married twice, he was associated with homosexuality from his youth onward and had close adult friendships with other men that suggested intense intimacy. His friend Hugh Walpole wrote to him, for example, "You can give yourself up to me and be perfectly safe; look on it as a kind of Jack-in-the-box spree to be indulged in once a year—and then back into your box you may go . . . I want to protect and help and care for [you] to the end of my days" (quoted in MacDonald, *James Branch Cabell and Richmond-in-Virginia,* p. 210).

58. Quoted in Pyron, *Southern Daughter,* p. 124.

59. Havelock Ellis, *Studies in the Psychology of Sex* (2d ed., rev. and enlarged, Philadelphia: F. A. Davis Co., 1928), vol. 3, Appendix B; the case study is on pp. 306–15, and the quotation is on p. 314.

60. See Joseph A. Boone, "Vacation Cruises; or, The Homoerotics of Orientalism," *PMLA* 110:1 (January 1995): 89–107; see also Boone, *Libidinal Currents: Sexuality and the Shaping of Modernism* (Chicago: University of Chicago Press, 1998), pp. 352–418. For a relevant discussion of Ellis, see Siobhan Somerville, "Scientific Racism and the Invention of the Homosexual Body," in *The Gender/Sexuality Reader,* edited by Roger N. Lancaster and Micaela di Leonardo (New York: Routledge, 1997): 37–52.

61. Mitchell, letter to Harvey Smith, 24 May 1933.

62. For an analysis of the literary complexities of the blush, see Mary Ann O'Farrell, *Telling Complexions: The Nineteenth-Century English Novel and the Blush* (Durham: Duke University Press, 1997).

63. Mitchell began researching and writing *Gone With the Wind* in 1926. For discussion of the novel's composition, see Pyron, *Southern Daughter,* pp. 220–37.

64. For another interpretations of Scarlett's "redness," see Roberts, *Myth of Aunt Jemima,* pp. 178–79; on her masculine traits, see Storace, "Look Away, Dixie Land," p. 34, and Jones, *Tomorrow Is Another Day,* pp. 341–43.

65. Peggy Mitchell, "Georgia's Empress and Women Soldiers," *Atlanta Journal,* 20 July 1923, p. 13; this article is discussed in Pyron, *Southern Daughter,* pp. 171–74. On "Private Bill," see Richard Hall, *Patriots in Disguise: Women Warriors of the Civil War* (New York: Paragon, 1993), pp. 100–101.

66. Peggy Mitchell, "Woman Doctor Decorated by Three Nations," *Atlanta Journal,* 2 August 1925, p. 9.

67. Jack Davis and Stan Hart, "Groan With the Wind," *Mad* 300, January 1991, p. 47. In a similar vein, Julie Burchill has observed that today, a remake of *Gone With the Wind* "would be retitled *Rhett and Ashley*" (quoted in Hawkins, "Shared Dreams," p. 133).

68. George Chauncey, *Gay New York: Gender, Urban Culture, and the Making of the Gay Male World, 1890–1940* (New York: Basic Books, 1994), pp. 12–23.

69. Taylor, *Scarlett's Women,* p. 110. These reactions were to Ashley in either his literary or cinematic incarnations, but Taylor emphasizes the negative impact of Howard's performance.

70. *Time,* 25 December 1939, p. 32. See also Howard's joking telegram to Mitchell on learning that he had been chosen for the part: "Dear Mrs Marsh, I am not at all envious of Rhett because thanks to you, it was Melanie, Ma'am, that I wanted. But seriously, I feel it a great honor to have been selected to enact one of the roles of your book" (quoted in *Letters,* p. 246).

71. I am indebted to Tania Modleski for this suggestion.

72. Quoted in Judy Cameron and Paul J. Christman, *The Art of "Gone With the Wind": The Making of a Legend* (New York: Prentice Hall, 1989), p. 186.

73. Richard Dyer, "White," *Screen* 29:4 (Autumn 1988): 59. See also Dyer, *White* (London: Routledge, 1997).

74. Mitchell, letter to Michael MacWhite, 27 January 1937, in *Letters*, pp. 113–14. For another interpretation of Irishness in *Gone With the Wind*, see James P. Cantrell, "Irish Culture and the War Between the States: *Paddy McGann* and *Gone With the Wind*," *Eire-Ireland* 27:2 (1992): 7–15.

75. Cullen, *Civil War in Popular Culture*, pp. 84–89.

76. Alexandra Ripley's sequel, *Scarlett* (1991) reopens the question of the story's "Irishness" by returning to Ireland, where Scarlett assumes control of her family's estate. As Cullen argues, in the sequel, the Irish setting displaces questions of race beyond American borders (*Civil War in Popular Culture*, pp. 103–7). On *Scarlett*, see also Harriett Hawkins, "The Sins of *Scarlett*," *Textual Practice* 6:3 (Winter 1992): 491–96; and Taylor, "Anniversaries, Sequels and Bandwagons."

77. Clinton uses this term to characterize white-authored apologias for slavery that purported to be slave autobiographies; see *Tara Revisited*, pp. 202–4.

78. Mitchell, letter to Stephen Vincent Benét, 9 July 1936, in *Letters*, p. 36. On daguerreotypes, see her letter of 9 July 1936 to Donald Adams: "I went through so many daguerreotypes . . . and that face and that type kept recurring . . . as a coastal, deep South face and type. Well, I needed him and I used him" (in *Letters*, p. 32).

79. Williamson, "How Black Was Rhett Butler?" p. 99.

80. Peggy Mitchell, " 'No Dumbbells Wanted,' Say Atlanta Debs," *Atlanta Journal Sunday Magazine*, 28 January 1923, p. 1; Peggy Mitchell, "Leave Latin Lovers on the Screen," *Atlanta Journal Sunday Magazine*, 8 March 1924, p. 1; and Peggy Mitchell, "Valentino Declares He Isn't a Sheik," *Atlanta Journal Sunday Magazine*, 1 July 1923, p. 11.

81. Pierpont, "A Study in Scarlett," p. 98.

82. Miriam Hansen, *Babel and Babylon: Spectatorship in American Silent Film* (Cambridge: Harvard University Press, 1991), p. 257. For discussion of Valentino, see also Bederman, *Manliness and Civilization*, pp. 232–33; Ella Shohat, "Gender and Culture of Empire: Toward a Feminist Ethnography of the Cinema," in *Visions of the East*, pp. 19–66; and Gaylyn Studlar, *This Mad Masquerade: Stardom and Masculinity in the Jazz Age* (New York: Columbia University Press, 1996), pp. 150–98.

83. See Bederman, *Manliness and Civilization*, pp. 218–32. On Tarzan and domestic anxieties about whiteness, see also Catherine Jurca, "Tarzan, Lord of the Suburbs," *Modern Language Quarterly* 57:3 (1996): 479–504.

84. On Gable's image, see Joe Fisher, "Clarke [*sic*] Gable's Balls: Real Men Never Lose Their Teeth," in *You Tarzan: Masculinity, Movies and Men*, edited by Pat Kirkham and Janet Thumin (New York: St. Martin's Press, 1993), pp. 35–51. On Fleming and Cukor, see Roland Flamini, *Scarlett, Rhett, and a Cast of Thousands: The Filming of "Gone With the Wind"* (New York: Collier Books, 1975), pp. 228–49.

85. Hansen, *Babel and Babylon*, pp. 259–60.

86. For interpretations of Rhett's "femininity," see also Charles Rowan Beye, who views Rhett as "almost a portrait of the stereotypical gay male who is so often presented

. . . as a woman's perfect companion" ("Gone With the Wind, and Good Riddance," *Southwest Review* 78 [1993]): 371), and Pyron, who sees him as maternal (*Southern Daughter,* pp. 263–65).

87. James Baldwin, *The Devil Finds Work,* in *Collected Essays,* edited by Toni Morrison (New York: Library of America, 1998), p. 506.

88. This plot is disputed among Mitchell's biographers. Farr states that the novella's heroine "was in love with a handsome mulatto" (*Margaret Mitchell of Atlanta,* p. 97); Edwards repeats this claim (*Road to Tara,* p. 130); and Williamson pursues the implications of a miscegenation plot ("How Black Was Rhett Butler?" pp. 102–4). Pyron, however, argues that the story was "Without anything to do with race or miscegenation" (*Southern Daughter,* p. 217).

89. Martha Hodes, *White Women, Black Men: Illicit Sex in the Nineteenth-Century South* (New Haven: Yale University Press, 1997); on the Civil War era, see pp. 125–46.

90. Anonymous [David Goodman Croly and George Wakeman], *Miscegenation: The Theory of the Blending of the Races, applied to the American White Man and Negro* (New York, 1864); subsequent page numbers are from this edition and cited parenthetically in the text. For discussion of this text, see Sidney Kaplan, "The Miscegenation Issue in the Election of 1864," *Journal of Negro History* 34:3 (July 1949): 274–343; David R. Roediger, *The Wages of Whiteness: Race and the Making of the American Working Class* (London: Verso, 1991), pp. 155–56; and Forrest G. Wood, *Black Scare: The Racist Response to Emancipation and Reconstruction* (Berkeley: University of California Press, 1968), pp. 53–79.

91. Quoted in Carlos E. Cortés, "Hollywood Interracial Love: Social Taboo as Screen Titillation," who surveys the ways filmmakers navigated this prohibition (in *Beyond the Stars II: Plot Conventions in American Popular Film,* edited by Paul Loukides and Linda K. Fuller [Bowling Green, OH: Bowling Green State University Popular Press, 1991], pp. 21–35). On the importance of miscegenation rhetoric to the revived Ku Klux Klan of the 1920s, see Nancy MacLean, *Behind the Mask of Chivalry: The Making of the Second Ku Klux Klan* (New York: Oxford University Press, 1994), pp. 141–48.

92. Interracial sex between black women and white men is cited only once, when Scarlett disdains Yankee women in postwar Atlanta who evidenced "a very nasty and ill-bred interest in slave concubinage. Especially did she resent this in view of the enormous increase in mulatto babies in Atlanta since the Yankee soldiers had settled in the town" (662). This comment transforms "slave concubinage" from a structural effect of white power under slavery to a feature of postwar Yankee invasion. On the contrast between perceptions of interracial sex involving black women and those involving white women, see Hodes, *White Women, Black Men,* esp. pp. 199–200.

93. Eve Kosofsky Sedgwick identifies the sexual implications of this passage in *Between Men: English Literature and Male Homosocial Desire* (New York: Columbia University Press, 1985), pp. 9–10.

94. Blanche H. Gelfant suggests that Peter and Pittypat are a married couple "in disguised form" ("*Gone With the Wind* and The Impossibilities of Fiction," *Southern Literary Journal* 13:1 [Fall 1980]: 28).

95. Shirley Temple Black, *Child Star: An Autobiography* (New York: McGraw-Hill,

1988), p. 91. James Snead, *White Screens/Black Images: Hollywood from the Dark Side,* edited by Colin MacCabe and Cornel West (New York: Routledge, 1994), pp. 47–66; Ann duCille, "The Shirley Temple of My Familiar," *Transition* 73 (1998): 10–32. See also Gubar, *Racechanges,* pp. 203–5, and Karen Orr Vered, "White and Black in Black and White: Management of Race and Sexuality in the Coupling of Child-Star Shirley Temple and Bill Robinson," *Velvet Light Trap* 39 (Spring 1997): 52–65.

96. Charlotte Brontë, *Jane Eyre* (New York: Oxford University Press, 1993), p. 119.

97. For an influential feminist analysis of sadomasochism, see Jessica Benjamin, *The Bonds of Love: Psychoanalysis, Feminism, and the Problem of Domination* (New York: Pantheon, 1988); on masochism in *Jane Eyre,* see Michelle A. Massé, *In the Name of Love: Women, Masochism, and the Gothic* (Ithaca: Cornell University Press, 1992), pp. 192–238. For an elaboration of parallels, although not interrelationships, between gothic romances and slave narratives, see Kari J. Winters, *Subjects of Slavery, Agents of Change: Women and Power in Gothic Novels and Slave Narratives, 1790–1865* (Athens: University of Georgia Press, 1992). See also Storace: "[T]he affair between Rhett and Scarlett . . . has inexplicably been taken for a love story, when it is almost entirely expressed through the imagery of slave and master" ("Look Away, Dixie Land," p. 36).

98. I am grateful to Lynn Wardley for this suggestion about New Orleans.

99. According to Alan David Vertrees, the censored scene was this: "The night lamp is burning on the table as Rhett enters with Scarlett. He drops her on the bed. She shrinks from him in terror. He looks at her for a moment and then, dropping on his knees beside the bed, reaches toward her and drags her to him. She fights him off with what strength she has left but can put up no defense against his power. His lips meet hers and she lies in his arm helpless. Fade out" (quoted in *Selznick's Vision: "Gone With the Wind" and Hollywood Filmmaking* [Austin: University of Texas Press, 1997], p. 40).

100. Tom Kuntz, "Rhett and Scarlett: Rough Sex or Rape? Feminists Give a Damn," *New York Times,* 19 February 1995, Week in Review Section, p. 7.

101. The racial metaphors of this scene have been noted by Fiedler, *Inadvertent Epic,* pp. 64–66; Williamson, "How Black Was Rhett Butler?" pp. 100–102; and Limon, *Writing After War,* pp. 189–90. For discussion of women's responses to the scene, see Taylor, *Scarlett's Women,* pp. 129–37.

102. On the set connection to *King Kong,* see Thomas Schatz, Foreword to *Selznick's Vision,* p. x; on *King Kong* in relation to images of African-American masculinity, see Snead, *White Screens/Black Images,* pp. 1–36. On *Frankenstein,* see my "Here Comes the Bride: Wedding Gender and Race in *Bride of Frankenstein,*" in *The Dread of Difference: Gender and the Horror Film,* edited by Barry Keith Grant (Austin: University of Texas Press, 1996), pp. 309–37. For a relevant theorization of couples who may function interracially even though they are not so designated, see Werner Sollors, *Neither Black Nor White Yet Both: Thematic Explorations of Interracial Literature* (New York: Oxford University Press, 1997), esp. pp. 16–24.

103. Fiedler, *Inadvertent Epic,* p. 66.

104. Modleski, *Loving With a Vengeance,* p. 41. On rape fantasies in romance novels, see also Radway, *Reading the Romance,* pp. 71–76, 141–44; for a relevant discussion of

fantasy in *Gone With the Wind* and other women's fiction, see Cora Kaplan, "*The Thorn Birds:* Fiction, Fantasy, Femininity," in *Sea Changes: Culture and Feminism* (London: Verso, 1986), pp. 117–46.

105. Mitchell, letter to Katharine Brown, 13 August 1937, in *Letters*, p. 163. For analysis of Scarlett's resemblance to Prissy, see Beye, "Gone With the Wind, and Good Riddance," p. 379.

106. This is the rendering of her lines in Sidney Howard's screenplay; see *GWTW: The Screenplay*, edited by Richard Harwell (New York: Macmillan, 1980), p. 196.

107. Roberts, *Myth of Aunt Jemima*, 181.

108. Lillian Smith, *Killers of the Dream*, introduction by Margaret Rose Gladney (1949; rpt. New York: W. W. Norton, 1994), pp. 83–84.

109. Mae West's novel of interracial sex is *The Constant Sinner* (1937; rpt. London: Virago, 1995). For discussion of West and race, see Ramona Curry, *Too Much of a Good Thing: Mae West as Cultural Icon* (Minneapolis: University of Minnesota Press, 1996), pp. 12–17, and Marybeth Hamilton, *When I'm Bad, I'm Better: Mae West, Sex, and American Entertainment* (New York: HarperCollins, 1995), pp. 153–72.

110. On the hostility between Mitchell and Smith, see Pyron, *Southern Daughter*, pp. 327, 341. For discussion of Smith, see Roberts, *Myth of Aunt Jemima*, pp. 181–92; and Jay Watson, "Uncovering the Body, Discovering Ideology: Segregation and Sexual Anxiety in Lillian Smith's *Killers of the Dream*," *American Quarterly* 49:3 (September 1997): 470–503. On Lumpkin, see Katharine Du Pre Lumpkin, *The Making of a Southerner*, foreword by Darlene Clark Hine (1946; rpt. Athens: University of Georgia Press, 1991), and Jacqueline Dowd Hall, "Open Secrets: Memory, Imagination, and the Refashioning of Southern Identity," *American Quarterly* 50:1 (March 1998): 109–24. On Durr, see Virginia Durr, *Outside the Magic Circle: The Autobiography of Virginia Foster Durr*, edited by Hollinger F. Barnard (Tuscaloosa: University of Alabama Press, 1985).

111. Selznick quoted in Cripps, "Winds of Change," p. 140. On the racial politics of the film's production, see also Cripps, *Slow Fade to Black: The Negro in American Film, 1900–1942* (New York: Oxford University Press, 1993), pp. 359–66, and Leonard J. Leff, "David Selznick's *Gone With the Wind:* 'The Negro Problem,'" *Georgia Review* 38:1 (Spring 1984): 146–64. On McQueen's protest and the bathroom desegregation campaign, see Flamini, *Scarlett, Rhett, and a Cast of Thousands*, p. 216.

112. Mitchell recounted the blackface audition in a letter to Katharine Brown, 8 March 1937: "I wish to God you could have seen the white woman who turned up last week with a can of blacking in her pocketbook and the determination of playing Mammy" (in *Letters*, pp. 131–32). On McDaniel, see Leonard J. Leff, "The Search for Hattie McDaniel," *New Orleans Review* 10:2–3 (1983): 91–98, and Carlton Jackson, *Hattie: The Life of Hattie McDaniel* (Lanham, MD: Madison Books, 1990). Discussions of the image of "Mammy" include Patricia Hill Collins, *Black Feminist Thought: Knowledge, Consciousness, and the Politics of Empowerment* (New York: Routledge, 1991), pp. 70–73; Cheryl Turner, "The Development of the Mammy Image and Mythology," in *Southern Women: Histories and Identities*, edited by Virginia Bernhard et al. (Columbia: University of Missouri Press, 1992), pp. 87–108; and Deborah Gray

White, *Ar'n't I a Woman? Female Slaves in the Plantation South* (New York: W. W. Norton, 1985), pp. 27–61.

113. Hazel V. Carby, "Ideologies of Black Folk: The Historical Novel of Slavery," in *Slavery and the Literary Imagination,* edited by Deborah E. McDowell and Arnold Rampersad (Baltimore: Johns Hopkins University Press, 1989), p. 132.

114. Donald Bogle, *Toms, Coons, Mammies, Mulattoes and Bucks: An Interpretive History of Blacks in American Films,* 3d ed. (New York: Continuum, 1994), p. 88. For other discussions of Mammy, see Clinton, *Tara Revisited,* pp. 212–13; Roberts, *Myth of Aunt Jemima,* pp. 175–77; and Taylor, *Scarlett's Women,* pp. 168–77.

115. On "antebellum Hollywood," see Cripps, *Making Movies Black: The Hollywood Message Movie from World War II to the Civil Rights Era* (New York: Oxford University Press, 1993), pp. 3–24.

116. See Cripps, *Making Movies Black,* pp. 24–26.

117. Most recently, J. California Cooper's novel, *The Wake of the Wind* (New York: Doubleday, 1998), which focuses on African-Americans in Reconstruction Texas, presents itself, as its title suggests, as a challenge to Mitchell's story.

118. For discussion of *Jubilee,* see Carby, "Ideologies of Black Folk"; Jacqueline Miller Carmichael, *Trumpeting a Fiery Sound: History and Folklore in Margaret Walker's "Jubilee"* (Athens: University of Georgia Press, 1998); Barbara Christian, "'Somebody Forgot to Tell Somebody Something': African-American Women's Historical Novels," in *Wild Women in the Whirlwind: Afra-American Culture and the Contemporary Literary Renaissance,* edited by Joanne M. Braxton and Andrée Nicola McLaughlin (New Brunswick: Rutgers University Press, 1990), pp. 326–41; Condé, "Some African-American Fictional Responses"; Charlotte Goodman, "From *Uncle Tom's Cabin* to Vyry's Kitchen: The Black Female Folk Tradition in Margaret Walker's *Jubilee,*" in *Tradition and the Talents of Women,* edited by Florence Howe (Urbana: University of Illinois Press, 1991), pp. 328–37; Minrose C. Gwin, *Black and White Women of the Old South: The Peculiar Sisterhood in American Literature* (Knoxville: University of Tennessee Press, 1985), pp. 151–70; Phyllis Rauch Klotman, "'Oh Freedom'—Women and History in Margaret Walker's *Jubilee,*" *Black American Literature Forum* 11:4 (Winter 1977): 139–45; Huang Songkang, "An Evaluation of *Gone With the Wind* and *Jubilee* from an Historical Point of View," in L. Moody Simms, Jr., ed., *"Gone With the Wind: The View from China," Southern Studies* 23:1 (Spring 1984): 15–19; Hortense Spillers, "A Hateful Passion, A Lost Love," *Feminist Studies* 9:2 (Summer 1983): 293–323; Eleanor Traylor, "Music as Theme: The Blues Mode in the Works of Margaret Walker," in *Black Women Writers (1950–1980): A Critical Evaluation,* edited by Mari Evans (Garden City, NY: Anchor Press/Doubleday, 1984), pp. 511–25; and Melissa Walker, *Down From the Mountaintop: Black Women's Novels in the Wake of the Civil Rights Movement, 1966–1989* (New Haven: Yale University Press, 1991), pp. 13–26. For Walker's own account of the novel, see "How I Wrote *Jubilee,*" in *How I Wrote Jubilee and Other Essays on Life and Literature* (New York: Feminist Press, 1990), pp. 50–65.

119. Margaret Walker, "Natchez and Richard Wright in Southern American Literature," in *On Being Female, Black, and Free: Essays by Margaret Walker, 1932–92,* edited by Maryemma Graham (Knoxville: University Press of Tennessee, 1997), p. 119.

120. Jacket copy, Margaret Walker, *Jubilee* (New York: Bantam, 1988). All subsequent quotations are from this edition and cited parenthetically in the text.

121. Charles H. Rowell, "Poetry, History and Humanism: An Interview With Margaret Walker," *Black World* 25:2 (December 1975): 10. For comparisons between *Jubilee* and *Gone With the Wind*, see Carby, "Ideologies of Black Folk," pp. 129–36; Carmichael, *Trumpeting a Fiery Sound*, pp. 26–28; Condé, "Some African-American Fictional Responses," pp. 212–14; Klotman, "'Oh Freedom,'" pp. 139–40; Huang, "An Evaluation of *Gone With the Wind* and *Jubilee* from an Historical Point of View"; and Taylor, *Scarlett's Women*, pp. 199–201.

122. Walker, "Reflections on Black Women Writers," in *On Being Female, Black, and Free*, p. 46.

123. See Condé, "Some African-American Fictional Responses," p. 212, and Taylor, *Scarlett's Women*, pp. 199–201.

124. Limon, *Writing After War*, p. 189.

125. See Walker, *Down From the Mountaintop*, on the novel's relation to racial politics in the 1960s.

126. In another well-known parody, television comedian Carol Burnett portrayed Scarlett wearing the dress made of curtains with the curtain rods still attached. Two more recent parodies are Missy D'Urberville, *Today Is Another Tomorrow: The Epic "Gone With the Wind" Parody* (New York: St. Martin's, 1991), and Beverly West and Nancy K. Peske, *Frankly Scarlett, I Do Give a Damn! Classic Romances Retold* (New York: HarperCollins, 1996), pp. 1–5. For a list of parodies, see Molt, *"Gone With the Wind" on Film: A Complete Reference*, pp. 443–44.

127. Quoted in Amy M. Spindler, "Is Fashion All Blond? A Spoof Takes Aim," *New York Times*, 7 April 1996, Styles section, p. 29.

128. André Leon Talley and Karl Lagerfeld, "Scarlett 'n the Hood," *Vanity Fair* May 1996: 182–91.

129. Quoted in Pierpont, "A Study in Scarlett," p. 102.

130. Quoted in Martin Arnold, "Rhett (and Pat Conroy) Aim to Have the Last Word," *New York Times*, 5 November 1998, p. E3.

AFTERWORD

1. *Cook v. Babbitt*, Civ. No. 91–0338 (D.D.C. 1993). The case was widely reported in both reenactor and mainstream media. For an excellent account of the controversy as it developed in the reenactment world, see Cathy Stanton, "Being the Elephant: The American Civil War Reenacted," M.A. thesis, Vermont College of Norwich University, 1997, chap. 6; I am indebted to Stanton for sharing her thesis and for further information on reenactments. Mainstream coverage includes the following: [Anon.], "Not Just Whistling Dixie: Lauren Cook Burgess Fights for a Woman's Right to Play Civil War," *People*, 5 October 1992, p. 103; [Anon.], "Woman Sues Over Exclusion From Events at National Park," *New York Times*, 25 February 1991, p. A7; Eugene Meyer, "A Civil War of the Sexes: Park Service Wanted Male Cast at Antietam,"

Washington Post, 9 June 1992, p. A1; Meyer, "Judge Admits Women to the Antietam Armies," *Washington Post,* 18 March 1993, p. B1; Lynda Robinson, "It's a Man's Job: A Woman's Fight to Be a Civil War 'Soldier,'" *San Francisco Chronicle* 13 October 1991, *Sunday Punch,* p. 2; and National Public Radio, story on "Morning Edition," 23 August 1991. On Burgess's work as an historian, see Lauren Cook Burgess, ed., *An Uncommon Soldier: The Civil War Letters of Rosetta Wakeman, alias Pvt. Lyons Wakeman, 153rd Regiment, New York State Volunteers, 1862–1864* (New York: Oxford University Press, 1994), and Eugene L. Meyer, "The Soldier Left a Portrait and Her Eyewitness Account," *Smithsonian* 24:10 (January 1994): 96–104.

For an introduction to reenactments, see R. Lee Hadden, *Reliving the War: A Reenactor's Handbook* (Mechanicsburg, PA: Stackpole Books, 1996). For assessments of this world, see Tony Horwitz, *Confederates in the Attic: Dispatches from the Unfinished Civil War* (New York: Pantheon, 1998), and the documentary film *Men of Reenaction* (directed by Jessica Yu, 1995). On the history of reenactments, see Jay Anderson, *Time Machines: The World of Living History* (Nashville: American Association for State and Local History, 1984), pp. 141–48; John Bodnar, *Remaking America: Public Memory, Commemoration, and Patriotism in the Twentieth Century* (Princeton: Princeton University Press, 1992), pp. 213–24; and Edward Tabor Linenthal, *Sacred Ground: Americans and Their Battlefields* (Urbana: University of Illinois Press, 1991), pp. 89–126. For analyses of contemporary reenactments, see Stanton, "Being the Elephant," and the following: Randal Allred, "Catharsis, Revision, and Re-enactment: Negotiating the Meaning of the American Civil War," *Journal of American Culture* 19:4 (Winter 1996): 1–13; Jack Barth, "The Red Badge of Make-Believe Courage," *Outside,* March 1996, pp. 88–92; Jim Cullen, *The Civil War in Popular Culture: A Reusable Past* (Washington: Smithsonian Institution Press, 1995), pp. 172–199; Dennis Hall, "Civil War Reenactors and the Postmodern Sense of History," *Journal of American Culture* 17:3 (Fall 1994): 7–12; Richard Handler and William Saxton, "Dyssimulation: Reflexivity, Narrative, and the Quest for Authenticity in 'Living History,'" *Cultural Anthropology* 3:3 (August 1988): 242–60; Phil Rubio, "Civil War Reenactments and Other Myths," in *Race Traitor,* edited by Noel Ignatiev and John Garvey (New York: Routledge, 1996), pp. 182–94; and Rory Turner, "Bloodless Battles: The Civil War Reenacted," *The Drama Review* 34:4 (1990): 123–36. The 40,000 figure is cited by James M. McPherson, who also states that some 250,000 people belong to Civil War societies, subscribe to Civil War magazines, or collect war memorabilia ("A War That Never Goes Away," in *Drawn With the Sword: Reflections on the American Civil War* (New York: Oxford University Press, 1996), p. 55. This estimate dates from 1990; numbers have almost certainly risen since then.

My comments on Civil War reenactments are based on these sources and on my own observations of reenactments and related events in Georgia, North Carolina, Virginia, and Massachusetts.

2. Meyer, "Judge Admits Women to the Antietam Armies," p. B3. On the demographics of the reenactment movement, see Stanton, "Being the Elephant," chap. 4.

3. Quotation sources, respectively: "If you're going to portray . . ." in "Woman Sues Over Exclusion"; "her lack of authenticity . . ." in "Morning Edition"; "There was no

hedging . . ." in "It's a Man's Job"; "I think I do a far better job . . ." in "Woman Sues Over Exclusion"; and judge's comments in "Judge Admits Women to the Antietam Armies." For an overview of current attitudes toward women soldiers, see Stanton, "Being the Elephant," chap. 6; for a profile of another women soldier, see Cullen, *Civil War in Popular Culture,* pp. 172–199.

4. On reenactment roles for women, see, for example, Hadden, *Reliving the Civil War,* who does not include "soldier" in a long list of suggested female roles (92–94), but concedes that "if women want to participate in this public activity, the law upholds their rights" (136).

5. On contemporary interest in cross-dressing, see Marjorie Garber, *Vested Interests: Cross-Dressing and Cultural Anxiety* (New York: Routledge, 1992); on transgender issues, see Leslie Feinberg, *Transgender Warriors: Making History from Joan of Arc to RuPaul* (Boston: Beacon Press, 1996).

6. See Judith Butler, *Gender Trouble: Feminism and the Subversion of Identity* (New York: Routledge, 1990), and "Imitation and Gender Insubordination," in *Inside/Out: Lesbian Theories, Gay Theories,* edited by Diana Fuss (New York: Routledge, 1991), pp. 13–31. For a variety of perspectives on gender and performance, see *The Routledge Reader in Gender and Performance,* edited by Lizbeth Goodman with Jane de Gay (London: Routledge, 1998).

7. On the connections between postmodernism and reenactments, see Hall, "Civil War Reenactors and the Postmodern Sense of History," and Handler and Saxton, "Dyssimulation."

8. See, for example, Horwitz's description of spooning: "'Spoon right!' someone shouted. Each man rolled onto his side and clutched the man beside him. Following suit, I snuggled my neighbor. A few bodies down, a man wedged between Joel and Rob began griping. 'You guys are so skinny you don't give off any heat. You're just sucking it out of me!'" (*Confederates in the Attic,* p. 13).

9. According to Stanton, such an assumption often accompanies attacks on cross-dressed reenactors, who are accused of being either lesbian or heterosexually promiscuous ("Being the Elephant," chap. 6).

10. On galvanizing, see Horwitz, *Confederates in the Attic,* pp. 134–35; Hadden, *Reliving the Civil War,* p. 106; and Stanton, "Being the Elephant," chap. 6.

11. On neo-Confederate activities, see Peter Applebome, *Dixie Rising: How the South Is Shaping American Values, Politics, and Culture* (New York: Times/Random House, 1996), pp. 116–47, and Horwitz, *Confederates in the Attic,* esp. pp. 66–70, 285–93.

12. On such fantasies, see John Shelton Reed, "U.S. Out of Dixie," in *Whistling Dixie: Dispatches from the South* (New York: Harcourt Brace Jovanovich, 1990), pp. 32–35.

13. These details are offered in "Not Just Whistling Dixie."

14. Rita Mae Brown, *High Hearts* (New York: Bantam, 1986). In her foreword, Brown invokes a tradition of Confederate cross-dressing women as context for her story (xv).

15. On the history of the flag, see John M. Coski, "The Confederate Flag in American History and Culture," and Kevin Thornton, "The Confederate Flag and the Meaning of Southern History," both in *Southern Cultures* 2:2 (1996): 195–231 and 233–45. For other extended commentaries on the flag, see also James Forman, Jr., "Driving Dixie Down: Removing the Confederate Flag from Southern State Capitols," *Yale Law Journal* 101:2 (November 1991): 505–26; Sanford Levinson, *Written in Stone: Public Monuments in Changing Societies* (Durham: Duke University Press, 1998); and George Schedler, *Racist Symbols and Reparations: Philosophical Reflections on Vestiges of the American Civil War* (Lanham, MD: Rowman and Littlefield, 1998).

16. Michael Andrew Grissom, *Southern by the Grace of God* (Gretna, LA: Pelican, 1995), p. 128.

17. See "The Black and the Gray: An Interview with Tony Horwitz," *Southern Cultures* 4:1 (1998): 5–15.

18. [Anon.], advertisement for Heritage Preservation Association, in *Camp Chase Gazette* 25:7 (June 1998): 52; this advertisement also circulates widely at Southern reenactments.

19. For discussion of the Klan and Confederate iconography, see Applebome, *Dixie Rising,* esp. pp. 136–39; for examples of neo-Nazi uses of the flag, see Forman, "Driving Dixie Down," pp. 513–14.

20. Horwitz, *Confederates in the Attic,* p. 389. For an approach that foregrounds racial issues more fully than Horwitz, see *Men of Reenaction;* for an analysis centered on reenactments as examples of "white culture," see Rubio, "Civil War Reenactments and Other Myths."

21. Robert Penn Warren, *The Legacy of the Civil War* (New York: Random House, 1961), p. 59.

22. For a critique of this episode, see Eric Foner, "Ken Burns and the Romance of Reunion," in *Ken Burns's "The Civil War": Historians Respond,* edited by Robert Brent Toplin (New York: Oxford University Press, 1996), pp. 103–18. See also the essays by Catherine Clinton and Leon F. Litwack in the same volume; Jeanie Attie, "Illusions of History: A Review of *The Civil War,*" *Radical History Review* 52 (Winter 1992): 95–104; and Bill Farrell, "All in the Family: Ken Burns's *The Civil War* and Black America," *Transition* 58 (1992): 169–73.

23. John Hope Franklin, "A Century of Civil War Observance," *Journal of Negro History* 47:2 (April 1962): 107. On the Civil War Centennial, see Bodnar, *Remaking America,* pp. 206–26, and Michael Kammen, *Mystic Chords of Memory: The Transformation of Tradition in American Culture* (New York: Vintage, 1991), pp. 590–610.

24. Allan Gurganus, *Oldest Living Confederate Widow Tells All* (New York: Alfred A. Knopf, 1989). For discussion of demythologizing the Civil War, see Tara McPherson, " 'Both Kinds of Arms': Remembering the Civil War," *Velvet Light Trap* 35 (Spring 1995): 3–18.

25. See *Men of Reenaction* for profiles of African-American reenactors. Events centered on African-American Civil War reenactors include the recent rededication of the Augustus Saint-Gaudens memorial to Col. Robert Gould Shaw and the Massa-

chusetts 54th Regiment in Boston (Boston, May 1997); a volume of essays generated by these events is forthcoming (*Hope and Glory: Essays on the Legacy of the 54th Massachusetts Regiment*, edited by Martin Blatt, Tom Brown, and Donald Yacovone [Amherst: University of Massachusetts Press/Boston: Massachusetts Historical Society]). A new African-American Civil War Memorial was dedicated in Washington, DC, in 1998.

26. By contrast, the popular Civil War novels of another African-American writer, Frank Yerby, do not share the overtly revisionist approaches of these later writers; novels like *The Foxes of Harrow* (1946) and *Captain Rebel* (1956) focus on white characters and experiences. For contrasting assessments of this underexamined writer, see James L. Hill, "Frank Yerby," in *The Oxford Companion to African American Literature*, edited by William L. Andrews, Frances Smith Foster, and Trudier Harris (New York: Oxford University Press, 1997), pp. 797–98, and Jack Temple Kirby, *Media-Made Dixie: The South in the American Imagination* (Baton Rouge: Louisiana State University Press, 1978), pp. 103–6. On Brown's important *Darktown Strutters*, see Eric Lott, Review, *African American Review* 31:1 (Spring 1997): 169–72, and W. T. Lhamon, Jr., *Raising Cain: Blackface Performance from Jim Crow to Hip Hop* (Cambridge: Harvard University Press, 1998), pp. 175–80.

27. Black women's novels with antebellum settings include Sherley Anne Williams's *Dessa Rose* (1986), Octavia E. Butler's *Kindred* (1979), and Gayl Jones's *Corregidora* (1975). For discussion of historical fiction by black women, see Barbara Christian, "'Somebody Forgot to Tell Somebody Something': African-American Women's Historical Novels," in *Wild Women in the Whirlwind: Afra-American Culture and the Contemporary Literary Renaissance*, edited by Joanne M. Braxton and Andrée Nicola McLaughlin (New Brunswick: Rutgers University Press, 1990), pp. 326–41, and Missy Dehn Kubitschek, *Claiming the Heritage: African-American Women Novelists and History* (Jackson: University Press of Mississippi, 1991).

28. See John Limon, *Writing After War: American War Fiction from Realism to Postmodernism* (New York: Oxford University Press, 1994), pp. 194–200. The critical literature on *Beloved* is extensive; for an introduction, see Barbara H. Solomon, ed., *Critical Essays on Toni Morrison's "Beloved"* (New York: G. K. Hall, 1998).

29. Toni Morrison, *Beloved* (New York: Alfred A. Knopf, 1987), p. 205.

30. Tom LeClair, "An Interview with Rosellen Brown," in *A Rosellen Brown Reader: Selected Poetry and Prose*, edited by Rosellen Brown (Hanover, NH: Middlebury College Press, 1992), pp. 293–94; Brown also assesses the novel in Melissa Walker, "An Interview with Rosellen Brown," *Contemporary Literature* 27:2 (Summer 1986): 145–59. For discussion of *Civil Wars*, see Nancy Porter, "Women's Interracial Friendships and Visions of Community in *Meridian, The Salt Eaters, Civil Wars*, and *Dessa Rose*," in *Tradition and the Talents of Women*, edited by Florence Howe (Urbana: University of Illinois Press, 1991), pp. 251–67.

31. Rosellen Brown, *Civil Wars* (New York: Penguin, 1984), p. 36. All subsequent quotations are from this edition and cited parenthetically in the text.

32. Brown, "Displaced Persons," in *A Rosellen Brown Reader*, p. 68.

33. Stephen L. Carter, *Civility: Manners, Morals, and the Etiquette of Democracy* (New York: Basic Books, 1998), pp. xi, 164. For a contrasting assessment of contemporary interest in civility, see Benjamin DeMott, "Seduced by Civility: Political Manners and the Crisis of Democratic Values," *The Nation,* 9 December 1996, pp. 11–19. For a relevant analysis of civility in the Civil Rights Movement, see William H. Chafe, *Civilities and Civil Rights: Greensboro, North Carolina, and the Black Struggle for Freedom* (New York: Oxford University Press, 1980).

34. June Jordan, "Declaration of an Independence I Would Just as Soon Not Have" (1976), in *Civil Wars* (Boston: Beacon Press, 1981), p. 118. Jordan cites the Civil War more directly in "Grand Army Plaza," a poem about two ex-lovers meeting at the Brooklyn memorial to the Union army (in *Passion: New Poems, 1977–1980* [Boston: Beacon Press, 1980], pp. 90–91).

35. June Jordan, "Civil Wars," in *Civil Wars,* p. 178. All subsequent quotations are from this edition and cited parenthetically in the text.

36. See "A New Politics of Sexuality" (1991), reprinted in Jordan, *Technical Difficulties: African-American Notes on the State of the Union* (New York: Pantheon, 1992), pp. 187–93.

Index

ADZ-436